PHILIP'S

C000262096

STREET ATLAS
East Yorkshire
Northern Lincolnshire

First published in 2002 by

Philip's, a division of
Octopus Publishing Group Ltd
2-4 Heron Quays, London E14 4JP

First edition 2002
Fourth impression with revisions 2004

ISBN-10   0-540-08145-0 (spiral)
ISBN-13   978-0-540-08145-5 (spiral)

© Philip's 2004

OS Ordnance Survey®

Contents

III **Key to map symbols**

IV **Key to map pages**

VI **Route planning**

VIII **Administrative and Postcode boundaries**

1 **Street maps** at 1¾ inches to 1 mile

122 **Street maps** at 3½ inches to 1 mile

154 **Street maps of centres of Beverley, Kingston-upon-Hull and York** at 7 inches to 1 mile

157 **Town maps** of Doncaster and Scarborough

158 **Index** of towns and villages

160 **Index** of streets, hospitals, industrial estates, railway stations, schools, shopping centres, universities and places of interest

Digital Data

The exceptionally high-quality mapping found in this book is available as digital data in TIFF format, which is easily convertible to other bitmapped (raster) image formats.

The index is also available in digital form as a standard database table. It contains all the details found in the printed index together with the National Grid reference for the map square in which each entry is named.

For further information and to discuss your requirements, please contact Philip's on 020 7644 6932 or james.mann@philips-maps.co.uk

(22a)	**Motorway** with junction number
	Primary route – dual/single carriageway
	A road – dual/single carriageway
	B road – dual/single carriageway
	Minor road – dual/single carriageway
	Other minor road – dual/single carriageway
	Road under construction
	Pedestrianised area
DY7	**Postcode boundaries**
	County and unitary authority boundaries
	Railway
	Railway under construction
	Tramway, miniature railway
	Rural track, private road or narrow road in urban area
	Gate or obstruction to traffic (restrictions may not apply at all times or to all vehicles)
	Path, bridleway, byway open to all traffic, road used as a public path

The representation in this atlas of a road, track or is no evidence of the existence of a of a right of way

187	
210	**Adjoining page indicators** (The colour of the arrow indicates the scale of the adjoining page - see scales below)
84	
211	**The map areas within the pink and blue bands are shown at a larger scale on the page, indicated by the red and blue blocks and arrows**
203	

Acad	**Academy**	Mkt	**Market**
Allot Gdns	**Allotments**	Meml	**Memorial**
Cemy	**Cemetery**	Mon	**Monument**
C Ctr	**Civic Centre**	Mus	**Museum**
CH	**Club House**	Obsy	**Observatory**
Coll	**College**	Pal	**Royal Palace**
Crem	**Crematorium**	PH	**Public House**
Ent	**Enterprise**	Recn Gd	**Recreation Ground**
Ex H	**Exhibition Hall**	Resr	**Reservoir**
Ind Est	**Industrial Estate**	Ret Pk	**Retail Park**
IRB Sta	**Inshore Rescue**	Sch	**School**
	Boat Station	Sh Ctr	**Shopping Centre**
Inst	**Institute**	TH	**Town Hall/House**
Ct	**Law Court**	Trad Est	**Trading Estate**
L Ctr	**Leisure Centre**	Univ	**University**
LC	**Level Crossing**	Wks	**Works**
Liby	**Library**	YH	**Youth Hostel**

Walsall	**Railway station**
	Private railway station
	Bus, coach station
	Ambulance station
	Coastguard station
	Fire station
	Police station
	Accident and Emergency entrance to hospital
H	**Hospital**
	Place of worship
i	**Information Centre** (open all year)
P	**Parking**
P&R	**Park and Ride**
PO	**Post Office**
	Camping site
	Caravan site
	Golf course
	Picnic site
Prim Sch	**Important buildings, schools, colleges, universities and hospitals**
River Medway	**Water name**
	River, stream
	Lock, weir
	Water
	Tidal water
	Woods
	Houses
Church	**Non-Roman antiquity**
ROMAN FORT	**Roman antiquity**

■ The small numbers around the edges of the maps identify the 1 kilometre National Grid lines ■ The dark grey border on the inside edge of some pages indicates that the mapping does not continue onto the adjacent page

The scale of the maps on the pages numbered in blue is 5.52 cm to 1 km • 3½ inches to 1 mile • 1: 18103

0	¼	½	¾	1 mile
0	250m	500m	750m	1 kilometre

The scale of the maps on pages numbered in green is 2.76 cm to 1 km • 1¾ inches to 1 mile • 1: 36206

0	¼	½	¾	1 mile
0	250m	500m	750m	1kilometre

The scale of the maps on pages numbered in red is 11.04 cm to 1 km • 7 inches to 1 mile • 1: 9051.4

0	220 yards	440 yards	660 yards	½ mile
0	125m	250m	375m	½ kilometre

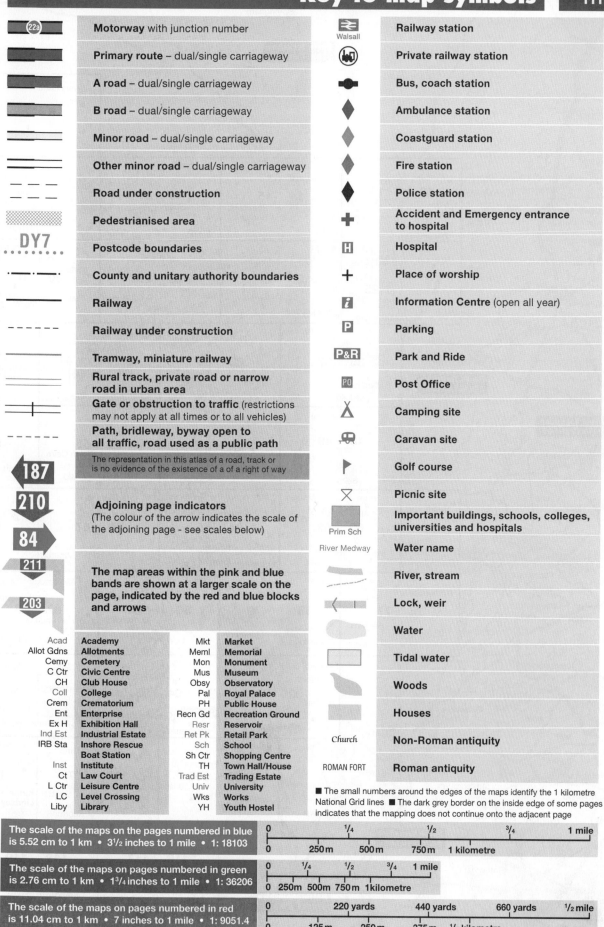

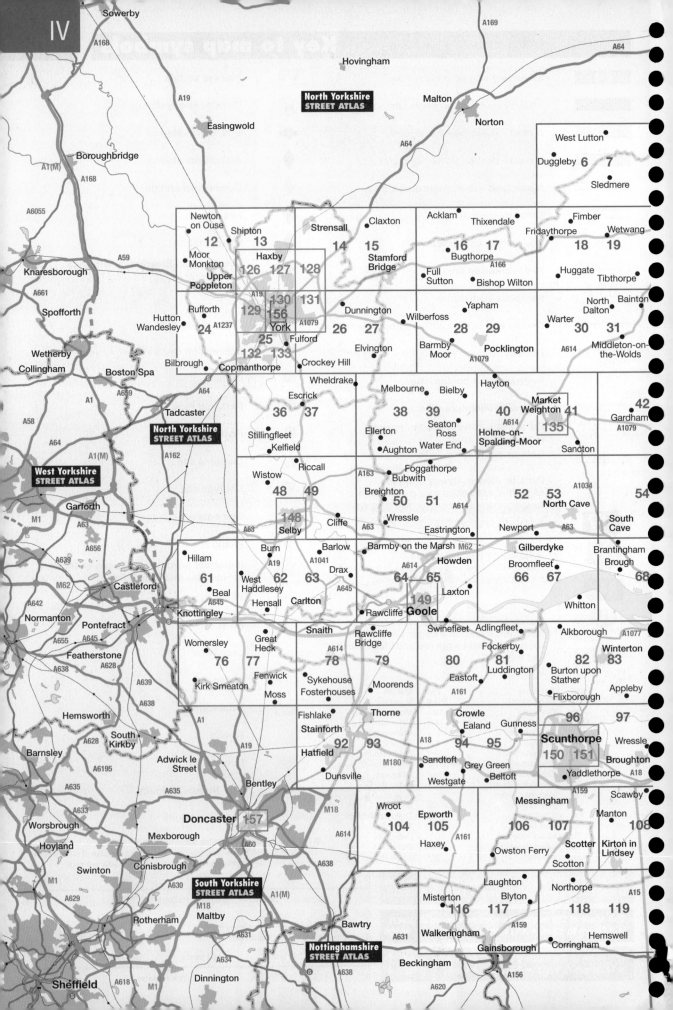

V

Key to map pages

156	Map pages at 7 inches to 1 mile
141	Map pages at 3½ inches to 1 mile
113	Map pages at 1¾ inches to 1 mile

Scale

0   5   10   15   20 km

0   5   10 miles

A1039

Filey

Hunmanby

Reighton

Fordon

1 **2** **3** A165

Foxholes

Butterwick

Grindale

4 **5**

Bempton

Flamborough

Langtoft

Rudston

Boynton

Bridlington

8 **9** **122** **123**

Kilham A614 **10** **11**

Burton Agnes

20 **21**

Gransmoor Fraisthorpe

Driffield Nafferton

124 **125** **22** **23**

Great Kelk

Kirkburn Skerne Skipsea

Church End A165

Hutton Dunnington

Cranswick

A164 **32** **33** **34** **35**

Bewholme

Beswick Brandesburton

134

Hornsea

Etton Leven Rolston

43 Leconfield Rise

Bishop **Beverley** Tickton **46** **47**

Burton **136** **137** **44** **45** A165 Withernwick

154 Skirlaugh Aldbrough

Walkington Swine

A1174 Dunswell Frinton Garton

55 A164 **56** **57** Sproatley **60**

Cottingham **58** **59** Hilston

Little **138** **139** **140** **141** Owstwick Tunstall

Weighton **Kingston** **142** Preston Burton Roos

upon Hull Pidsea

Kirk Ella A1105 **155** Hedon Burstwick Rimswell Withernsea

143 **144** **145** **146** **147** **74** **75**

Hessle A1033 **72** **73**

69 **70** **71** Paull Hollym Holmpton

North Keyingham Patrington

Ferriby New Holland

Barton-upon- Barrow upon Goxhill Patrington Skeffling Easington

Humber Humber Haven

Kingsforth **85** **86** **87** **88** **89** **90** **91**

84

Saxby Wootton A160 Kilnsea

All Saints Ulceby **Immingham**

Bonby

Worlaby A15 Croxton Habrough A180 **102** **103**

Elsham Kirmington Stallingborough **152** **153**

98 **99** **100** **101** **Grimsby**

Brigg Barnetby A18 Keelby Healing **Cleethorpes**

le Wold

Bigby Great Laceby A16 A1098

Limber

Grasby Irby upon **Humberston**

A1084 A1173 Humber Waltham New Waltham

Hibaldstow North Swallow Holton **114** **115**

109 Kelsey **110** **111** A46 **112** **113** le Clay North

Caistor A18 Coates

Redbourne South Rothwell Croxby Ashby North A1031

Kelsey cum Fenby Thoresby

Fulstow North

Somercotes

Lincolnshire Ludborough **120** **121** A1031

STREET ATLAS Binbrook

Utterby

A1103 Fotherby

A631 A46 Market Rasen

A631 A631 A16

A157 **Louth**

Route planning

Scale

0   5   10   15   20 km

0   5   10 miles

Administrative and Postcode boundaries

County and unitary authority boundaries

Postcode boundaries

Area covered by this atlas

Scale

| 0 | 5 | 10 | 15 | 20 | 25 | 30 | 35 | 40 km |

| 0 | 5 | 10 | 15 | 20 | 25 miles |

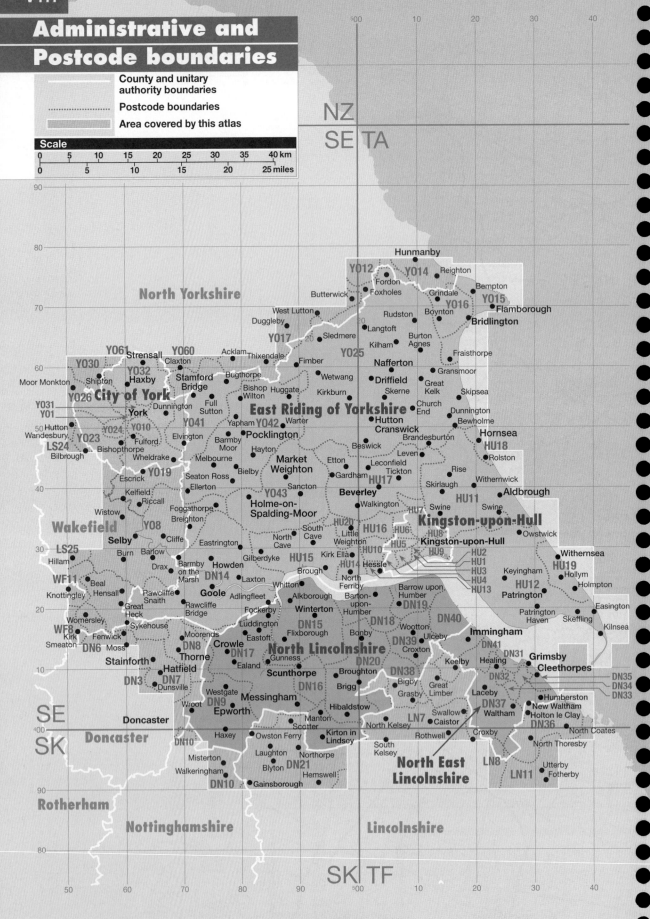

NZ

SE TA

North Yorkshire

Hunmanby

YO12   YO14   Reighton

Butterwick   Fordon   Bempton

West Lutton   Foxholes   Grindale   YO15   Bempton

Duggleby   Rudston   Boynton   Grindale   Flamborough

YO17   Sledmere   Langtoft   Burton Agnes   Bridlington

YO25   Kilham   Fraisthorpe

Acklam   Thixendale   Fimber

YO61   Strensall   YO60

YO30   Claxton   Nafferton   Gransmoor

Moor Monkton   Shipton   Haxby   Stamford Bridge   Bugthorpe   Wetwang   Driffield   Skipsea

YO32   Bishop Wilton   Huggate   Kirkburn   Skerne   Great Kelk

City of York   Dunnington   Full Sutton   Warter   Church End   Dunnington   Bewholme

YO31   York   YO41   YO42   Hutton Cranswick   Hornsea

YO01   Fulford   Elvington   Yapham   Pocklington   HU18

Hutton Wandesbury   YO24   YO10   Barmby Moor   Hayton   Beswick   Leven   Rolston

LS24   YO23   Bishopthorpe   Wheldrake   Melbourne   Bielby   Etton   Leconfield   Rise   Withernwick

Bilbrough   Seaton Ross   Ellerton   Gardham   HU17   Tickton   Skirlaugh   Aldbrough

YO19   Sancton   HU11

Escrick   Kelfield   Riccall   YO43   Holme-on-Spalding-Moor   Beverley   Walkington   Swine   Swine

Wistow   Foggathorpe   Breighton   South Cave   HU20   HU7   Kingston-upon-Hull   Owstwick

Wakefield   YO08   North Cave   Little Weighton   HU16   HU6   HU8   Kingston-upon-Hull

LS25   Selby   Cliffe   Eastrington   Gilberdyke   HU5   HU10   HU9   Withernsea

Hillam   Burn   Barlow   HU15   Kirk Ella   HU14   Hessle   HU2   Keyingham   HU19

WF11   Drax   Barmby on the Marsh   Howden   Brough   North Ferriby   HU3   HU1   Hollym

Beal   Rawcliffe   Laxton   Whitton   Barrow upon Humber   HU4   Holmpton

Knottingley   Hensall   Snaith   Goole   Adlingfleet   Alkborough   Barton-upon-Humber   HU13   HU12

Womersley   Great Heck   Rawcliffe Bridge   Fockerby   DN19   Patrington

WF8   Sykehouse   Luddington   Winterton   DN18   DN40   Patrington Haven   Easington

Kirk Smeaton   Fenwick   Moorends   DN15   Flixborough   Bonby   Wootton   Immingham   Skeffling   Kilnsea

DN6   Moss   DN8   Crowle   Eastoft   Croxton   DN39   DN41

Stainforth   Thorne   DN17   Gunness   North Lincolnshire   Ulceby   DN31   Grimsby

Hatfield   Ealand   DN20   Broughton   Keelby   Healing   Cleethorpes

DN3   DN7   DN16   Brigg   DN38   DN32   DN35

Dunsville   Westgate   Bigby   Great Limber   Laceby   DN34

Wroot   DN9   Messingham   Hibaldstow   Grasby   Humberston   DN33

Doncaster   Epworth   Manton   LN7   Swallow   DN37   New Waltham

Haxey   Scotter   Kirton in Lindsey   Caistor   Waltham   Holton le Clay   DN36

SE   DN10   Owston Ferry   North Kelsey   Rothwell   Croxby   North Coates

SK   Doncaster   Misterton   Laughton   Northorpe   South Kelsey   North Thoresby

Walkeringham   Blyton   DN21   Hemswell   North East Lincolnshire   LN8   LN11   Utterby   Fotherby

DN10   Gainsborough

Rotherham

Nottinghamshire   **Lincolnshire**

SK TF

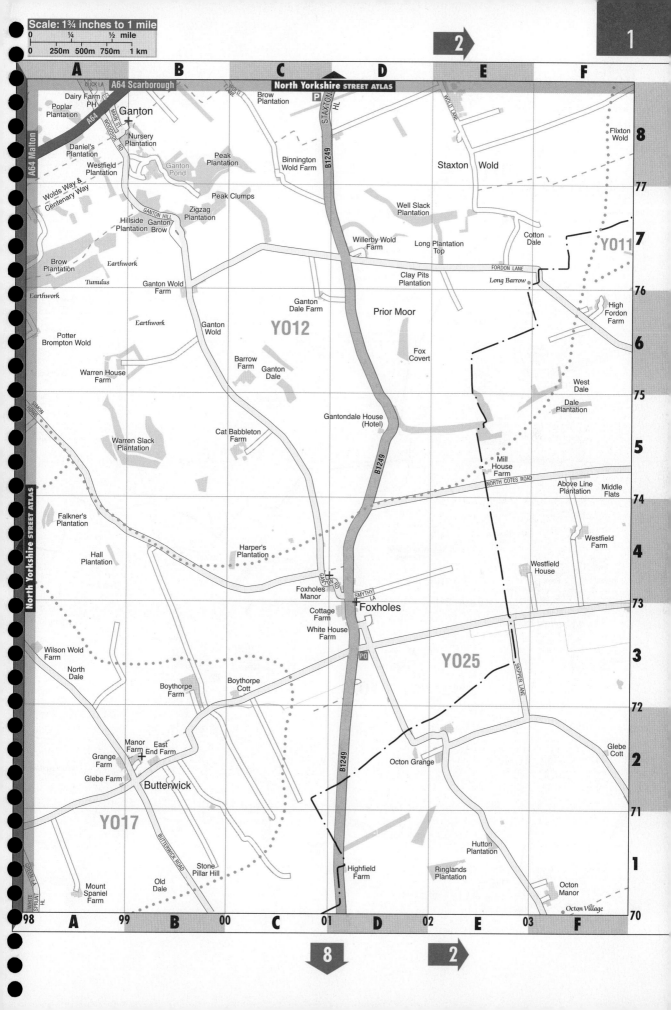

F8	7 HIGH CFT	14 BARDNEY RD
1 OWSTON RD	8 CASTLE HL	15 ROWEDALE CL
2 MITFORD RD	9 BOWLING GN LA	16 AMBREY CL
3 MITFORD CL	10 CHURCH HL	17 PARK RISE
4 OUTGAITS CL	11 HUNGATE CT	18 OLIVER'S CL
5 WENTWORTH WY	12 VICARAGE CL	19 ROSEMOOR CL
6 SIMPSON AV	13 FONTAYNE RD	20 HARBOROUGH CL

Scale: 1¾ inches to 1 mile

0   ¼   ½   mile
0   250m 500m 750m 1 km

North Yorkshire STREET ATLAS

A B C D E F

8

Sharpe Howe

Long Plantation

Kirk Heads

Folkton Wold

Wolds Way

Hunmanby

Sycamore Tree Farm

Foxhill Farm

CP Sch

Liby STONEGATE

Rec

MALTON RD

MUSTON RD

NORTHCOTE

HALL PK RD

BRIDLINGTON ST

Windmill Farm

Park House Farm

Hall Park

LAWSONS CL

Riding School

YO11

Camp Dale

YO14

77

Lang Dale

Danebury Manor

Kirk Heads

The Camp (Earthworks)

Field House Farm

Centenary Way

NEW ROAD

Hill Farm

7

North Fordon Farm

Five Firs Plantation

The Sheepwalks

South Dale

Quarry Farm

Saxdale House Farm

76

FORDON LANE

South Fordon Farm

Fordon

Hunmanby Grange

Cansdale Farm

Howe Farm

Bartindale Row

Dale Farm

6

Cans Dale

Highfield Farm

75

North Cotes Plantation

NORTH COTES RD

NORTH COTES ROAD

NORTH COTES RD

5

Wold Newton Field

Wold Newton Grange

Mill Flats

Hill Farm

74

Manor Farm

BACK LA

Highfield Farm

HIGHFIELD CL

FRONT ST

BACK ST

Wold Newton GM Sch

BRIDLINGTON

LAKING ROAD

BURTON FLEMING ROAD

Burton Fleming Grange

MILL ROAD

HUNMANBY RD

Far End

Hall Farm

Burton Fleming

WEST LA

73

LA PH

BUTT LA

Butt Hills

Wold Newton

The Ings

RAINSBURGH LA

Bridge Farm

WEST AV 1
THE CRESCENT 2
WOLD NEWTON RD 3
FRONT ST 4
BUTCHER'S LA 5

PO

SCHOOL LA

PH

Easter End

SOUTH ST

3

The Wold Cottage

Willy Howe

YO25

Willy Howe Farm

THWING ROAD

South End

72

West Field House

Eastfield Farm

Maidensgrave Farm

2

71

NINE DIKES ROAD

Refuge Farm

Maidensgrave Henge

1

Rectory Farm

Thwing

Eastgate Farm

PO

MAIN STREET

CHURCH

DIKES LA

ARGAM LANE

BURTON FLEMING RD

70

04   A   05   B   06   C   07   D   08   E   09   F

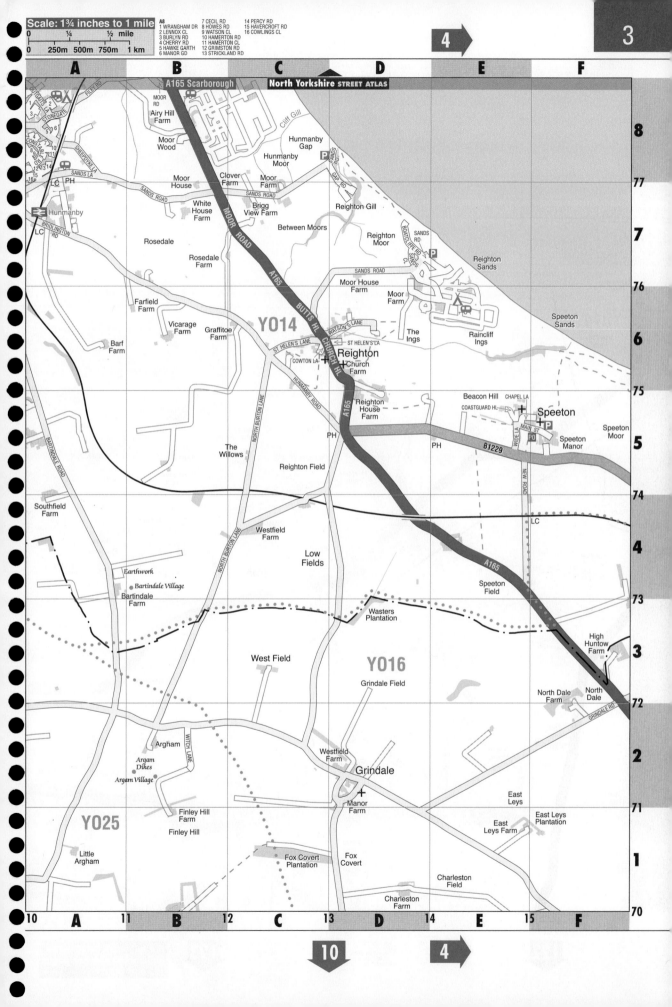

Scale: 1¾ inches to 1 mile

0   ¼   ½   mile
0   250m 500m 750m 1 km

A   B   C   D   E   F

8

76

7

75

King &
Queen Rocks

Speeton
Cliffs

Dulcey
Dock

Buckton
Cliffs

YO14

Speeton
Moor

Great
Moor

Crab
Rocks

74

B1229

Visitor Centre

Buckton
Hall

Standard
Hill

Bempton Cliffs
Nature Reserve

Scale
Nab

5

SPEETON GATE

Bempton
Grange

The
Moor

The Leys

Wandale
Farm

Cat Nab

Dykes
End

Grange
Farm

Norway
Farm

HODDY COWS LA

CLIFF LANE

73

Greenlands
Farm

B1229

BUCKTON GATE

White
House
Farm

Buckton

Bydales
Plantation

Metlands

Dykes
Plantation

Gull
Nook

Huntow

GRINDALE ROAD

PUMP LA

MAIN ST

SCARSEA WY

PH
GREEN

STONEPIT LA

YO15

Wold
Farm

4

LC

Primary
School

HIGH ST

PO

Bempton

72

BOLAM LANE

NEWSHAM HL LA

EDEN GD

LC

FLAMBOROUGH ROAD

Danes' Dyke

B1229

A165

Bempton

LC

Mill
Farm

Old Mill
Farm

Butterwicks
Farm

BEMPTON LANE

3

YO16

Newsham
Field

High Barn

Quarry
Farm

Lynhams

71

Norlands

OLD SYKES RD

East
Huntow

BEMPTON LANE

SHORT LANE

Field
House

Flamborough
Maltings

Long
Acres
Farm

Daneswood
Farm

Bream
Wood

The
Crofts

2

NORLANDS LA

North
Mount

JEWISON LANE

LC

FLAMBOROUGH RD

BRIDLINGTON RD

West
Huntow

Cote Walls
Plantation

Gell-spring
Plantation

Home
Farm

70

SCARBOROUGH ROAD

PINFOLD LANE

122

The
Grange

Stackyard
Plantation

SHEEPRAKE LA

PH

123

Marton

Dyke
Wood

1

122

Hill
Field

THORNTONDALE DR

KEPPEL DR

CRAY MORDACKS

THE LAWNS

SHEEPRAKE LA

MARTON GATE

Charity
Farm

Leys
Plantation

Long
Wood

HIGH
SEWERBY
RD

CHURCH LA

MOOR RD

Danes
Dyke
Farm

CH

123

Dykes
End

TRENTHAM DR

HADDON RD

B1255

Sewerby Hall
Museum & Art Gall

16   A   17   B   18   C   19   D   20   E   21   F

69

C4
1 WALMSLEY CL
2 GRANGE CL
3 COLLINGWOOD RD
4 THE MEADOWS
5 RINGLEY MS

D4
1 THE PADDOCK
2 SPRING LA
3 ST MICHAEL'S WK
4 BYEDALES
5 GILLUS LA
6 CHURCH LA
7 ACREDYKES
8 VICARAGE LA
9 CLARK CR

For full street detail of the
highlighted area see pages
122 and 123.

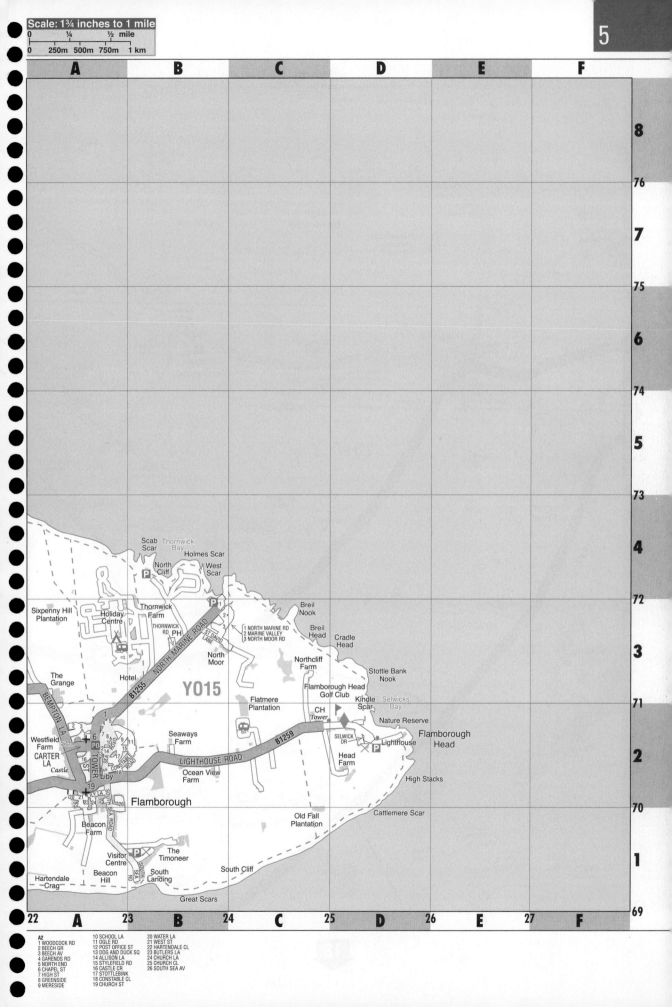

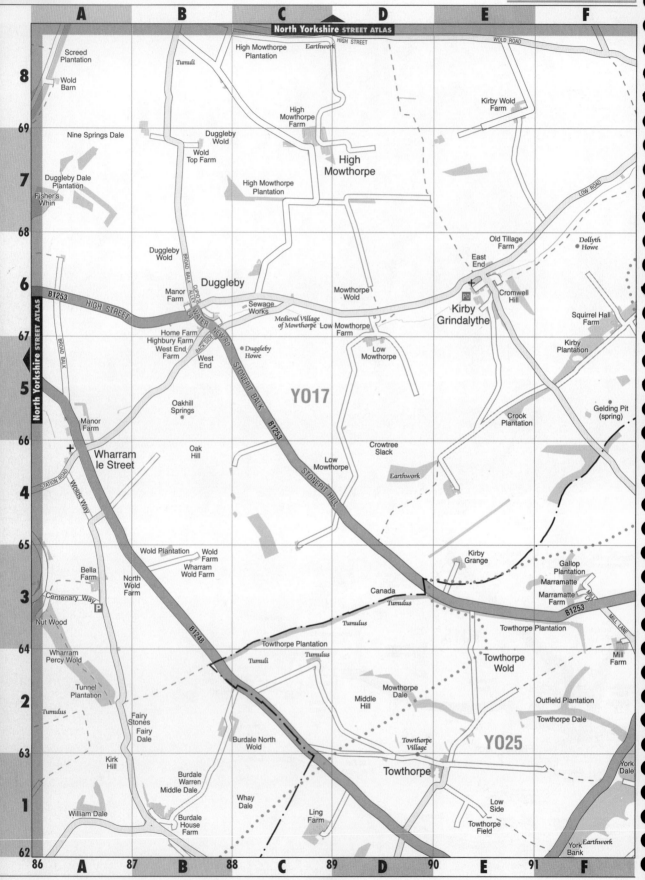

North Yorkshire STREET ATLAS

North Yorkshire STREET ATLAS

A **B** **C** **D** **E** **F**

HIGH STREET

WOLD ROAD

Screed
Plantation

Wold
Barn

Tumuli

High Mowthorpe
Plantation

Earthwork

High
Mowthorpe
Farm

Kirby Wold
Farm

8

Nine Springs Dale

Duggleby
Wold

Wold
Top Farm

High Mowthorpe
Plantation

High
Mowthorpe

LOW ROAD

69

7

Duggleby Dale
Plantation

Fisher's
Whin

Duggleby
Wold

Old Tillage
Farm

Dollyth
Howe

68

BROAD BALK

B1253

HIGH STREET

Manor
Farm

Duggleby

Sewage
Works

CUPIDS ALLEY

WATER LANE

NEW RD

Mowthorpe
Wold

East
End

Kirby
Grindalythe

PO

Cromwell
Hill

Squirrel Hall
Farm

6

BROAD BALK

Home Farm

Highbury Farm

West End
Farm

BACK SIDE

West
End

Duggleby
Howe

Medieval Village
of Mowthorpe

Low Mowthorpe
Farm

Low
Mowthorpe

Kirby
Plantation

67

STONEPIT BALK

Oakhill
Springs

YO17

Crook
Plantation

Gelding Pit
(spring)

5

STATION ROAD

Manor
Farm

Wharram
le Street

Oak
Hill

B1253

Low
Mowthorpe

Crowtree
Slack

Earthwork

66

WOLDS WAY

STONEPIT HILL

4

Bella
Farm

Centenary Way

Nut Wood

P

Wold Plantation

North
Wold
Farm

Wold
Farm

Wharram
Wold Farm

Kirby
Grange

Canada

Tumulus

Gallop
Plantation

Marramatte

Marramatte
Farm

MILL LANE

B1253

3

Wharram
Percy Wold

Tunnel
Plantation

Tumulus

B1248

Fairy
Stones

Fairy
Dale

Tumuli

Tumulus

Tumulus

Towthorpe Plantation

Towthorpe Plantation

Towthorpe
Wold

Outfield Plantation

Towthorpe Dale

Mill
Farm

65

64

2

Kirk
Hill

Burdale North
Wold

Tumulus

Middle
Hill

Mowthorpe
Dale

Towthorpe
Village

YO25

Towthorpe Dale

York
Dale

63

1

William Dale

Burdale
Warren
Middle Dale

Burdale
House
Farm

Whay
Dale

Ling
Farm

Towthorpe

Low
Side

Towthorpe
Field

York
Bank

Earthwork

62

A **B** **C** **D** **E** **F**

86 **87** **88** **89** **90** **91**

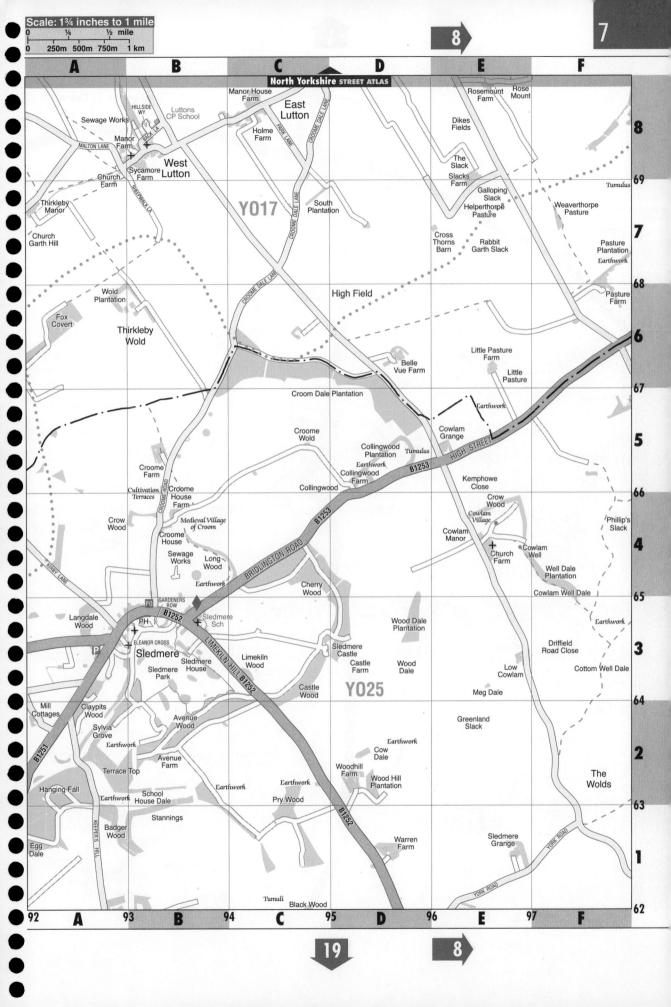

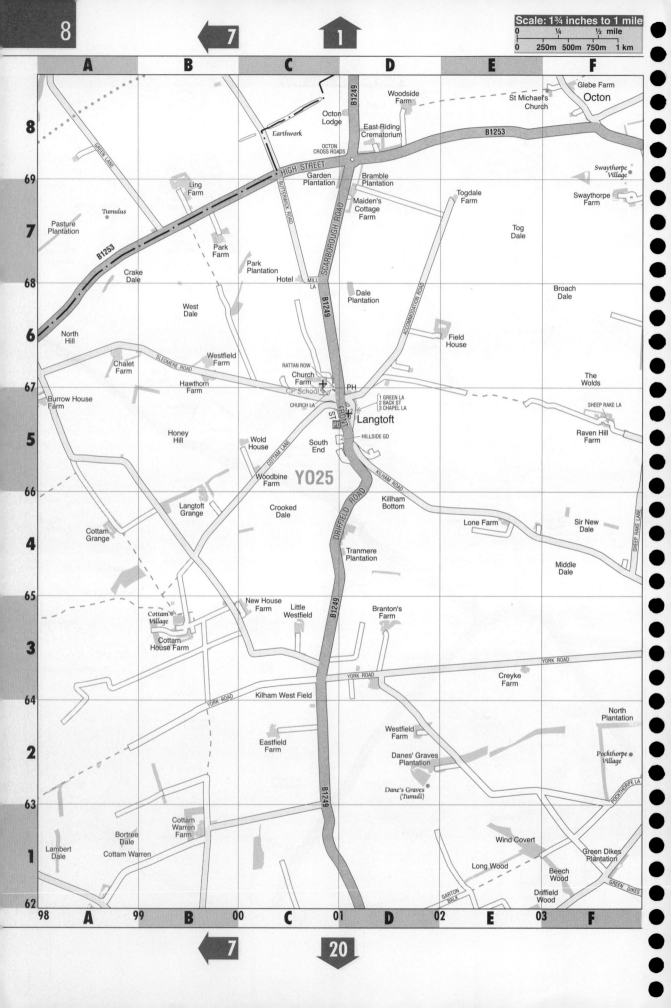

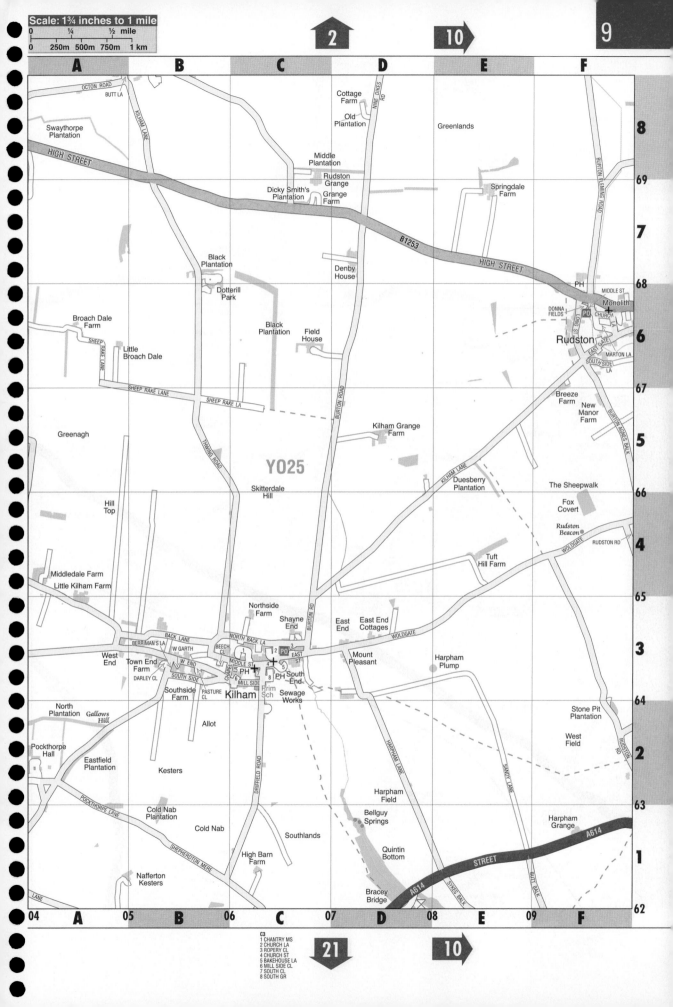

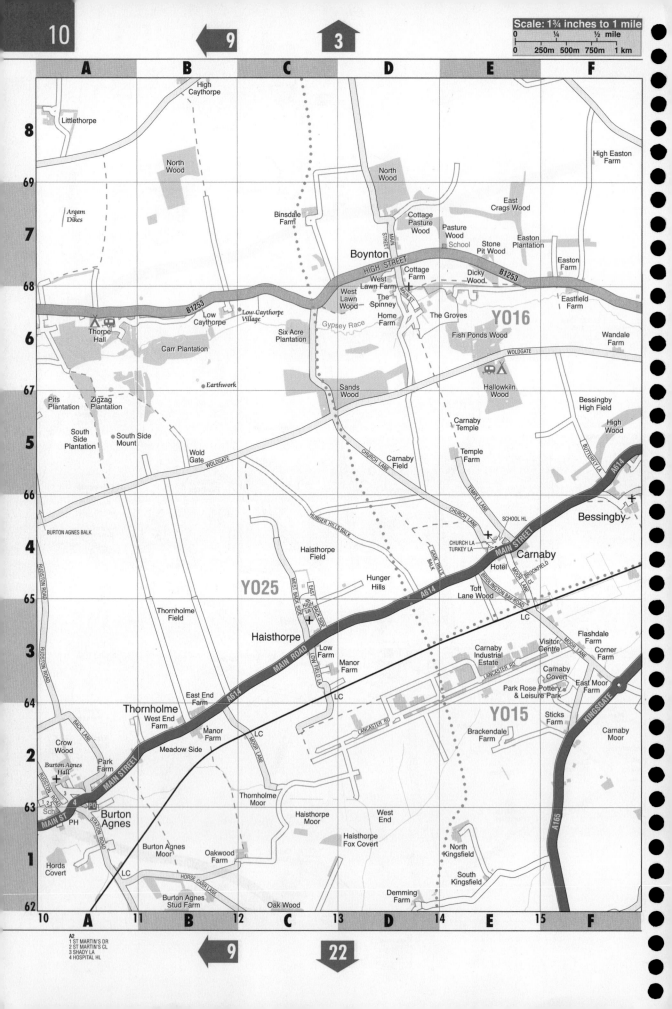

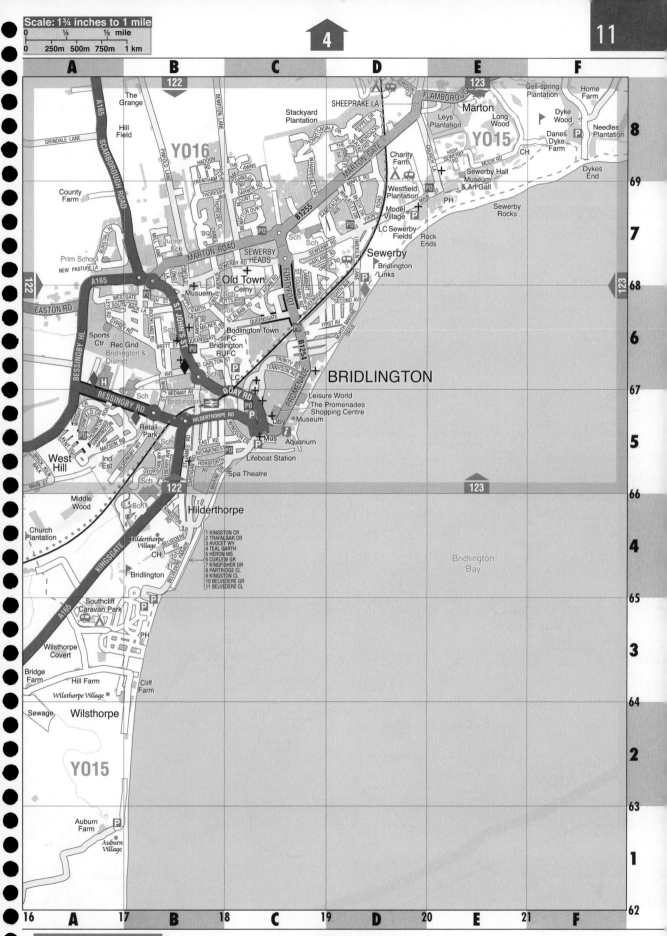

Scale: 1¾ inches to 1 mile

0   ¼   ½   mile
0   250m 500m 750m 1 km

A **B** **C** **D** **E** **F**

122

The Grange

Hill Field

GRINDALE LANE

County Farm

NEW PASTURE LA

Prim School

Y016

SCARBOROUGH ROAD

A165

EASTON RD

BESSINGBY HL

Sports Ctr

Rec Gnd
Bridlington & District

H

BESSINGBY RD

West Hill

BRICK KILN

MAIN ST

WRIGHT CR

CORNFIELD CR

HARRINGTON
MATSON RD

Ind Est

KENT RD

Sch

Retail Park

Sch

122

Middle Wood

Church Plantation

KINGSGATE

Hilderthorpe Village

CH

Bridlington

A165

Southcliff
Caravan Park

PH

Wilsthorpe Covert

Bridge Farm

Hill Farm

Wilsthorpe Village

Sewage

Wilsthorpe

Y015

Auburn Farm

P

Auburn Village

MARTON ROAD

SEWERBY HEADS

Old Town

Musuem

Cemy

Coll

Bridlington Town FC

Bridlington RUFC

Junior Sch

Sch

HIGH ST

ST JOHN'S ST

QUEENSGATE

Sch

P
LC

Sch

Sch

Bridlington

MIDWAY AV

QUAY RD

Sch

EAST RD

WINDSOR CR

HILDERTHORPE RD

P
PO

Liby

Mus

P

Aquarium

Lifeboat Station

Spa Theatre

HORSFORTH AV

RICHMOND ST

ST JAMES RD

CARDIGAN RD

GEORGE ST

MARINE DR

TERRY AV

Sch

Hilderthorpe

KINGSTON RD

BELVEDERE RD

BELVEDERE PARADE

1 KINGSTON CR
2 TRAFALGAR CR
3 AVOCET WY
4 TEAL GARTH
5 HERON MS
6 CURLEW GR
7 KINGFISHER DR
8 PARTRIDGE CL
9 KINGSTON CL
10 BELVEDERE GR
11 BELVEDERE CL

Cliff Farm

SHEEPRAKE LA

Stackyard Plantation

B1255

THORNDALE DR

MARTON GATE

MAPLE RD

VIKING RD

SEWERBY RD

HARLAND RD

LIMEKILN LANE

OMEGA RD

SANDSACRE AVE

Charity Farm

Westfield Plantation

Model Village

P

LC Sewerby Fields

Sewerby

Bridlington Links

P

FORTYFOOT

ST COLUMBA RD

LAMBERT RD

QUEENSGATE

FIRST AV

NORTH MARINE DRIVE

EIGHTH AVE

SECOND AV

TRINITY RD

TENNYSON AVE

B1254

PROMENADE

BRIDLINGTON

Leisure World

The Promenades
Shopping Centre

Museum

123

FLAMBOROUGH

Marton

Leys Plantation

Long Wood

Y015

HIGH SEWERBY RD

MOOR RD

Sewerby Hall
Museum & Art Gall

CH

PH

Sewerby Rocks

Rock Ends

Gell-spring
Plantation

Dyke Wood

P

Danes Dyke Farm

Home Farm

Needles Plantation

Dykes End

123

Bridlington Bay

16 **A** **17** **B** **18** **C** **19** **D** **20** **E** **21** **F**

8
69
7
68
6
67
5
66
4
65
3
64
2
63
1
62

For full street detail of the
highlighted area see pages
122 and 123.

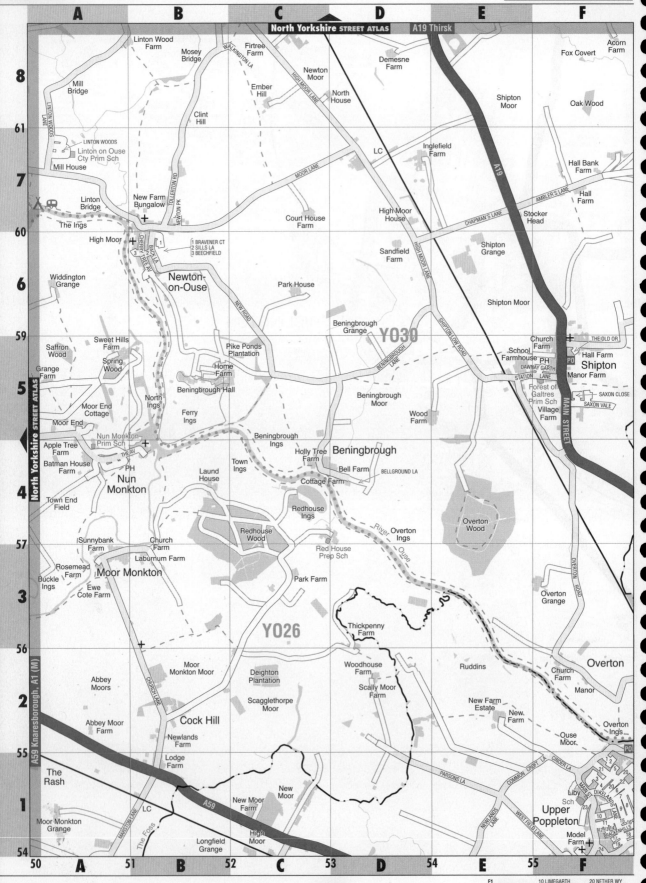

Scale: 1¾ inches to 1 mile

North Yorkshire STREET ATLAS

A19 Thirsk

North Yorkshire STREET ATLAS

A59 Knaresborough, A1(M)

YO30

YO26

Linton Wood Farm
Mosey Bridge
Firtree Farm
Newton Moor
Demesne Farm
Fox Covert
Acorn Farm
Mill Bridge
Ember Hill
North House
Shipton Moor
Oak Wood
Clint Hill
Linton Woods
Linton on Ouse Cty Prim Sch
LC
Inglefield Farm
Hall Bank Farm
Mill House
Moor Lane
Hall Farm
Linton Bridge
New Farm Bungalow
High Moor House
Ambler's Lane
Stocker Head
Chapman's Lane
The Ings
Court House Farm
High Moor
Newton-on-Ouse
1 BRAVENER CT
2 SILLS LA
3 BEECHFIELD
Park House
Sandfield Farm
Shipton Grange
Widdington Grange
Beningbrough Grange
Shipton Moor
Saffron Wood
Sweet Hills Farm
Pike Ponds Plantation
Church Farm
School Farmhouse
The Old Or
Hall Farm
Shipton
Grange Farm
Spring Wood
Home Farm
PH
PO
Manor Farm
Moor End Cottage
North Ings
Beningbrough Hall
Beningbrough Moor
Forest of Galtres Prim Sch
Saxon Close
Saxon Vale
Moor End
Ferry Ings
Wood Farm
Village Farm
Main Street
Apple Tree Farm
Nun Monkton Prim Sch
Beningbrough Ings
Holly Tree Farm
Beningbrough
Batman House Farm
PH
Nun Monkton
Town Ings
Laund House
Bell Farm
BELLGROUND LA
Town End Field
Cottage Farm
Overton Wood
Sunnybank Farm
Church Farm
Redhouse Ings
River Ouse
Overton Ings
Rosemead Farm
Laburnum Farm
Redhouse Wood
Red House Prep Sch
Buckle Ings
Moor Monkton
Park Farm
Overton Grange
Ewe Cote Farm
Thickpenny Farm
Overton
Moor Monkton Moor
Deighton Plantation
Woodhouse Farm
Ruddins
Church Farm
Manor
Abbey Moors
Scagglethorpe Moor
Scally Moor Farm
New Farm Estate
New Farm
Abbey Moor Farm
Cock Hill
Newlands Farm
New Farm
Overton Ings
Church Lane
Lodge Farm
Parsons La
Common Croft La
Cinder La
PO
The Rash
A59
New Moor Farm
New Moor
Newlands Lane
West Field Lane
Liby Sch
Upper Poppleton
Moor Monkton Grange
LC
High Moor
Model Farm
Longfield Grange
The Foss
Marston Lane

F1
1 RIVERSIDE WALK
2 RIVERSIDE GD
3 BANKSIDE CL
4 SPRINGFIELD RD
5 LITTLEFIELD CL
6 MONTAGUE WALK
7 EBOR WAY
8 PEAR TREE AV
9 ELM TREE AV
10 LIMEGARTH
11 CHANTRY GAP
12 GROVE GD
13 CHANTRY GR
14 CHANTRY AV
15 APPLE GARTH
16 CHERRY GROVE
17 SYCAMORE VIEW
18 FAIRWAY DR
19 DIKELANDS CL
20 NETHER WY
21 RIVERSVALE DR
22 ALLERTON DR
23 SCHOOL LA
24 STATION RD

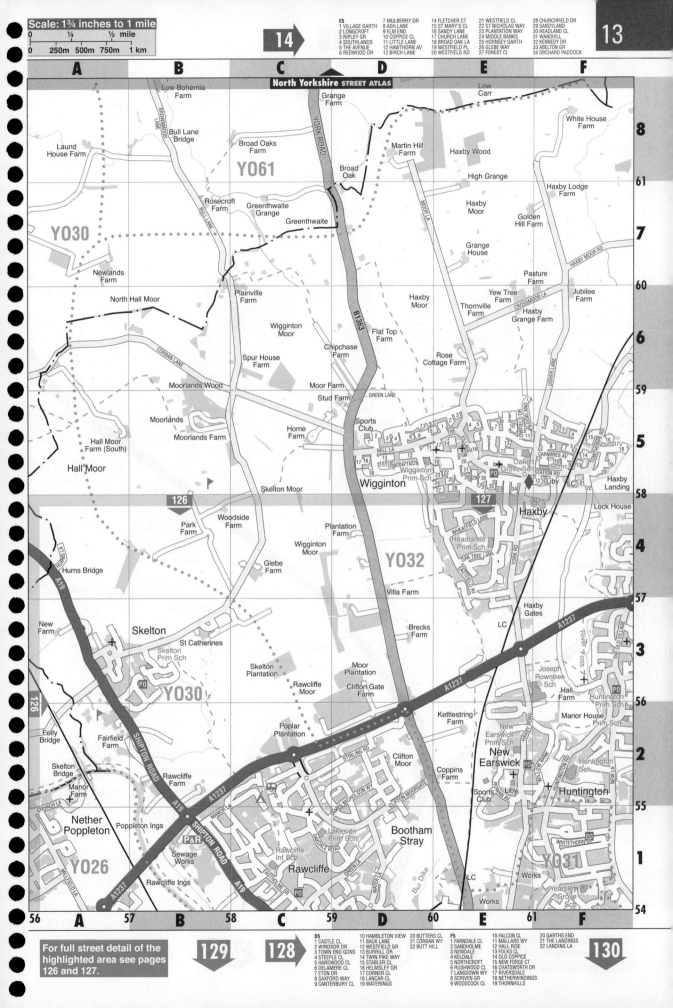

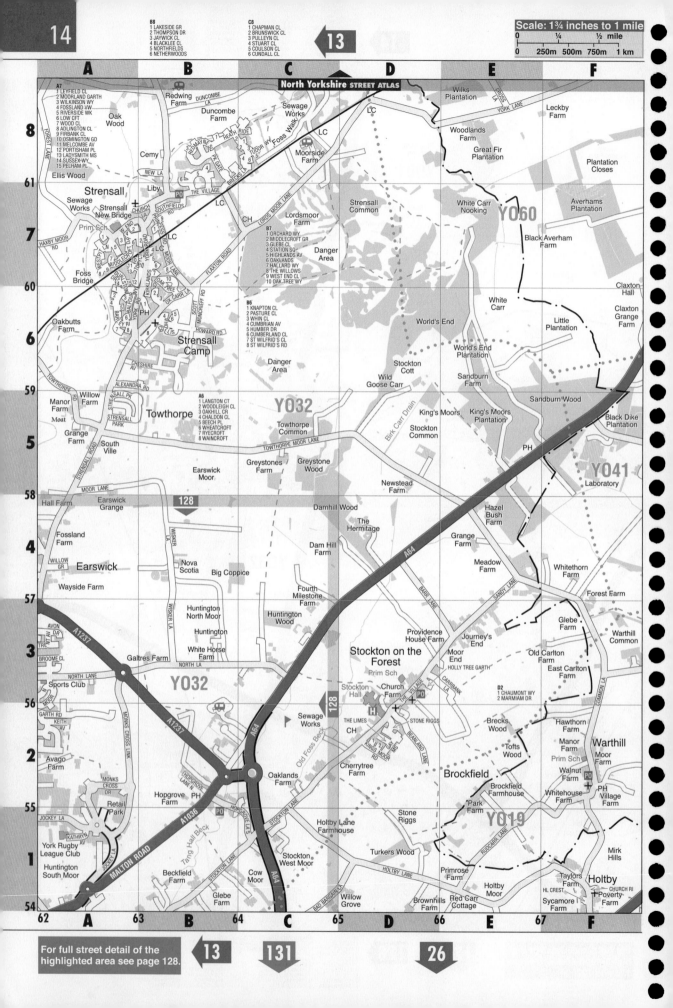

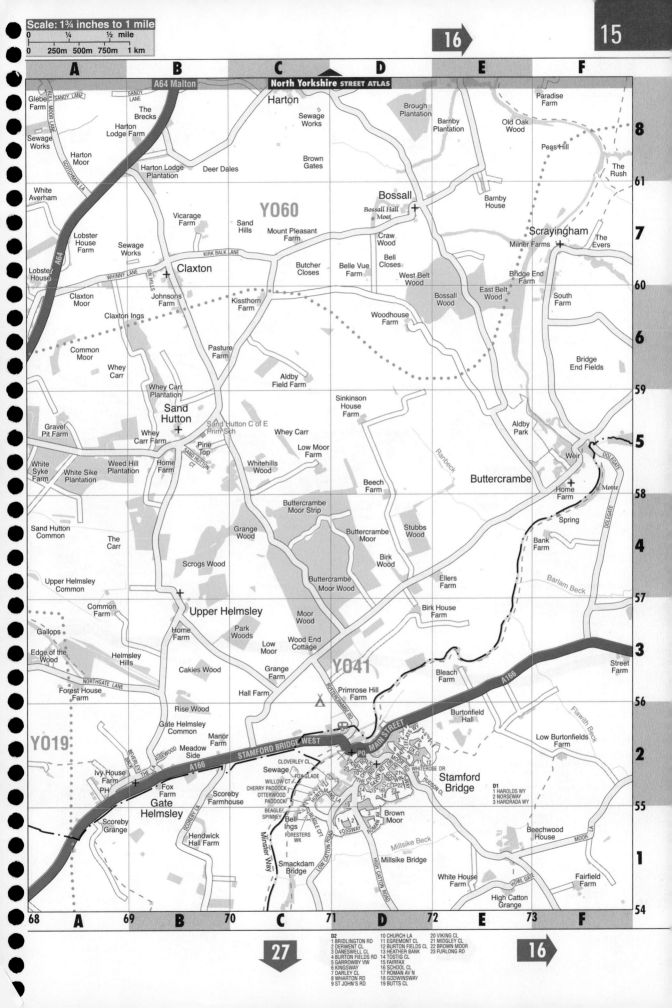

15

Scale: 1¾ inches to 1 mile
0 ¼ ½ mile
0 250m 500m 750m 1 km

North Yorkshire STREET ATLAS

A B C D E F

YO60

Low Ground Farm
The Farm
Whitecarr Beck
Plaster Pitts Farm
Hanging Cliffs
Poplar Farm
Ivy House Farm
Leppington Wood
Acklam Lodge
Wood Farm
Acklam
Acklam Wold Farm
Thuissendale Road
PH
Penty Wood
Highfield Farm
Spring Head
Manor Farm
Acklam Wold
Deepdale Spring
Deep Dale
Leppington
Manor Farm
Motte & Bailey
Pasture Hill Farm
Beckhouse Farm

8

Acres Lane
Low Field
Leppington Beck
Scrayingham Grange
Buskhill Plantation
Busk Hill
High Farm

YO17

Back Warren Plantation
Acklam Ings

61

Caradike Hill
Lowfield Lane
Dennings Plantation
Denn Ings
High Farm
High Sleights Farm

7

Kirk Gates
Wheathills Farm
Barthorpe Lodge Farm
Barthorpe Grange
Lower Sleights Farm
Sleights Lane
Greets Hill
Pasture Hill

60

Swallowpits Beck
Rush Hill
Low Farm
Bottoms Head
Gilder Beck
Baffham Plantation

6

Pasture Farm
Far Hillside Plantation
Baffham Farm
Salamanca Beck
East Ings
Bugthorpe La

59

Bridge End Fields
Bleaberry Lane
West Wood
Beck Plantation
Gorman Castle
Glebe Farm
Pasture Farm
Bugthorpe La Town E

Howl Beck
The Leys
Bugthorpe Grange
Thoralby Hall
Stubb's Plantation
Longhowes Plantation
Primrose Hill
Primrose Farm

YO41

5

Moat
Moat Farm

High Pasture Hill
Grange Plantation
Haybridge Mill Farm
Moat
Church Farm
PO
Bugthorpe
HIGH ROW
Lilac Farm
Preserve Plantation
Cheesecake House

58

Stephenwath La
Corner Farm
Minnees Plantation
Garden Plantation
Garrowby Hall

4

Manor House
PO
Doe Pk La
Haybridge Mill Farm
Bugthorpe Beck
Barf Lane
Barf Plantation
Home Farm
Ash Plantation
Old Wood

Skirpenbeck
Skirpen Beck
Crow Wood
Bluepaling Plantation
Garrowby Hill Plantation

57

Wallbank Farm
Poplar Farm
West Croft Farm
Broad Ings
West Ings
Keldsike Plantation
Garrowby Lodge
Garrowby Hill

Clayhill Plantation
Brickyard Farm
Clay Hill
A166
Kitty Hill (Tumuli)
Lodge Farm
Kitty Hill
GARROWBY STREET
GARROWBY HL
Garrowby Hill

3

A166
Jubilee Plantation
North Hill
North Field
Rush Plantation

56

Full Sutton
Grange Cl
Glebe Farm
Manor Farm
Clay Farm
Manor Farm
Awnhams Bridge
Vale Cr
Worsendale La
Bishop Wilton

2

Hart Hill Cr
Corner Farm
Moor Lane
Manor House Farm
Yew Tree Farm
White Cross Wy
Holly Cl
Kirklands Lane
East Farm
Youlthorpe
Awnhams Lane
Fox Covert
Bray Gate
Ings Lane
Moat
PO
PH
Park

Moor Lane
Glebe Ave
HM Prison
Pasture Farm
Youlthorpe Pasture Hill Farm
Providence Farm
Willow Tree Farm
Gowthorpe Farm
Grange Farm
Cautley Farm

YO42

South La
Park La Cl

55

Hatkel Lane
Highfield
Gowthorpe
Tynewood Farm
Gowthorpe
Belthorpe Lane
Bolton Lane
Thorny Lane

1

Airstrip (Disused)
Industrial Estate
Common La
The Flats
Belthorpe Whin
High Belthorpe

54

74 A 75 B 76 C 77 D 78 E 79 F

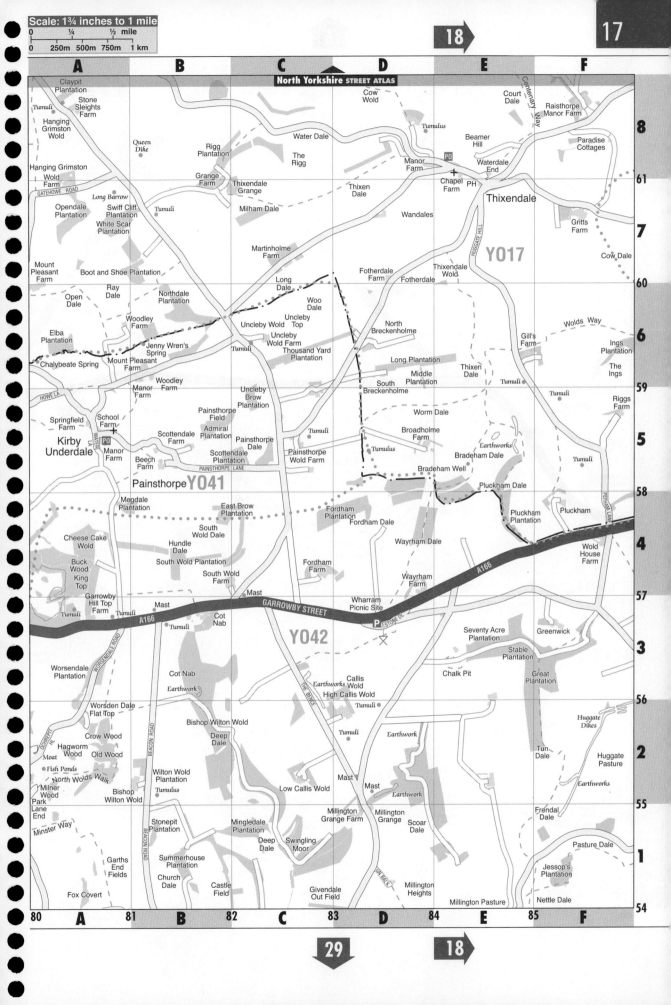

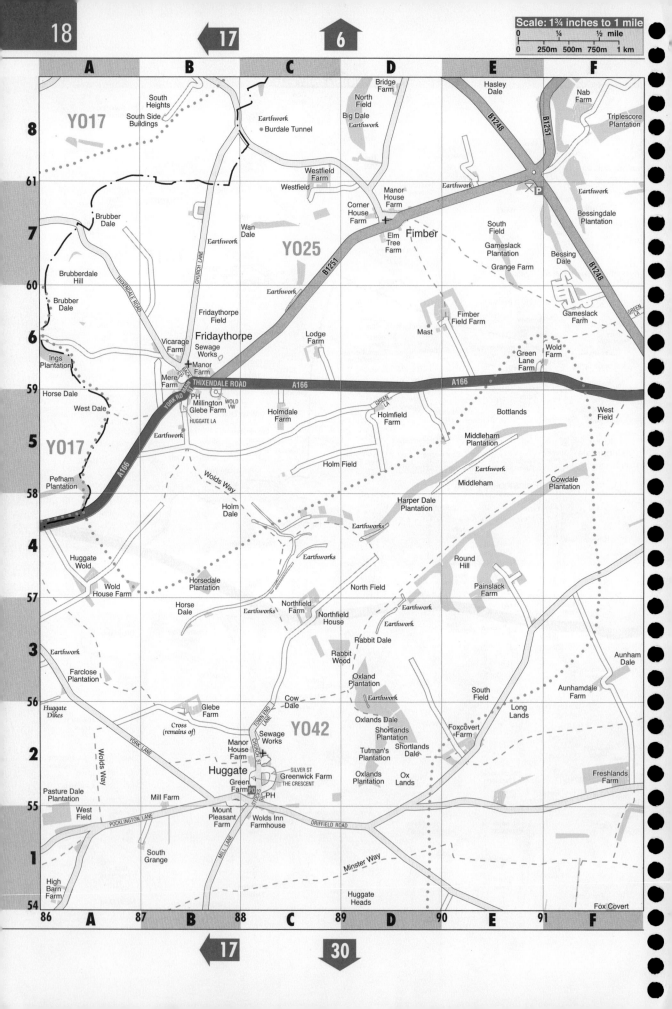

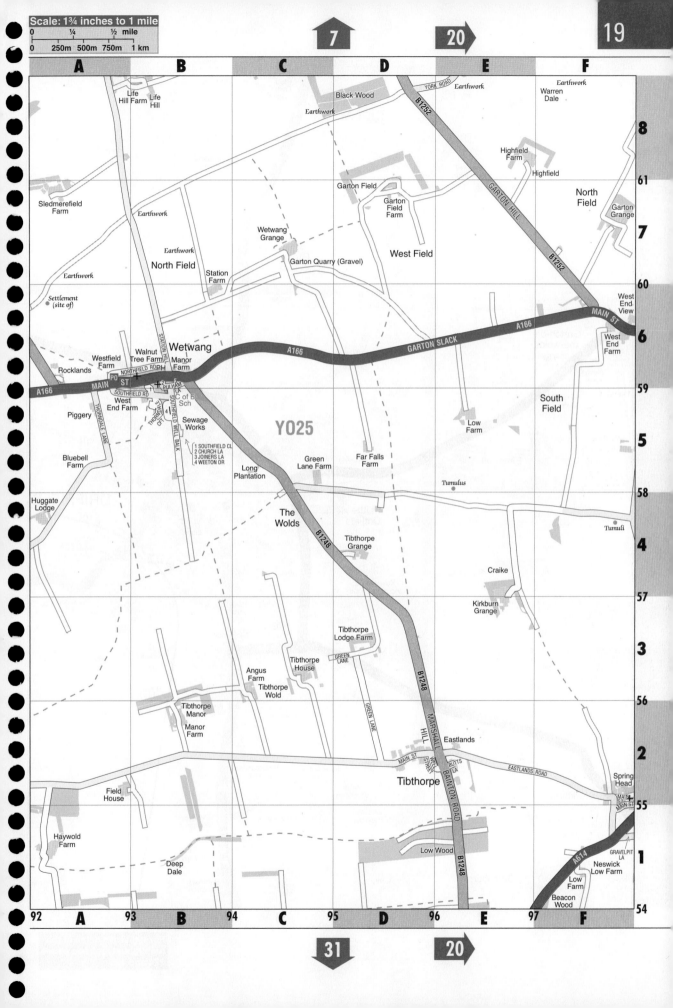

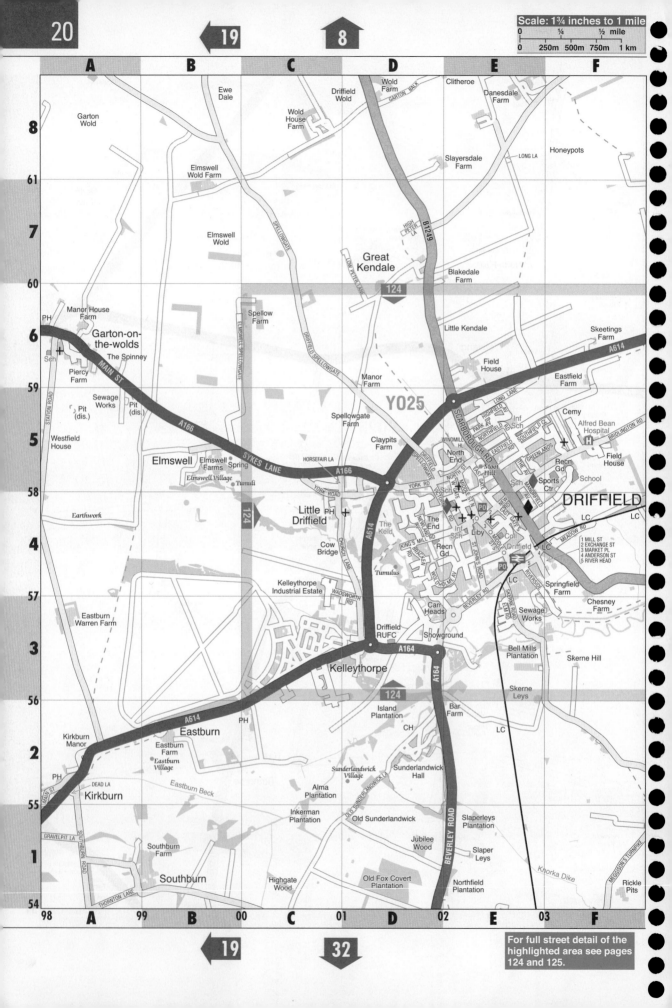

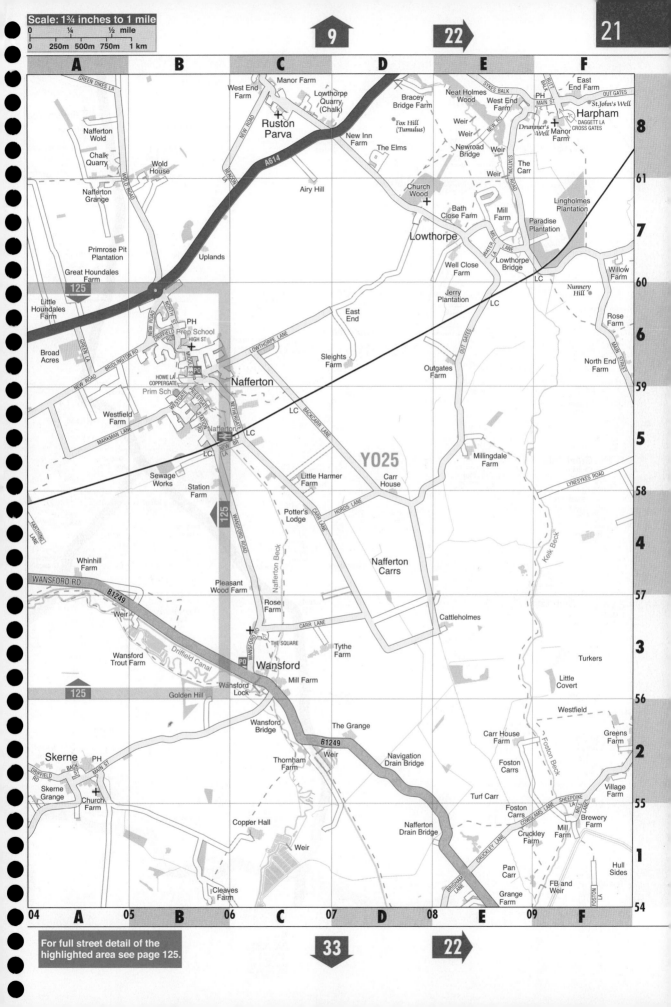

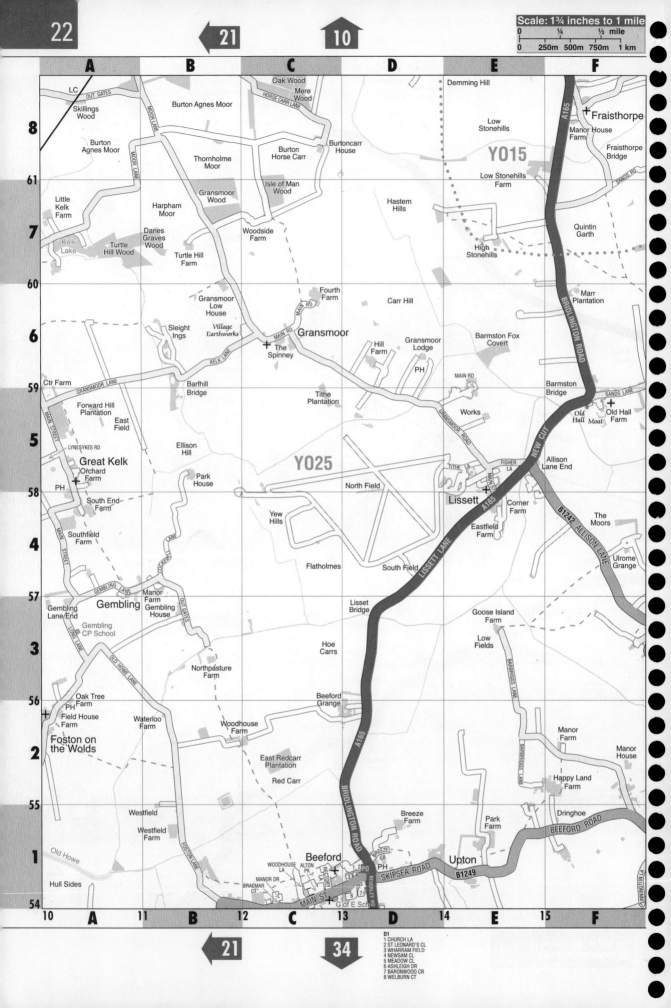

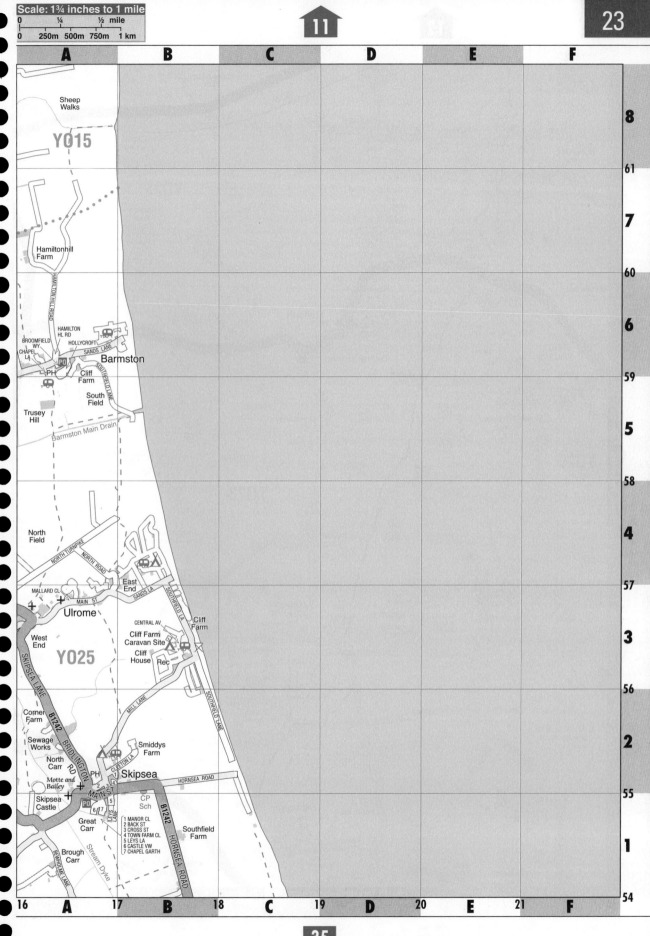

Scale: 1¾ inches to 1 mile

0 ¼ ½ mile
0 250m 500m 750m 1 km

A B C D E F

8
61
7
60
6
59
5
58
4
57
3
56
2
55
1
54

Sheep Walks

YO15

Hamiltonhill Farm

HAMILTON HILL ROAD

HAMILTON HL RD
BROOMFIELD WY
CHAPEL LA
HOLLYCROFT
SANDS LANE
PH Barmston
Cliff Farm
SOUTHFIELD LANE
South Field
Trusey Hill
Barmston Main Drain

North Field

NORTH TURNPIKE
NORTH ROAD
East End
SANDS LA
SOUTHFIELD LA
MALLARD CL
MAIN ST
Ulrome
CENTRAL AV
Cliff Farm
West End
YO25
Cliff Farm Caravan Site
Cliff House
Rec
SOUTHFIELD LANE
MILL LANE

SKIPSEA LANE
Corner Farm
B1242
BRIDLINGTON RD
Sewage Works
North Carr
Smiddys Farm
PH Skipsea
HORNSEA ROAD
Motte and Bailey
Skipsea Castle
PO
Great Carr
CLEETON LA
CP Sch
B1242
HORNSEA ROAD
Southfield Farm

1 MANOR CL
2 BACK ST
3 CROSS ST
4 TOWN FARM CL
5 LEYS LA
6 CASTLE VW
7 CHAPEL GARTH

Brough Carr
BEWHOLME LANE
Stream Dyke

16 A 17 B 18 C 19 D 20 E 21 F

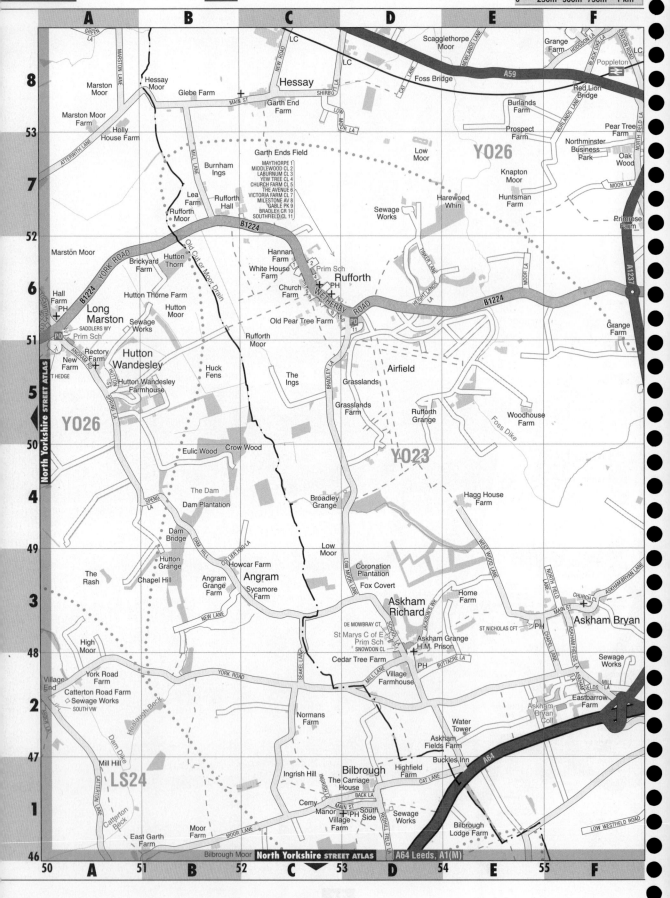

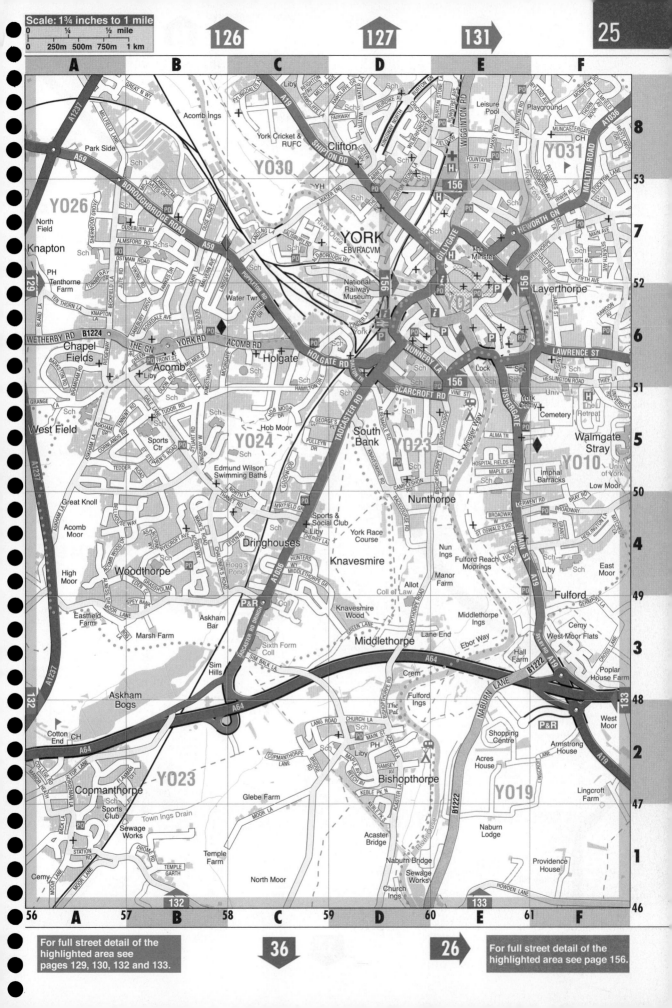

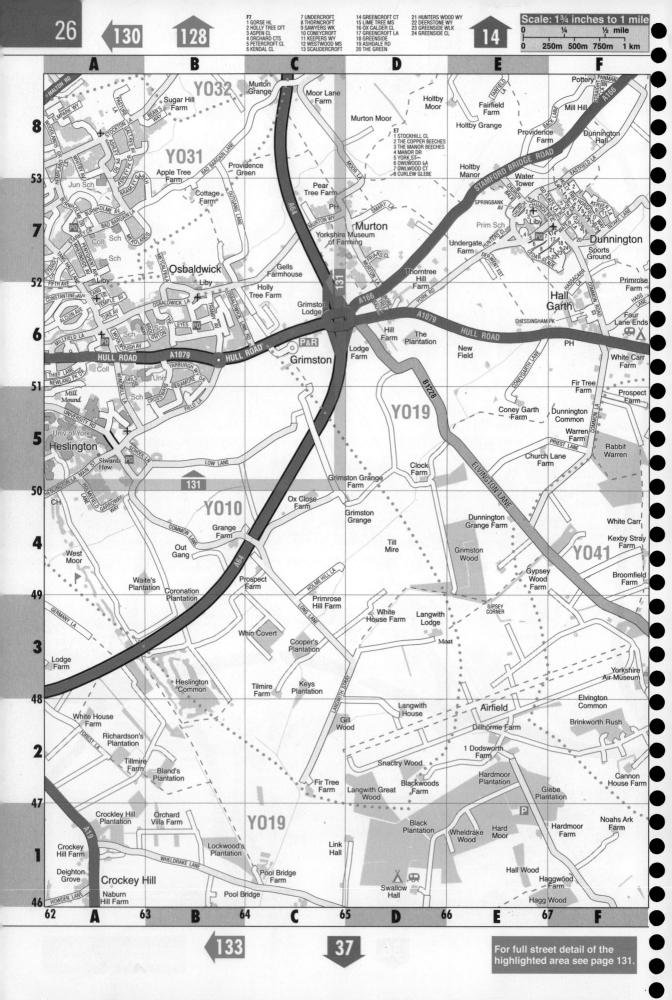

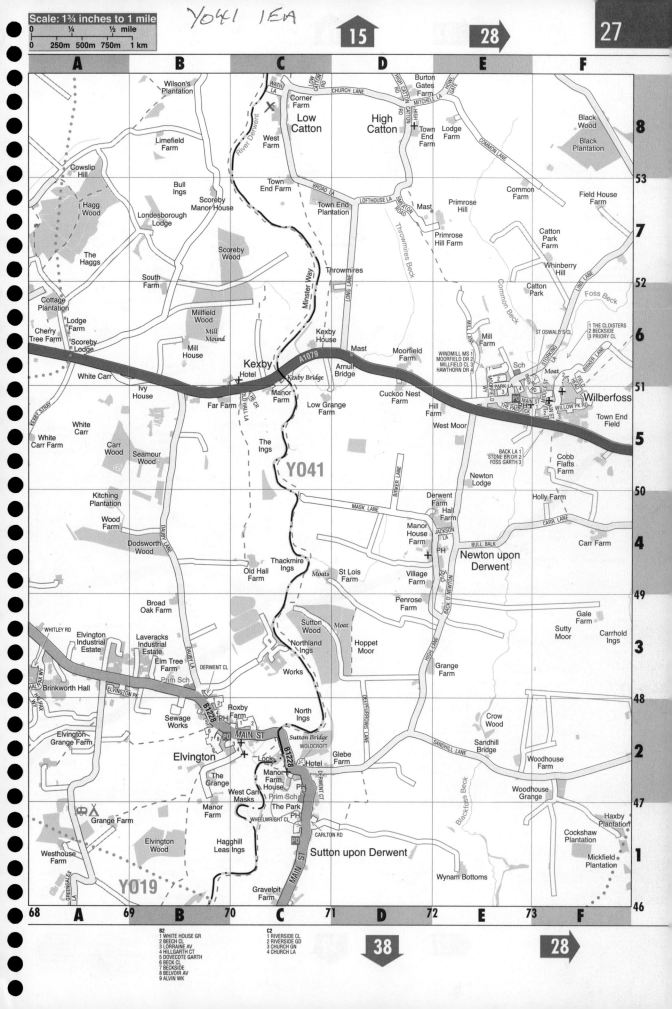

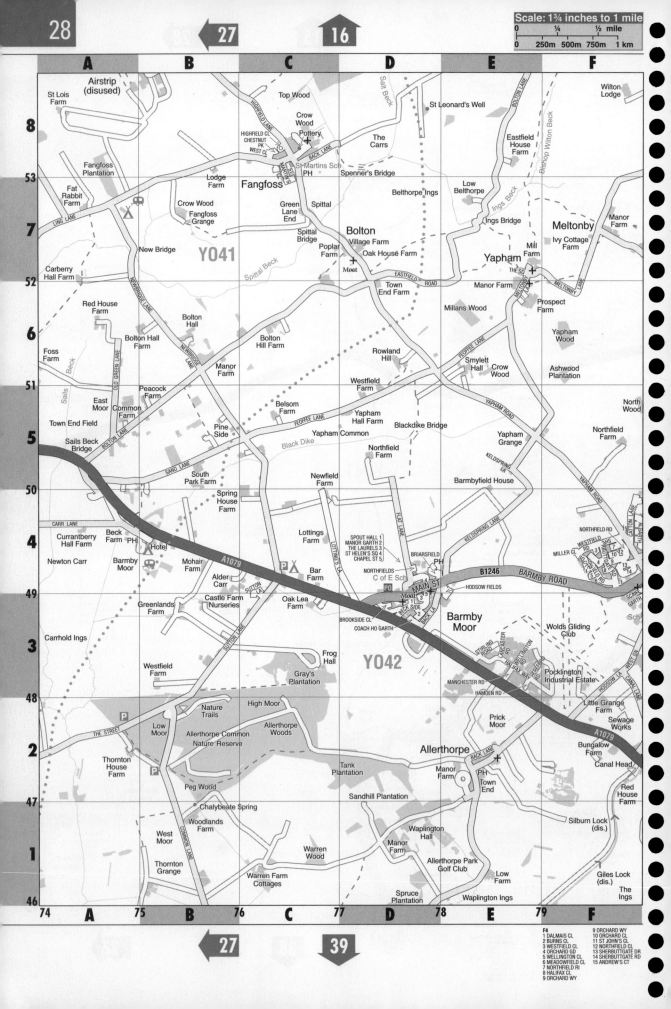

Scale: 1¾ inches to 1 mile
0   ¼   ½   mile
0   250m 500m 750m 1 km

St Lois Farm
Airstrip (disused)
Top Wood
Crow Wood
St Leonard's Well
Wilton Lodge

Fangfoss Plantation
Fat Rabbit Farm
HIGHFIELD CL
CHESTNUT PK
WEST CL
Pottery
The Carrs
Eastfield House Farm

Lodge Farm
Fangfoss
St Martins Sch PH
Spenner's Bridge
Belthorpe Ings
Low Belthorpe
Meltonby

Crow Wood
Fangfoss Grange
Green Lane End
Spittal
Bolton Village Farm
Ings Bridge
Ivy Cottage Farm
Manor Farm

YO41
New Bridge
Spittal Bridge
Poplar Farm
Oak House Farm
Yapham
Mill Farm
THE SQ

Carberry Hall Farm
Moat
EASTFIELD ROAD
Manor Farm
Prospect Farm

Red House Farm
Bolton Hall
Town End Farm
Millans Wood
Yapham Wood

Foss Farm
Bolton Hall Farm
Bolton Hill Farm
Rowland Hill
Smylett Hall
Crow Wood
Ashwood Plantation

Sails Beck
East Moor
Peacock Farm
Common Farm
Manor Farm
Westfield Farm
FEOFFEE LANE

Town End Field
Pine Side
Belsom Farm
Yapham Hall Farm
Yapham Common
Blackdike Bridge
Yapham Grange
North Wood

Sails Beck Bridge
Black Dike
Yapham Common
Northfield Farm
KELDSPRING LA
Northfield Farm

South Park Farm
SAND LANE
Newfield Farm
Barmbyfield House
YAPHAM ROAD

Spring House Farm
Lottings Farm
SPOUT HALL 1
MANOR GARTH 2
THE LAURELS 3
ST HELEN'S SQ 4
CHAPEL ST 5
Briarsfield
NORTHFIELD RD
WESTFIELD RD
MILLER CL

Currantberry Hall Farm
Beck Farm
PH
Hotel
Mohair Farm
Bar Farm
NORTHFIELDS
C of E Sch
PH
B1246
BARMBY ROAD

Newton Carr
Barmby Moor
Alder Carr
Oak Lea Farm
PO
MAIN ST
HODSOW FIELDS

Greenlands Farm
Castle Farm Nurseries
Moat
BECK SIDE
BACK LA
Barmby Moor
Wolds Gliding Club

Carrhold Ings
Westfield Farm
Frog Hall
Gray's Plantation
YO42
STIRLING ROAD
LANCASTER RD
WELLINGTON RD
HALIFAX WAY
Pocklington Industrial Estate

CARR LANE
THE STREET
Low Moor
Nature Trails
High Moor
MANCHESTER RD
HAMDEN RD
Little Grange Farm
Sewage Works

Thornton House Farm
Allerthorpe Common Nature Reserve
Allerthorpe Woods
Prick Moor
A1079
Bungalow Farm

Peg Wood
Tank Plantation
Allerthorpe
Manor Farm
PH
Town End
Canal Head

Chalybeate Spring
Sandhill Plantation
Red House Farm
Silburn Lock (dis.)

Woodlands Farm
West Moor
Warren Wood
Manor Farm
Waplington Hall
Allerthorpe Park Golf Club
Low Farm

Thornton Grange
Warren Farm Cottages
Spruce Plantation
Waplington Ings
Giles Lock (dis.)
The Ings

F4
1 DALMAIS CL
2 BURNS CL
3 WESTFIELD CL
4 ORCHARD GD
5 WELLINGTON CL
6 MEADOWFIELD CL
7 NORTHFIELD RI
8 HALIFAX CL
9 ORCHARD WY
9 ORCHARD WY
10 ORCHARD CL
11 ST JOHN'S CL
12 NORTHFIELD CL
13 SHERBUTTGATE DR
14 SHERBUTTGATE RD
15 ANDREW'S CT

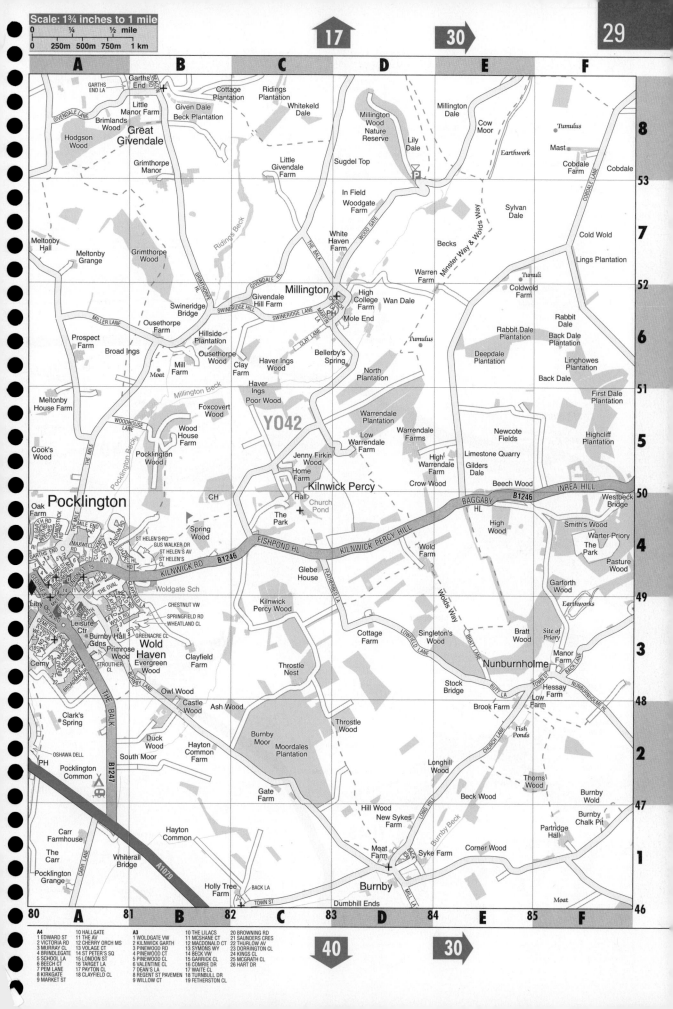

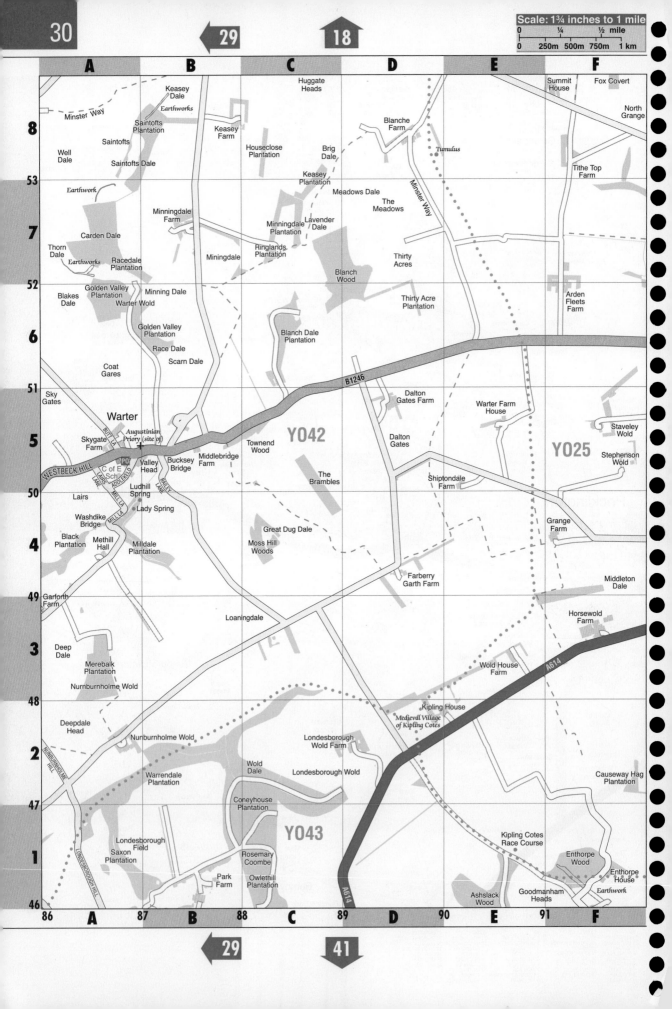

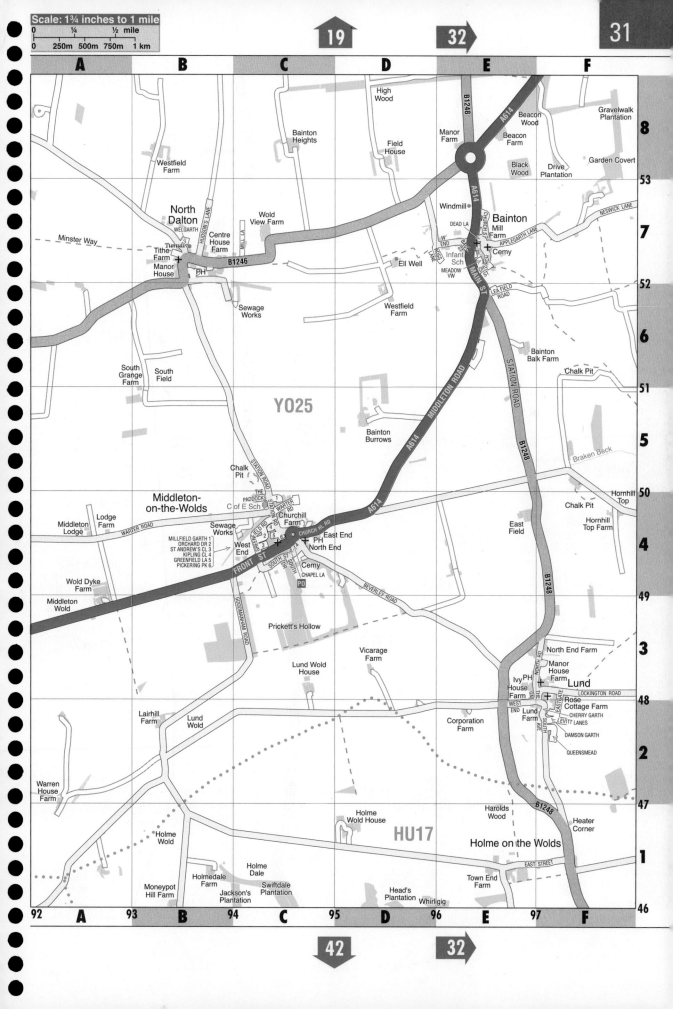

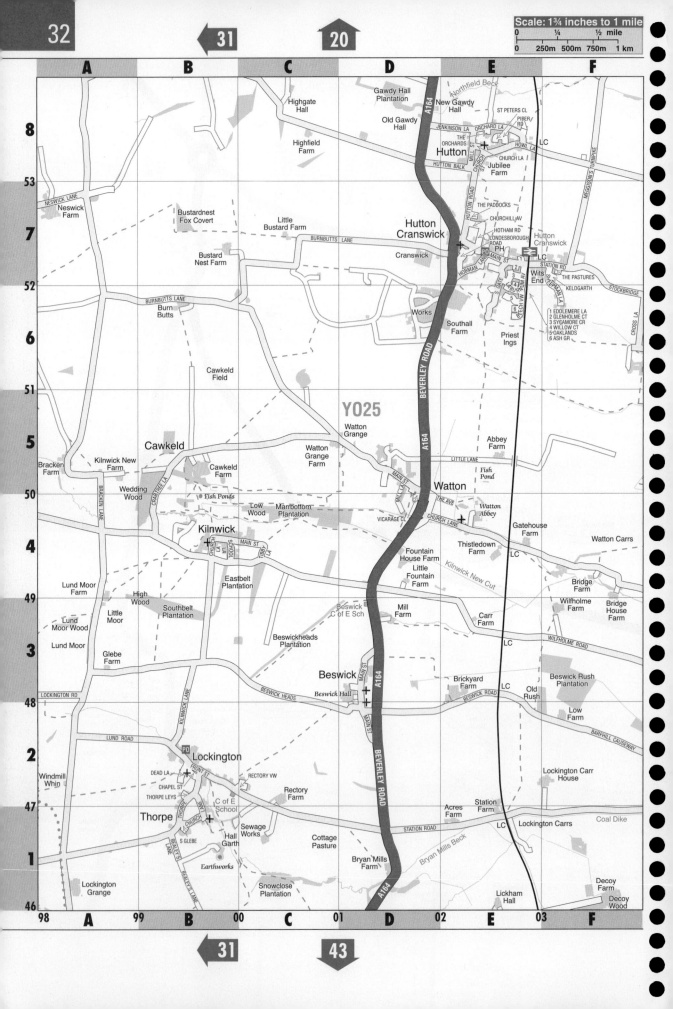

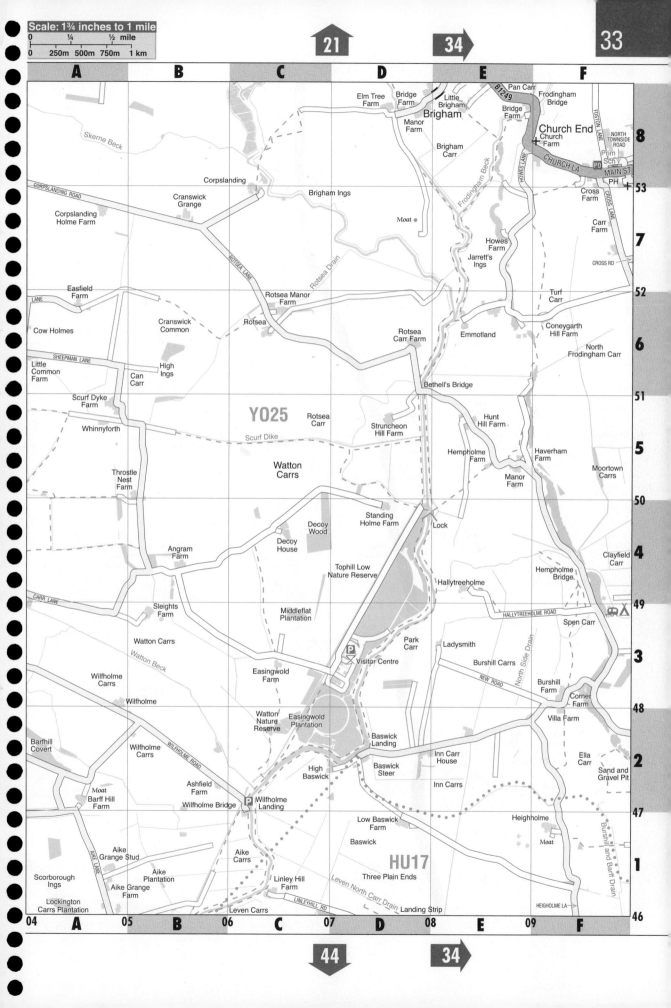

A   B   C   D   E   F

Hull Sides

NORTH TOWNSIDE RD

8 North Frodingham

Inholms Farm

WESTFIELD RISE

Braemar Ct

PARKLANDS

BEVERLEY ROAD

Syke Farm

Dunnington Grange

DUNNINGTON LANE

HIGH SIDE

PH
B1249   MAIN ST   BRIDLINGTON BALK

SOUTH TOWNSIDE RD   EASTFIELD CL

N FRODINGHAM RD

B1249

Bridge Farm

Wisefield Farm

53

Southfield Farm

DUNNINGTON LANE

MOUNT PLEASANT ROAD

7 Eastfield Farm

Manor Farm

Dunnington

CROSS RD

Mount Pleasant Farm

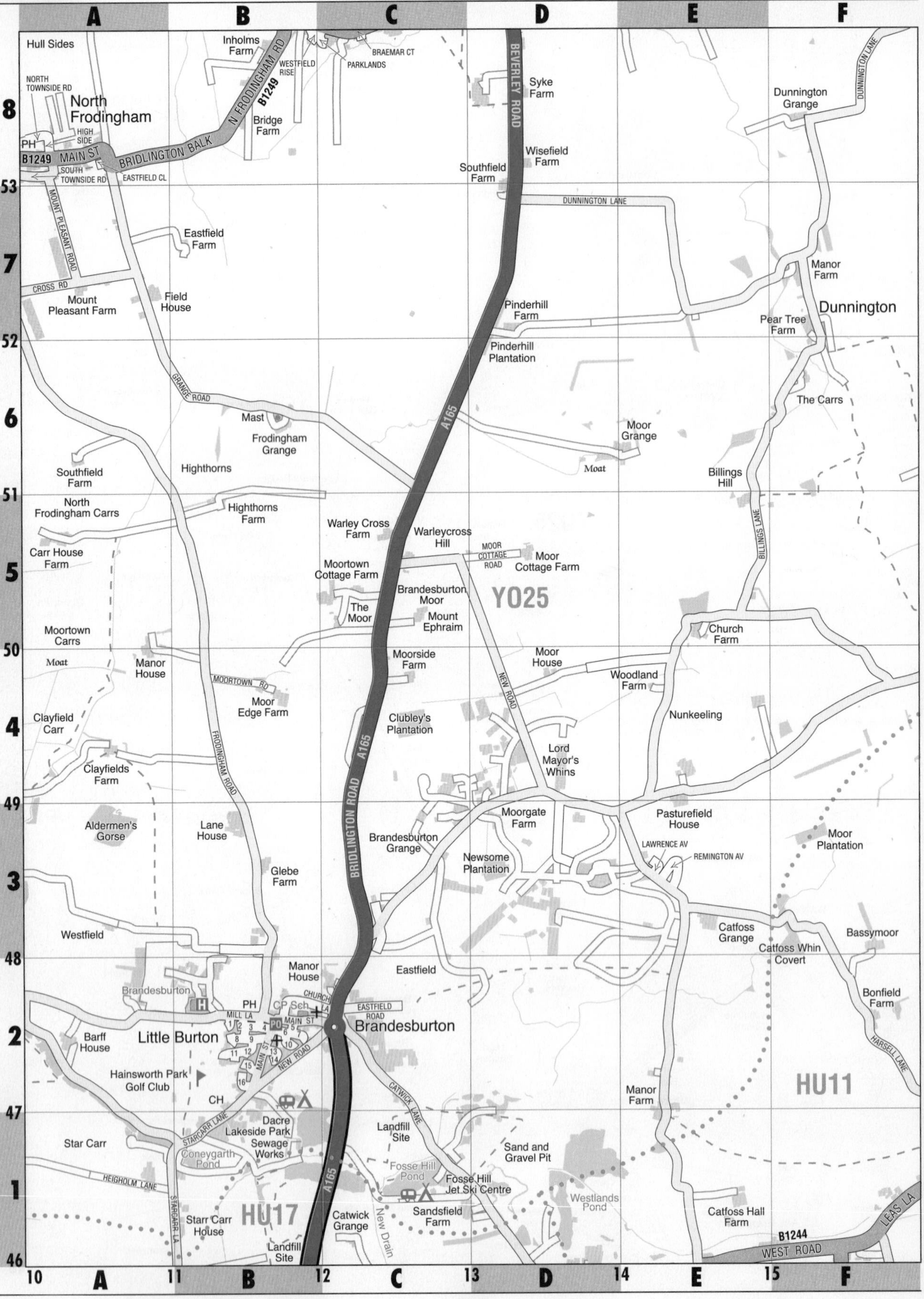

Field House

GRANGE ROAD

Pinderhill Farm

Pear Tree Farm

BILLINGS LANE

52

Pinderhill Plantation

6 Mast

Frodingham Grange

Highthorns

The Carrs

A165

Moor Grange

Moat

Southfield Farm

Billings Hill

51 North Frodingham Carrs

Highthorns Farm

Warley Cross Farm

Warleycross Hill

MOOR COTTAGE ROAD

Moor Cottage Farm

Carr House Farm

Moortown Cottage Farm

5

YO25

Church Farm

Moortown Carrs

The Moor

Brandesburton Moor

Mount Ephraim

Moor House

Moat

Manor House

MOORTOWN RD

Moorside Farm

Woodland Farm

50

FRODINGHAM ROAD

Moor Edge Farm

Nunkeeling

Clayfield Carr

Clubley's Plantation

4

A165

Clayfields Farm

Lane House

Lord Mayor's Whins

Aldermen's Gorse

Moorgate Farm

Pasturefield House

Moor Plantation

49

BRIDLINGTON ROAD

Glebe Farm

Brandesburton Grange

LAWRENCE AV

REMINGTON AV

3

Newsome Plantation

NEW ROAD

Westfield

Catfoss Grange

Bassymoor

Catfoss Whin Covert

48

Brandesburton

H

Manor House

CHURCH LA

Eastfield

Bonfield Farm

Barff House

PH

CP Sch

EASTFIELD ROAD

Manor Farm

HARSELL LANE

2 Little Burton

MILL LA

PO

MAIN ST

Brandesburton

HU11

Hainsworth Park Golf Club

CH

CATWICK LANE

47

Dacre Lakeside Park

Landfill Site

Sewage Works

STARCARR LANE

Sand and Gravel Pit

Star Carr

Coneygarth Pond

Fosse Hill Pond

Fosse Hill Jet Ski Centre

Westlands Pond

Catfoss Hall Farm

1

HEIGHOLM LANE

A165

Sandsfield Farm

B1244

LEAS LA

STARCARR LA

HU17

Starr Carr House

Catwick Grange

New Drain

WEST ROAD

46

Landfill Site

10   A   11   B   12   C   13   D   14   E   15   F

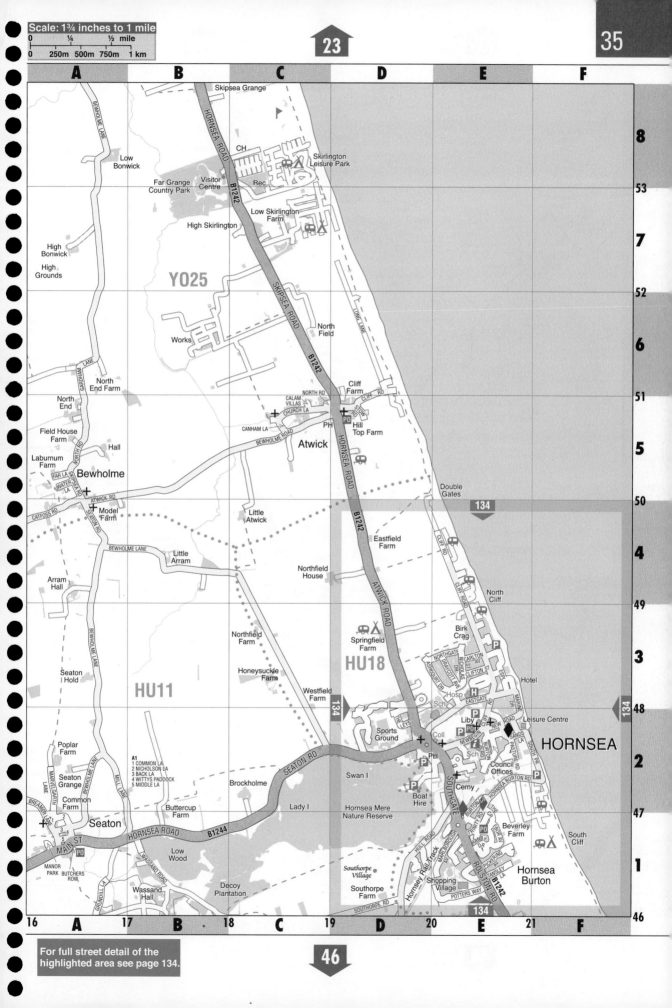

Scale: 1¾ inches to 1 mile

| 0 | ¼ | ½ mile |
| 0 | 250m 500m 750m | 1 km |

A   B   C   D   E   F

8

53

7

52

6

51

5

50

4

49

3

48

2

47

1

46

Skipsea Grange

CH

Skirlington Leisure Park

Far Grange Country Park

Visitor Centre

Rec

Low Skirlington Farm

High Skirlington

Low Bonwick

High Bonwick

High Grounds

YO25

Works

North Field

LONG LANE

North End Farm

GARDHAM LANE

North End

Cliff Farm

CLIFF RD

North RD

CALAM VILLAS

CHURCH LA

Field House Farm

Hall

CANHAM LA

Laburnum Farm

BEWHOLME ROAD

PH

PO

SEATON RD

Atwick

Hill Top Farm

FAR LA

WATER LA

Bewholme

ATWICK RD

Model Farm

Little Atwick

HORNSEA ROAD

Double Gates

134

CATFOSS RD

Eastfield Farm

CLIFF RD

North Cliff

BEWHOLME LANE

Little Arram

Northfield House

B1242

ATWICK ROAD

Arram Hall

Northfield Farm

Springfield Farm

HU18

Birk Crag

P

NORTHGATE

CARLTON AV

DRAYCOTT LANE

CLIFTON ST

Seaton Hold

Honeysuckle Farm

ASHCOURT DR

Hotel

HU11

Westfield Farm

134

Hosp

H

Sch

EASTGATE

ESPL

MARINE DR

Poplar Farm

MILL LANE

Sports Ground

THE LEYS

Coll

Liby

PO

P

SANDS

NEWBEGIN

Leisure Centre

A1
1 COMMON LA
2 NICHOLSON LA
3 BACK LA
4 WITTYS PADDOCK
5 MIDDLE LA

BEWHOLME LANE

MARKET PLACE

Seaton Grange

Brockholme

Swan I

PH

Sch

NEW

HORNSEA

PASTURE RD

BURTON

Council Offices

Common Farm

SOUTHGATE

Cemy

SOUTH PR

BREAMER LA

Buttercup Farm

Lady I

Boat Hire

Hornsea Mere Nature Reserve

THE

Beverley Farm

South Cliff

GRUNDILL LA

Seaton

HORNSEA ROAD

B1244

Low Wood

HULL ROAD

Hornsea Rail Track

MARLBOROUGH AV

Southorpe Village

TRINITY RD

RANBY

PICKERING LA

TANSLEY LA

Hornsea Burton

MAIN ST

PO

Manor Park

BUTCHERS ROW

WASSAND ROAD

Decoy Plantation

Southorpe Farm

Shopping Village

POTTERS WAY

FOLSTON RD

B1242

Wassand Hall

SOUTHORPE RD

134

134

16   A   17   B   18   C   19   D   20   E   21   F   46

For full street detail of the highlighted area see page 134.

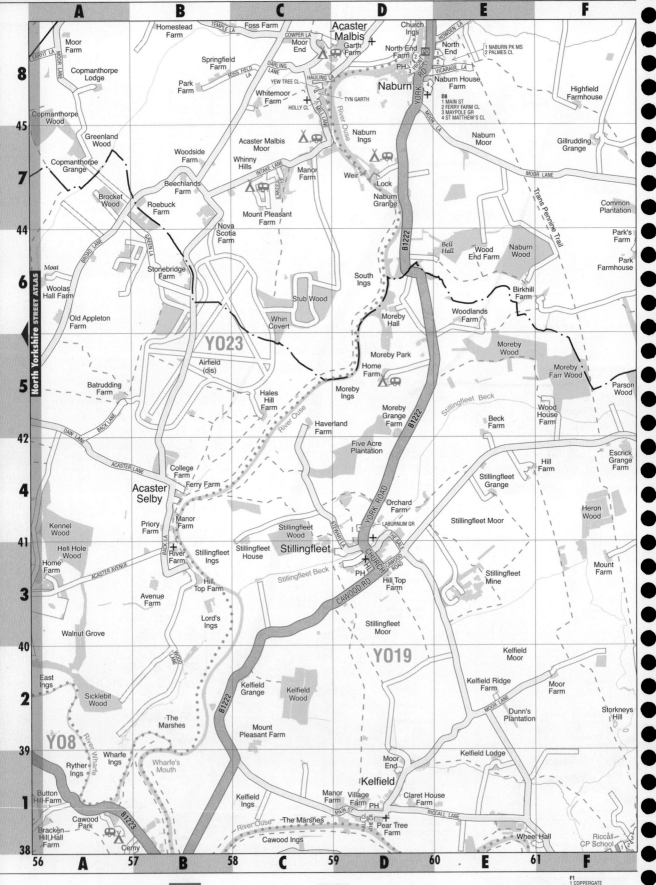

Scale: 1¾ inches to 1 mile

0   ¼   ½ mile

0 250m 500m 750m 1 km

North Yorkshire STREET ATLAS

A   B   C   D   E   F

8

45

7

44

6

5

42

4

41

3

40

2

39

1

38

Moor Farm

Copmanthorpe Lodge

Copmanthorpe Wood

Greenland Wood

Copmanthorpe Grange

Brocket Wood

Moat

Woolas Hall Farm

Old Appleton Farm

Batrudding Farm

Kennel Wood

Hell Hole Wood

Home Farm

Walnut Grove

East Ings

YO8

Ryther Ings

Button Hill Farm

Bracken Hill Hall Farm

Cemy

Homestead Farm

Springfield Farm

Park Farm

Woodside Farm

Beechlands Farm

Roebuck Farm

Stonebridge Farm

Sicklebit Wood

The Marshes

Wharfe Ings

Wharfe's Mouth

Cawood Park

Foss Farm

Moor End

Whitemoor Farm

Holly Cl

Whinny Hills

Mount Pleasant Farm

Nova Scotia Farm

Whin Covert

Airfield (dis)

Hales Hill Farm

College Farm

Ferry Farm

Acaster Selby

Priory Farm

Manor Farm

River Farm

Stillingfleet Ings

Avenue Farm

Hill Top Farm

Lord's Ings

Kelfield Grange

Mount Pleasant Farm

Kelfield Ings

YO23

Acaster Malbis

Garth Farm

Moor End

Acaster Malbis Moor

Manor Farm

Weir

Naburn Ings

Lock

Naburn Grange

South Ings

Stub Wood

Moreby Hall

Moreby Park

Moreby Ings

Home Farm

Moreby Grange Farm

Haverland Farm

Five Acre Plantation

Stillingfleet Wood

Stillingfleet House

Stillingfleet

Stillingfleet Beck

Orchard Farm

Laburnum Gr

Hill Top Farm

Stillingfleet Moor

YO19

Kelfield Wood

Moor End

Kelfield

Manor Farm

Village Farm

The Marshes

Pear Tree Farm

Church Ings

North End Farm

North End

1 NABURN PK MS
2 PALMES CL

Naburn

Naburn House Farm

D8
1 MAIN ST
2 FERRY FARM CL
3 MAYPOLE GR
4 ST MATTHEW'S CL

Naburn Moor

Bell Hall

Wood End Farm

Naburn Wood

Woodlands Farm

Birkhill Farm

Moreby Wood

Beck Farm

Stillingfleet Grange

Stillingfleet Moor

Stillingfleet Mine

Kelfield Moor

Kelfield Ridge Farm

Dunn's Plantation

Kelfield Lodge

Moor End

Claret House Farm

Highfield Farmhouse

Gillrudding Grange

Common Plantation

Park's Farm

Park Farmhouse

Moreby Farr Wood

Parson Wood

Wood House Farm

Hill Farm

Escrick Grange Farm

Heron Wood

Mount Farm

Moor Farm

Storkneys Hill

Wheel Hall

Riccall CP School

B1222

YORK ROAD

CAWOOD RD

CHURCH

THE GALE

STEWART LA

MAIN ST

RICCALL LANE

MOOR LANE

B1222

WOOD LANE

B1223

River Ouse

River Wharfe

Trans Pennine Trail

MOOR LANE

F1
1 COPPERGATE
2 ELMS CL
3 NORTHFIELD LA

A   B   C   D   E   F

Kirk's Rein

Sparrow Hall Farm   Hagg Wood

THE CRANBROOKS 1
MOOR CL 2
BRAITHEGAYTE 3
RUFFHAMS CL 4
DERWENT DR 5
RAKER CL 6
HARCOURT CL 7
WALKER LA 8
DYKELANDS CL 9
LOW WELL PK 10

Poplar Tree Farm

Rush Farm

Wigman Wood   Wigman Hall

Gothic House Farm

West Plantation

Low Well Farm

Wheldrake   8

Wincover Farm

Primrose Farm

Benjy Lane   45

Pasture Farm

Deighton

Sheepwalk Farm

Wharren House Farm

Brick Farm

Tile Farm

Millfield Farm   7

Swan Farm CT

Long Wood

New Road

North Selby Mine

Lacy Bottom Wood

Orchard Farm

Main Street   44

Swan Farm

Swan CL

Spring House Farm

Spring Wood

The Bottoms

Wheldrake Wrayst

South End   South Ruddings Lane

Moat

PH

Mill Hill Farm

Chequer Hall

Gravel Pitt Hill

Wheldrake Grange

Keld Carrs   6

43

1 DOWER CHASE
2 SOUTHLANDS CL
3 ESCRICK CT
4 WOODLANDS
5 ESCRICK PK GD

Crab Tree Farm

Gilbertson's Wood

Escrick

The Carrs

Tileshed Farm

Common Bottom Farm   Common Lane

Glebe Farm

Gashouse Plantation

Wheldrake Lane

Common Bottom Wood   5

Escrick C of E Prim Sch

Bridge Farm

Millfield Plantation

Y019

Grey Reins

Common Farm

42

Moons Plantation

Queen Margarets School

Kennel Plantation

Manor Farm

South Moor

Old Road Plantation

Fox Covert Plantation

Escrick Park

Escrick Park Home Farm

Mount Pleasant Farm

Low Cover Wood

West Grange

Dogs Leg Wood

Horn Farm   Gale La   4

Harrop's Plantation

Aviary Plantation

Whinchat Hall

Works

Roth Hill Lane   41

Hackings Wood

Duck Hole Plantation

West End   Park Farm

Menagerie Farm

Bridge Farm

Thornhill Farm

Manor Wood

Thorganby Lodge   3

Glade Farm

Common Wood

Crook Moor

Hunt Pease Carrs   Glade Road

40

Sheds Bell Farm

Hollicarrs Wood

Charity Farm

Field House Farm

Manor Farm

West End Farm

Duffield Wood   2

Hart Nooking

Nightingale Wood

Broomhill Plantation

Y08

Danes Hills (Tumuli)

Red Moors

Hollicarrs CL

Rainbows End

Black Tom Hill

Rider's Plantation

Hill Farm

Crook Moor

Redmoor Farm

Approach Farm

Little Skipwith

School Farm

Little Common   39

Scorce Bridge

Anne's Plantation

Church Farm

Park Farm   PH

Town End

Skipwith

Plantation House   1

The Ings

Moat

Bluebell Farm

Peel Hall Farm

South Moor Hill   South Moor

62   A   63   B   64   C   65   D   66   E   67   F   38

A1
1 MILL LA
2 HOLMES DR
3 CHAPEL LA
4 CHAPEL WK
5 PINFOLD CL

A | B | C | D | E | F

Y041

C of E Prim Sch
Mount Pleasant
Cheesecake Farm
Gravelpit Plantation
Mayfield Grange Farm
Four Beck Ends
Sutton Rush
Eller Carr
The Carr
Town's Ings
BROADLANDS
GREENGALES CT
BLUE SLATES CL
Sutton Farm
Hagg Bridge
Hagg Bridge Farm
Storwood Carr
Rossmoor Grange
Rossmoor Farm
The Grange
Frogs Nest Farm
Westfield Farm
Wheldrake
The Carr
South Wood
Broomhill Plantation
Storwood Grange
MARROW LA
HAGG LANE
B1228
Rossmoor Lodge
Oakland Farm
Park Wood
Grove Farm
1 DALTON HL
2 KITTY GARTH
3 ST HELEN'S RI
4 CHURCH CL
INGS LANE
GATEHEAD LANE
Farm Wood
Storwood
White House Farm
BALLHALL LANE
Quakers' Wood
Eastroad Plantation
Suss Carrs
Old Course of the River Derwent
Moat
West Farm
Park House Farm
Stackyard Plantation
Mattie Brown Wood
Thicket Priory
Wheldrake Ings Nature Reserve
Storwood Ings
Woodside Lodge Farm
The Rush
GENERAL LANE
South Wood
Ross Moor
Crinklety Wood
Whincover Wood
Home Farm
North Hills
POSTERN LANE
Ball Hall Farm
The Whin
Boundary Farm
Y019
Cottingwith Lock
PH
Langrickgate Field
Forest Farm
Acre Farm
North Moor
Common Lane
FERRY LANE
Cemy
CANAL RD
Langrickgate La
North Moor
Willow Tree Farm
B1228
Thornums Wood
ST MARYS CL
CHURCH LA
East Cottingwith
Grange Farm
South Acre Farm
East End PH
SOUTHMOOR ROAD
WESTFIELD LA
INGS LA
Green La
REDCAP LANE
East Cottingwith Common
South Moor
Glebe Farm
Thorganby Ings
Red Cap Farm
North Ross Farm
South Ross Farm
New Moor
Thorganby Hall Wood
Thorganby
HAG LANE
River Derwent
Mill House
BRIDGES LANE
Pond Farm
Ings View Farm
East Cottingwith Ings
FOG LANE
Spring House
Gale Farm
INGS RD
Yew Tree Farm
HAG LANE
Whitegate Bridge
WOODHOUSE RD
LONG RAMPART
B1228
Y042
Fox Covert
Woodfield Farm
East Lodge
Sike Bridge
Ellerton Common
New Lands
COW PASTURE LA
Scruton Wood
Priory Farm
Lofty Farm
South View Farm
Blue Slates Farm
BOWLAND
Ruddings Wood
East Grange Farm
MAIN ST
Main St
COTTAM LANE
North Grange
BOWLAND LANE
Far Woods
Ellerton Ings
Priory Farm
PH
Ellerton
Short Acre Farm
SHORTACRE LANE
RUDDINGS LANE
RUDDINGS LA
Aughton Ruddings
BACK LA
Hall Farm
Y08
Lawns House Farm
North Duffield Lodge
South Grange
Aughton Ruddings Grange
Red Moors
Great Wood
Lodge Farm
Aughton
Stud Farm
Wentsford House Farm
B1228
HANKINS LA
Longlane Plantation
Long Lane
Glebe Farm
HIGHFIELD LA
MAIN ST
LITTLE LA
Main St
Aughton Plantation
Common End Plantation
Park Farm
Aughton Ings
PASTURE LANE
BACK LA
Back Lane
York House Farm
TOWNEND RD
BIRK LA
Aughton Common
CH
Autherthaws Farm
North Duffield Carrs

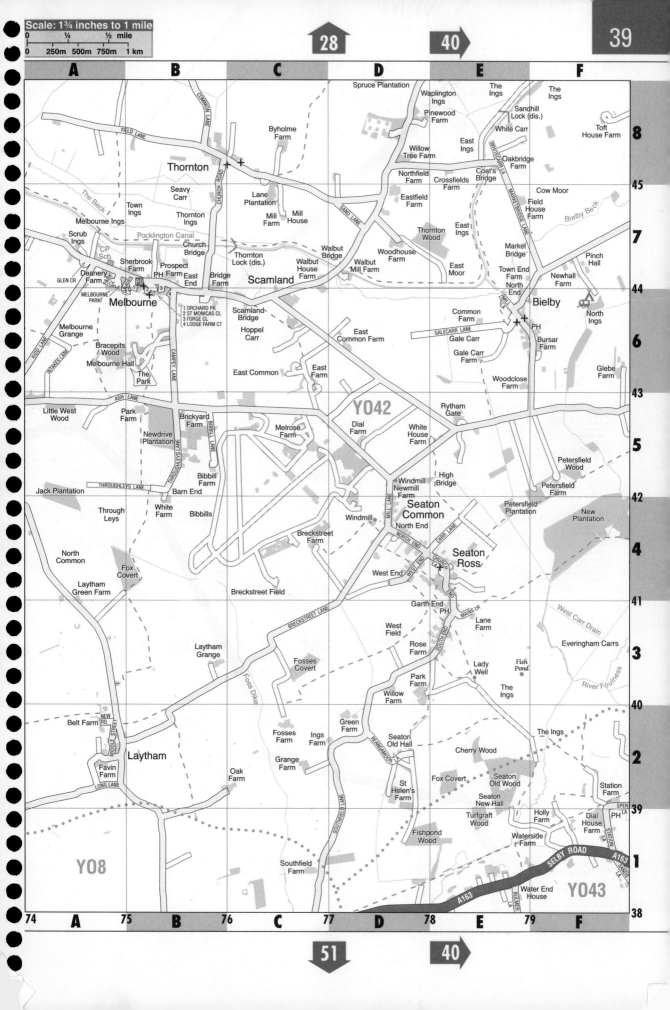

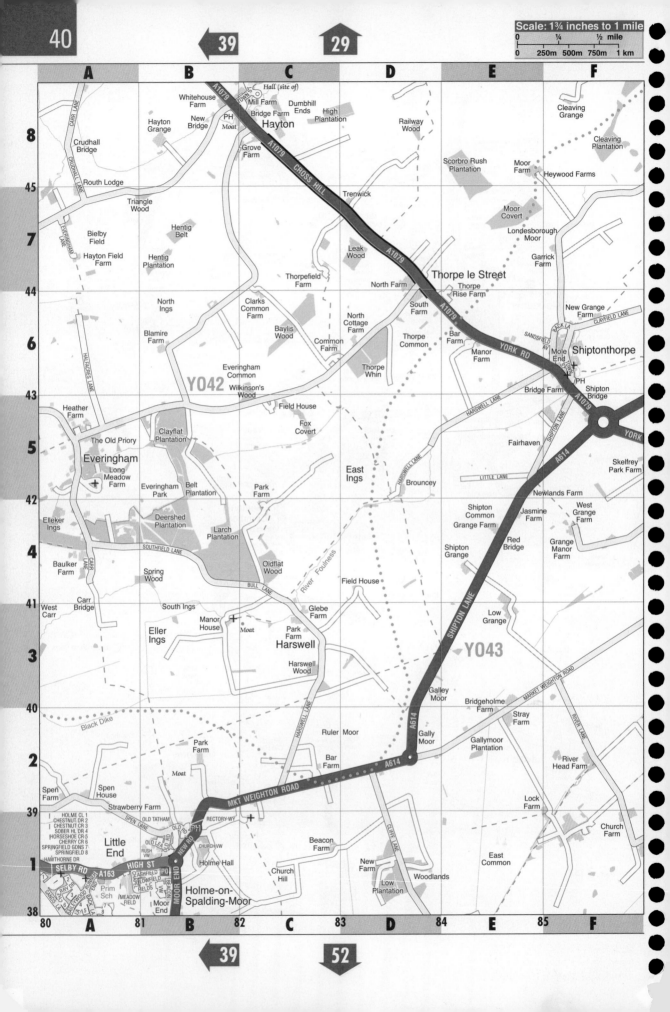

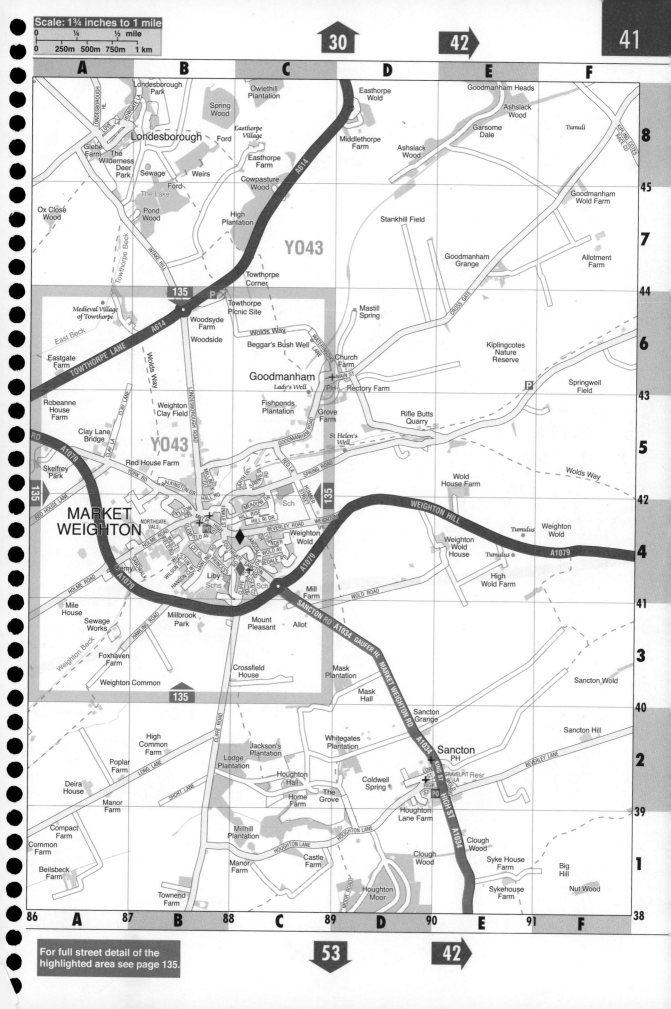

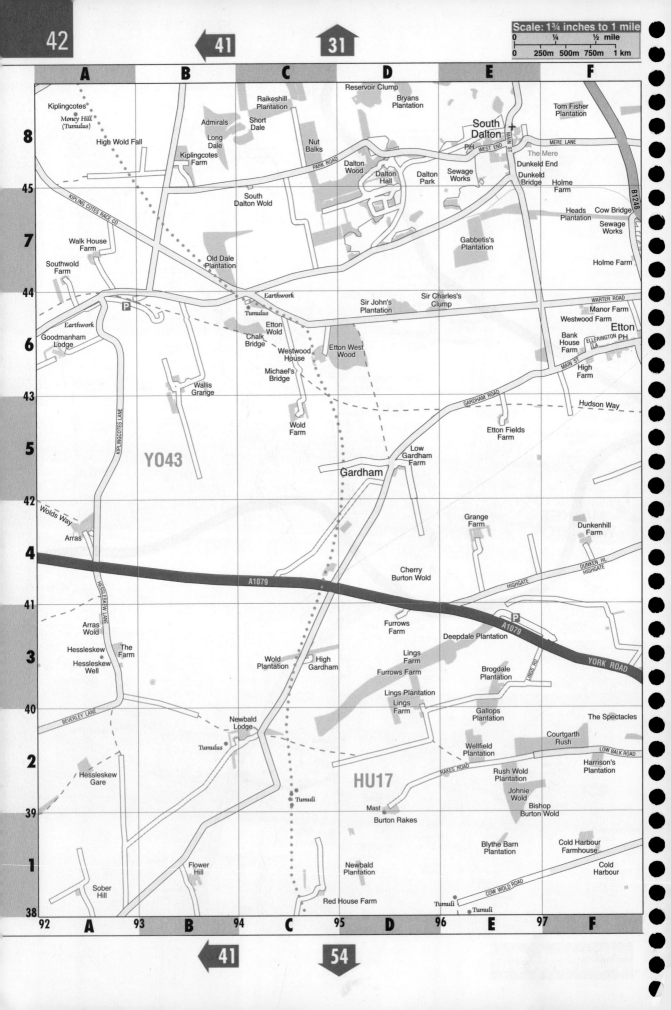

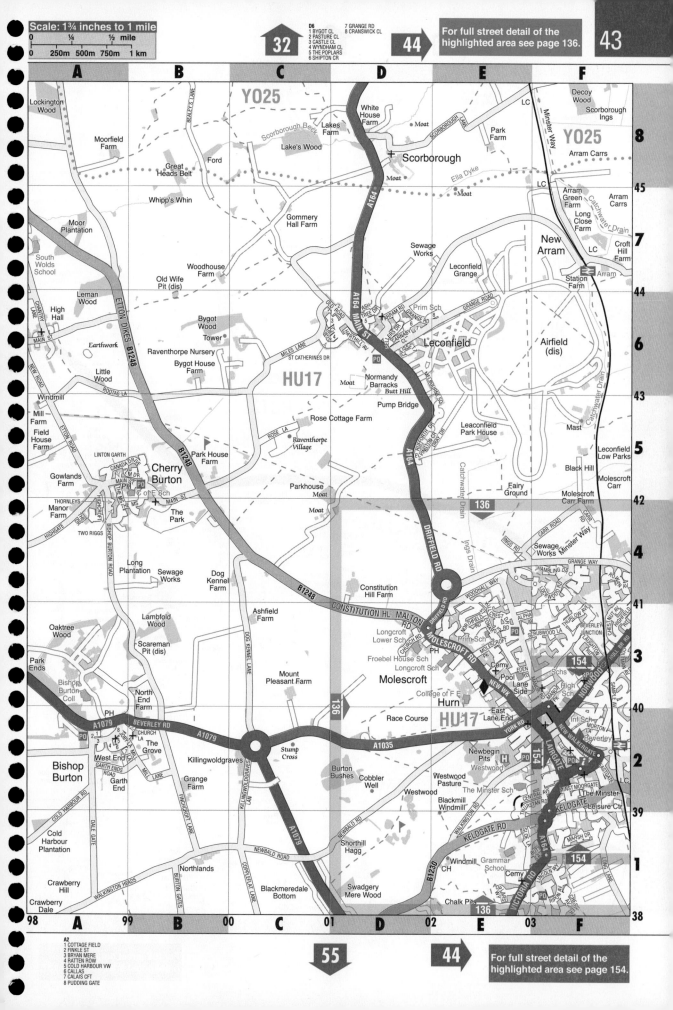

Scale: 1¾ inches to 1 mile
0   ¼   ½ mile
0 250m 500m 750m 1 km

A B C D E F

8

High Grange Farm New Farm
Laurel Farm Aike
YO25 Scorborough Ings
Aike Carrs
Leven South Carr Drain
Linleyhill Road
Landing Strip
Leven Carrs
Hall Garth
West Street
Heigholme Lane
Carr Lane

45

Arram Carrs
Far Fox Aqueduct
Leven Canal
Sandholme La
Sandholme Farm
Cross La

7

Arram
Eastfield Farm Beckend Farm
Eske Boundary Plantation
Waterloo Farm
Eske Boundary Plantation
Cross Drain
Glebe Farm
Eske Carrs Drain
Eske Carrs Drain

44

Lodge Farm
Arram Beck
Eske Plantation
Eske Carrs
Eske Wood
Eske Carrs Drain
Route Carrs

6

Moor Drain
Arram Grange
Eske Village
High Eske Farm
Eske Wood
Eske Plantation
Eske
Crowshore Plantation
High Farm
Quarry (Sand & Gravel)

43

North Bullock Dike
Pumping Station
HU17
PH
Park Farm
Cottage Farm
Butt Hills
Route Carrs

5

Molescroft Carr
Crookled Hill
Tickton Hall
Tickton Grange (Hotel)
Tickton Bridge
Hall Farm
A1035
Church Farm
Manor House Farm
Haver Fields
Route
Manor Farm

42

South Bullock Dike
Hull Bridge
137
Scotts Garth Dr
Scotts Garth Cl
Main St
PH
Tickton Carrs
Tickton Bridge Plantations
Fieldhouse Farm

4

Stork Hill Farm
Turf Gutter Bridge
Weel Rd
Eske River Side
Eske Cl
Tickton Carr Farm
Sewage Works
Tickton Carr Drain
Route Carrs
Little Storkhill Farm
Hull Bridge Road
Churchfields
Tickton
Tickton Carrs
Tickton Carr Drain
A1035

41

Grange Lane
Nursery
Fosters Bridge
Turf Gutter & Eske River Side
New Holland Drain
Dumble Pits Bridge
North Carrs
Sandhill Bottoms
Brigham Closes
Meaux Lane
Grange Way

3

Swine Moor
Swinemoor Bank
North Carr
Old Main Drain
The Decoy
Meaux Decoy
Little Decoy
Sand Hill
Fewsome Hill
Meaux Abbey Farm
Cote Bridge
Moat
North Grange
BEVERLEY
Sigston Road

40

HU17
Grovehill
Hoggard House Farm
Corporation Farm
Carr House Farm
Peartree Hill Plantation
Selley Carr
Stud Farm

2

Superstore
Chapel Farm
Weel Town's Drain
Weel Carr
Carr Lane
Weel Carr
Crown Farm
Moat
Site of Meaux Abbey
Meaux
Bridge Farm
154
Holme Church La
Annie Reed Rd
Bielby Dr
Waterside Rd
Sewage Works
Weel
Beverley Beck

39

Allot
Beverley Parklands
Figham
Beverley and Skidby Drain
Springdale Farm
Weel Stone Carr
Park Hill
Selley Carr
Halfpenny Hill
Meaux Bridge
Meaux Road
Spen Mill Lane

1

154
Cherry Tree Farm
Beverley & Skidby Drain
Tokenspire Park
Figham Clough Bridge
Figham Drain
Black Bank
Morris Carr
HU7
Stone Carr
Ash Dike Bank
Ash Dike Plantation
North Wray Closes
Wawne Grange
East Field

38

137
Figham Bridge
Carr Plantation
Carr House
Drove Lane

04 A 05 B 06 C 07 D 08 E 09 F

For full street detail of the highlighted area see page 154.

For full street detail of the highlighted area see page 137.

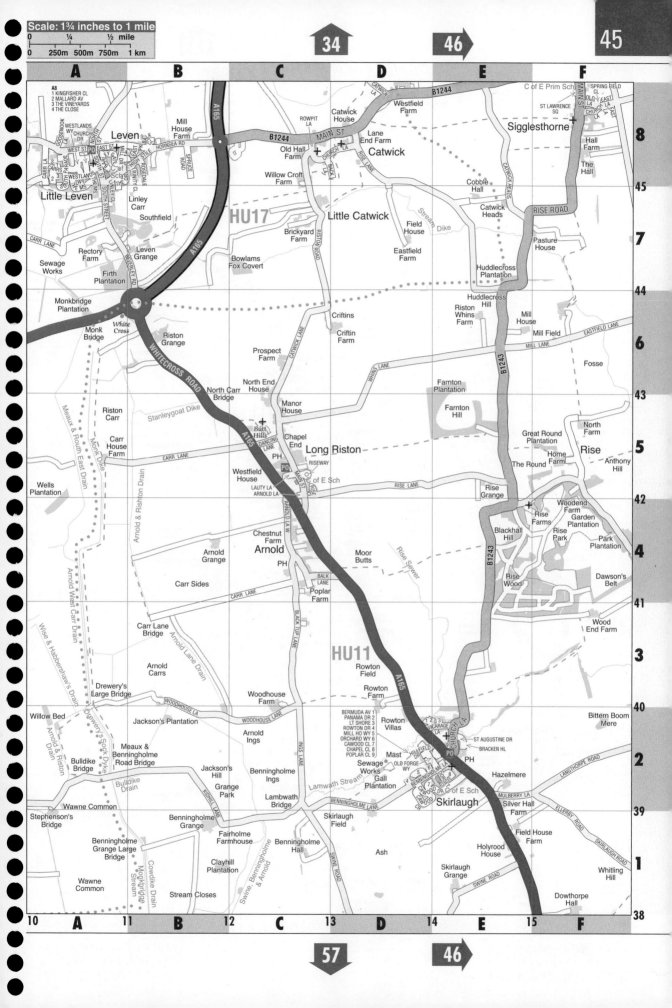

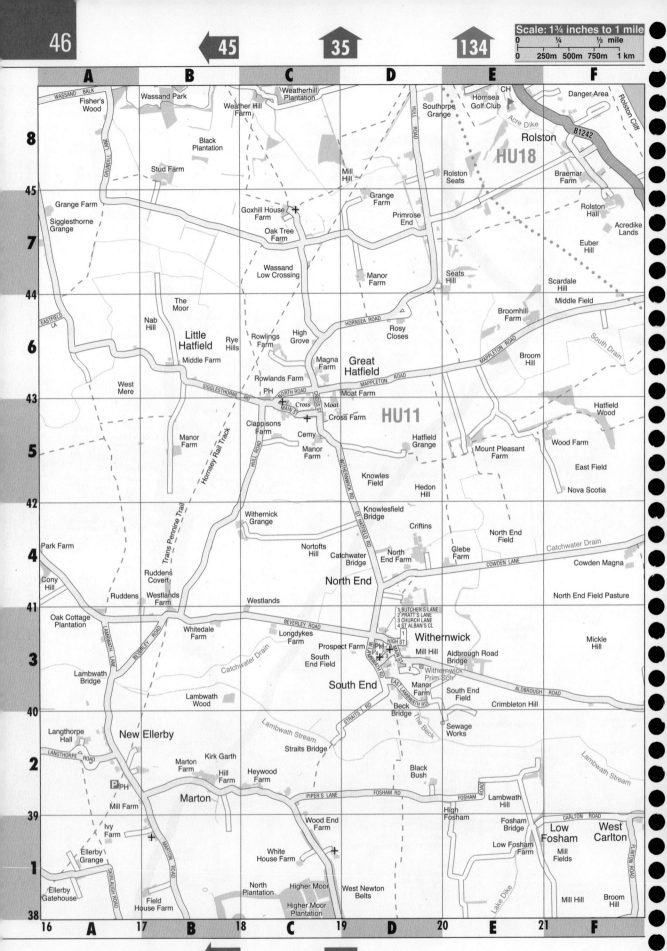

Scale: 1¾ inches to 1 mile

0 ¼ ½ mile

0 250m 500m 750m 1 km

A **B** **C** **D** **E** **F**

WASSAND BALK

Fisher's Wood

Wassand Park

Weatherhill Plantation

Weather Hill Farm

Southorpe Grange

Hornsea Golf Club

CH

Danger Area

Rolston Cliff

8

Black Plantation

Acre Dike

Rolston

B1242

GRIMSTON LANE

Stud Farm

Mill Hill Farm

Rolston Seats

HU18

Braemar Farm

45

Grange Farm

Goxhill House Farm

Oak Tree Farm

Grange Farm

Primrose End

Rolston Hall

Acredike Lands

Sigglesthorne Grange

Euber Hill

7

HULL ROAD

Wassand Low Crossing

Manor Farm

Seats Hill

Scardale Hill

44

EASTFIELD LA

The Moor

HORNSEA ROAD

Rosy Closes

Broomhill Farm

Middle Field

South Drain

Nab Hill

Little Hatfield

Rye Hills

Rowlings Farm

High Grove

Great Hatfield

MAPPLETON ROAD

Broom Hill

6

Middle Farm

Rowlands Farm

Magna Farm

MAPPLETON ROAD

West Mere

SIGGLESTHORNE RD

PH

NORTH ROAD

Moat Farm

Hatfield Wood

43

Cross

MAIN ST

Moat

Cross Farm

HU11

Manor Farm

Clappisons Farm

Cemy

Manor Farm

Hatfield Grange

Wood Farm

Hornsey Rail Track

Hatfield Grange

Mount Pleasant Farm

East Field

5

WITHERNWICK RD

Knowles Field

Hedon Hill

Nova Scotia

42

Trans Pennine Trail

Withernick Grange

GT HATFIELD RD

Knowlesfield Bridge

Criftins

North End Field

Catchwater Drain

Park Farm

Nortofts Hill

Catchwater Bridge

North End Farm

Glebe Farm

Cowden Magna

4

Cony Hill

COWDEN LANE

Ruddens Covert

North END

North End Field Pasture

Ruddens

Westlands Farm

Westlands

41

Oak Cottage Plantation

BEVERLEY ROAD

1 BUTCHER'S LANE
2 PRATT'S LANE
3 CHURCH LANE
4 ST ALBAN'S CL

Mickle Hill

Whitedale Farm

Longdykes Farm

Prospect Farm

HIGH ST

Withernwick

Mill Hill

Aldbrough Road Bridge

3

LAMBWATH LANE

BEVERLEY ROAD

PH

MAIN ST

Lambwath Bridge

South End Field

South End

Manor Farm

South End Field

ALDBROUGH ROAD

Lambwath Wood

Beck Bridge

Crimbleton Hill

40

Langthorpe Hall

Catchwater Drain

STRAITS RD

The Beck

Sewage Works

Lambwath Stream

LANGTHORPE ROAD

New Ellerby

Lambwath Stream

Straits Bridge

Black Bush

FOSHAM ROAD

Lambwath Hill

2

P PH

Marton Farm

Kirk Garth

Heywood Farm

PIPER'S LANE

FOSHAM RD

High Fosham

CARLTON ROAD

West Carlton

Mill Farm

MARTON ROAD

Marton

Fosham Bridge

Low Fosham

39

Ivy Farm

Wood End Farm

Low Fosham Farm

Mill Fields

FLINTON ROAD

Ellerby Grange

White House Farm

Mill Hill

Broom Hill

1

SKIRLAUGH ROAD

Ellerby Gatehouse

Field House Farm

North Plantation

Higher Moor

West Newton Belts

Lake Dike

38

Higher Moor Plantation

16 **17** **18** **19** **20** **21**

A **B** **C** **D** **E** **F**

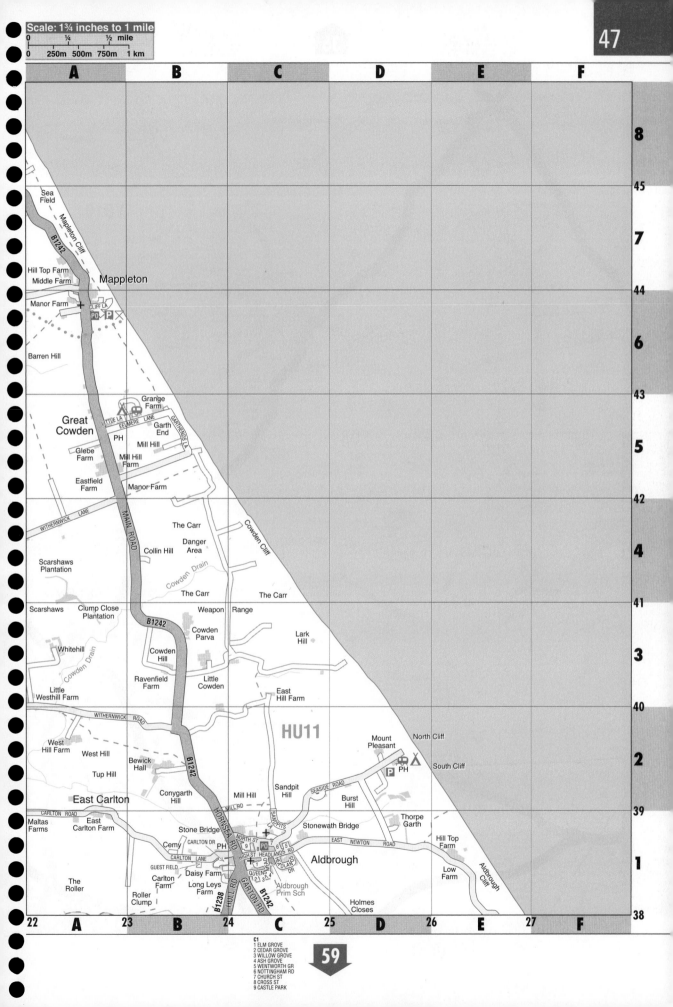

Scale: 1¾ inches to 1 mile

0   ¼   ½   mile
0   250m 500m 750m 1 km

A   **B**   **C**   **D**   **E**   **F**

Sea Field

Mapleton Cliff

B1242

Hill Top Farm
Middle Farm

Mappleton

Manor Farm

CLIFF LA

Barren Hill

Grange Farm

LITTLE LA
EELMERE LANE
GARTHENDS LA

Great Cowden

Garth End

PH

Mill Hill

Glebe Farm

Mill Hill Farm

Eastfield Farm

Manor Farm

WITHERNWICK LANE

MAIN ROAD

The Carr

Cowden Cliff

Danger Area

Collin Hill

Scarshaws Plantation

Cowden Drain

The Carr

The Carr

Scarshaws

Clump Close Plantation

Weapon   Range

B1242

Whitehill

Cowden Parva

Lark Hill

Cowden Drain

Cowden Hill

Little Westhill Farm

Ravenfield Farm

Little Cowden

East Hill Farm

WITHERNWICK ROAD

HU11

West Hill Farm

West Hill

Bewick Hall

B1242

Mount Pleasant

North Cliff

South Cliff

PH

Tup Hill

Conygarth Hill

Mill Hill

Sandpit Hill

SEASIDE ROAD

Burst Hill

East Carlton

Thorpe Garth

HORNSEA RD

MILL RD

SANDPITS

Maltas Farms

East Carlton Farm

CARLTON ROAD

Stone Bridge

CARLTON DR

PH

NORTH ST

PO

HIGH ST

HEADLANDS RD

Stonewath Bridge

EAST NEWTON ROAD

Hill Top Farm

Cemy

Guest Field

Daisy Farm

Carlton Farm

CARLTON LANE

QUEENS

GARTON RD

DR

Aldbrough

Low Farm

Aldbrough Cliff

The Roller

Long Leys Farm

Roller Clump

B1238

HULL RD

B1242

Aldbrough Prim Sch

Holmes Closes

22 **A** **23** **B** **24** **C** **25** **D** **26** **E** **27** **F** **38**

8
45
7
44
6
43
5
42
4
41
3
40
2
39
1

C1
1 ELM GROVE
2 CEDAR GROVE
3 WILLOW GROVE
4 ASH GROVE
5 WENTWORTH GR
6 NOTTINGHAM RD
7 CHURCH ST
8 CROSS ST
9 CASTLE PARK

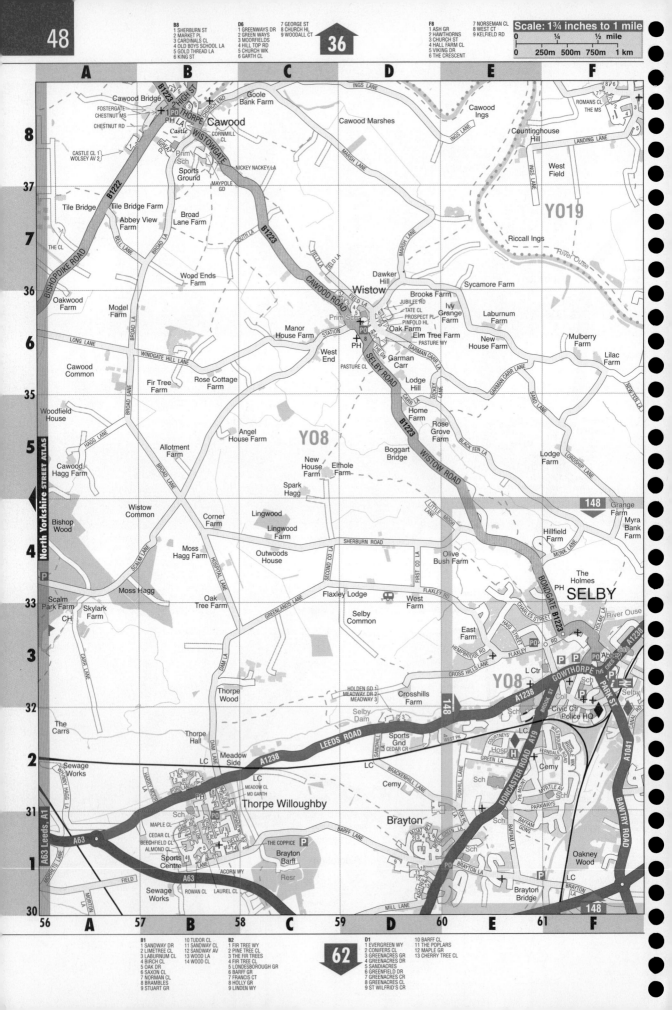

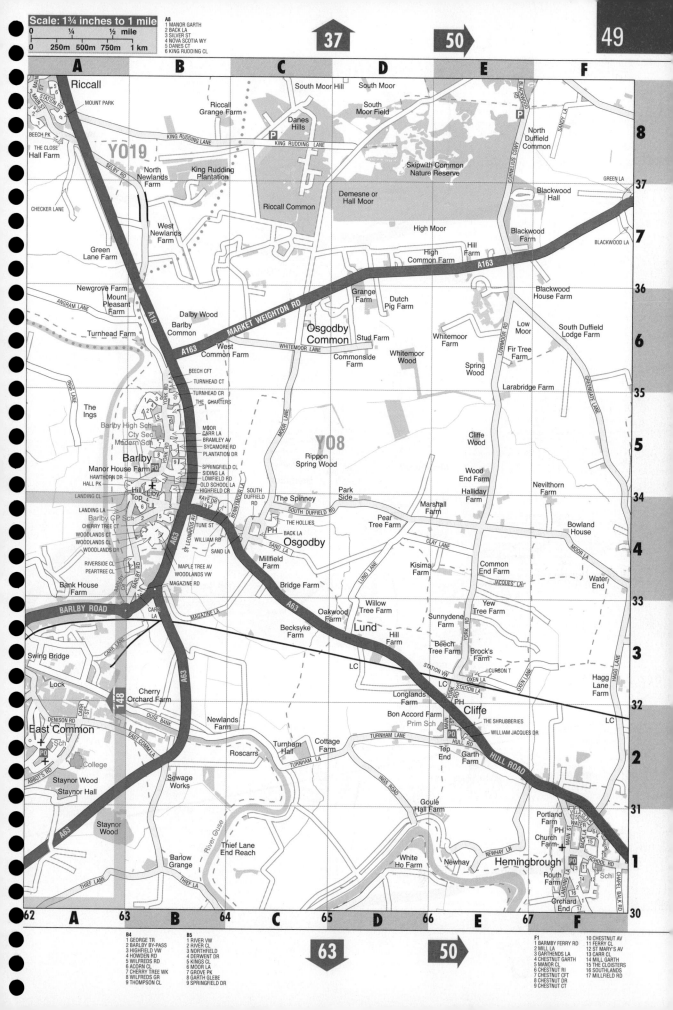

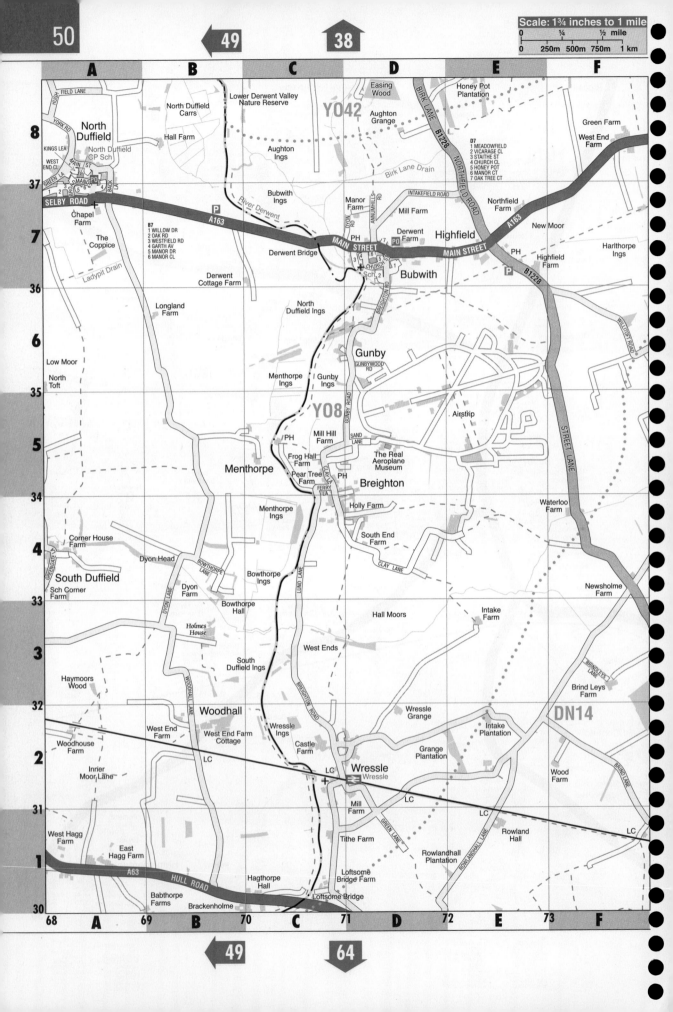

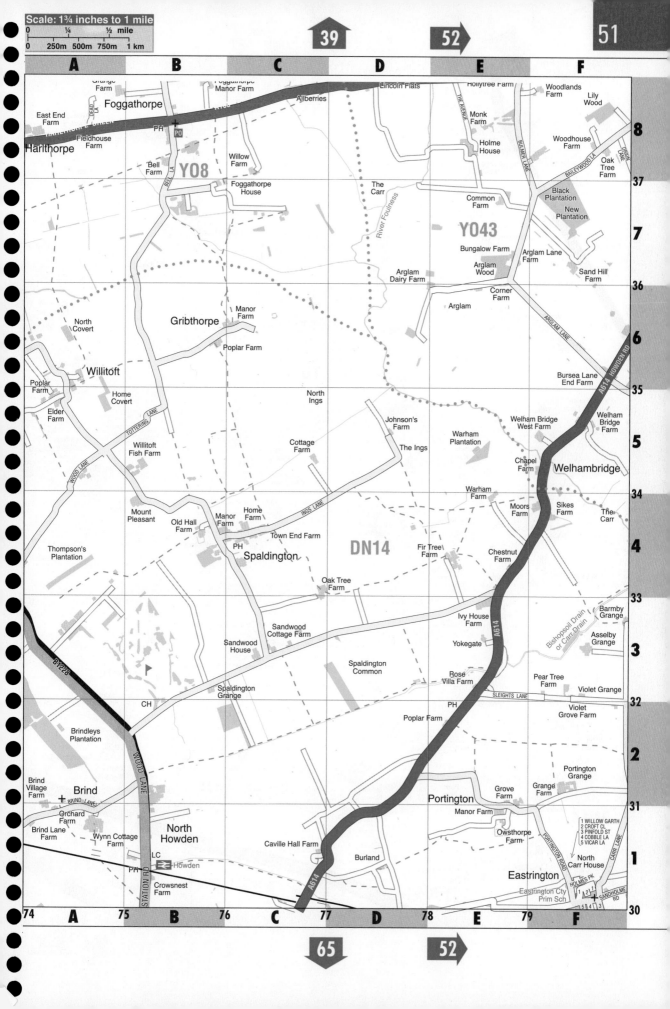

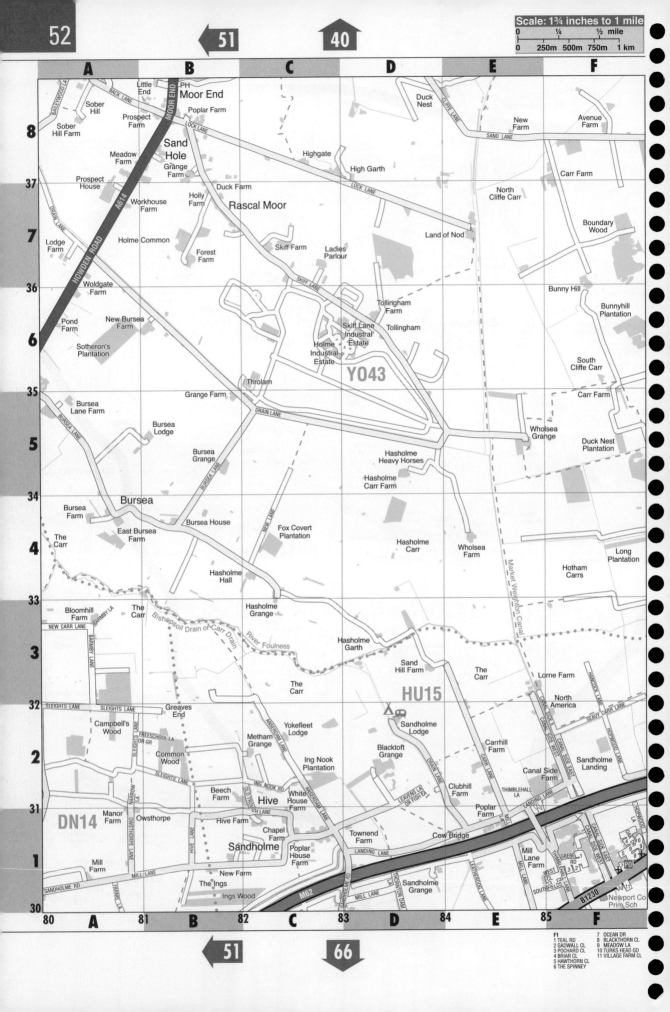

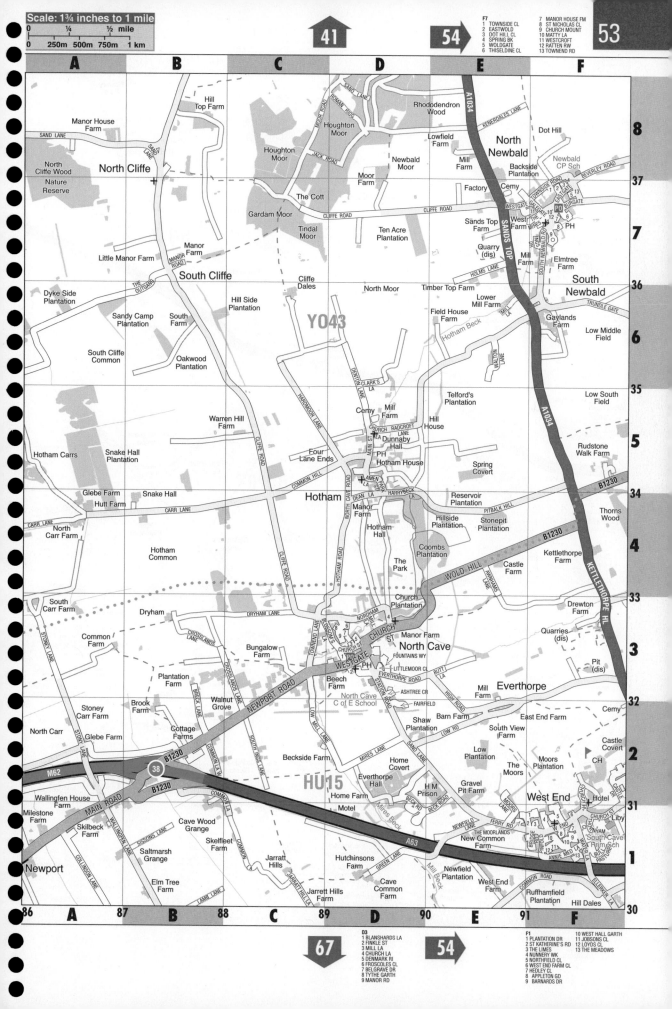

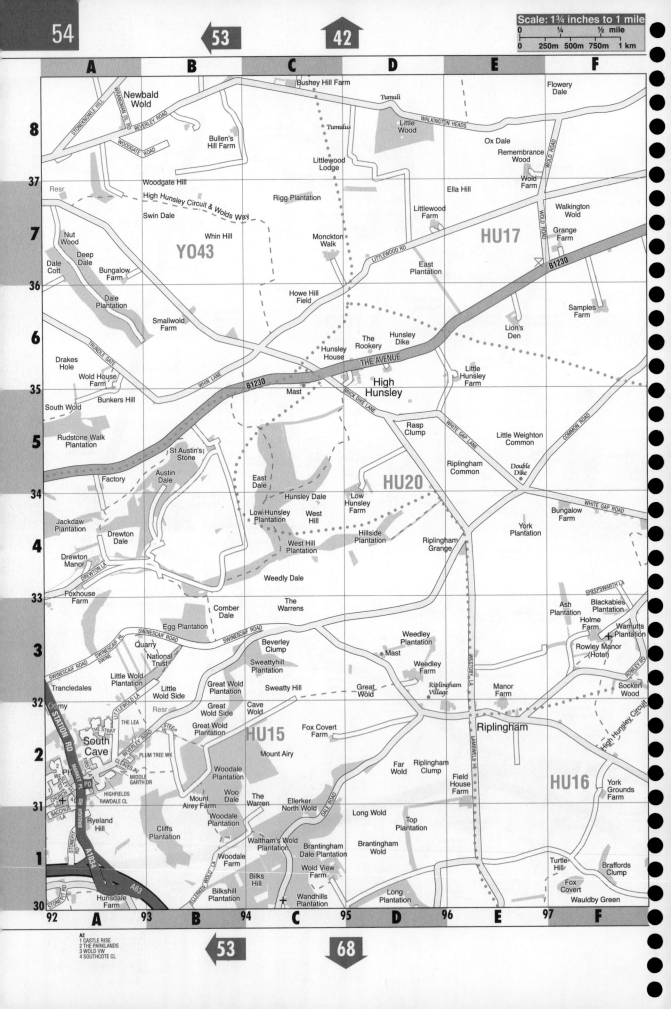

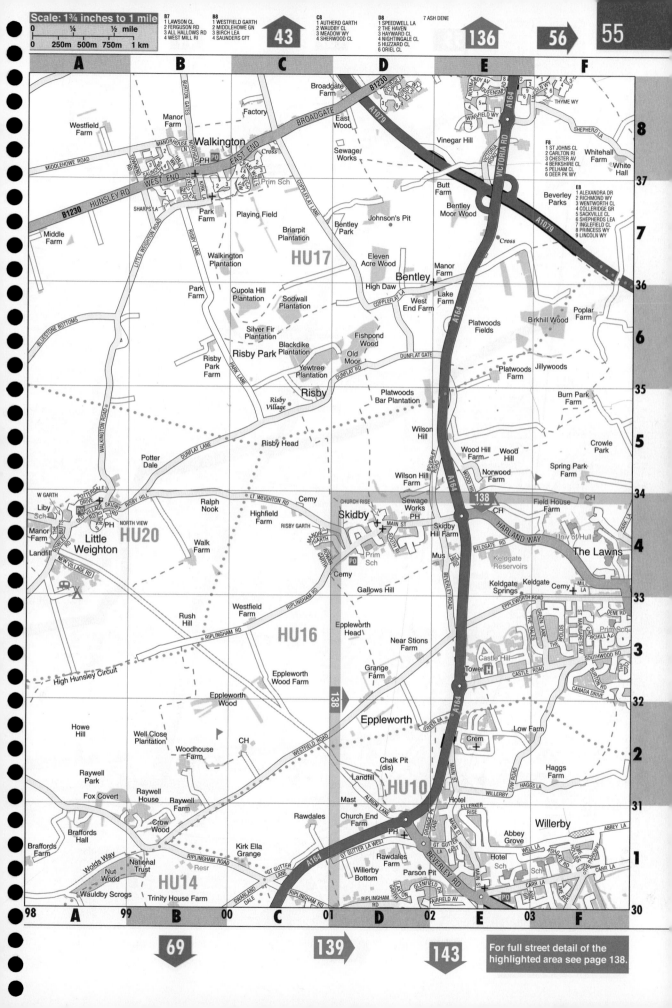

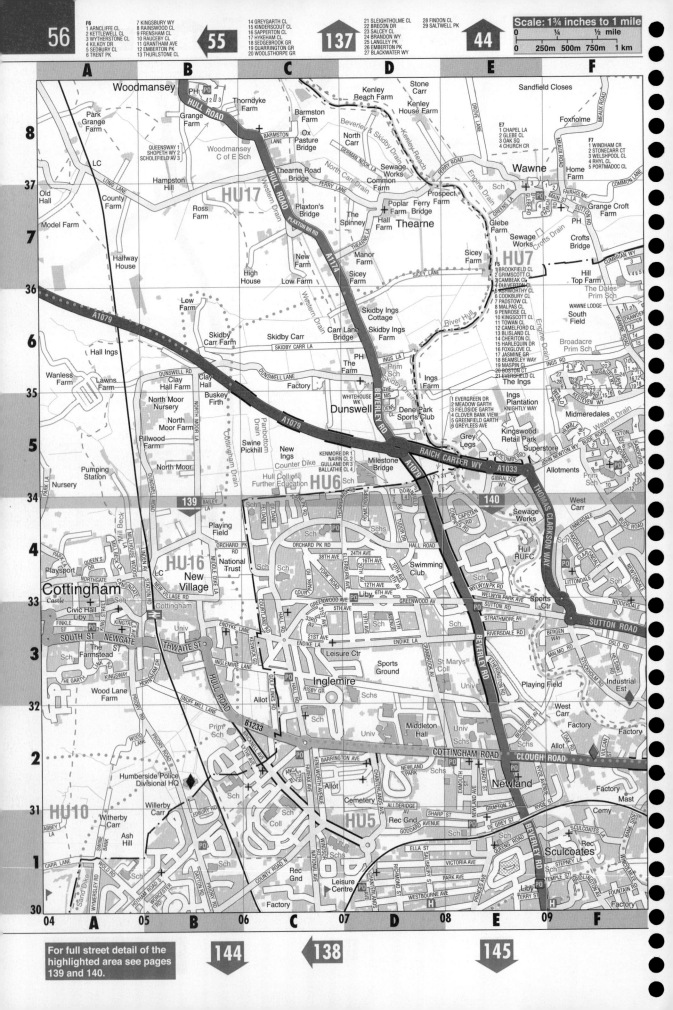

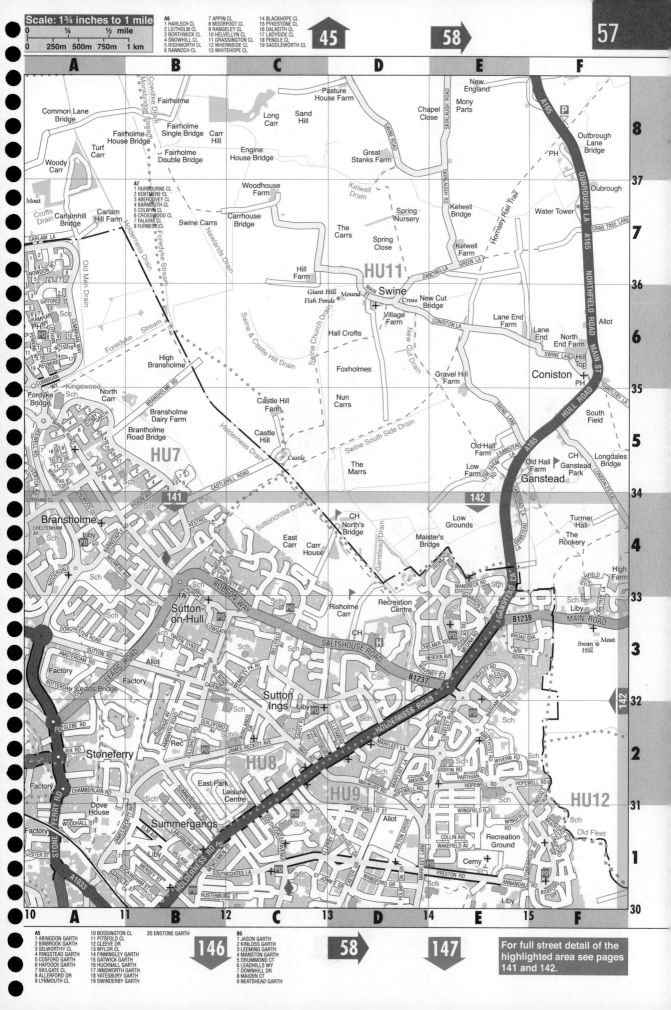

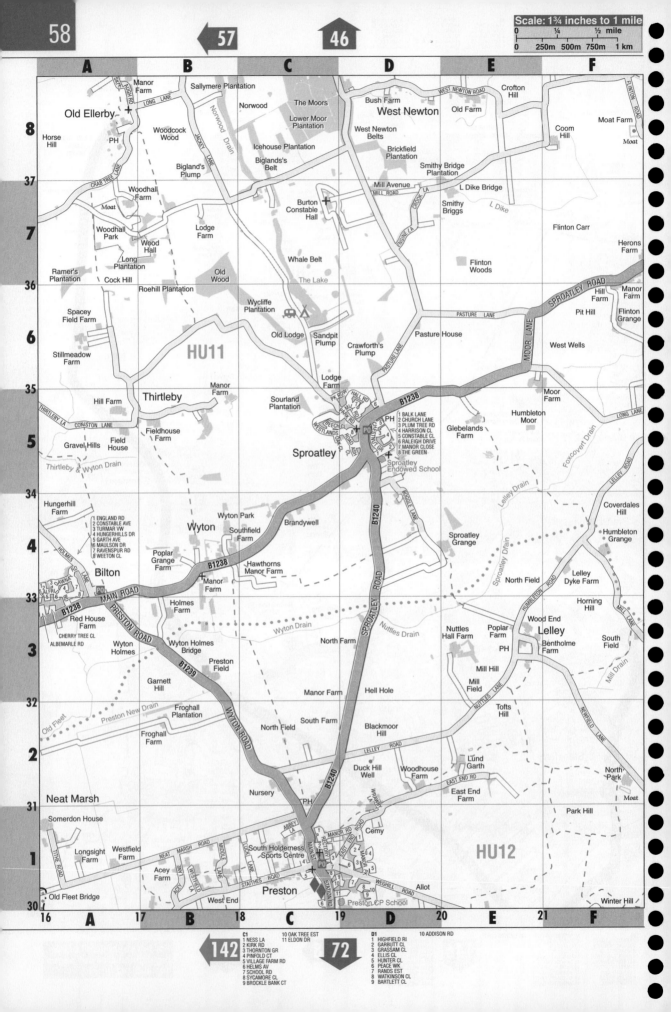

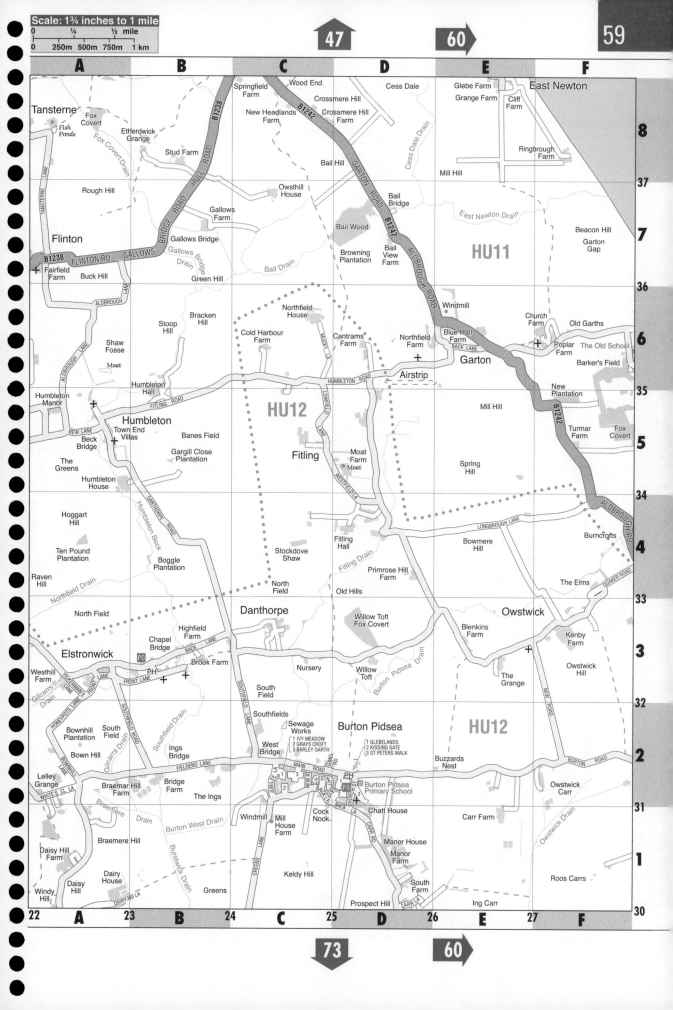

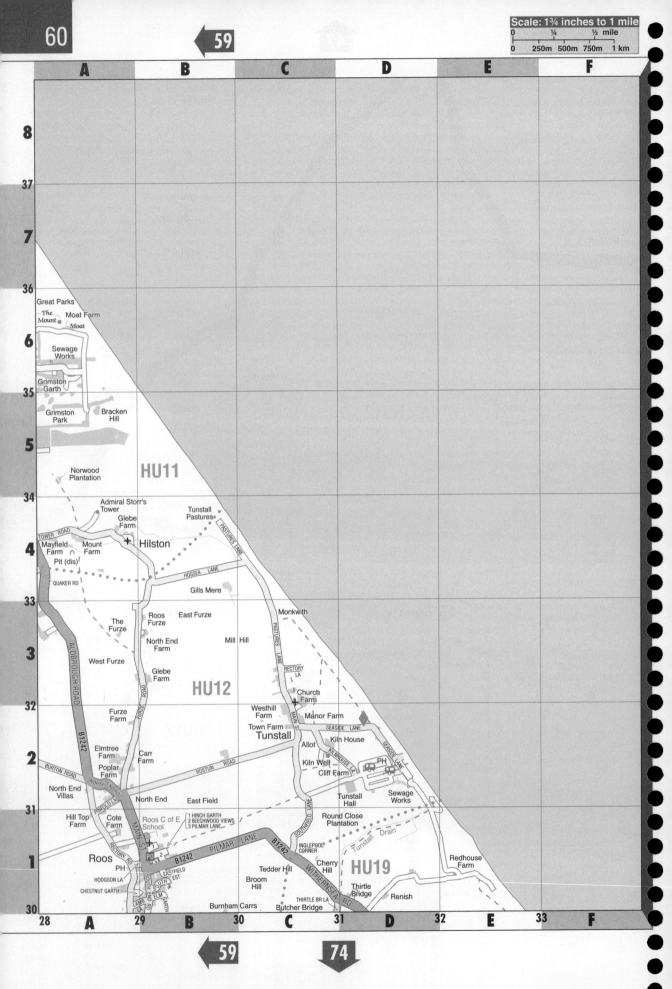

← 59

Scale: 1¾ inches to 1 mile

0   ¼   ½   mile
0   250m 500m 750m 1 km

A   B   C   D   E   F

8

37

7

36

Great Parks
The Mount   Moat Farm
            Moat

6   Sewage
     Works

     Grimston
     Garth

35   Grimston   Bracken
     Park   Hill

5

                 HU11
     Norwood
     Plantation

34   Admiral Storr's
     Tower
           Glebe   Tunstall
           Farm   Pastures

     Mayfield Mount   PASTURES LANE
4   Farm   Farm   + Hilston
     Pit (dis)
                    HOGSEA LANE
     QUAKER RD
                      Gills Mere

33   Monkwith

     The   Roos   East Furze
     Furze Furze

     North End   Mill Hill   PASTURES LANE
3   Farm
     West Furze   RECTORY LA

           Glebe
           Farm   HU12   + Church
                                 Farm

32   Furze   Westhill   Manor Farm
     Farm   Farm
                        Town Farm   SEASIDE LANE
     Elmtree   Tunstall
2   Farm   Carr   Allot   Kiln House
             Farm   KILNHOUSE LA
     Poplar   ROSTUN ROAD   Kiln Well   PH
     Farm
                                  Cliff Farm   Sewage
     North End   Works
     Villas   North End   East Field   Tunstall
                                          Hall
31   Hill Top   Cote   Round Close
     Farm   Farm   Roos C of E   1 HINCH GARTH   Plantation
                       School   2 BEECHWOOD VIEWS
                                     3 PILMAR LANE
                                              Tunstall   Drain
                        PO   PILMAR LANE   INGLEPOOL
1   Roos   B1242   B1242 CORNER
            PH   Redhouse
       HODGSON LA   EASTFIELD   Tedder Hill Cherry   HU19   Farm
                       EST   Hill
     CHESTNUT GARTH   Broom   Thirtle
                               Hill   Bridge   Renish
30   Burnham Carrs Butcher Bridge THIRTLE BR LA

28   A   29   B   30   C   31   D   32   E   33   F

ALDBROUGH ROAD
B1242
BURTON ROAD
NORTH END RD
PINFIELD LA
MAIN ST
RECTORY RD
SOUTH END RD
SOUTH ELM GARTH
LAMB END RD
FIRZE ROAD
SOUTHFIELD LANE
WITHERNSEA RD
SEASIDE LANE

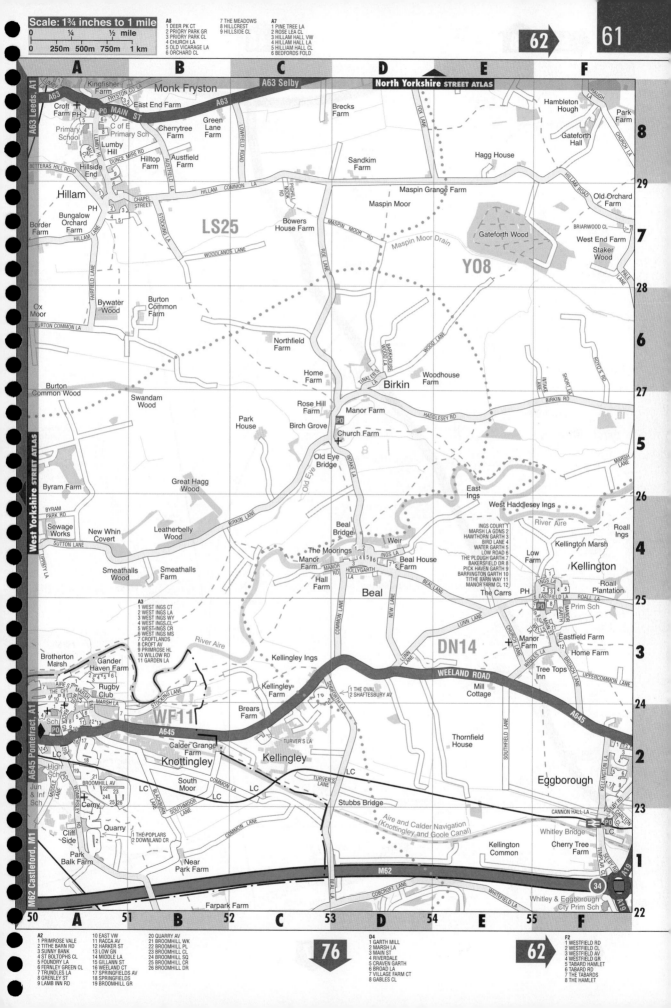

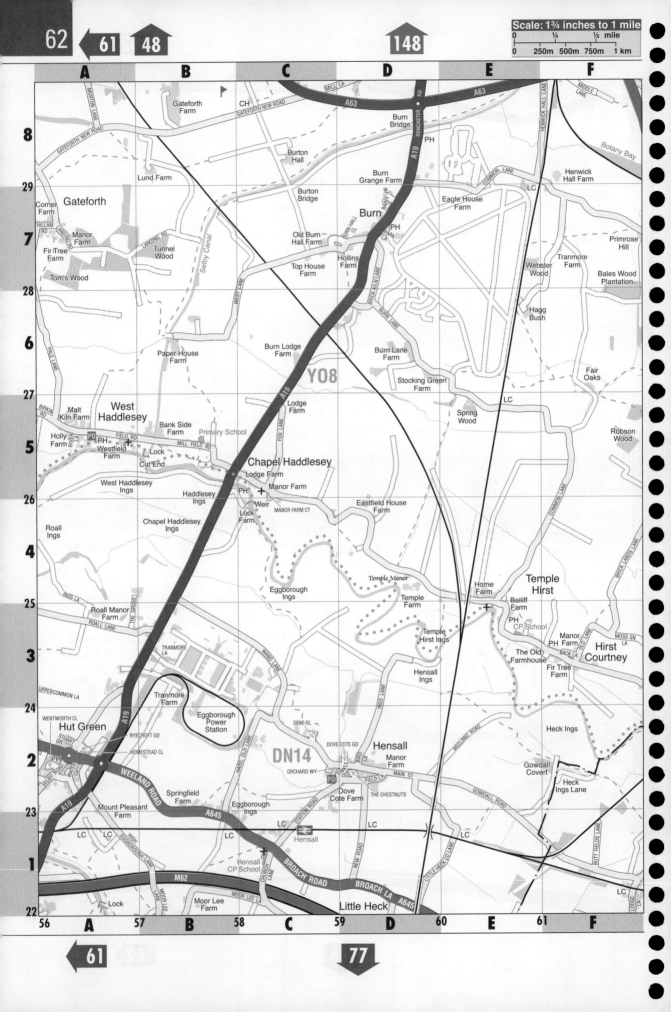

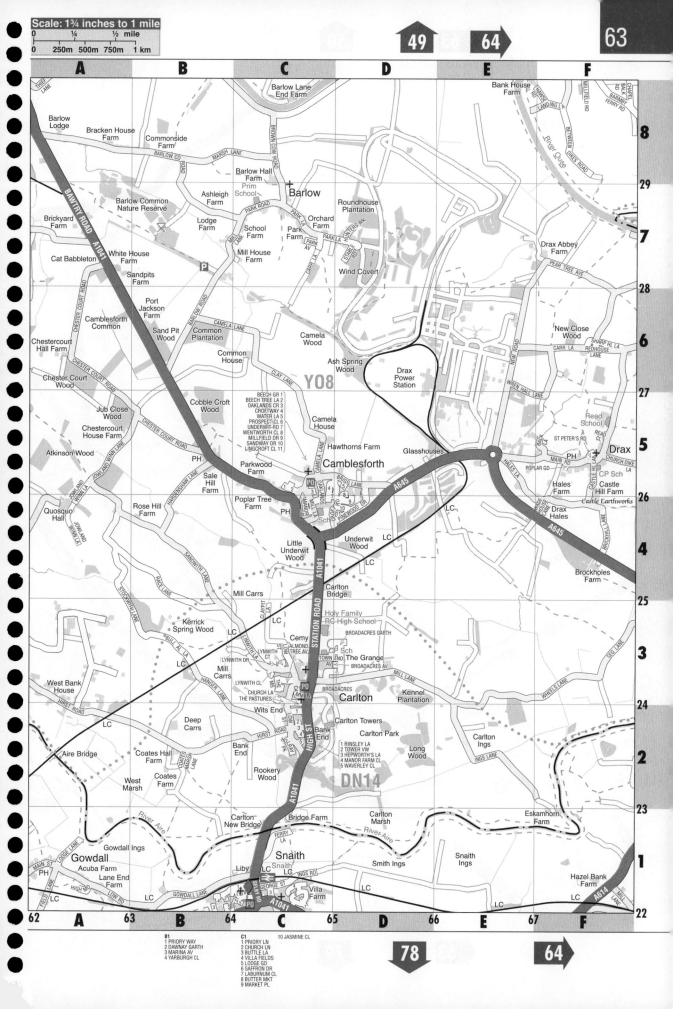

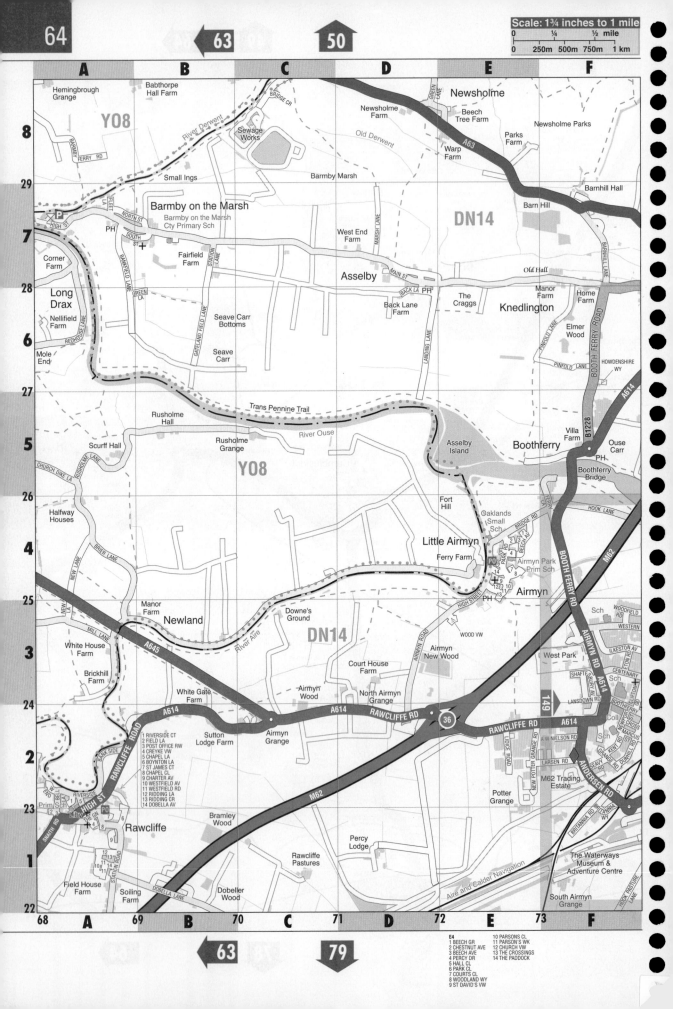

A B C D E F

Hemingbrough Grange

Babthorpe Hall Farm

YO8

8

River Derwent

Sewage Works

BRIDGE CR

Newsholme

Newsholme Farm

Beech Tree Farm

GREEN LANE

Parks Farm

Newsholme Parks

A63

29

Small Ings

Barmby Marsh

Warp Farm

Barnhill Hall

Barmby on the Marsh

Barmby on the Marsh Cty Primary Sch

P

FLEET LA

NORTH ST

PH

Barn Hill

DN14

BARNHILL LANE

7

High St

SOUTH ST

West End Farm

MARSH LANE

Old Hall

Corner Farm

BANKFIELD LANE

STATION LANE

Fairfield Farm

Asselby

MAIN ST

Manor Farm

Home Farm

28

Long Drax

GREEN LA

Nellifield Farm

Back La

PH

The Craggs

Knedlington

BOOTH FERRY ROAD

6

REDHOUSE LANE

GATELAND FIELD LANE

Seave Carr Bottoms

LANDING LANE

Back Lane Farm

Elmer Wood

PINFOLD LANE

HOWDENSHIRE WY

Mole End

Seave Carr

PINFOLD LANE

A614

27

Trans Pennine Trail

B1228

Rusholme Hall

River Ouse

Villa Farm

Scurff Hall

RUSHOLME LANE

Rusholme Grange

Asselby Island

Boothferry

Ouse Carr

5

CHURCH DIKE LA

YO8

Fort Hill

PH

Boothferry Bridge

26

Halfway Houses

BRIER LANE

Oaklands Small Sch

BRIDGE RD

FERRY

HOOK LANE

Little Airmyn

BEECH AV

4

NEW LANE

Ferry Farm

PO

Airmyn Park Prim Sch

BOOTH FERRY RD

M62

Sch

Woodfield Rd

Airmyn

WESTERN

25

NEW LA

Manor Farm

Newland

Downe's Ground

High Street

PH

WOOD VW

ILKESTON AV

MILL LANE

A645

River Aire

DN14

Airmyn Road

Airmyn New Wood

West Park

AIRMYN RD

A614

Sch

CENTENARY

SHAFTE

CLIFTON

3

White House Farm

Court House Farm

LANSDOWN RD

Coll

24

Brickhill Farm

White Gate Farm

Airmyn Wood

North Airmyn Grange

149

A W NIELSON RD

RAWCLIFFE ROAD

A614

Sutton Lodge Farm

Airmyn Grange

A614

36

RAWCLIFFE RD

RAWCLIFFE RD

A614

ANDERSEN RD

2

BANK SIDE

1 RIVERSIDE CT
2 FIELD LA
3 POST OFFICE RW
4 CREYKE VW
5 CHAPEL LA
6 BOYNTON LA
7 ST JAMES CT
8 CHAPEL CL
9 CHARTER AV
10 WESTFIELD AV
11 WESTFIELD RD
12 RIDDING LA
13 RIDDING CR
14 DOBELLA AV

LODGE ROAD

NEW POTTER GRANGE RD

LARSEN RD

M62 Trading Estate

RIVERSIDE

HIGH ST

M62

Potter Grange

23

Prim Sch

PO

Rawcliffe

Bramley Wood

Percy Lodge

The Waterways Museum & Adventure Centre

1

Field House Farm

Soiling Farm

DOBELLA LANE

Dobeller Wood

Rawcliffe Pastures

Aire and Calder Navigation

South Airmyn Grange

HOOK PASTURE LA

22

68 A 69 B 70 C 71 D 72 E 73 F

E4
1 BEECH GR
2 CHESTNUT AVE
3 BEECH AVE
4 PERCY DR
5 HALL CL
6 PARK CL
7 COURTS CL
8 WOODLAND WY
9 ST DAVID'S VW
10 PARSONS CL
11 PARSON'S WK
12 CHURCH VW
13 THE CROSSINGS
14 THE PADDOCK

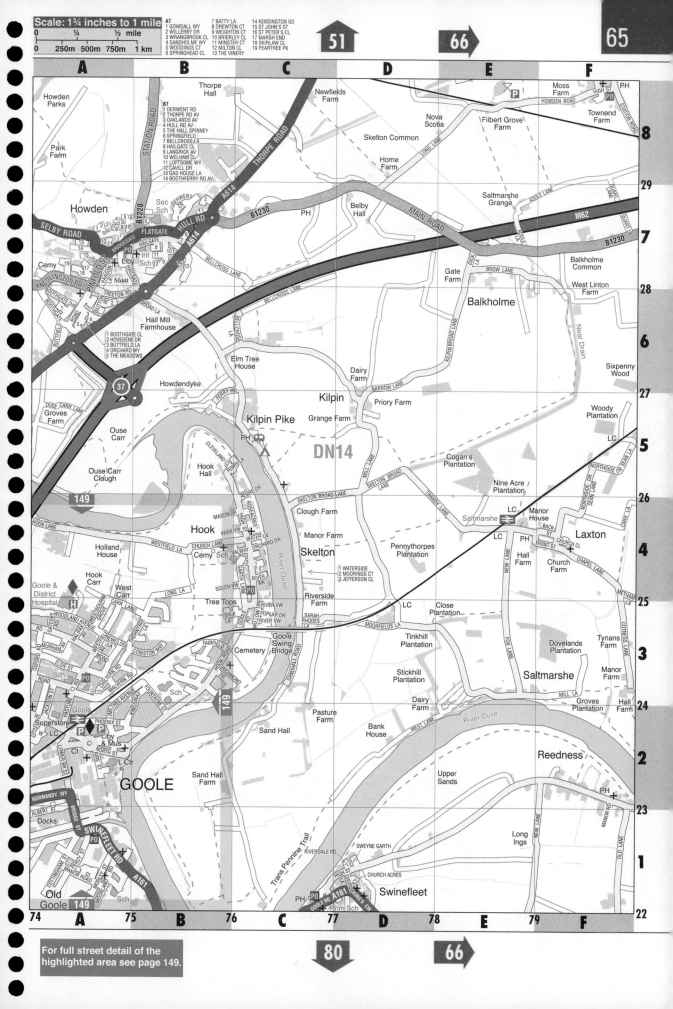

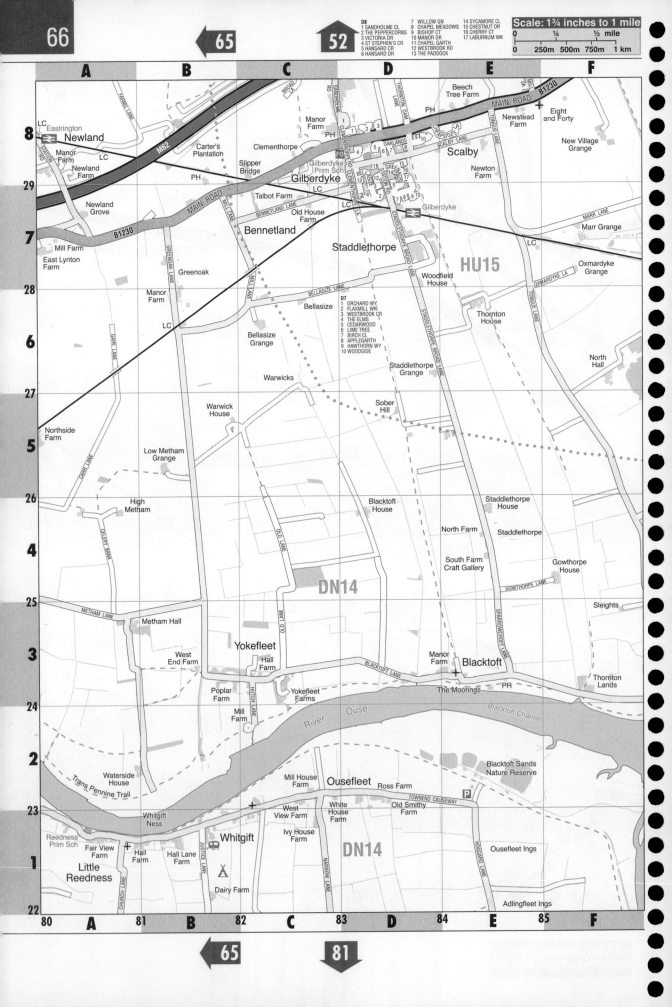

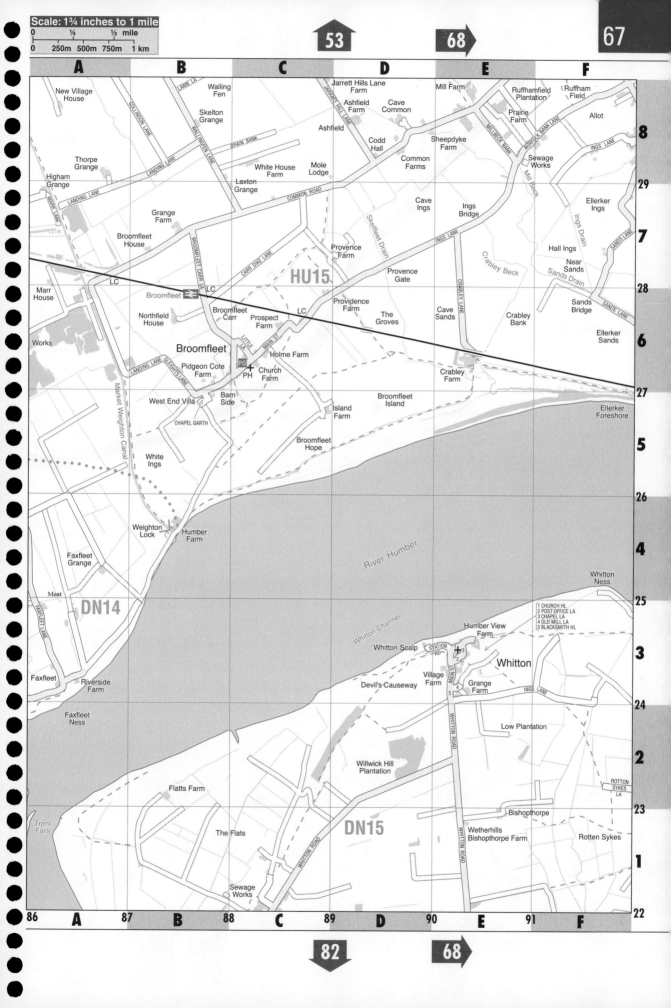

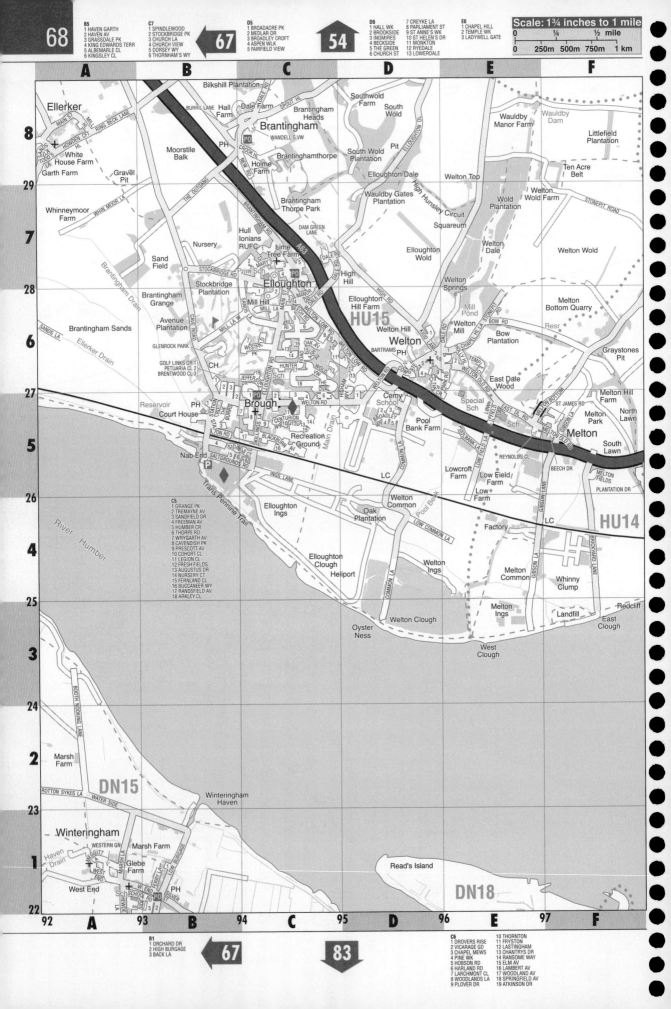

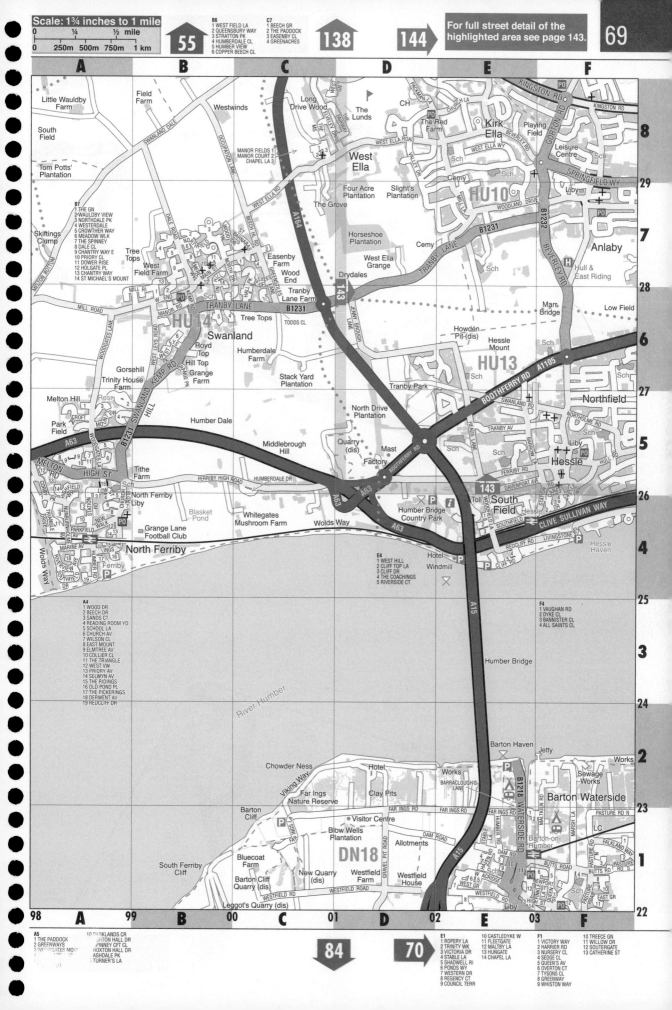

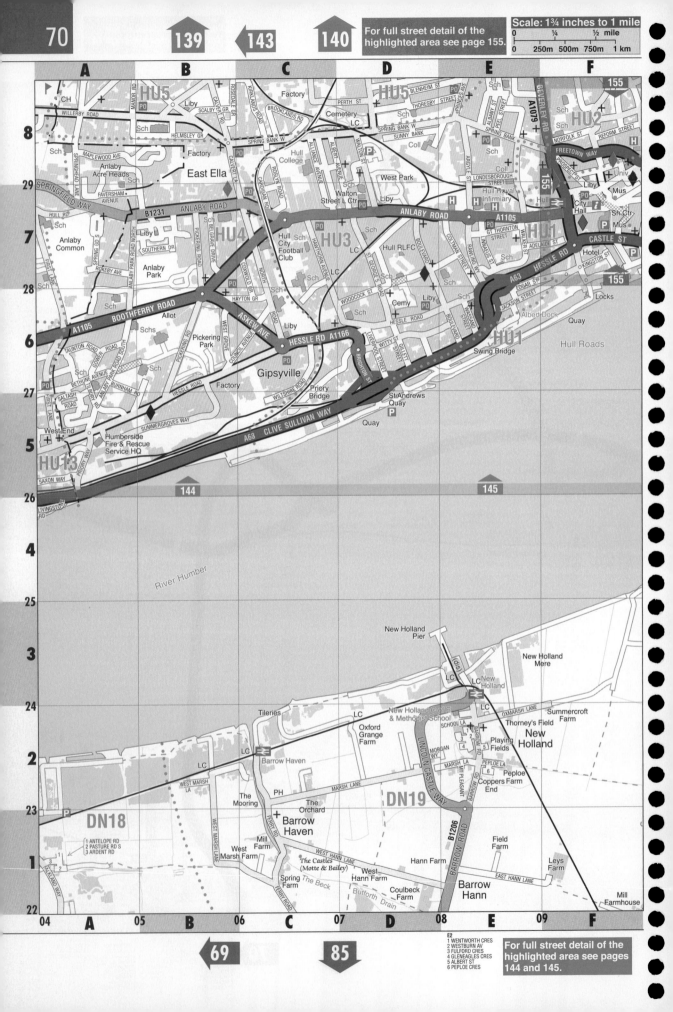

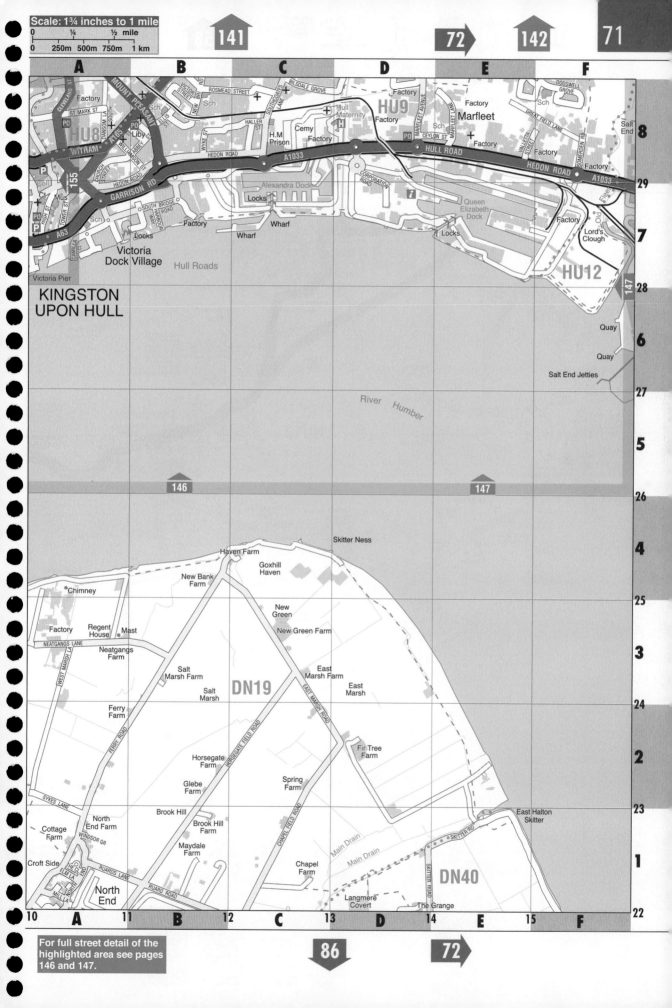

Scale: 1¾ inches to 1 mile

0   ¼   ½ mile
0 250m 500m 750m 1 km

A   B   C   D   E   F

Factory
CLEVELAND ST
ST MARK ST
Factory
VICTOR STREET
NEW BR RD
ROSMEAD STREET
Sch
BILSDALE GROVE
DODSWELL GROVE
MOUNT PLEASANT
Sch
Factory
HU9
GREAT FIELD LANE
Sch
Factory
Marfleet
Salt End
HU8
DANSOM LA SOUTH
ELLIS
Sch
HALLER
SOUTHCOATES LANE
Hull Maternity
MARFLEET AVENUE
MARFLEET LANE
Factory
B165
Liby
WYKE ST
H.M. Prison
Cemy
Factory
H
Factory
PO
CEYLON ST
Factory
WITHAM
PO
ABBEY
WILLIAMSON ST
HEDON ROAD
A1033
HULL ROAD
VALLETTA STREET
Factory
SOMERDEN RD
Factory
155
CHURCH STREET
HEDON ROAD
GARRISON RD
CORPORATION ROAD
HEDON ROAD
A1033
29
Coll
SOUTH BRIDGE ROAD
Factory
Alexandra Dock
i
Queen Elizabeth Dock
Factory
PO
Ct
Mus
Locks
Wharf
Locks
Lord's Clough
7
HIGH ST
TOWER ST
A63
Sch
Factory
Wharf
HU12
PO
CAMILLA CL
Locks
Victoria Dock Village
Hull Roads
147
28
Victoria Pier

KINGSTON
UPON HULL

Quay   6

Quay

Salt End Jetties   27

River   Humber   5

146
147
26

Skitter Ness   4
Haven Farm
Goxhill Haven
New Bank Farm
New Green   25
Chimney
New Green Farm
Factory
Regent House
Mast
Neatgangs Farm
Salt Marsh Farm
East Marsh Farm   3
NEATGANGS LANE
DN19
East Marsh
WEST MARSH LA
Salt Marsh
EAST MARSH ROAD
Ferry Farm   24
FERRY ROAD
Fir Tree Farm   2
Horsegate Farm
HORSEGATE FIELD ROAD
Glebe Farm
Spring Farm
Brook Hill   23
SYKES LANE
North End Farm
Brook Hill Farm
CHAPEL FIELD ROAD
East Halton Skitter
Cottage Farm
WINDSOR GR
Maydale Farm
Chapel Farm
Main Drain
Main Drain
SKITTER RD
1
Croft Side
RUARDS LANE
SKITTER ROAD
DN40
THE CL
ELM LA
North End
RUARD ROAD
Langmere Covert
The Grange   22
MILL LA

10   A   11   B   12   C   13   D   14   E   15   F   22

For full street detail of the highlighted area see pages 146 and 147.

86
72

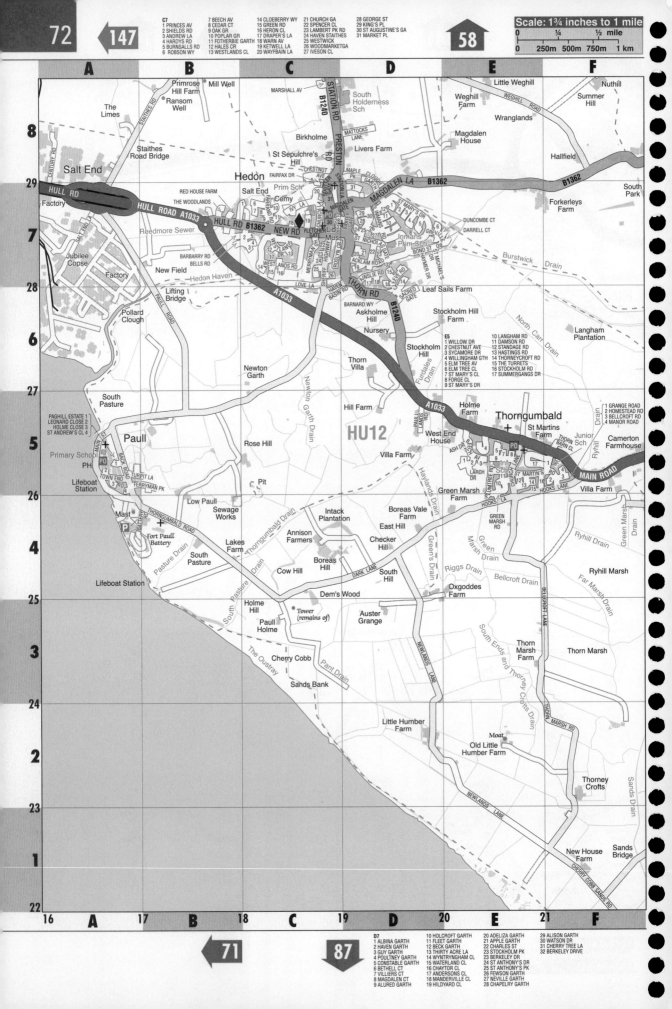

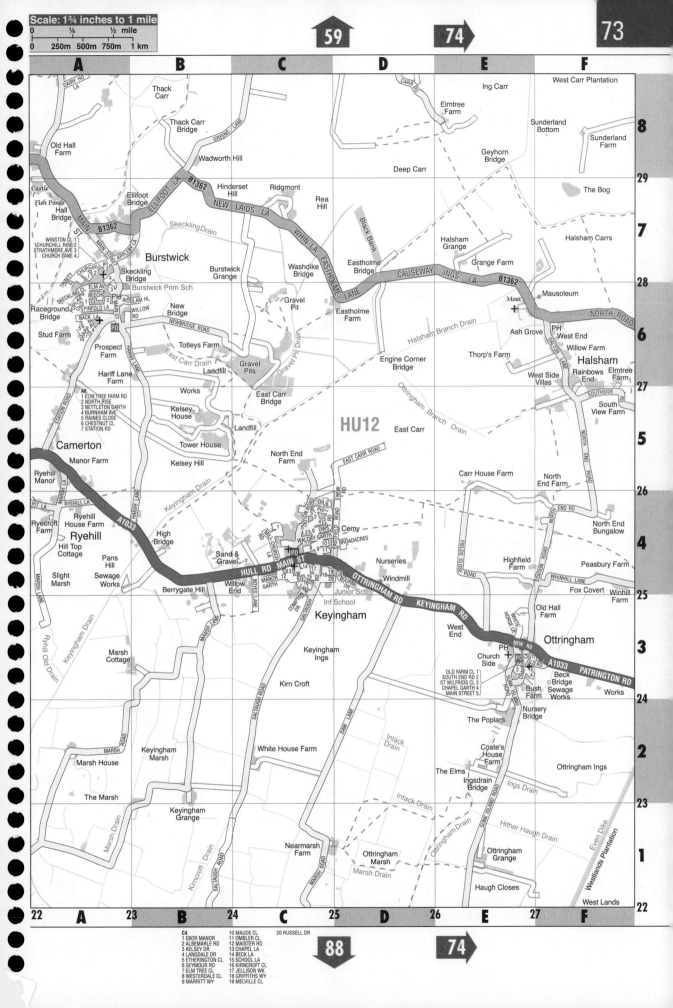

A   B   C   D   E   F

8
Roos Carrs
DOVE CL
CHERRY HL PK
ORCHARD CL
Dents Garth
Eastfield Plantation
Burnham Carrs
Elm Farm
Sewage Works
Moat
The Greens
Wood's Plantation
Rimswell Carrs
Carr Farm
North Farm
Sand Hills
Waxholme
Cliff Farm
Windmill
Craikham Hill
White Bridge
Roos Drain

29
Roos Bridge
Seathorne Holiday Village
Northfield House
Rimswell Valley
B1242
WAXHOLME RD
Halecote Farm
Hall Farm
Roos Drain
Fox Covert
Poplar Farm

7
Halsham Carrs
Southlands Farm
Hall Farm
Rimswell
Manor Farm
Shaw Farm
Foothead Garth
Withernsea High School
NORTHFIELD
OWTHORNE WK
Owthorne
Junior Sch
F7
1 HUBERT ST
2 CAMMIDGE ST
3 GEORGE ST
4 ALMA ST
5 WALTER ST
6 EDWARD ST

28
Hill Top Farm
Little Farm
Poplar Farm
PO
Tower Farm
Rimswell Lodge
Stock Bridge
The Lighthouse Mus
NORTHFIELD Inf School
CARAS

6
Bunker's Hill
B1362
NORTH ROAD
East End
Highfield Farm
Batty's Corner
B1362
North Field Farm
B1362
HULL ROAD
B1362
Cemy
Little England Hill
OWTHORNE GRANGE
CHELLSWAY
Leisure Ctr
Allot

27
Carr House Farm
Moate Farm
Eastfield Farm
SOUTHSIDE ROAD
CHUMLEY FIELD ROAD
CHANTRY LANE
Great England Hill
Catchwater Drain

5
Old Hall
HU12
Little Newsome
High Wood
Great Newsome Farm
Frodingham Hall
Moat
Central Farm
Willow House Farm
HU19
Dodd Hill
Jenny Carr Hill
North Carr Dales

26
Churchlands Farm
BADGER LANE
High Wood
Burgany Hall
Burgany Plantation
Winestead Hall
Dam Hill
Frodingham Lane
Town's Carr Hill
Hollym Carrs
NORTH CARR DALES RD

4
North Field
WINHILL LA
Churchlands Plantation
Sewage Works
West Field
Red Hall Farm
WINESTEAD LANE
Weldon's Plantation
Winestead Drain
Frodingham Carrs
Enholmes Hill
Garth Farm
SOUTH CARR DALES ROAD

25
Northfield Plantation
Westfield Plantation
ARABLES LANE
Bracken Hill
South Carr
Toffling Hill

3
Thorp's Plantation
BYDALES LANE
Winestead
Weldon's Plantation
Ring of Bright Water
CROFTS LANE
South Carr Dales
Toffling Farm
Fair View Farm
SOUTH CARR DALES RD

24
PATRINGTON ROAD   A1033
Hall Plantation
BYDALES LA
NICHOLSON'S LA
Fir Tree Farm
Whin Hill
Piper Hill
Piper Hill Clump
WINESTEAD L1
Mile House
HOLLYM ROAD

2
Park Farm
White Hall
Moat
STATION RD
Winestead Bridge
Whin Hill Clump
Winestead Carrs
Sewage Works
Patrington Carrs
Greenlands Farm

23
Winestead Ings
WINESTEAD INGS LANE
Red Enholmes
A1033
STATION RD
PH
Works
A1033
Windmill Hill
HOLMPTON ROAD
Eastfield House

1
Half Moon Plantation
Winestead West Lands
The Ings
Buckclose Plantation
Dunn Ings Plantation
INGS LANE
WESTFIELD
WESTGATE
PO MARKET PL
NORTHSIDE
EASTGATE
CHURCH
Patrington
Eastend Farm

Winestead Grange
Ingslane Bridge
Winestead Drain
Enholmes Hall
Enholmes Plantation
Cherry Plantation
HAVEN RD
Patrington C of E School
SALTMARSH LA
SOUTHSIDE
WELWICK ROAD
B1445
Cemy
Windmill
HU12

22

28   A   29   B   30   C   31   D   32   E   33   F

D1
1 HUNTER CL
2 GUARDIANS ROAD
3 FRANCIS WAY
4 WESTGATE MANOR
5 PUMP ROW
6 NORTHSIDE COURT
7 CHURCH VIEW
8 TITHE BARN LANE
9 TITHE BARN CL
10 CLARKS LANE
11 BEECH DRIVE
12 THE CLOSE
13 THE CRESCENT
14 ST PATRICK'S GN
15 SAFFRON GARTH

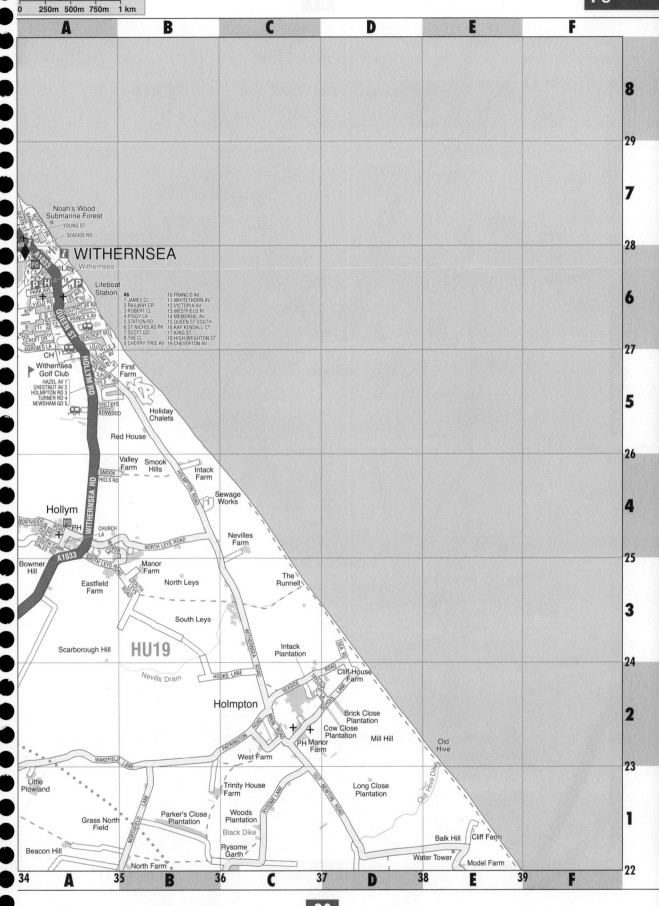

Scale: 1¾ inches to 1 mile
0   ¼   ½ mile
0   250m 500m 750m 1 km

A **B** **C** **D** **E** **F**

8

WF11

WHITEFIELD BUNGALOWS

WHITEFIELD LANE

Works

South Moor

DN14

21

LC

Cridling Stubbs

PH

COBCROFT LA

COBCROFT LANE

WRIGHTS LA

STUBBS LANE

Spring Lodge

Kelseycroft Wood

Grange Farm

GRAVEL HILL LANE

WHITLEY THORPE LA

CATHCART CL

7

Wake Wood

Wormersley Quarry

LC

NORTHFIELD LANE

Bell Lands Wood

Whitley Thorpe

BOOTY LANE

20

Beech House Farm

Scrombeck Farm

Rows Wood

Quarry (dis)

Womersley Common

Fulham House

FULHAM LANE

Hodgsoncroft Wood

Saulcroft Wood

6

Bank Wood

BANK WOOD ROAD

Well

Well

NORTHFIELD CL

LC

COLN LA

Ricketcroft Wood

Stapleton Park Farm

Manor Farm

Prim Sch

Clipsall Wood

BANK WOOD ROAD

Kingsland Wood

MILL LA

19

Sewage Works

Low Farm

Womersley

PARK LA

Grove Wood

STATION RD HIGHFIELD LA

LC

Stocking Green Farm

Ox Stocking Wood

Fishpond Wood

The Rookery

Wormesley Park

Womersley Beck

5

Stapleton Park

Belt Plantation

HIGHFIELD LANE

Brown Ings Wood

Dawland House Farm

Castle Hill Wood

Castle Farm

DN6

Birdspring Wood

Sod Wall Plantation

Quarry (dis)

18

Nutwood End

SMEATLEY'S LA

Little Grove Farm

Smeaton Leys

CHURCHFIELD LA

Smeaton Bridge

Grove Bridge

4

Brockadale Plantation

LEYS LANE

Long Crag

CHURCHFIELD LANE

Stubbs Common Farm

Smeaton Crags Quarry

River Went

Little Smeaton

WILLOWBRIDGE ROAD

Stubbs Bridge

Wells Farm

COMMON LA

17

WEST EDGE ROAD

Kirk Smeaton

CHAPEL LA

The Grove

LITTLE LA

Home Farm

LC

Walden Stubbs

3

WF8

PH

MALL LA

PO

WATER LA

MANOR CL

Willow Bridge

STUBBS ROAD

TANPIT LA

LC

Manor Farm

Little Bottom Plantation

Kirk Smeaton C of E Prim School

PINFOLD CROSS

PINFOLD LA

Sewage Works

16

MIDDLEFIELD LANE

LONG LANE

Norton Priory

Tanpit Bridge

WALDEN STUBBS ROAD

Sewage Works LC

Bradley's Spring

NORTON AND KIRK SMEAT

Norton

LINKWAY

BACK LANE

2

A1 Knottingley, M62

COAL PIT LA

Middle Field

Highfield Farm

WESTFIELD LANE

SPITTLERUSH LANE

BARNSDALE VW

BACK LANE

PRIORY RD

STATION RD

LC

CRAB TREE LANE

CLIFF HL RD

WEST END ROAD

PO

PINFOLD LA

NORTON CO LA

QUARRY RD

15

Sewage Works

A1

Hotel

Windhill Plantation

Fox Covert

GREENGATE ROAD

FOX COVERT RD

WHITELEY RD

Cliff Hill

West End

PH THE CLOSE

East End Villas

Norton Ings

A639 Pontefract

1

Shaft

Quarry

Barnsdale Wood

Windmill

WINDMILL LA

Campsmount School

STYGATE LA

Cemy

CHURCH FIELD ROAD

GLEBE RD

BEECH DR

P

Glebe Farm

A638 DONCASTER RD

Barnsdale

Campsmount Home Farm

WOODLAND RISE

CHURCH VW

Askern & Campsall Sports Ctr

14

Shaft

A1 Doncaster (A638)

Barnsdale Wood

South Yorkshire STREET ATLAS

50 **A** **51** **B** **52** **C** **53** **D** **54** **E** **55** **F**

West Yorkshire STREET ATLAS

C3
1 WENTDALE
2 STAN VALLEY
3 SPRINGFIELD CR

E2
1 BROC-O-BANK
2 NEWTHORPE RD
3 FORRESTER'S CL
4 TRAFFORD RD
5 ARUNDEL RD
6 ADELAIDE RD
7 HEADINGLEY RD
8 ORCHARD DR
9 ORCHARD CL
10 RYECROFT AV
11 FIR TREE DR
12 MANOR CL

E1
1 TENNYSON AV
2 SHAKESPEARE AV
3 BYRON AV
4 WORDSWORTH AV
5 WELLINGTONIA DR
6 LANGLEYS RD
7 EAST VW
8 GRANGE RD
9 WILLOW RD
10 VAUGHAN RD
11 CAMPSALL PK RD
12 CAMPSALL HALL RD
13 SHERWOOD CL

F2
1 LYNDHURST DR
2 LYNDHURST CL
3 LYNDHURST RI
4 ASHBURNHAM CL
5 ASHBURNHAM WK
6 DENVER RD
7 MANOR GARTH
8 SWAN SYKE DR
9 DRYHURST CL

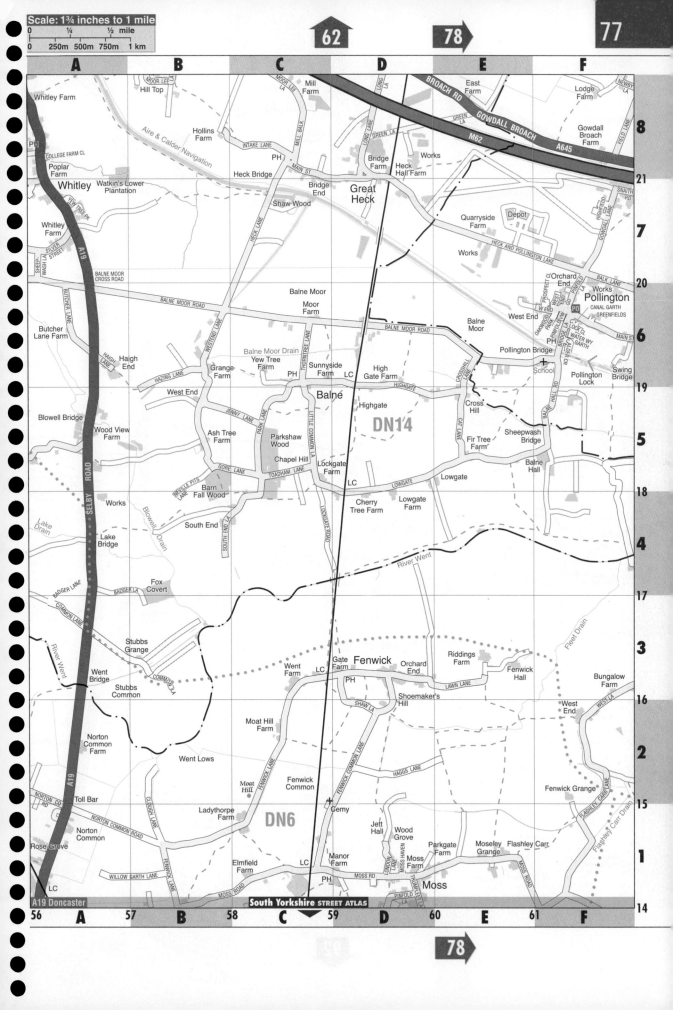

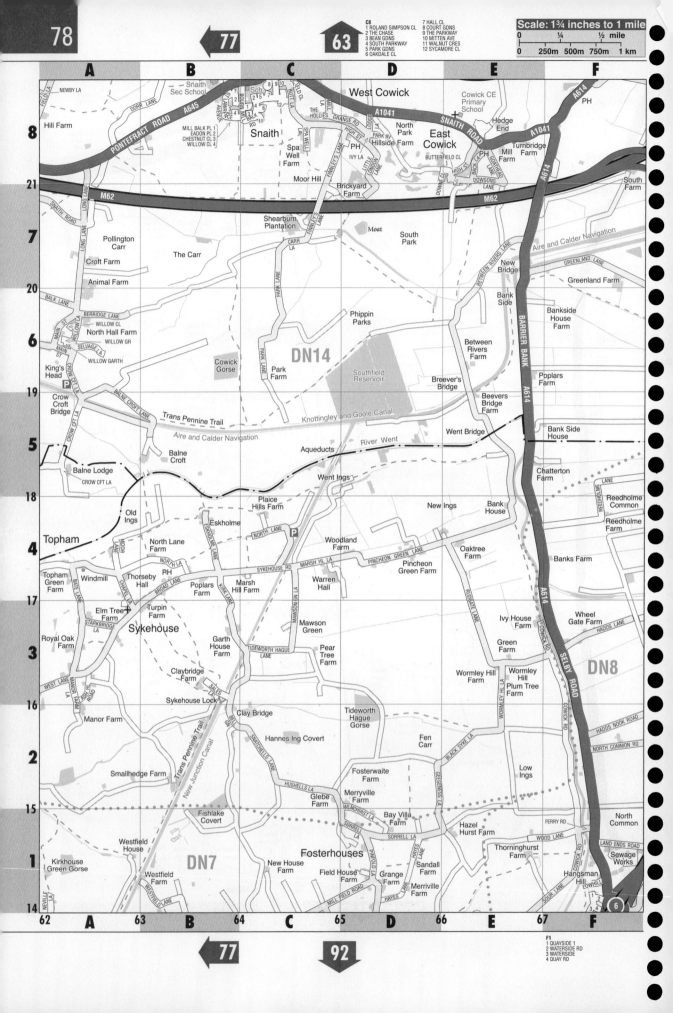

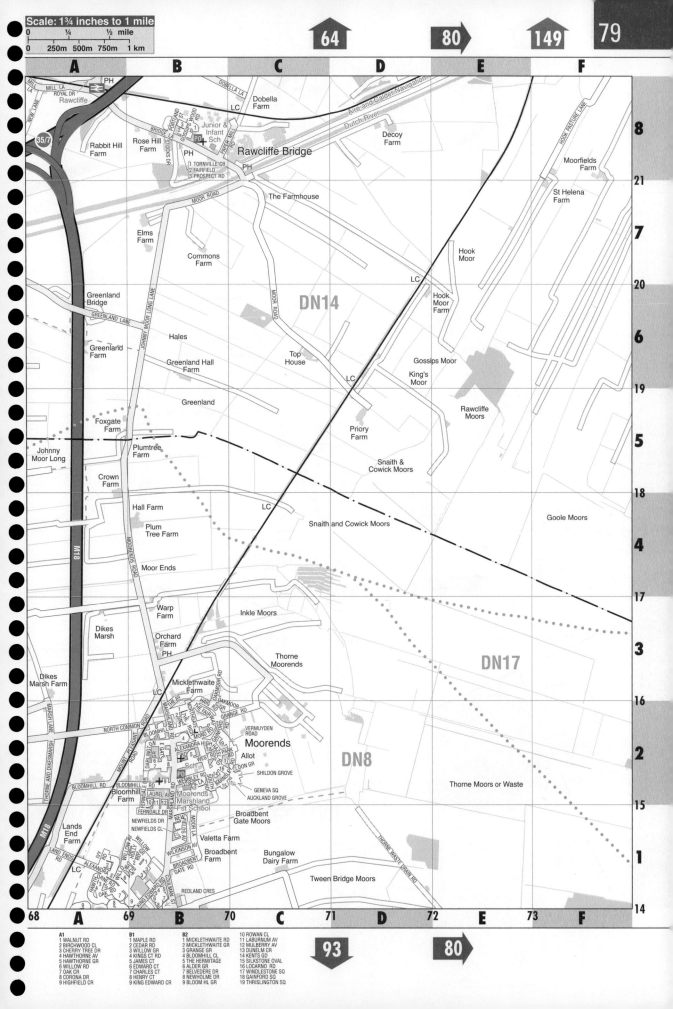

A   B   C   D   E   F

8
21
7
20
6
19
5
18
4
17
3
16
2
15
1
14

MILL LA
NEW LANE
ROYAL DR
Rawcliffe
PH
35/7
Rabbit Hill Farm
Rose Hill Farm
BRIDGE LA
STOCKS DR
PORTLAND ST
GOSSIP ST
PAPER MILL
PORTLAND ST
Junior & Infant Sch
PO
PH
LC
Dobella Farm
DOBELLA LA
Rawcliffe Bridge
PH
PH
1 TORNVILLE CR
2 FAIRFIELD
3 PROSPECT RD

Aire and Calder Navigation
Dutch River
Decoy Farm
Moorfields Farm
St Helena Farm

Elms Farm
MOOR ROAD
Commons Farm
The Farmhouse
Hook Moor

Greenland Bridge
GREENLAND LANE
JOHNNY MOOR LONG LANE
Hales
LC
Hook Moor Farm

DN14

Greenland Farm
Greenland Hall Farm
MOOR ROAD
Top House
Gossips Moor

Greenland
LC
King's Moor
Rawcliffe Moors

HOOK PASTURE LANE

Foxgate Farm
Plumtree Farm
Priory Farm
Snaith & Cowick Moors

Johnny Moor Long
Crown Farm

Hall Farm
LC
Snaith and Cowick Moors
Goole Moors

M18
Plum Tree Farm
MOORENDS ROAD
Moor Ends
Warp Farm
Inkle Moors

Dikes Marsh
Orchard Farm
PH
Thorne Moorends

DN17

Dikes Marsh Farm
LC
Micklethwaite Farm
MARSHLAND RD
NORTH COMMON ROAD
HAIG RD
THE AV
THE FAIRWAY
OAKMOOR RD
OAKMOOR RD
GRANGE RD
VERMUYDEN ROAD

MARSH LANE
THORNE AND DIKESMARSH
BLOOMHILL RD
MOUNT PLEASANT
DARLINGTON
ALEXANDRA HIGH ST
MOND RD
WEST RD
WEST RD
Allot
Moorends
Sch
PO
SHILDON GROVE
GENEVA SQ
AUCKLAND GROVE
ELDON GR

DN8
Thorne Moors or Waste

Lands End Farm
M18
LAND ENDS RD
LC
NEWFIELDS DR
NEWFIELDS CL
FERNDALE DR
LAUREL AV
Bloomhill Farm
BLOOMHILL RD
WILKINSON AV
Moorends Marshland Fst School
Valetta Farm
Broadbent Gate Moors

ALEXANDRA
HAWTHORNE RD
OAK RD
KING EDWARD RD
COLEMAN ST
WILLOW AV
WILLOW GR
HOLLY
IVY
BROADBENT GATE RD
REDLAND CRES
MOOR LA
Broadbent Farm
Bungalow Dairy Farm

THORNE WASTE DRAIN RD
Tween Bridge Moors

68   69   70   71   72   73
A   B   C   D   E   F

93 ▼   80 ►

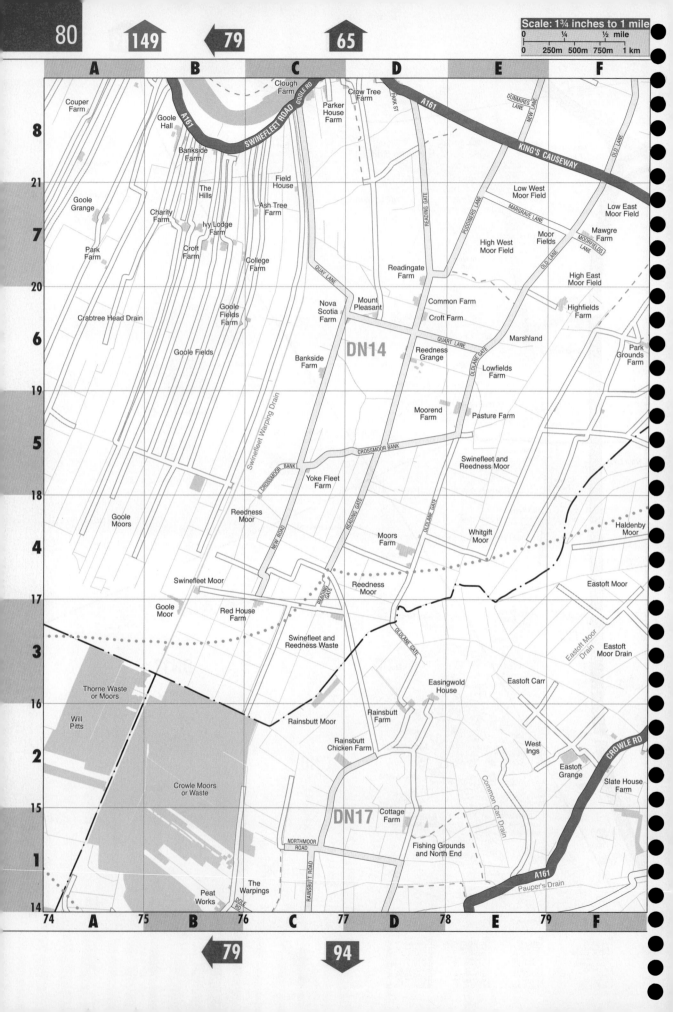

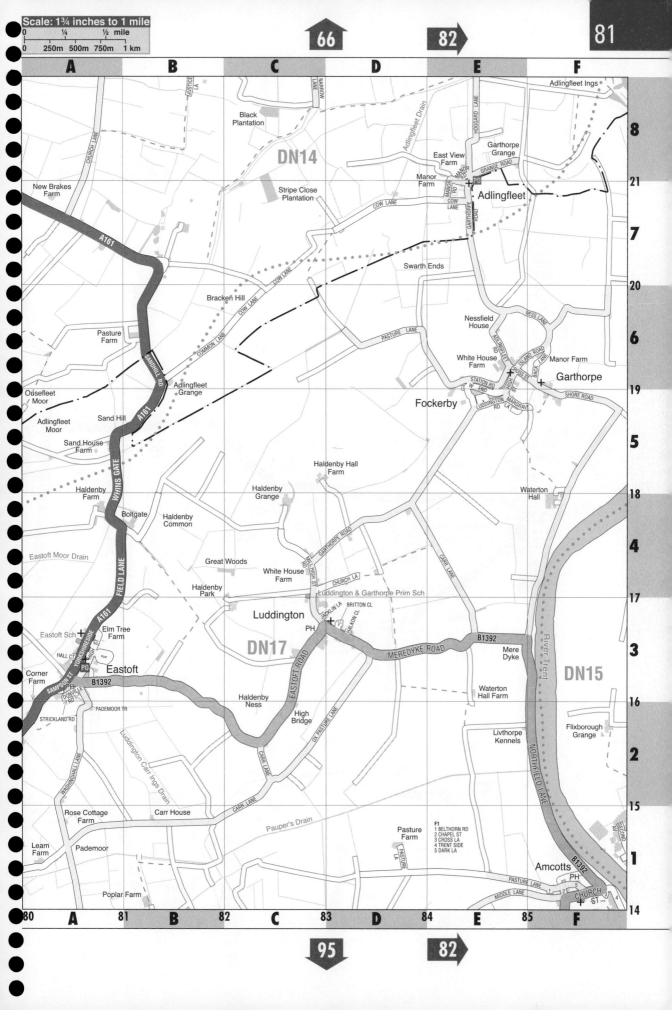

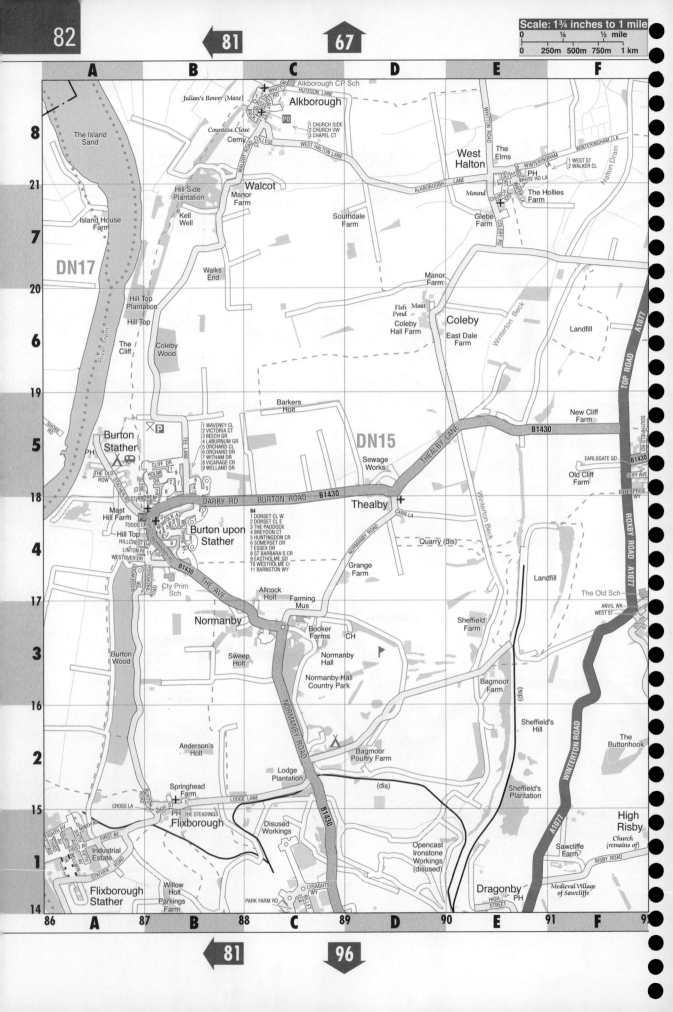

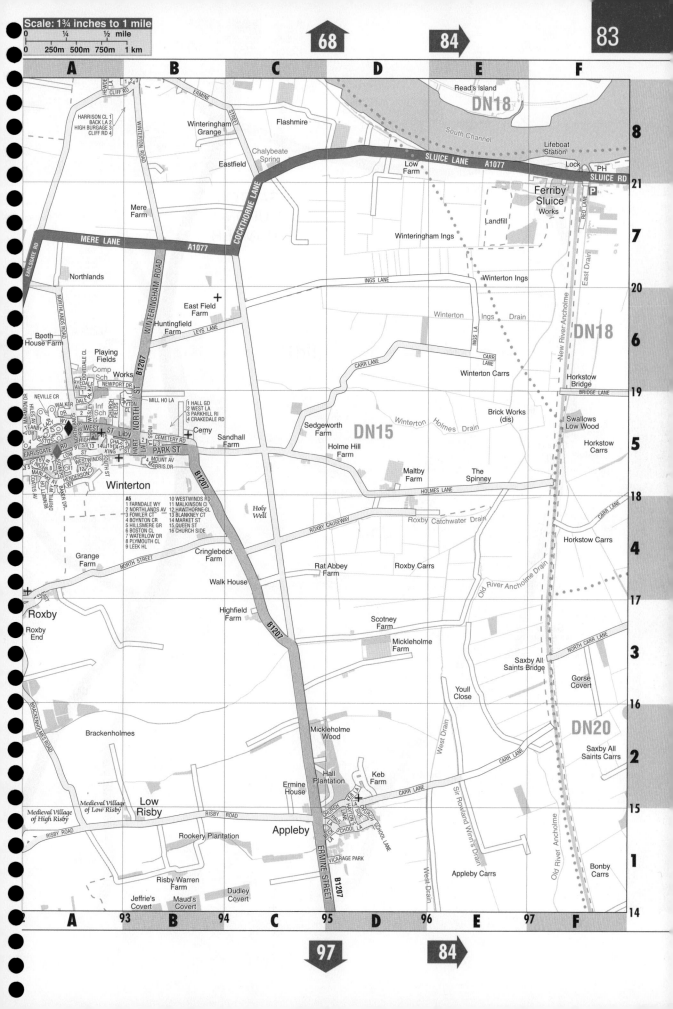

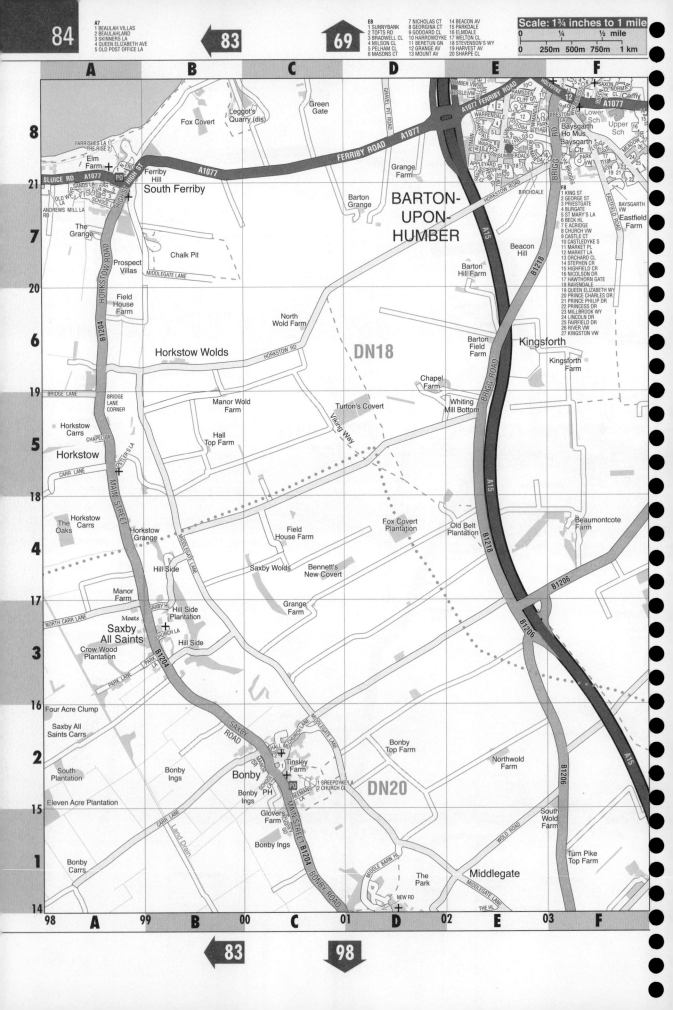

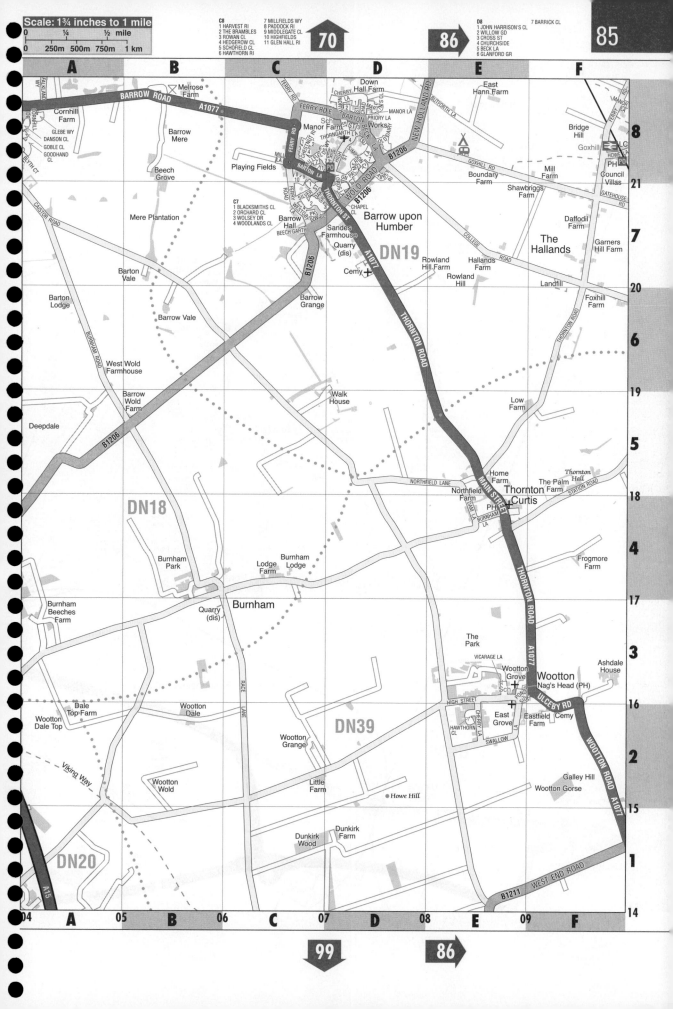

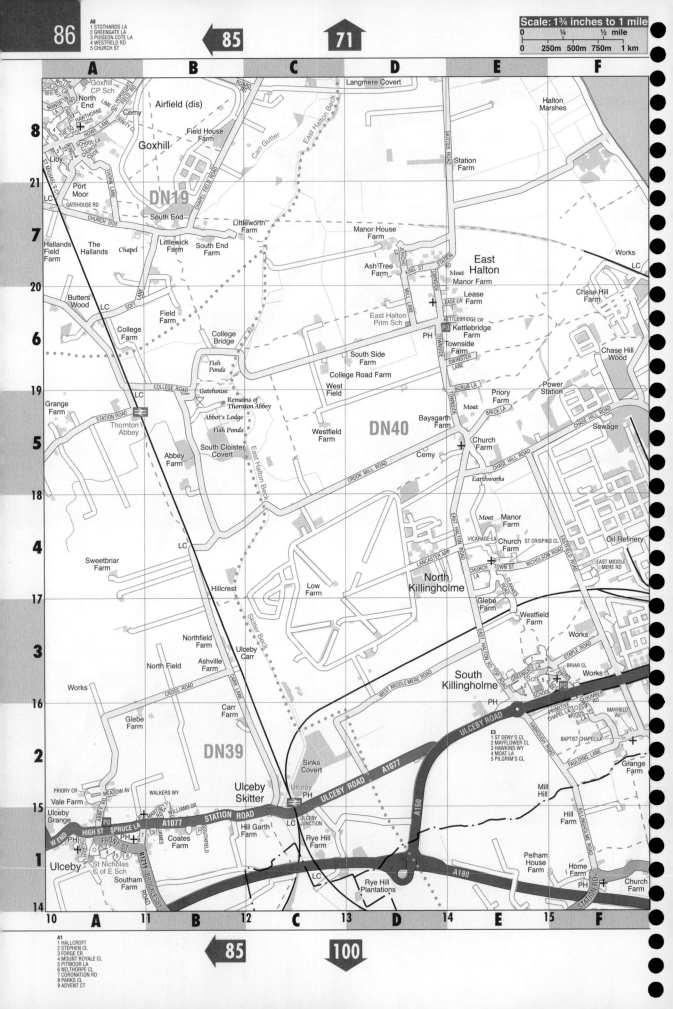

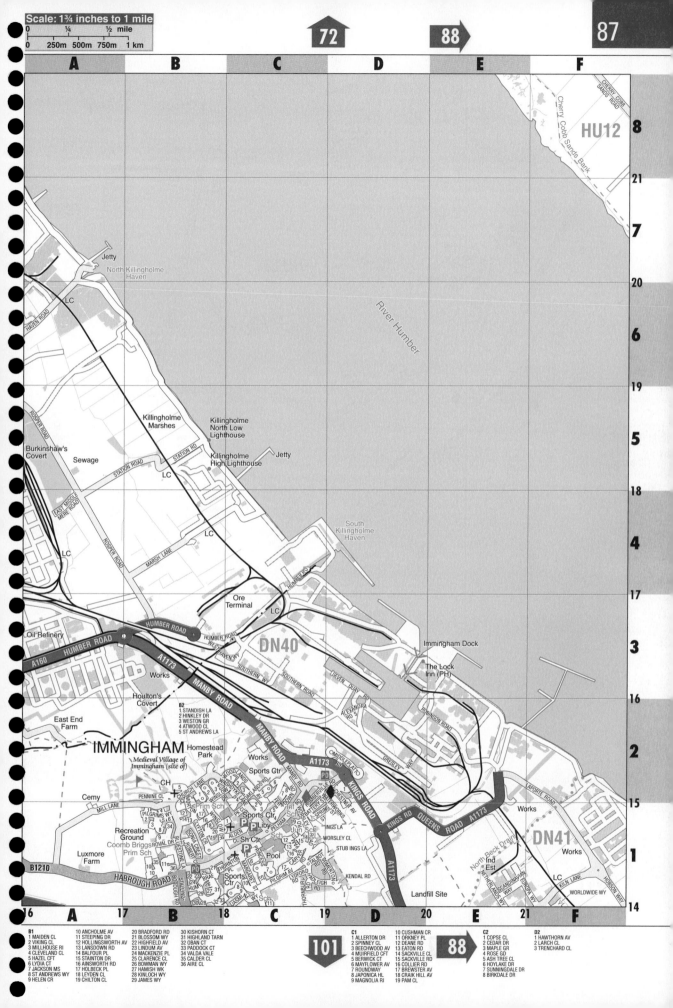

HU12

8

21

7

20

6

19

Jetty

North Killingholme
Haven

5

LC

River Humber

HAVEN ROAD

ROSPER ROAD

Burkinshaw's
Covert

Sewage

Killingholme
Marshes

Killingholme
North Low
Lighthouse

STATION ROAD

STATION RD

EAST MIDDLE
MERE ROAD

LC

Killingholme
High Lighthouse

Jetty

South
Killingholme
Haven

18

4

LC

MARSH LANE

ROSPER ROAD

LC

17

Ore
Terminal

LC

HUMBER RD

HUMBER ROAD

Oil Refinery

A160

HUMBER ROAD

HUMBER ROAD
WEST

A1173

DN40

Immingham Dock

The Lock
Inn (PH)

3

16

Works

SOUTHERN WY

SOUTHERN ROAD

MANBY ROAD

SEVEN QUAY RD

ALEXANDRA
RD

ROBINSON ROAD

Houlton's
Covert

East End
Farm

IMMINGHAM

Homestead
Park

Works

MANBY ROAD

A1173

GRESLEY WY

LAPORTE ROAD

DN41

Works

2

Medieval Village of
Immingham (site of)

Sports Ctr

CH

Cemy

PENNINE CL

MILL LANE

Prim Sch

Sports Ctr

Liby

KINGS ROAD

QUEENS ROAD

A1173

Works

15

Recreation
Ground

Coomb Briggs
Prim Sch

Luxmore
Farm

B1210

HABROUGH ROAD

Pool

Sports
Ctr

Worsley Cl

Stub Ings La

Kendal Rd

North Beck Drain

Ind
Est

Landfill Site

LC

KILN LANE

WORLDWIDE WY

1

14

A   B   C   D   E   F
16   17   18   19   20   21

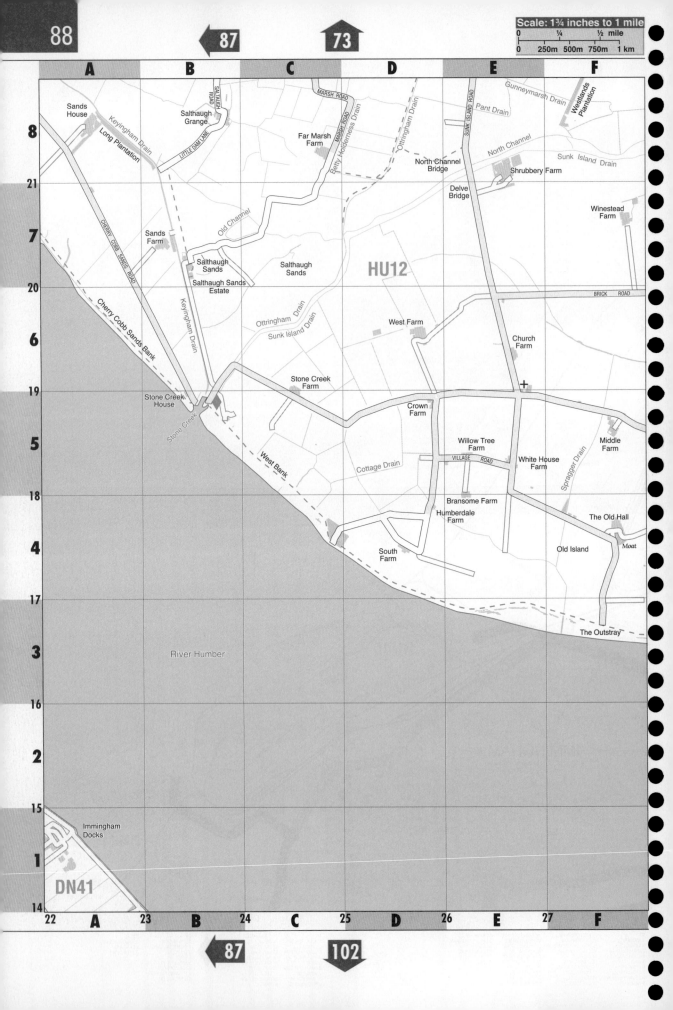

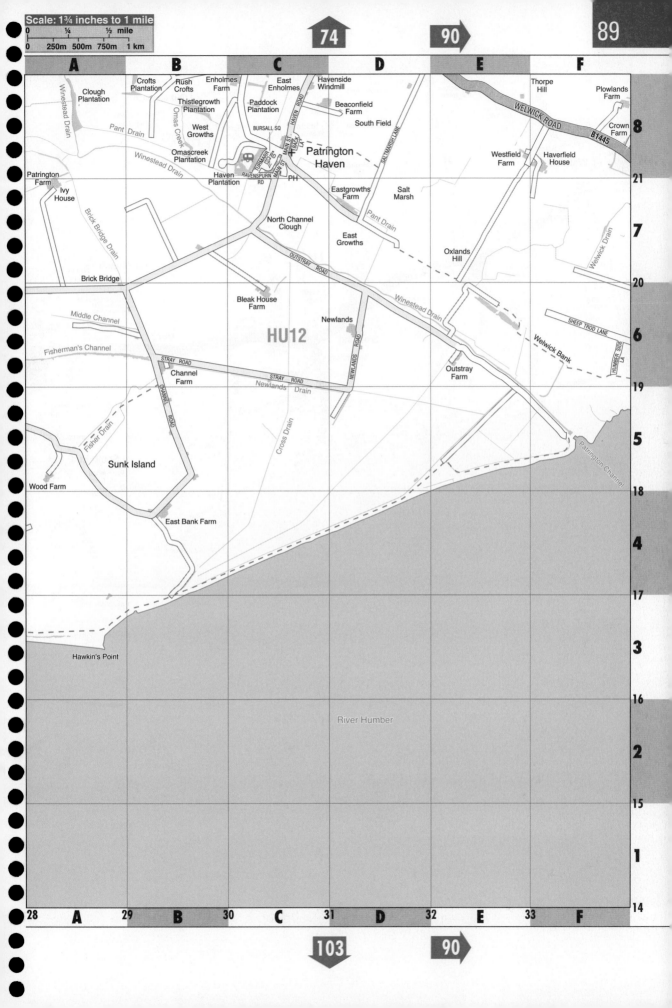

A   B   C   D   E   F

Clough Plantation
Winstead Drain
Pant Drain
Crofts Plantation
Rush Crofts
Thistlegrowth Plantation
Enholmes Farm
East Enholmes
Havenside Windmill
Thorpe Hill
Plowlands Farm
WELWICK ROAD
Omas Creek
West Growths
Paddock Plantation
BURSALL SQ
Beaconfield Farm
South Field
B1445
Crown Farm
8

Omascreek Plantation
Winstead Drain
HAVEN ROAD
MAIN ST
BACK LA
MAIN ST
Patrington Haven
Westfield Farm
Haverfield House
Patrington Farm
Ivy House
Haven Plantation
TURMASH RD
RAVENSPURN RD
PH
SKITMARSH LANE
21

Eastgrowths Farm
Salt Marsh
Brick Bridge Drain
North Channel Clough
Pant Drain
7

East Growths
Oxlands Hill
Brick Bridge
OUTSTRAY ROAD
Welwick Drain
20

Bleak House Farm
Winstead Drain
SHEEP TROD LANE
Middle Channel
Newlands
HU12
Welwick Bank
HUMBER SIDE LA
6

Fisherman's Channel
STRAY ROAD
NEWLANDS ROAD
Outstray Farm
19

Channel Farm
STRAY ROAD
Newlands   Drain
CHANNEL ROAD
Fisher Drain
Cross Drain
5

Sunk Island
Wood Farm
18

East Bank Farm
4

17

Hawkin's Point
3

16

River Humber
2

15

1

28   A   29   B   30   C   31   D   32   E   33   F   14

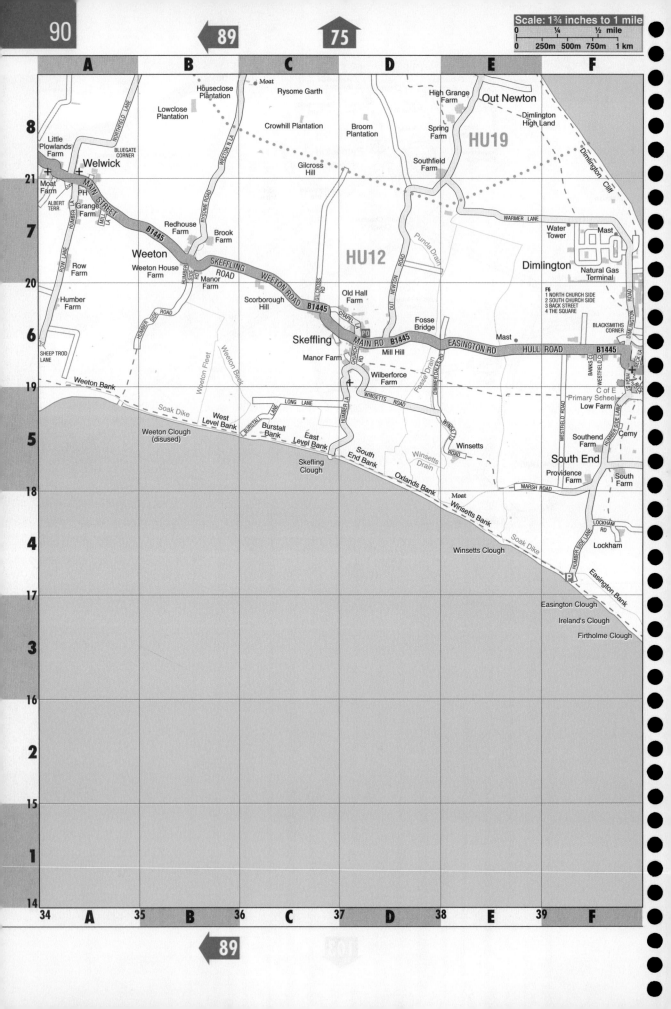

Scale: 1¾ inches to 1 mile

0 | ¼ | ½ mile
0 | 250m | 500m | 750m | 1 km

A **B** **C** **D** **E** **F**

Houseclose Plantation

Moat

Rysome Garth

High Grange Farm

Out Newton

8

Lowclose Plantation

Crowhill Plantation

Broom Plantation

Spring Farm

Dimlington High Land

HU19

Little Plowlands Farm

Gilcross Hill

Southfield Farm

21

Welwick

BLUEGATE CORNER

Dimlington Cliff

Moat Farm

PH

WARMER LANE

7

Grange Farm

Redhouse Farm

Brook Farm

Water Tower

Mast

B1445

Weeton

SKEFFLING ROAD

Dimlington

Natural Gas Terminal

Weeton House Farm

Manor Farm

WEETON ROAD

Punda Drain

20

Humber Farm

Scorborough Hill

HU12

Old Hall Farm

F6
1 NORTH CHURCH SIDE
2 SOUTH CHURCH SIDE
3 BACK STREET
4 THE SQUARE

B1445

6

Sheep Trod Lane

Skeffling

Fosse Bridge

Mast

EASINGTON RD

HULL ROAD

BLACKSMITHS CORNER

Manor Farm

MAIN RD

B1445

B1445

Mill Hill

Weeton Bank

19

Wilberforce Farm

WINSETTS ROAD

C of E Primary School

Low Farm

Soak Dike

LONG LANE

West Level Bank

Burstall Bank

East Level Bank

South End Bank

Winsetts

Southend Farm

Cemy

5

Weeton Clough (disused)

Skefling Clough

Winsetts Drain

South End

South Farm

18

Oxlands Bank

Moat

Providence Farm

MARSH ROAD

Winsetts Bank

LOCKHAM RD

4

Winsetts Clough

Soak Dike

Lockham

Easington Bank

17

Easington Clough

Ireland's Clough

3

Firtholme Clough

16

2

15

1

14

34 A **35** B **36** C **37** D **38** E **39** F

Scale: 1¾ inches to 1 mile

0   ¼   ½   mile

0   250m 500m 750m 1 km

A   B   C   D   E   F

40   41   42

8

21

13   13

7

Hawke Channel

20

HU12

12   12

6

Spurn Warren

Nature
Reserve

19

Jetty   P   Lighthouse

11   11

Lifeboat
Station

5

Spurn Head

18

40   41   42

Wyke Bight

VICAR'S LANE

Easington +

SEASIDE ROAD

PO
PH

St   Sewage
Works

SEASIDE RD

EASTFIELD RD

New Bank

FIRTHOLME ROAD

Long Bank

LOCKHAM
RD

Firtholme
Farm

Long Bank
Bridge

Long Bank

Kilnsea
Grange

Westmere
Farm

Black Moor
Well

Kilnsea +

P
PH   EASINGTON

NORTH MARSH ROAD

RD

Cliff Farm

Southfield
Farm

P   Visitor Centre

SPURN ROAD

P

Toll

Warren Head

Spurn Bird Observatory

Kilnsea Warren

17

4

3

16

2

15

1

14

40   A   41   B   42   C   43   D   44   E   45   F

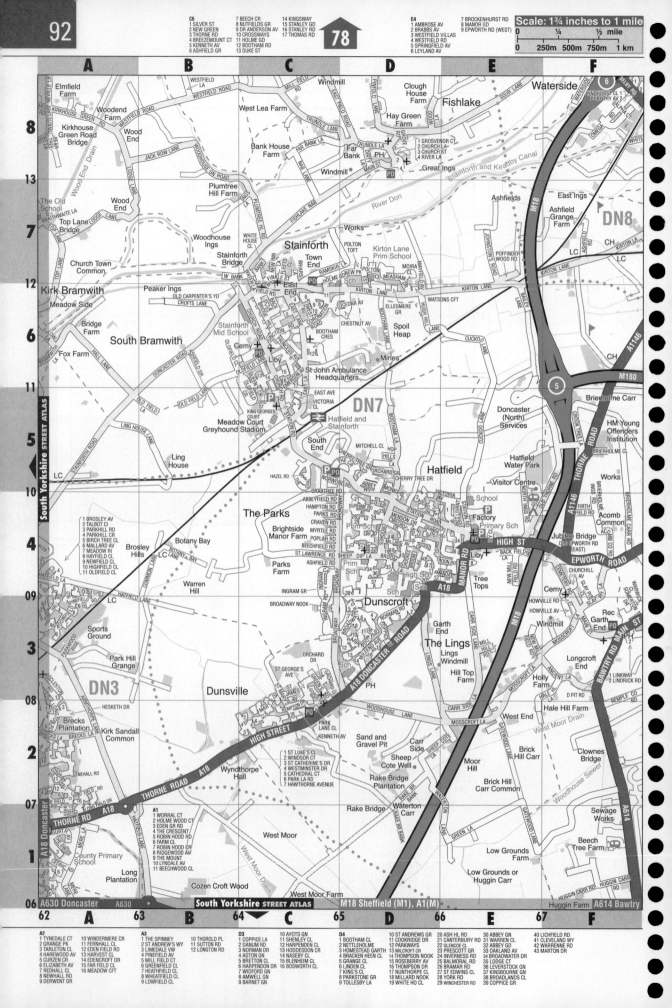

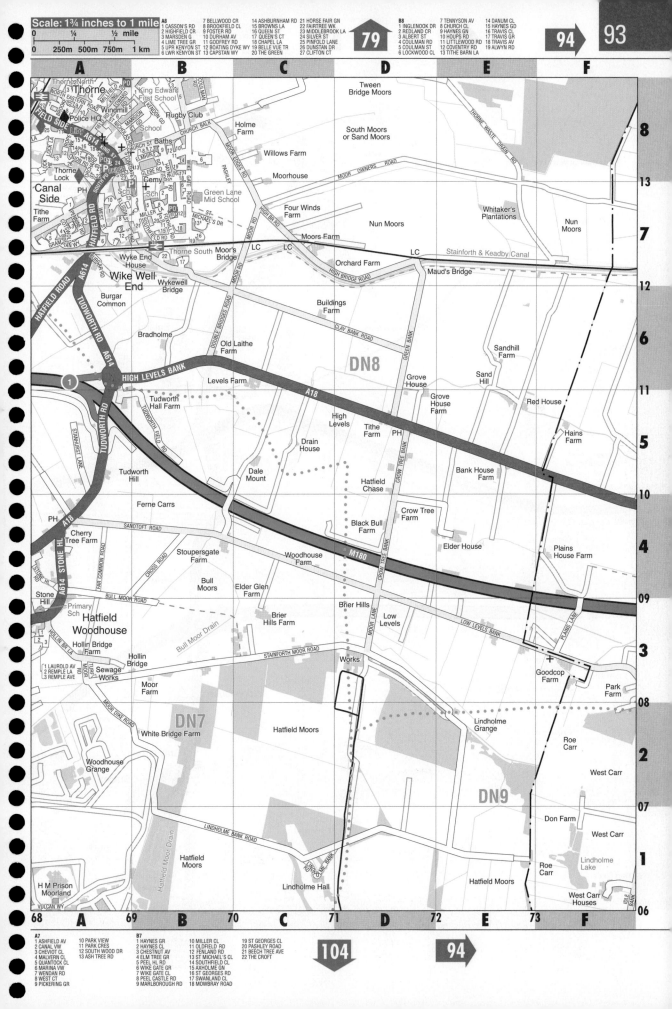

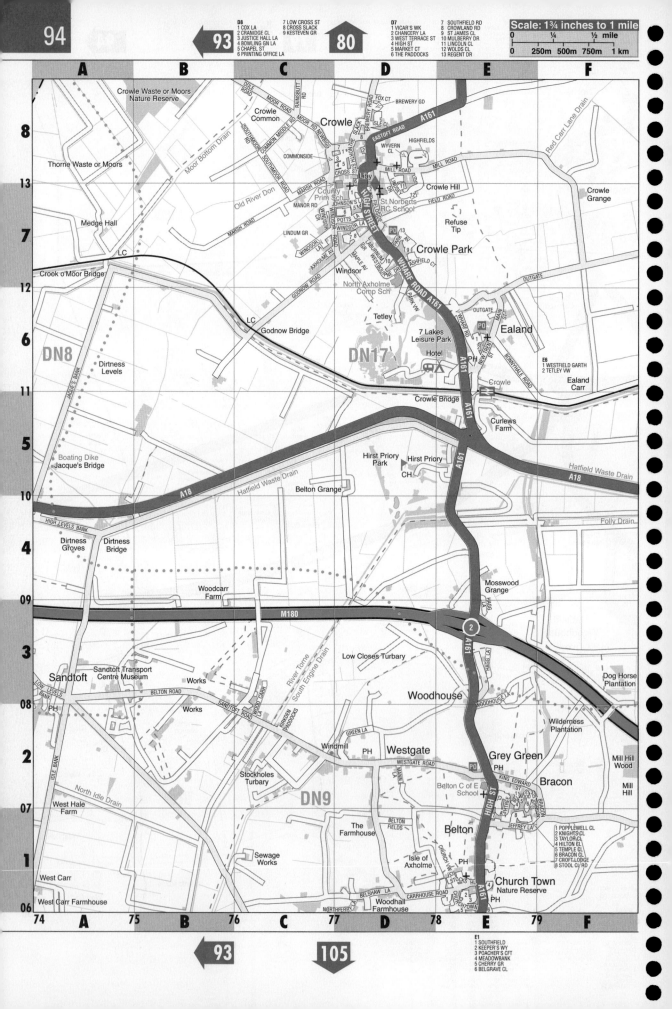

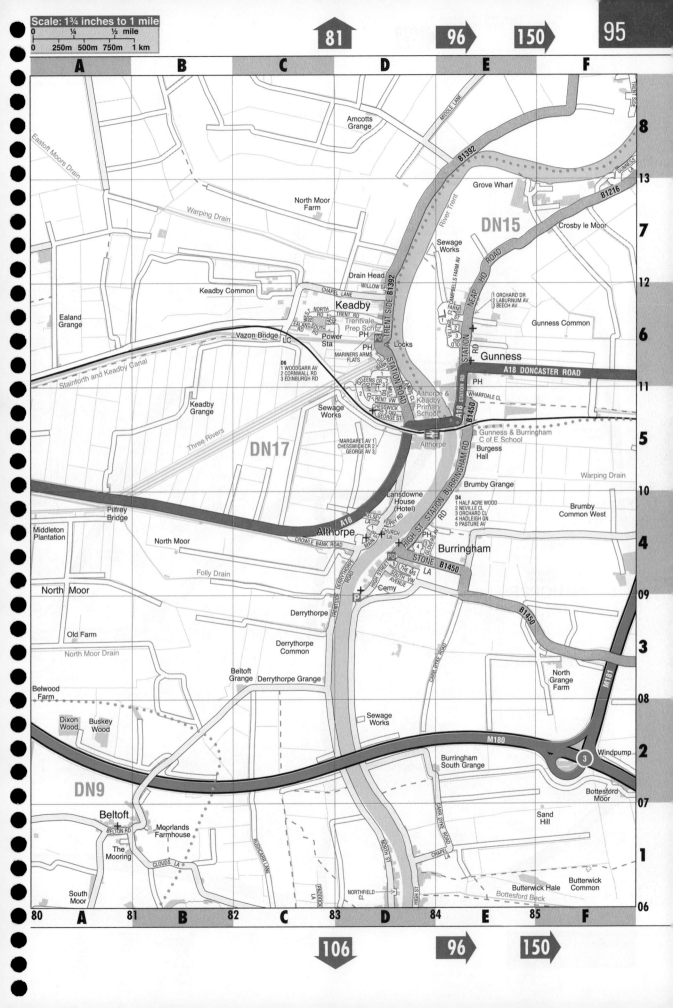

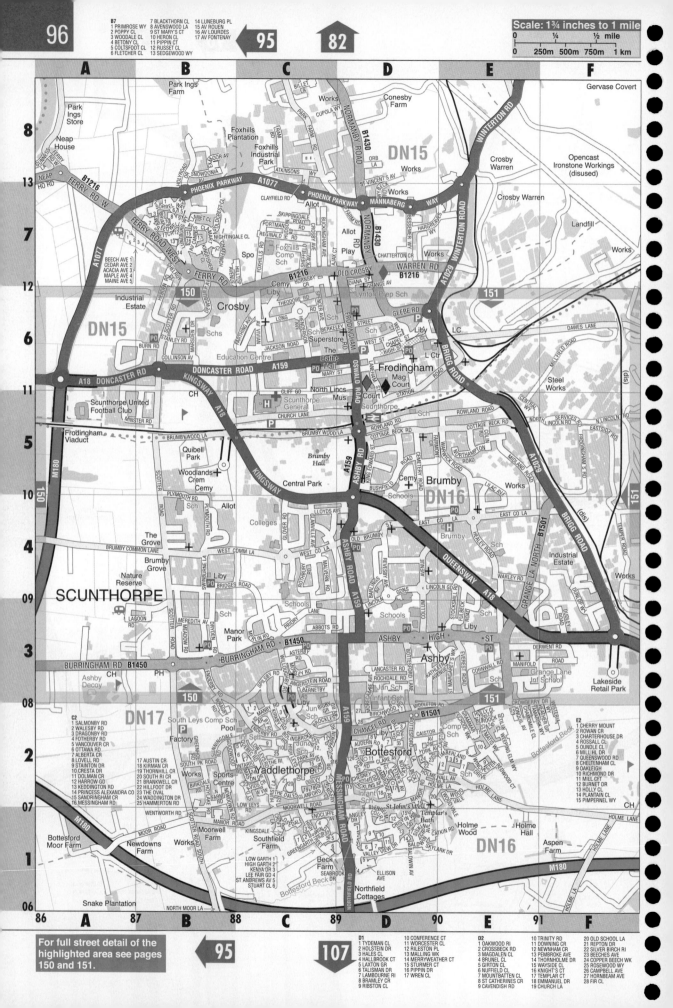

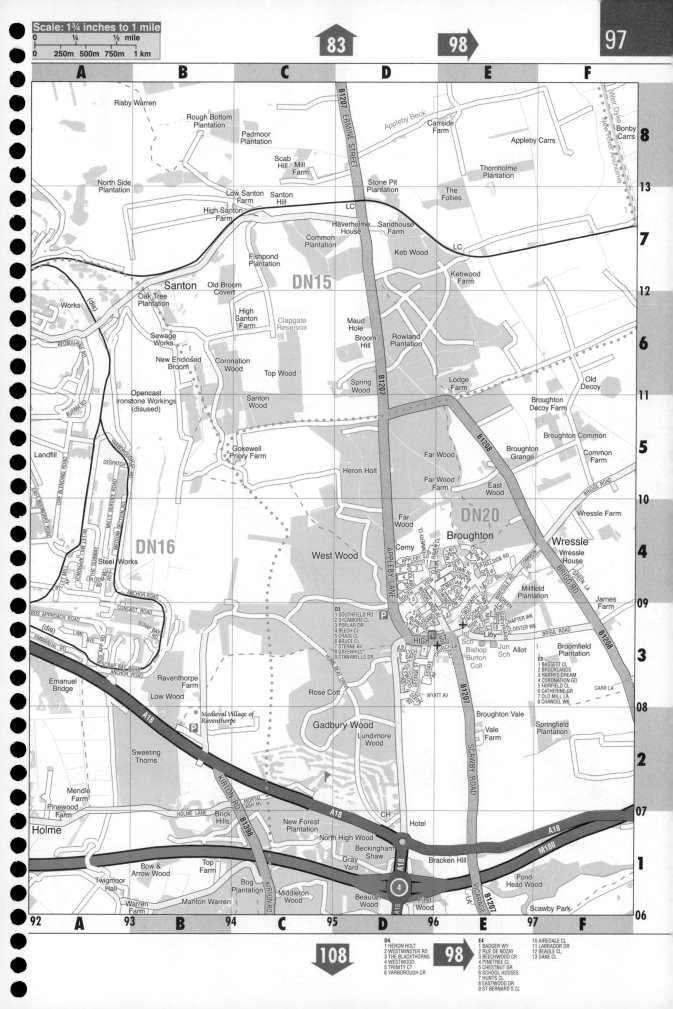

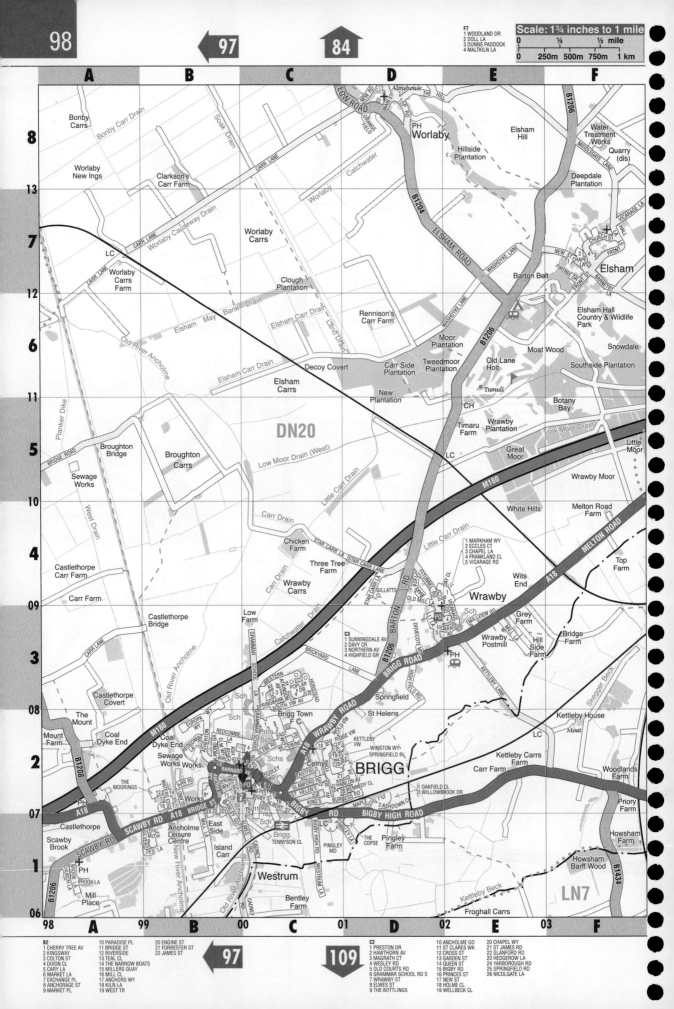

98

97

84

F7
1 WOODLAND DR
2 DOLL LA
3 DUNNS PADDOCK
4 MALTKILN LA

Scale: 1¾ inches to 1 mile
0   ¼   ½ mile
250m 500m 750m 1 km

A B C D E F

8
13
7
12
6
11
5
10
4
09
3
08
2
07
1
06

Bonby
Carrs

Bonby Carr Drain

Worlaby
New Ings

Clarkson's
Carr Farm

Soak Drain

CARR LANE

Worlaby Causeway Drain

LC

Carr Lane

Worlaby Carrs Farm

Worlaby
Carrs

CARR LANE

Worlaby

Clough
Plantation

Elsham   May   Bank   Drain

Land Drain

Elsham Carr Drain

Elsham Carr Drain

Rennison's
Carr Farm

Decoy Covert

Carr Side
Plantation

Elsham
Carrs

New
Plantation

Tweedmoor
Plantation

Moor
Plantation

ELSHAM ROAD

B1204

WASHDYKE LANE

Barton Belt

Old Lane
Holt

CH

Timaru
Farm

Wrawby
Plantation

Tumuli

B1206

Moat Wood

Snowdale

Southside Plantation

Botany
Bay

Almshouse
THE   HILL

LOW ROAD

NEW ST
MAIN ST
GRANGE
FIELD
TOP RD

Worlaby
PH

Hillside
Plantation

Elsham
Hill

Water
Treatment
Works

Quarry
(dis)

B1206

MIDDLEGATE LANE

Deepdale
Plantation

VICARAGE LA
HALL
CHURCH ST
NEW ST
CHAPEL
FIRTREE DR
FRONT ST
BARNETBY
FRONT ST

Elsham

Elsham Hall
Country & Wildlife
Park

DN20

Planker Dike

BRIDGE ROAD

Broughton
Bridge

Sewage
Works

Broughton
Carrs

West Drain

Old River Ancholme

Low Moor Drain (West)

Little Carr Drain

Carr Drain

Chicken
Farm

Three Tree
Farm

Wrawby
Carrs

STAR CARR LA
STAR CARR LANE

Carr Drain

Little Carr Drain

M180

LC

Great
Moor

White Hills

Wrawby Moor

Low Moor Drain

Little
Moor

Melton Road
Farm

Moor
Plantation

Wits
End

1 MARKHAM WY
2 ECCLES CT
3 CHAPEL LA
4 FRANKLAND CL
5 VICARAGE RD

Wrawby

MELTON ROAD

A18

Top
Farm

Castlethorpe
Carr Farm

Carr Farm

CARR LANE

Castlethorpe
Bridge

Old River Ancholme

Low
Farm

Catchwater   Drain

GRAMMAR
SCHOOL LANE

BRICKYARD
LANE

Gillatts
Cl

STAR CARR LA

Old Mill
BARTON RD
ETTUNE RD
DAY CL
VICARAGE RD

C3
1 SUNNINGDALE AV
2 DAVY CR
3 NORTHERN AV
4 HIGHFIELD GR

PO
ELMVIEW GD
VICARAGE
AV

Sch

Grey
Farm

Hill
Side
Farm

Bridge
Farm

Castlethorpe
Covert

The
Mount

Coal
Dyke End

M180

Coal
Dyke End

Sewage
Works Works

EUROPA
WY
REDCOMBE
LA
ATHERTON
WY

WESTERN
LA
ATKINS
CL
SPRINGBANK WY
SOUTH VW AV

POPLAR
DR

HORSTEAD
AV

Brigg Town
F C

St Helens

Springfield

B1206
BARTON RD

BRIGG ROAD

Wrawby
Postmill

PH

KETTLEBY LANE

WINSTON WY
Springfield Ri
KETTLEBY
VW

DOVECOTE LA
HIGHFIELD RD

Skegger Beck

Kettleby House

Moat

LC

Kettleby Carrs
Farm

Carr Farm

Woodlands
Farm

Mount
Farm

B1208

PH
A18

Castlethorpe

Scawby
Brook

SCAWBY RD

SCAWBY RD

B1206
BROOK LA
CHURCH LA

PH

Mill
Place

The
Moorings

Sewage
Works Works

BARNARD AV

WATERSIDE
CARR RD
SPRINGS

Ancholme
Leisure
Centre

East
Side

MILL LA

Island
Carr

Westrum

New River Ancholme

Old River Ancholme

CADNEY RD
ELWES RD

Prep
Sch

Brigg
Tennyson Cl

Bentley
Farm

BRIDGE ST

SCAWBY RD
A18

ALBERT ST
BIGBY ST

BIGBY
RD

PINGLEY
MD

Bigby High Rd

PINGLEY LA

BIGBY HIGH ROAD

The
Copse

Pingley
Farm

1 OAKFIELD CL
2 WILLOWBROOK DR

2 ASHDOWN CL
MAPLE
CL

Kettleby Beck

Froghall Carrs

LN7

B1434

Howsham
Barff Wood

Howsham
Farm

Priory
Farm

BRIGG

Westrum

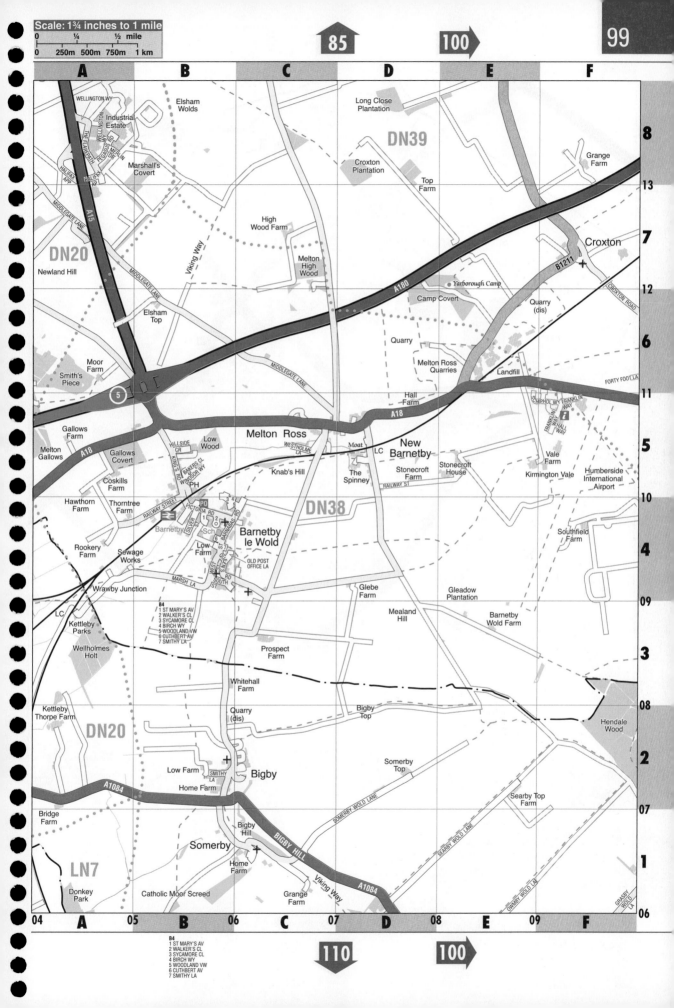

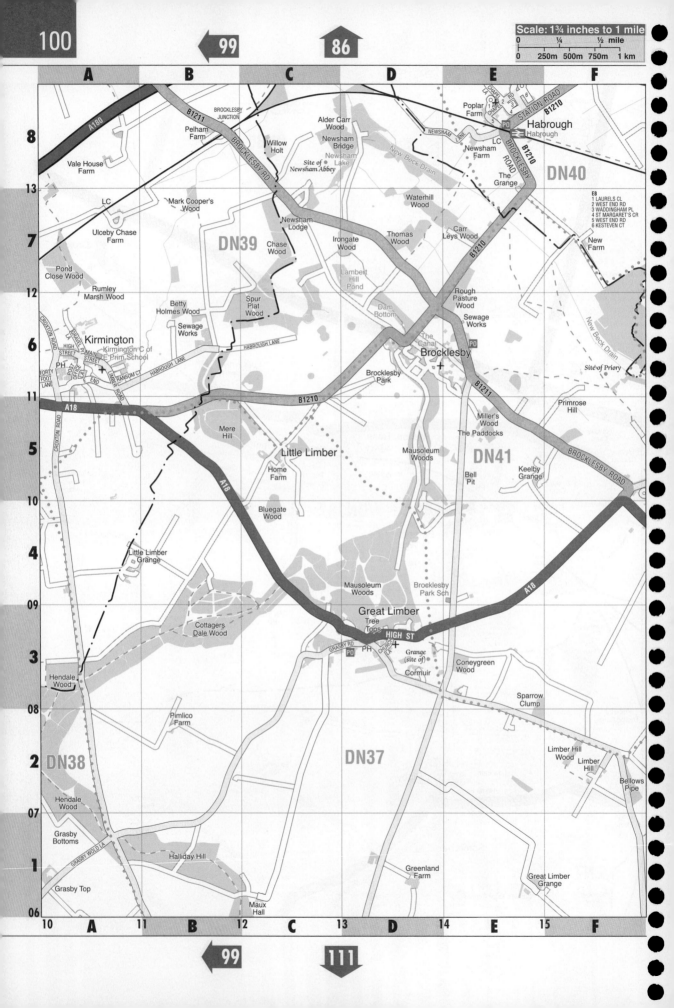

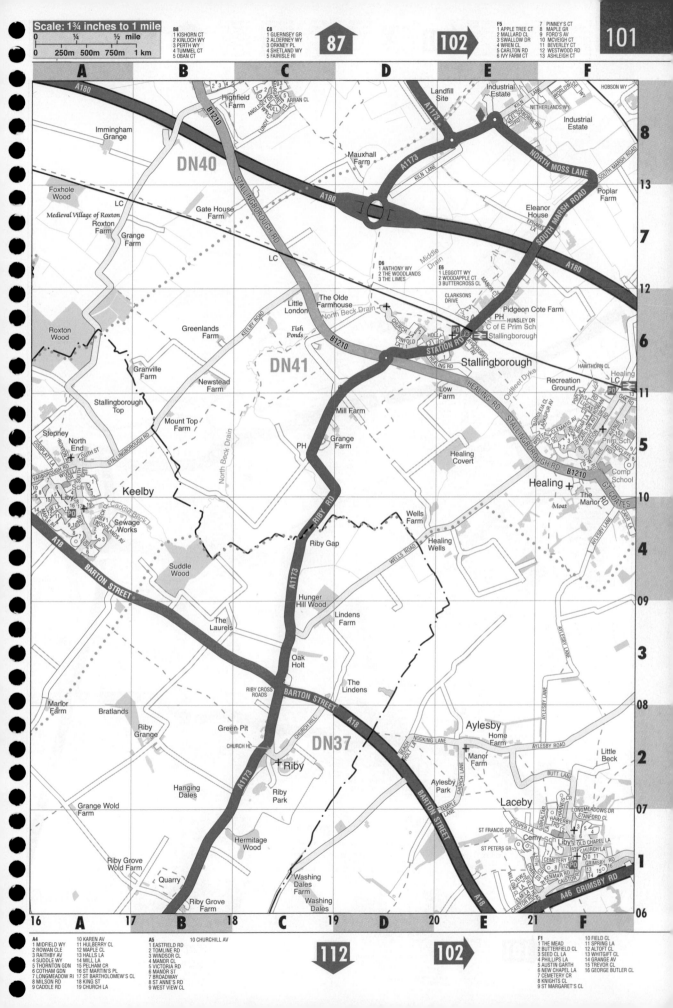

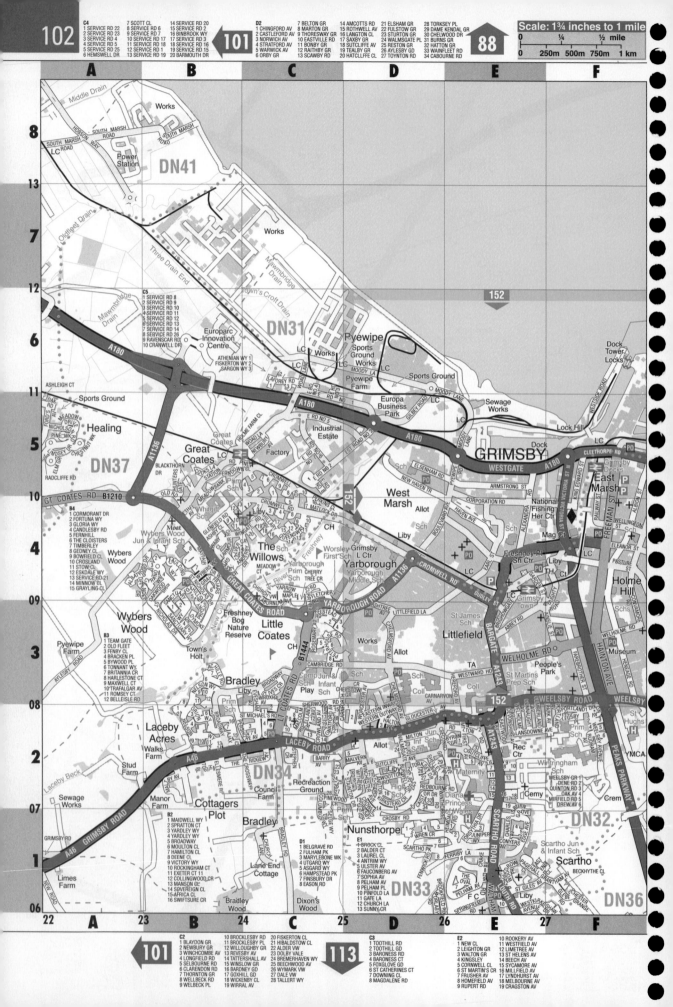

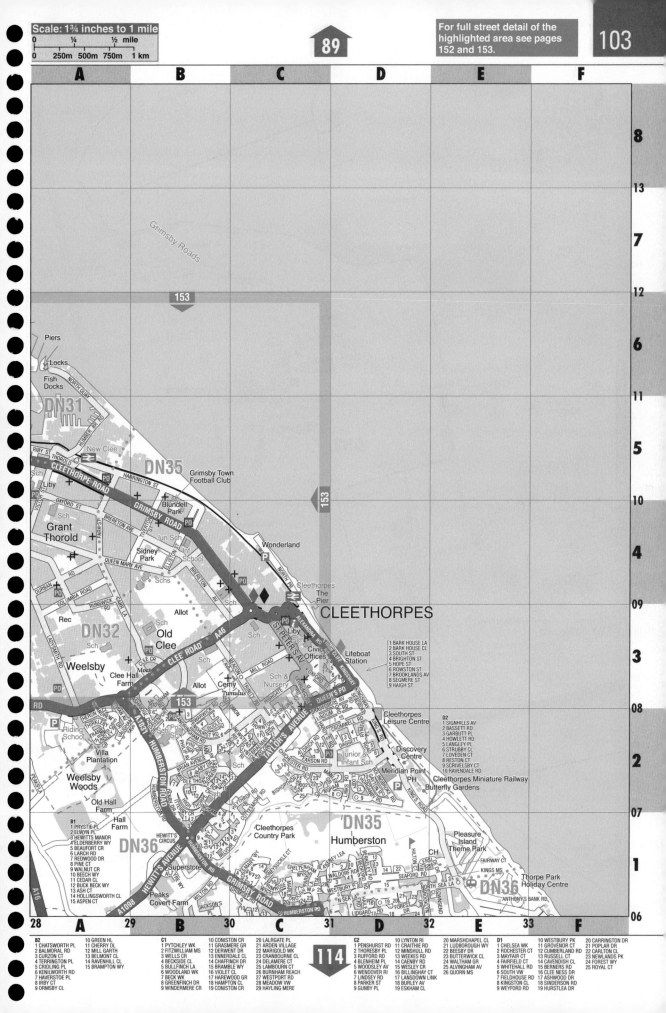

Scale: 1¾ inches to 1 mile

0   ¼   ½ mile
0 250m 500m 750m 1 km

89

For full street detail of the highlighted area see pages 152 and 153.

103

B2
1 CHATSWORTH PL
2 BALMORAL RD
3 CURZON CT
4 TERRINGTON PL
5 CRIDLING PL
6 KENILWORTH RD
7 HAVERSTOE PL
8 IRBY CT
9 ORMSBY CL
10 GREEN HL
11 CHERRY DL
12 MILL GARTH
13 BELMONT CL
14 RAVENHILL CL
15 BRAMPTON WY

C1
1 PYTCHLEY WK
2 FITZWILLIAM MS
3 WELLS CR
4 BECKSIDE CL
5 BULLFINCH LA
6 WOODLAND WK
7 BECK WK
8 GREENFINCH DR
9 WINDERMERE CR
10 CONISTON CR
11 GRASMERE GR
12 DERWENT DR
13 ENNERDALE CL
14 CHAFFINCH DR
15 BRAMBLE WY
16 VIOLET CL
17 HAREWOOD GR
18 HAMPTON CL
19 CONISTON CR
20 LALRGATE PL
21 ARDEN VILLAGE
22 MARIGOLD WK
23 CRANBOURNE CL
24 DELAMERE CT
25 LAMBOURN CT
26 BURNHAM REACH
27 WESTPORT CL
28 MEADOW VW
29 HAYLING MERE

C2
1 PENSHURST RD
2 THORESBY PL
3 RUFFORD RD
4 BLENHEIM PL
5 WOODSLEY AV
6 WENDOVER RI
7 LINDSEY RD
8 PARKER ST
9 GUNBY PL
10 LYNTON RI
11 CRAITHIE RD
12 MINSHULL RD
13 WEEKES RD
14 CAENBY RD
15 WESLEY CR
16 BILLINGHAY CR
17 LANSDOWN LINK
18 BURLEY AV
19 ESKHAM CL
20 MARSHCHAPEL CL
21 LUDBOROUGH WY
22 BEESBY DR
23 BUTTERWICK CL
24 WALTHAM GR
25 ALVINGHAM AV
26 QUORN MS

D1
1 CHELSEA WK
2 ROCHESTER CT
3 MAYFAIR CT
4 FAIRFIELD CT
5 WHITEHALL RD
6 SOUTH VW
7 FIELDHOUSE RD
8 KINGSTON CL
9 WEYFORD RD
10 WESTBURY PK
11 GROVENOR CT
12 CUMBERLAND RD
13 RUSSELL CT
14 CAVENDISH CL
15 BERNERS RD
16 CLEE NESS DR
17 ASHWOOD DR
18 SINDERSON RD
19 HURSTLEA DR
20 CARRINGTON DR
21 POPLAR DR
22 CARLTON CL
23 NEWLANDS PK
24 FOREST WY
25 ROYAL CT

B1
1 PRYSTIE PL
2 ELWYN PL
3 HEWITTS MANOR
4 ELDERBERRY WY
5 BEAUFORT CR
6 LARGH RD
7 REDWOOD DR
8 PINE CT
9 WALNUT CR
10 BEECH WY
11 CEDAR CL
12 BUCK BECK WY
13 ASH CT
14 HOLLINGSWORTH CL
15 ASPEN CT

D2
1 SIGNHILLS AV
2 BASSETT RD
3 GARBUTT PL
4 HOWLETT RD
5 LANGLEY PL
6 STRUBBY CL
7 LOVEDEN CT
8 RESTON CT
9 SCRIVELSBY CT
10 RAVENDALE RD

1 BARK HOUSE LA
2 BARK HOUSE CL
3 SOUTH ST
4 BRIGHTON ST
5 HOPE ST
6 ROWSTON ST
7 BROOKLANDS AV
8 SEGMERE ST
9 HAIGH ST

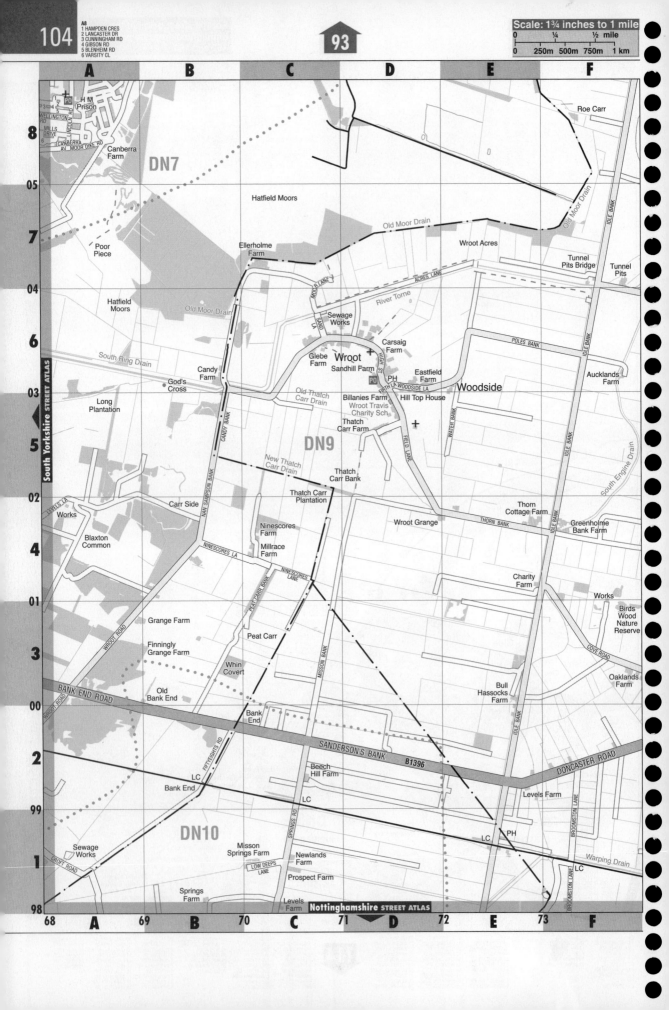

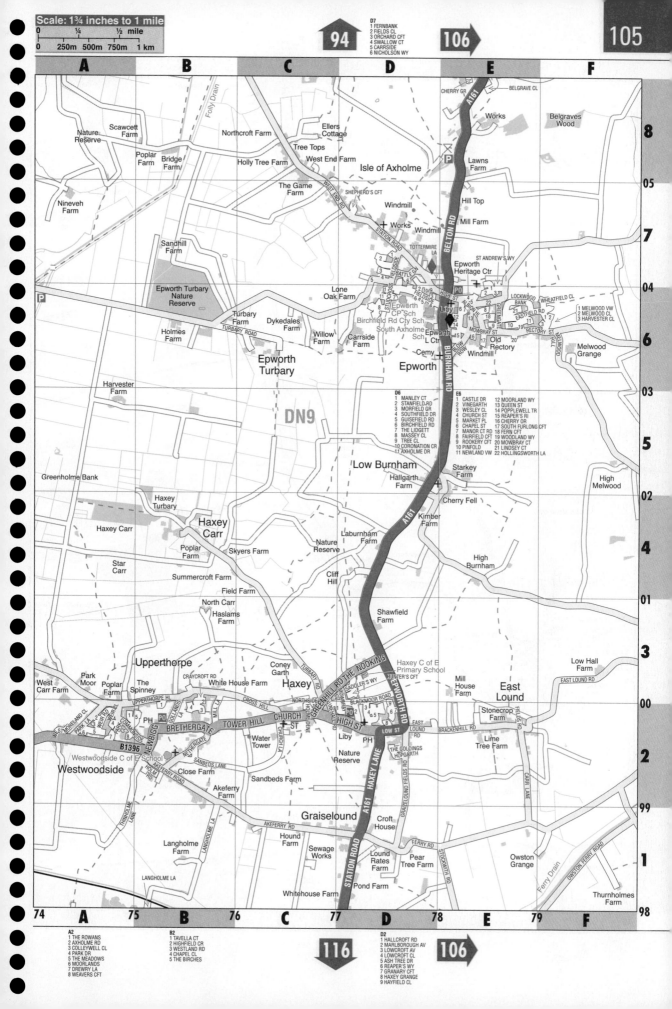

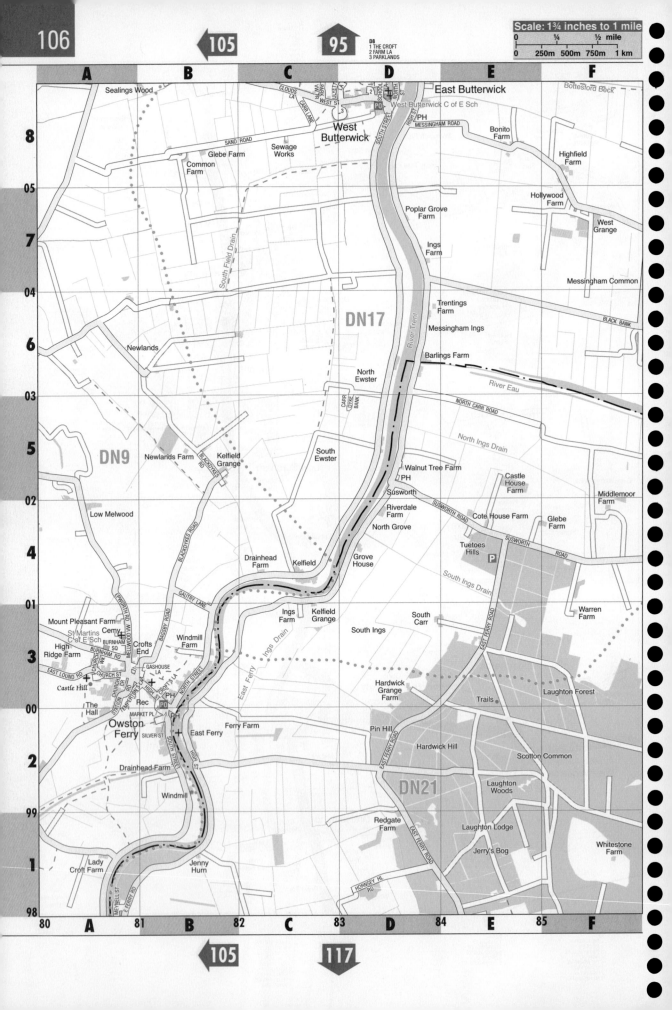

105
95

D8
1 THE CROFT
2 FARM LA
3 PARKLANDS

Scale: 1¾ inches to 1 mile

0   ¼   ½   mile
0 250m 500m 750m 1 km

A   B   C   D   E   F

Sealings Wood

Bottesford Beck

CLOUDS LA
CARR LANE
SAND ROAD
WEST ST
LILLYET LA
PARK
WALK
SCHOOL
NORTH
SOUTH STREET
HIGH ST

East Butterwick

West Butterwick C of E Sch
PO
West Butterwick
PH
Glebe Farm
Common Farm
Sewage Works
Bonito Farm
Highfield Farm
MESSINGHAM ROAD

05

Poplar Grove Farm
Hollywood Farm
West Grange

8

7
South Field Drain
Ings Farm
Messingham Common

04
River Trent
BLACK BANK

6
Newlands
DN17
Trentings Farm
Messingham Ings
Barlings Farm
River Eau

03
North Ewster
CARR DYKE BANK
NORTH CARR ROAD

5
DN9
Newlands Farm
Kelfield Grange
BLACKDYKES RD
South Ewster
North Ings Drain

02
Low Melwood
Walnut Tree Farm
PH
Susworth
SUSWORTH ROAD
Cote House Farm
Castle House Farm
Glebe Farm
Middlemoor Farm

4
Drainhead Farm
Kelfield
Riverdale Farm
North Grove
Grove House
Tuetoes Hills
P
SUSWORTH ROAD

01
GAUTRY LANE
Ings Farm
Kelfield Grange
South Ings Drain
Warren Farm

3
EPWORTH RD
MELLWOOD W
Mount Pleasant Farm
St Martins C of E Sch
Cemy
BURNHAM SQ
BAGSBY ROAD
Crofts End
Windmill Farm
East Ferry Ings Drain
South Carr
South Ings
East Ferry Road
Laughton Forest

High Ridge Farm
BURNHAM RD
CHURCH ST
STATION RD
IMPERIAL LA
CHURCH CR
GASHOUSE LA
NORTH STREET
CROFT'S LA
PH
Hardwick Grange Farm
Trails

EAST LOUND RD
Castle Hill
The Hall
Rec
PO
PH
MARKET PL
Owston Ferry
SILVER ST
SOUTH STREET
HIGH ST
Ferry Farm
Pin Hill
Hardwick Hill
Scotton Common

00

2
Drainhead Farm
East Ferry
DN21
Laughton Woods

99
Windmill
Redgate Farm
EAST FERRY ROAD
Laughton Lodge
Whitestone Farm

1
MEYNELL ST
EAST FERRY RD
Lady Croft Farm
Jenny Hurn
HORNSEY HL RD
Jerry's Bog

98
80   A   81   B   82   C   83   D   84   E   85   F

105
117

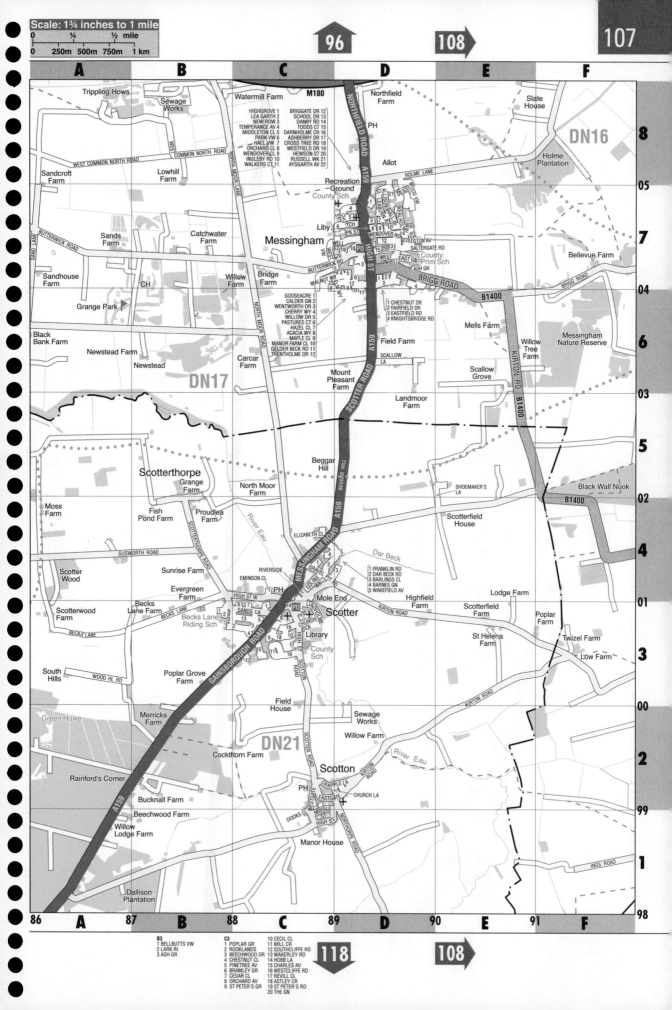

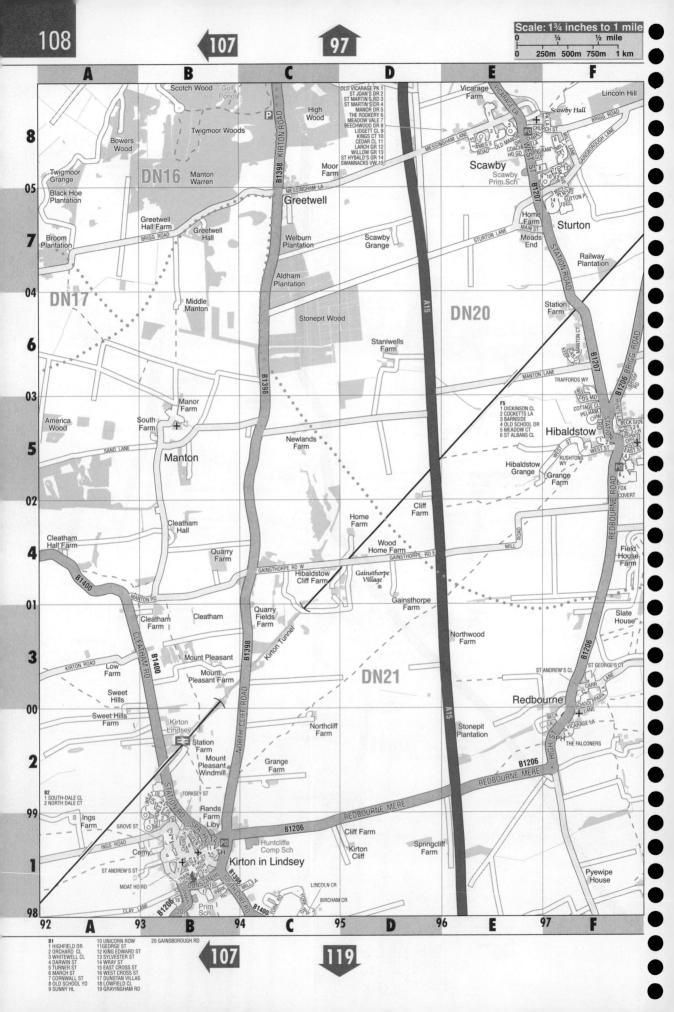

A   B   C   D   E   F

Scotch Wood
Gull Ponds

High Wood

OLD VICARAGE PK 1
ST JOAN'S DR 2
ST MARTIN'S RD 3
ST MARTIN'S CR 4
MANOR DR 5
THE ROOKERY 6
MEADOW VALE 7
BEECHWOOD DR 8
LIDGETT CL 9
KINGS CT 10
CEDAR CL 11
LARCH GR 12
WILLOW GR 13
ST HYBALD'S GR 14
SWANNACKS VW 15

Vicarage Farm

Lincoln Hill

Scawby Hall

Twigmoor Woods

8

Bowers Wood

DN16

Manton Warren

Moor Farm

Scawby

Scawby Prim Sch

05

Twigmoor Grange

Black Hoe Plantation

Greetwell Hall Farm

MESSINGHAM LA

Greetwell

Home Farm

Sturton

7

Broom Plantation

Greetwell Hall

BRIGG ROAD

Welburn Plantation

Scawby Grange

Sturton Lane

Meads End

Railway Plantation

04

DN17

Middle Manton

Aldham Plantation

Station Farm

Station Road

DN20

05

America Wood

Manor Farm

Stonepit Wood

Staniwells Farm

Manton Lane
TRAFFORDS WY

B1207

03

South Farm

SAND LANE

Newlands Farm

F5
1 DICKINSON CL
2 COCKETTS LA
3 BARNSIDE
4 OLD SCHOOL DR
5 MEADOW CT
6 ST ALBANS CL

Hibaldstow

Manton

B1398

Cliff Farm

Hibaldstow Grange

Grange Farm

FOX COVERT

02

Cleatham Hall

Home Farm

Wood Home Farm

MILL ROAD

Field House Farm

4

Cleatham Hall Farm

B1400

Quarry Farm

GAINSTHORPE RD W

Hibaldstow Cliff Farm

GAINSTHORPE RD E

Gainsthorpe Village

Gainsthorpe Farm

Northwood Farm

Slate House

01

MANTON RD

Quarry Fields Farm

Kirton Tunnel

DN21

B1206

3

KIRTON ROAD

Low Farm

Cleatham

Mount Pleasant

Mount Pleasant Farm

B1398

NORTH CLIFF ROAD

Redbourne

REDBOURNE ROAD

ST ANDREW'S CL

ST GEORGE'S CT

00

Sweet Hills

Sweet Hills Farm

Kirton Lindsey

Station Farm

Northcliff Farm

Stonepit Plantation

VICARAGE LA

THE FALCONERS

2

B2
1 SOUTH-DALE CL
2 NORTH DALE CT

Mount Pleasant Windmill

TORKSEY ST

Grange Farm

B1206

REDBOURNE MERE

99

Ings Farm

GROVE ST

INGS ROAD

Rands Farm Liby

SPA HL

PO

Redbourne Mere

Cliff Farm

Springcliff Farm

Pyewipe House

1

St Andrew's St

Cemy

MOAT HO RD

Kirton in Lindsey

Huntcliffe Comp Sch

Kirton Cliff

LINCOLN CR

BIRCHAM CR

98

CLAY LANE

B1206

Prim Sch

B1398

B1400

YORK RD

92   A   93   B   94   C   95   D   96   E   97   F

B1
1 HIGHFIELD DR
2 ORCHARD CL
3 WHITEWELL CL
4 DARWIN ST
5 TURNER ST
6 MARCH ST
7 CORNWALL ST
8 OLD SCHOOL YD
9 SUNNY HL
10 UNICORN ROW
11 GEORGE ST
12 KING EDWARD ST
13 SYLVESTER ST
14 WRAY ST
15 EAST CROSS ST
16 WEST CROSS ST
17 DUNSTAN VILLAS
18 LOWFIELD CL
19 GRAYINGHAM RD
20 GAINSBOROUGH RD

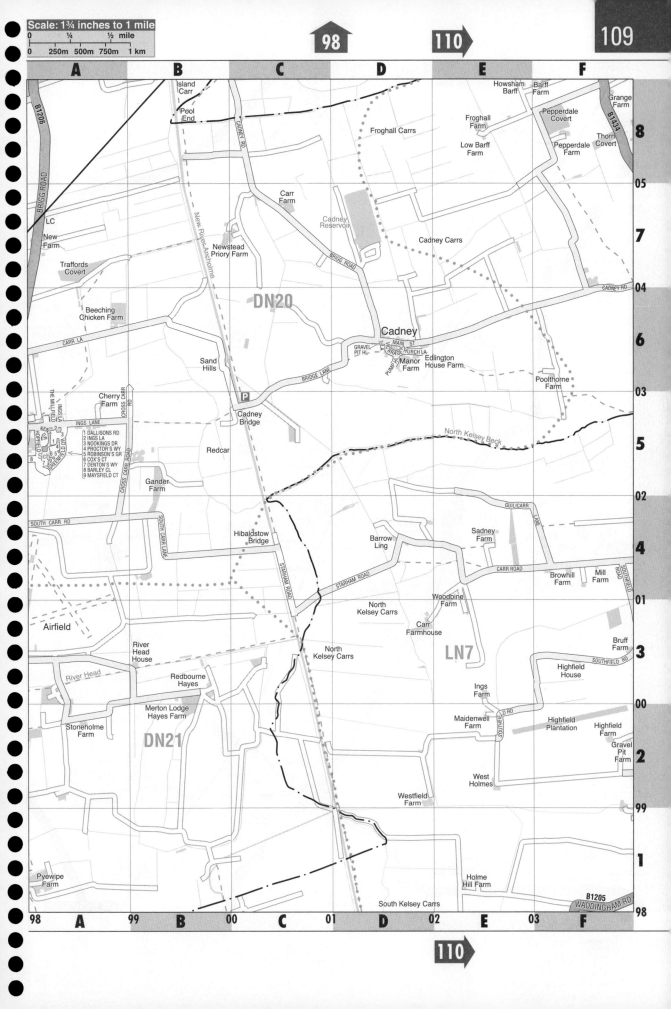

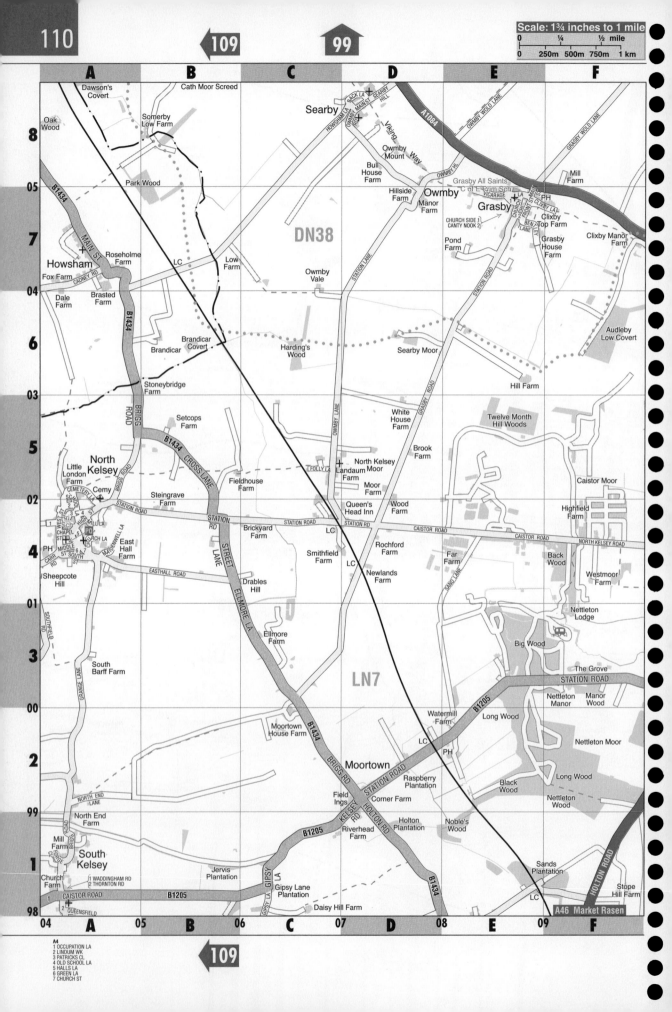

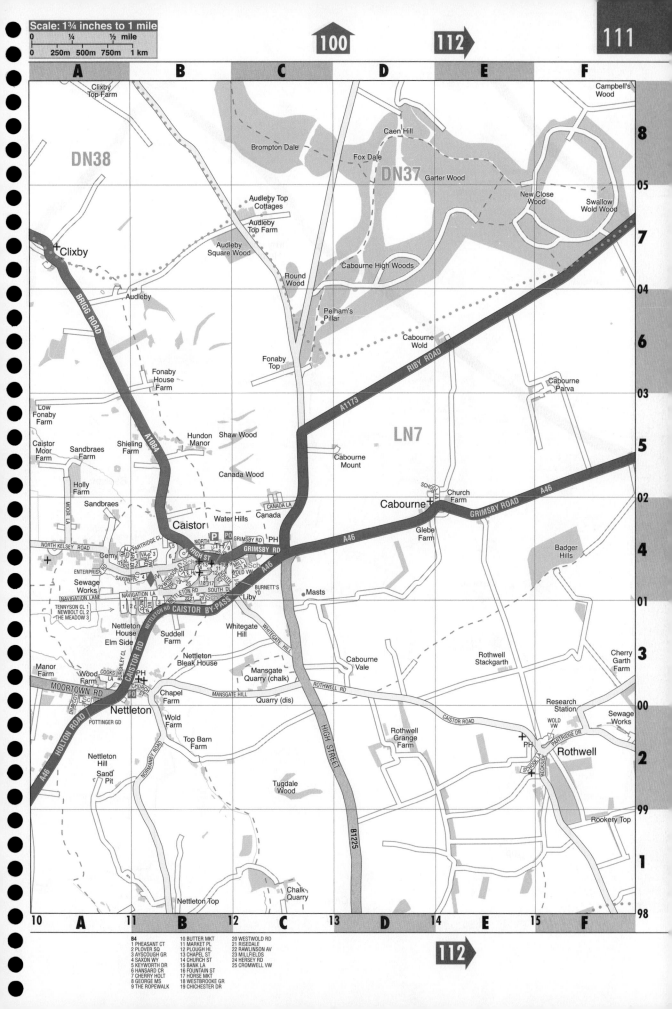

A | B | C | D | E | F

Clixby Top Farm

DN38

Campbell's Wood

Brompton Dale

Caen Hill

Fox Dale

DN37   Garter Wood

New Close Wood

Swallow Wold Wood

+Clixby

BRIG G ROAD

Audleby Top Cottages

Audleby Top Farm

Audleby Square Wood

Cabourne High Woods

Round Wood

05

Audleby

Pelham's Pillar

Cabourne Wold

RIBY ROAD

Cabourne Parva

04

Fonaby House Farm

Fonaby Top

A1173

07

Low Fonaby Farm

Hundon Manor

Shaw Wood

LN7

03

Caistor Moor Farm

Sandbraes Farm

Shieling Farm

A1084

Canada Wood

Cabourne Mount

Cabourne Parva

06

Holly Farm

Sandbraes

MOOR LA

Water Hills

CANADA LA

Canada

SCHOOL

Church Farm

Cabourne+

GRIMSBY ROAD   **A46**

Glebe Farm

Badger Hills

02

NORTH KELSEY ROAD

Cemy

ENTERPRISE

Sewage Works

NAVIGATION LANE

NAVIGATION LA

Caistor

P

PO

TH

GRIMSBY RD

PH

A46

A46

SCHOOL

MILL

Liby

Masts

04

TENNYSON CL 1
NEWBOLT CL 2
THE MEADOW 3

Nettleton House

Elm Side

Suddell Farm

Nettleton Bleak House

Whitegate Hill

WHITEGATE HILL

Cabourne Vale

Rothwell Stackgarth

Cherry Garth Farm

01

03

Manor Farm

Wood Farm

COOKS LA

BURGHLEY CL

PH

CHURCH ST

CAISTOR RD

Chapel Farm

Mansgate Quarry (chalk)

MANSGATE HILL

Quarry (dis)

Cabourne Vale

ROTHWELL RD

Research Station

WOLD VW

Sewage Works

Nettleton

MOORTOWN RD

SCH

PO ST

Wold Farm

Top Barn Farm

Rothwell Grange Farm

CAISTOR ROAD

PH

+Rothwell

BECKSIDE

SCHOOL

02

HOLTON ROAD

POTTINGER GD

A46

Nettleton Hill

Sand Pit

Top Barn Farm

Tugdale Wood

HIGH STREET

00

Rookery Top

99

Nettleton Top

Chalk Quarry

B1225

98

10 | A | 11 | B | 12 | C | 13 | D | 14 | E | 15 | F

→ **112**

B4
1 PHEASANT CT
2 PLOVER SQ
3 AYSCOUGH GR
4 SAXON WY
5 KEYWORTH DR
6 HANSARD CR
7 CHERRY HOLT
8 GEORGE MS
9 THE ROPEWALK

10 BUTTER MKT
11 MARKET PL
12 PLOUGH HL
13 CHAPEL ST
14 CHURCH ST
15 BANK LA
16 FOUNTAIN ST
17 HORSE MKT
18 WESTBROOKE GR
19 CHICHESTER DR

20 WESTWOLD RD
21 RISEDALE
22 RAWLINSON AV
23 MILLFIELDS
24 HERSEY RD
25 CROMWELL VW

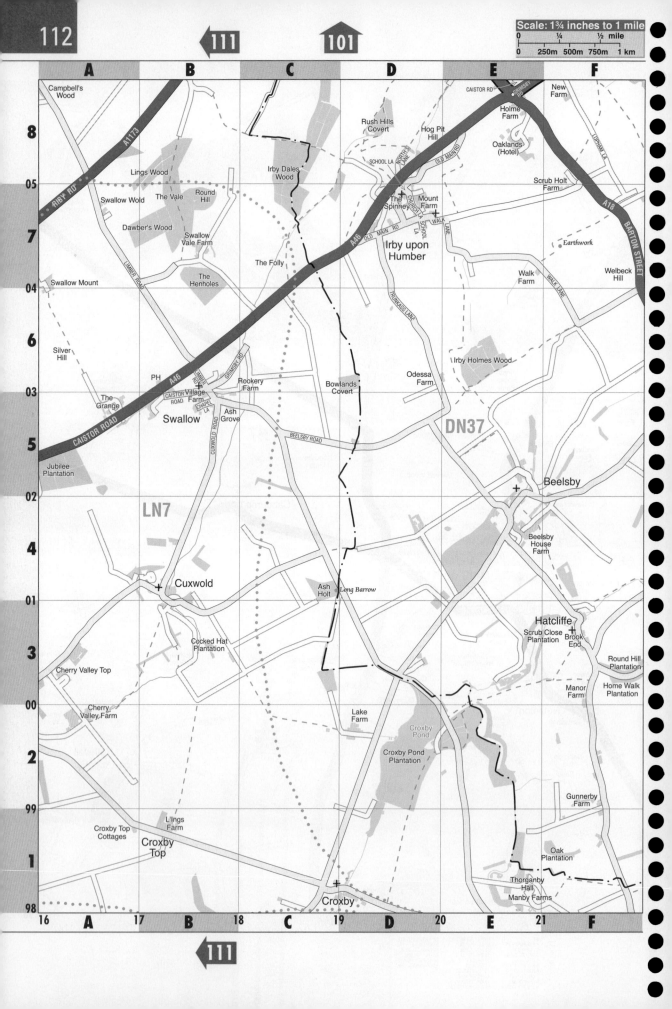

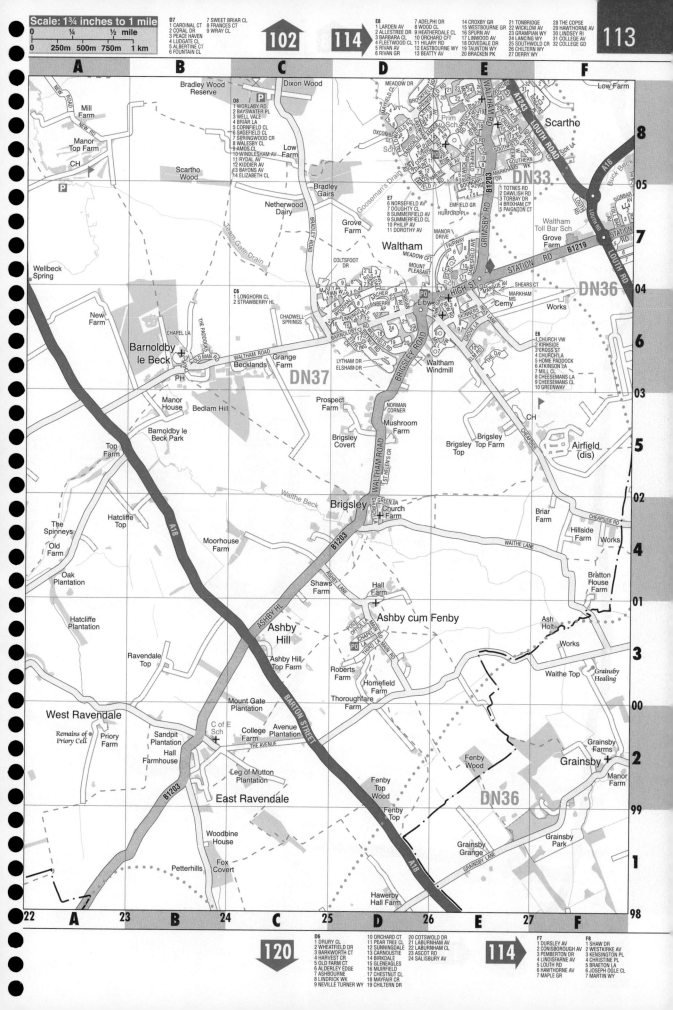

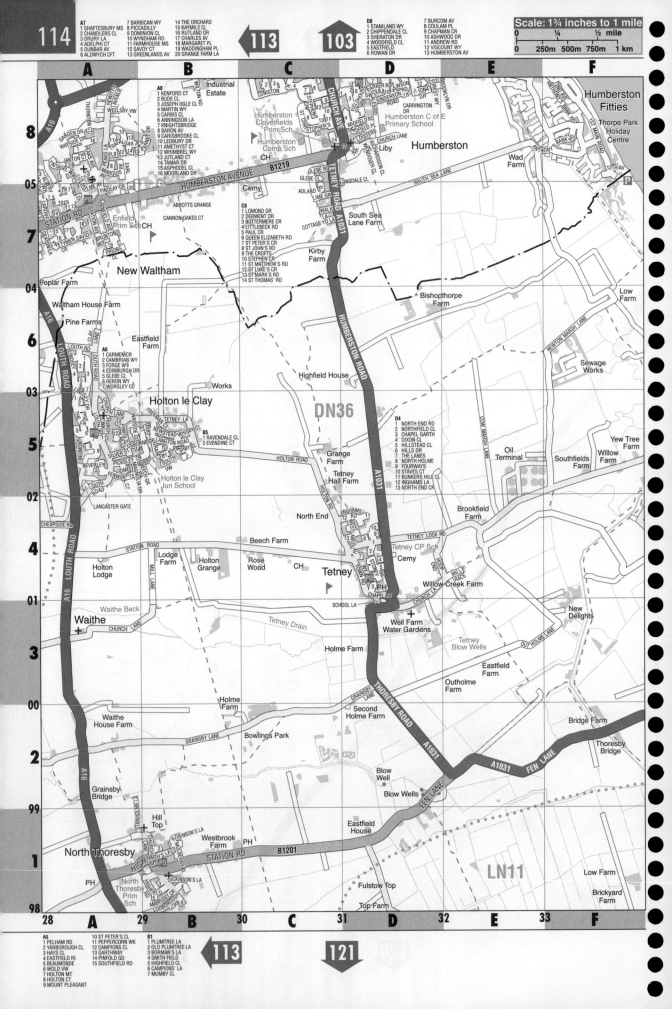

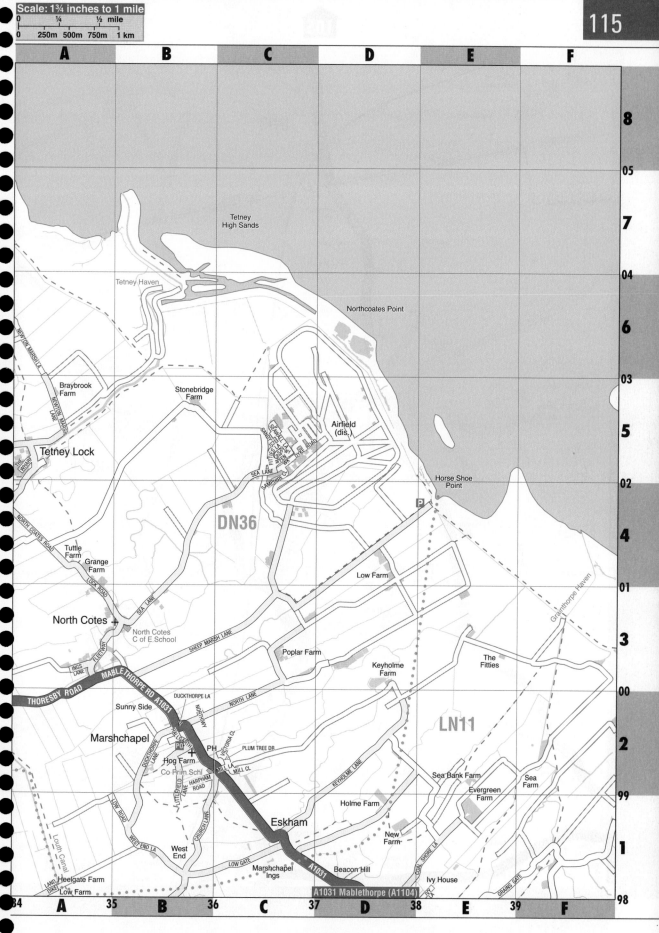

Scale: 1¾ inches to 1 mile

0 ¼ ½ mile
0 250m 500m 750m 1 km

A B C D E F

Tetney
High Sands

Tetney Haven

Northcoates Point

Braybrook
Farm

Stonebridge
Farm

Airfield
(dis.)

Tetney Lock

Horse Shoe
Point

DN36

Tuttle
Farm

Grange
Farm

Low Farm

Grainthorpe Haven

North Cotes

North Cotes
C of E School

SHEEP MARSH LANE

Poplar Farm

The Fitties

Keyholme
Farm

THORESBY ROAD

MABLETHORPE RD A1031

Sunny Side

DUCKTHORPE LA

NORTH LANE

LN11

Marshchapel

PH

PLUM TREE DR

Hog Farm

Co Prim Schl

HARPHAM
ROAD

MILL CL

Sea Bank Farm

Sea
Farm

Evergreen
Farm

Eskham

Holme Farm

LOW ROAD

WEST END LA

West
End

CHURCH LANE

LOW GATE

Marshchapel
Ings

New
Farm

Beacon Hill

Ivy House

Louth Canal

Heelgate Farm

Low Farm

A1031

A1031 Mablethorpe (A1104)

34 A 35 B 36 C 37 D 38 E 39 F 98

105

Nottinghamshire STREET ATLAS

A B C D E F

8

Langholme Wood Farm
Langholme Wood
Langholme

Poplar Farm
Bridge Farm

Ferry Drain

Intake House Farm

GUNTHORPE ROAD

DN9

97

TINDALE BANK RD

TINDALE BANK RD

Richmond Farm
LC

TINDALE BANK RD

North Carr

River Idle

LC

STATION ROAD A161

HAXEY GATE RD

OWSTON FERRY ROAD

STOCKWITH ROAD

GIPSY LANE

NORTH INTAKE LANE

7

Debdhill Farm

North Carr Farm

PH
Haxey Gate Bridge

Mother Drain Bridge

LC
North Carr Farm

SOUTH INTAKE LANE

HECKDYKE LANE

Mayfield Farm

96

CORNLEY ROAD

Cornley Farm
Cornley Carr Farmhouse

Cornley

Town End Farm

DEBDHILL

CORNLEY ROAD

Cemy

HAXEY ROAD A161

Carr Ings

North Carr Farm

North Carr Cottages

NORTH CARR ROAD

Misterton Soss

OWSTON ROAD

INGS LANE

ANTERSLEET LANE

Heckdyke

West Stockwith

Stockwith Ellers

6

C5
1 ASHLEA
2 WILLOW AV
3 CHURCH LA
4 OLD FORGE RD
5 DEANS CL
6 CHURCH DR
7 CHAPEL CL
8 CHAPEL LA

Misterton Carr

Carr Ings Drain

Cattle Farm

CATTLE ROAD

CARR LA 1½

CHURCH ST

Elm Misterton

HIGH ST

STATION ST

A167

Corner Farm

PH
Lock
Basin Bridge

PH

MAIN ST

Chestnut Farm

East Stockwith

5

MINSTER RD

MEADOW DR

ASHDOWN WAY

Cooper's Bridge

WHARF RD

Liby
Wharf Bridge

Lock
Swallow Bridge

Rec

YORK TR

ALBION TR

MARSH LANE

FRONT ST

BACK ST

ST PETERS CL

Sewage Works

N CARR RD

CANAL LA

DN21

4

TRENT VALLEY WAY

GRINGLEY RD

B1403

Gringley Road Farm

Fountain Hill

Manor Farm

G WOOD TR

GR PK

GRAVELHOLES LA

G WOOD RD

G WOOD DR

DN10

Misterton Prim Sch

GRANGE WK

GRANGE DR

AMCOTT

FOX COVERT LANE

Foundry

1 ORCHARD GR
2 GRANGE CL

STOCKWITH ROAD

A161

Lyne House Farm

Mole End

LINECROFT LANE

North Carr Farm

WALERITH ROAD

93

Gringley Carr

Smith's Bridge

FOUNTAIN HILL

BRICKYARD LA

CAVE'S LANE

Carrfield Farm

FOUNTAIN HL ROAD

Moor End

NORTH MOOR RD

C3
1 NORTH MOOR DR
2 SCHOOL HOUSE LA
3 MOORLAND AV
4 MOORLAND CL

Walkeringham City Prim Sch

MILL BAULK RD

STOCKWITH ROAD

Sewage Works

LC

STATION RD

MARSH ROAD

Walkerith

Point Farm

WALERITH ROAD

Jubilee Farm

INGS LANE

River Trent

BIRD LANE

3

Chesterfield Canal

Leys Farm

P

B1403

Nature Reserve

Highfield Farm

West Moor Fm
The Moor
West Moor

W MOOR RD

SOUTH MOOR ROAD

BRICKENHOLE

PO

1
4 3

PH
2

Church End

Cemy

92

Lowfield Farm

WALKERINGHAM RD

WOODEN BECK HL

Glebe Farm

GRINGLEY ROAD

MILL LANE

Highfield House

BECKINGHAM ROAD A161

D3
1 WRIGHTS GD
2 SIDSAPH HL
3 BIRDCROFT LA

2

HALL'S RD

WALKERINGHAM ROAD

OAKS LANE

Highfield Farm

91

BAWTRY RD

BEACON HL RD

GREEN HL RD

LC

BULSE FARM

1

A631 Bawtry

Beacon Hill
HIGH ST

Green Farm
PH

A631

LANCASTER ROAD

Gringley Grange

Sandy Furze

Pear Tree Farm

MUTTON LA

Beckingham Mill Farm

PO
CHURCH ST

The Hall

The Spinney

Fretwell Farm

D1
1 RAVENCROFT LA
2 THE LIMES
3 RECTORY GD
4 CHURCH VW

90

THE PADDOCKS

A631 Gainsborough (A159)

OLD TRENT RD

74 75 76 77 78 79

A B C D E F

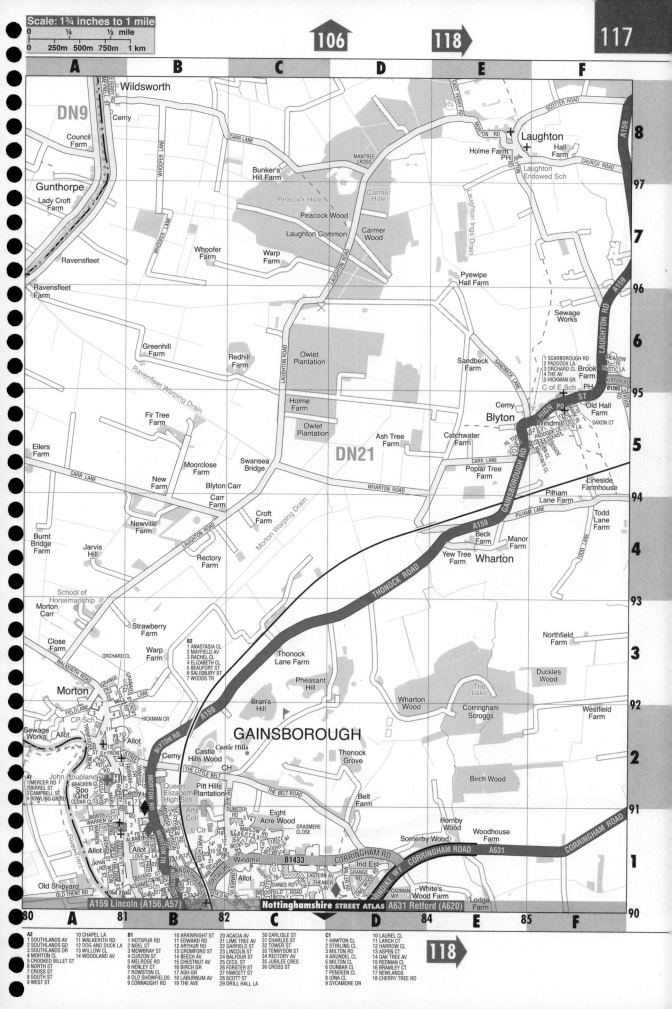

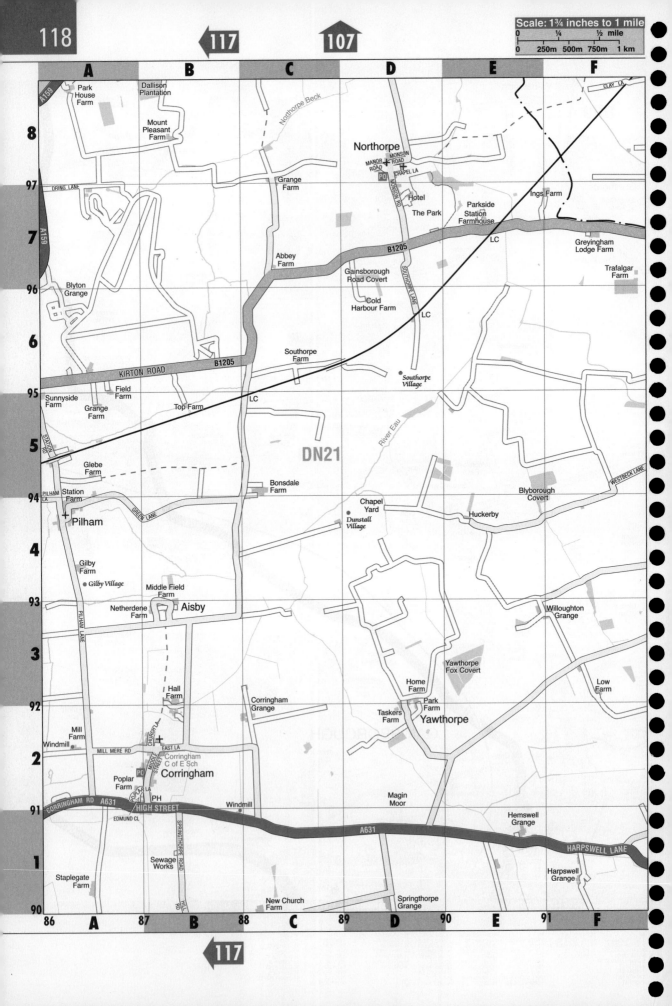

Scale: 1¾ inches to 1 mile

0   ¼   ½   mile

0   250m   500m   750m   1 km

A   B   C   D   E   F

A159

Park House Farm

Dallison Plantation

Mount Pleasant Farm

8

Northorpe Beck

Northorpe

MANOR ROAD   MONSON ROAD

PO   CHAPEL LA

97

DRING LANE

Grange Farm

Hotel

The Park

MONSON RD

Parkside Station Farmhouse

Ings Farm

7

A159

Abbey Farm

B1205

LC

Greyingham Lodge Farm

Trafalgar Farm

96

Blyton Grange

Gainsborough Road Covert

SOUTHORPE LANE

Cold Harbour Farm

LC

6

KIRTON ROAD   B1205

Southorpe Farm

Southorpe Village

5

Sunnyside Farm

Field Farm

Grange Farm

Top Farm

LC

STATION RD

River Eau

DN21

Glebe Farm

Bonsdale Farm

Chapel Yard

Blyborough Covert

WESTBECK LANE

94

PILHAM LA

Station Farm

Pilham

GREEN LANE

Dunstall Village

Huckerby

4

Gilby Farm

Gilby Village

Middle Field Farm

Netherdene Farm

Aisby

93

PILHAM LANE

Willoughton Grange

3

Yawthorpe Fox Covert

Low Farm

Hall Farm

Corringham Grange

Home Farm

Park Farm

92

Mill Farm

Windmill

CHURCH LA

Taskers Farm

Yawthorpe

MILL MERE RD

EAST LA

Corringham C of E Sch

MIDDLE STREET

Corringham

2

Poplar Farm

PO

POPLAR LA

Magin Moor

Hemswell Grange

CORRINGHAM RD   A631

PH

Windmill

91

HIGH STREET

EDMUND CL

SPRINGTHORPE ROAD

A631

HARPSWELL LANE

Sewage Works

1

Staplegate Farm

HILL RD

New Church Farm

Springthorpe Grange

Harpswell Grange

90

86   A   87   B   88   C   89   D   90   E   91   F

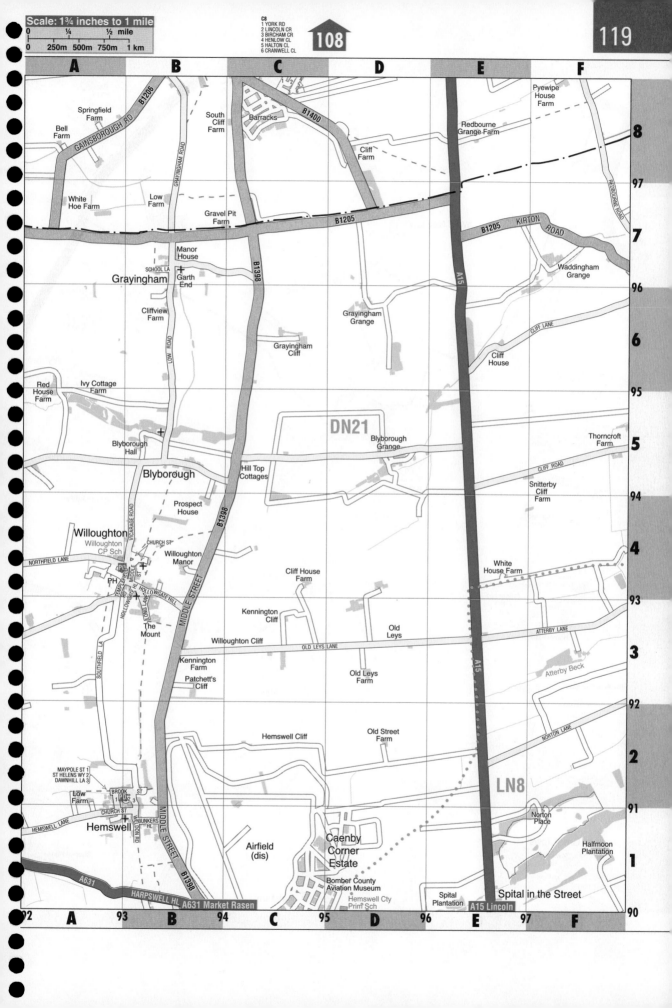

113

Scale: 1¾ inches to 1 mile
0 ¼ ½ mile
0 250m 500m 750m 1 km

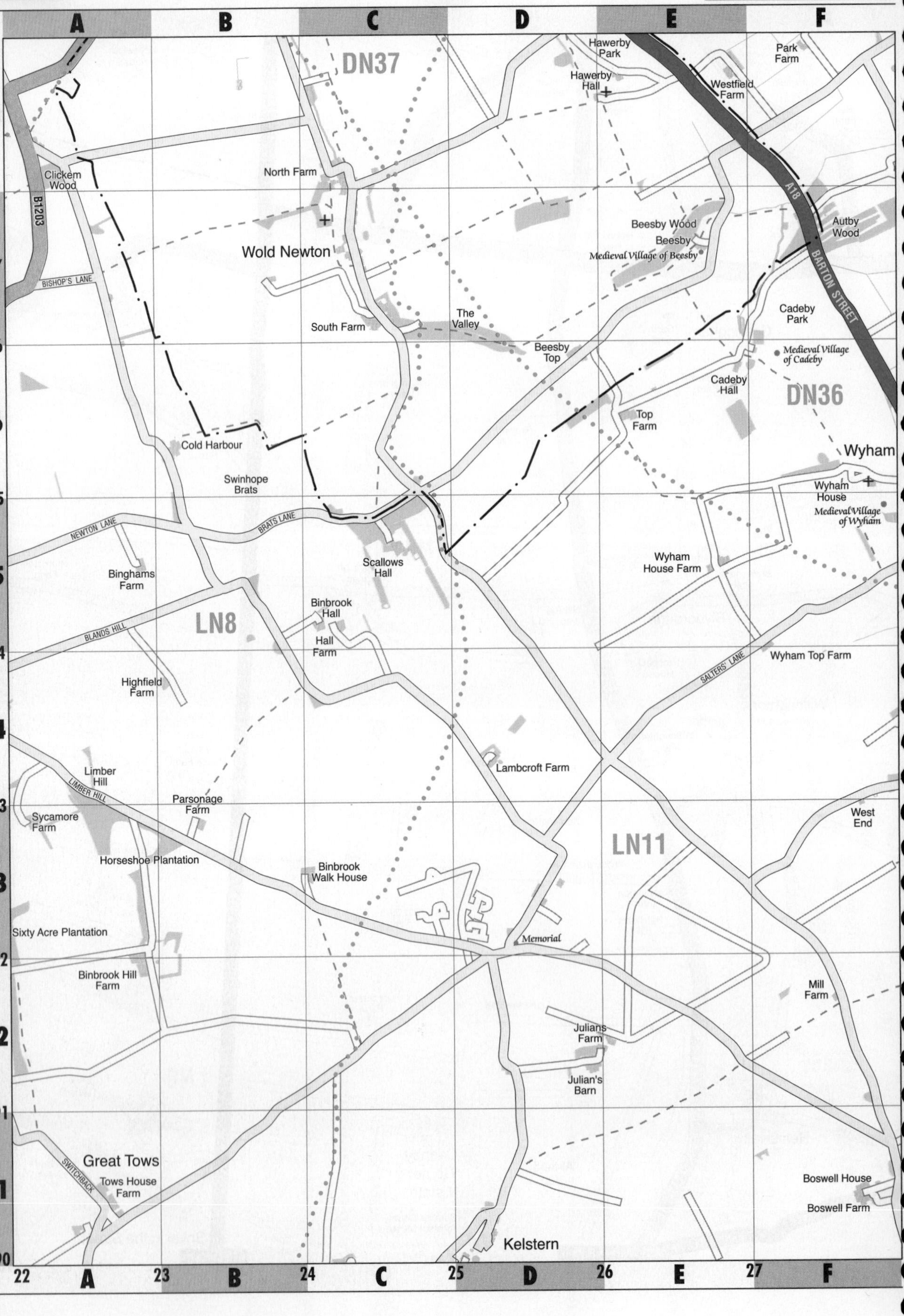

A
B
C
D
E
F
8
97
7
96
6
95
5
94
4
93
3
92
2
91
1
90
22
23
24
25
26
27
DN37
Hawerby Park
Hawerby Hall
Park Farm
Westfield Farm
Clickem Wood
B1203
North Farm
A18
Beesby Wood
Beesby
Medieval Village of Beesby
Autby Wood
Wold Newton
BISHOP'S LANE
BARTON STREET
South Farm
The Valley
Cadeby Park
Beesby Top
Medieval Village of Cadeby
Cadeby Hall
DN36
Top Farm
Cold Harbour
Wyham
Swinhope Brats
Wyham House
Medieval Village of Wyham
NEWTON LANE
BRATS LANE
Scallows Hall
Wyham House Farm
Binghams Farm
LN8
Binbrook Hall
BLANDS HILL
Hall Farm
Wyham Top Farm
SALTERS' LANE
Highfield Farm
Lambcroft Farm
Limber Hill
LIMBER HILL
Parsonage Farm
Sycamore Farm
West End
LN11
Horseshoe Plantation
Binbrook Walk House
Sixty Acre Plantation
Memorial
Binbrook Hill Farm
Mill Farm
Julians Farm
Julian's Barn
Great Tows
SWITCHBACK
Tows House Farm
Boswell House
Boswell Farm
Kelstern

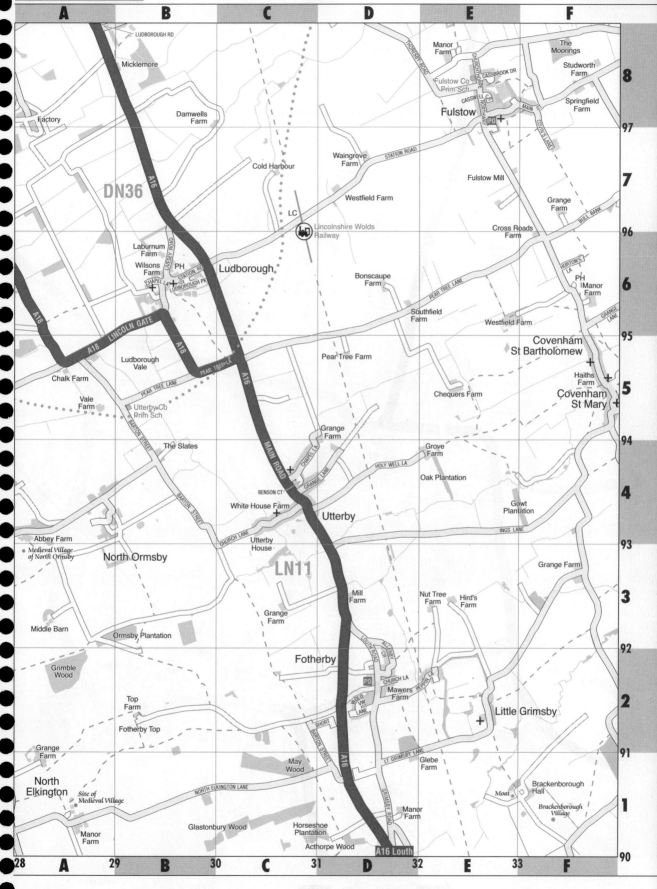

A B C D E F

8
97
7
96
6
95
5
94
4
93
3
92
2
91
1
90

LUDBOROUGH RD

Micklemore

Factory

Damwells Farm

DN36

A16

Cold Harbour

Waingrove Farm

STATION ROAD

Manor Farm

THORESBY ROAD

Fulstow Co Prim Sch

CASSBROOK DR

CHURCHDIKE NORTHWAY

CASSWELL CR

Fulstow

PO

MAIN ST

CASSWELL

COLINS LANE

The Moorings

Studworth Farm

Springfield Farm

Westfield Farm

LC

Lincolnshire Wolds Railway

Fulstow Mill

Grange Farm

BULL BANK

Cross Roads Farm

Laburnum Farm

Wilsons Farm

PH

LIVESEY ROAD

CHAPEL LA

STATION RD

Ludborough

LUDBOROUGH PK

A18

A18

LINCOLN GATE

Chalk Farm

A18

PEAR TREE LA

A16

Ludborough Vale

PEAR TREE LANE

Southfield Farm

PEAR TREE LANE

Bonscaupe Farm

HURTON'S LA

PH

Manor Farm

GRANGE LANE

Covenham St Bartholomew

Westfield Farm

Covenham St Mary

Haiths Farm

Vale Farm

BARTON STREET

Utterby Co Prim Sch

The Slates

Pear Tree Farm

Grange Farm

CHAPEL LA

GRANGE LANE

Grove Farm

HOLY WELL LA

Oak Plantation

Chequers Farm

MAIN ROAD

BENSON CT

White House Farm

BARTON STREET

CHURCH LANE

Utterby House

Utterby

INGS LANE

Gowt Plantation

Abbey Farm

Medieval Village of North Ormsby

North Ormsby

LN11

Mill Farm

Grange Farm

Grange Farm

Middle Barn

Ormsby Plantation

Grimble Wood

Fotherby

Nut Tree Farm

Hird's Farm

LOUTH ROAD

ALLENBY CR

PO

WOLD VW LANE

CHURCH LA

PEPPIN LA

Mawers Farm

Little Grimsby

Top Farm

Fotherby Top

SHORT BARTON STREET

A16

LT GRIMSBY LANE

Glebe Farm

Brackenborough Hall

Moat

Brackenborough Village

Grange Farm

North Elkington

Site of Medieval Village

NORTH ELKINGTON LANE

May Wood

GRIMSBY ROAD

Manor Farm

Manor Farm

Glastonbury Wood

Horseshoe Plantation

Acthorpe Wood

A16 Louth

28 A 29 B 30 C 31 D 32 E 33 F 90

A   B   C   D   E   F

D6
1 TRENTHAM MS
2 N PINFOLD WY
3 PINFOLD CT
4 PINFOLD CL
5 CHATSWORTH CL
6 SANDRINGHAM CL

7 THORESBY MS
8 BALMORAL CL

8

The Grange

Hill Field

YO16

ESKDALE DR

Stackyard Plantation

NEWTONDALE GARTH
AIREDALE DRIVE
THORNYTHWAITE GR

7

GRINDALE LANE

NOSTELL WAY

STUDLEY MEADOWS

MEADOW VIEW

THE ORCHARD

NORTH LEAS DRIVE

TROUTSDALE CLOSE

W CRAYKE
THE CRAYKE
WHARFEDALE DRIVE

DOVEDALE CT

69

FOUNTAINS AV

HADDON

RIDING DALE

TRENTHAM DR

N LEAS AV

RIBBLESDALE CLOSE

GLAISDALE CL

TEESDALE MS

WENSLEYDALE

6

County Farm

CLEETON WY

RAVENSPURN

D5
1 EVESHAM CFT
2 PINFOLD WY S
3 GRANGE RD
4 GT BARN ST
5 MALTHOUSE LA
6 SEWERBY CT
7 KIRKGATE MS
8 JUBILEE GR

PINFOLD GR

PINFOLD GD

HAREWOOD

NEWSTEAD

THORESBY AVE

DARWIN RD

REDWOOD WY

MOUNT CR

MOUNT DR

MOUNT AV

BEMPTON OVAL

ASGARTH

B1255

SANDSACRE WAY

Martengate County Prim Sch

HEADLANDS DRIVE

GREENWAY CL

W CRAYKE

SEWERBY HEADLANDS

Headlands School

YO16

5

BURSTALL HILL

SOUTHORPE CLOSE

New Pasture Lane County Primary School

NEW PASTURE LA

MILL GATE

RIPLEY CL

DANES CL

DANES CT

Burlington City Jun Sen

MARTON ROAD

B1255

WATSONS AV

SEWERBY CR

SEWERBY ROAD

BLADON

SEWERBY RI
SEWERBY RD

PRIORY CL

ST AUGUSTINE'S DR
ST AUGUSTINE'S GR

Cemetery

Old Town

PRIORY

BEMROSE

SEWERBY

HEADS

FORTYFOOT

HARLAND RD

HUSTLER RD
OMEGA

B1254

NIGHTINGALE DR

ST COLUMBA ROAD

LAMBERT RD

QUEENSGATE

EIGHTHGATE

FIRST AVENUE

LAMPLUGH

68

LOWOOD DR 1
EASTON RD 2
WAYSIDE CR 3
LEYS CT 4

B1253   EASTON ROAD

A165

PAXFIELD
AUBURN CL

A165

WELL LA

WELL LA

WESTGATE

MEDFORTH

SOUTH BACK LANE

GORDON RD

STEPNEY GR

HIGH STREET

HOLTBY'S YD

KIRKGATE

JUBILEE ST

Bayle Mus

CHURCH
WK

CHURCH CL

PRIORY
WK

ST AIDAN ST

RICKABY ST

ST ALBAN CL

ST ANTHONY RD

Girls Sch

ST ALBAN ROAD

CHAD

PRIORY RD

OSWALD RD

QUEENSGATE

CHAD

ST WILFRED RD

PO

PARK AV

SANDS LANE

ST ANNES RD

ALEXANDRA

4

NEW PASTURE LA

PASTURE RISE

LEYS RD

PRICKETT RD

WAYSIDE RD

LT BECK RD

GYPSEY ROAD

YO16

School

POSTILL SQUARE

ST JUDE GR

MARY'S WALK

MILNER RD

ST MARY'S SCH

College

ST THOMAS ST

ST ANDREW ST

ST CHAD

ST CHRISTOPHER

QUEENSGATE

Bridlington Town F C

CHAD

CREST

ST WILFRED GROVE

HOLYROOD

B1254

ALBION

FIRST AVENUE

3

WOLDGATE

BESSINGBY HILL

A165

Bridlington Sports Centre

Rec Ground

BRIDLINGTON

D4
1 BLYTHE WALK
2 NORTH BACK LA
3 THE BOLT
4 GRUNDELL'S YD
5 CHURCH GN
6 BAYLEGATE

BRETT ST

BOROUGH RD

ST JOHN'S WLK

PORTLAND

ORVILLE

ST JOHN'S AVENUE

Bridlington RUFC

Court House

D3
1 BURLINGTON GD
2 HAVELOCK ST
3 SWINDON ST
4 GILBERT ST
5 THOMPSON ST
6 HILL ST
7 MELBOURNE AV
8 WESTBOURNE AV
9 ASHBOURNE AV
10 STATION AV

CARLTON ST

OLIVERS LA

Sch

P

TENNYSON AVENUE

TRINITY ROAD

HASLEMERE

BLACKBURN

VERNON RD

PROMENADE

Leisure World

The Promenades Shopping Centre

Museum

Forum Centre

2

High Wood

BESSINGBY ROAD

A165

BESSINGBY ROAD

WRIGHT CRES

CARNABY AVE

THORNTON RD

RAMSEY CL

MATSON RD

Retail Park

BESSINGBY ST

ST JOHN'S AV

ST MARTINS

ELMA AVE

ELMA VILLAS

MIDWAY AVE

ST MARTINS DR

Bridlington

ADMIRALS MS

NEW BURLINGTON ROAD

HILDERTHORPE RD

A1038

A1038

STATION APP

STATION RD

VICTORIA RD

SPRINGFIELD

PROSPECT

NELSON ST

Cooks Gall

CHAPEL ST

CROSS ST

PRINCE ST

QUEEN ST

North Sea Aquarium

E2
1 BECK HILL
2 OLINDA RD
3 ST HILDA ST
4 SOUTH CLIFF RD
5 SAWMILL YD
6 MANOR ST
7 BRIDGE ST
8 PALANZA TR
9 THORPE ST
10 ALBERT ST
11 FERNDALE TR
12 GARDEN WK

67

A614

KENT RD

CRANBECK CL

Bridlington & District H

Bridlington School

MATSON ROAD

ST MARYS RC SCH

KINGSGATE

CARDIGAN RD

SAVAGE RD

HAMILTON RD

WINDSOR RD

YO15

Mus

P

Harbour

Lifeboat Station

SPA ROAD

P

DRIVE

E3
1 HARTLEY CT
2 BEDFORD GR
3 CLARENCE AV
4 FAIRFIELD RD
5 BOW ST
6 NEPTUNE ST
7 SOUTH ST

West Hill

EDWARDIAN DR 1
GEORGIAN MS 2
STUART CL 3
ELIZABETH CL 4
TUDOR CL 5
SHAFTESBURY RD 6

Bessingby Ind Est

GEORGIAN WAY

ROSEBERY AVE

ST JAMES ROAD

GEORGE ST

RICHMOND ST

WEST ST

PEMBROKE TR

Spa Royal Hall and Spa Theatre

1

BRICK KILN BALK

MAIN STREET

Manor Farm

Bessingby Enterprise Park

Jun Sch

Inf Sch

SHAFTESBURY RD

BELGRAVE

SUMMERFIELD RD

MAYFIELD RD

HORSFORTH AVE

ST MARTINS

MEADOWFIELD RD

66

16   A   B   17   C   D   18   E   F

C5
1 SEATHORNE RD
2 WYKEHAM CL
3 ELLERBURN RD
4 MILLFIELD RD
5 MILFORD CR
6 NEW PASTURE CL
7 SCARBOROUGH CR
8 SCARBOROUGH GR
9 THE HOLLOWS

10 MILL CT
11 MILLBANK
12 SHORT LA
13 STEPNEY AV

F2
1 CLARENCE RD
2 WESTMORLAND GR
3 WESTMORLAND AV
4 PRINCESS AV
5 PRINCESS TR
6 FORT TR
7 REGENT TR
8 MARLBOROUGH CRES
9 THE CRESCENT

F3
1 TRINITY GR
2 TRINITY MS
3 SWANLAND AV
4 ALEXANDRA CT
5 ALEXANDRA DR
6 GLADSTONE TR
7 BRIGHT ST
8 CARLISLE RD
9 LANSDOWNE CR

10 PROVIDENCE PL

F4
1 FORTYFOOT GR
2 PARK VW
3 SEVENTH AV
4 EDGECLIFFE VILLAS
5 CANTON VILLAS
6 LAMPLUGH SQ
7 LAMPLUGH LA

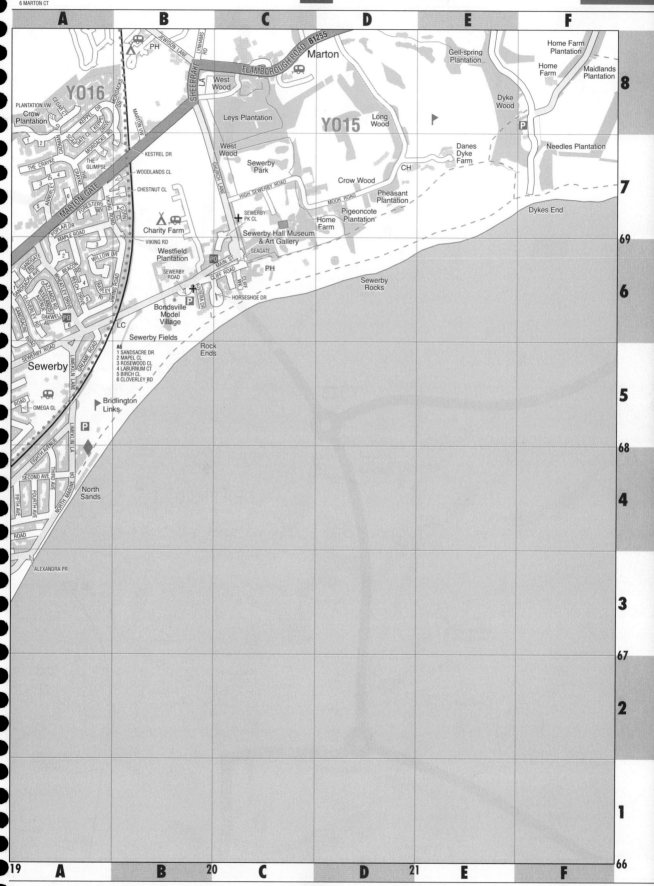

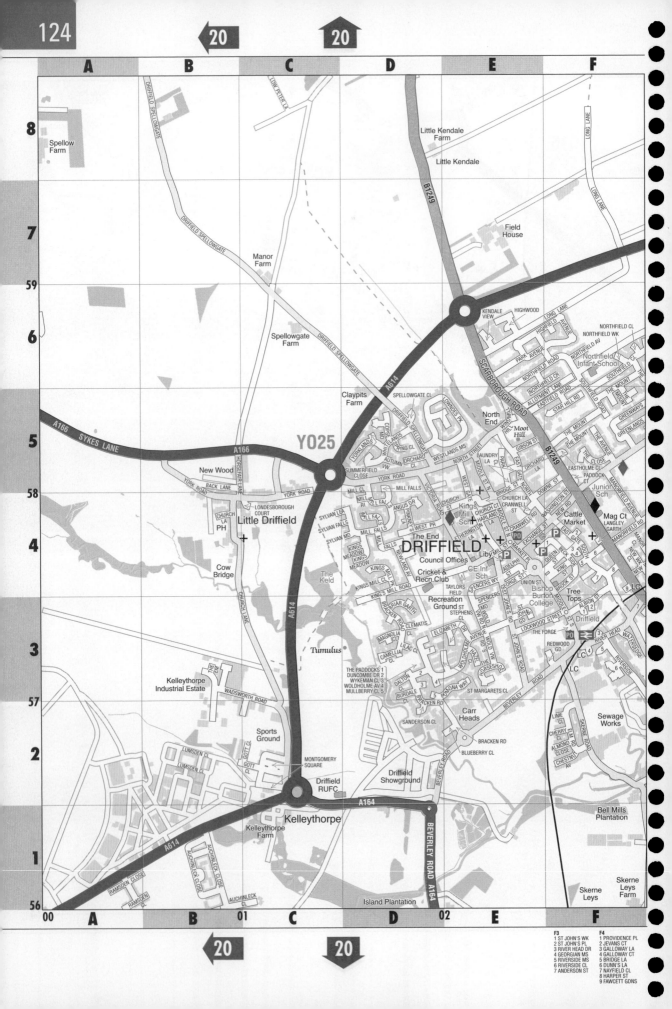

A B C D E F

8 Spellow Farm

Little Kendale Farm

Little Kendale

DRIFFIELD SPELLOWGATE

LOW PETER LA

7 Manor Farm

Field House

B1249

59

Spellowgate Farm

DRIFFIELD SPELLOWGATE

6 KENDALE VIEW HIGHWOOD

LONG LANE

Claypits Farm

Spellowgate CL

North End

NORTHFIELD CL
NORTHFIELD WK
Northfield Infant School

YO25

A166 SYKES LANE

Moot Hill

SCARBOROUGH ROAD

PARK AVENUE
HIGHFIELD
LONG LANE AVENUE

NORTHFIELD AV
Northfield Lane
EASTFIELD ROAD
SOUTHFIELD
STAR HILL RD
THE MOUNT
GREENWAYS
GREENLANDS

5 A166

Gibson St

THE AVENUE
THE CLOSE

B1249

New Wood

HORSEFAIR LANE

BACK LANE

York Road

A614

Summerfield Close

York Road

YORKLANDS
COPSE
WHITELANDS
AUTUMN CL
ORCHARD
CL

Westlands MS

North Park

LAUNDRY LA
EAST ORCHARD LA
MIDDLE ST N

EASTHOLME CL
PADDOCK

Junior Sch

58 CHURCH LA PH

LONDESBOROUGH COURT

Little Driffield

Mill Falls
Mill CL
MILL RT
7LL FA

Mill Falls

ANGUS DR
PINCKES ST

Church
HERINGTON

DOWNE ST

WASHINGTON RD

Mag Ct
LANGLEY GARTH

SYLVAN LEA
SYLVAN FALLS
SYLVAN MD

Kings Mill Sch

CHURCH LA N
HARLAND LA
CRANWELL ST

Cattle Market

MANORFIELD AVENUE

4 CHURCH LA PH

Cow Bridge

KINGS MEADOW
KINGS MEADOW

7LL FA

NEWLAND AV

WEST PR

The End

DRIFFIELD

Liby

CHURCH LA S
CRANWELL RD
EXCHANGE ST

PO

EAST GATE SOUTH

NEW TK
NEW

The Keld

KINGS MILL MLT

Council Offices

Cricket & Recn Club

GE Inf Sch

ADELPH

UNION ST
GEORGE ST

King

LC

KINGS MILL MLT

TAYLORS FIELD

SPENCERS WY
SPENCERS

Bishop Burton College

BROOK ST

Tree Tops

ALBION ST

3 Tumulus

King's Mill Road

BRIAR GARTH

BRACKEN ROAD

CLEMATIS

ST JOHN'S RD

ST STEPHENS

NEW YORK ST

LOCKWOOD STREET

THE FORGE

PO
Driffield

River Head

WATERSIDE

RIVERSIDE

LC

MAGNOLIA CT
CAMELLIA
LILAC CL

Elizabeth

WOODHOLME AVENUE

WOLD VW

THE HORSESHOE

REDWOOD GD

LC

THE PADDOCKS 1
DUNCOMBE DR 2
WYKEHAM CL 3
WOLDHOLME AV 4
MULLBERRY CL 5

DALTON
CL
BURDALE
CL

PONONA WAY

St Margarets Cl

BEVERLEY ROAD

LIME CL

57 Kelleythorpe Industrial Estate

WADSWORTH ROAD

SANDERSON CL

Bracken Rd

Carr Heads

Blueberry Cl

SKERNE ROAD

CHERRY CL
ELM CL
ALMOND CLOSE
CHESTNUT AV

Sewage Works

2 Sports Ground

LUMSDEN CL

LUMSDEN CL

THE ELMS
GOTT CL

Montgomery Square

Driffield RUFC

Driffield Showground

BEVERLEY ROAD

A164

Bell Mills Plantation

1 A614

RAMSDEN CLOSE

AUCHINLECK CLOSE

Kelleythorpe Farm

Kelleythorpe

A164

BEVERLEY ROAD A164

Skerne Leys

Skerne Leys Farm

56 RAMSDEN CL

AUCHINLECK CL

Island Plantation

A B C D E F

00 01 02

F3
1 ST JOHN'S WK
2 ST JOHN'S PL
3 RIVER HEAD DR
4 GEORGIAN MS
5 RIVERSIDE MS
6 RIVERSIDE CL
7 ANDERSON ST

F4
1 PROVIDENCE PL
2 JEVANS CT
3 GALLOWAY LA
4 GALLOWAY CT
5 BRIDGE LA
6 DUNN'S LA
7 NAYFIELD CL
8 HARPER ST
9 FAWCETT GDNS

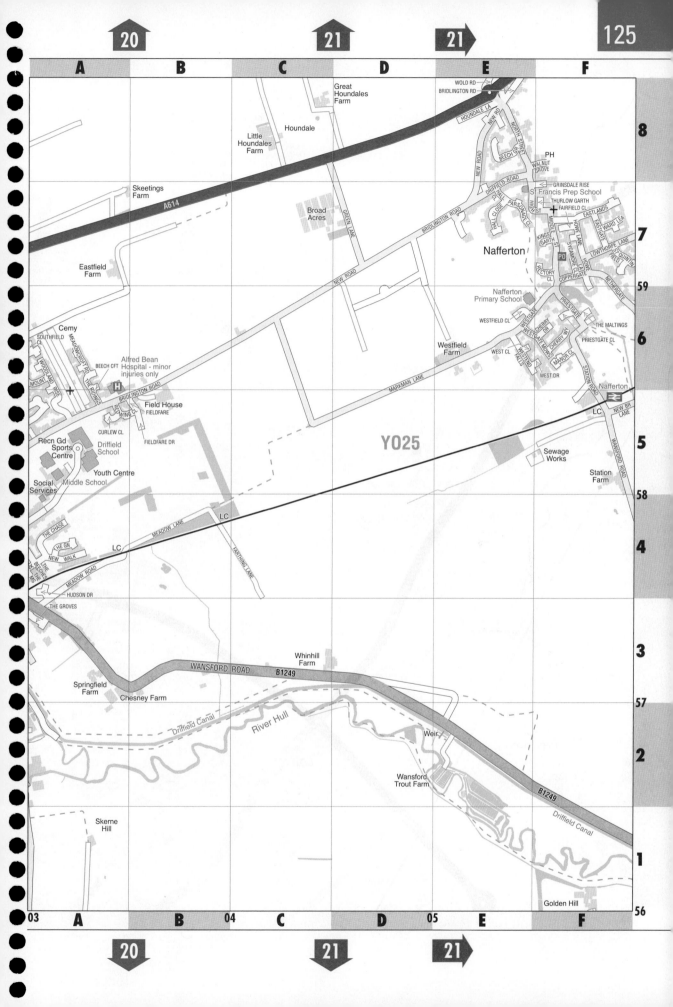

A B C D E F

8

Hall Moor

Wide Open Farm

CH

Woodside Farm

Park Farm

YO32

Wigginton Moor

7

Hurns Bridge

HURNS LA

Glebe Farm

Skelton Moor

57

Nova Scotia Plantation

A19

MOOR LANE

6

New Farm

THE VILLAGE

1ST GILES ROAD LANE

Skelton

St Catherines

Skelton Moor

MOORLANDS LANE

CHURCH LANE

Skelton Primary Sch

Skelton Plantation

Skelton Moor

BRECKSFIELD

B5
1 THE GREEN
2 THE MEADOWS
3 ORCHARD VIEW
4 THE WHEELHOUSE
5 THE DELL
6 ARTHUR PLACE

THE VILLAGE

YO30

5

PH

ST GILES CL

VILDALE

PASTURE CL

GRANGE CL

STRIPE LANE

FAIRFIELDS DR

PO

SYCAMORE CL

1 RATCLIFFE CT
2 GREGORY CL
3 ST CATHERINES CL

Rawcliffe Moor

CH

BIRTREE AV

56

Folly Bridge

Fairfield Farm

PARK CLOSE

1 THE ROWMANS
2 THE BEECHES

Rawcliffe Moor Farm

4

SHIPTON ROAD

FB

Poplar Plantation

A1237

Superstore

River Ouse

E3
1 CAITHNESS CL
2 CONWAY CL
3 HATFIELD CL
4 OSBOURNE DR
5 GRENWICH CL
6 SOMERSET CL
7 HIGHGROVE CL
8 LONGWOOD LINK
9 WINSCAR GR

Clifton Moor Retail Park

1 LANGSETT GR
2 RINGSTONE RD
3 BLAKELEY GR
4 ROSEBERRY CL

STIRLING RD

3

Overton Ings

Skelton Bridge

Rawcliffe Farm

BLENHEIM CT

MARLBOROUGH CL

A1237

HOLLYROOD RD

ST JAMES

Hurricane Way

LINDLEY WOOD GR

DEER HL GR

AVIATOR CL

Moat

Tom Cobleighs Riverside Farm

A19

MANOR LANE

Village Street

BROADSTONE WY

RIVELIN WAY

GRIMWITH GARTH

POPPLETON HALL GD

Manor Farm

CHURCH LANE

MANOR PK GR

DEANHEAD GR

BOOTHWOOD RD

MOREHALL CL 1
WHARNSCLIFFE DR 2
RYBURN CL 3

SOUTHWAITH CL

Lakeside Prim Sch

55

FOX GARTH

CHURCH LANE

HILLCREST AV

Nether Poppleton

HAREWOOD CL 1
KENSINGTON RD 2

FLORENCE GR

ELMA GR

RAWCLIFFE CL

ST MARK'S GR

ST MARK'S GR

BILSDALE

STAINDALE CL

BOTBY GR

ROUND HL LINK

DALE DIKE GR

THORNTON MOOR CL

STUBDEN GR

ELDWICK CL

LANGHAM CFT

2

NETHER WY

EBOR WAY

WHITTON CL

MILL FIELD RD

NURSERY CT

Rawcliffe Bar P&R

SHIPTON ROAD

MANOR LA

RONALD LINK

 INGS VIEW

HOWARD DRIVE

Rawcliffe Infant Sch

FURNESS DR

LOVELEY CT

SWINSTY CT

ANGRAM CL

LINLEY CT

ALLERTON DRIVE

MIDWAY AV

EASTHORPE DR

SANDYRIDGE

MILFRED LANE

Rawcliffe

BOWNESS DR

BUTTERMERE DR

PATERDALE DRIVE

EASTHOLME DR

GREYSTONE CT

KENTMERE DR

RISHWORTH

BORROWDALE

RAWCLIFFE LA

BEAVERDYKE

GAYLE CT

1

LONG RIDGE

LONG RIDGE LANE

ORCHARD RD

YO26

A1237

Sewage Works

Rawcliffe Ings

Hotel

WHITE ROSE CLOSE

WHITE ROSE WAY

INGS LA

Poppleton Ings

ALWYNE DRIVE

ALWYNE GR

NORTHOLME DRIVE

SHELLEY GR

A19

PO

54

56 A 57 B C 58 D E F

E1
1 CONISTON CL
2 WASDALE CL
3 GARBURN GR
4 SCAFELL CL
5 LOWESWATER RD
6 FYLINGDALES AV

F1
1 EMBLETON DR
2 COLEDALE CL
3 LEIGHTON CFT
4 BARMBY CL
5 GRASMERE GR
6 BARDEN CT
7 SOUTHOLME DR
8 MILTON CARR
9 FEWSTON DR

10 REIGHTON DR

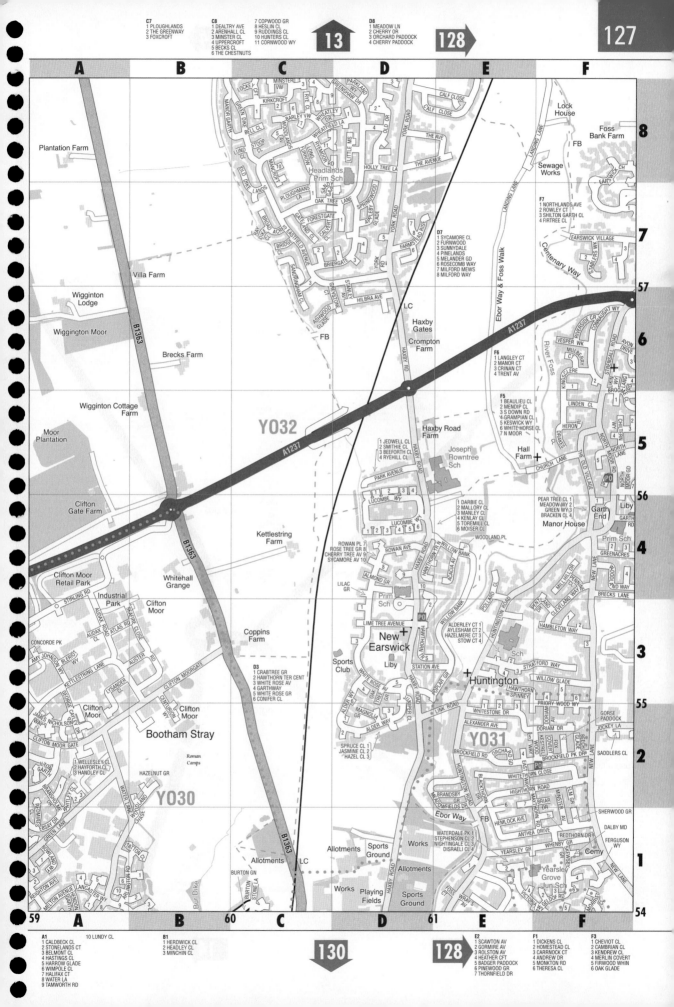

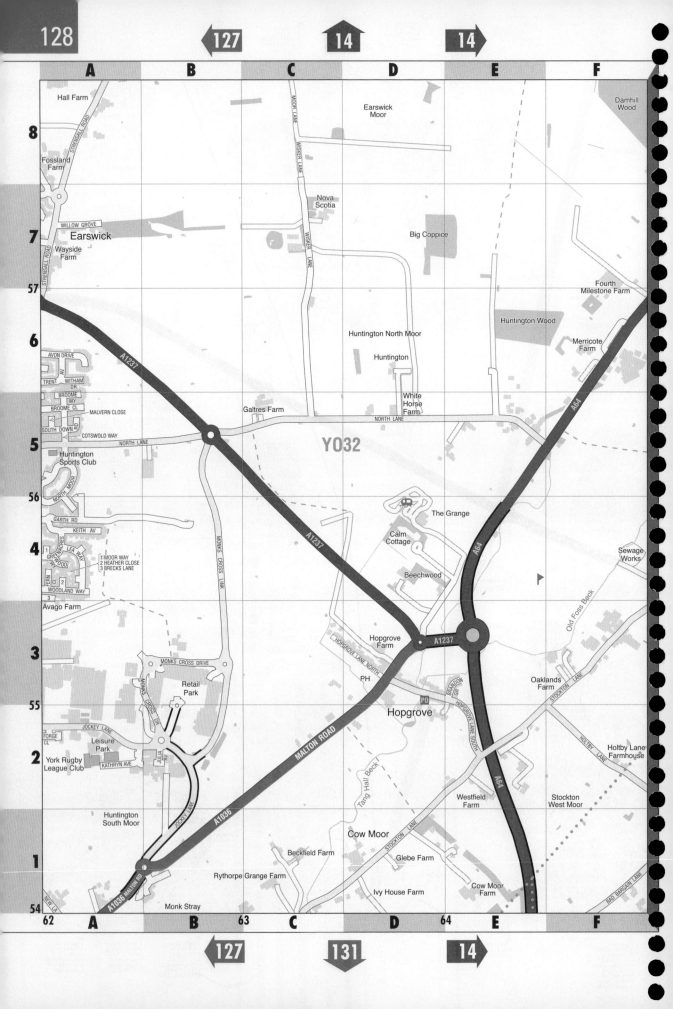

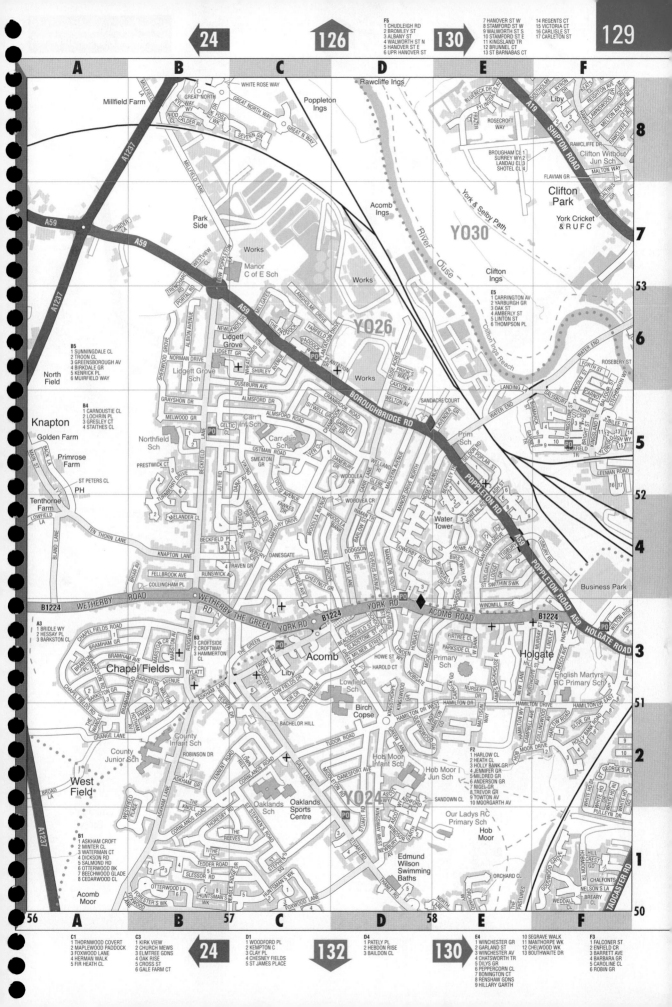

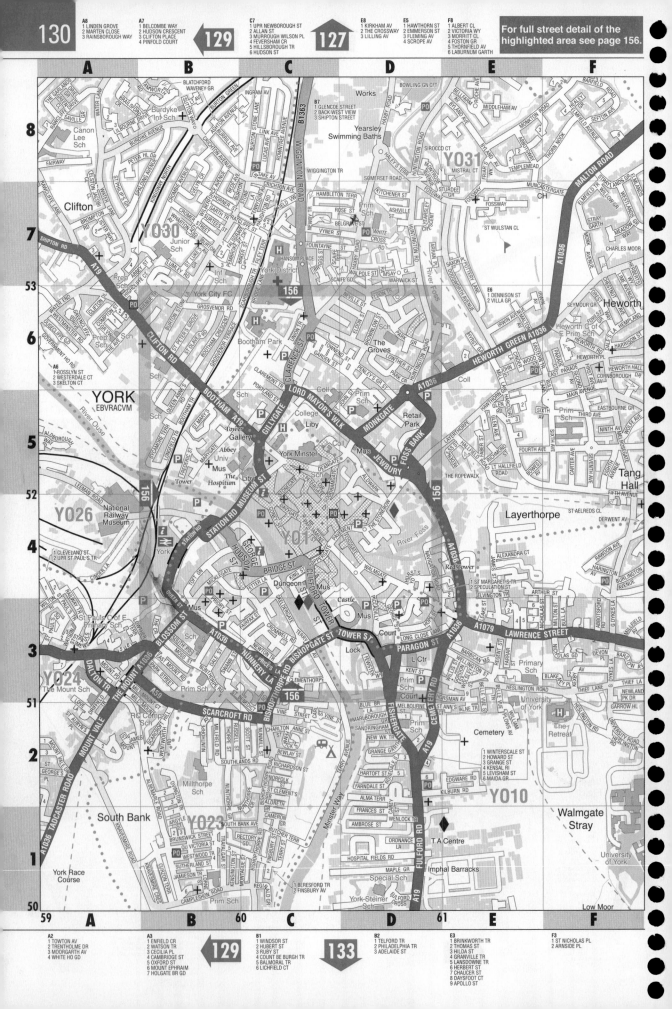

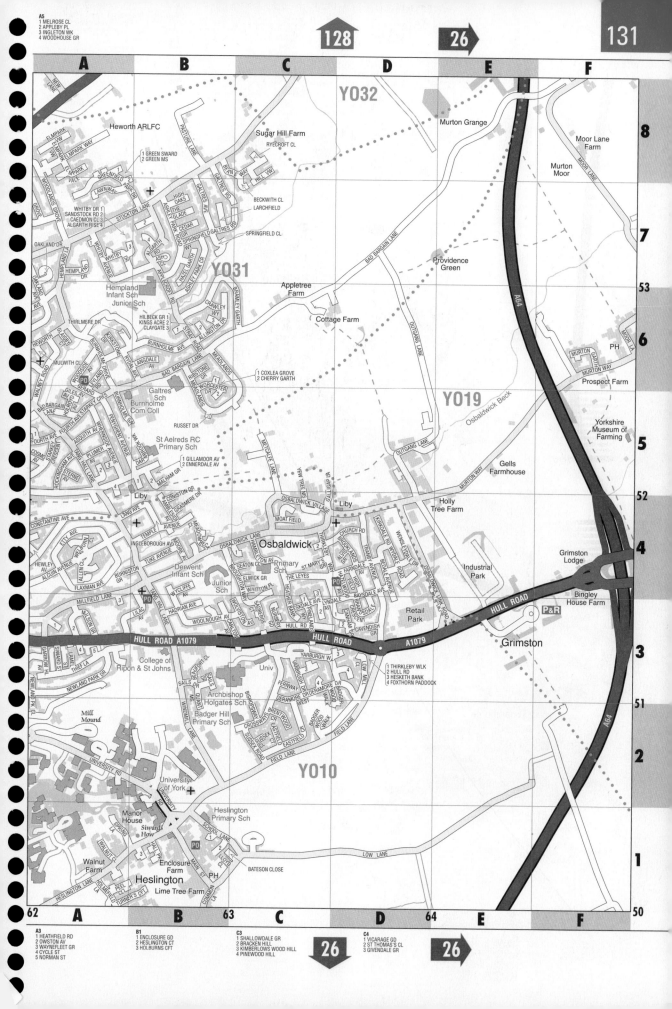

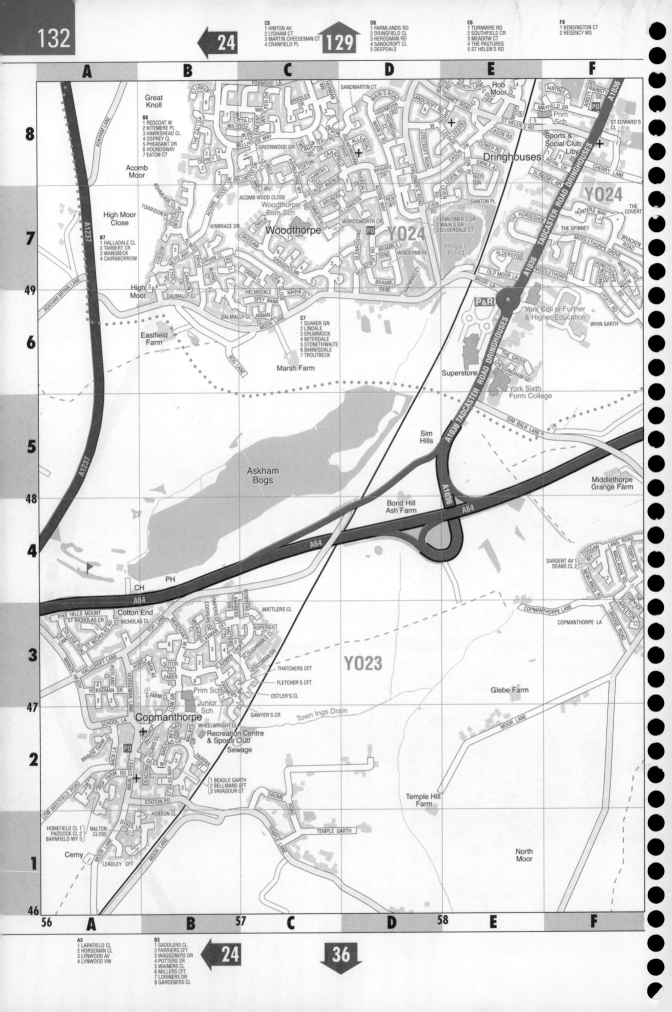

C8
1 HINTON AV
2 LYDHAM CT
3 MARTIN CHEESEMAN CT
4 CRANFIELD PL

D8
1 FARMLANDS RD
2 DRINGFIELD CL
3 HERDSMAN RD
4 SANDCROFT CL
5 DEEPDALE

E8
1 TURNMIRE RD
2 SOUTHFIELD CR
3 MEADOW CT
4 THE PASTURES
5 ST HELEN'S RD

F8
1 KENSINGTON CT
2 REGENCY MS

B8
1 REDCOAT W
2 KITEMERE PL
3 HAWKSHEAD CL
4 OSPREY CL
5 PHEASANT DR
6 HOUNDSWAY
7 EATON CT

B7
1 HALLADALE CL
2 TARBERT CR
3 WANSBECK
4 CAIRNBORROW

C7
1 QUAKER GN
2 LINDALE
3 CRUMMOCK
4 MITERDALE
5 STONETHWAITE
6 BANNISDALE
7 TROUTBECK

A3
1 LARKFIELD CL
2 HORSEMAN CL
3 LYNWOOD AV
4 LYNWOOD VW

B3
1 SADDLERS CL
2 FARRIERS CFT
3 WAGGONERS DR
4 POTTERS DR
5 WAINERS CL
6 MILLERS CFT
7 LORINERS DR
8 GARDENERS CL

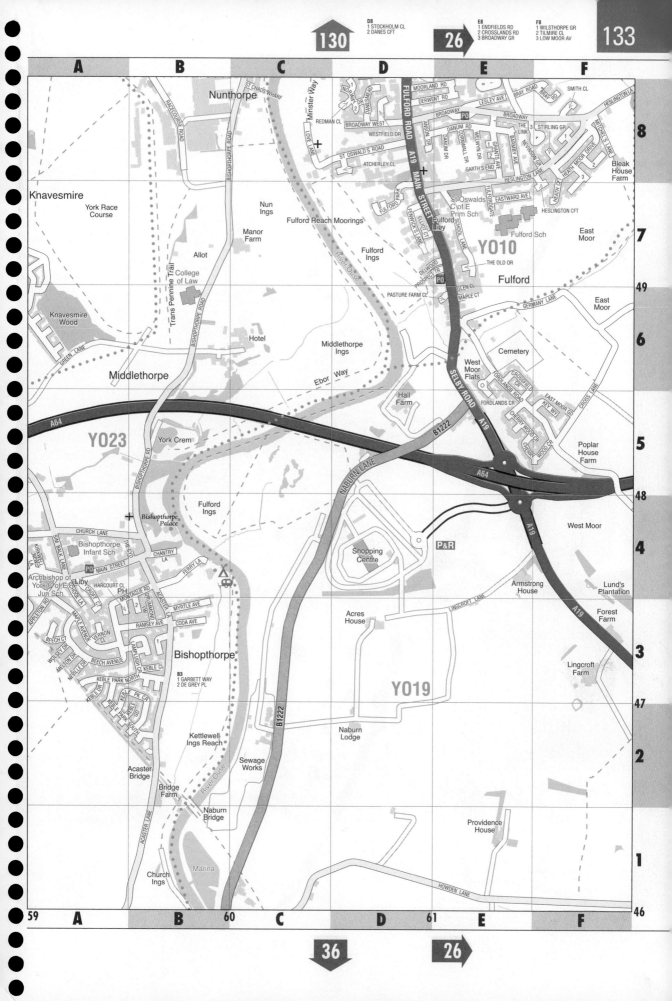

35
35

A B C D E F

8

Eastfield Farm

HORNSEA ROAD

7

Northfield House

B1242

ATWICK ROAD

49

Springfield Farm

6

North Cliff

CLIFF ROAD

Birk Crag

BAY VW AV

BELDEVERE PK

LOTEN DRI

LOTEN PRIOR

Victoria GD

HOLTBY GD

CARRINGTON AVENUE

ACKLAM DR

SANDPIPER CT

HU18

NORTHGATE

SAWLEY CL

DRAYCOTT ROAD

ST NICHOLAS DR

LANCASTER AVENUE

SHARDLOW ROAD

ARGBASTON RD

CARLTON AVE

CLIFFORD ST

CLIFTON STREET

Floral Hall

SHAFTESBURY AV

BELGRAVE DR

HARTLEY ST

HALL ROAD

ESPLANADE

Hotel

5

NORTHUMBERLAND AVENUE

COLLEGE GDS

DERWENT CLOSE

ASHCOURT DR

ASHCOURT DR

EASTGATE

Hornsea & Dist War Meml
H Cott

CHRYSTALS WALK

CONSTABLE DRIVE

MARINE DRIVE

DERWENT CL

48

CHEYNE GARTH

WESTWOOD AVE

B1242

Hornsea Sch

HORNSEA

CHRYSTAL'S RD

CARFSTALS RD

1 GROSVENOR RD
2 PARVA RD
3 STATION MS

CHEYNE GARTH

THE LEYS

Hollis Sports Ground

MILL LA

1

Liby

Meml Gdns

Leisure Centre

CHEYNE WK

SPRINGBANK AV

CINEMA ST

PARK ROW

BROADWAY

4

CHEYNE WALK

Beverley Coll

Moat

Hornsea Mus

P PO

P

NEWBEGIN

i

Town Co Offs

ALEXANDRA RD

EASTBOURNE RD

SANDS LANE

PASTURE RD

SOUTH PROMENADE

WESTGATE

MARKET PL

WILLOWS

Primary Sch

BURTON RD

STATION RD

FAIR PL

PH

P

SOUTHGATE

Low Wood

Football Green

GRAINGERS RD

MASCOTTE GDS

TRANMERE PK

P

SEATON ROAD

B1244

Swan I

MOUNT PLEASANT 1
HARTS CL 2
EASTGATE VW 3
EASTGATE 4
BACK WESTGATE 5
MERESIDE TR 6
SCALBY PL 7
HILLERBY LA 8

QUEENS RD

QUEENS GARDENS

BACK SOUTHGATE

Cemy

BECKSIDE

KING ST 1
SOUTHGATE GDS 2
WALLER LA 3

Hornsea Mere Nature Reserve

P

C4
CHAMBERS LA 1
QUAYLES MWS 2
BANK STREET 3
DESMOND AVE 4
THE WILLOWS 5
MERE WK 6

47

B1242

HORNSEA BURTON ROAD

BERESFORD AVENUE

Beverley Farm

HU11

BANK TR 1
WELLINGTON AV 2
TRINITY ROAD 3
LEYBURN AV 4
BEAUFORT AV 5
THE GREENWAY 6
SALISBURY AV 7
BROOKE DR 8
EDENFIELD AV 9

OLD BRIDGE RD

BURTON LANE

TRINITY RD

WHIMBREL AVE

EBOR AVENUE

1 ROWAN WK
2 THE HOLLIES
3 OAKLANDS

THE BIRCHES

South Cliff

2

HULL ROAD

LINDALE AVE

MERE VIEW

MARLBOROUGH AVENUE

STANLEY AVE

RANBY RD

RANBY CR

ROLSTON ROAD

PICKERING AVENUE

TANSLEY LANE

Hornsea Burton

Southorpe Village

1

Hornsey Rail Track

MARLBOROUGH AVENUE

Hornsea Freeport Shopping Village

GREENACRE PK

1 CEDAR CL
2 CHERRY CL

Southorpe Farm

HULL RD

SOUTHORPE ROAD

POTTERS WAY

B1242

STRAWBERRY GDNS

Hornsea Golf Club

CH

46

19 A B 20 C D 21 E F

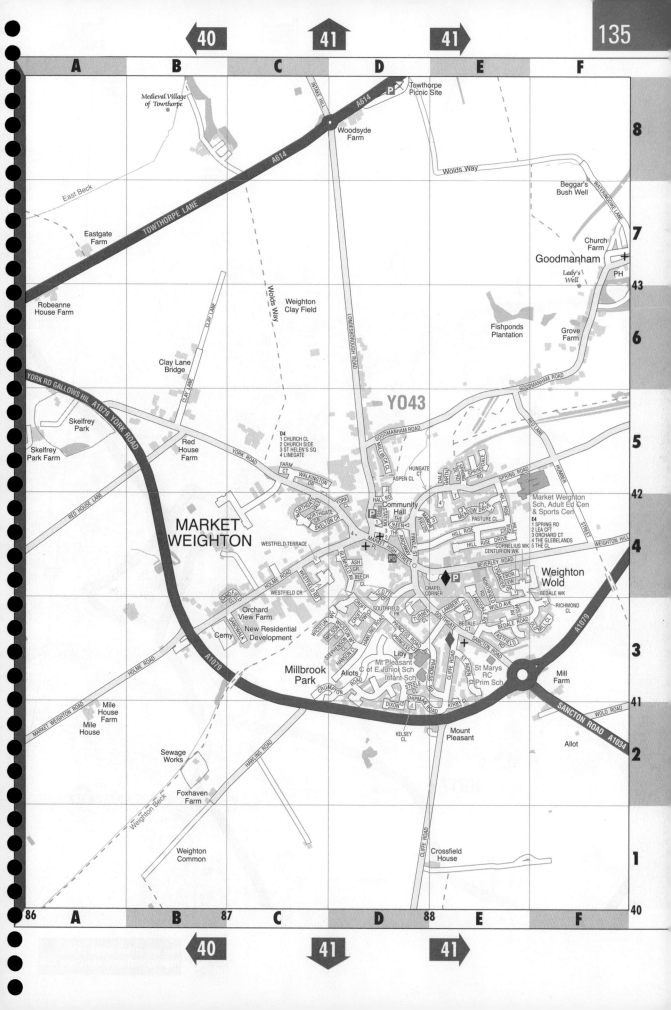

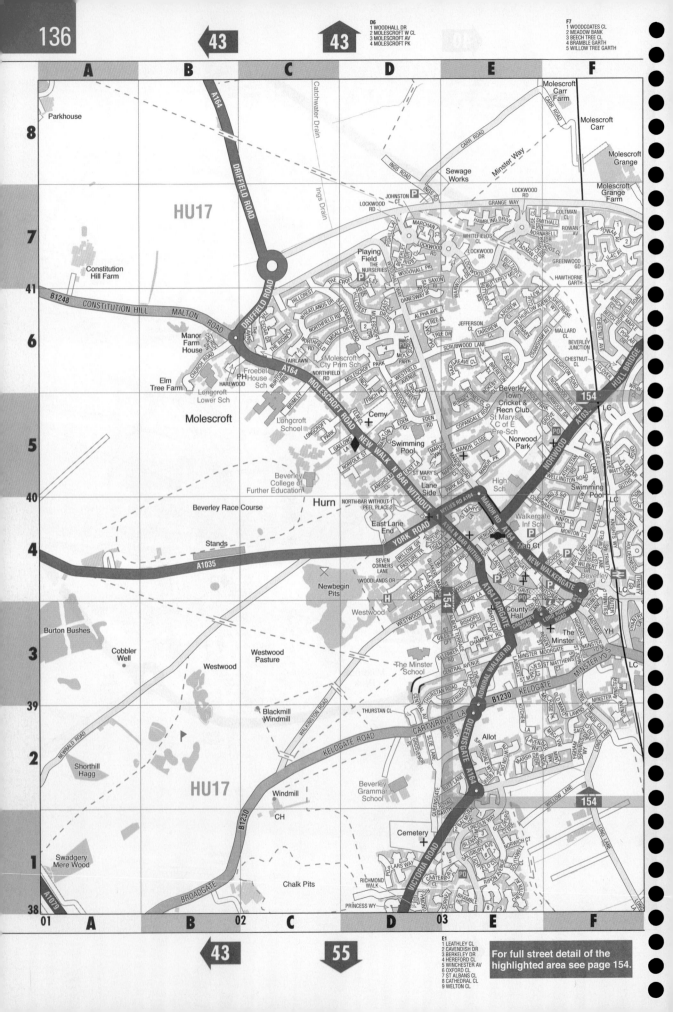

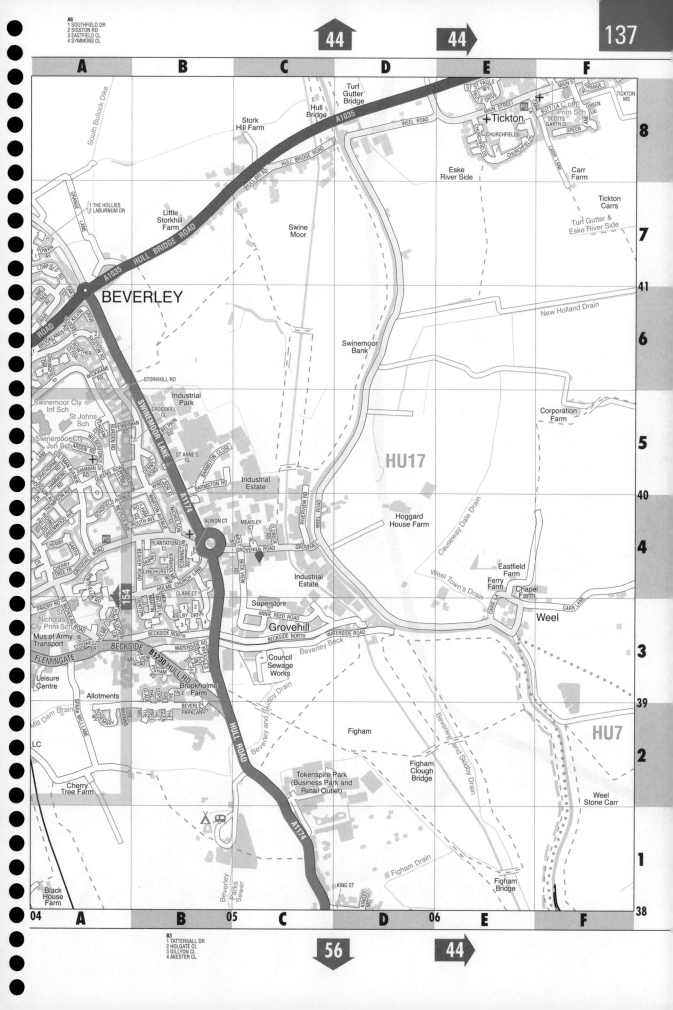

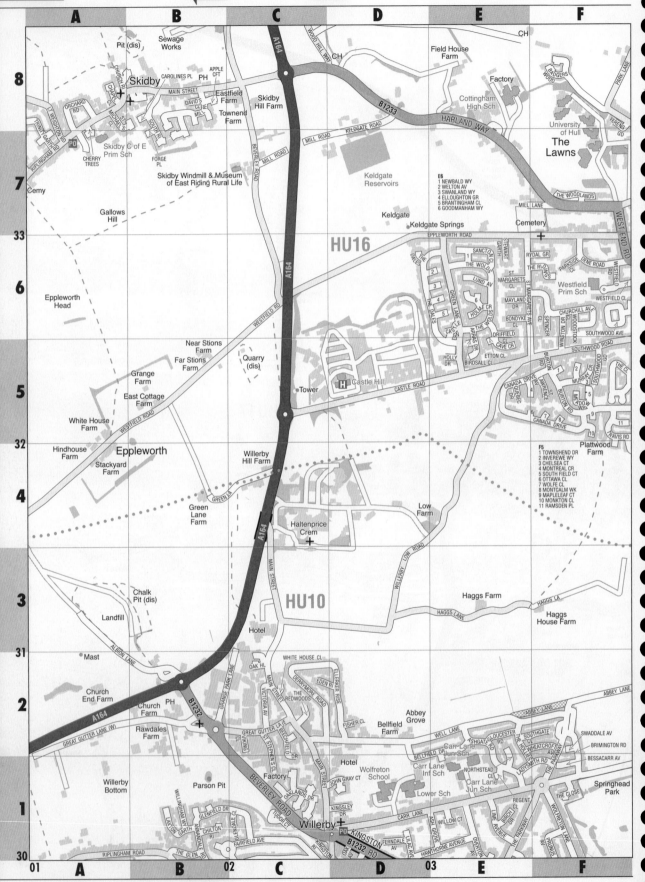

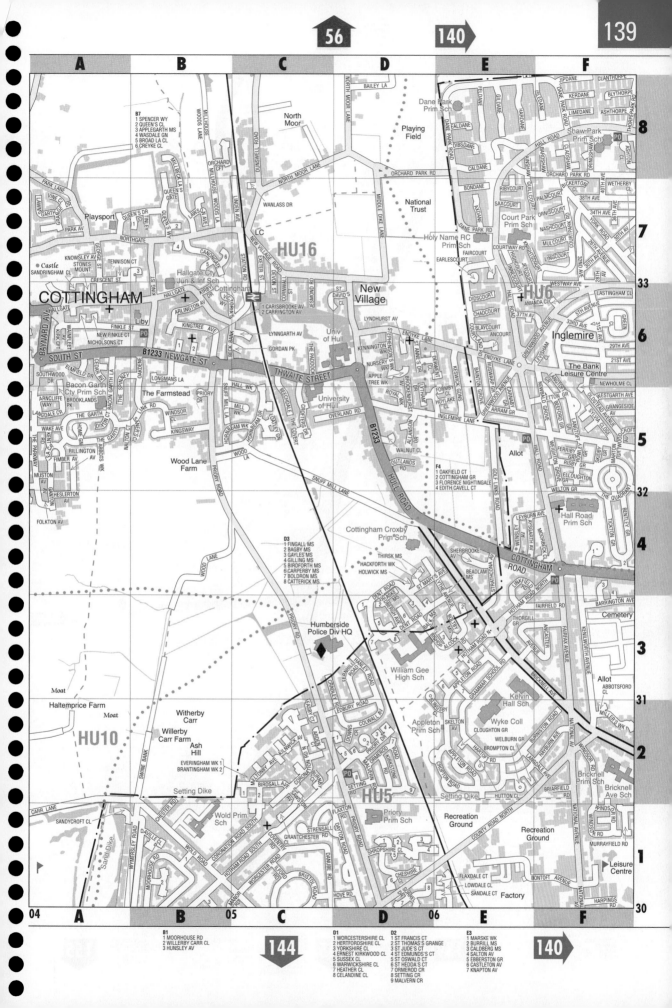

139

56

C8
1 FLAG WK
2 LARARD AV

C7
1 BEECHCLIFFE AV
2 CULLINGWORTH AV
3 DENHOLME AV
4 STEETON AV
5 SILSDEN AVE

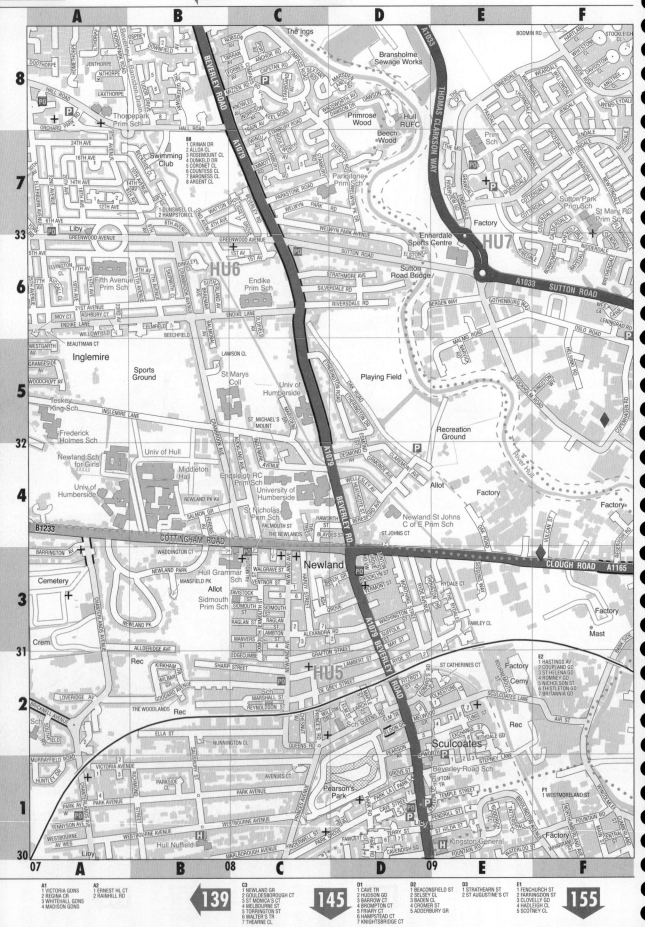

A1
1 VICTORIA GDNS
2 REGINA CR
3 WHITEHALL GDNS
4 MADISON GDNS

A2
1 ERNEST HL CT
2 RAINHILL RD

139

C3
1 NEWLAND GR
2 GOULDESBOROUGH CT
3 ST MONICA'S CT
4 MELBOURNE ST
5 TORRINGTON ST
6 WALTER'S TR
7 THEARNE CL

145

D1
1 CAVE TR
2 HUDSON GD
3 BARROW CT
4 BROMPTON CT
5 FRIARY CT
6 HAMPSTEAD CT
7 KNIGHTSBRIDGE CT

D2
1 BEACONSFIELD ST
2 SELSEY CL
3 BADEN CL
4 CROMER CL
5 ADDERBURY GR

D3
1 STRATHEARN ST
2 ST AUGUSTINE'S CT

E1
1 FENCHURCH ST
2 FARRINGDON ST
3 CLOVELLY GD
4 HADLEIGH CL
5 SCOTNEY CL

155

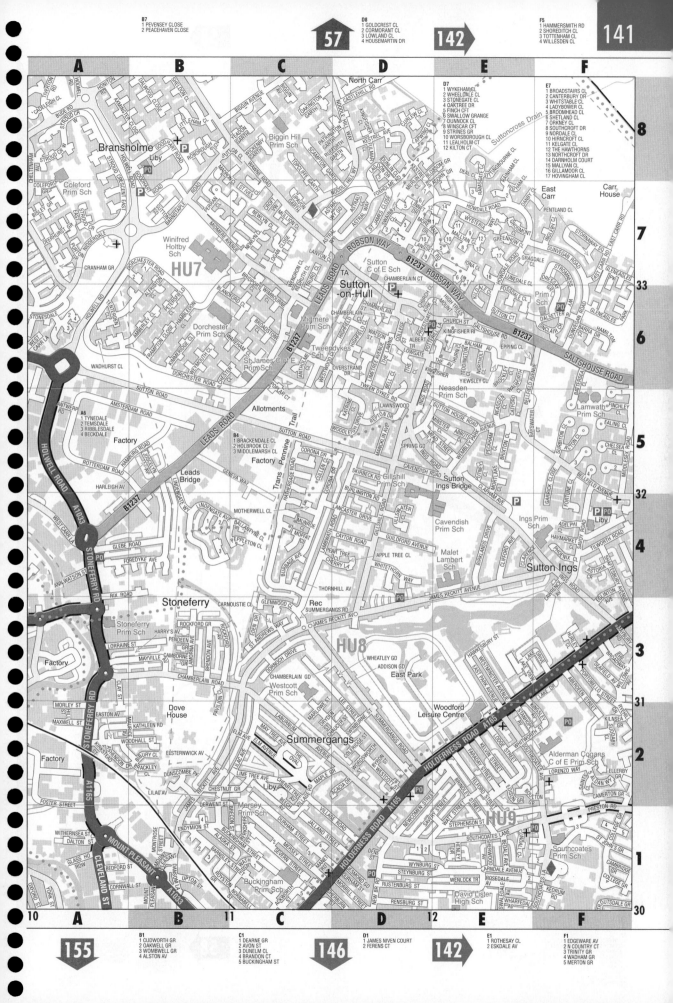

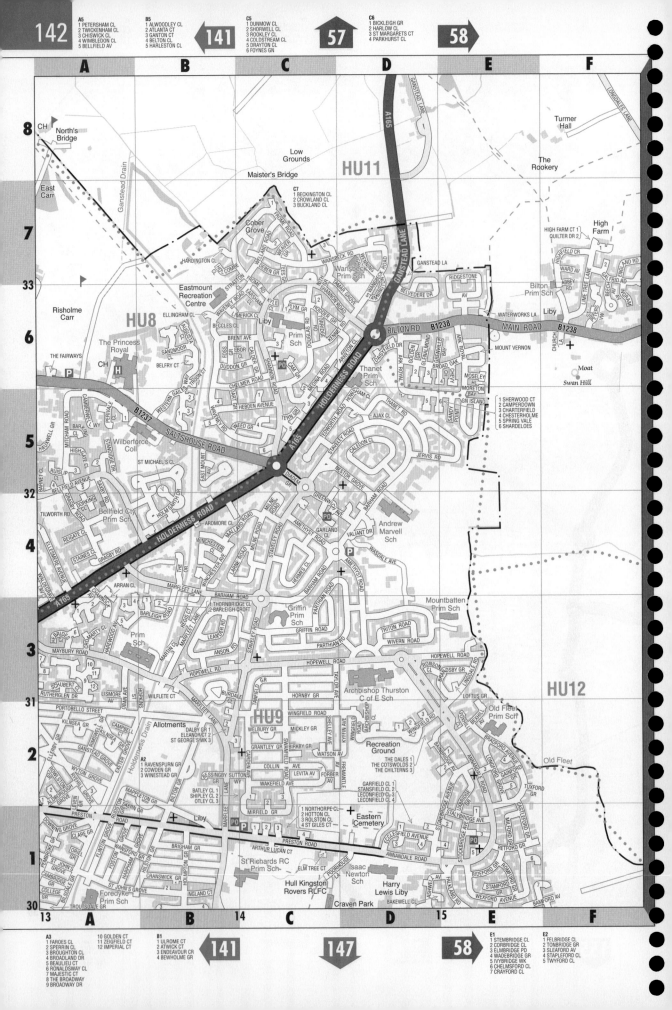

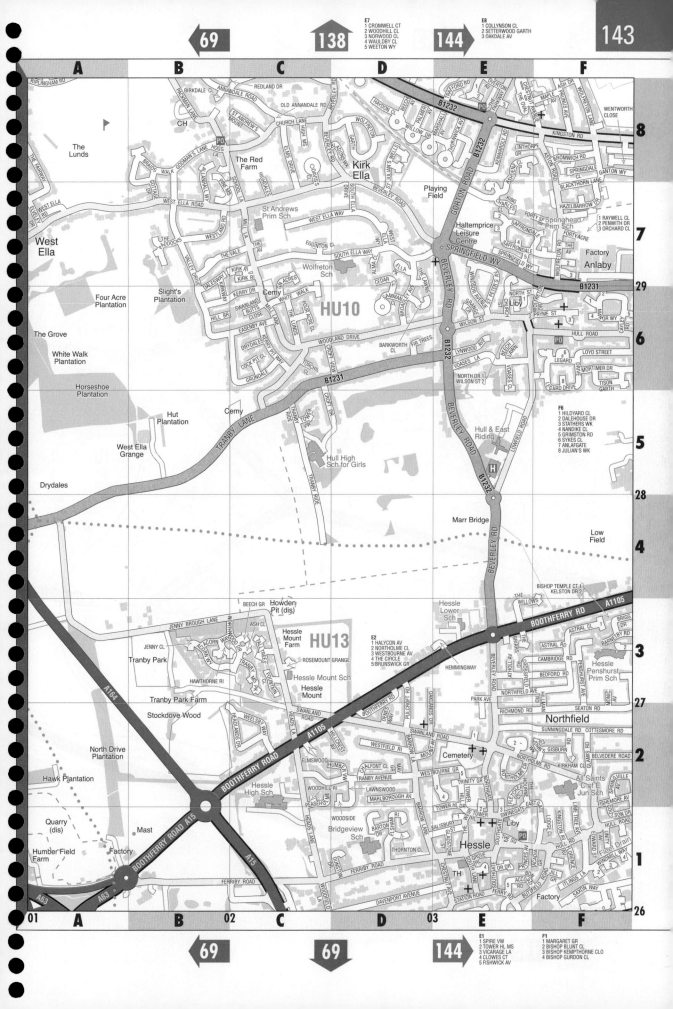

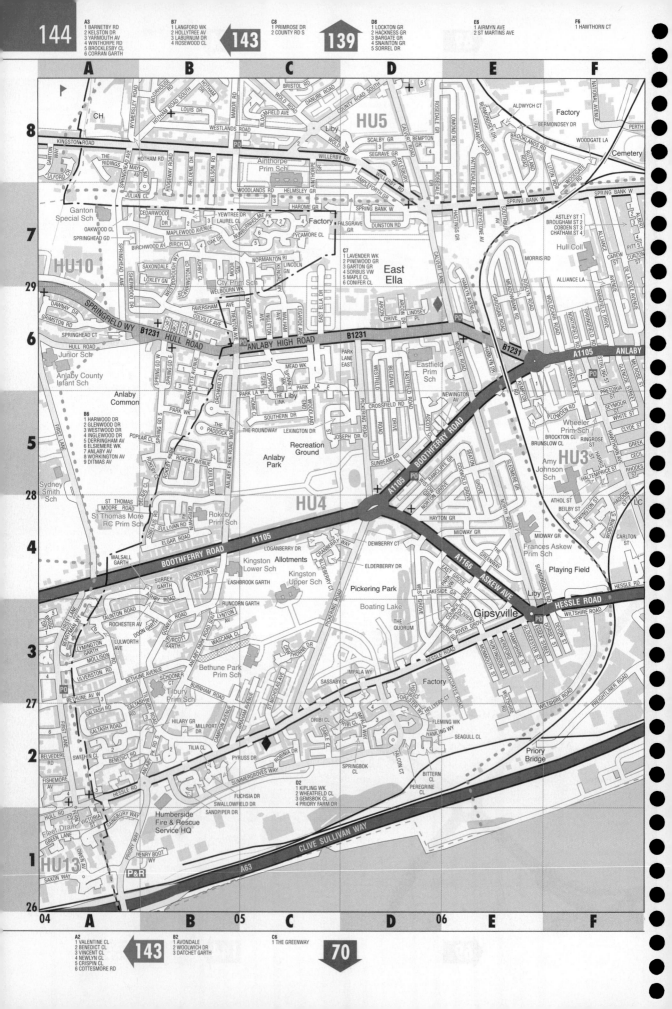

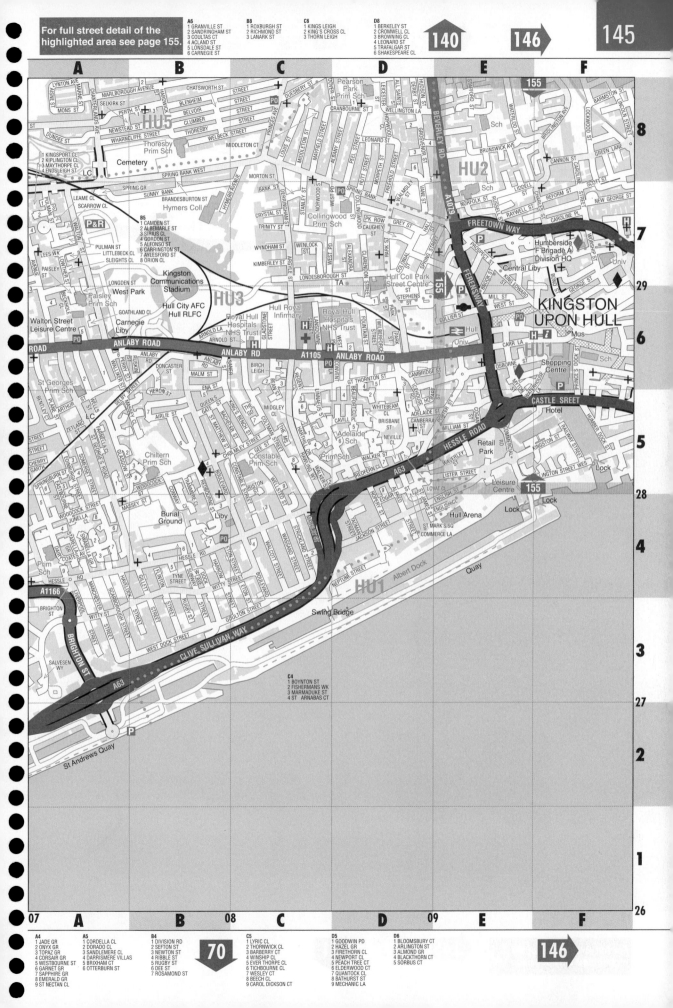

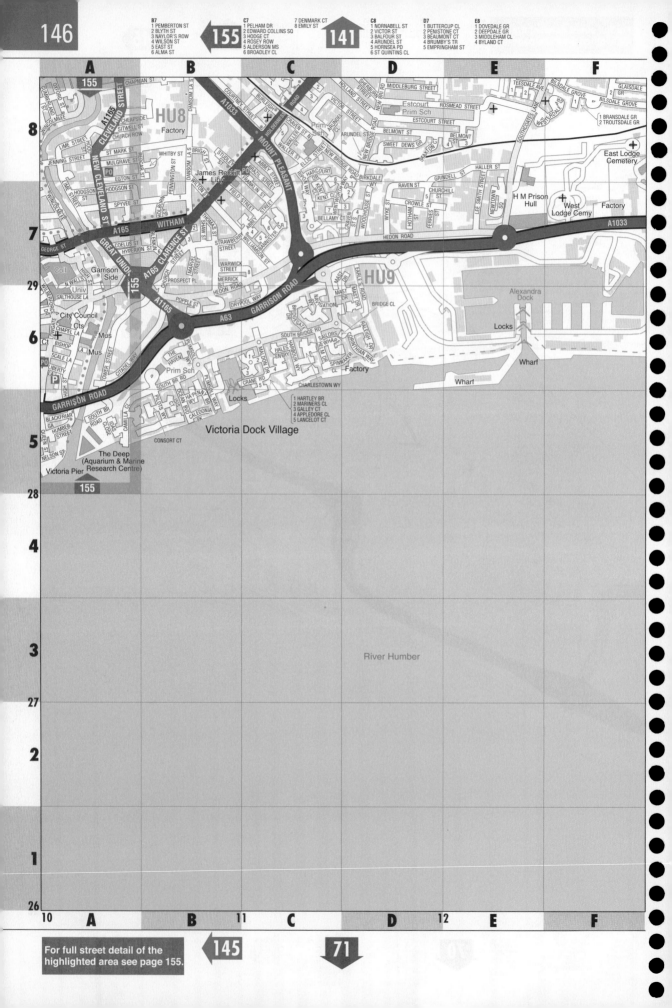

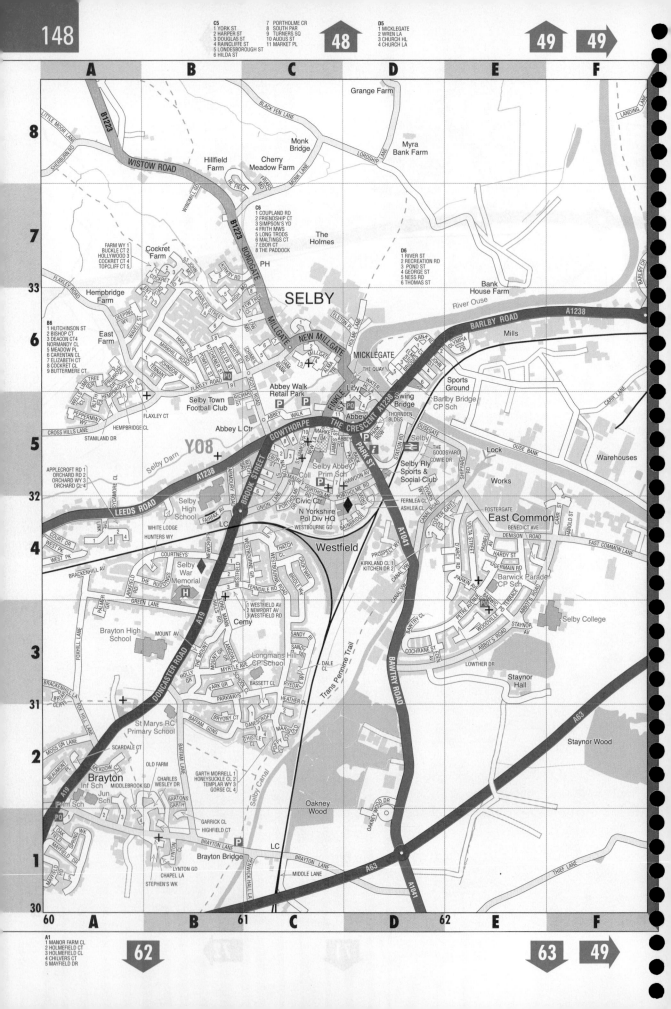

C5
1 YORK ST
2 HARPER ST
3 DOUGLAS ST
4 RAINCLIFFE ST
5 LONDESBOROUGH ST
6 HILDA ST

7 PORTHOLME CR
8 SOUTH PAR
9 TURNERS SQ
10 AUDUS ST
11 MARKET PL

D5
1 MICKLEGATE
2 WREN LA
3 CHURCH HL
4 CHURCH LA

Grange Farm

C6
1 COUPLAND RD
2 FRIENDSHIP CT
3 SIMPSON'S YD
4 FRITH MWS
5 LONG TRODS
6 MALTINGS CT
7 EBOR CT
8 THE PADDOCK

D6
1 RIVER ST
2 RECREATION RD
3 POND ST
4 GEORGE ST
5 NESS RD
6 THOMAS ST

B6
1 HUTCHINSON ST
2 BISHOP CT
3 DEACON CT
4 NORMANDY CL
5 MEADOW PL
6 CARENTAN CL
7 ELIZABETH CT
8 COCKRET CL
9 BUTTERMERE CL

FARM WY 1
BUCKLE CT 2
HOLLYWOOD 3
COCKRET CT 4
TOPCLIFF CT 5

SELBY

MICKLEGATE

YO8

APPLECROFT 1
ORCHARD RD 2
ORCHARD WY 3
ORCHARD CL 4

East Common

Westfield

1 WESTFIELD AV
2 NEWPORT AV
3 WESTFIELD RD

Selby College

KIRKLAND CL 1
KITCHEN DR 2

Staynor Hall

Staynor Wood

GARTH MORRELL 1
HONEYSUCKLE CL 2
TEMPLAR WY 3
GORSE CL 4

Brayton

Oakney Wood

Brayton Bridge

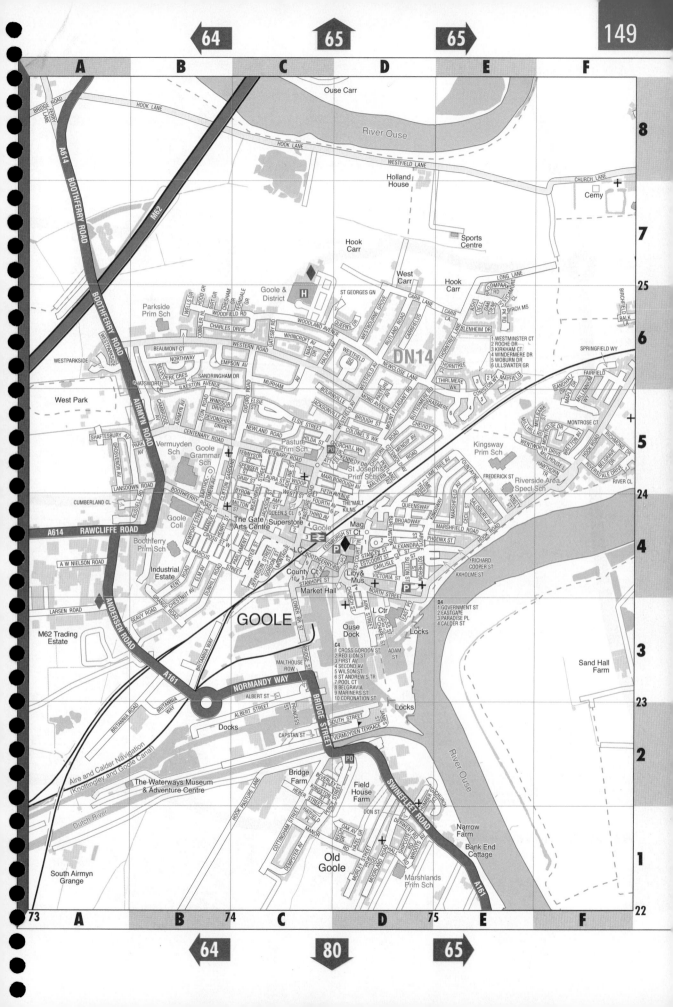

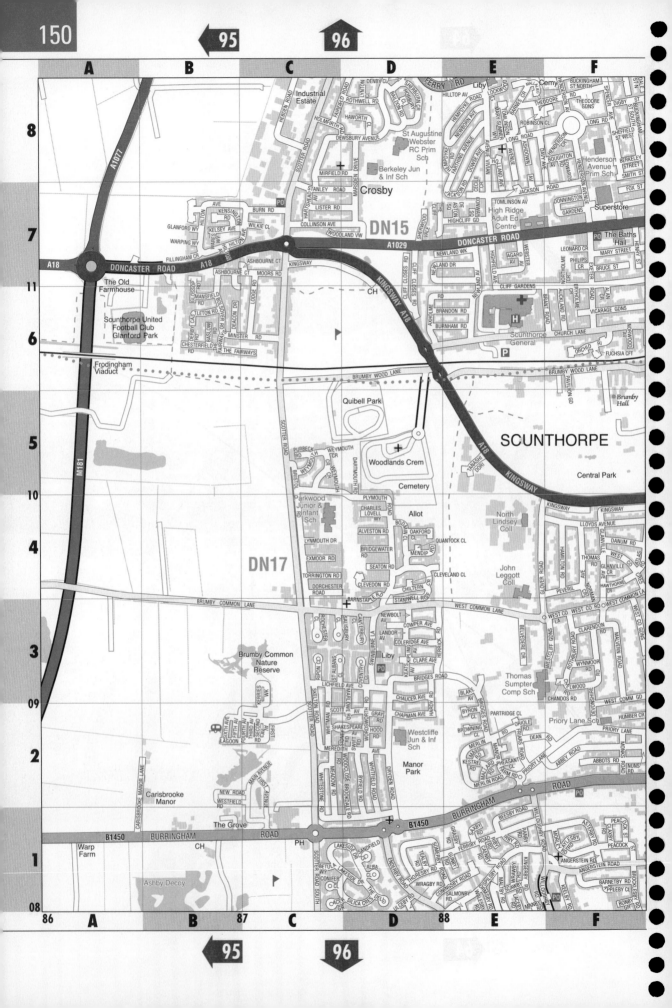

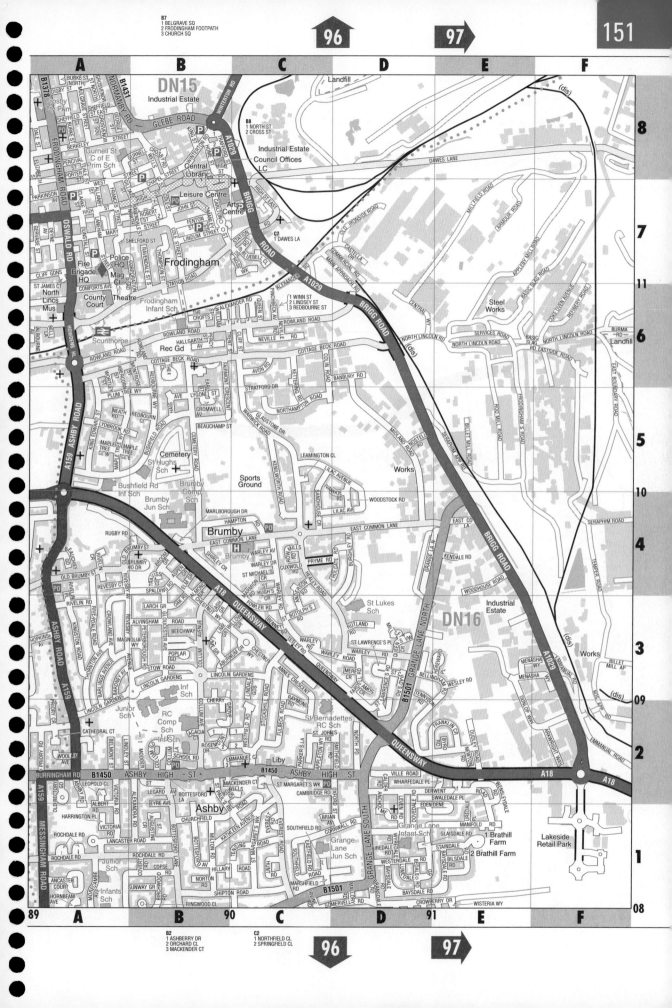

A B C D E F

8

River Humber

Pyewipe

Works
Works
Water Reclamation Works

7

Dock Tower Locks Locks

Works

Pyewipe Farm LC MOODY LANE
Sports Ground

BROWN ST 1
HENDERSON ST 2
SMITH ST 3
SIDEBOTTOM ST 4
SMITTON ST 5

11

Europa Business Park
LC
LC
Sewage Works
GATE WY

Royal Dock

STUART WORTLEY ST

ESTATE RD NO 1
VICTORIA WY
GILBY ROAD
ESTUARY WAY
MOODY LANE

DN31

Jetty

6

A180

LC

Lock Hill
ROWLANDSON ST

Marina

ESTATE RD NO 5 ESTATE ROAD NO 2
A180
WEST COATES ROAD
WESTSIDE RD
WESTSIDE ROAD
MOODY LANE

Alexandra Dock

LOCKHILL

MURRAYO

5

Little Coates Prim Sch

BIRCHIN WAY

A180

WESTGATE

CLEETHORPE RD

A180

Grimsby Docks
St Junier Sch
STRAND ST
NORTH BR ST
KENT
ALBERT ST
B1213

East Marsh

ADAM SMITH ST
WATKIN ST N
ANNES ST
EY ST
Retail Park

LWR SPRING ST
KING EDWARD ST
CRESSEY ST
NELSON ST
DUNCOMBE GD

CHURCH ST
SERVICE RD NO 1
SERVICE RD NO 2
ALBERT ST

West Marsh

ARMSTRONG ST
ARMSTRONG ST

10

LAWRENCE ST 1
SAUNDERS ST 2
CHAPMAN ST 3
FRESHNEY DRIVE 4

MILL AV
CORPORATION ROAD
CORPORATION ROAD

RAVENSPURN ST
CHARLTON ST
YORK ST
FREDERIC ST

TENNYSON ST
ALFRED ST
S PD

FREEPORT WHARF
Superstore
FREEPORT WHARF
LOWER BURGESS ST

PETC
NEWMARKET ST
HARLECH WY
WERNETH WY
WOOD ST

GARIBALDI ST
MILLOM WY
ALBION
BUTTERMERE WY

Allot

JACKSON ST

National Fishing Heritage Centre
MAG CT
GRIME MIDDLE ST

St Marys RC
COBDEN ST ST MARYS PRIM SCH
NORTH END
CLYDE ST

4

St LEONARD'S AV
St FRANCIS AV

SALAMANDER CLOSE
HAVEN AVE
HENRY ST
RICHARD ST
DOVER ST
HAVEN ST

YARBO ST
EDMONDS ST
GARTH LA

UPR BURGESS ST
Superstore

ELEANOR STREET

Macauley Jun & Infant Sch
MACAULAY STREET

Infant Sch
S PD
SOMERSBY ST

WELLINGTON ST

Grimsby Leisure Centre
CROMWELL ROAD

LANCASTER AVE
LISTER ST

FREDERICK WARD WAY

EASTGATE
HOLME ST

PASTURE ST
THOMAS ST
WRAGBY

3

THORNHILL
SPRING BANK
SPRINGWAY CR

Freshney Pl Sh Ctr
Mkt Hall Sh Ctr

Cty Ct
TOWN

BOWLING GN LA
SHEPPLD ST
ST

B1213
SIXHILLS STREET

Holme Hill

FANNYSTONE RD 1
ETHELSTONE RD 2
YARBOROUGH ROAD
A1136
FAIRFAX RD

CROMWELL RD

Welfare Service

Victoria Street
MANDELA LINK
A1136

Grimsby Town LC
OSBORNE ST
Liby
TH

Retail Park

Edward Heneage Primary Sch
MARGARET ST
CONNAMORE RD
ROPERY ST

Yarborough Middle Sch

Yarborough
A1136
DUDLEY ST

LC
Railway
P

MOSS ROAD
PEPPERCORN WALK
DUCHESS ST

PEAKS PARKWAY
CATHERINE ST

09

PO

WIMBORNE
PELHAM RD

West End Club

GRIMSBY

DE FRIGHT ST
BARGATE

A16

Welholme Fst Sch

2

Littlefield

St James Sch
COLLEGE ST
AUGUSTA ST

WINTRINGHAM

Welholme Mid Sch

PELHAM RD 1
THE SPINNEY 2
BISHOP'S WK 3
MALMESBURY DR 4
TEWKESBURY DR 5
THE LAWNS 6

CHELMSFORD PL

ABBEY PARK ROAD

WELHOLME RD
HARE STREET

GRANVILLE STREET
PATRICK STREET

DN34

Allotments

DN32

Welholme Mus & Gallery

1 PETERHOUSE RD
2 PEMBROKE RD
Works

WESTHILL RD
CAMBRIDGE RD

WELHOLME ROAD
B1212

People's Park
Wellow

PEAKS PARKWAY
HAINTON AVENUE
B1213

1

Cam Park Sch
Grange

WESTWARD HO
A1243
BARGATE AV

St Martins Preparatory Sch
A16

08

Franklin Sixth Form Coll
Hereford Sch
Grimsby Coll

WEELSBY ROAD A46 WEELSBY RD

25 A 26 B C 27 D E F

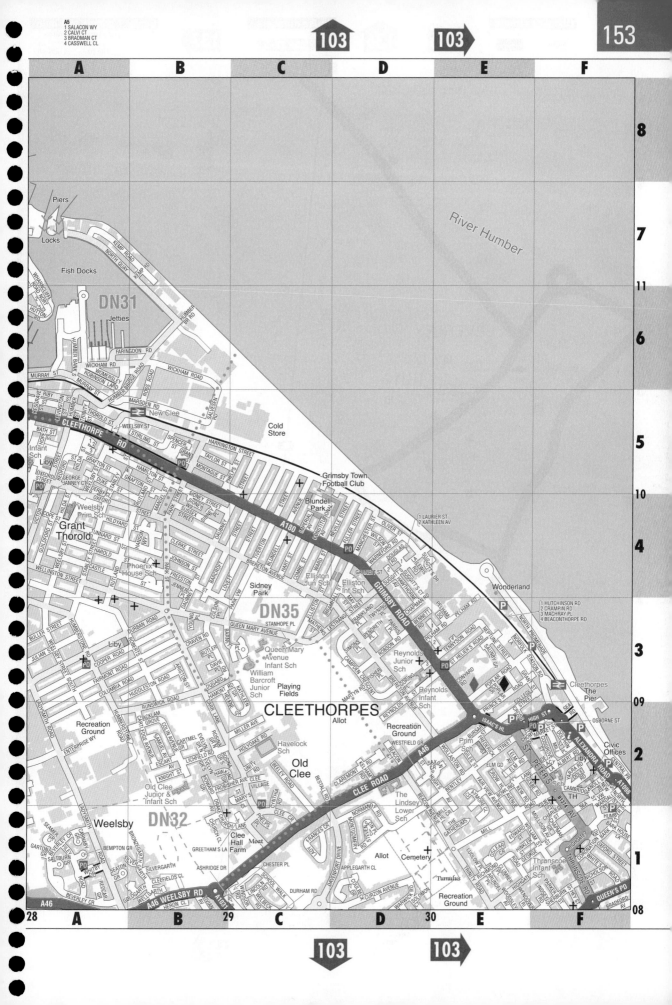

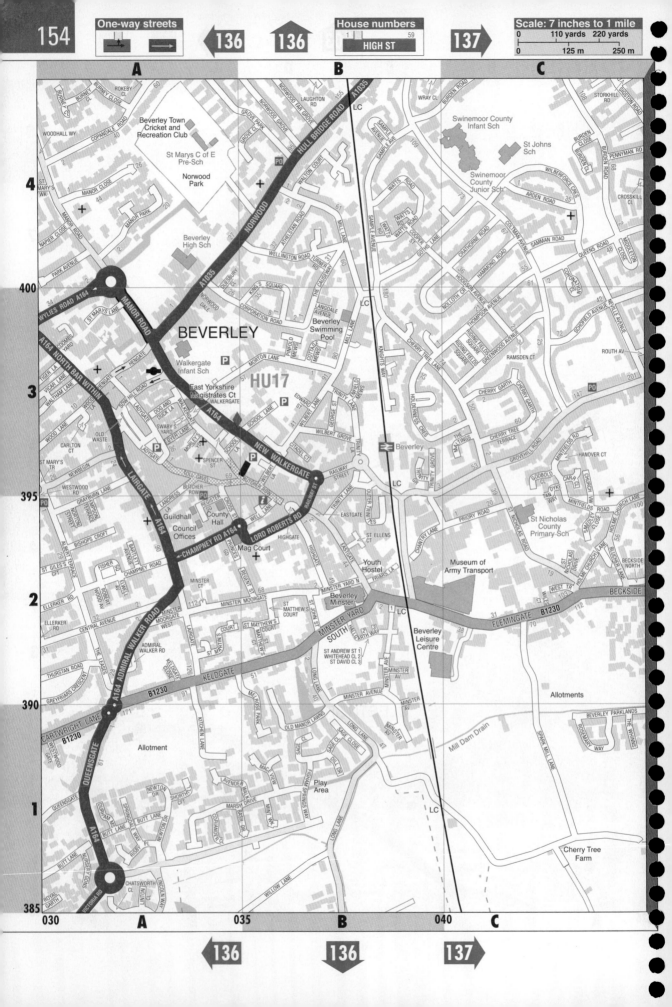

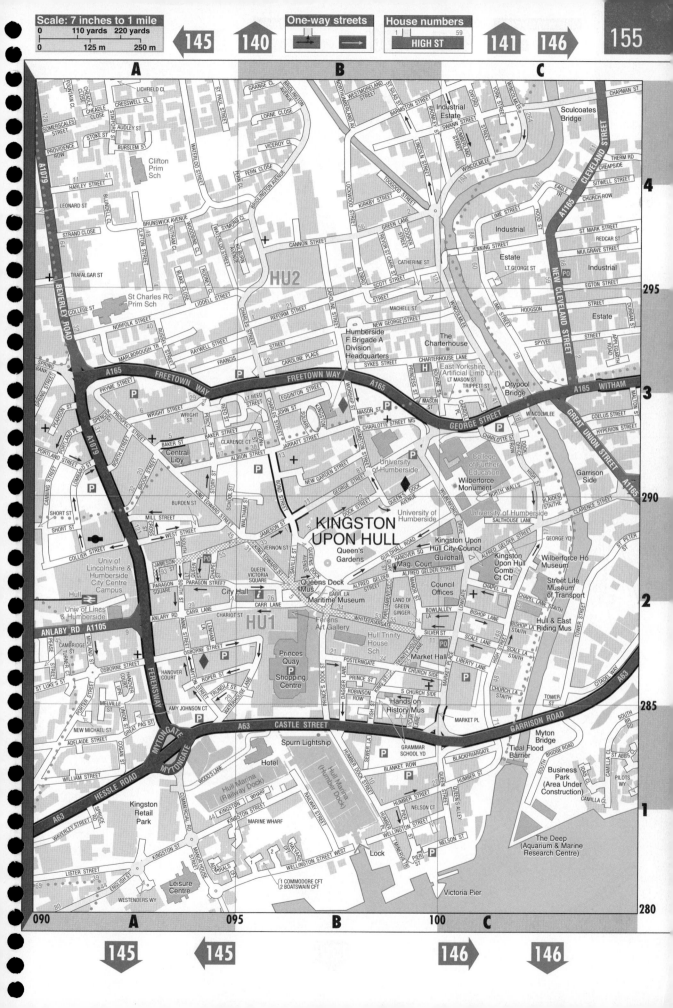

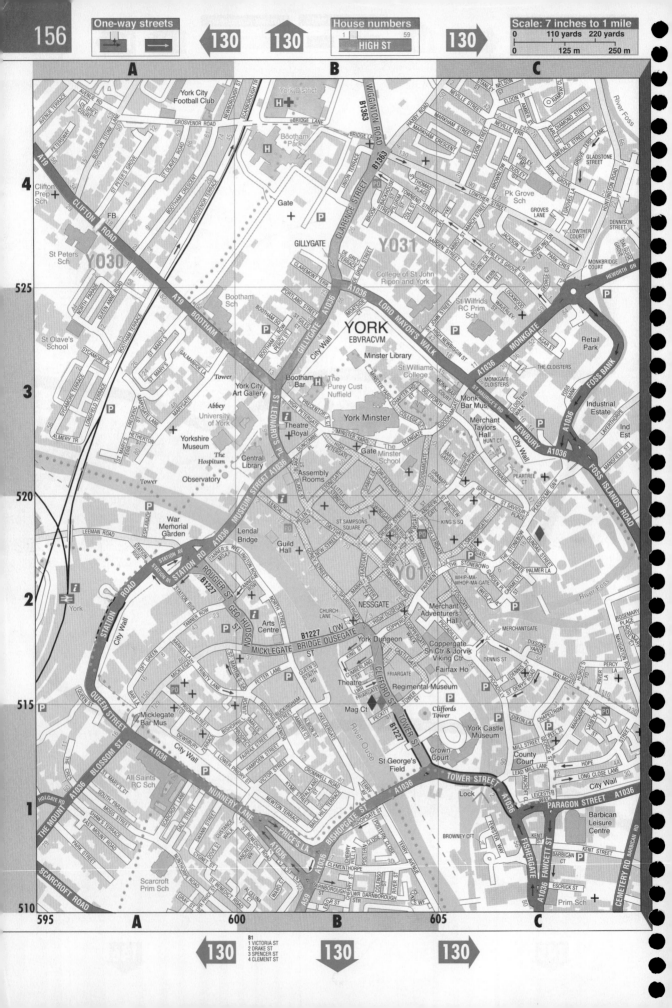

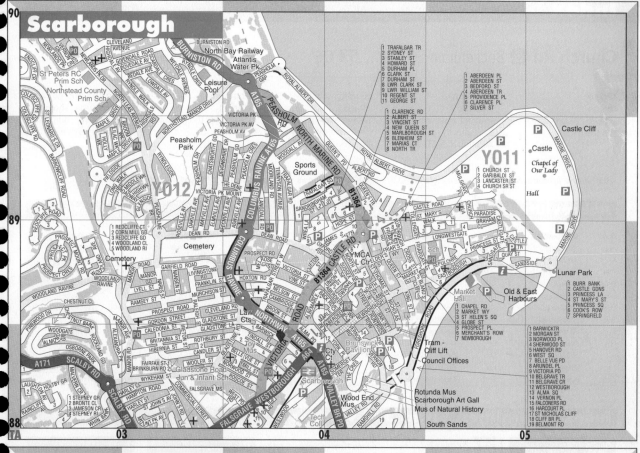

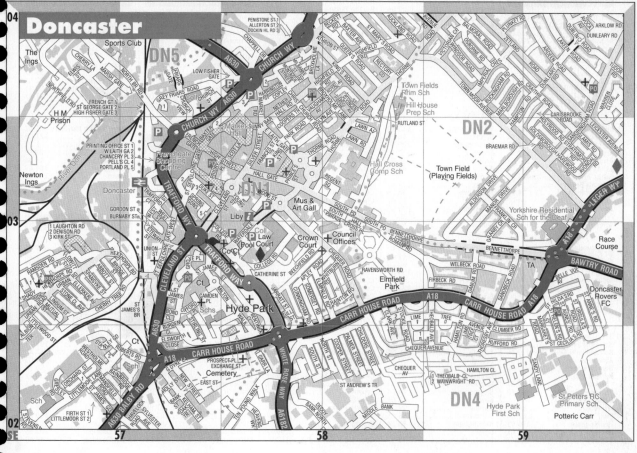

Index

Church Rd 6 Beckenham BR2..........**53** C6

Place name	**Location number**	**Locality, town or village**	**Postcode district**	**Page and grid square**
May be abbreviated on the map	Present when a number indicates the place's position in a crowded area of mapping	Shown when more than one place has the same name	District for the indexed place	Page number and grid reference for the standard mapping

Public and commercial buildings are highlighted in magenta   **Places of interest** are highlighted in blue with a star★

Abbreviations used in the index

Acad	Academy	Com	Community	Est	Estate	Int	International	Pas	Passage
App	Approach	Comm	Common	Ex	Exhibition	Intc	Interchange	Pk	Park
Arc	Arcade	Cott	Cottage	Gd	Ground	Junc	Junction	Pl	Place
Ave	Avenue	Cres	Crescent	Gdn	Garden	L	Leisure	Prec	Precinct
Bglw	Bungalow	Cswy	Causeway	Gn	Green	La	Lane	Prom	Prom
Bldg	Building	Ct	Court	Gr	Grove	Liby	Library	Rd	Road
Bsns, Bus	Business	Ctr	Centre	H	Hall	Mdw	Meadow	Recn	Recreation
Bvd	Boulevard	Ctry	Country	Ho	House	Meml	Memorial	Ret	Retail
Cath	Cathedral	Cty	County	Hospl	Hospital	Mkt	Market	Sh	Shopping
Cir	Circus	Dr	Drive	HQ	Headquarters	Mus	Museum	Sq	Square
Cl	Close	Dro	Drove	Hts	Heights	Orch	Orchard	St	Street
Cnr	Corner	Ed	Education	Ind	Industrial	Pal	Palace	Sta	Station
Coll	College	Emb	Embankment	Inst	Institute	Par	Parade	Terr	Terrace

Index of localities, towns and villages

A

Acaster Malbis 36 D8
Acaster Selby 36 B4
Acklam 16 E8
Acomb 129 C3
Adlingfleet 81 E7
Aike 44 A8
Airmyn 64 E4
Aisby 118 B3
Aldbrough 47 C1
Alkborough 82 C8
Allerthorpe 28 E2
Althorpe 95 D4
Amcotts 81 F1
Angram 24 C3
Anlaby 143 F7
Appleby 83 C1
Arnold 45 C4
Arram 44 A7
Ashby 151 B1
Ashby cum Fenby 113 D3
Ashby Hill 113 C3
Askham Bryan 24 F3
Askham Richard 24 D3
Asselby 64 D7
Atwick 35 C5
Aughton 38 C1
Aylesby 101 E2

B

Bainton 31 E7
Balkholme 65 E6
Balne 77 C5
Barlby 49 B5
Barlow 63 C7
Barmby Moor 28 E3
Barmby on
the Marsh 64 B7
Barmston 23 A6
Barnetby le Wold 99 C4
Barnoldby le Beck ...113 B6
Barrow Hann 70 E1
Barrow Haven 70 C1
Barrow upon
Humber 85 D7
Barton Waterside 69 F2
Barton-upon-
Humber 84 D7
Beal 61 D4
Beckingham 116 D1
Beeford 22 C1
Beelsby 112 F5

Beltoft 95 A1
Belton 94 E1
Bempton 4 D4
Beningbrough 12 D4
Bennetland 66 C7
Bentley 55 D7
Bessingby 10 F4
Beswick 32 D3
Beverley 154 A3
Bewholme 35 A5
Bielby 39 F6
Bigby 99 C2
Bilbrough 24 D1
Bilton 58 A4
Birkin 61 D6
Bishop Burton 43 A2
Bishop Wilton 16 F2
Bishopthorpe 133 B3
Blacktoft 66 E3
Blyborough 119 B5
Blyton 117 B5
Bolton 28 D7
Bonby 84 C2
Bootham
Stray 127 B2
Boothferry 64 E5
Bossall 15 D7
Bottesford 96 D2
Boynton 10 D7
Bracon 94 F2
Bradley 102 B3
Bradley 102 C1
Brandesburton 34 C2
Bransholme 141 A8
Brantingham 68 C8
Brayton 148 A2
Breighton 50 D5
Bridlington 122 B3
Brigg 98 D2
Brigham 33 E8
Brigsley 113 D4
Brind 51 A2
Brockfield 14 E2
Brocklesby 100 D6
Broomfleet 67 B6
Brough 68 C5
Broughton 97 E4
Brumby 151 B4
Bubwith 50 D7
Buckton 4 C4
Bugthorpe 16 D4
Burn 62 D7
Burnby 29 D1
Burnham 85 C3
Burringham 95 E4
Bursea 52 A4
Burstwick 73 B7

Burton Agnes 10 A1
Burton Fleming 2 E3
Burton Pidsea 59 D2
Burton Stather 82 A5
Burton upon
Stather 82 B4
Buttercrambe 15 E5
Butterwick 1 B2

C

Cabourne 111 D4
Cadney 109 D6
Caenby Corner Estate 119 D1
Caistor 111 B4
Camblesforth 63 D5
Camerton 73 A5
Canal Side 93 A7
Carlton 63 D3
Carnaby 10 E4
Catwick 45 D8
Cawkeld 32 B5
Cawood 48 B8
Chapel Fields 129 B3
Chapel
Haddlesey 62 C5
Cherry Burton 43 B5
Church End 33 F8
Church Town 94 E1
Claxton 15 B7
Cleethorpes 153 C2
Cliffe 49 E2
Clifton 130 A7
Clifton Park 129 F7
Clixby 111 A7
Cock Hill 12 B2
Coleby 82 E6
Coniston 57 F6
Copmanthorpe 132 B2
Corringham 118 B2
Cottages Plot 102 B2
Cottingham 139 A6
Covenham
St Bartholomew 121 F5
Covenham
St Mary 121 F5
Cridling Stubbs 76 C8
Crockey Hill 26 A1
Crosby 150 D7
Crowle 94 D8
Crowle Park 94 D7
Croxby 112 C1
Croxby Top 112 B1
Croxton 99 F7
Cuxwold 112 B4

D

Danthorpe 59 C3
Deighton 37 A7
Dimlington 90 F7
Dragonby 82 E1
Drax 63 F5
Driffield 124 D4
Dringhouses 132 E8
Duggleby 6 B6
Dunnington 26 F7
Dunnington 34 F7
Dunscroft 92 D3
Dunsville 92 B3
Dunswell 56 D5

E

Ealand 94 E6
Earswick 128 A7
Easington 91 A6
East Butterwick 106 E8
East Carlton 47 A2
East Common 148 E4
East
Cottingwith 38 C5
East Cowick 78 D8
East Ella 144 D7
East Halton 86 E7
East Lound 105 E3
East Lutton 7 C8
East Marsh 152 F5
East Newton 59 F8
East Ravendale 113 C2
East Stockwith 116 F5
Eastburn 20 B2
Eastoft 81 A3
Eastrington 51 F1
Eggborough 61 F2
Ellerker 68 A8
Ellerton 38 C2
Elloughton 68 C7
Elmswell 20 B5
Elsham 98 F7
Elstronwick 59 A3
Elvington 27 B2
Eppleworth 138 A4
Epworth 105 D6
Epworth Turbary ...105 C6
Escrick 37 B5
Eskham 115 C1
Etton 42 F6
Everingham 40 A5
Everthorpe 53 E3

F

Fangfoss 28 C7
Fenwick 77 D3
Ferriby Sluice 83 F7
Fimber 18 D7
Fishlake 92 E8
Fitling 59 C5
Flamborough 5 B2
Flinton 59 A7
Flixborough 82 B1
Flixborough Stather 82 A1
Fockerby 81 E5
Foggathorpe 51 B8
Fordon 2 A6
Fosterhouses 78 C1
Foston on the Wolds 22 A2
Fotherby 121 C2
Foxholes 1 D3
Fraisthorpe 22 F4
Fridaythorpe 18 B6
Frodingham 151 E2
Fulford 133 E7
Full Sutton 16 A2
Fulstow 121 E8

G

Gainsborough 117 C2
Ganstead 57 F5
Ganton 1 A8
Gardham 42 D5
Garthorpe 81 F6
Garton 59 E6
Garton-on-the-Wolds 20 A6
Gate Helmsley 15 B2
Gateforth 62 A7
Gembling 22 A3
Gilberdyke 66 C8
Gipsyville 144 E3
Goodmanham 135 F7
Goole 149 C3
Gowdall 63 A1
Gowthorpe 16 C1
Goxhill 86 B8
Grainsby 113 F2
Graiselound 105 C1
Grange 152 A1
Gransmoor 22 C6
Grant Thorold 153 A4
Grasby 110 F2
Grayingham 119 B7
Great Coates 102 B5
Great Cowden 47 A5

Great Givendale	29 B8	Kilpin Pike	65 C5	New Waltham	114 A7	Scawby	108 E8	Upton	22 E1
Great Hatfield	46 D6	Kingsforth	84 E6	Newland	64 B3	Scorborough	43 D8	Utterby	121 D4
Great Heck	77 D7	Kingston upon Hull	155 B2	Newland	66 A8	Scotter	107 D3	
Great Kelk	22 A5	Kirby Grindalythe	6 E6	Newland	140 C3	Scotterthorpe	107 B5	
Great Kendale	20 D7	Kirby Underdale	17 A5	Newport	53 A1	Scotton	107 D2	**V**
Great Limber	100 D3	Kirk Bramwith	92 A6	Newsholme	64 E8	Scrayingham	15 F7	
Great Tows	120 A1	Kirk Ella	143 D6	Newton upon Derwent	27 E4	Sculcoates	140 E2	Victoria Dock Village	146 B5
Greetwell	108 C7	Kirk Smeaton	76 B3	Newton-on-Ouse	12 B6	Scunthorpe	150 D5	
Grey Green	94 E2	Kirkburn	20 A2	Normanby	82 B3	Searby	110 C8	
Gribthorpe	51 B6	Kirmington	100 A6	North Cave	53 D3	Seaton	35 A1	**W**
Grimsby	152 E2	Kirton in Lindsey	108 B1	North Cliffe	53 B8	Seaton Common	39 D4	
Grimston	131 E3	Knapton	129 A5	North Cotes	115 A3	Seaton Ross	39 E4	Waithe	114 A3
Grindale	3 D2	Knavesmire	133 A7	North Dalton	31 B7	Selby	148 D2	Walcot	82 C7
Grovehill	137 C3	Knedlington	64 E6	North Duffield	50 A8	Sewerby	123 A5	Walden Stubbs	76 F3
Gunby	50 D6	Knottingley	61 B2	North Elkington	121 A1	Shipton	12 F5	Walkeringham	116 C3
Gunness	95 E6			North End	46 D4	Shiptonthorpe	40 F6	Walkerith	116 E3
Gunthorpe	117 A7			North End	71 A1	Sigglesthorne	45 F8	Walkington	55 B8
		L		North Ferriby	69 B4	Skeffling	90 C6	Walmgate Stray	130 F1
				North Frodingham	34 A8	Skelton	65 C4	Waltham	113 D7
H		Laceby	101 E2	North Howden	51 B1	Skelton	126 C6	Wansford	21 C3
		Laceby Acres	102 B2	North Kelsey	110 A5	Skerne	21 A2	Warter	30 A5
Habrough	100 E8	Langtoft	8 D5	North Killingholme	86 D4	Skidby	138 B8	Warthill	14 F2
Haisthorpe	10 C3	Laughton	117 F8	North Newbald	53 E8	Skipsea	23 B2	Waterside	92 F8
Hall Garth	26 F6	Laxton	65 F4	North Ormsby	121 B3	Skipwith	37 E1	Watton	32 D5
Halsham	73 F6	Layerthorpe	130 E4	North Thoresby	114 A1	Skirlaugh	45 E2	Wawne	56 E8
Harlthorpe	51 A8	Laytham	39 B2	Northfield	143 F2	Skirpenbeck	16 A4	Waxholme	74 E8
Harpham	21 F8	Leconfield	43 D6	Northorpe	118 D8	Sledmere	7 B3	Weel	137 F3
Harswell	40 C3	Lelley	58 F3	Norton	76 E2	Snaith	63 C1	Weelsby	153 A1
Harton	15 C8	Leppington	16 C8	Nun Monkton	12 A4	Somerby	99 B1	Weeton	90 B7
Hatcliffe	112 F3	Leven	45 A8	Nunburnholme	29 E3	South Bank	130 A1	Weighton Wold	135 F4
Hatfield	92 D5	Lissett	22 E4	Nunsthorpe	102 D1	South Bramwith	92 B6	Welhambridge	51 F5
Hatfield Woodhouse	93 A3	Little Airmyn	64 E4	Nunthorpe	133 C8	South Cave	54 A2	Wellow	152 D1
Haxey	105 C3	Little Burton	34 B2			South Cliffe	53 B7	Welton	68 D6
Haxey Carr	105 B4	Little Catwick	45 D7			South Dalton	42 E8	Welwick	90 A4
Hayton	40 C8	Little Coates	102 C3	**O**		South Duffield	50 A4	West Butterwick	106 D8
Healing	102 A5	Little Driffield	124 C4			South End	46 D3	West Carlton	46 F1
Hedon	72 C8	Little End	40 A1	Octon	8 F8	South End	90 F5	West Cowick	78 D8
Hemingbrough	49 F1	Little Grimsby	121 E2	Old Clee	153 C2	South Ferriby	84 B7	West Ella	143 A7
Hemswell	119 A1	Little Hatfield	46 B6	Old Ellerby	58 A8	South Field	69 E4	West End	53 F2
Hensall	62 D2	Little Heck	62 D1	Old Goole	149 C1	South Kelsey	110 A1	West Field	129 A2
Heslington	131 B1	Little Leven	45 A7	Old Town	122 E5	South Killingholme	86 E3	West Haddlesey	62 A5
Hessay	24 C8	Little Limber	100 C5	Osbaldwick	131 C4	South Newbald	53 F6	West Halton	82 E8
Hessle	143 E1	Little Reedness	66 A1	Osgodby	49 C4	Southburn	20 B1	West Hill	122 A1
Heworth	130 F6	Little Skipwith	37 D1	Osgodby Common	49 C6	Spaldington	51 C4	West Lutton	7 B8
Hibaldstow	108 F5	Little Smeaton	76 C3	Ottringham	73 F3	Speeton	3 F5	West Marsh	152 B5
High Catton	27 D8	Little Weighton	55 A4	Ousefleet	66 D2	Spital in the Street	119 E1	West Newton	58 D8
High Hunsley	54 D6	Littlefield	152 C2	Out Newton	90 E8	Sproatley	58 C5	West Ravendale	113 A2
High Mowthorpe	6 D7	Lockington	32 B2	Overton	12 F2	Staddlethorpe	66 D7	West Stockwith	116 F6
High Risby	82 F1	Londesborough	41 B8	Owmby	110 D7	Stainforth	92 C7	Westfield	148 C4
Highfield	50 E7	Long Drax	64 A6	Owston Ferry	106 A2	Stallingborough	101 E6	Westgate	94 D2
Hilderthorpe	11 B4	Long Marston	24 A6	Owstwick	59 E3	Stamford Bridge	15 E2	Westrum	98 C1
Hillam	61 A7	Long Riston	45 C5	Owthorne	74 F7	Stillingfleet	36 C3	Westwoodside	105 A2
Hilston	60 B4	Low Burnham	105 D5			Stockton on the Forest	14 D3	Wetwang	19 B6
Hirst Courtney	62 F3	Low Catton	27 C8			Stoneferry	141 B3	Wharram le Street	6 A4
Hive	52 C2	Low Fosham	46 F1	**P**		Strensall	14 A7	Wharton	117 E4
Holgate	129 F3	Low Risby	83 B1			Strensall Camp	14 B6	Wheldrake	38 A7
Hollym	75 A4	Lowthorpe	21 E7	Painsthorpe	17 B5	Sturton	108 F7	Whitgift	66 B1
Holme	97 A1	Ludborough	121 C6	Patrington	74 E1	Summergangs	141 C2	Whitley	77 A7
Holme Hill	152 F3	Luddington	81 C3	Patrington Haven	89 C8	Sutton Ings	141 F4	Whitley Thorpe	76 F7
Holme on the Wolds	31 E1	Lund	31 F3	Paull	72 B5	Sutton upon Derwent	27 C1	Whitton	67 E3
Holme-on-		Lund	49 D3	Pilham	118 A4	Sutton-on-Hull	141 D6	Wigginton	13 D5
Spalding-Moor	40 B1			Pocklington	29 A4	Swallow	112 B5	Wike Well End	93 B7
Holmpton	75 C2			Pollington	77 F6	Swanland	69 B6	Wilberfoss	27 F5
Holtby	14 F1	**M**		Portington	51 E2	Swine	57 D6	Wildsworth	117 A3
Holton le Clay	114 B5			Preston	58 C1	Swinefleet	65 D1	Willerby	138 C1
Hopgrove	128 D2	Manton	108 B5	Pyewipe	152 A8	Sykehouse	78 B3	Willitoft	51 A6
Horkstow	84 A5	Mappleton	47 A7					Willoughton	119 A4
Horkstow Wolds	84 B6	Marfleet	147 C8					Wilsthorpe	11 A2
Hornsea	134 C4	Market Weighton	135 B4	**R**		**T**		Winestead	74 C3
Hornsea Burton	134 C4	Marshchapel	115 B2					Winteringham	68 A1
Hotham	53 D4	Marton	46 B2	Rascal Moor	52 B7	Tang Hall	130 F5	Winterton	83 A5
Howden	65 A7	Marton	123 D8	Rawcliffe	64 A1	Tansterne	59 A8	Wistow	48 D6
Howsham	110 A7	Meaux	44 F2	Rawcliffe	126 E2	Temple Hirst	62 E4	Withernsea	75 A6
Huggate	18 B2	Melbourne	39 B6	Rawcliffe Bridge	79 C8	Tetney	114 D4	Withernwick	46 D3
Humberston	114 E4	Melton	68 F5	Redbourne	108 F3	Tetney Lock	115 A3	Wold Haven	29 B3
Humberston Fitties	114 F8	Melton Ross	99 C5	Reedness	65 F2	The Hallands	85 F7	Wold Newton	2 A3
Humbleton	59 B5	Meltonby	28 F7	Reighton	3 D6	The Lawns	138 F4	Wold Newton	120 B7
Hunmanby	2 F8	Menthorpe	50 C5	Riby	101 C2	The Lings	92 D3	Womersley	76 C6
Huntington	127 E3	Messingham	107 C7	Riccall	49 A8	The Parks	92 C4	Woodhall	50 B2
Hurn	136 C4	Middlegate	84 E1	Rimswell	74 D7	The Willows	102 C4	Woodhouse	94 E3
Hut Green	62 A2	Middlethorpe	133 B6	Riplingham	54 E2	Thealby	82 D4	Woodmansey	56 B8
Hutton	32 E8	Middleton-on-the-Wolds	31 B4	Risby	55 C5	Thearne	56 D7	Woodside	104 E6
Hutton Cranswick	32 D7	Millbrook Park	135 C3	Rise	45 F5	Thirtleby	58 B5	Woodthorpe	132 C7
Hutton Wandesley	24 A5	Millington	29 C6	Rolston	46 E8	Thixendale	17 E7	Wootton	85 F3
		Misterton	116 C5	Roos	60 A1	Thorganby	38 B4	Worlaby	98 D8
		Molescroft	136 B5	Rothwell	111 F2	Thorne	93 A8	Wrawby	98 E4
I		Monk Fryston	61 B8	Routh	44 F5	Thorngumbald	72 E5	Wressle	50 D2
		Moor End	52 B8	Roxby	83 A3	Thornholme	10 B2	Wressle	97 F4
Immingham	87 B3	Moor Monkton	12 A3	Rudston	9 F6	Thornton	39 B8	Wroot	104 D6
Inglemire	139 F6	Moorends	79 C2	Rufforth	24 C6	Thornton Curtis	85 E5	Wybers Wood	102 A3
Irby upon Humber	112 D7	Moortown	110 D2	Ruston Parva	21 C8	Thorpe	32 B1	Wyham	120 F6
		Morton	117 A3	Ryehill	73 A4	Thorpe le Street	40 D7	Wyton	58 B4
		Moss	77 D1			Thorpe Willoughby	48 C2	
K		Murton	26 D7			Thwing	2 B1	
				S		Tibthorpe	19 D2	**Y**
Keadby	95 D6					Tickton	137 E8	
Keelby	101 B5	**N**		Salt End	72 A8	Topham	78 A4	Yaddlethorpe	96 C2
Kelfield	36 D1			Saltmarshe	65 F3	Towthorpe	6 D1	Yapham	28 E1
Kelleythorpe	124 C1	Naburn	36 D8	Sancton	41 E2	Towthorpe	14 B5	Yarborough	152 A3
Kellingley	61 C2	Nafferton	125 E7	Sand Hole	52 B8	Tunstall	60 C2	Yawthorpe	118 D2
Kellington	61 F4	Neat Marsh	58 A2	Sand Hutton	15 B5			Yokefleet	66 C3
Kelstern	120 D1	Nether Poppleton	126 A2	Sandholme	52 C1			York	156 B3
Kexby	27 C6	Nettleton	111 A2	Sandtoft	94 A3	**U**		Youlthorpe	16 C2
Keyingham	73 D3	New Arram	43 F7	Santon	97 B7			
Kilham	9 C3	New Barnetby	99 D5	Saxby All Saints	84 A3	Ulceby	86 A1	
Kilnsea	91 B2	New Earswick	127 D3	Scalby	66 E8	Ulceby Skitter	86 C2	
Kilnwick	32 B4	New Ellerby	46 A2	Scamland	39 C7	Ulrome	23 A3	
Kilnwick Percy	29 C5	New Holland	70 E2	Scartho	102 F1	Upper Helmsley	15 B3	
Kilpin	65 D5	New Village	139 D6	Scawby	108 E8	Upper Poppleton	12 F1	
						Upperthorpe	105 B3	

1

1st Ave HU6	140 C6
1st Main Rd DN36	114 F8
10th Ave HU6	140 B7
11th Ave HU6	140 B6
12th Ave	
Humberston DN36	114 F8
Kingston upon Hull HU6	140 A7
14th Ave HU6	140 A6
15th Ave HU6	140 A6
16th Ave HU6	140 A7
17th Ave HU6	140 A7
18th Ave HU6	140 A7
19th Ave HU6	140 A6

2

2nd Ave	
Humberston DN36	114 F8
Kingston upon Hull HU6	140 B7
20-21 Visual Arts Ctr	
DN15	151 C7
20th Ave HU6	140 A7
21st Ave HU6	139 F6
22nd Ave HU6	140 A6
23rd Ave HU6	140 A6
24th Ave HU6	140 A7
25th Ave HU6	140 A6
26th Ave HU6	139 F7
27th Ave HU6	140 A6
28th Ave HU6	139 F7
29th Ave HU6	139 F6

3

30th Ave HU6	139 F7
31st Ave HU6	139 F6
32nd Ave HU6	139 F6
33rd Ave HU6	139 F6
34th Ave HU6	139 F7
36th Ave HU6	139 F6
37th Ave HU6	139 E6
38th Ave HU6	139 F7

4

| 4th Ave HU6 | 140 B7 |
| 40th Ave HU6 | 139 F7 |

5

| 5th Ave HU6 | 139 F6 |

6

| 6th Ave HU6 | 140 A7 |

7

| 7 Lakes L Pk★ DN17 | 94 D6 |
| 7th Ave HU6 | 140 B6 |

8

| 8th Ave HU6 | 140 A7 |

9

| 9th Ave HU6 | 140 B6 |

A

A W Nielson Rd DN14	149 A4
Abber La LS24	24 A2
Abbey Dr E DN32	152 D2
Abbey Dr W DN32	152 D2
Abbey Gdns 32 DN7	92 D4
Abbey Gn 30 DN7	92 D4
Abbey La	
Kingston upon Hull	
HU10	138 E2
Preston HU12	58 C1
Abbey Leisure Ctr	
YO8	148 C5
Abbey Pk Rd DN32	152 D2
Abbey Rd	
Bridlington YO16	122 B2
Grimsby DN32	152 D2
Hatfield DN7	92 D4
Kingston upon Hull	
HU11	142 F6
Scunthorpe DN17	150 F2
Ulceby DN39	86 A1
Abbey Rise DN19	85 D8
Abbey St	
Kingston upon Hull HU9	146 C7
York YO30	130 A7
Abbey Walk Ret Pk	
YO8	148 C6
Abbey Way DN7	92 D5
Abbey Wlk	
Grimsby DN32	152 D3
Selby YO8	148 C5

Abbey Yd YO8	148 C5
Abbeyfield Rd DN7	92 C4
Abbot St YO31	156 C4
Abbots Cl HU8	141 E5
Abbot's Lodge★ DN39	86 B5
Abbots Rd DN17	150 F2
Abbot's Rd YO8	148 E3
Abbots Wlk HU16	139 A5
Abbotsford Cl HU5	139 F3
Abbotsford Rd YO10	130 F3
Abbotsway	
Grimsby DN32	152 C1
York YO31	130 E8
Abbotts Grange DN36	114 B7
Abbotts Way YO16	122 D4
Abelton Gr 33 YO32	13 E5
Abercorn St DN16	151 A6
Aberdeen St HU3	141 F3
Aberdovey Cl 3 HU7	57 A7
Abingdon Garth 1 HU7	57 A5
Acacia	
Flixborough DN15	96 B7
Gainsborough DN21	117 B1
York YO32	127 E4
Acacia Ct DN16	151 B2
Acacia Dr HU8	141 D2
Acacia Way DN17	107 C6
Acadia Gr HU13	143 F1
Acaster Ave YO23	36 A3
Acaster La	
Acaster Malbis YO23	133 B1
Acaster Selby YO23	36 A4
Accommodation Rd	
YO25	8 D6
Acer Gr DN17	150 C1
Acey La HU12	58 B1
Achille Rd DN34	102 B3
Acklam Dr HU18	134 D6
Acklam Gr DN32	153 B2
Acklam Rd HU12	72 D7
Ackworth St HU8	141 C1
Acland St	
Gainsborough DN21	117 B3
4 Kingston upon Hull	
HU3	145 A6
Acomb Comm Rd DN7	92 F4
Acomb Prim Sch	
YO24	129 E3
Acomb Rd YO24	129 D3
Acomb Wood Cl YO24	132 C7
Acomb Wood Dr YO24	132 B7
Acorn Cl 6 Barlby YO8	49 B4
Bridlington YO16	123 B7
Acorn Gr HU8	141 E7
Acorn Way	
Gateforth YO8	48 B1
Hessle HU13	143 B3
York YO24	132 D7
Acredykes 7 YO15	4 D3
Acres La	
Scrayingham YO41	16 B8
Wroot DN9	104 D7
Acton Cl HU8	141 F5
Adam Smith St DN31	152 C5
Adam St DN14	149 D3
Adderbury Gr 5 HU5	140 D2
Addison Gdns HU8	141 D3
Addison Rd 10 HU12	58 D1
Addle La DN14	65 E7
Addlekeld YO42	30 A5
Adelaide Prim Sch	
HU3	145 D5
Adelaide Rd 6 DN6	76 E2
Adelaide Sch HU3	145 D5
Adelaide St	
Kingston upon Hull HU3	145 D5
Kingston upon Hull HU1	155 A1
3 York YO23	130 B2
Adeline St DN14	149 C5
Adeliza Garth 20 HU12	72 D7
Adelphi Cl HU8	141 F4
Adelphi Ct 4 DN36	114 C4
Adelphi Dr 7 DN33	113 E8
Adelphi St YO25	124 E4
Adlard Gr DN36	114 C7
Adlingfleet Rd DN17	81 E6
Adlington Cl 8 YO32	14 A7
Admiral Storr's Twr★	
HU11	60 A4
Admiral Walker Rd	
HU17	154 A2
Admirals Mews YO15	122 D2
Advent Ct 9 DN39	86 A1
Aegre Dr DN14	65 C4
Africa Cl 15 DN34	102 B2
Agar St YO31	156 C3
Agard Ave DN15	150 E7
Aike La YO25	33 A1
Ainshaw HU12	139 E8
Ainslie Rd HU12	72 D7
Ainslie St DN32	152 E2
Ainsty Ave YO24	132 F8
Ainsty Gr YO24	132 F8
Ainsty St DN14	149 E4
Ainsty View YO17	16 E8
Ainsworth Rd 16 DN40	87 B1
Ainthorpe Gr HU5	144 C7
Aintree Prim Sch	
HU5	144 C8
Aintree Cl YO24	132 F8
Air St HU5	140 F2
Aire Cl 38 DN40	87 B1
Aire St Goole DN14	149 D3
Knottingley WF11	61 A3
Airedale HU4	140 E6
Airedale Cl 10 DN20	97 E4
Airedale Dr YO16	122 F7

Airedale Rd DN16	151 D1
Airlie St HU3	145 B5
Airmyn Ave	
Goole DN14	149 B5
1 Kingston upon Hull	
HU3	144 E6
Airmyn Park Prim Sch	
DN14	64 E4
Airmyn Rd Airmyn DN14	64 D3
Goole DN14	149 B5
Aisne St HU3	145 A8
Ajax Cl Grimsby DN34	102 B2
Kingston upon Hull HU9	142 D5
Ajax Ct DN15	96 C7
Akeferry Rd	
Haxey DN9	105 C1
Westwoodside DN9	105 B2
Akester Cl 4 HU17	137 B3
Alan Cres DN15	150 F6
Alaska St HU8	141 B1
Alba Ct HU17	150 D1
Albany St	
Gainsborough DN21	117 B1
Kingston upon Hull HU3	145 D8
3 York YO26	129 F5
Albatross Dr DN37	102 A4
Albemarle Cl 5 HU15	68 B5
Albemarle Rd	
Bilton HU11	58 A1
2 Keyingham HU12	73 C4
York YO30	130 B2
Albemarle St 3 HU3	145 B5
Albert Ave HU3	145 A4
Albert Cl 1 YO32	130 F8
Albert Rd	
Cleethorpes DN35	153 F2
Scunthorpe DN16	151 A1
Albert St	
10 Bridlington YO15	122 E2
Brigg DN20	98 C2
Goole DN14	149 C2
5 New Holland DN19	70 E2
3 Thorne/Moorends DN8	93 B8
York DN15	156 C1
Albert St E DN32	152 F5
Albert St W DN32	152 F5
Albert Terr	
Beverley HU17	154 A2
Kingston upon Hull HU7	141 D6
Welwick HU12	90 A7
Albery Way DN36	114 A8
Albina Garth 1 HU12	72 D7
Albion Ave YO26	129 B6
Albion Ct HU17	137 B4
Albion Hill DN9	105 E6
Albion La HU10	138 A3
Albion St	
Great Driffield YO25	124 F3
Grimsby DN32	152 F4
Kingston upon Hull HU1	155 A3
York YO11	156 B1
Albion Terr	
Bridlington YO15	122 F3
Misterton DN10	116 D5
Albourne Ave DN15	151 A6
Alcelina Ct YO23	156 B1
Alcuin Ave YO10	131 A4
Aldborough Gr 9 HU12	142 A2
Aldborough Way YO26	129 F5
Aldbro' St HU2	155 B4
Aldbrough La HU11	59 A6
Aldbrough Prim Sch	
HU11	47 C1
Aldbrough Rd	
East Garton HU11	59 D7
Withernwick HU11	46 E3
Alden Cl DN40	87 C1
Alder Gr 6 DN8	79 B2
Alder View 22 DN33	102 C2
Alder Way YO32	127 D2
Alderley Ct YO32	127 E3
Alderley Edge 6 DN37	113 D6
Alderman Cogans C of E Prim	
Sch HU7	141 F2
Aldermans Way 10 YO25	34 B2
Alderney Way 2 DN40	101 C8
Alderson Ct YO16	122 D2
Alderson Mews 5 HU9	146 C7
Aldersyde YO24	132 E7
Aldreth Gr YO23	130 C2
Aldrich Rd DN35	103 C2
Aldwark YO1	156 C3
Aldwych Croft 6 DN36	114 A7
Aldwych Ct HU5	144 E8
Alexander Ave YO31	127 E2
Alexander Rd DN16	151 B6
Alexandra Ct	
4 Bridlington YO15	122 F3
York YO10	130 E4
Alexandra Dock DN31	152 D6
Alexandra Dr	
1 Beverley HU17	55 E8
5 Bridlington YO15	122 F3
Alexandra Prom YO15	123 A3
Alexandra Rd	
Cleethorpes DN35	153 F2
Grimsby DN31	152 D4
Hornsea HU18	134 C4
Kingston upon Hull HU5	140 C3
Scunthorpe DN16	151 B2
Strensall YO32	14 A6
Thorne/Moorends DN8	79 B2
Alexandra Rd S DN40	87 D2
Alexandra St	
Goole DN14	149 D4
Kingston upon Hull HU3	145 D7

Alexandra St continued	
Thorne DN8	79 A1
Alexandra Wlk YO15	122 F3
Alfonso St 5 HU3	145 B5
Alfred Bean Hospl	
YO25	125 A6
Alfred Gelder St HU1	155 B2
Alfred St	
Gainsborough DN21	117 B1
Grimsby DN31	152 D4
Kingston upon Hull HU3	145 B5
Alfriston Cl HU7	141 B6
Algarth Rd	
Pocklington YO42	29 A4
York YO31	131 B7
Algarth Rise	
Pocklington YO42	28 F4
York YO31	131 B7
Algernon St DN32	152 F1
Alison Garth 29 HU12	72 D7
Alkborough CP Sch	
DN15	82 C8
Alkborough La DN15	82 D7
All Hallows Rd 3 HU17	55 B7
All Saints C of E Jun Sch	
HU13	143 F2
All Saints Cl 4 HU13	69 F4
All Saints RC Comp Sch	
YO24	156 A1
All Saints' St HU3	145 D8
Allan St 2 YO30	130 C7
Allanby St DN15	151 A7
Allanhall Way HU10	143 B8
Allanson Dr HU16	139 D5
Allderidge Ave HU5	140 B3
Allen Cl YO10	131 A4
Allenby Ave DN34	152 A2
Allenby Cres LN11	121 D3
Allendale YO24	132 D8
Allerford Dr 8 HU7	57 A5
Allerton Dr	
1 Immingham DN40	87 C1
22 Poppleton YO26	12 F1
Poppleton YO26	126 A1
Allerton Prim Sch	
DN40	87 B1
Allestree Dr 2 DN33	113 E8
Alliance Ave HU3	144 F7
Alliance La HU3	144 F7
Allington Dr YO31	131 B6
Allison Cl DN17	107 D7
Allison La	
14 Flamborough YO15	5 A2
Ulrome YO25	22 F4
Alloa Cl 2 HU6	140 B8
Allotment La YO25	124 E5
Alma Cl HU10	143 D7
Alma St	
6 Kingston upon Hull	
HU9	146 B7
4 Withernsea HU19	74 F7
Alma Terr Selby YO8	148 C6
York YO10	130 D2
Almery Terr YO30	156 A3
Almond Cl	
Great Driffield YO25	124 F2
Hambleton YO8	48 B1
Almond Gr Brigg DN20	98 B2
3 Kingston upon Hull	
HU5	145 D6
Scunthorpe DN16	151 B4
York YO32	127 F6
Almond Tree Ave DN14	63 C3
Almsford Dr YO26	129 C5
Almsford Rd YO26	129 C5
Alne Terr YO10	130 E2
Alness Dr YO24	132 B7
Alpha Ave HU17	136 D6
Alpha Ct DN8	92 F8
Alston Ave 4 HU8	141 B1
Althorpe & Keadby Prim Sch	
DN17	95 D5
Althorpe Sta DN17	95 D5
Altoft Cl	
2 Brandesburton YO25	34 B2
12 Laceby DN37	101 F1
Alton Pk YO25	22 C5
Alton Rd YO16	122 D7
Altyre Way DN20	103 B1
Alured Garth 9 HU12	72 D7
Alveston Rd DN17	150 D4
Alvin Wlk 9 YO41	27 B2
Alvingham Ave 25 DN35	103 C2
Alvingham Rd DN16	151 B3
Alvis Gr YO10	131 D4
Alwoodley Cl 1 HU8	142 B5
Alwyn Rd 19 DN8	93 B8
Alwyne Dr YO30	126 E1
Alwyne Gr YO30	126 E1
Amanda Cl HU6	139 E6
Amanda Dr DN7	92 E4
Ambaston Rd HU18	134 C5
Amber St YO31	156 C4
Amberley Cl HU7	141 B6
Amberly St 4 YO26	129 E5
Ambleside Ave YO10	131 B4
Ambrey Cl 16 YO14	2 F8
Ambrose Ave 1 DN7	92 E4
Ambrose St YO10	130 D1
Amcotts Rd 14 DN33	102 D1
Amen La YO43	53 D5
Amesbury Ave DN33	113 D8
Amethyst Ct 11 DN36	114 A8
Amethyst Rd HU9	142 C4

Amos Cl 9 DN33	113 D8
Amos Cres DN16	151 D3
Ampleforth Gr HU5	144 D8
Amsterdam Rd HU7	141 A5
Amwell Gn 8 DN7	92 D3
Amy Johnson Ave	
YO16	122 E6
Amy Johnson Ct HU1	155 A1
Amy Johnson Sch	
HU3	144 F5
Amy Johnson Way	
YO30	127 A3
Amy St DN14	149 C4
Anastasia Cl 1 DN21	117 B2
Ancaster Ave	
Grimsby DN33	113 D8
Kingston upon Hull HU5	139 F3
Ancaster Ct DN16	151 A1
Ancholme Ave 10 DN40	87 B1
Ancholme Gdns 10 DN20	98 C2
Ancholme Rd DN16	151 D2
Ancholme Way DN20	98 B2
Anchor Rd	
Kingston upon Hull HU6	140 C8
Scunthorpe DN16	97 A3
Anchorage St 8 DN20	98 B2
Anchors Way 17 DN20	98 B2
Ancient La DN7	92 F3
Ancourt HU6	139 E6
Ancress Wlk YO23	156 B1
Ancroft Cl YO1	156 C1
Anderby Dr DN37	102 B4
Andersen Rd DN14	149 A3
Anderson Gr 6 YO24	129 F2
Anderson Rd DN16	151 C3
Anderson St	
7 Great Driffield YO25	124 F3
Grimsby DN31	152 D3
Andersons Cl 17 HU12	72 D7
Andrew Dr 4 YO32	127 F1
Andrew La 3 HU12	72 C7
Andrew Marvell Sch	
HU9	142 D4
Andrew Rd 11 DN36	114 D8
Andrew's Ct 15 YO42	28 F4
Andrews Rd DN18	84 A7
Andrews Way 8 DN40	87 B1
Angerstein Rd DN17	150 F1
Anglesey Dr DN40	101 C8
Angram Cl YO30	126 F1
Angram La YO19	49 A6
Angram Rd YO26	24 C3
Angus Dr YO25	124 D4
Anlaby Acre Head Cty Prim	
Sch HU4	144 B7
Anlaby Ave 7 HU4	144 B6
Anlaby Cty Inf Sch	
HU10	144 A6
Anlaby Cty Jun Sch	
HU10	144 A6
Anlaby High Rd HU4	144 C6
Anlaby Park Rd N	
HU4	144 B5
Anlaby Park Rd S HU4	144 B2
Anlaby Rd HU3	155 A2
Anlafgate 7 HU10	143 F6
Anlary Rd HU1	155 A2
Ann Gr DN35	103 B2
Ann Watson St HU7	141 B4
Annan Cl YO24	132 C6
Annandale Rd	
Kingston upon Hull	
HU10	138 B1
Kingston upon Hull HU9	142 E2
Anne St	
Kingston upon Hull HU1	155 A2
York YO30	130 C2
Annerley Dr YO16	123 A7
Annes Cres DN31	151 C3
Annesley St DN31	152 D5
Annie Med La HU15	53 F1
Annie Reed Rd HU17	137 C3
Anningson La 6 DN36	114 A8
Annumhills Rd YO8	50 D7
Ansaram La HU15	52 C2
Anson Dr YO10	133 D8
Anson Rd HU9	142 B3
Antelope Rd DN18	70 A1
Anthea Dr YO31	127 E1
Antholme Cl HU7	141 C6
Anthony Way 1 DN41	101 D6
Anthony's Bank Rd	
DN36	103 C1
Antrim Way 4 DN33	102 E1
Antwerp Rd HU7	141 A5
Anvil Wlk DN15	82 C7
Apollo St 9 YO30	130 E3
Appin Cl 7 HU7	57 A6
Apple Croft HU16	138 B8
Apple Garth	
21 Hedon HU12	72 D7
15 Poppleton YO26	12 F1
Apple Tree Cl HU8	141 D4
Apple Tree Ct 1 DN41	101 F5
Apple Tree Wlk HU16	139 D6
Appleby Cl DN17	150 F1
Appleby Gdns DN20	97 D4
Appleby Glade YO32	127 D6
Appleby La	
Broughton DN20	97 D4
Burstwick HU12	73 A7
Appleby Mill Rd DN16	151 E7
Appleby Pl 2 YO31	131 A5
Applecroft Rd	
Selby YO8	148 A5
York YO31	131 B7
Appledore Cl HU9	146 C6
Applegarth 8 HU15	66 D7

Applegarth Cl DN35 ...153 D1
Applegarth La
Bainton YO25 ...31 E7
Bridlington YO16 ...122 D4
Applegarth Mews 3 HU16 ...139 B7
Applegarth Rd HU8 ...155 C3
Appleton Ct YO23 ...132 F3
Appleton Gdns 8 HU15 ...53 F1
Appleton Prim Sch HU5 ...139 E2
Appleton Rd
Bishopthorpe YO23 ...133 A3
Kingston upon Hull HU5 ...139 E3
Appleton Way DN16 ...151 C2
Appleyard Dr DN18 ...84 E8
Arables La HU12 ...74 C4
Archbishop Cl HU9 ...142 D2
Archbishop Holgates Sch YO10 ...131 B3
Archbishop of York C of E Jun Sch YO23 ...133 A4
Archbishop Thurston C of E Sch HU9 ...142 D3
Archer Rd DN37 ...113 D6
Archway The YO43 ...135 D4
Arcon Dr HU4 ...144 D6
Arden Ct HU5 ...139 C2
Arden Rd HU17 ...154 C4
Arden Village 21 DN35 ...103 C1
Ardent Rd DN18 ...70 A1
Ardmore Cl HU9 ...142 B4
Arenhall Cl 2 YO32 ...127 C8
Argam Dikes*
Grindale YO25 ...3 B2
Rudston YO25 ...10 A7
Argam La YO25 ...2 F1
Argent Cl 8 HU6 ...140 B8
Arglam La YO43 ...51 F6
Argyle St Goole DN14 ...149 D4
Kingston upon Hull HU3 ...145 C7
York YO23 ...130 B1
Ariston St DN32 ...153 B3
Ark Royal HU11 ...142 E6
Arkley Cl 18 HU15 ...68 C5
Arkwright St 10 DN21 ...117 B1
Arkwright Way DN16 ...151 F2
Arlington Ave HU16 ...139 B6
Arlington Rd YO30 ...127 A1
Arlington St 2 HU3 ...145 D6
Armour Rd DN16 ...151 E7
Armoury Rd YO8 ...148 B5
Armstrong Pl E DN31 ...152 C5
Armstrong Pl W DN31 ...152 C5
Armstrong St DN31 ...152 C5
Armthorpe La DN3 ...92 A3
Arncliffe Cl 1 HU7 ...56 F6
Arncliffe Way HU16 ...139 A5
Arnold La
Kingston upon Hull HU3 ...145 B6
Riston HU11 ...45 C5
Arnold La W HU11 ...45 C4
Arnold St HU3 ...145 B6
Arnside Pl 2 YO10 ...130 F3
Arram Gr HU6 ...139 E5
Arram Rd HU17 ...43 D6
Arram Sta HU17 ...43 F7
Arran Cl
Immingham DN40 ...101 C8
Kingston upon Hull HU9 ...142 A4
Arran Pl YO31 ...130 D7
Arras Dr HU16 ...138 E6
Arreton Cl HU8 ...142 D6
Arthur Lucan Ct HU9 ...142 C1
Arthur Pl 6 YO30 ...126 B5
Arthur Rd 12 DN21 ...117 B1
Arthur St
Grimsby DN31 ...152 C4
Kingston upon Hull HU3 ...145 A5
Withernsea HU19 ...74 F7
York YO10 ...130 E4
Arundel Cl
4 Gainsborough DN21 ...117 C1
Kingston upon Hull HU9 ...146 C8
Arundel Gr YO24 ...132 C7
Arundel Pl DN35 ...153 E1
Arundel Rd 5 DN6 ...76 E2
Arundel St 4 HU9 ...146 C8
Ascot Rd 23 DN37 ...113 D6
Ascot Way YO24 ...129 D1
Ascott Cl HU4 ...144 D5
Asgard Way 5 DN33 ...102 D1
Ash Ave HU15 ...68 C6
Ash Cl Hessle HU13 ...143 C3
Newton on Derwent YO41 ...27 E4
Sproatley HU11 ...58 D5
York YO31 ...131 B7
Ash Ct 18 DN35 ...103 B1
Ash Dell DN14 ...149 E6
Ash Dene 7 HU17 ...55 D8
Ash Dr
Kingston upon Hull HU10 ...143 F8
Thorngumbald HU12 ...72 E5
Ash Gr 4 Aldbrough HU11 ...47 C1
Brigg DN20 ...98 B2
17 Gainsborough DN21 ...117 B1
Hutton Cranswick YO25 ...32 E6
Kingston upon Hull HU10 ...138 D1
Kingston upon Hull HU5 ...140 C3
Market Weighton YO43 ...135 D4
Messingham DN17 ...107 D7
1 Riccall YO19 ...48 F8
3 Scotter DN21 ...107 B3
Scunthorpe DN16 ...151 B3
Ash Hill Cres DN7 ...92 D4
Ash Hill Mid Sch DN7 ...92 D4
Ash Hill Rd
20 Hatfield DN7 ...92 D4
Sykehouse DN14 ...78 A3
Ash La 8 Haxby YO32 ...13 E5
Melbourne YO42 ...39 A5
Ash St YO26 ...129 E4
Ash Tree Cl 5 DN40 ...87 C2
Ash Tree Dr
5 Haxey DN9 ...105 D2
Leconfield HU17 ...43 D6
Ash Tree Rd 13 DN8 ...93 A7
Ashberry Dr
Messingham DN17 ...107 D7
1 Scunthorpe DN16 ...151 B2
Ashbourne 7 DN37 ...113 D6
Ashbourne Ct DN15 ...150 B7
Ashbourne Way YO24 ...132 C8
Ashburnham Cl 4 DN6 ...76 F2
Ashburnham Rd 14 DN8 ...93 A8
Ashburnham Wlk 5 DN6 76 F2
Ashbury Ct HU6 ...140 A6
Ashby Cl Grimsby DN37 ...102 B4
Holton le Clay DN36 ...114 B5
Kingston upon Hull HU4 ...144 B7
Ashby High St DN16 ...151 A2
Ashby Hill DN37 ...113 C3
Ashby Inf Sch DN16 ...151 B2
Ashby La DN37 ...113 C4
Ashby Rd
Cleethorpes DN35 ...103 B2
Kingston upon Hull HU4 ...144 B4
Scunthorpe DN16 ...151 A2
Ashcombe Rd HU7 ...56 E5
Ashcourt Cl HU18 ...134 C5
Ashcourt Dr HU18 ...134 B5
Ashdale Pk 14 HU14 ...69 A5
Ashdale Rd 19 YO19 ...26 F7
Ashdene Cl HU10 ...143 E7
Ashdown Ave DN15 ...150 E8
Ashdown Cl DN20 ...98 D2
Ashdown Way DN10 ...116 C5
Ashendon Dr HU8 ...141 A2
Ashfield YO43 ...40 A1
Ashfield Ave 1 DN8 ...93 A7
Ashfield Ct DN17 ...94 D7
Ashfield Gr 6 DN7 ...92 C6
Ashfield Rd Hatfield DN7 ...92 C4
Thorne DN8 ...92 F7
Ashford Pl YO24 ...129 D2
Ashgate Rd HU10 ...138 E2
Ashlea 1 DN10 ...116 C5
Ashlea Cl YO8 ...148 D4
Ashleigh Ct 13 DN41 ...101 F5
Ashleigh Dr 6 YO25 ...22 D1
Ashley Park Cres YO31 ...131 B6
Ashley Park Rd YO31 ...131 B7
Ashmeade Cl YO24 ...132 B8
Ashridge Dr DN32 ...153 B1
Ashthorpe HU6 ...139 F8
Ashton Ave YO30 ...130 B8
Ashton Cl HU6 ...139 F8
Ashtree Ave DN34 ...152 A2
Ashtree Cl DN9 ...94 E1
Ashtree Cres HU15 ...53 D3
Ashtree Dr YO8 ...48 D1
Ashville St
Bridlington YO16 ...122 D3
York YO31 ...130 D7
Ashwell Ave HU9 ...142 D1
Ashwood Dr
17 Humberston DN36 ...103 D1
10 Humberston DN36 ...114 D8
Ashwood Glade YO32 ...127 C6
Ashworthy Cl 5 HU7 ...56 F5
Aske Mews HU5 ...139 D3
Askern & Campsall Sports Ctr DN6 ...76 F1
Askew Ave HU4 ...144 E4
Askham Bryan Coll YO23 ...24 F2
Askham Bryan La YO23 ...132 A6
Askham Croft 1 YO24 ...129 B1
Askham Fields La YO23 ...24 F2
Askham Gr YO24 ...129 B2
Askham La
Askham Bryan YO24 ...132 A8
York YO24 ...129 B1
Aspen Cl
3 Dunnington YO19 ...26 F7
Market Weighton YO43 ...135 D5
Aspen Ct
15 Cleethorpes DN35 ...103 B1
13 Gainsborough DN21 ...117 C1
Aspen Gr DN16 ...151 B4
Aspen Wlk 4 HU15 ...68 D5
Asphodel Cl 15 DN36 ...114 B8
Asquith Ave YO31 ...131 A5
Asquith St DN21 ...117 A1
Asterby Rd DN17 ...150 F1
Astley Cres 18 DN21 ...107 C3
Astley St HU3 ...144 F7
Aston Gn 4 DN7 ...92 D3
Aston Hall Dr 11 HU14 ...69 A5
Aston Rd HU10 ...143 F8
Astoria Cres HU8 ...141 F4
Astral Cl
Kingston upon Hull HU7 ...141 D7
Kingston upon Hull HU13 ...143 F3
Astral Rd HU13 ...143 F3
Astral Way HU7 ...141 C7
Astral Way Gdns HU7 ...141 C7
Atcherley Cl YO10 ...133 D8
Athelstan Rd HU17 ...154 B4
Athenian Way DN37 ...102 C6
Atherton Way DN20 ...98 B2
Athol St HU3 ...144 F4
Atholl Ave HU13 ...143 E3
Atkinson Ave DN20 ...98 C3
Atkinson Dr 19 HU15 ...68 C6
Atkinson La 6 DN37 ...113 E6
Atkinsons Way DN15 ...96 C8
Atlanta Ct 2 HU8 ...142 B5
Atlas Rd
Scunthorpe DN17 ...150 F4
York YO30 ...127 A3
Atterby La LN8 ...119 F3
Atterwith La YO26 ...24 A7
Attlee Dr DN14 ...149 C5
Atwick Ct 2 HU9 ...142 B1
Atwick Rd
Bewholme YO25 ...35 A4
Hornsea HU18 ...134 B6
Atwood Cl 4 DN40 ...87 B2
Auburn Cl YO16 ...122 B5
Auchinleck Cl
Kelleythorpe YO25 ...124 B1
Kirkburn YO25 ...124 B1
Auckland Ave HU6 ...140 C5
Auckland Gr DN8 ...79 C2
Auckland Rd
Grimsby DN31 ...152 F6
Scunthorpe DN15 ...150 F6
Audax Cl YO30 ...127 A3
Audax Rd YO30 ...127 A3
Audern Rd DN16 ...96 D2
Audley St HU2 ...155 A4
Audus St 10 YO8 ...148 C5
Augusta Cl
Grimsby DN34 ...152 C2
Kingston upon Hull HU8 ...142 B6
Augusta Oaks DN34 ...152 C2
Augusta St DN34 ...152 B2
Augustinian Priory (site of)* YO42 ...30 B5
Augustus Dr 13 HU15 ...68 C5
Auster Rd YO30 ...127 B3
Austfield La LS25 ...61 B8
Austin Cres 17 DN17 ...96 C2
Austin Garth 5 DN37 ...101 F1
Autherd Garth 1 HU17 ...55 C8
Autumn View YO25 ...124 D5
Avenswood La 8 DN15 ...96 B7
Avenue Cannes DN15 ...96 B7
Avenue Clamart DN15 ...96 B7
Avenue Fontenay 17 DN15 ...96 B7
Avenue Lourdes 16 DN15 .96 B7
Avenue Nozay DN20 ...97 E4
Avenue Rd YO30 ...156 A4
Avenue Rouen 15 DN15 ...96 B7
Avenue Terr YO30 ...156 A4
Avenue The
Blyton DN21 ...117 E5
Burton upon Stather DN15 ...82 B4
Campsall DN6 ...76 E1
East Ravendale DN37 ...113 C2
19 Gainsborough DN21 ...117 B1
Great Driffield YO25 ...124 F5
Grimsby DN37 ...102 B4
5 Haxby YO32 ...13 E5
Haxby YO32 ...127 D8
Healing DN41 ...101 F5
Holme-on-Spalding-Moor YO43 ...51 E8
Kingston upon Hull HU7 ...141 E6
Kingston upon Hull HU10 ...143 C7
Kingston upon Hull HU10 ...143 F7
Nun Monkton YO26 ...12 A4
11 Pocklington YO42 ...29 A4
Rowley HU20 ...54 D6
Rufforth YO23 ...24 C6
Thorne/Moorends DN8 ...79 B3
Watton YO25 ...32 D4
York YO30 ...130 A6
Avenue Vivian DN15 ...150 E8
Avenues Ct HU5 ...140 C1
Aviator Ct YO30 ...126 F3
Avon Dr YO32 ...127 F6
Avon Rd DN16 ...151 C6
Avon St 2 HU8 ...141 C1
Avondale 1 HU4 ...144 B2
Awnhams La
Bishop Wilton YO42 ...16 D2
North Cave HU15 ...53 E4
Axdane HU6 ...139 E7
Axholme Ave DN17 ...94 C7
Axholme Dr 11 DN9 ...105 D6
Axholme Gn 15 DN8 ...93 B7
Axholme Rd
Scunthorpe DN15 ...150 D6
2 Westwoodside DN9 ...105 A2
Axholme St DN14 ...149 E4
Axminster Cl HU7 ...141 A8
Aylesbury Gr HU5 ...144 D8
Aylesby Gdns 26 DN33 ...102 D2
Aylesby La
Aylesby DN37 ...101 F2
Healing DN41 ...101 F4
Aylesby Rd
Aylesby DN37 ...101 E2
Scunthorpe DN17 ...150 F1
Aylesford St 7 HU3 ...145 B5
Aylesham Ct YO32 ...127 E3
Ayots Gn 10 DN7 ...92 D3
Ayscough Ave DN41 ...101 E6
Ayscough Gr 3 LN7 ...111 B4
Ayscough St DN31 ...152 C4
Aysgarth Ave
Kingston upon Hull HU6 ...139 E4
Messingham DN17 ...107 D7
Aysgarth Rise YO16 ...122 E6

B

Bacchus La HU15 ...54 A1
Bacheler St HU3 ...145 B5
Bachelor Hill YO24 ...129 C2
Back Field La DN7 ...92 E4
Back La
Acaster Selby YO23 ...36 B3
Allerthorpe YO42 ...28 E2
Appleton Roebuck YO23 ...36 A5
Asselby DN14 ...64 D6
Barlby with Osgodby YO8 ...49 C4
Bilbrough YO23 ...24 D1
Burstwick HU12 ...73 A6
Burton Agnes YO25 ...10 A2
Burton Pidsea HU12 ...59 C2
Catwick HU17 ...45 C8
Copmanthorpe YO23 ...132 A2
Cottingwith YO42 ...38 C5
Drax YO8 ...63 F5
Driffield YO25 ...124 B5
East Garton HU11 ...59 E6
Ellerton YO42 ...38 C1
Elstronwick HU12 ...59 B3
Fangfoss YO41 ...28 C8
Garthorpe & Fockerby DN17 ...81 F6
11 Haxby YO32 ...13 D5
Hayton YO42 ...29 C1
Hemingbrough YO8 ...49 F1
Hirst Courtney YO8 ...62 F3
Holme-on-Spalding-Moor YO43 ...40 A1
Holtby YO19 ...26 E8
Kilham YO25 ...9 B3
Luttons YO17 ...7 B8
Newton-on-Ouse YO30 ...12 B6
North Duffield YO8 ...50 A7
Norton DN6 ...76 E2
Nunburnholme YO42 ...29 F3
Patrington Haven HU12 ...89 C8
2 Riccall YO19 ...49 A8
Searby cum Owmby DN38 ...110 D8
3 Seaton HU11 ...35 A1
Shiptonthorpe YO43 ...40 F6
Snaith & Cowick DN14 ...78 E8
Stainforth DN7 ...92 C6
Wilberfoss YO41 ...27 F5
3 Winteringham DN15 ...68 B1
Winteringham DN15 ...83 B8
Wold Newton YO25 ...2 A4
York YO26 ...129 A5
Back La S YO19 ...37 F7
Back O' Newton YO41 ...27 E3
Back Park St YO8 ...148 D5
Back Rd HU12 ...72 A5
Back Side YO17 ...6 B5
Back Southgate HU18 ...134 C3
Back St Alkborough DN15 .82 C8
Bainton YO25 ...31 E7
Burton Fleming YO25 ...2 E3
3 Easington HU12 ...90 F6
East/West Stockwith DN21 ...116 E5
Fridaythorpe YO25 ...18 B6
Langtoft YO25 ...8 D5
Laxton DN14 ...65 F4
Skerne & Wansford YO25 ...21 A2
Skipsea YO25 ...23 A2
Wold Newton YO25 ...2 A4
Back West View 2 YO30 ...130 B7
Back Westgate HU18 ...134 B4
Backcarr La YO25 ...21 C5
Backhouse St YO31 ...156 B4
Bacon Garth Cty Prim Sch HU16 ...139 A5
Bacon Garth La HU16 ...139 A5
Bad Bargain La YO31 ...131 A5
Baden Cl 3 HU5 ...140 D2
Badger Hill Prim Sch YO10 ...131 B2
Badger La
Halsham HU12 ...74 B5
Walden Stubbs DN6 ...77 A3
Badger Paddock 5 YO31 ...127 E2
Badger Way 1 DN20 ...97 E4
Badger Wood Wlk YO10 ...131 D3
Badgers Wood HU16 ...138 F8
Baffam Gdns YO8 ...148 B2
Baffam La YO8 ...148 B2
Bagby Mews 2 HU5 ...139 D3
Baggaby Hill YO42 ...29 E4
Bagsby Rd DN9 ...106 B3
Baildon Cl 3 YO26 ...129 D4
Baildon Rd DN15 ...150 D8
Baile Hill Terr YO1 ...156 B1
Bailey La Hatfield DN7 ...92 E6
Kingston upon Hull HU16 ...139 D8
Warter YO42 ...30 B5
Baileywood La YO43 ...51 F8
Bainbridge Ave HU9 ...142 D2
Bainbridge Dr YO8 ...148 C4
Bainton Cl HU17 ...136 D5
Bainton Gr HU6 ...139 E6
Bainton Infant Sch YO25 ...31 E7
Bainton Rd YO25 ...19 E2
Bakehouse La 5 YO25 ...9 C3
Baker Dr DN15 ...83 A5
Baker St
Kingston upon Hull HU2 ...155 A3
York YO30 ...130 C7
Bakers Cl DN38 ...99 B5
Bakersfield DN20 ...98 D4
Bakersfield Dr DN14 ...61 F3
Bakewell Cl HU9 ...142 D1
Balder Ct 2 DN33 ...102 E1
Baldwin Ave DN16 ...96 D1
Balfour Pl 14 DN40 ...87 B1
Balfour St
24 Gainsborough DN21 ...117 B1
3 Kingston upon Hull HU9 ...146 C8
York YO26 ...129 F5
Balfour Way YO32 ...14 A6
Balham Ave HU8 ...141 E6
Balk Cl HU17 ...45 B8
Balk La Hook DN14 ...149 F6
Pollington DN14 ...77 F7
Riston HU11 ...45 C4
Sproatley HU11 ...58 D5
Balk Mews HU5 ...139 D3
Balk The
Bishop Wilton YO41 ...16 C2
Millington YO42 ...29 C7
Pocklington YO42 ...29 A3
Ballantyne Cl HU7 ...141 C4
Ballhall La YO42 ...38 E6
Balliol Dr DN16 ...96 D2
Balmoral Ave
Grimsby DN34 ...152 A3
Kingston upon Hull HU6 ...140 B6
Balmoral Cl 8 YO16 ...122 D6
Balmoral Dr HU17 ...136 E1
Balmoral Rd
2 Cleethorpes DN35 ...103 B2
25 Hatfield DN7 ...92 D4
Balmoral Terr 5 YO23 ...130 B1
Balne Croft La DN14 ...78 A6
Balne Hall Rd DN14 ...77 F5
Balne Moor Rd DN14 ...77 B6
Bamford Ave HU9 ...142 E1
Banbury Rd DN16 ...151 D6
Bank End Rd DN9 ...104 A3
Bank L Ctr The HU6 ...139 F6
Bank La 15 LN7 ...111 B4
Bank Rd YO8 ...148 D6
Bank Side
Kingston upon Hull HU5 ...140 F2
Rawcliffe DN14 ...64 A2
Bank St
3 Hornsea HU18 ...134 C4
Kingston upon Hull HU3 ...145 C7
Bank Terr HU18 ...134 C2
Bank Wood Rd WF8 ...76 A6
Bankfield La DN14 ...64 A7
Banks Cl HU12 ...90 F6
Bankside Cl 3 YO26 ...12 F1
Bannisdale 6 YO24 ...132 C7
Bannister Cl 3 HU13 ...69 F4
Bannister Dr HU9 ...146 C7
Bannister St HU19 ...75 A7
Baptist Chapel La DN40 ...86 F2
Baptist Pl YO16 ...122 D4
Bar La YO1 ...156 A2
Barbara Cl 3 DN33 ...113 E8
Barbara Gr 4 YO24 ...129 F3
Barbarry Rd HU12 ...72 B7
Barberry Ct 3 HU3 ...145 C5
Barbers Dr YO23 ...132 B4
Barbican Ct YO10 ...156 C1
Barbican L Ctr YO10 ...156 C1
Barbican Mews YO10 ...130 E3
Barbican Rd YO10 ...156 C1
Barbican Way 7 DN36 ...114 A7
Barbriggs La YO25 ...22 E2
Barcroft St DN35 ...153 B4
Barden Ct 6 YO30 ...126 F1
Bardney Ave DN16 ...151 A3
Bardney Gdns 16 DN34 ...102 C2
Bardney Rd 14 YO14 ...2 F8
Bardshaw HU6 ...139 F8
Barf La YO41 ...16 D4
Barff Cl 10 YO8 ...48 D1
Barff Gr 6 YO8 ...48 B2
Barff La YO8 ...48 C1
Barff View YO8 ...62 D7
Barfhill Cswy YO25 ...32 F2
Barfield Rd YO31 ...130 F8
Bargate DN34 ...152 C2
Bargate Ave DN32 ...152 D1
Bargate Gr 3 HU5 ...144 D8
Barham Rd HU9 ...142 B4
Bark House La DN35 ...153 F1
Bark St DN35 ...153 F1
Barker La YO1 ...156 A2
Barkhouse La DN35 ...153 F1
Barkhouse Wood La WF11 ...61 D6
Barking Cl HU8 ...142 A5
Barkston Ave YO26 ...129 B3
Barkston Cl 3 YO26 ...129 A3
Barkston Gr YO26 ...129 A3
Barkston Rd YO26 ...129 A3
Barkworth Cl HU10 ...143 D6
Barkworth Ct 3 DN37 ...113 D6
Barlby Bridge CP Sch YO8 ...148 D5
Barlby By-Pass 2 YO8 ...49 B4
Barlby CP Sch YO8 ...49 B4
Barlby Cres YO8 ...148 F7
Barlby High Sch YO8 ...49 B5
Barlby Rd YO8 ...148 E6
Barleigh Croft HU9 ...142 B3

Barleigh Rd HU9 142 B3
Barley Cl DN20 109 A5
Barley Garth
14 Brandesburton YO25 34 B2
Burton Pidsea HU12 59 C2
Barley Gate HU17 45 A8
Barley Rise
Bridlington YO16 123 A6
Strensall YO32 14 A6
Barley View YO32 127 C8
Barlings Ave DN16 151 A3
Barlings Cl DN21 107 D4
Barlow C of E Prim Sch YO8 63 C7
Barlow Comm Nature Reserve★ YO8 63 B7
Barlow Comm Rd YO8 63 B8
Barlow Rd YO8 63 B6
Barlow St YO26 129 D4
Barmby Ave YO10 133 E8
Barmby Cl 4 YO30 126 F1
Barmby Ferry Rd 1 YO8 49 F1
Barmby La DN14 52 A3
Barmby Moor C of E Sch YO42 28 D4
Barmby on the Marsh Cty Prim Sch DN14 64 B7
Barmby Rd YO42 28 E4
Barmouth Cl 4 HU7 57 A7
Barmouth Dr 20 DN37 102 C4
Barmston Cl HU17 137 B5
Barmston La HU17 56 C8
Barmston Rd HU17 137 B5
Barmston St HU2 155 B4
Barnard Ave DN20 98 C2
Barnard Way HU12 72 D6
Barnards Dr 9 HU15 53 F1
Barnes Cl HU17 137 B4
Barnes Cres DN15 150 E8
Barnes Gn DN21 107 C4
Barnet Cl HU8 142 A5
Barnet Dr DN36 114 B8
Barnet Gn 9 DN7 92 D3
Barnetby C of E Sch DN38 99 B4
Barnetby La DN20 98 F7
Barnetby Rd
1 Kingston upon Hull HU13 144 A3
Scunthorpe DN17 150 F1
Barnetby Sta DN38 99 B4
Barnett Pl DN35 153 B3
Barnfield Way YO23 132 A2
Barnhill La DN14 64 F7
Barnoldby Rd DN37 113 D6
Barnsdale View DN6 76 E2
Barnside DN20 108 F5
Barnsley Rd DN8 79 B2
Barnsley St HU8 141 B1
Barnstaple Rd
Kingston upon Hull HU7 141 B7
Scunthorpe DN17 150 D3
Barnston Way 11 DN15 82 B4
Baron Ave 8 DN36 114 A8
Baroness Cl 7 HU6 140 B8
Baroness Ct 4 DN34 102 C3
Baroness Rd
3 Grimsby DN34 102 C3
Grimsby DN34 152 A3
Barons Cres YO23 132 B2
Baronwood Cres 7 YO25 22 D1
Barr La YO32 14 D4
Barra Cl HU8 141 F6
Barraclough's La DN18 69 E2
Barrett Ave 3 YO24 129 F3
Barrick Cl 7 DN19 85 D8
Barrier Bank DN14 78 E6
Barrington Ave HU5 139 F3
Barrington Garth DN14 61 F3
Barrow Ct 3 HU3 140 D1
Barrow Haven Sta DN19 70 C2
Barrow La HU13 143 D2
Barrow Rd
Barrow upon Humber DN19 70 E1
Barton-upon-Humber DN18 85 A8
New Holland DN19 70 E2
Barry Ave DN34 102 C2
Barstow Ave YO10 130 F3
Bartholomew Ave DN14 149 B5
Bartindale Rd YO14 3 A5
Bartle Garth YO1 156 C3
Bartlett Ave HU17 154 A2
Bartlett Cl 9 HU12 58 D1
Barton Dr HU13 143 D1
Barton La DN19 85 C8
Barton Rd DN20 98 D3
Barton St
Barrow upon Humber DN19 85 D8
Irby DN37 112 F7
Keelby DN41 101 A4
Wyham cum Cadeby DN36 120 F7
Barton St Peters C of E Prim Sch DN18 69 F1
Barton-on-Humber Sta DN18 69 F1
Bartons Garth YO8 148 B2
Bartrams HU15 68 D6
Barwic Par YO8 148 E4
Barwick Parade CP Sch YO8 148 E4
Basic Slag Rd DN16 151 E6
Basil Dr HU17 154 A1
Baslow Rd DN15 150 B6
Bassett Cl
1 Broughton DN20 97 E3
Selby YO8 148 C3
Bassett Rd 2 DN35 103 D2
Bate La DN14 78 A4
Bateson Cl YO10 131 C1
Bath St DN32 153 A5
Baths Hall The DN15 150 F7
Bathurst St 8 HU3 145 D5
Batley Cl HU9 142 C2
Battersea Cl HU8 141 F5
Battery Rd HU12 72 A4
Battery St DN40 87 C1
Battle Gn DN9 105 D7
Battleflats Way YO41 15 D2
Batty La 7 DN14 65 A7
Bawtry Cl YO8 148 D3
Bawtry Rd Hatfield DN7 92 F3
Selby YO8 148 D3
Baxter Gate HU12 72 D7
Bay View Ave HU18 134 C6
Bayard St DN21 117 B1
Bayle Mus★ YO16 122 D4
Baylegate 6 YO16 122 D4
Baynard Ave HU16 139 A6
Bayons Ave 13 DN33 113 D8
Baysdale HU7 140 F6
Baysdale Ave YO10 131 D3
Baysdale Rd DN16 151 D1
Baysgarth L Ctr DN18 84 F8
Baysgarth Lower Sch DN18 84 F8
Baysgarth Mus★ DN18 84 F8
Baysgarth Upper Sch DN18 84 F8
Baysgarth View DN18 84 F7
Bayswater Ct HU8 141 E5
Bayswater Pl 2 DN33 113 D8
Baytree Ave DN34 152 A2
Beach Holt La DN37 101 D2
Beacon Ave
14 Barton-upon-Humber DN18 84 E8
Cleethorpes DN35 153 D2
Beacon Ct DN35 153 D2
Beacon Hill★ DN10 116 A1
Beacon Hill Rd DN10 116 A1
Beacon La YO25 21 B8
Beacon Rd
Bridlington YO16 123 A6
Millington YO42 17 B1
Beacon View YO43 40 B1
Beaconsfield HU19 74 F6
Beaconsfield St
1 Kingston upon Hull HU5 140 D2
York YO24 129 D3
Beaconthorpe Rd DN35 153 E3
Beadlam Mews HU5 139 E4
Beadle Garth YO23 132 B2
Beagle Cl 12 DN20 97 E4
Beagle Croft YO41 15 C1
Beagle Ridge Dr YO24 129 C1
Beagle Spinney YO41 15 C1
Beal La Beal DN14 61 D4
Cridling Stubbs WF11 61 C1
Bealey's La YO25 32 B1
Beamsley Way 18 HU7 56 F5
Bean Gdns 3 DN14 78 C8
Bean St HU3 145 C6
Beanland La YO32 14 D2
Bean's Way YO31 131 B8
Beatty Ave 13 DN33 113 E8
Beauchamp St DN16 151 B5
Beauchief Gdns DN16 151 A4
Beaufort Ave HU18 134 C2
Beaufort Cl
Kingston upon Hull HU3 145 D6
York YO10 131 B3
Beaufort Cres 5 DN35 103 B1
Beaufort St 5 DN21 117 B2
Beaulah Villas 1 DN18 84 A7
Beaulahland 2 DN18 84 A7
Beaulieu Cl 1 YO32 127 F5
Beaulieu Ct 5 HU9 142 A3
Beaumonde 5 DN36 114 A5
Beaumont Ct
Goole DN14 149 B6
3 Kingston upon Hull HU9 146 D7
Beaumont Pl YO8 148 A2
Beautiman Ct HU6 140 A5
Beaver Rd HU17 137 B4
Beaverdyke YO30 126 F1
Beccles Cl HU8 142 B6
Beck Bank HU16 139 C6
Beck Cl 6 Elvington YO41 27 B2
Keelby DN41 101 A4
Beck Garth 12 HU12 72 D7
Beck Hill
6 Barton-upon-Humber DN18 84 F8
1 Bridlington YO15 122 E2
Beck La Appleby DN15 83 D1
5 Barrow upon Humber DN19 85 D8
Broughton DN20 97 E3
Easington HU12 90 F6
Redbourne DN21 108 F2
Scunthorpe DN16 96 D2
Wheldrake YO19 38 A8
Beck Rd HU15 53 D2
Beck Row YO41 16 D5
Beck Side
Barmby Moor YO42 28 D3
Great Driffield YO25 124 F4
Hibaldstow DN20 108 F5
Beck St HU12 90 F6
Beck View 14 YO42 29 A3
Beck View Rd HU17 137 C4
Beck Wlk 7 DN35 103 C1
Beckdale 4 HU7 141 A6
Beckett Ave DN21 117 C1
Beckfield La YO26 129 B5
Beckfield Pl YO26 129 B4
Beckhole Cl HU3 145 A6
Beckhythe Cl DN33 102 F1
Beckingham Rd DN10 116 D2
Beckington Cl 1 HU8 142 C7
Becks Cl 5 YO32 127 C8
Becks La DN21 107 A3
Becks La Riding Sch DN21 107 B3
Beckside
Beverley HU17 154 C2
4 Brough HU15 68 D6
7 Elvington YO41 27 B2
Hornsea HU18 134 C3
Rothwell LN7 111 F2
Wilberfoss YO41 27 F6
Beckside Cl
4 Humberston DN35 103 C1
Kingston upon Hull HU6 140 B7
Beckside N HU17 154 C2
Beckwith Cl YO31 131 C7
Bedale Ave
Kingston upon Hull HU9 141 E1
York YO10 131 D4
Bedale Ct YO43 135 E3
Bedale Rd
Market Weighton YO43 135 E3
Scunthorpe DN16 151 D1
Bedale Wlk YO43 135 F4
Bede Ave YO30 130 B7
Bedford Gr YO15 122 D1
Bedford Rd
Humberston DN35 103 D1
Kingston upon Hull HU13 143 F3
Bedford St
Grimsby DN32 153 A5
Kingston upon Hull HU8 141 A1
Bedfords Fold 6 LS25 61 A7
Beech Ave
3 Airmyn DN14 64 E4
Beverley HU17 136 F6
Bishopthorpe YO23 133 A3
3 Flamborough YO15 5 A2
Flixborough DN15 96 A7
14 Gainsborough DN21 117 B1
14 Grimsby DN33 102 E2
Gunness DN15 95 E6
Kingston upon Hull HU8 141 C2
Kingston upon Hull HU11 142 F6
Kingston upon Hull HU10 143 D8
7 Preston HU12 72 C7
Thorngumbald HU12 72 E5
York YO24 129 F3
Beech Cl
4 Broughton DN20 97 D3
Burstwick HU12 73 A6
2 Elvington YO41 27 B2
Kilham YO25 9 B3
8 Kingston upon Hull HU3 145 C5
Market Weighton YO43 135 D4
Sproatley HU11 58 C5
Beech Cres 7 DN7 92 C6
Beech Croft
Barlby with Osgodby YO8 49 B6
Driffield YO25 125 A6
Beech Ct
Bishopthorpe YO23 133 A3
6 Pocklington YO42 29 A4
Beech Dr
Bridlington YO16 123 A6
2 North Ferriby HU14 69 A4
11 Patrington HU12 74 D1
Beech Garth DN19 85 C7
Beech Glade YO31 127 F2
Beech Gr 1 Airmyn DN14 64 E4
Burton upon Stather DN15 82 B5
Camblesforth YO8 63 C5
2 Flamborough YO15 5 A2
Goole DN14 149 D1
Holton le Clay DN36 114 B5
Kingston upon Hull HU5 140 C3
Kingston upon Hull HU13 143 C3
Nafferton YO25 125 E8
Selby YO8 148 C5
1 Swanland HU14 69 C7
York YO26 129 C4
Beech Hill Rd HU14 69 C7
Beech Lawn HU10 143 E6
Beech Pk YO19 49 A8
Beech Pl 5 YO32 14 A6
Beech Rd Brough HU15 68 C6
Campsall DN6 76 E1
Beech Tree Ave 21 DN8 93 B7
Beech Tree Cl 3 HU17 136 F7
Beech Tree La YO8 63 C5
Beech View
Hutton Cranswick YO25 32 E6
Walkington HU17 55 C8
Beech Way 10 DN36 103 B1
Beechcliffe Ave 1 HU6 140 C7
Beechdale HU16 139 C5
Beeches Ave 23 DN16 96 D2
Beeches The
Great Driffield YO25 125 A4
Pocklington YO42 29 A4
Skelton YO30 126 C4
Beechfield
Kingston upon Hull HU6 140 B6
Newton-on-Ouse YO30 12 B6
Beechfield Cl YO8 48 B1
Beechfield Dr HU10 138 C2
Beechfield Rd DN7 92 C4
Beechway DN16 151 B3
Beechwood Ave
25 Grimsby DN33 102 C2
3 Immingham DN40 87 C1
Beechwood Cl 11 DN3 92 A1
Beechwood Cres 3 DN20 97 E4
Beechwood Dr
Scawby DN20 108 E8
3 Scotter DN21 107 C3
Beechwood Glade 7 YO24 129 B1
Beechwood Views HU12 60 B1
Beeford C of E Sch YO25 22 C1
Beeford Gr HU6 139 F5
Beeford Rd YO25 22 F1
Beeforth Cl YO32 127 D5
Beeley Rd DN32 153 C2
Beel's Rd DN41 101 E8
Beelsby Rd DN37 112 C5
Beesby Dr 22 DN35 103 C2
Beesby Medieval Village★ DN36 120 E7
Beesby Rd DN17 150 E1
Beeson St DN31 152 C5
Beggar Hill DN21 107 D5
Beilby St HU3 144 F4
Belcombe Way 1 YO30 130 A7
Beldevere Pk HU18 134 C6
Belfry Ct HU8 142 B6
Belgrave Cl 6 Belton DN9 94 E1
Belton DN9 105 E8
Belgrave Dr
Goole DN14 149 F5
Hornsea HU18 134 C5
Kingston upon Hull HU4 144 D5
7 North Cave HU15 53 D3
Belgrave Rd
Bridlington YO15 122 D1
1 Grimsby DN33 102 D1
Belgrave Sq 1 DN15 151 B7
Belgrave St YO31 130 C7
Belgravia 8 DN14 149 C4
Bell Cl Haxby YO32 127 C8
Kingston upon Hull HU7 141 D5
Bell Gn DN14 78 B2
Bell Hall★ YO19 36 E6
Bell La Cawood YO8 48 A7
Foggathorpe YO8 51 B7
Rawcliffe DN14 64 A2
Scunthorpe DN15 151 A6
Bellamy Ct HU9 146 C7
Bellasize La HU15 66 C6
Bellasize Pk HU15 66 D8
Bellbutts View 1 DN21 107 B3
Bellcroft La HU12 72 E4
Bellcroft Rd HU12 72 F5
Bellcross La
7 Howden DN14 65 B7
Kilpin DN14 65 C6
Belle Vue St YO10 130 E3
Belle Vue Terr
19 Thorne/Moorends DN8 93 A8
York YO10 130 E3
Belleisle Rd 12 DN34 102 B3
Bellfarm Ave YO31 130 E8
Bellfield Ave 5 HU8 142 A5
Bellfield Cty Prim Sch HU8 142 A4
Bellfield Dr HU10 138 D1
Bellground La YO30 12 D4
Bellguy Springs★ YO25 8 F8
Bellhouse Way YO24 132 B8
Bellingham Rd DN16 151 D3
Bellmans Croft YO23 132 B2
Bells Rd HU12 72 B7
Bellwin Dr DN15 82 A1
Bellwood Cres 7 DN8 93 A8
Bellwood Dr YO24 132 B8
Belmont DN36 114 A5
Belmont Cl
13 Cleethorpes DN35 103 B2
3 York YO30 127 A1
Belmont St
Kingston upon Hull HU9 146 D8
Scunthorpe DN16 151 A2
Belprin Rd HU17 137 B5
Belshaw La DN9 94 D1
Belt Rd The DN21 117 C2
Belthorn Rd 1 DN17 81 F1
Belthorpe La YO42 16 E1
Belton C of E Sch DN9 94 E2
Belton Cl 4 HU8 142 B5
Belton Fields DN9 94 D1
Belton Gr 7 DN33 102 D2
Belton Rd Belton DN9 95 A1
Epworth DN9 105 E7
Sandtoft DN9 94 B3
Belvedere Cres DN14 149 B6
Belvedere Dr
Kingston upon Hull HU11 142 D6
Scunthorpe DN17 150 E3
7 Thorne/Moorends DN8 79 B2
Belvedere Par YO15 11 B4
Belvedere Rd
Bridlington YO15 11 B4
Kingston upon Hull HU13 143 F2
Belvoir Ave 8 YO41 27 B2
Belvoir Rd DN35 103 B1
Belvoir St HU5 145 C8
Belwood Dr DN9 94 E2
Bempton Cl YO16 122 E6
Bempton Cliffs Nature Reserve★ YO15 4 D4
Bempton Cres YO16 122 E6
Bempton Cty Prim Sch YO15 4 C3
Bempton Dr YO16 122 E6
Bempton Gdns YO16 122 E6
Bempton Gr
Grimsby DN32 153 A1
Kingston upon Hull HU5 144 D8
Bempton La
Bempton YO16 4 B1
Bridlington YO16 122 D8
Bempton Oval YO16 122 E6
Bempton Sta YO16 4 C2
Bemrose Gr YO16 122 E5
Bemrose Way DN31 152 C4
Bence The YO42 17 C3
Benedict Ave YO8 148 E4
Benedict Cl 2 HU4 144 A2
Benedict Rd HU4 144 A2
Beningbrough La YO30 12 D5
Benjy La YO19 37 E7
Bennetland La HU15 66 C7
Bennett Dr DN15 83 A4
Bennett Rd
Cleethorpes DN35 153 D3
Scunthorpe DN16 151 C3
Benningholme La HU11 45 D2
Bennymoor La YO8 49 C4
Benson Ct LN11 121 C4
Bentley Ct HU3 145 A5
Bentley Gr HU6 139 F4
Bentley La DN38 110 E7
Bentley St DN35 153 E2
Berea The DN34 152 C1
Beresford Ave
Hornsea HU18 134 D2
Kingston upon Hull HU6 140 D4
Beresford Terr YO23 130 C1
Beretun Gn 11 DN18 84 E8
Bergen Way HU7 140 D6
Berkeley Dr
8 Beverley HU17 136 E1
32 Hedon HU12 72 D7
Berkeley Jun & Inf Sch DN15 150 D8
Berkeley Rd DN35 103 D1
Berkeley St
1 Kingston upon Hull HU3 145 D8
Scunthorpe DN15 150 F8
Berkeley Terr YO26 129 E5
Berkshire Cl 4 HU17 55 F8
Berkshire St HU8 141 C1
Bermondsey Dr HU5 144 E8
Bermuda Ave HU11 45 D2
Bernadette Ave HU4 144 B5
Berners Rd 15 DN35 103 D1
Berridge La DN14 78 A6
Berriman's La YO25 9 B3
Berryman Way HU13 144 A3
Berwick Ct 5 DN40 87 C1
Bessacarr Ave HU10 138 F1
Bessemer Way DN15 96 D7
Bessingby Gate YO16 122 A2
Bessingby Gr HU9 142 B2
Bessingby Hill YO16 122 B3
Bessingby Rd YO16 122 C2
Bessingby Way YO16 122 C1
Bestall Rd DN32 153 C2
Beswick C of E Sch YO25 32 D3
Beswick Hall★ YO25 32 D3
Beswick Heads YO25 32 C3
Beswick Rd YO25 32 E2
Bethell Ct 6 HU12 72 D7
Bethlehem St DN32 152 D3
Bethune Ave HU4 144 A3
Bethune Ave W HU13 144 A3
Bethune Park Prim Sch HU4 144 C3
Betony Cl 4 DN15 96 B7
Betteras Hill Rd LS25 61 A8
Betula Way DN17 150 C1
Between Dikes Rd YO8 63 F8
Between Rivers La DN14 78 E7
Beverley Balk YO41 15 B2
Beverley Cl DN36 114 A5
Beverley Coll HU18 134 C4
Beverley Coll of F Ed HU17 136 C5
Beverley Cres DN32 153 A1
Beverley Ct 11 DN41 101 F5
Beverley Dr HU17 136 D7
Beverley Gram Sch HU17 136 D2
Beverley High Sch HU17 154 A4
Beverley L Ctr HU17 154 C2
Beverley La YO43 41 E2
Beverley Minster★ HU17 154 B2
Beverley Parklands HU17 154 C1

Beverley Race Course
  HU17 ....136 B4
Beverley Rd
  Beeford YO25 ....22 D1
  Bishop Burton HU17 ....43 B2
  Great Driffield YO25 ..124 E2
  Hutton Cranswick YO25 ..20 E1
  Kingston upon Hull HU6 .140 B8
  Kingston upon Hull
    HU13 ....143 E3
  Kingston upon Hull HU3 .155 A4
  Kirkburn YO25 ....124 D1
  Leven HU17 ....45 A7
  Market Weighton YO43 .135 E4
  Middleton YO25 ....31 D4
  Newbald YO43 ....53 F8
  Skidby HU16 ....138 C7
  South Cave HU15 ....54 A2
  Watton YO25 ....32 D5
  Withernwick HU11 ......46 A3
Beverley Road Sch
  HU5 ....140 E1
Beverley St DN14 ......149 C2
Beverley Sta HU17 ....154 B3
Beverley Swimming Pool
  HU17 ....154 B4
Beverley Town Cricket &
Recn Club HU17 ....154 A4
Bewholme Gr
  4 Kingston upon Hull
    HU9 ....142 B1
  Kingston upon Hull HU9 .147 B8
Bewholme La
  Bewholme YO25 ....35 A8
  Seaton HU11 ....35 A2
  Skipsea YO25 ....23 A1
Bewholme Rd YO25 ......35 C5
Bewlay St YO23 ....130 C4
Bexhill Ave HU9 ....142 E2
Bibbill La YO42 ....39 B5
Bibury Cl HU8 ....141 B2
Bickerton Cl HU6 ......139 F7
Bickleigh Gr 1 HU8 ...142 C6
Bideford Gr HU9 ....142 E1
Bielby Dr HU17 ....137 B3
Bigby Gr DN17 ....96 C2
Bigby High Rd DN20 ....98 C1
Bigby Hill DN38 ....99 C1
Bigby Rd 15 DN20 ......98 C2
Bigby St DN20 ....98 C2
Biggin Ave HU7 ....141 C8
Biggin Hill Prim Sch
  HU7 ....141 C8
Billet La DN15 ....96 C8
Billet Mill App DN16 ..151 F3
Billet Mill Rd DN16 ...151 E5
Billinghay Ct 16 DN35 .103 C2
Billings La YO25 ....34 E5
Bilsdale Cl YO30 ......126 E1
Bilsdale Gr HU9 ....146 F8
Bilsdale Rd DN16 ......151 E1
Bilton Gr HU9 ....142 B2
Bilton Prim Sch HU11 ...142 C6
Bilton Rd HU11 ....142 D6
Binbrook Garth 4 HU7 ..57 A5
Binbrook Way 16 DN37 .102 C4
Birch Ave Brigg DN20 ..98 B3
  Grimsby DN34 ....152 A2
Birch Cl Beverley HU17 136 F6
  5 Bridlington YO16 ...123 A6
  7 Gilberdyke HU15 .....66 D7
  Kingston upon Hull HU4 144 C6
  4 Thorpe Willoughby YO8 .48 B1
Birch Dr HU10 ....138 E1
Birch Gr 16 DN21 ......117 B1
Birch La 13 YO32 ....13 E5
Birch Lea 3 HU17 ....55 B8
Birch Mews DN14 ......149 E6
Birch Tree Cl DN3 ......92 A4
Birch Way 4 DN38 ....99 B4
Bircham Cres 3 DN21 ..119 C8
Birchdale DN18 ....84 E7
Birches The
  5 Haxey DN9 ....105 B2
  Hornsea HU18 ....134 D2
Birchfield DN14 ....149 F6
Birchfield Rd 6 DN9 ...105 D6
Birchfield Road Cty Sch
  DN9 ....105 D6
Birchin Way DN31 .....152 B5
Birchwood Ave HU4 ....144 A7
Birchwood Cl 2 DN8 ....79 A1
Birchwood Rd DN16 ....151 B5
Bird La Hensall DN14 ...62 D2
  Kellington DN14 ....61 F4
Birdcroft La 3 DN10 ...116 D3
Birdforth Mews 5 HU5 .139 D3
Birds Wood Nature Reserve★
  DN9 ....104 F3
Birdsall Ave HU5 ......139 C1
Birdsall Cl HU16 ......138 E5
Birk La YO42 ....50 D8
Birkby Gr HU9 ....142 C2
Birkdale 14 DN37 ......113 D6
Birkdale Cl HU10 ......143 B8
Birkdale Dr 8 DN40 .....87 C2
Birkdale Gr YO26 ......129 E5
Birkdale Rd DN17 ....96 B2
Birkdale Way HU5 ......146 D8
Birker La
  Newton on Derwent YO41 27 D4
  Wilberfoss YO41 ......27 F6
Birkin La WF11 ....61 B4
Birkin Rd YO8 ....61 F5
Birklands DN18 ....141 E4
Birrel St 2 DN21 ......117 A1
Birstwith Dr YO26 .....129 E4

Birt Gr DN14 ....149 B6
Bishop Alcock Rd
  HU5 ....139 D3
Bishop Blunt Cl 2
  HU13 ....143 F1
Bishop Burton Coll
  Bishop Burton HU17 ...43 A3
  Broughton DN20 ....97 E3
  Great Driffield YO25 ..124 F4
Bishop Burton Rd
  HU17 ....43 A4
Bishop Ct
  9 Gilberdyke HU15 ....66 D8
  2 Selby YO8 ....148 B6
Bishop Gurdon Cl 4
  HU13 ....143 F1
Bishop Kempthorne Clo 3
  HU13 ....143 F1
Bishop La HU1 ....155 C2
Bishop La Staith HU1 ..155 C1
Bishop Temple Ct
  HU13 ....143 F3
Bishop Witton Sch
  YO42 ....16 F2
Bishopdike Rd YO8 ......48 A6
Bishopgate St YO23 ....156 B1
Bishophill Jun YO1 ....156 A1
Bishophill Senior YO1 .156 B1
Bishops Croft HU17 ....154 A2
Bishop's La LN8 ....120 A7
Bishop's Wlk DN34 ....152 C2
Bishopsway YO10 ......131 C3
Bishopthorpe Inf Sch
  YO23 ....133 A4
Bishopthorpe Palace★
  YO23 ....133 B4
Bishopthorpe Rd
  Bishopthorpe YO23 ...133 B5
  Cleethorpes DN35 ....103 C2
Bisley Dr HU17 ....141 A7
Bismarck St YO26 ......129 E5
Bittern Cl HU4 ....144 D2
Black Bank DN17 ......106 F6
Black Dike La YO26 .....24 F8
Black Fen La YO8 ......148 C8
Black Syke La DN14 .....78 C2
Black Tup La HU11 ......45 C3
Blackburn Ave
  Bridlington YO15 .....122 F3
  Brough HU15 ....68 C5
Blackburn La WF11 .....61 B2
Blackdykes Rd DN9 ....106 B4
Blackfriargate HU1 ....155 C1
Blackhope Cl 14 HU7 ...57 A6
Blacklee Cl 4 YO32 .....14 B8
Blackmoor Rd DN9 .....105 D2
Blacksmith Hill DN15 ...67 B4
Blacksmiths Cl 1 DN19 .85 C7
Blackthorn Cl
  8 Newport HU15 ....52 F1
  7 Scunthorpe DN15 .....96 B7
Blackthorn Ct 4 HU3 ..145 D6
Blackthorn Dr
  Healing DN37 ....102 A3
  York YO31 ....127 C2
Blackthorn La HU10 ....143 F7
Blackthorns The 3
  DN20 ....97 D4
Blacktoft La DN14 ......66 D3
Blackwater Way 27 HU7 .56 F6
Blackwood Cl YO8 ......49 F7
Blackwood Rd YO8 ......49 E8
Bladon Rd YO16 ....122 C6
Bladons Wlk HU10 .....143 C8
Blaides Staithe HU1 ...155 C2
Blake Ave DN17 ....150 E3
Blake Cl HU2 ....155 A4
Blake Ct YO19 ....38 E4
Blake St YO1 ....156 B3
Blakeley Gr YO30 ......126 F3
Blakeney Lea DN35 ....103 C1
Blakeney Pl YO10 ......130 F3
Bland La YO26 ....129 A4
Blandford Cl HU7 ......141 B6
Blands Hill LN8 ....120 A3
Blanket Row HU1 ......155 B1
Blankney Ct 13 DN15 ...83 A5
Blanshards La 1 HU15 ..53 D3
Blatchford YO30 ....130 B8
Blaycourt HU6 ....139 E6
Blaydes St HU6 ....140 C4
Blaydon Gr 1 DN34 ....102 C2
Bleaberry La HU15 ......65 B5
Blenheim Cl 15 DN7 ....92 D3
Blenheim Ct
  Rawcliffe YO30 ....126 D3
  Scunthorpe DN16 ......96 D1
Blenheim Dr DN14 .....149 E6
Blenheim Pl 4 DN35 ...103 C2
Blenheim Rd
  Beverley HU17 ....136 E1
  Bridlington YO16 .....122 E3
  5 Moorland Prison DN7 .104 A8
Blenheim St HU5 ......145 C8
Blenkin St HU9 ....146 B7
Bleriot Way YO30 ......127 A3
Blisland Cl 13 HU7 .....56 F5
Bloom Hill Gr
  16 Thorne/Moorends DN8 .79 B4
  7 Thorne/Moorends DN8 .79 B5
Bloom Mill App Rd
  DN16 ....97 A4
Bloomfield Ave HU5 ...144 C8
Bloomhill Cl 8 DN8 .....79 B2
Bloomhill Ct DN8 ....79 B2
Bloomhill Gr DN8 ....79 B2
Bloomhill Rd DN8 ....79 A2
Bloomsbury Ct 1 HU3 ..145 D6
Blossom Gr HU8 ....141 D8

Blossom St YO24 ......156 A1
Blossom Way 21 DN40 ..87 B1
Blossom's La HU15 ......53 C3
Blow Row DN9 ....105 E6
Blucher La HU17 ....154 C2
Blue Bridge La YO10 ..130 D2
Blue Slates Cl YO19 ....38 A8
Bluebeck Dr YO30 .....129 E8
Bluebell Cl DN15 ......151 C7
Bluebell Ct HU4 ....144 C4
Blueberry Cl YO25 .....124 E2
Blueberry Ct HU4 .....144 C4
Bluestone Bottoms
  HU17 ....55 A6
Bluestone La DN40 ......87 B1
Blundell Ave DN35 ....153 C4
Blundell Cl HU2 ....155 A4
Blyth Cl YO8 ....148 B5
Blyth Ct DN18 ....85 A8
Blyth St HU9 ....146 B7
Blythe Wlk 1 YO16 ....122 B4
Blythorpe HU6 ....139 F8
Blyton C of E Sch
  DN21 ....117 F6
Blyton Rd
  Gainsborough DN21 ...117 B2
  Laughton DN21 ....117 B8
Boardman La 6 YO25 ....34 C2
Boardman Pk 7 YO25 ....34 C2
Boatcliffe Rd YO14 ......3 C7
Boating Dyke Way 12
  DN8 ....93 A8
Boatswain Croft HU1 ..155 B1
Bodiam Way DN33 .....152 F4
Bodmin Cl DN17 ....150 D4
Bodmin Rd HU7 ....140 E8
Bog La YO24 ....132 B6
Bolam La YO16 ....4 C2
Boldron Mews 7 HU5 ..139 D3
Bolingbroke Rd
  Cleethorpes DN35 ....103 D2
  Scunthorpe DN17 ......96 C2
Bolsover Rd DN15 .....150 B6
Bolt The 3 YO16 ......122 D4
Boltby Mews HU5 ......139 E3
Boltby Rd YO30 ....126 F2
Bolton La
  Bishop Wilton YO42 ...16 E1
  Wilberfoss YO41 ......28 A5
Bomber Cty Aviation Mus★
  DN21 ....119 D1
Bon Accord Rd HU13 ..143 E1
Bonby Gr
  11 Grimsby DN33 .....102 D2
  Scunthorpe DN17 ....150 F1
Bonby La YO8 ....37 E2
Bonby Rd DN20 ....84 C1
Bond St Hedon HU12 ....72 D7
  Kingston upon Hull HU1 155 B3
Bondane HU6 ....139 E7
Bondgate 18 DN7 ......148 B7
Bonington Ct 7 YO26 ..129 E4
Bonnyhale Rd DN17 .....94 E6
Bontoft Ave HU5 ......139 E1
Booth Ferry Rd HU4 ....64 F6
Booth Nooking La
  DN15 ....68 A3
Bootham YO30 ....156 A3
Bootham Bar★ YO31 ....156 B3
Bootham Cl 1 DN7 ......92 D4
Bootham Cres
  Stainforth DN7 ....92 C6
  York YO30 ....156 A4
Bootham La
  Hatfield DN7 ....92 D5
  Stainforth DN7 ....92 D6
Bootham Park Hospl
  YO31 ....156 B4
Bootham Rd 12 DN7 ....92 C6
Bootham Row YO31 ....156 B3
Bootham Sch YO31 ....156 A3
Bootham Sq YO31 .....156 B3
Bootham Terr YO30 ....156 A3
Boothferry Prim Sch
  DN14 ....149 B4
Boothferry Rd
  Airmyn DN14 ....149 A8
  Hessle HU13 ....143 B2
Boothferry Rd Ave 14
  DN14 ....65 A7
Boothgate DN14 ....65 A6
Boothgate Cl DN14 .....65 A6
Boothgate Dr DN14 .....65 A6
Boothwood Rd YO30 ...126 E2
Booty La DN14 ....93 A7
Bore Tree Baulk YO19 ..26 D6
Borman's La 3 DN36 ....11 A1
Borough Rd YO16 ......122 C3
Boroughbridge Rd
  YO26 ....129 D5
Borrowdale HU7 ....140 F6
Borrowdale Dr YO30 ...126 E1
Borthwick Cl 3 HU7 ....57 A6
Bos App Rd DN16 ....151 F3
Bossall Hall★ YO60 .....15 D7
Bossington Cl 10 HU7 ..57 A5
Boston Cl 6 DN15 ......83 A5
Boston Rd 20 HU7 ......56 F5
Bosworth St 16 DN17 ...92 D3
Botany Bay DN3 ....92 B4
Bothwell Gr HU9 ......147 D8
Bottesford Ave DN16 ...151 B1
Bottesford Inf Sch
  DN16 ....96 D2

Bottesford La DN16 ....151 B1
Bottesford Town Football &
Cricket Club DN17 ......96 B2
Bottlings The 9 DN20 ..98 C2
Boughton Ave DN15 ...150 F8
Boulevard HU3 ....145 B5
Boulevard Ave DN31 ..152 B4
Boulsworth Ave HU6 ..140 C7
Boulton Gr HU9 ....141 E2
Boundary Rd
  Bridlington YO15 .....122 C1
  Grimsby DN33 ....113 C8
Bourn Mill Balk Rd
  DN14 ....78 B8
Bourne St HU2 ....155 B3
Bournemouth St HU5 ..140 E2
Bournville DN14 ......149 C5
Bouthwaite Dr 18 YO26 129 E4
Bow Rd HU15 ....68 E6
Bow St YO15 ....122 D1
Bowers Ave DN34 .....152 B3
Bowes Ave YO31 ......130 E5
Bowfield Cl 9 DN37 ...102 B4
Bowlalley La HU1 .....155 B2
Bowland La YO42 ....38 E2
Bowland Way YO30 ...127 A1
Bowling Green Ct
  YO31 ....130 D8
Bowling Green La
  4 Crowle DN17 ....94 D8
  Grimsby DN32 ....152 E3
  9 Hunmanby YO14 ......2 F8
  York YO31 ....156 C4
Bowling Green Rd 4
  DN21 ....117 A1
Bowling La DN35 ......153 E2
Bowman Way 26 DN40 ..87 B1
Bowmandale DN18 ......84 E8
Bowmandale Prim Sch
  DN18 ....84 E8
Bowness Dr YO30 .....126 E1
Bownhill La HU17 ......59 A2
Bowthorpe La YO8 ......50 B4
Bowyers Cl YO23 .....132 C4
Boyes Ave HU12 ....73 C4
Boynton Ave YO16 ....122 B4
Boynton Cres 4 DN15 ...83 A5
Boynton La DN14 ....64 A1
Boynton Sch YO16 ......10 E7
Boynton St 1 HU3 .....145 C4
Brabbs Ave 2 DN7 ......92 A4
Bracken Cl
  Gainsborough DN21 ...117 A2
  York YO32 ....127 D3
Bracken Heen Cl 4 DN7 .92 D4
Bracken Hill
  Skirlaugh HU11 ....45 A3
  2 York YO31 ....131 C3
Bracken La YO25 ....32 A5
Bracken Pk 20 DN33 ...113 E8
Bracken Pl 4 DN37 ....102 B3
Bracken Rd
  Great Driffield YO25 ..124 D3
  York YO24 ....132 C4
Brackendale 1 DN14 ...141 B4
Brackendale Ave YO8 ..148 A4
Brackenhill La YO8 ....148 A3
Brackenhill La DN9 ....105 E2
Brackenhills YO26 ......12 F1
Brackenholmes Rd
  DN15 ....83 A2
Brackley Cl 3 HU7 ....141 B2
Bracon DN9 ....94 F2
Bracon Cl DN9 ....94 F2
Bradford Ave
  Cleethorpes DN35 ....103 C2
  Kingston upon Hull HU9 142 E2
Bradford Rd 20 DN40 ...87 B1
Bradley Cres DN37 .....24 D6
Bradley Dr YO24 ......132 C8
Bradley La YO23 ....24 C5
Bradley Rd 12 DN7 ....102 C1
Bradley St DN32 ......152 E4
Bradman St 3 DN34 ...153 A5
Bradwell Cl 3 DN18 ....84 E8
Braemar Ave HU6 .....140 B6
Braemar Ct YO25 ....34 C8
Braemar Rd DN35 .....103 C2
Braeside Gdns YO24 ..129 C3
Braeton La 5 DN33 ....113 F8
Braids Wlk YO10 ......143 B8
Brailsford Cres YO30 .130 A8
Braithegayte YO19 .....37 F8
Braithwaite La DN7 ....92 A7
Bramar Rd 26 DN7 ......92 D4
Bramble Dene YO24 ...132 D7
Bramble Garth 4 HU17 136 F7
Bramble Hill HU17 ....136 E1
Bramble Way 15 DN35 .103 C1
Brambles 8 DN8 ....48 B1
Brambles The 2 DN19 ..85 C8
Bramhall St DN35 .....153 C3
Bramham Ave YO26 ...129 A3
Bramham Gr YO26 .....129 A3
Bramham Rd YO26 .....129 A2
Bramley Ave YO8 ....49 B6
Bramley Cres 8 DN16 ..96 D1
Bramley Cl 5 DN21 ....117 C1
Bramley Garth YO31 ...131 B6
Bramley Gr 6 DN21 ....107 C3
Brampton Way DN35 ..103 C2
Bramwith La DN7 ....92 A6

Brandesburton CP Sch
  YO25 ....34 B2
Brandesburton Hospl
  YO25 ....34 B2
Brandesburton St
  HU3 ....145 B7
Brandon Ct 4 HU8 ....141 C1
Brandon Gr YO32 .....128 E3
Brandon Rd DN15 .....150 D6
Brandon Way 24 HU7 ...56 F6
Brandsby Gr
  Kingston upon Hull HU9 142 E3
  York YO31 ....127 E2
Brandsdale Cres
  YO10 ....131 D3
Brankwell Cres 21 DN17 96 C2
Bransdale Gr HU9 .....146 F8
Bransdale Rd DN16 ....151 D1
Bransholme Dr YO30 ..127 A2
Bransholme Rd HU7 ....57 B5
Brant Rd DN15 ....150 E6
Brantingham Cl 5
  HU16 ....138 E6
Brantingham Rd HU15 ..68 C7
Brantingham Wlk
  HU5 ....139 C3
Branton Pl YO26 ......129 A3
Brats La LN8 ....120 B5
Bratt La YO42 ....29 E3
Bravener Ct YO30 ......12 B6
Bray Gate YO42 ....16 E2
Bray Rd YO10 ....133 F8
Brayton C of E Prim Sch
  YO8 ....148 A2
Brayton Cty Inf Sch
  YO8 ....148 A2
Brayton Cty Jun Sch
  YO8 ....148 A2
Brayton High Sch
  YO8 ....148 A1
Brayton La YO8 ....148 B1
Brazil St HU9 ....146 C8
Breamer La HU11 ....35 A2
Breary Cl YO24 ....129 F1
Breck La HU15 ....53 B3
Brecks La
  Kirk Sandall DN3 ......92 A3
  Strensall YO32 ....14 B7
  York YO32 ....127 F4
Brecksfield YO30 ......126 C5
Breckstreet La YO42 ...39 C3
Brecon Dr 22 HU7 ......56 F6
Brecon St HU8 ....141 B1
Breeze La YO25 ....22 D1
Breezemount Ct 4 DN7 .92 C6
Breighton Rd
  Bubwith YO8 ....50 D6
  Wressle YO8 ....50 C3
Bremerhaven Way 24
  DN33 ....102 C2
Brendon Ave HU8 .....141 B3
Brent Ave HU8 ....142 B6
Brentwood Cl HU15 .....68 B6
Brentwood Cres YO10 .131 C2
Brereton Ave DN35 ....153 C4
Brereton Cl HU17 .....136 E6
Bretherdale HU7 ......140 F6
Brethergate DN9 ......105 B2
Brett St DN14 ....149 F5
Bretton Ave DN14 .....149 F5
Bretton Cl 5 DN7 ......92 C3
Brewery Gdns DN17 ....94 D8
Brewery Rd DN17 ......94 D8
Brewster Ave 17 DN40 ..87 C1
Breydon Ct 4 DN15 ....82 B4
Brian Ave
  Cleethorpes DN35 ....103 B2
  Scunthorpe DN16 .....151 C1
  Waltham DN37 ....113 D6
Briar Ave YO26 ......129 B4
Briar Cl 4 Newport HU15 52 F1
  South Killingholme DN40 .86 F3
Briar Cliffe YO8 ......148 A3
Briar Dr YO31 ....127 F2
Briar Garth YO25 .....124 D3
Briar La
  4 Grimsby DN33 ......113 D8
  Healing DN41 ....101 A3
Briar Way DN15 ....96 B7
Briars The HU13 ......143 E3
Briarfield Rd HU5 .....139 F2
Briars La DN7 ....92 C7
Briars The HU13 ......143 E3
Briarsfield YO42 ....28 D4
Briarwood YO8 ....61 F7
Brick Dike La HU20 ....54 C5
Brick Kiln Balk YO16 .122 A1
Brick Kiln La YO8 ......62 D6
Brick La DN40 ....86 E5
Brick Lands La YO8 .....62 F4
Brick Rd HU12 ....88 F4
Brickenhole La DN10 ..116 C3
Brickhill La YO8 ....63 F4
Bricknell Ave HU5 ....139 E3
Bricknell Ave Sch
  HU5 ....139 F2
Bricknell Prim Sch
  HU5 ....139 F2
Brickyard La
  Melton HU14 ....68 F4
  Walkeringham DN10 ..116 B3
  Wrawby DN20 ....98 C3
Bridge Cl Haxby YO32 .127 C7
  Kingston upon Hull HU9 142 D6
Bridge Cres DN14 ......64 C8
Bridge Gdns DN31 .....152 A5
Bridge Hill DN7 ....92 C6
Bridge La Cadney DN20 109 C6
  5 Great Driffield YO25 124 F4
  Horkstow DN18 ....83 F5
  Pollington DN14 ....77 F6
  Rawcliffe DN14 ....79 B8

Bridge La continued
  York YO30 ....**156** B4
Bridge Rd Airmyn DN14 ..**149** A8
  Bishopthorpe YO23 .....**132** F3
  Broughton DN20 ....**97** F5
  South Cave HU15 ....**53** F1
Bridge St
 7 Bridlington YO15 .....**122** E2
 11 Brigg DN20 ....**98** B2
  Goole DN14 ....**149** C3
  Great Driffield YO25 ....**124** E4
  Pocklington YO42 ....**29** A4
  Thorne/Moorends DN8 ..**93** A8
  York YO1 ....**156** B2
Bridgegate DN14 ....**65** A7
Bridgegate Dr HU9 ....**146** C6
Bridges Ct YO8 ....**148** D6
Bridges La YO42 ....**38** E4
Bridges Rd DN17 ....**150** E3
Bridges The DN18 ....**84** F8
Bridgeview Sch HU13 ..**143** D1
Bridgewater Rd DN17 ..**150** D4
Bridle Way **1** YO26 ....**129** A3
Bridle Wlk YO8 ....**148** C4
Bridlington & District Hospl
  YO16 ....**122** B3
Bridlington Ave HU2 ...**155** B4
Bridlington Balk YO25 ..**34** A8
Bridlington Bay Rd
  YO16 ....**10** E4
Bridlington Harbour
  Museum★ YO15 ....**122** F2
Bridlington Leisure World★
  YO15 ....**122** F2
Bridlington New Pasture
  Lane Prim Sch YO16 ..**122** B5
Bridlington Rd
  Barmston YO25 ....**22** F6
  Brandesburton YO25 ....**34** C3
  Driffield YO25 ....**125** A5
  Flamborough YO15 ......**4** F1
  Hunmanby YO14 ....**3** A7
  Sledmere YO25 ....**7** C4
 1 Stamford Bridge YO41 ..**15** D2
  Ulrome YO25 ....**23** A4
  Wold Newton YO25 ......**2** A4
Bridlington RUFC
  YO16 ....**122** D3
Bridlington Sch YO16 ..**122** D3
Bridlington Sports Ctr
  YO16 ....**122** B4
Bridlington St YO14 ......**2** F8
Bridlington Sta YO15 ...**122** D2
Bridlington Town Football
  Club YO16 ....**122** E4
Bridport Cl HU7 ....**141** C7
Brier La YO8 ....**64** A4
Briergate YO32 ....**127** C7
Brierholme Carr Rd
  DN7 ....**92** F5
Brierholme Cl DN7 ......**92** F5
Brierholme Ings Rd
  DN7 ....**92** F5
Brierley Cl **10** DN14 ....**65** A7
Brigg Cty Prim Sch
  DN20 ....**98** C2
Brigg Dr HU13 ....**143** F3
Brigg La YO8 ....**63** D5
Brigg Prep Sch DN20 ...**98** C1
Brigg Rd
  Barton-upon-Humber
   DN18 ....**84** E5
  Broughton DN20 ....**97** F3
  Cadney DN20 ....**109** C7
  Grasby LN7 ....**111** A6
  Hibaldstow DN20 ......**108** F6
  Messingham DN17 ......**107** D7
  North Kelsey LN7 ......**110** A5
  Scunthorpe DN15 ......**151** C7
  South Kelsey LN7 ......**110** A1
  Wrawby DN20 ....**98** D3
Brigg Sta DN20 ....**98** C1
Brigg Town Football Club
  DN20 ....**98** C2
Briggate Dr DN17 ......**107** D7
Briggs St YO31 ....**130** C7
Brigham Gr HU9 ....**142** B1
Brigham La YO25 ....**21** E1
Brighowgate DN34 .....**152** D2
Bright Cres **7** YO15 ...**122** F3
Bright St
  Kingston upon Hull HU8 ..**146** B8
  York YO15 ....**129** F5
Brighton St HU3 ....**145** A3
Brigsley Rd DN37 ....**113** D6
Brimington Rd HU10 ...**138** F7
Brimley HU17 ....**136** C5
Brind La DN14 ....**50** F2
Brindlegate **4** YO42 ....**29** A4
Brindley St HU9 ....**141** E2
Brindleys La DN14 ......**50** F3
Brinkworth Terr **1**
  YO10 ....**130** E3
Brisbane St HU3 ....**145** D5
Bristol Rd
  Kingston upon Hull HU5 ..**144** C8
  Scunthorpe DN17 ......**150** E3
Britannia Cres **7** DN34 ..**102** B3
Britannia Gdns **7** HU5 ..**140** E2
Britannia Rd DN14 .....**149** A2
Britannia Way DN14 ...**149** B3
Britton Cl DN17 ....**81** D3
Brixham Ct
 5 Kingston upon Hull
   HU3 ....**145** A5

Brixham Ct continued
  Waltham DN33 ....**113** E7
Brixton Cl HU8 ....**141** E5
Broach La Heck DN14 ....**62** D1
  Kellington DN14 ....**61** F3
Broach Rd Heck DN14 ....**77** D8
  Hensall DN14 ....**62** C1
Broad Acres YO32 ......**127** C7
Broad Balk YO17 ....**6** A5
Broad Highway YO19 ....**37** F8
Broad La
  Appleton Roebuck YO23 ..**36** A6
 6 Beal DN14 ....**61** D4
  Catton YO41 ....**27** C7
  Cawood YO8 ....**48** A6
  Gilberdyke HU15 ....**66** C8
  Howden DN14 ....**65** B6
  Rufforth YO23 ....**129** A3
  Sykehouse DN14 ....**78** B4
  Wistow YO8 ....**48** A5
Broad La Cl **5** HU16 ...**139** B7
Broad Manor YO42 ......**29** A3
Broad Oak
  Kingston upon Hull
   HU11 ....**142** D6
  Sutton-on-the-Forest
   YO61 ....**13** D8
Broad Oak La **18** YO32 ..**13** E5
Broadacre Pk **1** HU15 ..**68** D5
Broadacre Prim Sch
  HU7 ....**56** F6
Broadacres
  Carlton DN14 ....**63** D3
  Keyingham HU12 ....**73** D4
Broadacres Ave DN14 ...**63** D3
Broadacres Garth
  DN14 ....**63** D3
Broadbent Gate Rd
  DN8 ....**79** B1
Broadgate DN17 ....**136** B1
Broadland Dr **4** HU9 ...**142** A3
Broadlands YO19 ....**38** A8
Broadlands Cl **38** DN7 ..**92** A3
Broadley Ave HU10 .....**143** D6
Broadley Cl **6** HU9 ....**146** C7
Broadley Croft **3** HU15 ..**68** D5
Broadley Way HU15 .....**68** D5
Broadmanor
  North Duffield YO8 ....**50** A7
  Pocklington YO42 ....**29** A3
Broadstairs Cl **1** HU8 ..**141** E7
Broadstone Cl HU7 .....**141** C6
Broadstone Way YO30 ..**126** E3
Broadwater Dr **34** DN7 ..**92** C4
Broadway Goole DN14 ..**149** D4
 5 Grimsby DN34 ....**102** B2
  Hatfield DN7 ....**92** C3
  Hornsea HU18 ....**134** D4
 7 Keelby DN41 ....**101** A5
  York YO10 ....**133** E8
Broadway Dr **3** HU9 ...**142** A3
Broadway Gr **3** YO10 ..**133** E8
Broadway Nook DN7 ....**92** C3
Broadway The **6** HU9 ..**142** A3
Broadway W YO10 ......**133** D8
Brock Cl **1** DN33 ......**102** E1
Brockenhurst Ave
  HU16 ....**139** D6
Brockenhurst Rd **7** DN7 ..**92** E4
Brockfield Pk Dr YO31 ..**127** F2
Brockfield Rd YO31 ....**127** E2
Brockle Bank Ct **9** HU12 ..58 C1
Brocklesby Cl **5** HU13 ..**144** A3
Brocklesby Park Sch
  DN41 ....**100** E4
Brocklesby Pl **11** DN34 ..**102** C2
Brocklesby Rd
 10 Grimsby DN34 ......**102** C2
  Scunthorpe DN17 ......**150** F1
  Ulceby DN39 ....**100** B8
Brockley Cl HU8 ....**141** E6
Brockton Cl HU3 ....**144** F5
Broc-o-Bank **1** DN6 ....**76** E2
Bromley St
  Kingston upon Hull HU2 ..**155** B4
 2 York YO26 ....**129** F5
Brompton Cl HU5 ......**139** E2
Brompton Ct **4** HU3 ...**140** D1
Brompton Rd YO30 ....**130** A7
Bromwich Rd HU10 ....**143** D6
Bronzegarth DN32 .....**153** B1
Brook St
  Great Driffield YO25 ....**124** F4
  Hemswell DN21 ....**119** A2
  Kingston upon Hull HU2 ..**155** A3
  Selby YO8 ....**148** C4
  York YO31 ....**156** B4
Brookdale Rd DN17 .....**150** D2
Brooke Dr HU18 ....**134** C2
Brooke St DN8 ....**93** A8
Brookfield Cl
  Carnaby YO16 ....**10** E4
 1 Kingston upon Hull HU7 ..**56** F5
 8 Thorne/Moorends DN8 ..**93** A8
Brookfield Rd DN33 ....**102** D1
Brookland Rd YO16 ....**122** C4
Brooklands
 2 Broughton DN20 ......**97** E3
  York YO10 ....**131** D4
Brooklands Ave
  Broughton DN20 ....**97** D4
  Cleethorpes DN35 .....**103** D3
Brooklands Cl HU17 ...**137** A6
Brooklands Pk HU16 ...**139** A5
Brooklands Rd HU5 ....**144** E8
Brooklyn Dr DN36 .....**114** D8
Brooklyn St HU5 ....**140** D3

Brookside **2** HU15 ....**68** D6
Brookside Cl YO42 ....**28** D3
Brookside DN16 ....**151** B4
Broome Cl YO32 ....**127** F5
Broome Way YO32 ......**128** A5
Broomfield Way YO25 ...**23** A6
Broomfleet Carr La
  HU15 ....**67** B7
Broomfleet Sta HU15 ....**67** B6
Broomhead Cl **5** HU7 ..**141** E7
Broomhill Cl **23** WF11 ...**61** A2
Broomhill Cres **25** WF11 ..**61** A2
Broomhill Dr **26** WF11 ...**61** A2
Broomhill Gr **19** WF11 ...**61** A2
Broomhill Pl **22** WF11 ...**61** A2
Broomhill Sq **24** WF11 ...**61** A2
Broomhill Wlk **21** WF11 ..**61** A2
Broompark Rd DN14 ...**149** E6
Broomston La DN9 .....**104** F1
Brosley Ave DN3 ....**92** A4
Brough County Prim Sch
  HU15 ....**68** C7
Brough Cty Prim Sch
  HU15 ....**68** C6
Brough Rd HU15 ....**54** A1
Brough St DN14 ....**149** D5
Brougham Cl YO30 .....**129** F8
Brougham St HU3 ......**144** F7
Broughton **3** HU7 ......**142** A3
Broughton Inf Sch
  DN20 ....**97** E3
Broughton Jun Sch
  DN20 ....**97** E3
Broughton Way YO10 ..**131** B4
Brow La HU17 ....**65** E7
Brown Cow Rd YO8 ......**63** C8
Brown Moor **22** YO41 ...**15** D2
Browney Croft YO1 ....**156** C1
Browning Cl
 3 Kingston upon Hull
   HU3 ....**145** D8
  Scunthorpe DN17 ......**150** E2
Browning Rd **20** YO42 ...**29** A3
Brownlow St YO31 .....**156** C4
Brownmoor La YO61 .....**13** B8
Browns La **15** DN8 ....**93** A8
Browns Orch DN32 .....**152** D2
Bruce Cl **6** DN20 ....**97** D3
Bruce St DN15 ....**150** F7
Brumby Comm La
  DN17 ....**150** C3
Brumby Common Nature
  Reserve★ DN17 ......**150** C3
Brumby Comp Sch
  DN16 ....**151** B5
Brumby Hall★ DN17 ...**150** F3
Brumby Hospl DN16 ...**151** C4
Brumby House Dr
  DN16 ....**151** A4
Brumby Jun Sch
  DN16 ....**151** B4
Brumby Wood La
  DN15 ....**150** D6
Brumby's Terr **4** HU9 ..**146** D7
Brunel Cl **4** HU5 ....**96** D2
Brunel Ct **12** YO26 .....**129** F5
Brunslow Cl HU3 ....**144** E5
Brunswick Ave HU2 ....**155** A4
Brunswick Cl **2** YO32 ...**14** C8
Brunswick Gr **5** HU13 ..**143** C4
Brunswick St YO23 ....**130** B1
Brunton Way DN36 ....**114** A7
Bryan Mere **3** HU17 ....**43** A2
Bryony Cl YO8 ....**148** B2
Bubwith Cty Prim Sch
  YO8 ....**50** D7
Buccaneer Way **16** HU15 ..68 C5
Buck Beck Way **12**
  DN36 ....**103** B1
Buckingham Ave DN15 ..**96** C7
Buckingham Prim Sch
  HU8 ....**141** C1
Buckingham St
 5 Kingston upon Hull
   HU8 ....**141** C1
  York YO1 ....**156** B1
Buckingham St N
  DN15 ....**150** F8
Buckingham St S
  DN15 ....**150** F8
Buckland Cl **3** HU8 ....**142** C7
Buckle Ct YO8 ....**148** B7
Buckton Gate YO15 ......**4** C3
Buddleia Cl DN41 ......**101** F5
Bude Cl **2** DN36 ....**114** A8
Bude Park Prim Sch
  HU7 ....**56** F5
Bude Rd HU7 ....**140** F8
Bugthorpe YO41 ....**16** D5
  Kirby Underdale YO41 ....**16** F5
Bugthorpe La Town E
  YO41 ....**16** E5
Bull Alley La DN14 ......**63** B3
Bull Balk YO41 ....**27** E4
Bull Bank LN11 ....**121** F7
Bull La Everingham YO42 ..**40** C4
  Huby YO61 ....**13** B7
  York YO1 ....**130** F3
Bull Moor La YO60 ......**15** A8
Bull Moor Rd DN7 ....**93** A4
Bull Pasture HU15 ......**53** F1
Buller St Grimsby DN32 ..**153** A3
  Selby YO8 ....**148** B6
Bullfinch La **5** DN35 ...**103** C1
Bullivant Rd DN7 ....**92** E4
Bulmer La YO43 ....**51** E8

Bulwick Ave DN33 .....**113** E8
Bunkers Hill DN21 .....**119** B1
Bunkers Hill Cl **11** DN36 ..114 D4
Burbage Ave HU8 ......**141** C4
Burcom Ave **7** DN36 ...**114** D8
Burcott Garth HU4 .....**144** B3
Burdale Cl
  Great Driffield YO25 ....**124** D3
  Kingston upon Hull HU9 ..**142** B3
Burden Cl HU17 ....**154** C4
Burden Rd HU17 ....**154** C4
Burden St HU1 ....**155** A2
Burdike Ave YO30 ......**130** A8
Burdock Rd DN16 ....**96** E2
Burdyke Inf Sch YO30 ..**130** B8
Burgar Rd DN8 ....**93** A7
Burgate
 4 Barton-upon-Humber
   DN18 ....**84** F8
  North Newbald YO43 ....**53** F7
Burgess Rd DN20 ....**98** C2
Burghley Cl LN7 ....**111** A3
Burghley Rd DN16 .....**151** D4
Burke St DN15 ....**151** A8
Burke St N DN15 ......**151** A8
Burlands La YO26 ....**24** F7
Burleigh St HU8 ....**146** C8
Burley Ave **18** DN35 ...**103** C2
Burlington Ave YO10 ...**130** F4
Burlington Cres DN14 ..**149** C4
Burlington Cty Jun Sch
  YO16 ....**122** D5
Burlington Gdns YO16 ..**122** D3
Burlington Rd HU8 .....**141** D5
Burlyn Rd **3** YO14 ......**3** A8
Burma Dr HU9 ....**147** B8
Burma Rd DN16 ....**151** F6
Burn Hall Cl YO8 ....**62** D7
Burn La YO8 ....**62** D6
Burn Rd DN15 ....**150** C7
Burnaby Cl HU17 ......**136** E6
Burnbutts La
  Hutton Cranswick YO25 ..**32** C3
  Watton YO25 ....**32** B6
Burnby Cl HU5 ....**139** C2
Burnby Hall Gdns★
  YO42 ....**29** A3
Burnby La YO42 ....**29** A3
Burnet Dr **12** DN16 .....**96** E2
Burnett's Yd LN7 ......**111** C4
Burney Cl HU17 ....**154** A4
Burnham Ave **4** HU12 ..**73** A6
Burnham La DN39 ....**85** E4
Burnham Rd
  Barton-upon-Humber
   DN18 ....**85** A6
  Epworth DN9 ....**105** E6
  Kingston upon Hull HU4 ..**144** B3
  Owston Ferry DN9 .....**106** A3
  Scunthorpe DN15 ......**150** D6
Burnham Reach **28**
  DN35 ....**103** C1
Burnham Sq DN35 .....**106** A3
Burnholme Ave YO31 ..**131** B6
Burnholme Com Coll
  YO31 ....**131** A5
Burnholme Dr YO31 ...**131** A6
Burnholme Gr YO31 ...**131** A5
Burniston Gr YO10 ....**131** A4
Burniston Rd HU5 .....**139** E2
Burns Cl **2** YO42 ....**28** E4
Burns Ct YO24 ....**132** B7
Burns Gr **31** DN33 ....**102** D2
Burns St DN21 ....**117** A1
Burnsall Dr YO26 .....**129** E4
Burnsalls Rd **5** HU12 ...**72** C7
Burnside DN20 ....**97** D3
Burrill Ave YO30 ......**130** B8
Burrill Dr **13** YO32 ......**13** D5
Burrill La HU15 ....**68** B8
Burrill Mews **2** HU5 ...**139** E3
Burringham Rd DN17 ..**150** B1
Burrs The HU15 ....**68** B5
Bursall Sq HU12 ....**89** C8
Bursar Prim Sch
  DN35 ....**153** E2
Bursar St DN35 ....**153** E2
Bursea La YO43 ....**52** A5
Burslem St HU2 ....**155** A4
Burstall Hill DN15 ....**122** B5
Burstall La HU12 ....**90** C5
Burstwick Prim Sch
  HU12 ....**73** B6
Burton Agnes Balk YO25 ..**9** F5
Burton Agnes Hall★
  YO25 ....**10** A2
Burton Agnes Sch
  YO25 ....**10** A1
Burton Ave YO30 ......**130** B7
Burton Comm La LS25 ..**61** A6
Burton Constable Hall★
  HU11 ....**58** C7
Burton Fields Cl YO41 ..15 D2
Burton Fields Rd **4**
  YO41 ....**15** D2
Burton Fleming Rd
  Rudston YO25 ....**9** F8
  Wold Newton YO25 ......**2** B3
Burton Gates HU17 .....**55** B8
Burton Gn YO30 ......**130** B8
Burton La HU18 ....**134** C2
Burton Pidsea Prim Sch
  HU12 ....**59** D2
Burton Rd
  Beverley HU17 ....**136** C6
  Flixborough DN15 ....**82** B2
  Hornsea HU18 ....**134** D4
  Kilham YO25 ....**9** C3

Burton Rd continued
  Kingston upon Hull
   HU16 ....**138** F5
  Roos HU12 ....**59** F2
Burton Stone La YO30 ..**156** A4
Burton upon Stather Cty
  Prim Sch DN15 ....**82** B4
Burtree Ave YO30 .....**126** B4
Burwell Dr DN33 ......**102** D2
Bush Cl HU4 ....**144** D3
Bushfield Rd DN16 ....**151** B5
Bushfield Rd Inf Sch
  DN16 ....**151** A5
Butcher La DN14 ....**77** A6
Butcher Row HU17 ....**154** A3
Butcher Terr YO23 ....**130** C1
Butcher's La
  Burton Fleming YO25 .....**2** E3
  Withernwick HU11 ......**46** D3
Butchers Row HU11 .....**35** A1
Butforth La DN19 ....**85** E8
Butler Pl DN35 ....**153** B3
Butlers La **23** YO15 ......**5** A2
Butt Balk YO25 ....**9** E1
Butt Fields La DN14 .....**62** F1
Butt Hedge YO26 ....**24** A5
Butt Hill **22** Haxby YO32 ..**13** D5
  Leconfield HU17 ....**43** D6
Butt Hills★ Riston HU11 ..**45** C5
  Routh HU17 ....**44** F5
  Wold Newton YO25 ......**2** A3
Butt La Beverley HU17 ..**154** A1
  Laceby DN37 ....**101** F2
  North Cave HU15 ....**53** E3
  Nunburnholme YO42 ....**29** E3
  Snaith DN14 ....**78** C8
  Thwing YO25 ....**9** A8
  Tickton HU17 ....**137** F8
  Warter YO42 ....**30** A1
  Wold Newton YO25 ......**2** A3
Buttacre La YO23 ....**24** D2
Butter Mkt
 10 Caistor LN7 ....**111** B4
 8 Snaith DN14 ....**63** C1
Buttercrambe Rd YO41 ..**15** A3
Buttercross Cl **3** DN41 ..**101** E6
Buttercup Cl **1** HU9 ...**146** D7
Butterfield Cl
 2 Laceby DN37 ....**101** F1
  Snaith DN14 ....**78** D8
Butterfly Gdns★
  DN35 ....**103** D2
Butterfly La YO16 ....**10** F5
Butterfly Mdws HU17 ..**136** E6
Buttermere Cres **3**
  DN36 ....**114** C8
Buttermere Ct **9** YO8 ..**148** B6
Buttermere Dr YO30 ...**126** E1
Buttermere Rd DN14 ..**149** D5
Buttermere Way DN32 ..**152** D4
Butters St **20** YO32 ......**13** D5
Butterwick Cl **28** DN35 ..**103** C2
Butterwick Rd
  Foxholes YO17 ....**1** B1
  Langtoft YO25 ....**8** C7
  Messingham DN17 ......**107** A7
Buttfield La DN14 ....**65** A6
Buttfield Rd
  Howden DN14 ....**65** A6
  Kingston upon Hull
   HU13 ....**143** E1
Buttle La **3** DN14 ....**63** C1
Butts Cl
  Bridlington YO16 ....**122** D4
 19 Stamford Bridge YO41 ..**15** D2
Butts Hill YO14 ....**3** C6
Butts La YO25 ....**19** E2
Butts Rd DN18 ....**69** E1
Butts The HU20 ....**55** A4
Byass Ave DN14 ....**122** E4
Bycroft Rd DN21 ......**117** B3
Bydales La HU12 ....**74** B3
Byedales **4** YO15 ....**4** D3
Byfield Rd DN17 ....**150** D2
Bygot Cl **1** HU17 ....**43** D6
Byland Ave YO31 ......**130** E8
Byland Ct **4** HU9 ......**146** E8
Byram Park Rd WF11 ...**61** A4
Byrd Rd DN16 ....**151** E2
Byron Ave **3** DN6 ......**76** E1
Byron Cl DN17 ....**150** E2
Byron Dr YO30 ....**129** F8
Byron Gr DN33 ....**102** E2
Byron St Goole DN14 ...**149** C5
  Kingston upon Hull HU8 ..**141** D2
Bywood Pl **5** DN37 ....**102** B3

C

Cabourne Rd **34** DN33 ..**102** D2
Caddle Rd **9** DN41 ....**101** A4
Cadeby Medieval Village★
  DN36 ....**120** F6
Cadeleigh Cl HU7 .....**141** A8
Cadman Rd YO16 ......**123** A7
Cadney Rd Bigby DN20 ..**98** C1
  Cadney DN20 ....**109** C8
  Cadney LN7 ....**109** F6
Caedmon Cl YO31 .....**131** A7
Caenby Rd
 14 Cleethorpes DN35 ....**103** C2
  Scunthorpe DN17 ......**150** E1
Cairnborrow **4** YO24 ..**132** B7
Caistor Ave DN16 ....**96** D2
Caistor By-Pass LN7 ...**111** B3
Caistor Dr DN33 ......**102** D2

Caistor Joint C of E &
Methodist Prim Sch
LN7 . . . . .111 B4
Caistor Rd
Barton-upon-Humber
DN18 . . . . .85 A7
Laceby DN37 . . . . .112 E8
Nettleton LN7 . . . . .111 A3
North Kelsey LN7 . . . . . .110 D4
Rothwell LN7 . . . . .111 E2
South Kelsey LN7 . . . . . .110 A1
Swallow LN7 . . . . .112 A5
Caistor Yarborough Sch
LN7 . . . . .111 C4
Caithness Cl ◻1 YO30 . . . .126 E5
Calais Croft ◻7 HU17 . . . .43 A2
Calam Villas YO25 . . . . . .35 C5
Caldane HU6 . . . . .139 E8
Caldbeck Cl ◻1 YO32 . . . .127 E3
Caldberg Mews ◻3 HU5 . .139 E6
Calder Ave YO26 . . . . . . .129 B8
Calder Cl ◻35 DN40 . . . . . .87 B1
Calder Cres DN14 . . . . . .77 F6
Calder Gn DN17 . . . . . . .107 D7
Calder Gr HU8 . . . . .142 C6
Calder Rd DN16 . . . . . . .151 D2
Calder St ◻4 DN14 . . . . .149 D4
Calderdale HU7 . . . . . . .140 F6
Calderdale Cl ◻2 YO16 . .123 A7
Caledon Cl HU9 . . . . . . .142 D5
Caledonia Pk HU9 . . . . .146 B5
Calf Cl YO32 . . . . .127 D8
Callas ◻6 HU17 . . . . .43 A2
Calver Cres DN37 . . . . . .102 B4
Calvert Cl YO32 . . . . . . .127 C7
Calvert La HU4 . . . . .144 C7
Calvert Rd HU5 . . . . . . .144 D8
Calvi Ct ◻2 DN32 . . . . . .153 A5
Cam Gr HU8 . . . . .142 C6
Camargue Ave DN37 . . .113 E7
Cambeak Cl ◻3 HU7 . . . .56 F5
Camberwell Way HU8 . . .142 A5
Camblesforth CP Sch
YO8 . . . . .63 C4
Camborne Gr HU8 . . . . .141 B3
Cambrian Cl ◻2 YO32 . . .127 F3
Cambrian Way ◻2 DN36 .114 A6
Cambridge Ave
Goole DN14 . . . . .149 B5
Scunthorpe DN16 . . . . . .96 D2
Cambridge Gr HU9 . . . . .141 F1
Cambridge Park Sch
DN34 . . . . .152 A1
Cambridge Rd
Grimsby DN34 . . . . .152 A1
Kingston upon Hull
HU13 . . . . .143 F3
Scunthorpe DN16 . . . . . .151 C2
Cambridge St
Bridlington YO16 . . . . . .122 D3
Cleethorpes DN35 . . . . .153 F2
Kingston upon Hull HU1 .155 A2
◻4 York YO24 . . . . .130 A3
Camden St ◻1 HU3 . . . .145 B5
Camela La YO8 . . . . .63 B6
Camelford Cl ◻12 HU7 . .56 F5
Camellia Cl YO25 . . . . . .124 D3
Cameron Gr ◻2 YO24 . . .130 C1
Camerton Gr HU9 . . . . .141 F1
Camilla Cl HU9 . . . . .155 C1
Camm La DN14 . . . . . . .63 C3
Cammidge St ◻2 HU19 . .74 F7
Camp The (Earthworks)★
YO11 . . . . .2 C7
Campbell Ave
◻26 Scunthorpe DN16 . . . .96 D2
York YO24 . . . . .129 E2
Campbell Ct HU9 . . . . . .142 E6
Campbell St ◻3 DN21 . . .117 A1
Campbells Farm Ave
DN15 . . . . .95 E6
Camden Cres DN35 . . . .153 C3
Camperdown HU11 . . . .142 D6
Campey La YO42 . . . . . . .39 B6
Campion Ave HU4 . . . . .144 B2
Campions Cl ◻12 DN36 . .114 B1
Campions' La ◻6 DN36 . .114 B1
Campleshon Rd YO23 . . .130 B1
Campsall Balk DN6 . . . . .76 E1
Campsall Hall Rd ◻12 DN6 76 E1
Campsall Park Rd ◻11
DN6 . . . . .76 E1
Campsmount Sch DN6 . .76 D1
Canada Dr
Cherry Burton HU17 . . . .43 A5
Kingston upon Hull
HU16 . . . . .138 E5
Canada La LN7 . . . . .111 C4
Canal Garth DN14 . . . . .77 F6
Canal La
Barmby Moor YO42 . . . . .28 F3
West Stockwith DN10 . . .116 E5
Canal Rd
Cottingham YO42 . . . . . .38 C5
Selby YO8 . . . . .148 D4
Canal Side E HU15 . . . . .52 E3
Canal Side W HU15 . . . . .52 E3
Canal View Selby YO8 . . .148 D3
◻2 Thorne/Moorends DN8 .93 A7
Canberra Ave DN7 . . . . .104 A8
Canberra St HU3 . . . . . .145 D5
Candlesby Rd ◻4 DN37 .102 B4
Candy Bank DN9 . . . . . .104 B5
Canham Gr YO10 . . . . . .131 D3
Canham La YO25 . . . . . .35 C5
Canning St HU1 . . . . . . .155 A2
Cannon Hall La DN14 . . .61 F1

Cannon Oakes Ct
DN36 . . . . .114 B7
Cannon St ◻2 HU2 . . . . .155 B4
Canon Lee Sch YO30 . . .130 A8
Canongate HU16 . . . . . .139 B7
Canterbury Cl
Beverley HU17 . . . . .136 D1
◻9 Haxby YO32 . . . . .13 D5
Scunthorpe DN17 . . . . . .150 D3
Canterbury Dr
Grimsby DN34 . . . . .152 C2
◻2 Kingston upon Hull
HU8 . . . . .141 E7
Canterbury Rd ◻21 DN7 .92 D4
Canton Villas ◻5 YO15 . .122 F4
Canty Nook DN38 . . . . .110 E7
Capstan Rd HU6 . . . . . .140 C8
Capstan St DN14 . . . . . .149 C2
Capstan Way ◻18 DN8 . . .93 A8
Carbis Cl ◻5 DN36 . . . . .114 A8
Carden Ave HU9 . . . . . .142 C2
Cardigan Rd
Bridlington YO15 . . . . . .122 D1
Kingston upon Hull HU3 .144 E6
Cardinal Cl ◻21 DN7 . . . .113 D7
Cardinals Cl ◻3 YO8 . . . .48 B8
Carentan Cl ◻6 YO8 . . . .148 B6
Carew St HU3 . . . . .144 F7
Carey St YO10 . . . . .130 D1
Carisbrooke Ave
HU16 . . . . .139 B5
Carisbrooke Cl ◻8 DN36 114 A8
Carisbrooke Manor La
DN17 . . . . .150 A1
Carl St YO23 . . . . .130 C1
Carlam La HU7 . . . . .57 A7
Carleton St ◻17 YO26 . . .129 F5
Carlisle Rd ◻8 YO15 . . . .122 F3
Carlisle St
◻30 Gainsborough DN21 . .117 B1
Goole DN14 . . . . .149 D4
◻16 York YO26 . . . . .129 F5
Carlton Ave
Healing DN41 . . . . .101 F5
Hornsea HU18 . . . . .134 C5
York YO10 . . . . .131 B3
Carlton Cl
Eggborough DN14 . . . . .61 F1
◻22 Humberston DN35 . . .103 D1
Carlton Ct HU17 . . . . . . .154 A3
Carlton Dr HU17 . . . . . . .47 B1
Carlton La HU11 . . . . . . .47 B1
Carlton Rd
Aldbrough HU11 . . . . . . .46 F1
Grimsby DN34 . . . . .152 B2
◻5 Healing DN41 . . . . . . .101 F5
Sutton upon Derwent
YO41 . . . . .27 C1
Carlton Rise ◻2 HU17 . . .55 F8
Carlton St
Bridlington YO16 . . . . . .122 D3
Kingston upon Hull HU3 .144 F4
Scunthorpe DN15 . . . . . .151 B7
Carlton Twrs ★ DN14 . . .63 D2
Carlton-in-Snaith CP Sch
DN14 . . . . .63 C3
Carmelite St YO1 . . . . . .156 C2
Carmen Cres ◻1 DN14 . .114 A6
Carmires Ave YO32 . . . . .13 F5
Carnaby Ave YO16 . . . . .122 B2
Carnaby Cl HU17 . . . . . .43 C6
Carnaby Gr
Grimsby DN32 . . . . .153 A1
Kingston upon Hull HU6 .139 E5
Carnaby Ind Est YO15 . . .10 C3
Carnegie St ◻6 HU3 . . . .145 A6
Carnforth Cres DN34 . . .152 A1
Carnot St YO26 . . . . .129 F5
Carnoustie ◻18 DN37 . . .113 D6
Carnoustie Cl
Kingston upon Hull HU8 .141 C3
◻1 York YO26 . . . . .129 B4
Carol Dickson Ct ◻9
HU3 . . . . .145 C5
Caroline Cl ◻5 YO24 . . . .129 F3
Caroline Pl HU2 . . . . . . .155 B3
Caroline St HU2 . . . . . . .155 B4
Carolines Pl HU16 . . . . .138 B8
Carperby Mews ◻6 HU5 139 D3
Carr Cl Beverley HU17 . . .154 C3
◻13 Hemingbrough YO8 . . .49 F1
Carr Dike La HU15 . . . . .67 C7
Carr Dyke Bank DN17 . . .106 C5
Carr Dyke Rd DN17 . . . . .95 C3
Carr Inf Sch YO26 . . . . . .129 C5
Carr Jun Sch YO26 . . . . .129 C5
Carr La Appleby DN15 . . .83 D2
Barlby with Osgodby
YO8 . . . . .148 F5
Barlow YO8 . . . . .63 C7
Blyton DN21 . . . . .117 A5
Bonby DN20 . . . . .84 B1
Broughton DN20 . . . . . .97 F3
Burton Pidsea HU12 . . . .59 D1
Burton upon Stather
DN15 . . . . .82 D4
Eastrington DN14 . . . . . .51 F1
Escrick YO19 . . . . .37 B5
Everingham HU17 . . . . . .40 A4
Garthorpe & Fockerby
DN17 . . . . .81 E4
Goole DN14 . . . . .149 D6
Grimsby DN32 . . . . .153 B3
Haxey DN9 . . . . .105 A4
Healing DN41 . . . . .101 F4
Hibaldstow DN20 . . . . . .109 A6
Horkstow DN18 . . . . . . .83 F4

Carr La continued
Hotham YO43 . . . . .53 A4
Kingston upon Hull
HU10 . . . . .138 D1
Kingston upon Hull HU1 .155 A2
Laxton DN14 . . . . .65 F4
Leven HU17 . . . . .44 E8
Long Drax YO8 . . . . .63 F6
Luddington & Haldenby
DN17 . . . . .81 C1
Misterton DN10 . . . . . . .116 C5
Nafferton YO25 . . . . . . .21 C4
Newport HU15 . . . . .52 E2
Newton on Derwent YO41 .27 F4
Pocklington YO42 . . . . . .40 A8
Redbourne DN21 . . . . . .108 F3
Riston LN8 . . . . .45 B5
Seaton Ross YO42 . . . . . .39 A4
Snaith & Cowick DN14 . .78 C7
Stallingborough DN41 . . .101 E7
Tickton HU17 . . . . .137 E3
Tickton HU17 . . . . .137 E8
Ulceby DN39 . . . . .86 B3
Watton YO25 . . . . .33 A4
West Butterwick DN17 . .106 C8
Wildsworth DN21 . . . . . .117 C8
Winterton DN15 . . . . . . .83 D6
Wistow YO8 . . . . .48 A3
Worlaby DN20 . . . . .98 A7
York YO26 . . . . .129 D5
Carr Lane Infants Sch
HU10 . . . . .138 D1
Carr Lane Jun Sch
HU10 . . . . .138 D1
Carr Rd
Burton Pidsea HU12 . . . .59 D1
Molescroft HU17 . . . . . .136 E8
North Kelsey LN7 . . . . . .109 E4
Carr Side La DN7 . . . . . . .92 E2
Carr St
Kingston upon Hull HU2 .155 B4
Selby YO8 . . . . .148 F4
Carrbank La YO32 . . . . . .14 E3
Carrfield YO24 . . . . .132 C8
Carrfields DN14 . . . . . . .149 D6
Carrhouse Rd DN9 . . . . .94 D1
Carrick Gdns YO24 . . . . .129 C3
Carrington Ave
Hornsea HU18 . . . . .134 C6
Kingston upon Hull
HU16 . . . . .139 B6
◻1 York YO26 . . . . .129 E5
Carrington Dr
◻20 Humberston DN36 . . .103 D1
Humberston DN36 . . . . .114 D8
Carrington St ◻6 HU3 . . .145 B5
Carrnock Ct ◻3 YO32 . . .127 F1
Carroll Pl HU1 . . . . .155 C3
Carron Cres YO24 . . . . . .132 B2
Carroway Cl ◻4 YO16 . . .123 A7
Carrs Mdw Escrick YO19 . .37 B5
Carrside ◻5 DN9 . . . . . .105 D7
Carson Ave DN34 . . . . . .152 B2
Carson Rd DN21 . . . . . . .117 B1
Carter Ave YO31 . . . . . . .130 F5
Carter Dr HU17 . . . . .136 E7
Carter La YO15 . . . . .5 A2
Carter St DN14 . . . . .149 C4
Cartergate DN31 . . . . . .152 D3
Cartledge Ave DN32 . . . .153 B2
Cartmel Dr DN32 . . . . . .153 B2
Cartwright La HU17 . . . .154 A1
Carver Rd DN40 . . . . . . .87 C1
Cary La ◻5 DN17 . . . . . .98 B2
Cassbrook Dr LN11 . . . .121 B7
Casson's La ◻1 DN8 . . . .93 A8
Caswell Cl ◻4 DN21 . . . .153 A5
Caswell Cres LN11 . . . . .121 E8
Castella Dr DN16 . . . . . .151 D7
Castle Cl Cawood YO8 . . .48 A8
◻1 Haxby YO32 . . . . .13 D5
◻3 Leconfield HU17 . . . . .43 D6
Castle Cres ◻16 YO15 . . .5 A2
Castle Ct ◻8 DN18 . . . . .84 F8
Castle Dr
◻1 Epworth DN9 . . . . . .105 E6
South Cave HU15 . . . . . .53 F2
Castle Earthworks★
YO8 . . . . .63 F4
Castle Gn HU16 . . . . . . .138 E6
Castle Hill Caistor LN7 . .111 B4
◻8 Hunmanby YO14 . . . . .3 A8
★ Owston Ferry DN9 . . . .106 A3
Castle Hill Hospl
HU16 . . . . .138 D5
Castle Hill La YO8 . . . . . .63 F5
Castle Hills★ DN21 . . . . .117 C2
Castle Keep DN20 . . . . . .108 F6
Castle Pk HU11 . . . . .47 C1
Castle Rd HU16 . . . . .138 D5
Castle Rise ◻1 HU15 . . . .54 A2
Castle St Grimsby DN32 . .153 A4
Kingston upon Hull HU1 .155 A1
Castle View YO25 . . . . . .23 A1
Castle Way HU13 . . . . . .69 F4
Castledyke Prim Sch
DN18 . . . . .69 E1
Castledyke S ◻10 DN18 . .84 F8
Castledyke W ◻5 DN18 . .69 E1
Castleford Ave ◻2 DN34 102 D2
Castleford Gr HU9 . . . . .142 E2
Castlegate YO1 . . . . .156 B2
Castlehill Rd HU7 . . . . . .141 D8
Castlehills Com Arts Coll
DN21 . . . . .117 B1
Castleton Ave ◻6 HU5 . .139 E3
Castleton Rd DN15 . . . . .150 B6

Cat La Balne DN14 . . . . .77 E5
Bilbrough YO23 . . . . .24 D1
Upper Poppleton YO26 . .24 D8
Catford Cl HU8 . . . . .141 E5
Catfoss Rd YO25 . . . . . . .35 A4
Cathcart Cl DN14 . . . . . .76 F7
Cathedral Cl ◻8 HU17 . .136 E1
Cathedral Ct
Hatfield DN7 . . . . .92 C2
Scunthorpe DN16 . . . . . .151 A2
Catherine Gr ◻6 DN20 . .97 E3
Catherine St
◻13 Barton-upon-Humber
DN18 . . . . .69 E1
Grimsby DN32 . . . . .152 E3
Kingston upon Hull HU2 .155 B4
Catkin Rd DN16 . . . . . . .96 D2
Catterick Mews ◻8 HU5 139 D3
Catterton La LS24 . . . . . .24 A1
Cattle Rd DN10 . . . . . . .116 A5
Catton La HU17 . . . . . . .28 F4
Catwick Heads HU11 . . . .45 E8
Catwick La
Brandesburton YO25 . . . .34 C2
Catwick HU17 . . . . .45 D8
Riston LN8 . . . . .45 C6
Caughey St HU3 . . . . . . .145 D7
Causeway Ings La
HU12 . . . . .73 E7
Causewy The HU17 . . . . .154 B3
Cave Cres HU16 . . . . . . .138 E5
Cave St HU5 . . . . .140 D1
Cave Rd HU15 . . . . .68 B6
Cave Terr ◻1 HU5 . . . . .140 D1
Cavendish Ave ◻35 DN35 .103 D1
Cavendish Dr ◻2 HU17 .136 E1
Cavendish Gr YO10 . . . . .131 D3
Cavendish Pk HU15 . . . .68 C5
Cavendish Prim Sch
HU8 . . . . .141 E4
Cavendish Rd
Kingston upon Hull HU8 .141 D5
◻9 Scunthorpe DN16 . . . .96 D2
Cavendish Sq HU3 . . . . .140 D1
Cavendish Way DN32 . . .152 F3
Cave's La DN10 . . . . .116 B3
Cavill Dr ◻12 DN14 . . . . .65 B7
Cavill Pl HU3 . . . . .145 D5
Cawood C of E Prim Sch
YO8 . . . . .48 B8
Cawood Cl HU11 . . . . . .45 D2
Cawood Cres HU11 . . . . .45 D2
Cawood Dr HU11 . . . . . .45 D2
Cawood Rd
Stillingfleet YO19 . . . . . .36 D3
Wistow YO8 . . . . .48 C7
Cawthorne Dr HU4 . . . . .144 C3
Caxton Ave YO26 . . . . . .129 D6
Cayley Cl YO30 . . . . .126 F1
Cayley Rd HU10 . . . . . . .143 F6
Cayton Rd HU8 . . . . .141 D4
Cecil Cl ◻10 DN21 . . . . .107 C3
Cecil Rd ◻7 YO14 . . . . . .3 A8
Cecil St
◻25 Gainsborough DN21 . .117 B1
Goole DN14 . . . . .149 E4
Kingston upon Hull HU3 .144 F5
Cecile Cres DN15 . . . . . .150 E7
Cecilia Pl ◻3 YO24 . . . . .130 A3
Cedar Ave
Flixborough DN15 . . . . . .96 A7
Kingston upon Hull
HU16 . . . . .139 A6
Stainforth DN7 . . . . .92 D6
Cedar Cl
◻11 Cleethorpes DN35 . . .103 B1
Gainsborough DN21 . . . .117 A2
Hambleton YO8 . . . . .48 B1
Hornsea HU18 . . . . .134 C1
Kingston upon Hull
HU10 . . . . .143 D7
Scawby DN20 . . . . .108 F8
◻7 Scotter DN21 . . . . . .107 C3
Cedar Cres YO8 . . . . .48 D2
Cedar Ct
Bridlington YO16 . . . . . .123 A8
◻8 Hedon HU12 . . . . . . .72 C7
Cedar Dr ◻2 DN40 . . . . .87 C2
Cedar Glade YO19 . . . . . .26 C7
Cedar Gr
◻2 Aldbrough HU11 . . . .47 C1
York YO31 . . . . .131 B5
Cedar Gr The HU17 . . . . .136 C6
Cedar Rd ◻2 DN8 . . . . . .79 B1
Cedarwood ◻5 HU15 . . .66 D7
Cedarwood Cl ◻8 YO24 .129 B1
Cedarwood Dr HU4 . . . . .144 B7
Cedric Rd DN21 . . . . . . .92 A1
Celandine Cl ◻8 HU5 . . .139 D1
Celery Bank DN14 . . . . . .64 A4
Celtic Cl YO26 . . . . .129 B5
Cemetery Cres ◻7 DN37 .101 F1
Cemetery La
North Kelsey LN7 . . . . . .110 A5
Pocklington YO42 . . . . . .29 A3
Cemetery Rd
Hatfield DN7 . . . . .92 F4
Laceby DN37 . . . . .101 F1
Scunthorpe DN16 . . . . . .151 B5
Winterton DN15 . . . . . . .83 B5
York YO10 . . . . .156 C1
Centenary Rd DN14 . . . .149 B5
Central Ave
Beverley HU17 . . . . .154 A2
Ulrome YO25 . . . . .23 B3
Central Par DN34 . . . . . .152 A3
Central Prom DN35 . . . . .153 F2
Central St HU2 . . . . .140 F1

Central Way DN16 . . . . .151 D6
Centurion Way
Brough HU15 . . . . .68 C5
Clifton YO30 . . . . .127 B3
Centurion Wlk YO43 . . . .135 E4
Century Rd HU12 . . . . . .72 A8
Ceylon St ◻9 HU9 . . . . . .147 C2
Chadcourt HU6 . . . . .139 E6
Chadwell Springs
DN37 . . . . .113 C6
Chaffinch Cl DN15 . . . . .96 B7
Chaffinch Dr ◻14 DN35 .103 C1
Chaldon Cl ◻4 YO32 . . .14 A6
Chalfont Cl HU13 . . . . . .143 D2
Chalfonts YO24 . . . . .129 F1
Chaloner's Cres YO24 . . .132 D7
Chaloner's Rd YO24 . . . .132 D8
Chamberlain Cl HU7 . . . .141 D6
Chamberlain Ct HU7 . . . .141 D7
Chamberlain Gdns
HU8 . . . . .141 C3
Chamberlain Rd HU8 . . .141 B3
Chamberlain St HU7 . . . .141 D6
Chambers La ◻1 HU18 . .134 C4
Chamomile Cl DN16 . . . .96 E2
Champney Rd HU17 . . . .154 A2
Chancel Rd DN16 . . . . . .96 D2
Chancel Wlk ◻8 DN20 . .97 E3
Chancery Ct YO24 . . . . . .129 C3
Chancery La ◻2 DN17 . . .94 D7
Chandlers Cl ◻2 DN36 . .114 A7
Chandos Rd DN17 . . . . . .150 F3
Channel Rd HU12 . . . . . .89 B6
Chanterlands Ave
HU5 . . . . .140 A1
Chantreys Dr ◻13 HU15 .68 C6
Chantry Ave ◻14 YO26 . .12 F1
Chantry Cl
Grimsby DN31 . . . . .152 C3
York YO24 . . . . .132 C8
Chantry Gap ◻11 YO26 . .12 F1
Chantry Gr ◻13 YO26 . . .12 F1
Chantry La
Beverley HU17 . . . . .154 B2
Bishopthorpe YO23 . . . . .133 B4
Etton HU17 . . . . .43 A6
Grimsby DN31 . . . . .152 C3
Rimswell HU12 . . . . .74 C5
Chantry Mdws ◻1 YO25 . .9 C3
Chantry Way HU14 . . . . .69 B7
Chantry Way E ◻9 HU14 .69 B7
Chapel Balk Rd YO8 . . . .49 F1
Chapel Cl
Barrow upon Humber
DN19 . . . . .85 D7
◻7 Misterton DN10 . . . . .116 C5
Rawcliffe DN14 . . . . .64 A1
Skidby HU16 . . . . .138 A8
Skirlaugh HU11 . . . . .45 E2
◻4 Westwoodside DN9 . .105 B2
Chapel Cnr YO43 . . . . . .135 D4
Chapel Ct DN15 . . . . . . .82 C8
Chapel Field Rd DN19 . . .86 B7
Chapel Fields YO43 . . . . .40 A1
Chapel Fields Rd
YO26 . . . . .129 A3
Chapel Garth
Broomfleet HU15 . . . . . .67 B5
◻11 Gilberdyke HU15 . . . .66 D8
Ottringham HU12 . . . . . .73 E3
Skipsea YO25 . . . . .23 A1
◻3 Tetney DN36 . . . . . .114 D4
Chapel Haddlesey C of E
Prim Sch YO8 . . . . .62 B5
Chapel Hill ◻1 HU15 . . . .68 E6
Chapel Hill La HU15 . . . .68 E6
Chapel Hill Rd YO42 . . . .29 A4
Chapel La
Ashby cum Fenby DN37 . .113 D3
Askham Bryan YO23 . . . .24 F3
Barmston YO25 . . . . .23 A6
Barnoldby le Beck DN37 . .113 B6
◻14 Barton-upon-Humber
DN18 . . . . .69 E1
Brayton YO8 . . . . .148 B1
Broughton DN20 . . . . . .97 E3
Elsham DN20 . . . . .98 F7
◻10 Gainsborough DN21 . .117 A2
Habrough DN40 . . . . . . .100 E8
Horkstow DN18 . . . . . . .84 A5
Keadby with Althorpe
DN17 . . . . .95 C6
◻13 Keyingham HU12 . . . .73 C4
Kilham YO25 . . . . .9 B3
Kingston upon Hull HU1 .69 C8
Kingston upon Hull HU1 .155 C2
Langtoft YO25 . . . . .8 D5
Laxton DN14 . . . . .65 F4
Little Smeaton WF8 . . . .76 B3
Ludborough DN36 . . . . .121 B6
Middleton YO25 . . . . . . .31 C4
◻8 Misterton DN10 . . . . .116 C5
Northorpe DN21 . . . . . . .118 D8
Ottringham HU12 . . . . . .73 E3
Rawcliffe DN14 . . . . .64 A2
Reighton YO14 . . . . .3 E5
◻3 Riccall YO19 . . . . . . .37 A1
Scawby DN20 . . . . .108 E8
Skeffling HU12 . . . . .90 C6
Swallow LN7 . . . . .112 A5
Sykehouse DN14 . . . . . .78 A4
◻18 Thorne/Moorends DN8 .93 A8
Utterby LN11 . . . . .121 C4
◻1 Wawne HU7 . . . . . . .56 E7

Chapel La continued
West/East Butterwick
 DN17 . . . .**.95** D1
Whitton DN15 . . . .**.67** E3
Winterton DN15 . . . .**.83** A5
Wrawby DN20 . . . .**.98** D4
Chapel La Staith HU1 .**155** C2
Chapel Mdws 8 HU15 .**.66** D8
Chapel Mews 3 HU15 . .**.68** C6
Chapel Rd
Broughton DN20 . . . .**.97** E3
Habrough DN40 . . . .**100** E8
Tetney DN36 . . . .**114** D4
Chapel Row YO10 . . . .**156** C1
Chapel St
2 Amcotts DN17 . . . . . .**.81** F1
Barmby Moor YO42 . . . . .**.28** D3
Bridlington YO15 . . . . . .**122** E2
13 Caistor LN7 . . . .**111** B4
5 Crowle DN17 . . . .**.94** D8
6 Epworth DN9 . . . .**105** E6
6 Flamborough YO15 . . . . .**5** A2
Goole DN14 . . . .**149** D3
Goxhill DN19 . . . .**.86** A8
Hillam LS25 . . . .**.61** B7
Kingston upon Hull HU1 .**155** A2
Lockington YO25 . . . .**.32** B2
North Kelsey LN7 . . . . . .**110** A4
Scunthorpe DN15 . . . . . .**151** B7
Chapel Way 20 DN20 . .**.98** C2
Chapel Wlk 4 YO19 . . .**.37** A1
Chapelry Garth 28 HU12 .**72** D7
Chapman Ave DN17 . . .**150** F1
Chapman Cl 1 YO32 . . .**.14** C8
Chapman Ct DN31 . . . .**152** D4
Chapman Gr DN35 . . . .**153** F1
Chapman Rd DN33 . . . .**153** D3
Chapman St HU8 . . . . .**155** C4
Chapmans Ct YO24 . . . .**132** D6
Chapman's La YO30 . . .**.12** E7
Chapter House St YO1 .**156** B3
Chapter Wk DN20 . . . . .**.97** E3
Chariot St HU1 . . . . . .**155** A2
Charles Ave
Grimsby DN33 . . . .**102** E1
Laceby DN37 . . . .**101** E1
17 New Waltham DN36 . . .**114** A7
15 Scotter DN21 . . . .**107** C3
Charles Ct 7 DN8 . . . . .**.79** B1
Charles Dr DN14 . . . . .**149** B6
Charles Lovell Way
 DN17 . . . .**150** D4
Charles Moor YO31 . . .**130** F7
Charles St
Cleethorpes DN35 . . . . . .**153** F1
31 Gainsborough DN21 . . .**117** B1
22 Hedon HU12 . . . .**.72** D7
Kingston upon Hull HU2 .**155** B3
Selby YO8 . . . .**148** B6
Charles Wesley Dr
 HU9 . . . .**148** B2
Charlestown Way
 HU9 . . . .**146** C6
Charlotte St HU1 . . . . .**155** C3
Charlotte St Mews
 HU1 . . . .**155** B3
Charlton St
Grimsby DN31 . . . .**152** C4
York YO23 . . . .**130** C2
Charnock Ave HU9 . . . .**142** A4
Charter Ave DN14 . . . . .**.64** A1
Charterfield HU11 . . . .**142** D6
Charterhouse Dr 3
 DN16 . . . .**.96** E2
Charterhouse La HU2 .**155** B3
Charterhouse The★
 HU2 . . . .**155** C3
Charter's La 4 YO25 . .**.34** B2
Charters The YO8 . . . . .**.49** B5
Chase Hill Rd DN40 . . .**.86** C8
Chase Side Ct YO24 . . .**132** E8
Chase The
Driffield YO25 . . . .**125** A4
2 Snaith DN14 . . . .**.78** C8
Chatham St HU3 . . . . .**144** F7
Chatsworth Cl
Beverley HU17 . . . .**154** A1
5 Bridlington YO16 . . . . .**122** D6
Chatsworth Dr
Goole DN14 . . . .**149** B6
16 Haxby YO32 . . . .**.13** F5
Chatsworth Pl 1 DN35 .**103** B2
Chatsworth St HU5 . . .**145** B8
Chatsworth Terr 4
 YO26 . . . .**129** E4
Chatterton Cres DN17 .**.96** D7
Chaucer Ave DN17 . . . .**150** D3
Chaucer St
Kingston upon Hull HU8 .**141** C2
7 York YO10 . . . .**130** E3
Chaumont Way 1 YO32 .**.14** D2
Chaytor Cl 16 HU12 . . .**.72** D6
Cheadle Cl HU5 . . . . . .**155** A4
Cheapside
Kingston upon Hull HU8 .**155** C4
Waltham DN37 . . . .**113** E5
Cheapside Rd DN37 . . .**113** F4
Cheapsides La HU15 . . .**.66** D8
Checker La YO19 . . . . . .**.49** A7
Cheesemans Cl 9
 DN37 . . . .**113** E6
Cheesemans La 8
 DN37 . . . .**113** E6
Chelkar Way YO30 . . . .**126** F1
Chellsway HU19 . . . . . .**.74** F6

Chelmer Rd HU8 . . . . .**142** B5
Chelmsford Ave DN34 .**152** A1
Chelmsford Cl 6 HU9 .**142** E1
Chelmsford Pl DN34 . .**152** B2
Chelsea Cl HU8 . . . . . .**141** F5
Chelsea Ct 3 HU16 . . .**138** F5
Chelsea Wlk 1 DN35 . .**103** D1
Cheltenham Ave HU7 . .**141** B6
Cheltenham Cl 8 DN16 .**.96** E2
Cheltenham Way
 DN35 . . . .**103** C1
Chelwood Dr 30 DN33 .**102** D2
Chelwood Rd DN17 . . . .**150** F3
Chelwood Wlk 12 YO26 .**129** E4
Chepstow Gr DN34 . . . .**152** A1
Cheriton Cl 14 HU7 . . .**.56** F5
Cherry Burton C of E Sch
 HU17 . . . .**.43** B5
Cherry Cl
Great Driffield YO25 . . . .**124** F2
Hornsea HU18 . . . .**134** D1
Cherry Cobb Sands Rd
 HU12 . . . .**.87** F8
Cherry Cres YO43 . . . . .**40** A1
Cherry Ct 16 HU15 . . . .**66** D8
Cherry Dale 11 DN35 . .**103** B2
Cherry Dr
Holme-on-Spalding-Moor
 YO43 . . . .**40** A1
Nafferton YO25 . . . .**125** F6
Cherry Garth
Beverley HU17 . . . .**154** C3
Kingston upon Hull HU3 .**145** A5
Lund YO25 . . . .**.31** F2
York YO31 . . . .**131** B5
Cherry Gr 5 Belton DN9 .**94** E1
Belton DN9 . . . .**105** E8
16 Poppleton YO26 . . . . .**.12** F1
Scunthorpe DN16 . . . . . .**151** B2
Cherry Hill La YO23 . . .**156** B1
Cherry Hill Pk HU12 . . .**.74** B8
Cherry Holt 7 LN7 . . . .**111** B4
Cherry La
Barrow upon Humber
 DN19 . . . .**.85** D8
Kingston upon Hull HU8 .**141** C4
Wootton DN39 . . . .**.85** C2
York YO24 . . . .**132** F8
Cherry Mount 1 DN16 .**.96** E2
Cherry Orch
16 Epworth DN9 . . . . . .**105** E6
2 Haxby YO32 . . . .**127** D8
Cherry Orch Mews 12
 YO42 . . . .**29** A4
Cherry Paddock
4 Haxby YO32 . . . .**127** D8
Kexby YO41 . . . .**.15** C2
Cherry Rd 4 YO14 . . . . .**.3** A8
Cherry St YO23 . . . . . .**156** B1
Cherry Tree Ave
1 Brigg DN20 . . . .**.98** B2
Kingston upon Hull HU8 .**141** C2
Newton-on-Ouse YO30 . . .**.12** B6
9 Withernsea HU19 . . . .**.75** A6
York YO32 . . . .**127** D4
Cherry Tree Cl
Bilton HU11 . . . .**.58** A3
13 Brayton YO8 . . . .**.48** D1
Cherry Tree Cres
 DN34 . . . .**102** C4
Cherry Tree Dr
Hatfield DN7 . . . .**.92** D5
3 Thorne/Moorends DN8 .**.79** A1
Cherry Tree Gr DN7 . . .**.92** C5
Cherry Tree La
Beverley HU17 . . . .**154** B3
31 Hedon HU12 . . . .**.72** D7
Cherry Tree Rd 18
 DN21 . . . .**117** C1
Cherry Tree Terr
 HU17 . . . .**154** C3
Cherry Tree Wlk 7 YO8 .**49** B4
Cherry Trees HU16 . . . .**138** A7
Cherry Way
Messingham DN17 . . . . . .**107** D7
Nafferton YO25 . . . .**125** F6
Cherry Wood Cres
 YO19 . . . .**133** E5
Chesham Gr DN14 . . . .**149** B6
Cheshire Ave YO32 . . . .**.14** A6
Cheshire Cl HU5 . . . . . .**139** D1
Chesney Dr DN16 . . . . .**.96** D2
Chesney Fields 4 YO24 .**129** D1
Chesnut Ave HU5 . . . . .**140** C2
Chesnut Way DN19 . . . .**.86** A8
Chessingham Gdns
 YO24 . . . .**132** E6
Chessingham Pk YO19 . .**.26** F6
Chesswick Ave DN17 . . .**.95** D5
Chesswick Cres DN17 . .**.95** D5
Chester Ave
3 Beverley HU17 . . . . . .**.55** F8
Beverley HU17 . . . .**136** E1
Chester Ct Rd YO8 . . . .**.63** A6
Chester Grange DN33 . .**102** F1
Chester Pl DN35 . . . . . .**153** C1
Chester Rd HU5 . . . . . .**139** B1
Chesterfield Rd DN15 .**150** B6
Chesterholme HU11 . . .**142** E6
Chestnut Ave
2 Airmyn DN14 . . . .**.64** E4
Beverley HU17 . . . .**136** F6
15 Gainsborough DN21 . . .**117** B1
Goole DN14 . . . .**149** B3
Great Driffield YO25 . . . .**124** F2
Hedon HU12 . . . .**.72** C8
10 Hemingbrough YO8 . . .**.49** F1
Immingham DN40 . . . . . .**.87** D2

Chestnut Ave continued
Kingston upon Hull
 HU13 . . . .**143** E1
Kingston upon Hull
 HU10 . . . .**143** E8
Stainforth DN7 . . . .**.92** D6
3 Thorne/Moorends DN8 .**.93** B7
2 Thorngumbald HU12 . . .**72** E5
Withernsea HU19 . . . .**75** A5
York YO31 . . . .**130** F6
Chestnut Cl
Beverley HU17 . . . .**136** F6
Bridlington YO15 . . . . . .**123** B7
6 Burstwick HU12 . . . . .**.73** A6
4 Scotter DN21 . . . .**107** C3
Snaith DN14 . . . .**.78** B8
17 Waltham DN37 . . . . .**113** D6
Chestnut Cres YO43 . . . .**40** A1
Chestnut Croft 7 YO8 . .**.49** F1
Chestnut Ct 9 YO8 . . . .**.49** F1
Chestnut Dr
15 Gilberdyke HU15 . . . .**.66** D8
8 Hemingbrough YO8 . . .**.49** F1
Holme-on-Spalding-Moor
 YO43 . . . .**40** A1
Messingham DN17 . . . . . .**107** D7
Chestnut Garth
Burton Pidsea HU12 . . . . .**59** C2
4 Hemingbrough YO8 . . .**.49** F1
Roos HU12 . . . .**60** A1
Chestnut Gr
5 Broughton DN20 . . . . .**.97** E4
Kingston upon Hull HU8 .**141** B2
Sproatley HU11 . . . .**58** D5
York YO26 . . . .**129** C4
Chestnut Mews YO8 . . .**.48** A8
Chestnut Pk YO41 . . . . .**.28** C8
Chestnut Rd
Cawood YO8 . . . .**48** A8
Waltham DN37 . . . .**113** D6
Chestnut Rise
Barrow upon Humber
 DN19 . . . .**.85** C8
6 Hemingbrough YO8 . . .**.49** F1
Chestnut View YO42 . . . .**29** B3
Chestnut Way DN16 . . .**151** B3
Chestnut Wlk DN41 . . .**102** A5
Chestnuts The
6 Haxby YO32 . . . .**127** C8
Hensall DN14 . . . .**.62** D2
Cheverton Ave 19 HU19 .**75** A6
Cheviot Ave DN14 . . . .**149** D5
Cheviot Cl
3 Thorne/Moorends DN8 .**.93** A7
1 York YO32 . . . .**127** F3
Cheviotdale HU7 . . . . .**140** F6
Chevy Chase HU11 . . . .**142** E6
Cheyne Garth HU18 . . .**134** A4
Cheyne Wlk HU18 . . . .**134** A4
Chichester Dr 19 LN7 . .**111** B4
Chichester Rd DN35 . . .**103** C2
Chiltern Cres DN17 . . . .**150** D4
Chiltern Dr 19 DN37 . . .**113** D6
Chiltern Prim Sch
 HU3 . . . .**145** B5
Chiltern Rd DN14 . . . . .**149** D5
Chiltern Way
26 Grimsby DN33 . . . . . .**113** E8
York YO32 . . . .**127** F5
Chilterns The HU9 . . . .**142** D2
Chilton Cl 19 DN40 . . . .**.87** B1
Chilton Rise HU10 . . . .**138** B1
Chilvers Ct 4 YO8 . . . . .**148** A1
Chimes Rd YO8 . . . .**148** C6
Chimney Field Rd HU7 . .**74** B6
Chingford Ave 1 DN34 .**102** C2
Chippendale Cl 2
 DN36 . . . .**114** D8
Chiswick Cl 3 HU8 . . . .**142** A5
Cholmley St HU3 . . . . .**145** B5
Christine Pl 4 DN33 . . .**113** F8
Chrystals Rd HU18 . . . .**134** D5
Chrystals Wlk HU18 . . .**134** D5
Chudleigh Rd 1 YO26 . .**129** F5
Church Acres DN14 . . . .**.65** D1
Church Ave
Humberston DN36 . . . . . .**114** C8
6 North Ferriby HU14 . . .**.69** A4
Church Balk
Dunnington YO19 . . . .**26** E7
Thorne/Moorends DN8 . . . .**93** B8
Church Cl
Askham Bryan YO23 . . . . .**24** F3
Bonby DN20 . . . .**84** C2
Bridlington YO16 . . . . . .**122** D4
4 Bubwith YO8 . . . .**50** D7
25 Flamborough YO15 . . . .**5** A2
Goole DN14 . . . .**149** E2
Grimsby DN32 . . . .**153** B1
Kingston upon Hull HU7 .**141** D6
Laxton DN14 . . . .**65** F4
1 Market Weighton
 YO43 . . . .**135** D4
8 Thorne/Moorends DN8 .**.93** B8
Wheldrake YO19 . . . .**.38** A7
Church Cres
Owston Ferry DN9 . . . . . .**106** A3
4 Wawne HU7 . . . .**56** E7
Church Ct YO25 . . . . . .**124** E4
Church Dike La YO8 . . . .**63** F5
Church Dr Leven HU17 . .**45** A8
6 Misterton DN10 . . . . .**116** C5
Church End YO8 . . . .**48** B8
Church Farm Cl YO23 . .**24** C6
Church Field Rd DN6 . . .**.76** E1
Church Fields DN15 . . . .**83** A5
Church Gate 21 HU12 . .**.72** C7

Church Gn
Beverley HU17 . . . .**136** B6
5 Bridlington YO16 . . . . .**122** D4
3 Elvington YO41 . . . . . .**27** C2
Church Hill
Grasby DN38 . . . .**110** E7
10 Hunmanby YO14 . . . . . .**2** F8
Reighton YO14 . . . .**3** C6
Riby DN37 . . . .**101** B2
3 Selby YO8 . . . .**148** D5
South Cave HU15 . . . .**53** F2
Stillingfleet YO19 . . . .**36** D3
Whitton DN15 . . . .**67** E3
8 Wistow YO8 . . . .**48** D6
Church Hill Rd YO25 . . .**.31** C4
Church La Appleby DN15 .**83** C1
Atwick YO25 . . . .**35** C5
Aylesby DN37 . . . .**101** E2
Barnetby Le Beck DN37 . .**113** B6
1 Beeford YO25 . . . .**22** D1
Beswick YO25 . . . .**32** B4
Bilton HU11 . . . .**142** F6
Bishop Burton HU17 . . . . .**43** B3
Bishopthorpe YO23 . . . . .**133** A4
Blyton DN21 . . . .**117** F5
Bonby DN20 . . . .**84** C2
Bradley DN37 . . . .**102** C1
Brandesburton YO25 . . . . .**34** B2
Bridlington YO15 . . . . . .**123** B7
Brigsley DN37 . . . .**113** D4
3 Brough HU15 . . . .**68** C7
Broughton DN20 . . . .**.97** E3
6 Buckton/Bempton YO15 . .**4** D3
Burstwick HU12 . . . .**73** A7
Cadney DN20 . . . .**109** D6
Carlton DN14 . . . .**63** C3
Carnaby YO16 . . . .**10** D1
Catton YO41 . . . .**27** D8
Catwick HU17 . . . .**45** C8
Corringham DN21 . . . . . .**118** B2
Driffield YO25 . . . .**124** B4
Dunnington YO19 . . . .**26** E7
4 Elvington YO41 . . . . . .**27** C2
Fishlake DN7 . . . .**92** D8
Fotherby LN11 . . . .**121** D2
Fridaythorpe YO25 . . . . . .**18** B7
Garton YO25 . . . .**124** B4
Gateforth YO8 . . . .**61** F8
Great Driffield YO25 . . . .**124** B4
Great Limber DN37 . . . . .**100** D3
Grimsby DN32 . . . .**152** D3
Grimsby DN32 . . . .**153** B1
17 Haxby YO32 . . . .**13** E5
Haxey DN9 . . . .**105** C2
Hedon HU12 . . . .**72** C7
Hensall DN14 . . . .**62** C1
Hollym HU19 . . . .**75** A4
Holton le Clay DN36 . . . .**114** A5
Hook DN14 . . . .**149** F7
Hotham YO43 . . . .**53** D5
Humberston DN36 . . . . . .**114** D8
Hutton Cranswick YO25 . . .**32** E8
Immingham DN40 . . . . . .**.86** E4
Immingham DN40 . . . . . .**.87** B2
Irby DN37 . . . .**112** D7
Keadby with Althorpe
 DN17 . . . .**.95** D4
Kellington DN14 . . . .**.61** E3
Keyingham HU12 . . . .**73** C4
2 Kilham YO25 . . . .**9** C4
Kingston upon Hull
 HU10 . . . .**143** C8
Kingston upon Hull HU9 .**147** C8
Laceby DN37 . . . .**101** F1
Langtoft YO25 . . . .**8** C5
Lockington YO25 . . . .**32** B1
Luddington & Haldenby
 DN17 . . . .**.81** D4
Marsh Chapel DN36 . . . . .**115** B1
Millington YO42 . . . .**29** D6
3 Misterton DN10 . . . . .**116** C5
4 Monk Fryston LS25 . . .**61** A8
Moor Monkton YO26 . . . . .**12** B2
Nether Poppleton YO26 . . .**126** B3
New Earswick YO32 . . . . .**127** F5
North Frodingham YO25 . . .**33** F8
North Kelsey LN7 . . . .**110** A4
North Thoresby DN36 . . . .**114** B1
Nunburnholme YO42 . . . . .**29** E2
Patrington HU12 . . . .**74** D1
Poppleton YO26 . . . .**126** A3
Rudston YO25 . . . .**9** F6
Saxby All Saints DN20 . . . .**84** B3
Scawby DN20 . . . .**98** A1
Scotter DN21 . . . .**107** C3
19 Scunthorpe DN16 . . . .**.96** D2
Scunthorpe DN15 . . . . . .**150** F6
Seaton Ross YO42 . . . .**39** E4
4 Selby YO8 . . . .**148** D5
Sigglesthorne HU11 . . . . . .**45** F8
Skelton YO30 . . . .**126** B5
Skirlaugh HU11 . . . .**45** E2
2 Snaith DN14 . . . .**63** C1
Sproatley HU11 . . . .**58** D5
Stallingborough DN41 . . . .**101** D6
10 Stamford Bridge YO41 . .**15** D2
Strensall YO32 . . . .**14** A7
Swinefleet DN14 . . . .**65** D1
Tetney DN36 . . . .**114** D3
Thorngumbald HU12 . . . . .**72** E5
Thwing YO25 . . . .**2** A1
Twin Rivers DN14 . . . .**81** A8
Ulceby DN39 . . . .**86** A1
Utterby LN11 . . . .**121** C3
Waithe DN36 . . . .**114** A3

Church La continued
4 Waltham DN37 . . . . . .**113** E6
Watton YO25 . . . .**32** A4
Wetwang YO25 . . . .**19** B6
Wheldrake YO19 . . . .**38** A7
Withernwick HU11 . . . .**46** D3
York YO1 . . . .**156** B2
Church La Staith HU1 .**155** C2
Church Mews 2 YO26 .**129** C3
Church Mount 9 YO43 . .**53** F7
Church Rd
Beverley HU17 . . . .**136** B6
Laughton DN21 . . . .**117** F8
North Ferriby HU14 . . . . . .**69** A4
Rimswell HU19 . . . .**74** D7
Skeffling HU12 . . . .**90** D6
Stainforth DN7 . . . .**92** C6
Stamford Bridge YO41 . . . .**15** D2
Thornton YO42 . . . .**39** B7
Wawne HU7 . . . .**56** E7
York YO10 . . . .**131** D4
Church Rise Holtby YO19 .**14** C1
Skidby HU16 . . . .**138** A8
Church Row HU8 . . . . .**155** C4
Church Side
Alkborough DN15 . . . .**82** C8
Appleby DN15 . . . .**83** D2
Goxhill DN19 . . . .**86** A7
Grasby DN38 . . . .**110** E7
2 Market Weighton
 YO43 . . . .**135** D4
West Halton DN15 . . . . . .**82** E7
16 Winterton DN15 . . . . .**83** A5
Church Sq 3 DN15 . . . .**151** B7
Church St
7 Aldbrough HU11 . . . . . .**47** C1
Amcotts DN17 . . . .**81** F1
Bainton YO25 . . . .**31** E7
Beckingham DN10 . . . . . .**116** D1
6 Brough HU15 . . . .**68** D6
Bubwith YO8 . . . .**50** D7
Burton Pidsea HU12 . . . . .**59** D1
14 Caistor LN7 . . . .**111** B4
Copmanthorpe YO23 . . . .**132** B2
Dunnington YO19 . . . .**26** E7
Elsham DN20 . . . .**98** F7
4 Epworth DN9 . . . .**105** E6
Fishlake DN7 . . . .**92** D8
19 Flamborough YO15 . . . .**5** A2
Gainsborough DN21 . . . . .**117** B1
Goole DN14 . . . .**149** D4
5 Goxhill DN19 . . . .**86** A8
Great Driffield YO25 . . . .**124** F4
Grimsby DN32 . . . .**152** F5
Haxey DN9 . . . .**105** C2
Hemswell DN21 . . . .**119** A1
Hibaldstow DN20 . . . . . .**108** F5
Hutton Cranswick YO25 . . .**32** E7
4 Kilham YO25 . . . .**9** C3
Kingston upon Hull HU7 .**141** E6
Kingston upon Hull
 HU10 . . . .**143** E6
Kingston upon Hull HU9 .**146** B6
Kirton in Lindsey DN21 . .**108** B1
Messingham DN17 . . . . . .**107** D7
Misterton DN10 . . . .**116** C5
Nettleton LN7 . . . .**111** B3
North Cave HU15 . . . .**53** D3
North Kelsey LN7 . . . .**110** A4
Owston Ferry DN9 . . . . . .**106** A3
Scawby DN20 . . . .**108** E8
South Cave HU15 . . . .**53** F1
Thorne/Moorends DN8 . . . .**93** A8
Willoughton DN21 . . . . . .**119** B4
York YO1 . . . .**156** B2
Church View
12 Airmyn DN14 . . . .**64** E4
Alkborough DN15 . . . .**82** C8
8 Barton-upon-Humber
 DN18 . . . .**.84** F8
4 Beckingham DN10 . . . .**116** D1
Beverley HU17 . . . .**154** C3
4 Brough HU15 . . . .**68** C7
Grimsby DN34 . . . .**102** C4
Norton DN6 . . . .**76** E1
7 Patrington HU12 . . . . .**74** D1
1 Waltham DN37 . . . . . .**113** E6
Church View Cl DN9 . . .**.94** E1
Church Wlk
Bridlington YO16 . . . . . .**122** D5
Holton le Clay DN36 . . . .**114** A5
Owston Ferry DN9 . . . . . .**106** A3
5 Wistow YO8 . . . .**48** D6
Churchfield Dr 28 YO32 .**13** C8
Churchfield La
Little Smeaton DN6 . . . . . .**76** C4
Womersley DN6 . . . .**76** D4
Churchfield Rd DN16 . .**151** B1
Churchfields HU17 . . . .**137** E8
Churchill Ave
Brigg DN20 . . . .**98** C2
Burstwick HU12 . . . .**73** A7
Hatfield DN7 . . . .**92** F4
Hutton Cranswick YO25 . . .**32** E7
10 Keelby DN41 . . . .**101** A5
Kingston upon Hull
 HU16 . . . .**138** F6
Churchill Rise HU12 . . .**.73** A7
Churchill St HU9 . . . . .**146** D7
Churchill Way DN32 . . .**152** F3
Churchill Wlk DN14 . . .**149** C5
Churchside 4 DN19 . . . .**85** D8
Churchthorpe LN11 . . .**121** E8
Churchtown DN9 . . . . . .**94** E1
Cinder La
Upper Poppleton YO26 . . . .**12** F1
Upper Poppleton YO26 . . .**129** A7

Cinder La continued
York YO26 . . . .**130** A4
York YO31 . . . .**130** E6
Cinema St HU18 . . . .**134** C4
Circle The 4 HU13 . . . . .**143** E2
Cissplatt La DN41 . . . .**101** A4
Citadel Ct HU17 . . . .**154** B3
Citadel Way HU9 . . . .**155** C2
Cladshaw HU6 . . . .**139** F8
Clanthorpe HU6 . . . .**139** F8
Clapham Ave HU8 . . . .**141** E4
Clare Ave HU17 . . . .**150** D3
Clare Ct Beverley HU17 . . .**137** B4
Grimsby DN34 . . . .**152** A4
Clare Gr HU9 . . . .**142** A1
Claremont Ave HU6 . . . . . .**140** D4
Claremont Rd DN32 . . . . . .**153** D2
Claremont Terr YO31 . . . . .**156** B4
Clarence Ave
Bridlington YO15 . . . .**122** D1
Kingston upon Hull HU6 . . .**141** E4
Clarence Cl 25 DN40 . . . . . .**87** B1
Clarence Ct HU2 . . . .**155** A3
Clarence Rd 1 YO15 . . . . . .**122** F2
Clarence St
Kingston upon Hull HU9 . . .**155** C2
York YO31 . . . .**156** B4
Clarendon Rd
6 Grimsby DN34 . . . .**102** C2
Scunthorpe DN17 . . . .**150** F3
Clarendon St HU3 . . . .**145** B7
Clark Ave DN34 . . . .**152** A3
Clarke Cres 9 YO15 . . . . . . .4 D3
Clarke St DN15 . . . .**151** A7
Clarkes Rd DN32 . . . .**86** E4
Clark's La YO43 . . . .**53** D6
Clarks La 10 HU12 . . . .**74** D1
Clarksons Dr DN41 . . . .**101** E6
Clarondale HU7 . . . .**140** E7
Clavering St DN31 . . . .**152** B5
Claxby Rd DN17 . . . .**150** F1
Clay Bank Rd DN8 . . . .**93** C6
Clay Hill YO41 . . . . .16 C3
Clay La Bubwith YO8 . . . . . .50 C5
Camblesforth YO8 . . . . .63 C6
Cliffe YO8 . . . . .49 D4
Holton le Clay DN36 . . . . . .**114** A6
Kirton in Lindsey DN21 . . . .**118** F8
Market Weighton YO43 . . . .**135** B5
Millington YO42 . . . . .29 C6
Clay Pl 3 YO24 . . . .**129** D1
Clay St HU8 . . . .**141** A3
Clayden St DN31 . . . .**152** B5
Clayfield Cl 18 YO42 . . . . . . .29 A3
Clayfield La
Pocklington YO42 . . . . .29 A4
Shipton Thorpe YO43 . . . . . .40 F3
Clayfield Rd
Pocklington YO42 . . . . .29 A3
Scunthorpe DN15 . . . . .96 C7
Claygate YO31 . . . .**131** B6
Claymore Cl DN35 . . . .**153** E2
Claypit La DN14 . . . . .63 C3
Cleatham Rd DN21 . . . .**108** A3
Cleaves Ave HU15 . . . . .54 A2
Clee Cres DN32 . . . .**153** C1
Clee Ness Dr 18 DN36 . . . . .**103** D1
Clee Rd DN35 . . . .**153** D2
Clee Village DN32 . . . .**153** C2
Cleefields Cl DN32 . . . .**153** B1
Cleethorpe Rd DN32 . . . . . .**153** A5
Cleethorpes Ctry Pk★
DN35 . . . .**103** C1
Cleethorpes L Ctr
DN35 . . . .**103** D2
Cleethorpes Miniature Rly★
DN35 . . . .**103** C2
Cleethorpes Sta DN35 . . . . .**153** F3
Cleeton La YO25 . . . . .23 A2
Cleeton Way YO16 . . . .**122** B6
Cleeve Dr 12 HU7 . . . . .57 A5
Cleeve Prim Sch HU7 . . . . .57 A5
Cleeve Rd HU12 . . . . .72 D6
Clematis Ave DN41 . . . .**101** F5
Clematis Cl YO25 . . . .**124** D3
Clematis Way DN16 . . . . . . .96 E2
Clement St 4 YO23 . . . . . .**156** B1
Clementhorpe YO23 . . . . . .**156** B1
Clementhorpe La HU15 . . . .66 D8
Clementhorpe Rd
HU15 . . . . .66 D8
Clerke St DN35 . . . .**153** E1
Clevedon Rd DN17 . . . .**150** D4
Cleveland Cl Hook DN14 . . .65 B5
4 Immingham DN40 . . . . .87 B1
Scunthorpe DN17 . . . .**150** D4
Cleveland Gdns DN31 . . . . .**152** B5
Cleveland St
Grimsby DN31 . . . .**152** B5
Kingston upon Hull HU8 . . .**141** A4
Kingston upon Hull HU8 . . .**155** C4
York YO24 . . . .**130** A4
Cleveland Way
41 Hatfield DN7 . . . . .92 D4
York YO32 . . . .**127** F3
Cliff Ave DN15 . . . . .82 F5
Cliff Closes Rd DN15 . . . . .**150** D6
Cliff Dr
Burton upon Stather
DN15 . . . . .82 A5
3 Kingston upon Hull HU13 69 E4
Cliff Gdns DN15 . . . .**150** E6
Cliff Gr DN18 . . . . .84 E8
Cliff Hill Rd DN6 . . . . .76 D2
Cliff La Bempton YO15 . . . . .4 D4
Mappleton HU18 . . . . .47 A6
Waddingham DN21 . . . . . .**119** F6
Cliff Rd Atwick YO25 . . . . . .35 D5

Cliff Rd continued
Bridlington YO15 . . . .**123** B6
Hessle HU13 . . . . .69 E4
Hornsea HU18 . . . .**134** C6
Snitterby DN21 . . . .**119** F5
Winteringham DN15 . . . . . .83 A8
Cliff St Bridlington YO15 . . .**123** B6
Scunthorpe DN16 . . . .**151** C6
Cliff Top La 2 HU13 . . . . . . .69 E4
Cliff Wlk YO15 . . . .**123** C6
Cliffe La YO43 . . . . .52 D8
Cliffe Prim Sch YO8 . . . . . .49 E2
Cliffe Rd
Market Weighton YO43 . . . .**135** D1
Newbald YO43 . . . . .53 C7
North Cave HU15 . . . . .53 C4
Clifford Ave HU8 . . . .**141** E4
Clifford St
Hornsea HU18 . . . .**134** C5
York YO1 . . . .**156** B2
Cliffords Twr★ YO1 . . . . . .**156** B1
Clifton Ct 27 DN8 . . . . .93 A8
Clifton Dale YO30 . . . .**130** A6
Clifton Gdns DN14 . . . .**149** B4
Clifton Moor Gate
YO30 . . . .**127** A2
Clifton Moor Ret Pk
YO30 . . . .**126** E3
Clifton Moorgate
YO30 . . . .**127** B3
Clifton Pl 3 YO30 . . . .**130** A7
Clifton Prep Sch
YO30 . . . .**156** A4
Clifton Prim Sch HU2 . . . . .**155** A4
Clifton Rd
Grimsby DN34 . . . .**152** A2
York YO30 . . . .**156** A4
Clifton St
Hornsea HU18 . . . .**134** C5
Kingston upon Hull HU2 . . .**155** A4
Clifton Terr HU5 . . . .**140** E1
Clifton Without Jun Sch
YO30 . . . .**129** F8
Clive Gr YO24 . . . .**129** F2
Clive Sullivan Way
HU4 . . . .**144** C4
Clixby Cl DN35 . . . .**103** D2
Clixby La DN38 . . . .**110** E7
Clockmill La YO42 . . . . .29 A4
Cloeberry Way 14 HU12 . . .72 C7
Cloister Wk DN20 . . . . .97 E3
Cloisters The
6 Grimsby DN37 . . . .**102** B4
15 Hemingbrough YO8 . . . .49 F1
Humberston DN36 . . . .**114** D8
Wilberfoss YO41 . . . . .27 F6
Cloisters Wlk YO31 . . . .**156** C3
Close The Cawood YO8 . . . . .48 A7
Goxhill DN19 . . . . .71 A1
Great Driffield YO25 . . . . . .**124** F5
Grimsby DN34 . . . .**152** A3
Kingston upon Hull
HU10 . . . .**138** F1
Kingston upon Hull
HU16 . . . .**138** F5
Kingston upon Hull HU7 . . .**141** D6
4 Leven HU17 . . . . .45 A8
5 Market Weighton YO43 . .**135** E4
Norton DN6 . . . . .76 E2
12 Patrington HU12 . . . . . . .74 D1
Riccall YO19 . . . . .49 A8
Scunthorpe DN16 . . . .**151** B6
8 Withernsea HU19 . . . . . .75 A4
York YO30 . . . .**129** F8
Clouds La Belton DN9 . . . . .95 B1
West Butterwick DN17 . . . .**106** C8
Clough Garth HU12 . . . . . . .72 D8
Clough La DN6 . . . . .77 B2
Clough Rd HU5 . . . .**140** F3
Cloughton Gr HU5 . . . .**139** E2
Clovelly Gdns 3 HU5 . . . . .**140** E1
Clover Bank View HU6 . . . .56 F5
Cloverley Cl YO41 . . . . .15 C2
Cloverley Rd 6 YO16 . . . . . .**123** A6
Clowes Ct HU4 . . . .**143** E1
Clumber Pl DN35 . . . .**153** E1
Clumber St HU5 . . . .**145** C8
Clyde St Grimsby DN32 . . . .**152** F4
Kingston upon Hull HU3 . . .**144** F5
Clyfton Cres DN40 . . . . .87 B1
Coach House Garth
YO42 . . . . .28 D3
Coach House Gdns
DN20 . . . .**108** E8
Coachings The 4 HU13 . . . .69 E4
Coal Pit La WF8 . . . . .76 A2
Coal Shore La LN11 . . . . . .**115** E1
Coastguard Hill YO14 . . . . . .3 E5
Coates Ave DN15 . . . . .83 A5
Coates Marsh La DN14 . . . .63 B2
Cobble La DN14 . . . . .51 F1
Cobbler Hill DN14 . . . .**149** B6
Cobcroft La WF11 . . . . .76 B8
Cobdale La YO42 . . . . .29 F7
Cobden St HU3 . . . .**144** F4
Cobden St North End
DN32 . . . .**152** F4
Cochrane St YO8 . . . .**148** D3
Cock Pit Cl HU10 . . . .**143** C6
Cockerell La YO25 . . . . .22 B4
Cocketts La DN20 . . . .**108** F5
Cockret Cl 8 YO8 . . . .**148** B6
Cockret Ct YO8 . . . .**148** B7
Cockret Rd YO8 . . . .**148** B7
Cockthorne La DN15 . . . . . .83 C7
Coda Ave YO23 . . . .**133** B3

Coelus St HU9 . . . .**155** C3
Coeside YO24 . . . .**132** B7
Cogan St HU1 . . . .**155** A1
Coggan Way YO23 . . . .**132** F4
Cohort Cl 10 HU15 . . . . .68 C5
Coke Oven Ave DN16 . . . . .**151** F6
Cold Harbour Rd HU17 . . . .43 A1
Cold Harbour View 5
HU17 . . . . .43 A2
Coldstream Cl 4 HU8 . . . . .**142** C5
Cole St
Scunthorpe DN15 . . . .**151** B7
York YO31 . . . .**156** B4
Coleby Rd DN15 . . . . .82 E7
Coledale Cl 2 YO30 . . . . . .**126** F1
Coleford Gr HU7 . . . .**141** A7
Coleford Prim Sch
HU7 . . . .**141** A7
Colenso St YO23 . . . .**156** B1
Coleridge Ave DN17 . . . . . .**150** D3
Coleridge St HU8 . . . .**141** D2
Colin Ave DN32 . . . .**153** B2
Colin Rd DN16 . . . .**151** C6
Colins Wlk DN21 . . . .**107** C4
Coll of St John The
YO31 . . . .**156** B3
College Ave 31 DN33 . . . . . .**113** E8
College Cl DN15 . . . . .82 C8
College Farm Cl DN14 . . . . .77 A8
College Gdns
32 Grimsby DN33 . . . .**113** E8
Hornsea HU18 . . . .**134** C5
College Gr HU9 . . . .**141** F1
College of Law YO23 . . . . .**133** B7
College of Ripon & St Johns
YO10 . . . .**131** B3
College of Ripon & York St
Johns YO31 . . . .**156** B3
College Rd
Barrow upon Humber
DN19 . . . . .85 E7
Copmanthorpe YO23 . . . . .**132** A3
Thornton Curtis DN39 . . . . .86 B6
College St
Cleethorpes DN35 . . . .**153** E2
Grimsby DN34 . . . .**152** C2
Kingston upon Hull HU1 . . .**141** D6
Kingston upon Hull HU2 . . .**155** A4
York YO1 . . . .**156** B3
Colleridge Gr 4 HU17 . . . . .55 E8
Colleys HU19 . . . . .75 A5
Colleywell Cl 3 DN9 . . . . . .**105** A2
Collier Cl 10 HU14 . . . . .69 A4
Collier Hag La YO23 . . . . . . .24 B3
Collier Rd 16 DN40 . . . . .87 C1
Collier St HU1 . . . .**155** A2
Colliergate YO1 . . . .**156** B2
Collin Ave HU9 . . . .**142** C2
Collingwood Ave
YO24 . . . .**129** F2
Collingwood Cres 12
DN34 . . . .**102** B2
Collingwood Prim Sch
HU3 . . . .**145** C7
Collingwood Rd 3 YO15 . . . .4 C3
Collingwood St HU3 . . . . . .**145** D7
Collinson Ave DN15 . . . . . .**150** D4
Collinson La HU15 . . . . .67 A8
Collum Ave DN16 . . . .**151** B3
Collum Gdns DN16 . . . .**151** B2
Collum La DN16 . . . .**151** B3
Collynson Cl 1 HU10 . . . . .**143** E8
Colonel's Wlk DN14 . . . . . .**149** D5
Colonial St HU2 . . . .**145** D7
Colson Pl DN35 . . . .**153** B3
Coltman Ave HU17 . . . .**154** C4
Coltman Cl HU17 . . . .**136** F7
Coltman St HU3 . . . .**145** C5
Colton St 3 Brigg DN20 . . . .98 B2
Misterton DN10 . . . .**116** C5
Coltsfoot Cl 5 DN15 . . . . . .96 B7
Coltsfoot Dr DN37 . . . .**113** D7
Columbia Rd DN32 . . . .**153** C4
Columbus Way DN33 . . . . .**102** C2
Colville Ave HU4 . . . .**144** B6
Colwall Ave HU5 . . . .**139** D2
Colwyn Cl 5 HU7 . . . . .57 A7
Combe St DN35 . . . .**153** C4
Comforts Ave DN15 . . . . . .**151** A6
Commerce La HU1 . . . .**145** D4
Commercial Rd
Kingston upon Hull HU1 . . .**155** B1
Scunthorpe DN16 . . . .**151** C7
Commodore Croft
HU1 . . . .**155** B1
Common Croft La YO26 . . .12 E1
Common Hill YO43 . . . . .53 C5
Common La
Barnby Dun with Kirk Sandall
DN3 . . . . .92 B4
Beal DN14 . . . . .61 D3
Burn YO8 . . . . .62 F7
Catton YO41 . . . . .27 E8
Dunnington YO19 . . . . .26 E5
Fangfoss YO41 . . . . .16 B1
Knottingley WF11 . . . . .61 B1
North Cave HU15 . . . . .53 B2
Norton DN6 . . . . .76 E2
1 Seaton HU11 . . . . .35 A1
Sutton upon Derwent
YO41 . . . . .38 C8
Temple Hirst YO8 . . . . .62 F4
Thorganby YO19 . . . . .37 F5
Thornton YO42 . . . . .39 B8
Twin Rivers DN17 . . . . .81 B6
Walden Stubbs DN6 . . . . . .76 A4
Warthill YO19 . . . . .14 F2
Wawne HU7 . . . . .56 F7

Common La continued
Welton HU15 . . . . .68 D4
York YO31 . . . .**131** B1
Common La W HU15 . . . . . .53 D4
Common Mid Rd DN17 . . . .94 C8
Common Rd
Broughton DN20 . . . . .97 E4
Dunnington YO19 . . . . .26 F7
Rowley HU20 . . . . .54 F5
Skipwith YO8 . . . . .37 E1
South Cave HU15 . . . . .67 C7
Commonside
Crowle DN17 . . . . .94 C8
Westwoodside DN9 . . . . . .**105** A2
Compass Rd HU6 . . . .**140** C8
Compton Dr
Grimsby DN34 . . . .**152** C3
Keyingham HU12 . . . . .73 C3
Compton St YO30 . . . .**130** A6
Comrie Dr 16 YO42 . . . . . . .29 A3
Concast Rd DN16 . . . . .97 A3
Concorde Pk YO30 . . . .**127** A3
Coney St YO1 . . . .**156** B2
Coneycroft 10 YO19 . . . . . . .26 F7
Coneygarth La YO19 . . . . . .26 E5
Conference Ct 10 DN16 . . . .96 D1
Conifer Cl
6 Kingston upon Hull
HU4 . . . .**144** C7
Scunthorpe DN17 . . . .**150** C1
6 York YO32 . . . .**127** D3
Conifers Cl 2 YO8 . . . . .48 C1
Coningsby Dr DN34 . . . .**152** A1
Coningsby Rd DN17 . . . . . .**150** D1
Conington Ave HU17 . . . . . .**137** B4
Conisborough Ave 2
DN36 . . . .**113** F7
Coniston Ave DN33 . . . .**113** D8
Coniston Cl 1 YO30 . . . . . .**126** F1
Coniston Cres
19 Humberston DN36 . . . . .**103** C1
10 Humberston DN36 . . . . .**103** C1
Humberston DN36 . . . .**114** C8
Coniston Dr YO10 . . . .**131** B4
Coniston La
Coniston HU11 . . . . .58 A5
Swine HU11 . . . . .57 E6
Coniston Way DN14 . . . . . .**149** E5
Connaught Ave DN32 . . . . .**152** D1
Connaught Rd 9 DN21 . . . .**117** B1
Connaught Way YO32 . . . . .**127** F6
Consort Ct HU9 . . . .**146** B5
Constable Ave HU11 . . . . . .58 A4
Constable Cl
18 Flamborough YO15 . . . . .5 A2
Sproatley HU11 . . . . .58 D5
Constable Garth 5 HU12 72 D7
Constable Prim Sch
HU3 . . . .**145** C5
Constable Rd
Flamborough YO15 . . . . . . .5 A2
Hornsea HU18 . . . .**134** D5
Hunmanby YO14 . . . . .3 A8
Constable St HU3 . . . .**145** C5
Constantine Ave YO10 . . . .**131** A4
Constitution Hill
HU17 . . . .**136** A6
Constitutional Ave
DN35 . . . .**153** C4
Convamore Rd DN32 . . . . . .**152** D1
Convent La HU3 . . . .**145** D6
Conway Ave DN34 . . . .**152** A3
Conway Cl
Kingston upon Hull HU3 . . .**145** B5
2 York YO30 . . . .**126** E3
Conway Sq DN15 . . . .**150** E7
Conyard Rd DN35 . . . .**153** E3
Conyers Ave DN33 . . . .**102** E1
Cookbury Cl 6 HU7 . . . . . . .56 F5
Cookridge Dr 11 DN7 . . . . .92 D4
Cooks La Grimsby DN37 . . .**102** B5
Nettleton LN7 . . . .**111** A3
Coombs Yd HU17 . . . .**154** C4
Cooper La DN37 . . . .**101** E1
Cooper Rd DN32 . . . .**153** A3
Cooper St
Beverley HU17 . . . .**154** B4
Kingston upon Hull HU2 . . .**155** B4
Coopers Dr YO23 . . . .**132** B3
Copandale Rd HU17 . . . . . .**154** C4
Cope St DN32 . . . .**153** A4
Copenhagen Rd HU7 . . . . .**140** F5
Copmanthorpe Jun Sch
YO23 . . . .**132** B3
Copmanthorpe La
YO23 . . . .**132** E3
Copmanthorpe Prim Sch
YO23 . . . .**132** B3
Copmanthorpe Recn Ctr &
Sports Club YO23 . . . . . .**132** B2
Copper Beech Cl 6
HU14 . . . . .69 B6
Copper Beech Wlk 24
DN16 . . . . .96 D2
Copper Beeches The 2
YO19 . . . . .26 E7
Coppergate
Nafferton YO25 . . . .**125** F7
1 Riccall YO19 . . . . .36 F1
York YO1 . . . .**156** B2
Coppergate Wlk YO1 . . . . .**156** B2
Coppice Ave DN7 . . . . .92 D3
Coppice Cl 10 YO32 . . . . . .**127** C8
Coppice Gr 39 DN7 . . . . . . .92 D3
Coppice La 1 DN7 . . . . .92 D3
Coppice Side HU4 . . . .**144** C6

Coppice The
Bishopthorpe YO23 . . . . . .**132** F4
Brayton YO8 . . . . .48 C1
Coppleflat La
Rowley HU17 . . . . .55 D6
Walkington HU17 . . . . .43 C1
Copse Cl 1 DN40 . . . . .87 C2
Copse Mead YO25 . . . .**124** D5
Copse Rd DN16 . . . .**151** B1
Copse The
Beverley HU17 . . . .**137** B3
Bigby DN20 . . . . .98 D1
28 Grimsby DN33 . . . .**113** E8
Copwood Gr 7 YO32 . . . . . .**127** C8
Coral Dr 2 DN37 . . . .**113** D7
Corban La YO32 . . . . .13 B6
Corban Way 21 YO32 . . . . . .13 D5
Corbridge Cl 2 HU9 . . . . . .**142** E1
Corby Pk HU14 . . . . .69 A5
Cordella Cl 1 HU3 . . . .**145** A5
Coriander Cl HU17 . . . .**154** A1
Corinthian Ave DN34 . . . . .**152** B2
Corinthian Way HU5 . . . . . .**146** D6
Cormorant Cl 2 HU7 . . . . .**141** D8
Cormorant Dr 1 DN37 . . . .**102** B4
Cornborough Av YO31 . . . .**130** F6
Cornelius Cswy YO8 . . . . . .49 E8
Cornelius Wlk YO43 . . . . . .**135** E4
Corner Cl 17 YO32 . . . . .13 D5
Cornfield Cl 5 DN33 . . . . . .**113** D8
Cornfield Cres YO16 . . . . . .**122** B2
Cornhill Dr DN18 . . . . .85 A8
Cornlands Rd YO24 . . . .**129** B1
Cornley Rd DN10 . . . .**116** A6
Cornmill Cl YO8 . . . . .48 B8
Cornwall Dr YO10 . . . .**133** E8
Cornwall Rd
2 Keadby DN17 . . . . .95 D6
Scunthorpe DN16 . . . .**151** C1
Cornwall St
Kingston upon Hull
HU16 . . . .**139** C6
Kingston upon Hull HU8 . . .**141** A1
7 Kirton in Lindsey DN21 108 B1
Cornwell Cl 3 DN33 . . . . . .**102** E2
Cornwood Way 11 YO32 127 C8
Corona Dr
Kingston upon Hull HU8 . . .**141** C4
8 Thorne/Moorends DN8 . . .79 A1
Coronation Cl HU17 . . . . . .**154** C3
Coronation Cres 10
DN9 . . . .**105** D6
Coronation Gdns 4
DN20 . . . . .97 E3
Coronation Rd
Cleethorpes DN35 . . . .**153** F1
Stainforth DN7 . . . . .92 C6
7 Ulceby DN39 . . . . .86 A1
Coronation Rd N HU5 . . . . .**139** C2
Coronation Rd S HU5 . . . . .**139** B1
Coronation St 10 DN15 . . . .**149** C4
Coronet Cl 5 HU6 . . . .**140** B8
Corporation Rd
Beverley HU17 . . . .**154** A3
Grimsby DN31 . . . .**152** C5
Kingston upon Hull HU9 . . .**147** A7
Scunthorpe DN15 . . . .**151** A7
Corpslanding Rd YO25 . . . .33 A7
Corran Garth 6 HU4 . . . . . .**144** A3
Corringham C of E Sch
DN21 . . . .**118** B2
Corringham Rd
Corringham DN21 . . . .**117** D1
Gainsborough DN21 . . . . . .**117** D1
Corsair Gr 4 HU3 . . . .**145** A4
Cosford Garth 5 HU7 . . . . .57 A5
Cosgrove St DN35 . . . .**153** F2
Cosmo Ave YO31 . . . .**131** A5
Cotham Gdns 4 DN41 . . . .**101** A4
Cotness La DN14 . . . . .65 F3
Cotswold Ave DN14 . . . . . .**149** D5
Cotswold Dr 20 DN37 . . . . .**113** D6
Cotswold Rd DN8 . . . . .93 A7
Cotswold Way DN32 . . . . . .**128** C3
Cotswolds The HU9 . . . . . .**142** D2
Cottage Beck Rd
DN16 . . . .**151** B6
Cottage Cl DN20 . . . .**108** F5
Cottage Dr HU10 . . . .**143** B8
Cottage Field 1 HU17 . . . . .43 A2
Cottage Mews HU17 . . . . . .**154** B3
Cottage Yard La DN36 . . . .**114** C7
Cottam La YO25 . . . . .8 C5
Cotterdale HU7 . . . .**140** E7
Cottesmore Rd
Cleethorpes DN35 . . . .**103** C1
6 Kingston upon Hull
HU13 . . . .**144** A2
Cottingham Croxby Prim Sch
HU5 . . . .**139** D4
Cottingham Gr 2 HU6 . . . . .**139** F4
Cottingham High Sch
HU16 . . . .**138** E8
Cottingham Playsport
HU16 . . . .**139** A7
Cottingham Rd HU5 . . . . . .**139** E4
Cottingham St DN32 . . . . . .**149** C1
Cottingham Sta HU16 . . . . .**139** B6
Cottom La YO42 . . . . .38 C2
Coulam Pl 8 DN36 . . . .**114** D8
Coulbeck Dr DN35 . . . .**153** D1
Coulman Rd 4 DN8 . . . . . . .93 B8
Coulman St 5 DN8 . . . . . . .93 B8
Coulson Cl 5 YO32 . . . . . . .14 C8
Coulson Dr HU13 . . . .**143** F2

Crescent St continued
Kingston upon Hull
HU16 ....139 A6
Crescent The
Beckingham DN10 ....116 E1
9 Bridlington YO15 ......122 F2
Brough HU15 ....68 D6
Burton Fleming YO25 ......2 E3
Hatfield DN7 ....92 C5
Holton le Clay DN36 ....114 A5
Hornsea HU18 ....134 D3
Huggate YO42 ....18 C2
Kelfield YO19 ....36 D1
Kexby HU5 ....27 C5
4 Kirk Sandall DN3 .....92 A1
13 Patrington HU12 ......74 D1
6 Riccall YO19 ....48 F8
Stamford Bridge YO41 ...15 D2
York YO24 ....156 A1
Cressey St DN31 ......152 E5
Cresswell Cl HU2 ......155 A4
Cresta Dr 10 DN17 .....96 C2
Cresta The DN34 ....152 C1
Creyke Cl 6 HU16 .....139 B7
Creyke La 7 HU15 ......68 D6
Creyke View DN14 ....64 A1
Crichton Ave YO30 ....130 B8
Cridling Gdns DN6 ......76 F2
Cridling Pl 5 DN35 ....103 B2
Crinan Ct 3 YO32 .....127 F6
Crinan Dr 1 HU6 ......140 B8
Crispin Cl 5 HU4 .....144 A2
Crispin Way DN16 ....96 D1
Croft Ave 8 WF11 ......61 A3
Croft Cl
Eastrington DN14 ....51 F1
Market Weighton YO43 ..135 D3
Croft Ct YO23 ....133 A4
Croft Dr HU10 ....143 C5
Croft Farm Cl YO23 ...132 B3
Croft La DN17 ....96 C1
Croft Lodge DN9 ....94 E1
Croft Pk HU14 ....69 A5
Croft Rd
Camblesforth YO8 ....63 D4
Finningley DN10 ....104 A1
Croft The
Beverley HU17 ....136 C7
Kingston upon Hull HU7 .140 E8
Knottingley WF11 ....61 A3
22 Thorne/Moorends DN8 .93 B7
1 West/East Butterwick
DN17 ....106 D8
Croft View
Kingston upon Hull HU7 .141 C7
Kingston upon Hull
HU10 ....143 C6
Market Weighton YO43 ..135 D3
Crofters Dr HU16 ......139 C5
Croftlands 7 WF11 .....61 A3
Crofts La HU19 ....74 F4
Croft's La DN9 ....106 D3
Croft's La DN7 ....92 B6
Crofts The
9 Humberston DN36 ....114 C8
Scunthorpe DN16 ....151 B6
Croftside 1 YO26 .....129 B3
Croftway
Camblesforth YO8 ....63 C5
Selby YO8 ....148 C4
2 York YO26 ....129 B3
Cromarty Cl HU9 ....142 A3
Crombie Ave YO30 .....130 B7
Cromer Ave DN34 ......152 A1
Cromer St
4 Kingston upon Hull
HU5 ....140 D2
York YO30 ....130 B7
Cromford St 13 DN21 ..117 B1
Cromwell Ave DN16 ....151 B5
Cromwell Cl 2 HU3 ....145 D8
Cromwell Ct 1 HU10 ..143 E7
Cromwell Rd
Cleethorpes DN35 ......103 D2
Grimsby DN31 ....152 A4
York YO1 ....156 B1
Cromwell View 25 LN7 .111 B4
Crook Hill HU15 ....68 C8
Crook La HU11 ....58 D7
Crook Mill Rd DN40 .....86 D5
Crook Tree La DN7 ......92 F5
Crooked Billet St 5
DN21 ....117 A2
Crookes Broom Ave
DN7 ....92 D4
Crookes Broom La
DN7 ....92 D4
Crookland La YO32 .....13 F5
Croom Medieval Village ★
YO25 ....34 B1
Croome Dale La YO17 ...7 C6
Croome Rd YO25 ....7 B4
Cropton Rd HU5 ....139 E2
Crosby Ave DN15 ....96 C7
Crosby Inf & Jun Sch
DN15 ....151 A8
Crosby Rd
Grimsby DN33 ....102 D1
Scunthorpe DN15 ......151 B8
Crosland Rd DN37 .....102 E4
Cross Carr Rd DN20 ...109 A5
Cross Coates Rd
DN34 ....152 A2
Cross Gate YO43 ....41 E6
Cross Gates YO25 ......21 F8
Cross Gordon St 1
DN14 ....149 C4

Cross Hill
5 Brandesburton YO25 ..34 B2
Haxey DN9 ....105 C3
Hayton YO42 ....40 C8
Cross Hills La YO8 ....148 A5
Cross La
Alkborough DN15 ....82 C8
3 Amcotts DN17 ....81 F1
Flaxton YO60 ....14 E8
Flixborough DN15 ....82 A2
Fulford YO19 ....133 F5
Hutton Cranswick YO25 ..32 F6
Leven HU17 ....44 F7
North Frodingham YO25 ..33 F7
North Kelsey LN7 ......110 B5
Cross Rd Hatfield DN7 ...93 B4
North Frodingham YO25 ..33 F7
Ulceby DN39 ....86 B3
Cross Slack 8 DN17 ....94 D8
Cross St
8 Aldbrough HU11 ......47 C1
3 Barrow upon Humber
DN19 ....85 D8
Beverley HU17 ....154 A2
Bridlington YO15 ......122 F2
12 Brigg DN20 ....98 C2
Cleethorpes DN35 .....153 E2
Crowle DN17 ....94 D8
7 Gainsborough DN21 ..117 A2
36 Gainsborough DN21 ..117 B1
Garthorpe & Fockerby
DN17 ....81 E6
Goole DN14 ....149 D3
Grimsby DN31 ....152 F6
Hatfield DN7 ....46 C6
Kingston upon Hull HU1 .155 A2
2 Scunthorpe DN15 ....151 B8
Skipsea YO25 ....23 A2
3 Waltham DN37 ......113 E6
West Halton DN15 ......82 E8
5 York YO24 ....129 C3
Cross St W DN14 ......149 B4
Cross Tree Rd DN17 ...107 D7
Crossbeck Rd 2 DN16 ..96 D2
Crossfield Cres YO19 ..133 E6
Crossfield Rd
Kingston upon Hull
HU13 ....143 D1
Kingston upon Hull HU4 .144 D5
Crosshill La DN14 ....77 C6
Crossings The 13 DN14 .64 E4
Crosskill Cl HU17 .....154 C4
Crosslands La HU15 ....53 B3
Crosslands Rd 2 YO10 .133 E8
Crossmoor Bank DN14 ...80 C5
Crossmoor La YO32 .....13 E6
Crossway The
Grimsby DN34 ....102 B2
2 York YO31 ....130 E8
Crossways
10 Stainforth DN7 ......92 C6
York YO10 ....131 C1
Crosswood Cl 6 HU7 ...57 A7
Crow Croft La
Balne DN14 ....78 A5
Pollington DN14 ....78 A5
Crow Hill Ave DN35 ...153 E2
Crow Tree Bank DN8 ....93 D4
Crowberry Dr DN16 ....151 D1
Crowland Ave
Grimsby DN34 ....102 C2
Scunthorpe DN16 ......151 A3
Crowland Cl 2 HU8 ....142 C7
Crowland Rd 8 DN17 ....94 D7
Crowle Bank Rd DN17 ..95 C4
Crowle County Prim Sch
DN17 ....94 C7
Crowle Dr DN33 ....102 D2
Crowle Rd DN17 ....80 F2
Crowle St HU9 ....146 D7
Crowle Sta DN17 ....94 E6
Crowle Waste or Moors
Nature Reserve ★
DN17 ....94 B8
Crowther Cl HU17 .....137 A6
Crowther Way 5 HU14 ..69 B7
Croxby Ave DN33 ......113 E8
Croxby Gr 14 DN33 ....113 E8
Croxton Rd
Croxton DN39 ....99 F7
Kirmington DN39 ......100 A5
Cruckley La YO25 ....21 E1
Crudhall La YO42 ....40 A8
Crummock 3 YO24 .....132 C7
Crumpton Rd YO43 ....135 C3
Crystal St HU3 ....145 C7
Cuckoo La DN7 ....92 E6
Cudworth Gr 1 HU8 ...141 B1
Cullen Cl HU8 ....141 C5
Cullingworth Ave 2
HU6 ....140 C7
Cumberland Ave
DN32 ....152 D1
Cumberland Cl
Goole DN14 ....149 A4
6 Strensall YO32 ......14 B6
Cumberland Rd DN35 ..103 D1
Cumberland St
Kingston upon Hull HU2 .155 A3
York YO1 ....156 B2
Cumbrian Ave 4 YO32 ..14 B6
Cumbrian Way HU7 .....56 F7
Cundall Cl
Kingston upon Hull HU9 .141 E1
6 Strensall YO32 ......14 C6
Cunningham Rd 3 DN7 .104 A8
Cupid's Alley YO17 ......6 B6
Cupola Way DN15 ....96 C8

Curlew Cl
Beverley HU17 ....136 E6
Driffield YO25 ....125 A5
Kingston upon Hull HU7 .141 D8
Curlew Glebe 8 YO19 ..26 E7
Curry Rd DN34 ....102 A2
Curson Terr YO8 ....49 E3
Curzen Cres 5 DN3 ....92 A2
Curzon Ave DN35 ......153 D1
Curzon Ct 3 DN35 .....103 B2
Curzon St
4 Gainsborough DN21 ..117 B1
Kingston upon Hull HU3 .144 F7
Curzon Terr YO23 .....130 B1
Cushman Cres 10 DN40 .87 C1
Custance Wlk YO23 ....156 A1
Cuthbert Ave 6 DN38 ...99 B4
Cuxwold Rd
Scunthorpe DN16 ......151 C4
Swallow LN7 ....112 B5
Cycle St 4 YO10 ......131 A3
Cygnet St YO23 ....156 A1
Cynthia Rd DN32 ......153 C1
Cyprus St HU9 ....147 B8
Cyrano Way DN37 .....102 B4

D

Dacre Lakeside Pk ★
YO25 ....34 B1
Dagger La HU1 ....155 B2
Daggett La YO25 ....21 F8
Daggett Rd DN35 ......103 D2
Dairy House La HU12 ...73 A8
Dairycoates Ave HU3 ..145 A4
Dairycoates Rd HU4 ...144 E3
Daisyfield Dr HU9 .....142 D6
Dalby Gr HU9 ....142 B2
Dalby Mead YO32 ......127 F1
Dale Cl Selby YO8 .....148 C3
8 Swanland HU14 ....69 B7
Dale Dike Gr YO30 .....126 F2
Dale Garth YO43 ......135 E5
Dale Gate HU17 ....43 A1
Dale Pit Rd DN7 ....92 F3
Dale Pk Ave DN15 ......83 A5
Dale Rd
Brantingham HU15 ......68 C8
Bridlington YO16 ......122 D4
Elloughton-cum-Brough
HU15 ....68 C6
Swanland HU14 ....69 B7
Welton HU15 ....68 E6
Dale St
Scunthorpe DN15 ......151 A8
York YO23 ....156 A1
Dale St N DN15 ....150 F8
Dale View 27 DN33 ....102 C2
Dalehouse Dr 2 HU10 .143 F6
Dale's La YO31 ....130 F6
Dales Prim Sch The
HU7 ....56 F6
Dales The
Kingston upon Hull
HU16 ....138 D6
Kingston upon Hull HU9 .142 D2
Scunthorpe DN17 ....96 C2
Dalesway HU10 ....143 B6
Dalguise Gr YO31 .....156 C4
Dalkeith Cl 16 HU7 .....57 A6
Dallisons Rd DN20 .....109 A5
Dalmais Cl 1 YO42 .....28 E4
Dalmally Cl YO24 ......132 B6
Dalmatian Way DN20 ...97 E4
Dalsetter Rise HU8 ....141 F6
Dalton Cl YO25 ....124 D3
Dalton Hill YO19 ....38 A8
Dalton La HU12 ....73 F6
Dalton St HU8 ....141 A1
Dalton Terr YO24 ......130 A3
Dalwood Cl HU7 ....141 C8
Dam Bank YO8 ....148 C6
Dam Green La HU15 ....68 C2
Dam Hill YO23 ....24 B4
Dam La Ottringham HU12 .73 D2
Selby YO8 ....48 B3
Thornton Curtis DN39 ...85 E4
Dam Rd DN18 ....69 E1
Dame Kendal Gr 29
DN33 ....102 D2
Damson Garth YO25 ....31 F2
Danby Cl HU8 ....141 E2
Danby Rd DN17 ....107 D7
Dancing La Riston HU11 ..45 C5
Swine HU11 ....57 D7
Dane Ave
Thorpe Willoughby YO8 ..48 B1
York YO26 ....129 C5
Dane Cl 13 DN20 ....97 E4
Dane Park Prim Sch
HU6 ....139 E8
Dane Park Rd HU6 .....139 E7
Danebury Cres YO26 ..129 C5
Danebury Dr YO26 ....129 C4
Danes Croft
Bridlington YO16 ......122 D5
2 York YO10 ....133 D7
Danes Ct 5 YO19 ....49 A8
Danes Dr HU13 ....69 F4
Danes' Dyke ★ YO15 ...4 F2
Dane's Graves (Tumuli) ★
YO25 ....8 D2
Danes Hills (Tumuli) ★
YO8 ....37 E2
Danes Rd DN21 ....117 C1
Danescroft YO8 ....148 C2
Danesfield Ave DN37 ..113 E7

Danesfort Ave YO24 ...129 D2
Danesgate YO26 ....129 C4
Danesmead YO10 ......133 D8
Danesway HU17 ....136 D6
Daneswell Cl 3 YO41 ..15 D2
Dansom La HU8 ....141 B1
Dansom La S HU8 .....146 B8
Danson Cl DN18 ....85 A8
Danthorpe Rd HU11 ....59 B4
Danube Rd HU5 ....144 C8
Danum Cl 14 DN8 ......93 B8
Danum Dr YO10 ....133 E8
Danum Rd
2 Hatfield DN7 ....92 D3
Scunthorpe DN17 ......150 F4
York YO10 ....133 E8
Dar Beck Rd DN21 ....107 C4
Darbie Cl YO32 ....127 D4
Darby Rd DN15 ....82 B4
D'arcy Rd YO8 ....148 E4
Dark La 5 Amcotts DN17 .81 F1
Paull HU12 ....72 D4
Darley Cl Kilham YO25 ...9 B3
7 Stamford Bridge YO41 .15 D2
Darling La YO23 ....36 C8
Darlington Gr DN8 ......79 B2
Darnborough St YO23 ..156 B1
Darnbrook Wlk YO31 ..131 B5
Darnholm Ct 14 HU11 ..141 E7
Darnholme Cres
DN17 ....107 D7
Darrismere Villas 4
HU3 ....145 A5
Dart Gr HU8 ....142 B5
Dartmouth Rd DN17 ...150 D5
Darwin Rd YO16 ......122 E6
Darwin St 4 DN21 ....108 B1
Datchet Garth 3 HU4 ..144 B2
Daubney St DN35 .....153 B4
Dauby La YO41 ....27 B3
Davenport Ave HU13 ..143 D1
Davenport Dr DN35 ...153 D1
David Lister High Sch
HU9 ....141 E1
David Pl DN36 ....114 A7
David St DN32 ....152 F1
David's Cl HU16 ......138 B8
Davidstow Cl HU7 .....140 F8
Davie Pl DN35 ....153 B3
Daville Cl HU5 ....139 B1
Davis's Cl HU13 ......143 C8
Davy Ave DN15 ....150 E8
Davy Cres 2 DN20 .....98 C3
Davygate YO1 ....156 B2
Daw La YO23 ....36 A5
Dawes La 1 DN15 .....151 C7
Dawlish Rd DN33 .....113 E7
Dawnay Dr HU10 .....144 E4
Dawnay Garth
Shipton YO30 ....12 E5
2 Snaith DN14 ....63 B1
Dawnay Rd HU11 ....58 A4
Dawnhill La DN21 .....119 B2
Dawson Dr HU6 ....140 D8
Day Cl Keadby DN17 ....95 D6
Wrawby DN20 ....98 E4
Daysfoot Ct 8 YO10 ..130 E3
Dayton Rd HU5 ....139 D1
De Aston Sq DN15 ....150 E7
De Grey Ct YO30 .....156 A4
De Grey Pl 2 YO23 ...133 B3
De Grey St
Kingston upon Hull HU5 .140 C2
York YO31 ....156 B4
De Grey Terr YO31 ....156 B4
De La Pole Ave HU3 ..144 F7
De Lacy La DN35 ......153 F2
De Lacy Way DN15 .....83 A5
De Mowbray Ct YO23 ..24 D3
Deacon Cl 3 YO8 .....148 B6
Deacon Dr DN15 ......150 B6
Deacons Ct YO23 .....132 B2
Dead La Bainton YO25 ..31 E7
Foggathorpe YO8 ....51 A8
Kirkburn YO25 ....20 A2
Lockington YO25 ....32 B2
Deal Cl HU8 ....141 E8
Dealtry Ave 1 YO32 ..127 C8
Dean La YO43 ....53 D4
Dean Rd DN15 ....150 E2
Deane Rd 12 DN40 .....87 C1
Deangate YO1 ....156 B3
Deanhead Gr YO30 ....126 E2
Deans Cl
Bishopthorpe YO23 ....132 F4
5 Misterton DN10 ....116 C5
Dean's La 7 YO42 .....29 A3
Deansgate DN34 ......152 C2
Dearne Gr 1 HU8 .....141 C1
Deaton La DN36 ......114 A7
Debdhill Rd DN10 .....116 C6
Deben Gr HU8 ....142 C7
Dee Cl DN14 ....132 B7
Dee St 6 HU3 ....145 B4
Deene Cl 3 DN34 .....102 B2
Deep The (Aquarium &
Marine Research Ctr) ★
.....................155 C1
Deepdale 5 YO24 .....132 D8
Deepdale Gr 2 HU9 ...146 E8
Deepfurrows La YO41 ..27 D3
Deeping Way YO8 .....148 A6
Deer Hill Gr YO30 ....126 F3
Deer Park Cl 1 LS25 ..61 F8
Deer Park Way 6 HU17 .55 F8
Deerhurst Gr HU7 .....141 A8
Deerstone Way 22 YO19 .26 F7
Defender Dr DN37 .....102 A4

Del Pyke YO31 ... 156 C4
Delamere Cl 6 YO32 ... 13 D5
Delamere Ct 24 DN35 ... 103 C1
Delhi St HU9 ... 147 B7
Delius Cl HU4 ... 144 B4
Dell The Beverley HU17 ... 137 B2
Scunthorpe DN17 ... 150 D1
5 Skelton YO30 ... 126 B5
Delwood YO10 ... 133 D7
Dempster Ave DN14 ... 149 C1
Denby Cl DN15 ... 150 D8
Denby Dr DN36 ... 103 B2
Dene Cl Dunswell HU6 ... 56 D5
Hensall DN14 ... 62 C2
Dene Park Sports Club HU6 ... 56 D5
Dene Rd Grimsby DN32 ... 102 F2
Kingston upon Hull HU16 ... 138 F6
Dene St HU9 ... 141 D1
Denehall Rd DN3 ... 92 A2
Denesway HU13 ... 143 D2
Denholme Ave 3 HU6 ... 140 C7
Denison Rd
Pocklington YO42 ... 29 A4
Selby YO8 ... 148 E4
Denmark Ct 7 HU9 ... 146 C7
Denmark Rise 5 HU15 ... 53 D3
Dennett Rd HU17 ... 137 B5
Dennis St YO1 ... 156 C2
Dennison St
1 York YO31 ... 130 E6
York YO31 ... 156 C4
Dent Rd HU5 ... 139 D3
Denton La YO43 ... 53 D6
Denton St HU17 ... 137 B3
Denton's Way DN20 ... 109 A5
Denver Rd 6 DN6 ... 76 F2
Deramore Dr YO10 ... 131 C3
Deramore Dr W YO10 ... 131 C3
Derby Cl DN32 ... 153 A5
Derby Rd DN15 ... 150 B6
Derby St HU3 ... 145 D8
Derringham Ave 5 HU4 144 B6
Derringham St HU3 ... 145 C7
Derry Way 27 DN33 ... 113 E8
Derrymore Rd HU10 ... 138 C2
Derrythorpe Rd DN17 ... 95 D4
Derwent Ave
18 North Ferriby HU14 ... 69 A4
York YO31 ... 130 F4
Derwent Cl
Elvington YO41 ... 27 B3
Hornsea HU18 ... 134 C5
Kingston upon Hull HU6 ... 139 D6
2 Stamford Bridge YO41 ... 15 D2
Derwent Cres DN14 ... 65 B7
Derwent Ct YO41 ... 27 C2
Derwent Dr 4 Barlby YO8 49 B5
12 Humberston DN36 ... 103 C1
2 Humberston DN36 ... 114 C8
9 Kirk Sandall DN3 ... 92 A2
Wheldrake YO19 ... 37 F7
Derwent Est YO19 ... 26 E7
Derwent Inf Sch YO10 ... 131 B4
Derwent Jun Sch YO10 ... 131 B4
Derwent Pk YO19 ... 38 A8
Derwent Rd
Goole DN14 ... 149 D1
1 Howden DN14 ... 65 B7
Scunthorpe DN16 ... 151 D2
York YO10 ... 133 D8
Derwent St HU8 ... 141 B1
Desmond Ave
4 Hornsea HU18 ... 134 C4
Kingston upon Hull HU6 ... 140 D4
Despatch Rd DN16 ... 97 A5
Detuyll St W DN15 ... 96 C7
Deveron Way YO24 ... 132 B7
Devon Pl YO10 ... 130 F3
Devon St
Kingston upon Hull HU16 ... 139 C7
Kingston upon Hull HU4 ... 144 F3
Devonshire Ave DN32 ... 102 E2
Devonshire Dr DN14 ... 149 B5
Devonshire Rd DN17 ... 150 F2
Dewberry Ct HU4 ... 144 D4
Dewsbury Ave DN15 ... 150 C8
Dewsbury Terr YO1 ... 156 A1
Deyne Ave DN15 ... 151 A7
Diadem Gr HU9 ... 142 C5
Dial Sq DN31 ... 152 E3
Diamond St YO31 ... 156 C4
Diana Princess of Wales Hospl DN33 ... 102 E2
Diana St DN15 ... 96 D7
Dibsdane HU6 ... 139 E8
Dick La DN14 ... 65 E7
Dickens Cl 1 YO32 ... 127 F1
Dickey La YO8 ... 48 D5
Dickinson Cl DN20 ... 108 F5
Dickinson's La DN36 ... 114 B1
Dickson Rd 4 YO24 ... 129 B1
Didscourt HU6 ... 139 E6
Digby Garth HU7 ... 57 A5
Digby Gdns DN34 ... 152 A1
Digby St DN15 ... 150 F8
Dijon Ave YO24 ... 129 C2
Dikelands Cl 19 YO26 ... 12 F1
Dikelands La YO26 ... 12 F1
Dill Dr HU17 ... 154 B1
Dilys Gr 5 YO26 ... 129 E4
Dimlington Rd HU12 ... 90 F6
Dimmer Dales Rd HU12 ... 90 D5
Dingley Cl HU6 ... 140 B6
Dirty La DN7 ... 92 D8
Discovery Ctr★ DN35 ... 103 D2
Disraeli Cl YO32 ... 127 E1
Ditmas Ave 9 HU4 ... 144 B6
Division Rd 1 HU3 ... 145 B4
Dixon Ave
Broughton DN20 ... 97 D3
Grimsby DN32 ... 102 F2
Dixon Cl 4 Brigg DN20 ... 98 C2
Market Weighton YO43 ... 135 D2
4 Tetney DN36 ... 114 D4
Dixon Ct HU16 ... 139 A5
Dixon La YO1 ... 156 C1
Dixsons Yd YO1 ... 156 C2
Dobella Ave DN14 ... 64 A1
Dobella La DN14 ... 79 B8
Dock Office Row HU1 ... 155 C3
Dock St HU1 ... 155 B2
Dodgson Terr YO26 ... 129 D4
Dodswell Gr HU9 ... 147 E8
Dodsworth Ave YO31 ... 130 E7
Dodthorpe HU6 ... 140 A8
Doe Park La YO41 ... 16 B4
Doe Pk YO30 ... 126 F2
Dog & Duck La
Beverley HU17 ... 154 A3
12 Gainsborough DN21 ... 117 A2
Dog & Duck Sq 13 YO15 ... 5 A2
Dog Kennel La HU17 ... 43 C3
Dolby Vale 23 DN34 ... 102 C2
Dole Rd DN17 ... 80 B1
Dolegate YO41 ... 15 F4
Doll La 2 DN20 ... 98 F7
Dollyth Howe★ YO17 ... 6 F6
Dolman Cres 11 DN17 ... 96 C2
Dolphin St DN35 ... 153 F2
Dominion Cl 9 DN36 ... 114 A7
Don Ave YO24 ... 132 E8
Don St DN14 ... 149 D1
Doncaster Rd
Brayton YO8 ... 148 B3
Gunness DN15 ... 95 E6
Hatfield DN7 ... 92 D3
Haxey DN9 ... 104 F2
North Elmsall WF8 ... 76 A1
Scunthorpe DN15 ... 150 A4
Stainforth DN7 ... 92 B6
Doncaster St HU3 ... 145 B6
Donna Fields YO25 ... 9 F6
Donnington Gdns DN15 ... 150 F7
Donnington St DN32 ... 152 F3
Donville Rd DN17 ... 81 A3
Dooks Cl DN21 ... 107 C1
Doon Garth HU4 ... 144 A3
Dorado Cl 2 HU3 ... 145 A5
Dorchester Prim Sch HU7 ... 141 B6
Dorchester Rd
Kingston upon Hull HU7 ... 141 B7
Scunthorpe DN17 ... 150 C4
Doriam Ave YO31 ... 127 F2
Doriam Dr YO31 ... 127 F2
Dorking Cl HU8 ... 142 A4
Dornoch Dr HU8 ... 141 C3
Dorothy Ave
Thorne/Moorends DN8 ... 92 F8
6 Waltham DN37 ... 113 E7
Dorr La DN14 ... 78 A8
Dorrington Cl 23 YO42 ... 29 A3
Dorset Ave HU11 ... 45 E2
Dorset Cl E 2 DN15 ... 82 B4
Dorset Cl W 1 DN15 ... 82 B4
Dorset St HU4 ... 144 F3
Dorsey Way 5 HU15 ... 68 C7
Dot Hill Cl 3 YO43 ... 53 F7
Double Bridges Rd DN8 ... 93 B6
Double Dike★ HU20 ... 54 E5
Doughty Cl 2 DN37 ... 113 E7
Doughty Rd DN32 ... 152 E3
Douglas Ave DN34 ... 152 A4
Douglas Rd
Cleethorpes DN35 ... 153 D4
Kingston upon Hull HU8 ... 142 C6
Douglas St 3 YO8 ... 148 C5
Dove Cl HU12 ... 74 A8
Dove Cote Gdns DN14 ... 62 D2
Dove La HU12 ... 74 B8
Dove St YO23 ... 156 A1
Dovecote Garth 5 YO41 27 B2
Dovecote Mdws DN20 ... 98 D3
Dovedale Cl DN15 ... 83 A6
Dovedale Ct YO16 ... 122 F7
Dovedale Dr 18 DN33 ... 113 E8
Dovedale Gr 1 HU9 ... 146 E8
Dovedale Rd DN16 ... 151 D1
Dover St Grimsby DN31 ... 152 C4
Kingston upon Hull HU3 ... 145 C8
Dower Chase YO19 ... 37 A6
Dower Pk YO19 ... 37 B6
Dower Rise 11 HU14 ... 69 B7
Downe Cl DN14 ... 78 D7
Downe St YO25 ... 124 E4
Downfield Ave HU6 ... 140 B8
Downhill Dr 7 HU7 ... 57 B5
Downing Cl 7 DN34 ... 102 C3
Downing Cres 11 DN16 ... 96 D2
Downing Gr HU9 ... 142 A1
Downland Cres WF11 ... 61 A1
Downs Cres HU5 ... 139 D2
Dowse Ave DN15 ... 150 E8
Dowsons La DN14 ... 78 E8
Dr Anderson Ave 9 DN7 92 C6
Dragon La YO16 ... 122 C5
Dragonby Rd 3 DN17 ... 96 C2
Drain Bank HU15 ... 67 B8
Drain La
Gilberdyke HU15 ... 52 D2
Holme-on-Spalding-Moor YO43 ... 51 F8
Drake Ave DN32 ... 153 B2
Drake St 2 YO23 ... 156 B1
Drakes Cl YO32 ... 127 F5
Drapers Croft YO23 ... 132 B4
Draper's La 17 HU12 ... 72 C7
Drax CP Sch YO8 ... 63 F5
Dray Dr HU17 ... 43 E5
Draycot LN7 ... 111 A2
Draycott Ave HU18 ... 134 C5
Drayton Cl 5 HU8 ... 142 C5
Dressay Gr HU8 ... 141 F7
Drew Ave DN32 ... 102 F2
Drewry La 7 DN9 ... 105 A2
Drewton Ct 8 DN14 ... 65 A7
Drewton La HU15 ... 54 A4
Driffield C of E VC Inf Sch YO25 ... 124 E4
Driffield Cl HU16 ... 138 E6
Driffield Cricket & Recn Club YO25 ... 124 D4
Driffield Cty Jun Sch YO25 ... 124 F5
Driffield Rd
Beverley HU17 ... 136 C6
Huggate YO42 ... 18 C1
Kilham YO25 ... 9 C2
Langtoft YO25 ... 8 C4
Molescroft HU17 ... 136 B8
Nafferton YO25 ... 125 E7
Skerne & Wansford YO25 ... 21 A2
Driffield RUFC YO25 ... 124 C2
Driffield Sch YO25 ... 125 A5
Driffield Showground★ YO25 ... 124 D2
Driffield Spellowgate YO25 ... 124 B7
Driffield Sports Ctr YO25 ... 125 A5
Driffield Sta YO25 ... 124 F3
Driffield Terr YO24 ... 130 A2
Driffil Way DN15 ... 83 A4
Drill Hall La 29 DN21 ... 117 B1
Dring La DN21 ... 118 A7
Dringfield Cl 2 YO24 ... 132 D8
Dringhouses Prim Sch YO24 ... 132 F8
Dringhouses Sports & Social Club YO24 ... 132 F8
Dringshaw HU6 ... 139 F8
Dringthorpe Rd YO24 ... 132 F7
Drive The
Cherry Burton HU17 ... 43 A4
Kirk Sandall DN3 ... 92 A1
Waltham DN37 ... 113 E6
Drome Rd YO23 ... 132 C2
Drove La HU7 ... 44 E1
Drovers Rise 1 HU15 ... 68 C6
Drummer's Well★ YO25 ... 21 F8
Drummond Ct 5 HU7 ... 57 B5
Drummond View YO23 ... 133 B4
Drury Cl 1 DN37 ... 113 D6
Drury La 3 DN36 ... 114 A7
Drydales HU10 ... 143 C6
Dryden Rd DN17 ... 150 D2
Dryden St HU8 ... 141 C2
Dryham La HU15 ... 53 C3
Dryhurst Cl 9 DN6 ... 76 F2
Drypool Way HU9 ... 146 B6
Duchess St DN32 ... 152 D2
Duck La YO12 ... 1 A8
Duckthorpe La DN36 ... 115 B2
Duddon Gr HU8 ... 142 B6
Dudley Mews YO31 ... 156 C4
Dudley Pl DN35 ... 103 B2
Dudley Rd Brigg DN20 ... 98 C2
Scunthorpe DN16 ... 151 E2
Dudley St
Grimsby DN34 ... 152 C3
York YO31 ... 156 C4
Duesbery St HU5 ... 145 C8
Duesbury Cl HU17 ... 154 A3
Dugard Rd DN32 ... 153 B3
Duggleby Howe★ YO17 ... 6 C5
Duke St Grimsby DN32 ... 153 A5
13 Stainforth DN7 ... 92 C6
Duke's La YO25 ... 2 A1
Dukes Wharf YO23 ... 156 B1
Dulverton Cl 4 HU7 ... 56 F5
Dunbar Ave 5 DN36 ... 114 A7
Dunbar Cl 6 DN21 ... 117 C1
Dunce Mire Rd LS25 ... 61 A8
Duncombe Ct HU12 ... 72 E7
Duncombe Dr YO25 ... 124 D3
Duncombe Gdns DN32 ... 152 F5
Duncombe La YO32 ... 14 B8
Duncombe Pl YO1 ... 156 B3
Duncombe St DN32 ... 152 F4
Dundas St YO1 ... 156 C2
Dundee St HU5 ... 145 A8
Dunelm Cl 3 HU8 ... 141 C1
Dunelm Cres 13 DN8 ... 79 B2
Dunflat Gate HU17 ... 55 D6
Dunflat La HU20 ... 55 B5
Dunflat Rd HU17 ... 55 D6
Dunhill Rd DN14 ... 149 B4
Dunkeld Dr 4 HU6 ... 140 B8
Dunken Hill Highgate HU17 ... 42 F4
Dunlin Cl HU7 ... 141 D8
Dunlop Way DN16 ... 151 E3
Dunmires La DN14 ... 80 E8
Dunmow Cl 1 HU8 ... 142 C5
Dunmow St DN31 ... 152 B5
Dunnington C of E Prim Sch YO19 ... 26 E7
Dunnington La
Beeford YO25 ... 34 D7
Skipsea YO25 ... 22 F1
Dunnock Cl 7 HU8 ... 141 D7
Dunn's La 6 YO25 ... 124 F4
Dunns Paddock 3 DN20 98 F7
Dunscombe Pk HU8 ... 141 B2
Dunstall St DN15 ... 151 A7
Dunstan Dr 26 DN8 ... 93 A8
Dunstan Hill DN21 ... 108 B1
Dunstan Villas 17 DN21 108 B1
Dunster Rd DN21 ... 117 C1
Dunston Dr HU13 ... 143 D1
Dunston Rd HU4 ... 144 D7
Dunswell Cl HU6 ... 140 A7
Dunswell La HU6 ... 56 C6
Dunswell Prim Sch HU6 ... 56 D6
Dunswell Rd
Cottingham HU16 ... 56 B6
Kingston upon Hull HU16 ... 139 C8
Dunvegan Rd HU8 ... 141 F6
Durban Rd DN32 ... 153 B3
Durban St HU8 ... 155 C3
Durham Ave
Grimsby DN34 ... 152 A3
10 Thorne/Moorends DN8 93 A8
Durham Mews HU17 ... 154 A1
Durham Rd
Cleethorpes DN35 ... 153 C1
Hatfield DN7 ... 92 D4
Durham St HU8 ... 141 C1
Durlston Dr YO32 ... 14 A7
Dursley Ave 1 DN36 ... 113 F7
Dyer La HU17 ... 154 A3
Dyke Cl 2 HU13 ... 69 F4
Dyke Rd DN36 ... 115 C5
Dykelands Cl YO19 ... 37 F7
Dykes La YO23 ... 132 A1
Dymoke Dr DN37 ... 102 B3
Dyon La YO8 ... 50 B3
Dyon Rd YO8 ... 50 D7

E

Eadon Pl DN14 ... 78 B8
Eagle Terr HU8 ... 155 C4
Ealand Rd DN17 ... 95 C6
Ealdane HU6 ... 139 E8
Ealing Cl HU8 ... 141 F5
Earfit La YO23 ... 36 A8
Earl Ave DN36 ... 114 A8
Earl St Grimsby DN31 ... 152 C3
Scunthorpe DN16 ... 151 B6
Earle St YO31 ... 156 C4
Earle's Rd HU9 ... 146 D7
Earlescourt HU6 ... 139 E7
Earlsgate Gdns DN15 ... 82 F5
Earlsgate Rd DN15 ... 83 A5
Earsham Cl HU8 ... 142 C6
Earswick Chase YO32 ... 127 F7
Earswick Village YO32 ... 127 F7
Easby Ct HU5 ... 139 C2
Easenby Ave HU10 ... 143 C6
Easenby Cl 3 HU14 ... 69 C7
Easington C of E Prim Sch HU12 ... 90 F5
Easington Rd
Easington HU12 ... 91 B2
Skeffling HU12 ... 90 E6
Eason Rd
8 Grimsby DN33 ... 102 D1
York YO24 ... 132 E8
Eason View YO24 ... 132 E8
East Acridge 7 DN18 ... 84 F8
East Back Side YO25 ... 10 C3
East Bank DN7 ... 92 C7
East Boundary Rd DN16 ... 151 F6
East Carr Rd
Keyingham HU12 ... 73 D5
Kingston upon Hull HU8 ... 141 F7
East Cl HU17 ... 136 D6
East Comm La
Scunthorpe DN16 ... 151 B4
Selby YO8 ... 148 F4
East Cross St 15 DN21 ... 108 B1
East Dale Dr DN21 ... 108 B2
East Dale Rd HU14 ... 68 E5
East Ella Dr HU4 ... 144 C6
East End
Humberside Airport DN39 ... 100 A6
Walkington HU17 ... 55 C8
East End Cl DN33 ... 102 E1
East End Rd HU12 ... 58 D1
East Ferry Rd
Laughton DN21 ... 106 D1
Wildsworth DN21 ... 117 A8
East Field Rd DN7 ... 92 C8
East Gate Rudston YO25 ... 9 F6
Thorne/Moorends DN8 ... 79 B2
East Gate N YO25 ... 124 E5
East Gate S YO25 ... 124 F4
East Gn DN17 ... 107 D7
East Gr
Barton-upon-Humber DN18 ... 69 F1
Kingston upon Hull HU4 ... 144 D4
East Halton Prim Sch DN40 ... 86 D6
East Halton Rd DN40 ... 86 E3
East Hann La DN19 ... 70 E1
East La Beverley HU17 ... 136 D5
Corringham DN21 ... 118 B2
Sigglesthorne HU11 ... 45 F8
Stainforth DN7 ... 92 C6
East Lambwath Rd HU11 ... 46 D3
East Lound Rd
Haxey DN9 ... 105 D2
Owston Ferry DN9 ... 106 A3
East Marsh Rd DN19 ... 71 C3
East Mid Mere Rd DN40 ... 86 F4
East Moor Gdns YO19 ... 133 F5
East Mount 8 HU14 ... 69 A4
East Mount Ave HU8 ... 142 B5
East Mount Rd YO24 ... 156 A1
East Newton Rd HU11 ... 47 D1
East Par Brigg DN20 ... 98 C2
Goole DN14 ... 149 D3
York YO31 ... 130 F6
East Park Ave HU8 ... 141 E3
East Pk HU17 ... 45 B8
East Ravendale C of E Sch DN37 ... 113 B2
East Rd
Bridlington YO15 ... 122 D1
Keadby with Althorpe DN17 ... 95 C6
East St
Dalton Holme HU17 ... 31 E1
Grimsby DN32 ... 152 E3
Hibaldstow DN20 ... 108 F5
Kilham YO25 ... 9 C3
5 Kingston upon Hull HU9 ... 146 B7
Leven HU17 ... 45 A8
Roxby cum Risby DN15 ... 83 A4
East St Mary's Gate 3 DN31 ... 152 D3
East View
7 Campsall DN6 ... 76 E1
10 Knottingley WF11 ... 61 A2
East Way YO31 ... 127 E2
East Yorkshire Coll YO16 ... 122 D4
East Yorkshire Hospl (Artificial Limb Unit) HU2 ... 155 C3
Eastbourne Gr YO31 ... 130 F5
Eastbourne Rd HU18 ... 134 D4
Eastbourne St HU3 ... 145 A5
Eastbourne Way 12 DN33 ... 113 E8
Eastern Ave DN21 ... 117 C1
Eastern Inway DN34 ... 152 A1
Eastern Terr YO31 ... 130 E6
Eastfield 5 DN36 ... 114 D8
Eastfield Ave
Grimsby DN33 ... 113 E8
Haxby YO32 ... 127 C7
Eastfield Cl
3 Beverley HU17 ... 137 A6
North Frodingham YO25 ... 34 A8
Eastfield Cres YO10 ... 131 C2
Eastfield Ct YO10 ... 131 C2
Eastfield Cty Inf Sch DN40 ... 87 C1
Eastfield Est HU12 ... 60 B1
Eastfield La
Dunnington YO19 ... 26 F8
Kellington DN14 ... 61 F4
Rise HU11 ... 45 F6
Eastfield Prim Sch HU4 ... 144 D6
Eastfield Rd
Barton-upon-Humber DN18 ... 84 F7
Brandesburton YO25 ... 34 C2
Bridlington YO16 ... 122 E5
Brigg DN20 ... 98 C2
Easington HU12 ... 91 A5
Epworth DN9 ... 105 E6
Fangfoss YO41 ... 28 D7
Great Driffield YO25 ... 124 E5
1 Keelby DN41 ... 101 A5
Keyingham HU12 ... 73 D4
Kingston upon Hull HU4 ... 144 D6
Market Weighton YO43 ... 135 E3
Messingham DN17 ... 107 D7
North Killingholme DN40 ... 86 F4
Scunthorpe DN16 ... 151 C1
Eastfield Rise 4 DN36 114 A5
Eastgate Beverley HU17 ... 154 B2
2 Goole DN14 ... 149 D4
Grimsby DN32 ... 152 E4
4 Hornsea HU18 ... 134 B4
Kingston upon Hull HU13 ... 143 E2
Lund YO25 ... 31 F2
Nafferton YO25 ... 125 F7
North Newbald YO43 ... 53 F7
Patrington HU12 ... 74 D1
Scotton DN21 ... 107 C2
Eastgate View HU18 ... 134 B4
Easthall Rd LN7 ... 110 B4
Eastholme Cl YO25 ... 124 F5
Eastholme Dr YO30 ... 126 E1
Eastholme Gdns 9 DN15 82 B4
Eastholme La HU12 ... 73 C7
Easthorpe Dr YO26 ... 126 A1
Eastlands YO25 ... 125 F7
Eastlands Rd YO25 ... 19 E2
Eastmount Recn Ctr HU8 ... 142 B6
Eastoft Rd Crowle DN17 ... 94 D8

Eastoft Rd continued
Luddington & Haldenby
DN17 ....81 C3
Eastoft Sch DN17 ......81 A3
Easton Ave HU8 ....141 A2
Easton Rd YO16 ......66 A8
Eastrington Cty Prim Sch
DN14 ....51 F1
Eastrington Sta DN14 ..66 A8
Eastside Rd
Grimsby DN31 ....152 F5
Scunthorpe DN16 .....151 F6
Eastville Rd DN33 ....102 C2
Eastward Ave YO10 ...133 E7
Eastwold [2] YO43 .....53 F7
Eastwood Ave DN32 ..102 E2
Eastwood Dr [8] DN20 ..97 E4
Eaton Ct Grimsby DN34 ..152 C2
[7] York YO24 ....132 B8
Eaton Rd [18] DN40 ....87 C1
Ebberston Gr [5] HU4 .139 E3
Ebor Ave HU18 ....134 D2
Ebor Cl HU8 ....142 B6
Ebor Ct [7] YO8 ....148 C6
Ebor Manor [1] HU12 ...73 C4
Ebor Prep Sch YO30 ..130 A1
Ebor St Selby YO8 ....148 C5
York YO23 ....156 B1
Ebor View YO43 ......135 E4
Ebor Way
[7] Poppleton YO26 .....12 F1
Poppleton YO26 ....126 A2
Ebsay Dr YO30 ....127 A1
Eccles Ct DN20 ....98 D4
Ecclesfield Ave HU9 ..142 D1
Eccleston Rd DN3 ....92 A3
Eddlemere La YO25 .....32 E7
Eden Ave YO8 ....148 D3
Eden Cl Beverley HU17 .136 D5
York YO24 ....132 C7
Eden Dene DN16 ......151 D1
Eden Dr HU8 ....141 C3
Eden Field Rd [12] DN3 ..92 A2
Eden Rd HU17 ....136 D5
Eden Gdns YO15 ....4 D2
Eden Gr Rd [3] DN3 ....92 A1
Eden Rise HU10 ....138 C2
Edencroft Dr [14] DN3 ..92 A2
Edendale HU7 ....140 F6
Edenfield Ave HU18 ..134 C2
Edenthorpe Hall Prim Sch
DN3 ....92 A1
Edgar St HU3 ....145 D5
Edge Ave DN33 ....102 E1
Edgecliffe Villas [4]
YO15 ....122 F1
Edgecumbe St HU5 ...140 C2
Edgeware Ave [1] HU9 .141 F1
Edgware Rd YO10 .....130 E2
Edinburgh Dr [4] DN36 .114 A6
Edinburgh Rd [3] DN17 ..95 D6
Edinburgh St
Goole DN14 ....149 C4
Kingston upon Hull HU3 .145 A5
Edison Gr HU9 ....141 E2
Edith Cavell Ct [4] HU5 .139 F4
Edmonds Way DN31 ...152 D4
Edmund Cl DN21 ......118 A1
**Edmund Wilson Swimming
Baths** YO24 ....129 D1
Edward Collins Sq [2]
HU9 ....146 D2
Edward Ct [6] DN8 .....79 B1
Edward Heneage Prim Sch
DN32 ....152 D2
Edward Rd [11] DN21 ..117 B1
Edward St
Beverley HU17 ....154 B3
Cleethorpes DN35 ....153 C4
Grimsby DN32 ....152 F3
Kingston upon Hull
HU13 ....143 F1
[1] Pocklington YO42 ...29 A4
[6] Withernsea HU19 ...74 F7
Edwardian Dr YO15 ...122 C1
Edwards La HU11 ......47 A5
Eelmere La HU11 ......47 A5
Egginton Cl HU10 .....143 C7
Egginton St HU2 ......155 B3
Eglinton Ave HU8 .....141 F3
Egremont Cl [11] YO41 ..15 D2
Egrom's La HU19 ....75 A5
Egton Ave DN17 ......107 D7
Egton St HU8 ....155 C4
Egypt St HU9 ....147 B7
Eighth Ave
Bridlington YO15 .....122 F4
Fixborough Ind Est. DN15 ..82 A1
York YO31 ....130 F5
Elba St HU9 ....147 C2
Elderberry Dr HU4 ....144 D4
Elderberry Way [4]
DN35 ....103 B1
Elderwood Ct [6] HU3 .145 D5
Eldon Dr [11] HU12 .....58 C1
Eldon Gr
Kingston upon Hull HU5 .140 D2
Thorne/Moorends DN8 ..79 C2
Eldon St YO31 ....156 C4
Eldon Terr YO31 ......156 C4
Eldwick Cl YO30 ......126 F2
Eleanor Cl HU9 ....142 B2
Eleanor St DN32 ......152 F4
Elgar Rd HU4 ....144 B4
Elizabeth Ave [6] DN3 ..92 A2

Elizabeth Cl
Bridlington YO15 .....122 C1
[4] Gainsborough DN21 ..117 B2
[14] Grimsby DN33 ....113 D8
Scotter DN21 ....107 C4
Elizabeth Ct [7] YO8 ..148 B6
Elizabeth Dr YO25 ....124 D3
Elizabeth St DN15 ....151 A8
Ella Pk HU10 ....143 D7
Ella St HU5 ....140 E2
Ellerburn Ave HU6 ...140 A7
Ellerburn Dr [3] YO16 .122 C5
Ellerby Gatehouse★
HU11 ....46 A1
Ellerby Gr HU9 ....141 F2
Ellerby Rd HU11 ......45 F2
Ellerington La HU17 ...42 F6
Ellerker La HU15 ......53 F1
Ellerker Rd HU17 .....154 A2
Ellerker Rise HU10 ...138 D2
Ellerker Wold La HU15 .54 B1
Ellesmere Ave HU8 ...142 A4
Ellesmere Gr DN7 .....92 D6
Ellesmere Rise DN34 .102 B2
Ellifoot La HU12 ....73 B7
Ellingham Cl HU8 .....142 B6
Elliot Ct YO10 ....133 D7
Ellis Cl [4] HU12 ....58 C1
Ellis Way DN31 ....152 E4
Ellison Ave DN16 ....96 D1
Ellison St DN8 ....93 A7
Elliston Inf Sch DN35 .153 D4
Elliston Jun Sch DN35 .153 C4
Elliston St DN35 ......153 C3
Ellmore La LN7 ....110 B4
Elloughton Dale HU15 ..68 D8
Elloughton Gr [4] HU16 .138 E6
Elloughton Rd HU15 ...68 C6
Elm Ave [15] Brough HU15 .68 C6
Burstwick HU12 ....73 A6
Cleethorpes DN35 .....153 E2
Goole DN14 ....149 B4
Grimsby DN34 ....152 C2
Kingston upon Hull HU8 .141 C2
Elm Cl HU17 ....136 D5
Elm Dr HU17 ....43 A5
Elm End [9] YO32 ....13 E5
Elm Garth HU12 ....60 B1
Elm Gdns DN35 ......153 E2
Elm Gr [1] Aldbrough HU11 .47 C1
Healing DN41 ....102 A5
Scunthorpe DN16 .....151 B4
York YO31 ....127 F2
Elm La Goxhill DN19 ...71 A1
Laceby DN37 ....101 C1
Elm Rd
Cleethorpes DN35 ....153 E2
Great Driffield YO25 ..124 F2
Waltham DN37 ....113 E6
Elm St
Kingston upon Hull HU5 .140 D2
Selby YO8 ....148 D6
Elm Terr HU5 ....140 D2
Elm Tree Ave
[9] Poppleton YO26 .....12 F1
[5] Thorngumbald HU12 .72 E5
Elm Tree Cl
Keyingham HU12 ......73 C4
[1] Thorngumbald HU12 .72 E5
Elm Tree La HU9 ......142 E1
Elm Tree Farm Rd [1]
HU12 ....73 A6
Elm Tree Gr [4] DN8 ....93 B7
Elm Way Brigg DN20 ...98 B2
Messingham DN17 ....107 C7
Elma Ave YO16 ....122 D2
Elma Gr YO30 ....126 E2
Elma Villas YO16 .....122 D2
Elmbridge Par [3] HU9 .142 E1
Elmdale [16] DN18 ......84 E8
Elmfield HU6 ....140 B6
Elmfield Ave YO31 ...130 F8
Elmfield Dr
[16] Brandesburton YO25 .34 B2
Kingston upon Hull
HU16 ....139 A6
Elmfield Terr YO31 ...130 F7
Elmhirst Rd DN8 ....93 B8
Elmlands Gr YO31 ....130 F8
Elmpark Vale YO31 ...131 A8
Elmpark View YO31 ...131 A8
Elmpark Way YO31 ...131 A8
Elms Cl [2] YO19 ....36 F1
Elms Dr HU10 ....143 C8
Elms The [4] HU15 .....66 D7
Elmsall Dr HU17 ......136 C6
Elmswell Spellowgate
YO25 ....20 B6
Elmswood HU13 ....143 C2
Elmtree Ave [9] HU14 ..69 A4
Elmtree Gdns [3] YO26 .129 C2
Elsenham Rd DN31 ....152 B5
Elsham Dr DN37 ......113 D6
Elsham Gr [21] DN33 ...102 D2
**Elsham Hall Ctry & Wildlife
Pk**★ DN20 ....98 F6
Elsham Rd DN20 ....98 D7
Elsham Rise HU13 ....143 D1
Elsie St DN14 ....149 C5
Elsiemere Wlk [6] HU4 .144 B6
Elsternwick Ave HU8 .141 B2
Elston Cl
Kingston upon Hull HU6 .140 D6
York YO30 ....130 A8
Elston Pl YO8 ....148 C6
Elvaston Ave HU18 ....134 C5
Elveley Dr HU10 ......143 A7

Elvington C of E Prim Sch
YO41 ....27 B3
Elvington Cl HU6 .....140 A6
Elvington Cres HU17 ...43 D5
Elvington Ind Est YO41 .27 A3
Elvington La YO19 .....26 E5
Elvington Pk YO41 .....27 A3
Elvington Terr YO10 ..130 E4
Elwell Ave HU17 ......154 A2
Elwes St [8] DN20 ......98 C2
Elwick Gr YO10 ....131 C4
Elwyn Pl [2] DN35 ....103 B1
Embankment The
YO25 ....124 B3
Emberton Pk
[26] Kingston upon Hull HU7 .56 F6
[12] Kingston upon Hull HU7 .56 F6
Embleton Dr [7] YO30 .126 F1
Emerald Gr [8] HU3 ...145 A4
Emerald St YO31 .....156 C4
Emerson Ave DN7 ......92 C5
Emfield Gr DN33 ......113 E7
Emfield Rd DN33 ......113 D8
Emily St [8] HU9 ......146 C7
Eminson Cl DN21 .....107 C4
Emmanual Rd DN16 ...151 F2
Emmanuel Ct DN16 ...151 B2
Emmanuel Dr [18] DN16 .96 D2
Emmerson St [2] YO31 .130 E5
Emmery Cl DN20 ....97 D4
Emmott Rd HU6 ......140 C7
Empringham St [5] HU9 .146 D7
Empson Ave DN14 ....149 B6
Empson Terr HU17 ....154 A2
Ena St HU3 ....145 B6
Enclosure Gdns [1]
YO10 ....131 B1
Endcliffe Ave DN17 ....96 C1
Endeavour Cres [3] HU9 .142 B1
Enderby Rd DN17 .....150 D1
Enderby Rd Inf Sch
DN17 ....96 C2
Endfields Rd [1] YO10 .133 E8
Endike La HU5 ....140 A6
Endike Prim Sch HU6 .140 C6
Endsleigh RC Prim Sch
HU6 ....140 C4
Endsleigh St HU3 .....145 A7
Endyke La HU5 ....139 D6
Endymion St HU8 .....141 B1
Enfield Ave DN36 .....114 A7
Enfield Cres
[2] York YO24 ....129 F3
[1] York YO24 ....130 A3
Enfield Mews HU17 ...154 B3
Enfield Prim Sch
DN36 ....114 A7
Engine La HU11 ....58 D7
Engine St [20] DN20 ....98 B2
England Rd HU11 .....142 F7
English Cl HU3 ....145 A4
English Martyrs RC Prim Sch
YO24 ....129 F3
English St HU1 ....155 A1
Ennerdale HU7 ....140 E7
Ennerdale Ave YO31 ..131 B5
Ennerdale Cl [18] DN36 .103 C1
Ennerdale Sports Ctr
HU7 ....140 E6
Enstone Garth [20] HU7 .57 A5
Enterprise Rd LN7 ....111 A4
Enterprise Way
Grimsby DN32 ....153 A2
Winterton DN15 ....82 F5
Ephams La DN41 .....101 E7
Epping Cl HU8 ....141 E6
Eppleworth Rd HU16 .138 D6
Epworth Cty Prim Sch
DN9 ....105 C6
Epworth Heritage Ctr★
DN9 ....105 E7
Epworth L Ctr DN9 ...105 D6
Epworth Rd Hatfield DN7 .92 F4
Haxey DN9 ....105 D3
Owston Ferry DN9 ....106 A4
Epworth Rd W [9] DN7 ..92 E4
Epworth St HU5 ......140 D1
**Epworth Turbarg Nature
Reserve**★ DN9 ....105 B6
Ermine St Appleby DN15 .97 D8
Winteringham DN15 ....83 B8
Ernest Hill Ct [1] HU5 .140 A2
Ernest Kirkwood Cl [4]
HU5 ....139 D1
Eryholme Cres DN15 .150 F7
Escart Ave DN32 .....153 B2
Escrick C of E Prim Sch
YO19 ....37 A5
Escrick Ct YO19 ....37 B5
Escrick Park Gdns
YO19 ....37 B5
Escrick St YO10 ......156 C1
Esk Dr YO26 ....129 B8
Eskdale Ave
[2] Kingston upon Hull
HU9 ....141 E1
York YO16 ....131 C3
Eskdale Dr YO16 .....122 F8
Eskdale Way [12] DN37 .102 B4
Eske Cl HU17 ....44 C5
Eske La HU17 ....44 C5
Eskham Cl [19] DN35 ..103 C2
Eskholme La DN14 .....78 B4
Esmond St HU6 ....140 D5
Esplanade
Hornsea HU18 ....134 D5
York YO26 ....156 A2
Essex Dr [7] DN15 ......82 B4

Essex St HU4 ....144 E3
Estate Ave DN20 ......97 D3
Estate Rd No 1 DN31 ..152 A6
Estate Rd No 2 DN31 ..152 A5
Estate Rd No 3 DN31 ..102 C5
Estate Rd No 4 DN31 ..102 C5
Estate Rd No 5 DN31 ..152 A6
Estate Rd No 6 DN37 ..102 C5
Estate Rd No 7 DN37 ..102 C5
Estate Rd No 8 DN37 ..102 C5
Estcourt Prim Sch
HU9 ....146 D8
Estcourt St
Goole DN14 ....149 D4
Kingston upon Hull HU9 .146 D8
Estcourt Terr DN14 ...149 D4
Estuary Way DN31 ....152 B6
Ethelstone Rd DN34 ..152 A3
Etherington Cl [5] HU12 .73 C4
Etherington Dr HU6 ..140 D5
Etherington La HU17 ..124 E4
Etherington Rd HU6 ..140 C5
Etive Pl YO24 ....132 B7
Eton Dr [7] Haxby YO32 .13 D1
Scunthorpe DN17 ......96 C2
Eton Rd DN14 ....149 B5
Eton St HU3 ....145 C4
Etton Cl HU16 ....138 E5
Etton Dikes HU17 ......43 A6
Etton Gr HU6 ....139 F5
Etton Rd HU17 ....43 A5
Etty Ave YO10 ....131 A4
Europa Bsns Pk DN31 .152 A6
Europa Way Brigg DN20 .98 B2
Immingham DN41 ......87 C1
Europarc Innovation Ctr
DN37 ....102 B6
Eva Ave YO30 ....126 D2
Evelyn Cres YO30 ....130 B7
Evelyn Gr N DN32 ....153 B2
Evelyn Gr S DN32 ....153 B2
Evendine Ct [2] DN36 .114 B5
Ever Thorpe Cl [5] HU3 .145 C5
Everest Rd DN16 .....151 C1
Evergreen Dr HU6 .....56 D5
Evergreen Way [1] YO8 .48 D1
Everingham La YO42 ...40 A7
Everingham Wlk HU5 .139 C2
Eversfield Cl [21] HU7 ..56 F5
Everthorpe Rd HU15 ...53 D3
Evesham Ave DN34 ...102 C3
Evesham Croft [1] YO16 .122 C5
Exchange Pl [7] DN20 ..98 B2
Exchange St
Great Driffield YO25 ..124 E4
Kingston upon Hull HU5 .140 E2
Exeter Ct [11] DN34 ...102 B2
Exeter Gr HU9 ....142 A2
Exeter Rd DN15 ......150 F7
Exeter St HU16 ....139 C7
Exmoor Ave DN15 .....96 B8
Exmoor Rd DN17 .....150 C4
Exmouth St HU5 ......140 C3
Exton Cl HU7 ....56 F5
Eyre Ave DN16 ....151 B1

F

Faber Cl YO23 ....132 B3
Faber St YO31 ....130 E5
Fair Pl HU18 ....134 B4
Fair View Ave DN35 ..153 E2
Fairbourne Cl [1] HU7 ..57 A7
Faircourt HU6 ....139 E7
Fairfax [15] YO41 ......15 D2
Fairfax Ave
Kingston upon Hull HU5 .139 F3
Selby YO8 ....148 B4
Fairfax Croft YO23 ...132 B2
Fairfax Dr HU12 ....72 C8
Fairfax Rd DN34 .....152 B3
Fairfax St YO1 ....156 B1
Fairfield Goole DN14 ..149 F6
North Cave HU15 ......53 D2
Rawcliffe DN14 ....79 B8
Fairfield Ave
Grimsby DN33 ....113 E8
Kingston upon Hull
HU13 ....138 C1
Fairfield Cl
[5] Broughton DN20 ....97 E3
Nafferton YO25 ....125 E7
Fairfield Croft [8] DN9 .105 E6
Fairfield Ct [4] DN35 ..103 D1
Fairfield Dr
[25] Barton-upon-Humber
DN18 ....84 F8
Messingham DN17 ....107 D7
Fairfield La LS25 ......61 A6
Fairfield Rd
Bridlington YO15 .....122 D1
Grimsby DN33 ....113 E8
Kingston upon Hull HU5 .139 F3
Scunthorpe DN15 .....150 D8
Fairfield View [5] HU15 .68 D5
Fairfields Dr YO30 ....126 B5
Fairholme La HU7 ....136 C6
Fairisle Rise [5] DN40 .101 C8
Fairlawn HU17 ....136 C6
Fairmont Cres DN16 ..151 B6
Fairmont Rd DN32 ....153 A3
Fairtree Wlk [21] DN8 ..93 A8
Fairway Waltham DN37 .113 E7
York YO30 ....130 B7
Fairway Ave DN21 ....117 B2
Fairway Ct DN35 .....103 E1

Fairway Dr [18] YO26 ...12 F1
Fairway The
Kingston upon Hull
HU10 ....143 A8
Thorne/Moorends DN8 ..79 B2
Fairways The
Kingston upon Hull HU8 .142 A6
Scunthorpe DN15 .....150 B6
Falcon Cl [10] YO32 .....13 F5
Falcon Ct HU4 ....144 D2
Falconer St [1] YO24 ..129 F3
Falconers The DN21 ..108 F2
Falkirk Cl [7] HU7 ......57 A7
Falkland Rd HU9 .....147 E8
Falkland St YO1 ......156 B1
Falkland Way DN18 ....69 F1
Fallowfield Rd DN33 ..113 D8
Falmouth St HU5 .....140 C3
Falsgrave Cres YO30 ..130 B7
Falsgrave Gr HU4 ....144 D7
Fannystone Rd DN34 .152 B3
Far Bank La DN7 ....92 C8
Far Comm Rd DN7 ....93 A4
Far Field Cl [15] DN3 ...92 A2
Far Field Rd DN3 ......92 A2
Far Ings Cl HU18 ......69 C1
Far Ings Rd DN18 ......69 C1
Far La YO25 ....35 A5
Faraday St HU9 ....141 E2
Fardell Rd DN16 ......151 D3
Farebrother St DN32 .152 E1
Farfield YO26 ....129 C6
Farfield La YO19 ....26 E8
Faringdon Rd DN31 ...153 A6
Farm Cl
[6] Edenthorpe DN3 ....92 A1
Gunness DN15 ....95 E6
Farm Ct YO43 ....135 C5
Farm La [2] DN7 .....106 D8
Farm Way YO8 ....148 B7
Farmers Way YO23 ..132 B3
Farmhouse Mews [11]
DN36 ....114 A7
Farmlands Rd [1] YO24 .132 D8
Farms La DN14 ....66 A8
Farmstead Rise YO32 .127 D7
Farndale Ave
Kingston upon Hull HU9 .141 E1
York YO10 ....131 D4
Farndale Cl [1] YO32 ...13 F5
Farndale St YO10 .....130 D2
Farndale Way [1] DN15 .83 A5
Farnella Cl HU3 ......145 A5
Faroes Cl [1] HU9 ....142 A3
Farrand Rd HU12 ......72 C7
Farrar St YO10 ....130 E3
Farriers Croft [2] YO23 .132 B3
Farringdon St [2] HU5 .140 E1
Farrishes La DN18 ......84 A8
Farthing Ave DN15 ...150 E8
Farthing La YO25 .....125 C4
Fauconberg Ave [6]
DN33 ....102 E1
Faulding La DN40 ......86 F2
Faulding Way DN37 ..102 B4
Faversham Ave HU4 ..144 B6
Fawcett Cl HU5 ....140 E1
Fawcett Gdns [9] YO25 .124 F4
Fawcett St
[27] Gainsborough DN21 .117 B1
York YO10 ....156 C1
Fawkes Dr YO26 .....129 C4
Fawley Cl HU5 ....140 E3
Faxfleet La DN14 ......67 A3
Feasegate YO1 ....156 B2
Featherbed La YO42 ...29 C4
Felbridge Cl [1] HU9 ..142 E2
Feldane HU6 ....139 E8
Fellbrook Ave YO26 ..129 B4
Felstead Rd DN34 ....102 C3
Fen La DN36 ....114 D1
Fen Wlk DN36 ....115 C5
Fenby Cl [3] DN37 ....102 B3
Fenchurch St [1] HU5 .140 E1
Fenland Rd [12] DN8 ...93 B7
Fenton St DN15 ......151 B7
Fenwick Comm La DN6 .77 D2
Fenwick Ct DN36 .....114 A5
Fenwick La DN6 ....77 B1
Fenwick Rd DN33 .....102 D1
Fenwick St YO23 .....130 C2
Fenwick's La YO10 ...133 D7
Feoffee La YO42 ......28 C5
Ferens Art Gall★ HU1 .155 B2
Ferens Ave HU6 ......140 B4
Ferens Ct [2] HU9 ....141 D1
Ferens Gdns HU16 ...138 F8
Ferensway HU2 ......155 A3
Ferguson Rd [2] HU17 ..55 B7
Ferguson Way YO32 ..127 D7
Fern Cl
Kingston upon Hull HU2 .155 A4
York YO32 ....128 A4
Fern Croft [18] DN9 ...105 E6
Fern Ct HU13 ....144 A1
Fern St YO31 ....156 C4
Fenbank [1] DN9 ......105 D7
Ferndale Ave HU10 ...138 D1
Ferndale Dr DN8 ....79 B1
Ferndale Gr DN14 ....149 C6
Ferndale Rd YO8 .....148 C4
Ferndale Terr [11] YO15 .122 E2
Ferndown DN37 ......102 B5
Ferndown Dr DN40 ....87 C2
Fernhall Cl [11] DN3 ....92 A2
Fernhill DN37 ....102 B4
Fernhill Rd HU5 ......139 D3
Fernland Cl [15] HU15 ..68 C5

Fernlea Cl YO8 148 D4
Fernley Gn Cl 6 WF11 61 A2
Fernway YO10 131 C3
Ferriby Gr HU6 139 F5
Ferriby High Rd HU14 69 B5
Ferriby La DN33 102 E1
Ferriby Rd
Barton-upon-Humber DN18 84 E8
Hessle HU13 143 B1
Scunthorpe DN17 150 E1
Ferriby Sta HU14 69 A4
Ferries St HU9 146 D7
Ferry Cl 11 YO8 49 F1
Ferry Farm Cl 2 YO19 36 D8
Ferry La Airmyn DN14 149 A8
Bishopthorpe YO23 133 B4
Bubwith YO8 50 C5
Goole DN14 65 B5
Snaith & Cowick DN14 63 C1
Thorganby YO19 38 B5
Winteringham DN15 68 B1
Woodmansey HU17 56 C7
Ferry Rd
Barrow upon Humber DN19 70 C1
Fishlake DN8 78 F1
Goxhill DN19 85 F8
Haxey DN9 105 D1
Keadby with Althorpe DN17 95 D4
Kilpin DN14 65 B5
Kingston upon Hull HU13 143 E1
Scunthorpe DN15 150 D8
South Cave HU15 53 E1
Wawne HU7 56 D8
Ferry Rd E DN19 85 C8
Ferry Rd W DN15 96 A7
Ferryman Pk HU12 72 A5
Fetherston Cl 19 YO42 29 A3
Fetter La YO1 156 B2
Feversham Cres 4 YO31 130 C7
Fewson Garth 26 HU12 72 D7
Fewster Way YO10 156 C1
Fewston Dr 9 YO30 126 F1
Field Ave YO8 48 B1
Field Cl 10 Laceby DN37 101 F1
Snaith DN14 78 C8
Field Head
Laceby DN37 101 E1
Wilberfoss YO41 27 F6
Field La Eastoft DN17 81 A4
Gowdall DN14 77 F8
Hambleton YO8 48 B1
Hensall DN14 62 D2
Heslington YO10 131 C2
Morton DN21 116 F3
Rawcliffe DN14 64 A1
Thornton YO42 39 A8
Wistow YO8 48 C7
Wroot DN9 104 D5
Field Lane Sports Ctr YO8 48 B1
Field Rd
Bridlington YO16 122 C4
Crowle DN17 94 D7
Stainforth DN7 92 C6
Thorne/Moorends DN8 93 A8
West Haddlesey YO8 62 A5
Field Side DN8 93 A8
Field St HU9 146 B7
Field View YO31 130 C7
Fieldend La HU12 59 B2
Fieldfare YO25 125 B5
Fieldfare Dr YO25 125 B5
Fieldhouse Rd
7 Humberston DN36 103 D1
Humberston DN36 114 D8
Fields Cl 2 DN9 105 D7
Fields Cl Rd HU12 73 E4
Fields Rd DN9 105 E2
Fieldside Blyton DN21 117 F5
Crowle DN17 94 D7
Epworth DN9 105 D6
Fieldside Garth HU6 56 D5
Fifth Ave
Bridlington YO15 123 A4
Fixborough Ind Est. DN15 82 A1
Goole DN14 149 C5
Scunthorpe DN17 150 B2
York YO31 130 F4
Fifth Avenue Prim Sch HU6 140 A6
Fiftyeights Rd DN10 104 B2
Figham Rd HU17 137 B3
Figham Springs Way HU17 154 B1
Fildes St DN31 152 D3
Filey Rd Grimsby DN32 153 A1
Hunmanby YO14 3 A8
Filey Terr YO30 130 C7
Fillingham Cres
Cleethorpes DN35 103 C2
Gunness DN15 150 B7
Fimber Ave HU16 139 A5
Finch Croft 5 HU7 141 D7
Finch Pk HU17 136 D5
Finchcroft La HU17 43 B2
Finchley Cl HU8 141 F5
Findlay Cres DN36 114 A7
Findon Cl 28 HU7 56 F6
Fingall Mews 1 HU5 139 D3
Finkle La DN18 69 F1
Finkle St
2 Bishop Burton HU17 43 A2
Hensall DN14 62 D2
Finkle St continued
Kingston upon Hull HU16 139 A6
Market Weighton YO43 135 D4
2 North Cave HU15 53 D3
Selby YO8 148 C5
Stainforth DN7 92 C7
Finningley Garth 14 HU7 57 A5
Finnley's La DN14 78 C7
Finsbury Ave YO23 130 C1
Finsbury Dr 7 DN33 102 D1
Finsbury St YO23 130 C1
Fir Cl DN16 96 D2
Fir Heath Cl 5 YO24 129 C1
Fir Tree Cl YO8 48 B2
Fir Tree Dr 11 DN6 76 E2
Fir Tree La YO8 48 B2
Fir Tree Way YO8 48 B2
Fir Trees HU10 143 D6
Fir Trees The YO8 48 B2
Firbank Cl 9 YO32 14 A7
Firethorn Cl 3 HU3 145 D5
Firsby Cres DN33 102 D1
First Ave
Bridlington YO15 122 F4
Flixborough DN15 82 A1
3 Goole DN14 149 C4
Grimsby DN33 102 E2
Scunthorpe DN17 150 C2
York YO31 130 F6
First Comm La YO8 48 D4
First La
Kingston upon Hull HU10 144 A5
South Cave HU15 54 A2
Firth Field Rd DN7 92 F4
Firth La DN9 104 D5
Firtholme Rd HU12 91 A4
Firtree Cl
4 Earswick YO32 127 F7
York YO24 129 E3
Firtree Dr DN20 98 F7
Firwood Whin 5 YO32 127 F3
Fish Dock Rd DN31 152 F6
Fish La HU15 52 D2
Fish St HU1 155 B1
Fishemore Ave HU13 143 F2
Fisher Cl HU10 138 D2
Fisher La YO25 22 E5
Fisher Pl DN35 153 D3
Fisher Sq HU17 154 A2
Fishergate YO10 156 C1
Fishergate Prim Sch YO10 156 C1
Fisherman's Wharf DN31 152 D4
Fishermans Wlk 2 HU3 145 C4
Fishlake Nab DN7 92 C7
Fishpond Hill YO42 29 C4
Fishwick Ave 5 HU13 143 E1
Fiskerton Cl 20 DN34 102 C2
Fiskerton Way DN31 102 C6
Fitling Rd HU11 59 B5
Fitties La DN36 115 C5
Fitzroy St HU5 140 D2
Fitzwilliam Mews 2 DN35 103 C1
Flag Wlk 1 HU6 140 C8
Flag Yd YO16 122 C4
Flamborough Head Nature Reserve★ YO15 5 D2
Flamborough Rd
Bempton YO15 4 E1
Bridlington YO15 122 F4
Bridlington YO15 123 C8
Flamborough Sch YO15 5 A2
Flarepath The DN20 99 A8
Flashley Carr La DN6 77 F1
Flat La YO42 28 D4
Flatgate DN14 65 B7
Flavian Gr YO30 129 F8
Flaxdale Ct HU5 139 E1
Flaxley Ct YO8 148 B5
Flaxley Rd YO8 148 A7
Flaxman Ave YO10 131 A4
Flaxman Croft YO23 132 B3
Flaxmill Wlk 2 HU15 66 D7
Flaxton Rd
Kingston upon Hull HU5 139 D1
Strensall YO32 14 B7
Fleet Garth 11 HU12 72 D7
Fleet La DN14 64 A7
Fleetgate 11 DN18 69 E1
Fleets Cl DN7 92 C7
Fleetway DN36 115 A3
Fleetwood Cl 4 DN33 113 E8
Fleming Ave 3 YO31 130 E5
Fleming Wlk HU4 144 D2
Flemingate HU17 154 C2
Flemingdale HU7 140 F7
Fletcher Cl
Kingston upon Hull HU13 143 E2
6 Scunthorpe DN15 96 B7
Fletcher Ct 14 YO32 13 E5
Fletcher Gate HU12 72 C7
Fletcher Rd DN34 102 C4
Fletcher's Croft YO23 132 C3
Flinton Gr HU9 142 A1
Flinton Rd
Aldbrough HU11 58 F8
Humbleton HU11 59 A7
Flinton St HU3 145 B3
Flixborough Rd DN15 82 A4
Floral Hall HU18 134 D5
Florence Ave HU13 143 F1
Florence Gr YO30 126 D2
Florence Nightingale 3 HU5 139 F4
Florence St DN32 152 E1
Flour Sq DN31 152 E5
Fog La YO42 38 E4
Folkestone St HU5 140 D2
Folks Cl 13 YO32 13 F5
Folkton Ave HU16 139 A4
Follies The DN15 97 E7
Folly La LN7 110 C5
Football Gn HU18 134 C3
Forber Ave HU9 142 C2
Forbes Ave HU6 140 C8
Ford La DN20 108 F5
Fordlands YO8 48 B2
Fordlands Cres YO19 133 E5
Fordlands Rd YO19 133 E6
Fordon La Willerby YO12 1 E7
Wold Newton YO25 2 A6
Ford's Ave 9 DN41 101 F5
Foredyke Ave HU7 141 A4
Foredyke Prim Sch HU9 142 A1
Forest Cl 27 YO32 13 E5
Forest Dr DN36 103 D1
Forest Gr YO31 130 F6
Forest La Fulford YO19 26 A2
Strensall YO32 14 A8
Forest of Galtres Prim Sch YO30 12 F5
Forest Way
24 Humberston DN36 103 D1
Humberston DN36 114 D8
York YO31 130 F6
Forester Way HU4 144 D3
Foresters Way YO16 123 A7
Foresters Wlk YO41 15 C1
Forester's Wlk YO24 129 B1
Forestgate YO32 127 C7
Forge Cl
Huntington YO32 128 A2
Melbourne YO42 39 B6
South Kelsey LN7 110 A1
8 Thorngumbald HU12 72 E5
Forge Cres 3 DN39 86 A1
Forge La YO19 37 A7
Forge Pl HU16 138 B7
Forge The YO25 124 E3
Forge Way 3 DN36 114 A6
Forkedale DN18 84 E8
Formby Cl HU6 139 E5
Forrester St 21 DN20 98 B2
Forrester's Cl 3 DN6 76 E2
Forster St 26 DN21 117 B1
Forsythia Dr DN33 102 E1
Fort Paull Battery★ HU12 72 B4
Fort Terr 6 YO15 122 F2
Forth St YO26 129 F6
Fortuna Way 2 DN37 102 B4
Fortune Cl HU8 141 F4
Forty Acre HU10 143 F7
Forty Foot La DN39 99 F6
Forty Steps HU10 143 F7
Fortyfoot YO16 122 F4
Fortyfoot Ct YO16 122 E4
Fortyfoot Gr 1 YO16 122 F4
Forum Ctr★ YO15 122 F2
Fosham Rd HU11 46 D2
Foss Bank YO31 156 C3
Foss Ct YO31 127 E1
Foss Field La YO23 36 B8
Foss Garth YO41 27 F5
Foss Gr HU8 142 B6
Foss Islands Rd YO31 156 C3
Foss Wlk YO26 129 B8
Fossdale Cl HU8 141 E6
Fosse Hill Jet Ski Ctr★ YO25 34 C1
Fossgate YO1 156 C2
Fossland View 4 YO32 14 A7
Fossway
Stamford Bridge YO41 15 D1
York YO31 130 D7
Foster Gate YO8 148 D4
Foster Rd 9 DN8 93 A8
Foster St HU8 141 A2
Fostergate YO8 48 A8
Foston Gr
Kingston upon Hull HU9 142 A1
4 York YO31 130 F8
Foston La Beeford YO25 22 B1
North Frodingham YO25 21 F1
Fotherbie Garth 11 HU12 72 C7
Fotherby Rd 4 DN17 96 C2
Fotherby St DN31 152 E5
Foundry La 5 WF11 61 A2
Fountain Cl
Kingston upon Hull HU13 143 C3
Kingston upon Hull HU2 155 A4
6 Waltham DN37 113 D7
Fountain Hill DN10 116 B3
Fountain Hill Rd DN10 116 B4
Fountain Rd HU2 140 E1
Fountain St
16 Caistor LN7 111 B4
Kingston upon Hull HU3 145 D6
Fountains Ave YO16 122 D7
Fountains Way HU15 53 D3
Fountayne Rd
13 Hunmanby YO14 2 F8
13 Hunmanby YO14 2 F8
Fountayne St
Goole DN14 149 E5
York YO31 130 C7
Four Acre Cl HU10 143 C6
Fourth Ave
Bridlington YO15 123 A4
Fixborough Ind Est. DN15 82 A1
Goole DN14 149 C4
Scunthorpe DN17 150 C2
York YO31 130 E5
Fourways 9 DN36 114 D4
Fowler Ct 3 DN15 83 A5
Fowler Rd DN16 151 C3
Fox Covert
Hibaldstow DN20 108 F5
York YO31 127 F2
Fox Covert La DN10 116 D4
Fox Covert Rd WF8 76 C1
Fox Ct DN17 94 D8
Fox Garth YO26 126 A3
Fox Glade YO41 15 C2
Fox Hill (Tumulus)★ YO25 21 D8
Fox Hill La YO8 148 A3
Fox La
Chapel Haddlesey YO8 62 C5
Hambleton LS25 61 D8
Laxton DN14 65 E3
Thorpe Willoughby YO8 48 B1
Fox St DN15 150 F7
Foxcroft 3 YO32 127 C7
Foxdale Ave YO8 48 B1
Foxglove Cl 16 HU7 56 F5
Foxglove Gdns 5 DN34 102 C3
Foxhill DN37 102 B4
Foxhill Cl HU9 142 E2
Foxhill La YO8 148 A3
Foxhill Rd DN8 93 B7
Foxhills Comp Sch DN15 96 C7
Foxhills Ind Pk DN15 96 C8
Foxhills Rd DN15 96 C7
Foxholme Rd HU7 141 D7
Foxthorn Paddock YO10 131 D3
Foxton Cl YO24 132 C8
Foxwood La York YO24 129 A1
3 York YO24 129 C1
York YO24 132 C8
Foynes Gn 6 HU8 142 C5
Frampton Cl HU7 141 B6
Frances Askew Prim Sch HU4 144 E4
Frances Ct 8 DN37 113 D7
Frances St
Scunthorpe DN15 151 A7
York YO10 130 D1
Francis Ave 10 HU19 75 A6
Francis Ct 7 YO8 48 B2
Francis St HU2 155 B3
Francis Way 3 HU12 74 D1
Frankland Cl DN20 98 E3
Frankland Pl DN35 153 D3
Franklin Cres DN16 151 E2
Franklin Rd DN21 107 C4
Franklin Sixth Form Coll DN34 152 B1
Franklin St HU9 146 C8
Franklin Way DN38 99 F5
Fraser St DN32 152 F3
Frazer Ct YO30 129 E8
Frederic St YO30 156 A3
Frederick Gough Comp Sch DN16 96 E2
Frederick Holmes Sch HU6 140 A5
Frederick St
Cleethorpes DN35 153 E2
Goole DN14 149 E5
Grimsby DN31 152 D4
Frederick Ward Way DN31 152 D3
Freehold St HU3 145 D7
Freeman Ave 4 HU15 68 C5
Freeman Ct DN36 114 B5
Freeman St DN32 152 F4
Freemans La DN20 84 C2
Freeport Wharf DN31 152 E4
Freeschool La or Gr DN14 52 A2
Freeston St DN35 153 B4
Freetown Way HU2 155 A3
Freightliner Rd HU3 144 F2
Fremantle Ave HU9 142 D2
Frensham Cl 9 HU7 56 F6
Fresh Fields 12 HU15 68 C5
Freshney Bog Nature Reserve★ DN34 102 B3
Freshney Dr DN31 152 C4
Freshney Places Sh Ctr DN31 152 D3
Friargate YO1 156 B2
Friars Cl YO19 26 D7
Friars La HU17 154 B2
Friars Mdw YO8 148 C8
Friars Rd DN17 150 E2
Friar's Wlk YO31 130 E8
Friary Ct 5 HU3 140 D1
Friendship Ct 2 YO8 148 C6
Frith Mews 4 YO8 148 C6
Frobisher Ave DN32 153 B2
Frodingham Footpath 2 DN15 151 B7
Frodingham Inf Sch DN15 151 B6
Frodingham La HU12 74 D4
Frodingham Rd
Brandesburton YO25 34 B4
Scunthorpe DN15 151 A8
Frodingham S Rd DN16 151 E5
Frodsham St HU9 147 B7
Froebel House Sch HU17 136 C6
Frome Rd HU8 142 C7
Front La HU12 59 A3
Front St
Alkborough DN15 82 C8
Burton Fleming YO25 2 E3
East Stockwith DN21 116 E5
Elsham DN20 98 F7
Gainsborough DN21 117 A2
Grasby DN38 110 E7
Langtoft YO25 8 C5
Laxton DN14 65 E4
Lockington YO25 32 B2
Middleton YO25 31 C4
Naburn YO19 36 D8
Ulceby DN39 86 A1
Wold Newton YO25 2 A4
York YO24 129 C3
Froscoles Cl 6 HU15 53 D3
Frusher Ave 7 DN33 102 E2
Fryston 11 HU15 68 C6
Fryston Comm La LS25 61 A8
Fuchsia Croft DN15 150 F6
Fuchsia Dr HU4 144 B2
Fulbeck Rd DN16 151 C2
Fulford Cres
Kingston upon Hull HU10 144 A8
3 New Holland DN19 70 E2
Fulford Cross YO10 130 D1
Fulford Cross Specl Sch YO10 130 D1
Fulford Pk YO10 133 D7
Fulford Rd YO10 133 D8
Fulford Sch YO10 133 E7
Fulfordgate YO10 133 E7
Fulham La DN14 76 E7
Fulham Pk 2 DN33 102 D1
Fuller St DN35 153 D4
Fulmar Cl HU7 141 D8
Fulstow Cty Prim Sch LN11 121 E8
Fulstow Gr 22 DN33 102 D2
Furlong Rd 23 YO41 15 D2
Furness Cl 8 HU7 57 A7
Furness Dr YO30 126 E1
Furnwood 2 YO32 127 D7
Furze Rd HU12 60 B2
Fussey Gdns DN20 84 C1
Fylingdales Ave
6 York YO30 126 E1
York YO30 129 E8

G

Gable Pk YO23 24 C6
Gables Cl 8 DN14 61 D4
Gadwall Cl 2 HU15 52 F1
Gain Hills Balk YO16 10 D4
Gainas Ave DN21 117 B1
Gainford Gr HU9 142 E2
Gainford Rd DN8 79 B2
Gainford Sq 18 DN8 79 B2
Gainsborough La DN20 108 F8
Gainsborough Rd
Blyton DN21 117 E4
20 Kirton in Lindsey DN21 108 B1
Kirton in Lindsey DN21 119 A8
Scotter DN21 107 B3
Gainsthorpe Rd E DN21 108 D4
Gainsthorpe Rd W DN21 108 C4
Gale Farm Ct 6 YO24 129 C3
Gale La Thorganby YO19 37 F4
York YO24 129 C2
Gale The YO19 36 D4
Galecarr La YO42 39 E6
Galegate YO43 53 E7
Galfrid Rd HU11 142 F7
Galley Ct HU9 146 C6
Galligap La YO10 131 C4
Gallops The YO24 132 B8
Galloway Ct 4 YO25 124 F4
Galloway La 3 YO25 124 F4
Gallows Bridge Rd HU11 59 A7
Gallows Hill★ YO25 9 A2
Gallows La HU17 136 D5
Galmanhoe La YO30 156 A3
Galtres Ave YO31 131 B7
Galtres Gr YO30 129 F7
Galtres Rd YO31 131 B7
Galtres Sch YO31 131 B5
Ganstead Gr HU9 142 A2
Ganstead La HU11 142 D6
Ganton Ave HU16 139 A5
Ganton Ct 3 HU8 142 B5
Ganton Hill YO12 1 B7
Ganton Pl YO24 132 E7
Ganton Rd YO25 1 C4
Ganton Specl Sch HU10 144 A7
Ganton Way HU10 143 F8
Gap Rd YO14 3 D8
Garbett Way 1 YO23 133 B3
Garburn Gr 3 YO30 126 E1
Garbutt Cl 2 HU12 58 D1
Garbutt Gr YO26 129 D5
Garbutt Pl 3 DN35 103 D2
Garden Dr DN36 114 A8
Garden Flats La YO19 26 E7

Garden La 11 WF11 . . . . . .61 A3
Garden Pl YO1 . . . . .156 C2
Garden St 13 Brigg DN20 . .98 C2
　Grimsby DN32 . . . . .152 D3
　York YO31 . . . . .156 B4
Garden Wlk 12 YO15 . . . .122 C2
Gardeners Cl 8 YO23 . . . .132 B3
Gardeners Row YO25 . . . . . .7 B3
Gardens The HU3 . . . . . .145 C5
Gardham La YO25 . . . . . . .35 A6
Gardham Rd HU17 . . . . . . .42 E5
Gare La DN14 . . . . .66 A6
Garends Rd 4 YO15 . . . . . .5 A2
Garfield Cl HU9 . . . . .142 D1
Garfield St 22 DN21 . . . . .117 B1
Garfield Terr YO26 . . . . . .129 F5
Garibaldi St DN32 . . . . . .152 F5
Garland Cl HU3 . . . . .142 C4
Garland St 2 YO26 . . . . . .129 E4
Garlands The YO30 . . . . . .130 A8
Garman Carr La YO8 . . . . .48 D6
Garner St DN32 . . . . .152 E2
Garnet Gr 6 HU3 . . . . . . .145 A4
Garnet Terr YO26 . . . . . . .129 E5
Garnett St DN35 . . . . . . .153 D4
Garrick Cl Brayton YO8 . . .148 B1
　Kingston upon Hull HU8 . . .141 F4
　15 Pocklington YO42 . . . . .29 A4
Garrison Rd HU9 . . . . . . .155 C1
Garrison St YO15 . . . . . . .122 F2
Garrow Hill YO10 . . . . . . .130 F2
Garrow Hill Ave YO10 . . . .131 A3
Garroway Way YO10 . . . . .26 A4
Garrowby Hill YO41 . . . . . .16 F3
Garrowby Rd YO42 . . . . . .16 F2
Garrowby St YO41 . . . . . . .16 E3
Garrowby View 5 YO41 . . .15 D2
Garth Ave
　Kingston upon Hull HU11 . . .58 A3
　4 North Duffield YO8 . . . . .50 A7
Garth Cl 6 YO8 . . . . .48 D6
Garth Ends Rd HU17 . . . . .43 A2
Garth Glebe 8 YO8 . . . . . .49 B5
Garth La Goole DN14 . . . . .65 C4
　Grimsby DN31 . . . . .152 D4
Garth Mill 1 DN14 . . . . . . .61 D4
Garth Morrell YO8 . . . . . .148 C2
Garth Rd YO32 . . . . .127 F4
Garth Terr YO30 . . . . .130 B7
Garth The HU16 . . . . .139 A5
Garthends La
　3 Hemingbrough YO8 . . . . .49 F1
　Mappleton HU11 . . . . .47 B5
Garthorpe Rd
　Luddington & Haldenby
　　DN17 . . . . .81 C3
　Twin Rivers DN14 . . . . . . .81 E7
Garths End 20 Haxby YO32 .13 D3
　Pocklington YO42 . . . . .29 A4
Garth's End YO10 . . . . . . .133 E8
Garths End La YO42 . . . . . .29 A8
Garthway
　13 Holton le Clay DN36 . . .114 A5
　4 York YO32 . . . . .127 D3
Garton Balk YO25 . . . . . . .20 D8
Garton Gr
　Grimsby DN32 . . . . .153 A1
　3 Kingston upon Hull
　　HU4 . . . . .144 C7
Garton Hill YO25 . . . . .19 E7
Garton Rd HU11 . . . . .47 C1
Garton Sch YO25 . . . . .20 A4
Garton Slack YO25 . . . . . . .19 D6
Gas House La 13 DN14 . . . .65 B7
Gashouse La DN9 . . . . . . .106 B3
Gate Arts Ctr The ★
　DN14 . . . . .149 C4
Gate La 11 DN33 . . . . . . .102 C1
Gate Way DN31 . . . . .152 C6
Gateforth New Rd YO8 . . . .62 A8
Gatehead La YO42 . . . . . . .38 D7
Gatehouse ★ DN39 . . . . . .86 B5
Gatehouse Rd DN19 . . . . . .85 F7
Gatehowe Rd YO17 . . . . . . .17 A4
Gateland Cl YO32 . . . . . . .127 C2
Gateland Field La DN14 . . . .64 B6
Gatesby Rd DN14 . . . . . . .149 C6
Gatewood La DN7 . . . . . . .92 E1
Gatherums The DN35 . . . . .153 E1
Gatwick Garth 15 HU7 . . . .57 A5
Gaufer Hill YO43 . . . . .41 D3
Gautry La DN9 . . . . .106 B4
Gay Mdws YO25 . . . . .14 D2
Gayles Mews 3 HU5 . . . . .139 D3
Gayton Rd DN35 . . . . .103 D2
Gedney Cl 8 DN37 . . . . . .102 B4
Gee St HU3 . . . . .145 C5
Geeseness La DN14 . . . . . .78 D2
Geldof Rd YO12 . . . . .127 F1
Gembling CP Sch YO25 . . . .22 A3
Gembling La YO25 . . . . . . .22 A4
Gemel Rd HU12 . . . . .59 C2
Gemsbok Cl 3 HU4 . . . . . .144 D2
General La HU12 . . . . .38 E6
Geneva Sq DN8 . . . . .79 C2
Geneva Way HU7 . . . . . . .141 B5
George Ave DN17 . . . . .95 D5
George Butler Cl 16
　DN37 . . . . .101 F1
George Cayley Dr
　YO30 . . . . .127 A3
George Ct YO31 . . . . .156 C4
George Hudson St
　YO1 . . . . .156 B2

George Janney Ct
　DN32 . . . . .153 A5
George La HU17 . . . . .55 D8
George Mews 8 LN7 . . . . .111 B4
George St
　2 Barton-upon-Humber
　　DN18 . . . . .84 F8
　Beverley HU17 . . . . .154 B3
　Bridlington YO15 . . . . . . .122 C1
　Broughton DN20 . . . . .97 D3
　Cleethorpes DN35 . . . . . .153 E1
　Gainsborough DN21 . . . . .117 A1
　Great Driffield YO25 . . . . .124 E4
　Grimsby DN31 . . . . .152 D3
　28 Hedon HU12 . . . . .72 C7
　Keadby DN17 . . . . .95 D5
　Kingston upon Hull
　　HU16 . . . . .139 A7
　Kingston upon Hull HU1 . . .155 B2
　11 Kirton in Lindsey DN21 .108 B1
　Pocklington YO42 . . . . . . .29 A4
　Scunthorpe DN15 . . . . . . .151 A8
　4 Selby YO8 . . . . .148 D6
　Snaith DN14 . . . . .63 C1
　7 Wistow YO8 . . . . .48 D6
　3 Withernsea HU19 . . . . . .74 F7
　York YO1 . . . . .156 C1
George Terr 1 YO8 . . . . . .49 B4
George Yd HU1 . . . . .155 B2
Georgian Mews
　Bridlington YO15 . . . . . . .122 C1
　4 Great Driffield YO25 . . . .124 F3
Georgian Way YO15 . . . . .122 C1
Georgina Ct 8 DN18 . . . . .84 E8
Gerard Ave YO31 . . . . . . .131 A5
Germain Rd YO8 . . . . .148 E4
German Nook La HU7 . . . . .56 B8
Germany La YO19 . . . . . . .133 E6
Gershwin Ave HU4 . . . . . .144 B4
Gertrude St DN32 . . . . . . .152 E1
Gervase St DN15 . . . . . . .151 A7
Giant Hill ★ HU11 . . . . . . .57 D6
Gibraltar 8 DN37 . . . . . . .101 F1
Gibraltar Way HU7 . . . . . . .56 E5
Gibson La HU14 . . . . .68 E4
Gibson Rd 4 DN7 . . . . . . .104 A8
Gibson St YO25 . . . . .124 E5
Gifford Cl HU7 . . . . .57 A6
Gilberdyke Prim Sch
　HU15 . . . . .66 D8
Gilberdyke Sta HU15 . . . . .66 D7
Gilbert St YO16 . . . . .122 C1
Gilbey Rd DN31 . . . . .152 B5
Gilcross Rd HU12 . . . . .90 C6
Gildane HU6 . . . . .139 E8
Giles Ave YO31 . . . . .131 A5
Giles St DN35 . . . . .153 E2
Gillamoor Ave YO31 . . . . .131 B5
Gillamoor Cl 16 HU8 . . . . .141 E7
Gillann St 15 WF11 . . . . . . .61 A2
Gillatts Cl DN20 . . . . .98 D4
Gillett St HU3 . . . . .145 B4
Gilliatt St DN15 . . . . .151 A7
Gilling Mews 4 HU5 . . . . .139 D3
Gillingwood Rd YO30 . . . .126 F3
Gillshill Prim Sch
　HU8 . . . . .141 D5
Gillshill Rd HU8 . . . . .141 D4
Gillus La 5 YO15 . . . . .4 D3
Gillygate YO31 . . . . .156 B3
Gillyon Ct 3 HU17 . . . . . .137 B3
Gipsey Cnr YO19 . . . . .26 E3
Gipsy La
　Holton le Moor LN7 . . . . .110 C1
　Owston Ferry DN9 . . . . . .116 F8
Girton Cl 5 DN16 . . . . .96 D2
Girvan Cl YO24 . . . . .132 B7
Gisburn Rd HU13 . . . . . . .143 F2
Givendale Gr 3 YO10 . . . .131 C4
Givendale Hill YO42 . . . . . .29 C6
Givendale Rd YO42 . . . . . . .29 A8
Glade Rd YO19 . . . . .37 B2
Glade The
　Beverley HU17 . . . . .137 D8
　Escrick YO19 . . . . .37 A6
　York YO31 . . . . .131 B7
Gladstone Dr DN16 . . . . . .151 C5
Gladstone St
　Kingston upon Hull
　　HU13 . . . . .143 E1
　Kingston upon Hull HU3 . . .145 C6
　York YO31 . . . . .156 C4
Gladstone Terr 6 YO15 . . .122 F3
Glaisby Ct YO31 . . . . .131 A6
Glaisdale Cl YO16 . . . . . . .122 F7
Glaisdale Gr HU9 . . . . . . .146 F8
Glaisdale Rd DN16 . . . . . .151 E1
Glamis Rd HU13 . . . . .143 F2
Glanford Gr 6 DN19 . . . . .85 D8
Glanford Rd
　22 Brigg DN20 . . . . .98 C2
　Scunthorpe DN17 . . . . . . .96 C2
Glanford Way DN15 . . . . . .150 B7
Glanville Ave DN17 . . . . . .150 F4
Glanville Cres DN17 . . . . .150 F4
Glasgow St HU3 . . . . .145 A5
Glass House Row HU8 . . . .141 A1
Glebe Ave
　Full Sutton YO41 . . . . .16 A2
　York YO26 . . . . .129 D5
Glebe Cl
　Burton upon Stather
　　DN15 . . . . .82 A5
　5 Holton le Clay DN36 . . .114 A6
　Humberston DN36 . . . . . .114 C8
　3 Strensall YO32 . . . . .14 B7
　2 Wawne HU7 . . . . .56 E7

Glebe Lands The 4
　YO43 . . . . .135 E4
Glebe Rd Brigg DN20 . . . . .98 C2
　Campsall DN6 . . . . .76 E1
　Cleethorpes DN35 . . . . . .153 E2
　Grimsby DN33 . . . . .102 F1
　Humberston DN36 . . . . . .114 C8
　Kingston upon Hull HU7 . . .141 A4
　Scunthorpe DN15 . . . . . . .151 B8
　Thorne/Moorends DN8 . . . .93 B8
　Wawne HU7 . . . . .56 E7
Glebe Way
　Barton-upon-Humber
　　DN18 . . . . .85 A8
　26 Haxby YO32 . . . . .13 D5
Glebelands HU12 . . . . .59 D2
Glen Almond HU11 . . . . . .142 D6
Glen Ave YO31 . . . . .130 E5
Glen Cl YO10 . . . . .133 E6
Glen Cres YO42 . . . . .39 A7
Glen Hall Rise 11 DN19 . . .85 C8
Glen Rd YO31 . . . . .130 E5
Glen The
　Beverley HU17 . . . . .137 B2
　Kingston upon Hull
　　HU10 . . . . .138 B1
Glencoe Cl 22 DN7 . . . . . .92 D4
Glencoe St
　Kingston upon Hull HU3 . . .144 F6
　1 York YO30 . . . . .130 B7
Glendale Cl HU10 . . . . . . .138 C1
Gleneagles 15 DN37 . . . . .113 D6
Gleneagles Cres 4 DN19 .70 E2
Gleneagles Pk HU8 . . . . . .141 F6
Glenfield Ave YO43 . . . . . .135 D4
Glenfield Dr HU10 . . . . . . .138 B1
Glenfield Rd DN37 . . . . . . .102 B4
Glenholme Ct YO25 . . . . . .32 E7
Glenriding YO24 . . . . .132 D7
Glenrock Pk HU15 . . . . . . .68 B6
Glenwood Dr 2 HU4 . . . . .144 B6
Glimpse The YO23 . . . . . . .123 A4
Gloria Way 3 DN37 . . . . . .102 B4
Glossop Rd DN15 . . . . . . .150 B6
Gloucester Ave
　Grimsby DN34 . . . . .102 D2
　Scunthorpe DN16 . . . . . . .151 B4
Gloucester Rd HU10 . . . . .138 C2
Gloucester St HU4 . . . . . .144 C5
Glover Rd DN17 . . . . .150 E4
Glovers Ave DN17 . . . . . . .95 D4
Goathead La HU11 . . . . . . .78 E8
Goathland Cl HU3 . . . . . . .145 A6
Goble Cl DN18 . . . . .85 A8
Godbold Cl HU17 . . . . . . .154 C3
Goddard Ave HU5 . . . . . . .140 B2
Goddard Cl 9 DN18 . . . . . .84 E8
Godfrey Rd 11 DN8 . . . . . .93 A8
Godman's La HU10 . . . . . .143 B8
Godnow Rd DN17 . . . . .94 C6
Godric's Cross ★ DN9 . . . .104 B6
Godwinsway 18 YO41 . . . . .15 C2
God's Cross ★ DN9 . . . . . .104 B6
Gold Thread La 5 YO8 . . . .48 B8
Goldcrest Cl
　1 Kingston upon Hull
　　HU7 . . . . .141 D8
　Scunthorpe DN15 . . . . . . .96 B7
Golden Ct 10 HU9 . . . . . . .142 A3
Golden Gr HU11 . . . . .142 D6
Goldgarth DN32 . . . . .153 A1
Goldings The DN9 . . . . . . .105 D2
Golf Links Dr HU15 . . . . . . .68 B6
Golf Links Rd HU6 . . . . . . .139 E5
Gollands La DN9 . . . . .105 B2
Goodfell Rd HU17 . . . . . . .137 A6
Goodhand Cl DN18 . . . . . . .85 A8
Goodhart Rd HU7 . . . . . . .141 B8
Goodmanham Rd
　Market Weighton YO43 . . .135 D5
　Middleton YO25 . . . . .31 C3
Goodmanham Way 6
　HU16 . . . . .138 E6
Goodramgate YO1 . . . . . . .156 B2
Goodrich Cl HU3 . . . . .140 C1
Goodsyard The YO8 . . . . . .148 D5
Goodwin Par 1 HU3 . . . . .145 D5
Goodwood DN17 . . . . .96 B2
Goodwood Gr YO24 . . . . . .129 F1
Goole & District Hospl
　DN14 . . . . .149 C6
Goole Coll DN14 . . . . .149 B4
Goole Gram Sch DN14 . . . .149 B5
Goole L Ctr DN14 . . . . . . .149 D3
Goole Rd Goole DN14 . . . . .65 C3
　Swinefleet DN14 . . . . .80 C8
Goole Sta DN14 . . . . .149 C4
Gooseacre DN17 . . . . .107 D7
Goosenook La HU17 . . . . . .45 A4
Gordan Pk HU16 . . . . .139 C6
Gordon Gdns DN33 . . . . . .113 E8
Gordon Rd YO16 . . . . .122 C4
Gordon St Goole DN14 . . . .149 C4
　4 Kingston upon Hull
　　HU3 . . . . .145 B5
　York YO10 . . . . .130 E3
Gore La DN14 . . . . .77 B5
Goring Pl DN35 . . . . .153 D3
Gormire Ave 2 YO31 . . . . .127 E2
Gorse Cl Hatfield DN7 . . . . .92 C3
　Selby YO8 . . . . .148 C2
Gorse Hill 1 YO19 . . . . . . .26 F7
Gorse Paddock YO32 . . . . .127 E2
Gorsedale HU7 . . . . .140 E7
Gorton Cl HU10 . . . . .143 C7
Gorton St DN31 . . . . .152 F6
Gosport Rd DN34 . . . . . . .152 A2
Gossips Wood Rd DN14 . . .79 B8

Gothenburg Way HU7 . . . .140 E6
Goths La HU17 . . . . .154 B4
Gott Cl YO25 . . . . .124 C2
Gouldesborough Ct 2
　HU5 . . . . .140 C3
Goulton St HU3 . . . . .145 B3
Gouthwaite Cl YO30 . . . . .126 F2
Government House Rd
　YO30 . . . . .130 A6
Government St 1 DN14 . . .149 D4
Gowdall Broach DN14 . . . . .77 E8
Gowdall La
　Pollington DN14 . . . . .77 F7
　Snaith & Cowick DN14 . . . .63 B1
Gowdall Rd DN14 . . . . .62 E2
Gowdall Way 1 DN14 . . . . .65 A7
Gower Rd
　Kingston upon Hull HU4 . . .144 B3
　York YO24 . . . . .132 E8
Gowthorpe YO8 . . . . .148 C5
Gowthorpe La HU11 . . . . . .66 E4
Goxhill Airport DN19 . . . . . .86 B8
Goxhill CP Sch DN19 . . . . . .86 A8
Goxhill Gdns 17 DN34 . . . .102 C2
Goxhill Rd DN19 . . . . .85 E8
Goxhill Sta DN19 . . . . .85 F8
Grafton St
　Grimsby DN32 . . . . .153 A5
　Kingston upon Hull HU5 . . .140 C2
Gragdale Cl HU8 . . . . .141 E7
Graham Ave HU4 . . . . .144 C2
Graingers Rd HU18 . . . . . .134 D3
Grains Gate LN11 . . . . . . .115 E1
Grainsby Ave
　Cleethorpes DN35 . . . . . .103 B2
　Holton le Clay DN36 . . . . .114 B5
Grainsby Healing ★
　DN36 . . . . .113 F3
Grainsby La
　Grainsby DN36 . . . . .113 E1
　Tetney DN36 . . . . .114 D3
Graizelound Fields Rd
　DN9 . . . . .105 D1
Grammar Sch La DN20 . . . .98 C3
Grammar Sch Rd
　Brigg DN20 . . . . .98 C2
　Kingston upon Hull HU5 . . .139 E2
Grammar Sch Rd S 6
　DN20 . . . . .98 C2
Grammar Sch Wlk
　HU1 . . . . .96 E2
Grammar Sch Yd HU1 . . . .155 B1
Grampian Cl 4 YO32 . . . . .127 F5
Grampian Way
　23 Grimsby DN33 . . . . . . .113 E8
　Kingston upon Hull HU7 . . .57 A6
　Thorne/Moorends DN8 . . . .93 A7
Granary Cl DN21 . . . . .117 B3
Granary Croft 7 DN9 . . . . .105 D2
Granary Ct YO1 . . . . .156 B3
Grandale HU7 . . . . .140 E7
Grange Ave
　12 Barton-upon-Humber
　　DN18 . . . . .84 E8
　Hatfield DN7 . . . . .92 D4
　14 Laceby DN37 . . . . . . .101 F1
　Misterton DN10 . . . . .116 D5
Grange Cl
　2 Buckton/Bempton YO15 . . .4 C3
　Full Sutton YO41 . . . . .16 A2
　5 Hatfield DN7 . . . . .92 D4
　Kingston upon Hull HU2 . . .155 B4
　Misterton DN10 . . . . .116 D4
　Skelton YO30 . . . . .126 B5
Grange Cres
　Kingston upon Hull
　　HU10 . . . . .143 E6
　Tickton HU17 . . . . .137 F8
Grange Dr
　Kingston upon Hull
　　HU16 . . . . .139 A7
　Misterton DN10 . . . . .116 D4
Grange Farm La 20
　DN36 . . . . .114 A7
Grange Field DN20 . . . . . . .98 D8
Grange Garth YO10 . . . . . .130 D2
Grange Gr 3 DN8 . . . . .79 B2
Grange Jun & Inf Sch
　DN34 . . . . .102 C3
Grange La
　Covenham St Bartholomew
　　LN11 . . . . .121 F6
　Molescroft HU17 . . . . .137 A7
　North Kelsey LN7 . . . . . . .110 A3
　Rufforth YO26 . . . . .129 A2
　Utterby LN11 . . . . .121 C4
Grange La Football Club
　HU14 . . . . .69 B4
Grange La Inf Sch
　DN16 . . . . .151 D1
Grange La Jun Sch
　DN16 . . . . .151 D1
Grange La N DN16 . . . . . .151 D3
Grange La S DN16 . . . . . .151 D1
Grange Park La HU10 . . . . .138 B2
Grange Pk
　1 Brough HU15 . . . . .68 C5
　Gainsborough DN21 . . . . .117 A3
　2 Kirk Sandall DN3 . . . . . .92 A2
　Swanland HU14 . . . . .69 B6
Grange Rd
　3 Bridlington YO16 . . . . .122 D5
　8 Campsall DN6 . . . . .76 E1
　Gainsborough DN21 . . . . .117 D1
　Garthorpe & Fockerby
　　DN17 . . . . .81 D8
　Goole DN14 . . . . .149 B4
　7 Leconfield HU17 . . . . . . .43 D6

Grange Rd continued
　North Frodingham YO25 . . .34 A8
　Snaith DN14 . . . . .78 C8
　Thorne/Moorends DN8 . . . .79 B2
　Thorngumbald HU12 . . . . . .72 F5
Grange St YO10 . . . . .130 D2
Grange Way HU17 . . . . . . .136 E7
Grange Wlk
　Grimsby DN34 . . . . .152 A2
　Misterton DN10 . . . . .116 D5
Granger Ave YO26 . . . . . . .129 C4
Grangeside Ave HU6 . . . . .139 F5
Gransmoor La YO25 . . . . . .22 A5
Gransmoor Rd YO25 . . . . . .22 D5
Grant St
　Cleethorpes DN35 . . . . . .153 E3
　Grimsby DN31 . . . . .153 B5
Grantchester Cl HU5 . . . . .139 C1
Grantham Ave
　Grimsby DN33 . . . . .102 E1
　11 Kingston upon Hull HU7 .56 F6
Grantham Dr YO26 . . . . . .129 E4
Grantley Gr HU9 . . . . .142 C2
Grants Ave YO10 . . . . .133 E8
Granville St
　Grimsby DN32 . . . . .152 F2
　1 Kingston upon Hull
　　HU3 . . . . .145 A6
Granville Terr 4 YO10 . . . .130 E3
Grape La YO1 . . . . .156 B3
Grasby All Saints C of E Prim
　Sch DN38 . . . . .110 E8
Grasby Cres DN37 . . . . . . .102 B4
Grasby Rd
　Great Limber DN37 . . . . .100 C3
　Kingston upon Hull HU8 . . .142 A4
　North Kelsey LN7 . . . . . . .110 D5
　Scunthorpe DN17 . . . . . . .150 C5
Grasby Wold La DN38 . . . .110 F8
Grasmere Ave
　Gainsborough DN21 . . . . .117 C1
　Goole DN14 . . . . .149 D5
Grasmere Dr YO10 . . . . . .131 B4
Grasmere Gr
　11 Humberston DN36 . . . .103 C1
　5 York YO30 . . . . .126 F1
Grassam Cl 3 HU12 . . . . . .58 D1
Grassdale Pk 3 HU15 . . . . .68 B5
Grassholme YO24 . . . . . . .132 C7
Grassington Cl 11 HU7 . . . .57 A6
Gravel Pit Hill DN20 . . . . .109 D6
Gravel Pit La DN39 . . . . . .100 A6
Gravel Pit Rd
　Barton-upon-Humber
　　DN18 . . . . .84 D8
　Scotter DN21 . . . . .107 C4
Gravelhill La DN14 . . . . . . .76 F7
Gravelholes La DN10 . . . . .116 C4
Gravelpit La
　Kirkburn YO25 . . . . .19 F1
　Sancton YO43 . . . . .41 E2
Graves La YO42 . . . . .39 B6
Gray Friars DN37 . . . . . . .102 B4
Gray Rd DN17 . . . . .150 D2
Gray St Goole DN14 . . . . .149 C5
　York YO31 . . . . .156 A1
Grayburn La HU17 . . . . . . .154 B3
Grayingham Rd
　19 Kirton in Lindsey DN21 .108 B1
　Kirton in Lindsey DN21 . . .119 B7
Grayling Cl 15 DN37 . . . . .102 B4
Grays Croft HU12 . . . . .59 C2
Grayshon Dr YO26 . . . . . .129 B5
Greame Rd YO16 . . . . .123 A5
Great Barn St 4 YO16 . . . .122 D5
Great Cl YO8 . . . . .48 B8
Great Coates Prim Sch
　DN37 . . . . .102 B4
Great Coates Rd
　Grimsby DN37 . . . . .102 B4
　Healing DN41 . . . . .101 F5
Great Coates Sta
　DN37 . . . . .102 B5
Great Field La 17 HU10 . . . .55 C1
Great Gutter La HU10 . . . . .55 C1
Great Gutter La E
　HU10 . . . . .138 C2
Great Gutter La W
　HU10 . . . . .138 A2
Great Hatfield Rd HU11 . . .46 D4
Great Meadow Rd
　YO16 . . . . .122 E5
Great North Way
　YO26 . . . . .129 B8
Great Passage St HU1 . . . .155 A2
Great Thornton St
　HU3 . . . . .145 D6
Great Union St HU9 . . . . . .155 C3
Grebe Rd HU15 . . . . .52 F1
Greek St HU3 . . . . .144 F5
Green Acres HU10 . . . . . . .143 C6
Green Balk YO42 . . . . .17 D1
Green Bank DN8 . . . . .93 D6
Green Cl
　Kingston upon Hull HU6 . . .139 F6
　York YO30 . . . . .130 A8
Green Dike YO32 . . . . .127 C8
Green Dikes La YO25 . . . . . .8 F1
Green Dykes La YO10 . . . .130 F3
Green Hill 10 DN35 . . . . . .103 B4
Green Hills YO60 . . . . .15 B7
Green Island HU9 . . . . . . .142 E5
Green La
　Appleton Roebuck YO23 . . .36 B4
　Barmby on the Marsh
　　DN14 . . . . .64 A4
　Barrow upon Humber
　　DN19 . . . . .85 D8

Green La continued
Barton-upon-Humber
DN18 . . . .**84** F8
Belton DN9 . . . .**94** D2
Bishopthorpe YO24 . . .**133** A6
Brigsley DN37 . . . .**113** D4
Broughton DN20 . . . . . .**97** E3
Buckton/Bempton YO15 . .**4** D3
Cottingwith YO42 . . . . .**38** C5
Fimber YO25 . . . .**18** F6
Hatfield DN7 . . . .**92** E1
Heck DN14 . . . .**77** D8
Kingston upon Hull
HU16 . . . .**138** E6
Kingston upon Hull
HU13 . . . .**144** A1
Langtoft YO25 . . . .**8** D5
Moor Monkton YO26 . . . .**24** A8
Nafferton YO25 . . . . . .**125** D7
North Duffield YO8 . . . . .**49** F8
North Kelsey LN7 . . . . .**110** A4
Pilham DN21 . . . .**118** A4
Selby YO8 . . . .**148** A3
Skidby HU10 . . . .**138** B4
South Cave HU15 . . . . . .**53** D1
Swine HU11 . . . .**57** E7
Tibthorpe YO25 . . . .**19** D2
Tickton HU17 . . . .**137** F8
Weaverthorpe YO25 . . . . .**8** A8
Wetwang YO25 . . . .**18** D5
Wigginton YO32 . . . .**13** D5
Wressle DN14 . . . .**64** D8
York YO30 . . . .**127** A1
York YO24 . . . .**129** D2
Green Lane Mid Sch
DN8 . . . .**93** B7
Green Marsh Rd HU12 . .**72** E4
Green Mdws YO31 . . . .**131** A7
Green Rd
Gringley on the Hill
DN10 . . . .**116** A1
15 Hedon HU12 . . . . . .**72** C7
Green Sward YO31 . . . .**131** A8
Green The
5 Brough HU15 . . . .**68** D6
20 Dunnington YO19 . . . .**26** F7
Great Driffield YO25 . . .**125** A4
Lund YO25 . . . .**31** F3
Market Weighton YO43 . .**135** D4
Rawcliffe DN14 . . . .**64** A1
20 Scotter DN21 . . . . . .**107** C3
1 Skelton YO30 . . . . . .**126** B5
Sproatley HU11 . . . .**58** D5
1 Swanland HU14 . . . . . .**69** B7
20 Thorne/Moorends DN8 . .**93** A8
Wistow YO8 . . . .**48** D6
York YO26 . . . .**129** C3
Green Top Fst Sch DN8 . .**93** A7
Green Way YO32 . . . . .**127** F4
Green Ways 2 YO8 . . . . .**48** D6
Greenacre Cl YO42 . . . . .**29** B3
Greenacre Pk
Gilberdyke HU15 . . . . . .**66** D8
Hornsea HU18 . . . .**134** C1
Greenacres
4 Swanland HU14 . . . . . .**69** C7
York YO32 . . . .**127** F4
Greenacres Cl 8 YO8 . . .**48** A8
Greenacres Cres 7 YO8 .**48** D1
Greenacres Dr 4 YO8 . . .**48** D1
Greenacres Gr 3 YO8 . . .**48** D1
Greencliffe Dr YO30 . . . .**130** A6
Greencroft Cl 26 YO19 . . .**26** F7
Greencroft La 17 YO19 . . .**26** F7
Greenfield Cl 6 DN3 . . .**92** A3
Greenfield Dr
6 Brayton YO8 . . . .**48** D1
Hibaldstow DN20 . . . . .**109** A5
Greenfield Garth HU6 . . .**56** D5
Greenfield La YO25 . . . .**31** C4
Greenfield Pk Dr
YO31 . . . .**131** A7
Greenfield Rd
Bridlington YO16 . . . . . .**122** B2
Middleton-on-the-Wolds
YO25 . . . .**31** C4
Greenfields DN14 . . . . . .**77** F6
Greenfinch Dr 8 DN35 . .**103** C1
Greengales Ct YO19 . . . .**38** A8
Greengales La YO19 . . . .**38** A8
Greengarth DN17 . . . . . .**96** C1
Greengate DN9 . . . .**105** E6
Greengate La Cliffe YO8 . .**49** F6
2 Goxhill DN19 . . . .**86** A8
South Killingholme DN40 . .**86** E3
Greengate Rd WF8 . . . . .**76** C1
Greenhill 8 DN20 . . . . . .**97** D3
Greenhill Rd DN9 . . . . .**105** C2
Greenhoe Rd DN17 . . . . .**96** B2
Greenhow Cl HU8 . . . . .**141** E6
Greenland La DN14 . . . . .**78** F7
Greenlands YO25 . . . . . .**124** F5
Greenlands Ave 13
DN36 . . . .**114** A7
Greenlands La YO8 . . . . .**48** C3
Greenoak La DN14 . . . . .**66** B7
Greens La
Burstwick HU12 . . . .**73** B8
Burton Pidsea HU12 . . . .**59** C5
Wawne HU7 . . . .**56** E7
Green's Rd DN7 . . . .**92** C3
Greensborough Ave 3
YO26 . . . .**129** B5
Greenshaw Dr YO32 . . . .**127** C8
Greenshaw La HU12 . . . .**74** D1
Greenside
18 Dunnington YO19 . . . .**26** F7

Greenside continued
8 Flamborough YO15 . . . .**5** A2
Greenside Cl 24 YO19 . . .**26** F7
Greenside Wlk 23 YO19 . .**26** F7
Greenstiles La HU14 . . . .**69** C7
Greenway
8 Barton-upon-Humber
DN18 . . . .**69** F1
10 Waltham DN37 . . . . .**113** E6
Greenway The
2 Haxby YO32 . . . .**127** C7
Hornsea HU18 . . . .**134** C2
1 Kingston upon Hull
HU4 . . . .**144** C6
Greenways
Great Driffield YO25 . . . .**124** F5
2 North Ferriby HU14 . . . .**69** A5
Greenways Cl YO16 . . . .**122** F6
Greenways Dr 1 YO8 . . . .**48** D6
Greenwich Ave HU8 . . . .**142** C4
Greenwood Ave
Beverley HU17 . . . .**154** C3
Kingston upon Hull HU6 . .**139** E5
Greenwood Gdns
HU17 . . . .**136** F7
Greenwood Gr YO24 . . .**132** C8
Greetham's La DN32 . . . .**153** B1
Greet's Hill YO17 . . . . . .**16** E7
Gregory Cl YO30 . . . . . .**126** C5
Grenley St 8 WF11 . . . . .**61** A2
Grenville Bay HU17 . . . .**142** D6
Grenwich Cl 5 YO30 . . .**126** E3
Gresley Ct 3 YO26 . . . .**129** B4
Greville Rd HU12 . . . . . .**72** D7
Grey St
Gainsborough DN21 . . . .**117** A1
Kingston upon Hull HU2 . .**145** D7
Greyfriars Cres HU17 . . .**154** A1
Greyfriars Rd 20 DN20 . . .**97** E3
Greygarth Cl 14 HU7 . . . .**56** F6
Greystoke Rd YO30 . . . .**126** E1
Greystone Ave HU4 . . . .**144** E1
Greystone Ct 3 YO24 . . .**132** C8
Greystones Rd DN21 . . .**117** A2
Griffin Prim Sch HU9 . . .**142** C3
Griffiths Way 18 HU12 . . .**73** C4
Grime St DN31 . . . .**152** E4
Grimsby Coll DN34 . . . .**152** C1
Grimsby Docks Sta DN32 .**152** F4
Grimsby L Ctr DN34 . . . .**152** A4
Grimsby Maternity Hospl
DN33 . . . .**102** E2
Grimsby Rd
Caistor LN7 . . . .**111** C4
Cleethorpes DN35 . . . . .**153** D4
Fotherby LN11 . . . .**121** D1
Humberston DN36 . . . . .**103** B1
Laceby DN37 . . . .**101** F1
Swallow LN7 . . . .**112** B6
Waltham DN37 . . . .**113** E7
Grimsby RUFC DN33 . . .**102** E1
Grimsby Town Football Club
DN35 . . . .**153** C5
Grimsby Town Sta
DN32 . . . .**152** D3
Grimscott Cl 2 HU7 . . . .**56** F5
Grimston Rd
12 Hunmanby YO14 . . . . .**3** A8
5 Kingston upon Hull
HU10 . . . .**143** F6
Grimston St HU1 . . . . . .**155** B3
Grimthorpe Hill YO42 . . . .**29** B7
Grimwith Garth YO30 . . .**126** F2
Grindale La YO16 . . . . . .**122** A7
Grindale Rd
Bempton YO16 . . . .**4** A3
Grindale YO16 . . . .**122** A8
Grindell St HU9 . . . . . .**146** D8
Gringley Rd
Misterton DN10 . . . .**116** B4
Walkeringham DN10 . . . .**116** C2
Grinsdale Rise YO25 . . . .**125** F7
Grizedale HU7 . . . .**140** F7
Grosmont Cl HU8 . . . . .**141** E7
Grosvenor Ave DN14 . . .**149** A5
Grosvenor Cres 1
DN32 . . . .**152** D3
Grosvenor Ct DN7 . . . . .**92** D8
Grosvenor Pl HU17 . . . .**136** D2
Grosvenor Rd
Hornsea HU18 . . . .**134** D4
York YO30 . . . .**156** A4
Grosvenor St
Grimsby DN32 . . . .**152** D2
Kingston upon Hull HU3 . .**145** D8
Grosvenor St N DN15 . . .**151** A8
Grosvenor St S DN15 . . .**151** A8
Grosvenor Terr YO30 . . .**156** A4
Grove Cl HU17 . . . .**154** B4
Grove Gdns 2 YO26 . . . .**12** F1
Grove Hill HU13 . . . . . .**143** E1
Grove House View
HU5 . . . .**140** D3
Grove La DN7 . . . .**113** E6
Grove Pk 7 Barlby YO8 . . . .**49** B5
Beverley HU17 . . . .**154** A4
Misterton DN10 . . . .**116** C5
Grove Rd DN7 . . . .**92** D8
Grove St
Kingston upon Hull HU5 . .**140** D1
Kirton in Lindsey DN21 . .**108** A1
Grove Terr La YO31 . . . .**156** C4
Grove The
Barrow upon Humber
DN19 . . . .**85** D8
Beckingham DN10 . . . . .**116** D1

Grove The continued
Kellington DN14 . . . .**62** A3
York YO24 . . . .**132** E6
Grove View YO30 . . . . .**130** A6
Grove Wharf ★ DN15 . . . .**95** E7
Grove Wood Rd DN10 . . .**116** C5
Grove Wood Terr
DN10 . . . .**116** C5
Grovehill HU17 . . . .**137** C4
Grovehill Rd HU17 . . . . .**154** C3
Grovenor Ct 11 DN35 . . .**103** D1
Groves La YO31 . . . . . .**156** C4
Groves The YO25 . . . . .**125** A3
Grundale HU10 . . . .**143** C6
Grundell's Yd 4 YO16 . . .**122** D4
Grundill La
Hatfield HU11 . . . .**46** A8
Seaton HU11 . . . .**35** A1
Guardians Rd 2 HU12 . . .**74** D1
Guernsey Gr 1 DN40 . . .**101** C8
Guest Hall HU11 . . . . . .**47** B1
Guildford Ave HU8 . . . . .**141** D4
Guildford Cl HU17 . . . . .**136** E1
Guildford St DN32 . . . . .**153** A4
Guildhall Rd HU1 . . . . . .**155** B2
Guilcarr La LN7 . . . . . .**109** E4
Guisefield Rd 5 DN9 . . .**105** D6
Gullane Dr HU6 . . . .**56** D5
Gunby Pl 9 DN35 . . . . .**103** C2
Gunby Rd Bubwith YO8 . . .**50** D5
Scunthorpe DN17 . . . . .**150** E1
Gunbywood Rd YO8 . . . .**50** D6
Gunness & Burringham C of
E Sch DN15 . . . .**95** A5
Gunness La DN15 . . . . . .**95** F8
Gunthorpe Rd DN9 . . . .**116** F8
Gurnell St DN15 . . . . . .**151** A8
Gurnell Street C of E Sch
DN15 . . . .**151** A8
Gurth Ave DN3 . . . .**92** A1
Gus Walker Dr YO42 . . . .**29** B4
Guy Garth 3 HU12 . . . . .**72** D7
Gypsey Rd YO16 . . . . . .**122** B4

H

Habrough La
Brocklesby DN39 . . . . . .**100** C6
Kirmington DN39 . . . . . .**100** B6
Habrough Rd
Immingham DN40 . . . . . .**87** A1
South Killingholme DN40 . .**86** E2
Habrough Sta DN40 . . . .**100** E8
Hackforth Wlk HU5 . . . .**139** D4
Hackness Gr 2 HU5 . . . .**144** D8
Haddlesey Rd WF11 . . . .**61** D1
Haddon Rd YO16 . . . . . .**122** D7
Haddon St HU3 . . . .**144** F4
Hadds La DN8 . . . .**78** F3
Hadds Nook Rd DN8 . . . .**78** F2
Hadleigh Cl 4 HU3 . . . .**140** E1
Hadleigh Gn 4 DN7 . . . . .**95** D4
Hadleigh Rd DN40 . . . . .**87** C1
Hadrian Ave HU13 . . . . .**131** B3
Hag La YO42 . . . .**38** C4
Hagg La Belton DN17 . . . .**94** B3
Cottingwith YO42 . . . . . .**38** E8
Dunnington YO19 . . . . . .**26** F6
Hemingbrough YO8 . . . . .**49** F3
Haggs La Fenwick DN6 . . .**77** D2
Kingston upon Hull
HU10 . . . .**138** E3
Haig Ave DN16 . . . .**151** B5
Haig Rd DN8 . . . .**79** B2
Haig St YO8 . . . .**148** B6
Haigh La DN14 . . . .**77** A6
Haigh St DN35 . . . .**103** D3
Haile Rd DN36 . . . .**103** D1
Hailgate DN14 . . . .**65** A7
Hailgate Cl 8 DN14 . . . .**65** B7
Hainton Ave DN32 . . . . .**152** F2
Haith's La DN36 . . . . . .**114** B1
Haldane St DN21 . . . . . .**117** A1
Hale Hill La DN7 . . . . . .**92** E3
Hales Cl 3 DN16 . . . .**96** D1
Hales Cres 12 HU12 . . . .**72** C7
Hales La YO8 . . . .**63** E5
Haley's Terr YO31 . . . . .**130** D8
Half Acre Wood 1 DN17 .**95** D4
Halfacres La YO42 . . . . . .**40** A6
Halfax Rd DN20 . . . .**99** A8
Halifax Ave DN16 . . . . .**149** C6
Halifax Cl 8 YO42 . . . . . .**28** F4
Halifax St 7 YO30 . . . . .**127** A1
Halifax Way
Elvington Airfield YO41 . . .**27** A3
Pocklington Ind Est YO42 . .**28** E3
Halkon Cl DN17 . . . .**81** D3
Hall Cl 5 Airmyn DN14 . . .**64** E4
Cawood YO8 . . . .**36** D1
Nafferton YO25 . . . .**125** E7
7 Snaith DN14 . . . .**78** C8
Hall Ct DN7 . . . .**81** A3
Hall Farm Cl 4 YO19 . . . .**48** F8
Hall Gdns DN15 . . . .**83** B5
Hall La Elsham DN20 . . . .**98** F7
Stainforth DN7 . . . .**92** A6
Hall Mdw DN20 . . . .**84** C2
Hall Pk Swanland HU14 . . .**69** C6
Wistow YO8 . . . .**49** A5
York YO10 . . . .**131** B1
Hall Rd Goole DN14 . . . .**149** D1
Hornsea HU18 . . . .**134** D5
Kingston upon Hull HU6 . .**139** E5
Market Weighton YO43 . .**135** D4

Hall Rd continued
Sproatley HU11 . . . .**58** D5
Messingham DN17 . . . . .**107** D7
Hall Road Prim Sch
HU6 . . . .**139** F4
Hall Spinney The 5
DN14 . . . .**65** B7
Hall St HU2 . . . .**145** D7
Hall View DN17 . . . .**107** D7
Hall Way DN38 . . . .**99** F5
Hall Wlk 1 Brough HU15 . .**68** D6
Kingston upon Hull
HU16 . . . .**139** B6
Walkington HU17 . . . . . .**55** B8
Halladale Cl 1 HU4 . . . .**132** B7
Hallard Way 7 YO32 . . . .**14** B7
Hallbrook Ct 4 DN16 . . . .**96** D1
Hallcroft 1 DN39 . . . . . .**86** A1
Hallcroft La YO23 . . . . .**132** A3
Hallcroft Rd 1 DN9 . . . .**105** D2
Haller St HU9 . . . .**146** B8
Hallfield Rd YO31 . . . . .**130** E5
Hallgarth DN36 . . . .**115** B2
Hallgarth Ave DN16 . . . .**151** B6
Hallgarth Way HU17 . . . .**154** B2
Hallgate
Kingston upon Hull
HU16 . . . .**139** A6
10 Pocklington YO42 . . . .**29** A3
Hallgate Cty Jun & Inf Sch
HU16 . . . .**139** B5
Halliwell Cl HU9 . . . . . .**147** E8
Halls La 13 Keelby DN41 .**101** A4
North Kelsey LN7 . . . . . .**110** A4
Hall's Rd DN10 . . . .**116** A2
Hallytreeholme Rd
YO25 . . . .**33** C3
Haltemprice L Ctr
HU10 . . . .**143** E7
Haltemprice St HU3 . . . .**144** F5
Halton Cl 5 DN21 . . . . .**119** C8
Halton Pl DN35 . . . .**103** B2
Halton Way DN34 . . . . .**102** C2
Halyard Croft HU1 . . . . .**155** B1
Halycon Ave 1 HU13 . . .**143** E2
Hambleton Cl HU7 . . . . .**141** B6
Hambleton Ave YO10 . . .**131** C4
Hambleton Terr YO31 . . .**130** C7
Hambleton View 10
YO32 . . . .**13** D5
Hambleton Way YO32 . . .**127** C8
Hambling Dr HU17 . . . . .**136** E7
Hamburg Rd HU7 . . . . . .**141** A5
Hamden Rd YO42 . . . . . .**28** E3
Hamerton Cl 11 YO14 . . . .**3** A8
Hamerton Rd 10 YO14 . . . .**3** A8
Hamilton Cl 7 DN34 . . . .**102** B2
Hamilton Dr
Kingston upon Hull HU8 . .**141** F6
York YO24 . . . .**129** E2
Hamilton Dr E YO24 . . . .**129** F2
Hamilton Dr W YO24 . . . .**129** D2
Hamilton Hill Rd YO25 . . .**23** A4
Hamilton Rd
Bridlington YO15 . . . . . .**122** D2
Scunthorpe DN17 . . . . .**150** F4
Hamilton St DN32 . . . . .**153** B1
Hamilton Way DN32 . . . .**129** E2
Hamish Wlk 27 DN40 . . . .**87** B1
Hamlet The 8 DN14 . . . . .**61** F2
Hamling Way HU4 . . . . .**144** D2
Hamlyn Ave HU4 . . . . . .**144** C6
Hamlyn Dr HU4 . . . .**144** C6
Hammersike Rd YO8 . . . .**48** A4
Hammersmith Rd 1
HU8 . . . .**141** F5
Hammerton Cl 3 YO26 . .**129** B3
Hammerton Rd 25 DN17 . .**96** C2
Hammond Rd DN14 . . . .**154** C4
Hamont Rd DN32 . . . . .**153** B3
Hampden Cres 1 DN7 . .**104** A8
Hampden St YO1 . . . . . .**156** B1
Hampshire St HU4 . . . . .**144** E3
Hampstead Ct 6 HU3 . . .**140** F1
Hampstead Pk 6 DN33 . .**102** D1
Hampston Cl HU6 . . . . .**140** A7
Hampton Cl 18 DN35 . . .**103** C1
Hampton Rd
Hatfield DN7 . . . .**92** C4
Scunthorpe DN16 . . . . .**151** B4
Hancock La HU15 . . . . . .**52** F3
Handel House Sch
DN21 . . . .**117** B1
Handley Cl 8 HU3 . . . . .**145** D8
Hands on History Mus ★
HU1 . . . .**155** B2
Hanger La DN14 . . . .**63** B3
Hankins La HU42 . . . . . .**38** D1
Hanley Rd HU5 . . . .**139** D3
Hanover Ct
Beverley HU17 . . . .**154** C3
Kingston upon Hull HU1 . .**155** A2
Hanover Sq HU1 . . . . . .**155** B2
Hanover St E HU9 . . . . .**129** F5
Hanover St W 7 HU9 . . .**129** F5
Hansard Cres
6 Caistor LN7 . . . .**111** B4
5 Gilberdyke HU15 . . . . .**66** D8
Hansard Dr 6 HU15 . . . .**66** D8
Hansom Pl YO31 . . . . . .**130** C7
Hanson Cl YO43 . . . . . .**135** D3
Hanson Way DN32 . . . . .**153** B4
Ha'penny Bridge Way
HU9 . . . .**146** B5
Harborough 20 YO14 . . . . .**2** F8
Harbour Rd YO15 . . . . . .**122** F2
Harbour Way HU9 . . . . .**146** C6

Gre - Har **173**

Harcourt Cl
Bishopthorpe YO23 . . . .**133** A4
Wheldrake YO19 . . . . . .**37** F7
Harcourt Dr HU9 . . . . . .**146** C8
Harcourt St YO31 . . . . .**130** E5
Hardane HU6 . . . .**139** E8
Harden Cl YO43 . . . . . .**126** F2
Hardenshaw La YO8 . . . .**63** B4
Hardington Cl HU8 . . . . .**142** B7
Hardmoor La YO43 . . . . .**53** C5
Hardrada Way 3 YO41 . . .**15** D1
Hardwick St HU5 . . . . . .**145** B8
Hardy Rd DN17 . . . .**150** D2
Hardy St
Kingston upon Hull HU5 . .**140** C3
Selby YO8 . . . .**148** E4
Hardy's Rd DN35 . . . . .**103** C2
Hardys Rd 4 HU12 . . . . .**72** C7
Hare St DN32 . . . .**152** F2
Harewood HU17 . . . . . .**136** B6
Harewood Ave
Bridlington YO16 . . . . . .**122** D6
Kingston upon Hull HU4 . .**144** A3
4 Kirk Sandall DN3 . . . . .**92** A2
Harewood Cl
Rawcliffe YO30 . . . .**126** D2
5 Wigginton YO32 . . . . .**13** D5
Harewood Gr 17 DN35 . .**103** C1
Hargrave St DN31 . . . . .**152** B5
Hargreave Cl HU17 . . . .**136** E6
Hargreaves Way HU15 . . .**96** D7
Hariff La HU12 . . . .**73** B4
Harington Ave YO10 . . . .**130** F4
Harker St 12 WF11 . . . . .**61** A2
Harland La YO25 . . . . . .**124** E4
Harland Rd
Bridlington YO16 . . . . . .**122** F5
6 Brough HU15 . . . .**68** C6
Harland Way HU16 . . . . .**138** E8
Harlech Cl 1 HU7 . . . . . .**57** A6
Harlech Way DN32 . . . . .**152** F4
Harleigh Ave HU7 . . . . .**141** A5
Harlequin Dr 18 HU7 . . . .**57** A5
Harlestone Cl 5 HU8 . . .**142** B5
Harlestone Ct 8 DN34 . .**102** B3
Harley St HU2 . . . .**155** A4
Harlow Cl
2 Kingston upon Hull
HU8 . . . .**142** C6
1 York YO24 . . . .**129** F2
Harlow Rd DN7 . . . .**129** F2
Harlow St DN31 . . . . . .**152** B5
Harlthorpe Gn YO8 . . . . .**51** A8
Harneis Cres DN37 . . . .**101** F1
Harold Ct YO24 . . . .**129** D3
Harold St
Grimsby DN32 . . . .**153** A4
Selby YO8 . . . .**148** F4
Harolds Way 1 YO41 . . . .**15** D1
Harome Gr HU4 . . . .**144** C2
Harpenden Cl 12 DN7 . . .**92** D3
Harpendon Dr 6 DN7 . . . .**92** D3
Harper Cl YO42 . . . .**29** A3
Harper St
8 Great Driffield YO25 . . .**124** F4
2 Selby YO8 . . . .**148** C5
Harpham Cl HU9 . . . . . .**142** A1
Harpham Gr HU9 . . . . . .**142** A1
Harpham Rd DN36 . . . . .**115** B2
Harpings Rd HU5 . . . . . .**139** F1
Harpswell Hill DN21 . . . .**119** B1
Harpswell La DN21 . . . .**118** F1
Harrier Rd 2 DN18 . . . . .**69** F1
Harrington Pl DN16 . . . .**151** A1
Harrington Rd YO16 . . . .**122** B2
Harrington St DN35 . . . .**153** B5
Harris St HU3 . . . .**144** F5
Harrison Cl
Sproatley HU11 . . . .**58** D5
Winteringham DN15 . . . .**83** B8
Harrison St
Grimsby DN31 . . . .**152** C3
York YO31 . . . .**130** F6
Harrow Cl 12 DN21 . . . .**117** C1
Harrow Gdns 12 DN17 . . .**96** C2
Harrow Glade 5 YO30 . . .**127** A1
Harrow St HU3 . . . .**145** B4
Harrowdyke 10 DN18 . . . .**84** E8
Harry Moor La YO8 . . . . .**48** B2
Harrybeck La YO43 . . . . .**53** D4
Harry's Ave HU8 . . . . . .**141** B3
Harrys Dream 3 DN20 . . .**97** E3
Harsell La HU11 . . . .**34** F7
Harswell La
Everingham YO43 . . . . . .**40** D5
Holme-on-Spalding-Moor
YO42 . . . .**40** C2
Hart Dr 28 YO42 . . . .**29** A3
Hart Hill Cres YO41 . . . . .**16** A2
Hart La DN15 . . . .**83** B5
Hart St DN35 . . . .**153** C4
Hartendale Cl 22 YO15 . . . .**5** A2
Harthill Ave HU17 . . . . . .**43** D6
Harthill Dr HU3 . . . .**145** C5
Hartland Cl HU7 . . . . . .**140** F8
Hartley Bridge HU9 . . . .**146** C6
Hartley Cl YO15 . . . . . .**122** D1
Hartley St HU18 . . . . . .**134** D5
Hartoft Rd HU5 . . . .**139** E2
Hartoft St YO10 . . . . . .**130** D2
Harts Cl HU18 . . . .**134** B4
Hartshead Ave DN15 . . .**150** C7
Harvest Ave HU18 . . . . . .**84** E8
Harvest Cl 13 DN3 . . . . .**92** A2
Harvest Cres 4 DN37 . . .**113** D6

Harvest Rise **1** DN19 ...85 C8
Harvester Cl DN9 ......105 F6
Harwood Dr **1** HU4 ..144 B6
Haslemere Ave YO15 ..122 E3
Hassacarr La YO19 ......26 F6
Hastings Ave **1** HU5 ..140 E2
Hastings Cl **4** YO30 ..127 A1
Hastings Gr HU4 ......144 E7
HatcIiffe CI **20** DN33 ..102 D2
Hatfield & Dunsville Cty Prim Sch DN7 ....92 D3
Hatfield & Stainforth Sta DN7 ....92 C5
Hatfield CI **3** YO30 ..126 E3
Hatfield Comp Sch DN7 ....92 D4
Hatfield Cty Prim Sch DN7 ....92 D4
Hatfield High Sch DN7 .92 D4
Hatfield La
  Barnby Dun DN3 ......92 A4
  Edenthorpe DN3 ......92 A1
Hatfield Pl DN14 ......149 C1
Hatfield Rd Hatfield DN7 .93 A6
  Thorne/Moorends DN8 .93 A7
Hatfield Water Pk*
  DN7 ....92 E5
Hatfield Woodhouse Cty Prim Sch DN7 ....93 A3
Hathersage Rd HU7 ....141 C4
Hatkill La YO41 ....16 B1
Hatters CI YO23 ......132 B3
Hatton Gr **32** DN33 ..102 D2
Haugh La YO8 ....61 F8
Haughton Rd YO30 ....130 C7
Hauling La YO23 ....36 C8
Hauxwell Gr HU8 ......142 A5
Havelock Cres YO16 ..122 C3
Havelock Pl YO16 ....122 D3
Havelock Sch DN32 ..153 C2
Havelock St
  Bridlington YO16 ....122 D3
  Kingston upon Hull HU3 .145 A4
Haven Ave
  2 Brough HU15 ......68 B5
  Grimsby DN31 ....152 C4
Haven Basin Rd HU12 ..72 C4
Haven CI DN21 ....117 F5
Haven Garth
  Barton-upon-Humber DN18 ....69 E1
  North Killingholme DN40 .87 A6
  Patrington HU12 ......89 C8
Haven Staithes **24** HU12 .72 C7
Haven Terr DN31 ......152 C4
Haven The
  Kingston upon Hull HU9 .146 B6
  2 Walkington HU17 ..55 D8
Havercroft Rd **15** YO14 ..3 A8
Haverstoe Pl **7** DN35 ..103 B2
Hawdon Ave YO8 ......148 D5
Hawerby Rd DN37 ....101 F1
Hawke Garth **5** YO14 ..3 A8
Hawkesbury St HU8 ..141 E3
Hawkins Gr DN32 ....153 B2
Hawkins Way **3** DN40 ..86 E3
Hawkshead CI **3** YO24 .132 B8
Hawling Rd YO43 ....135 C2
Haworth CI DN15 ....150 E8
Haworth St HU6 ......140 C4
Hawse Rd YO8 ....63 E8
Hawthorn Ave
  2 Brigg DN20 ....98 C2
  Gainsborough DN21 ..117 B1
  1 Immingham DN40 ..87 D2
  Kingston upon Hull HU3 .144 F5
Hawthorn CI
  Healing DN41 ....101 F4
  5 Newport HU15 ......52 F1
  Wootton DN39 ....85 E2
Hawthorn Ct **1** HU3 ..144 F5
Hawthorn Dr
  Wilberfoss YO41 ......27 C5
  Wistow YO8 ....49 A5
Hawthorn Garth DN14 ..61 F4
Hawthorn Gate **17** DN18 .84 F8
Hawthorn Gr
  Gainsborough DN21 ..117 B1
  York YO31 ....130 E5
Hawthorn Rise **6** DN19 .85 C8
Hawthorn Spinney
  YO32 ....127 E3
Hawthorn St **1** YO31 .130 E5
Hawthorn Terr DN14 ..149 F5
Hawthorn Terr Cent **2**
  YO32 ....127 D3
Hawthorn Terr N
  YO32 ....127 D4
Hawthorn Terr S
  YO32 ....127 D3
Hawthorn Way **9** HU15 ..66 D7
Hawthorne Ave
  Cleethorpes DN35 ....153 D4
  29 Grimsby DN33 ....113 E8
  Hatfield DN7 ....92 C2
  12 Haxby YO32 ......13 E5
  Kingston upon Hull HU10 ....138 D1
  6 New Waltham DN36 .113 F7
  Scunthorpe DN17 ....150 F4
  4 Thorne/Moorends DN8 .79 A1

Hawthorne CI **12** DN15 ..83 A5
Hawthorne Cres DN17 ..150 F4
Hawthorne Dr YO43 ....40 A1
Hawthorne Garth
  HU17 ....136 F7
Hawthorne Gdns DN19 ..86 A8
Hawthorne Gr **5** DN8 ..79 A1
Hawthorne Rd DN8 ....79 A1
Hawthorne Rise HU13 .143 B3
Hawthorns **3** Riccall YO19 .48 F8
  2 Riccall YO19 ......48 F8
Hawthorns The **12** HU8 .141 E7
Hawton CI **1** DN21 ..117 C1
Haxby Moor Rd
  Haxby YO32 ....13 F7
  Towthorpe YO32 ......14 A7
Haxby Rd Clifton YO31 .127 D1
  New Earswick YO32 ..127 D6
  York YO31 ....156 B4
Haxby Rd Prim Sch
  YO31 ....130 D7
Haxey C of E Prim Sch
  DN9 ....105 D3
Haxey Gate Rd DN10 ..116 C7
Haxey Grange **8** DN9 .105 D2
Haxey La DN9 ....105 D2
Haxey Rd DN10 ....116 C6
Hayburn Ave HU5 ....139 F2
Haycroft Ave DN31 ..152 C3
Haycroft St DN31 ....152 C3
Haydock Garth **6** HU7 ..57 A5
Haydon CI HU10 ......143 D8
Hayfield CI
  Barnby Dun DN3 ......92 A4
  9 Haxey DN9 ....105 D2
Hayforth CI YO30 ....127 A2
Hayling Mere **29** DN35 .103 C1
Haymarket CI HU8 ....141 F4
Haymer Dr HU12 ......72 D7
Haynes CI **2** DN8 ....93 B7
Haynes Gdns **15** DN8 ..93 B8
Haynes Gn **2** DN8 ....93 B8
Haynes Gr **1** DN8 ....93 B7
Haynes Rd DN8 ....93 B8
Hays CI **3** DN36 ....114 A5
Hayton CI DN15 ......83 A5
Hayton Gr HU4 ......144 D4
Hayton's La DN15 ....83 D2
Hayward CI **3** HU17 ..55 D8
Hazel Ave HU19 ......75 A5
Hazel CI
  Great Driffield YO25 .124 E3
  Messingham DN17 ....107 C7
  York YO32 ....127 D2
Hazel Croft **5** DN40 ..87 B1
Hazel Garth YO31 ....131 B7
Hazel Gr Goole DN14 .149 D1
  2 Kingston upon Hull HU3 ....145 D5
Hazel Old La DN14 ....62 C2
Hazel Rd DN7 ....92 C5
Hazelbarrow Dr HU10 .143 F7
Hazelmere La YO32 ..127 E3
Hazelnut Gr YO30 ....127 B2
Hazelwood Ave YO10 .131 D4
Hazing La DN14 ....77 B6
Headingley Rd DN6 ....76 F2
Headland CI **30** YO32 ..13 E5
Headlands CI YO16 ..122 F6
Headlands Dr
  Aldbrough HU11 ......47 C1
  Bridlington YO16 ....122 F6
  Kingston upon Hull HU13 ....143 C2
Headlands Lower Sch
  YO16 ....122 E4
Headlands Prim Sch
  YO32 ....127 D8
Headlands Rd HU11 ..47 C1
Headlands Sch YO16 ..122 F5
Headley CI **2** YO30 ..127 B1
Heads La HU13 ....143 C1
Healey Gr YO31 ......130 F8
Healey Rd DN16 ......151 C4
Healing Comp Sch
  DN41 ....101 F5
Healing Prim Sch
  DN41 ....101 F5
Healing Rd DN41 ....101 D6
Healing Sta DN41 ....101 F6
Heapham Rd DN21 ....117 C1
Heath CI **2** YO24 ....129 F2
Heath Croft YO10 ....133 F7
Heath Moor Dr YO10 .133 F8
Heath Ride YO32 ......14 B8
Heathcote St HU6 ....140 D4
Heather Bank
  13 Stamford Bridge YO41 .15 D2
  York YO10 ....131 C4
Heather CI
  7 Kingston upon Hull HU5 ....139 D1
  Selby YO8 ....148 C3
  York YO32 ....128 A4
Heather Croft **4** YO41 .127 E2
Heather Gr DN16 ......96 F2
Heatherdale Cl **8** DN33 .113 E8
Heathfield Cl **8** DN3 ..92 A3
Heathfield Ct DN34 ..152 B1
Heathfield Rd **1** YO10 .131 A3
Hebden Ave HU8 ......142 C5
Hebden Rd DN15 ......150 C8
Hebden Rise **2** YO26 .129 D4
Hebrides Cl HU9 ......142 A3
Heck & Pollington Lake
  DN14 ....77 E7

Heck La DN14 ....77 C7
Heckdyke La DN10 ....116 F7
Hedgerow CI **4** DN19 ..85 C8
Hedgerow La **28** DN20 ..98 C2
Hedley CI **7** HU15 ....53 F1
Hedon Museum*
  HU12 ....72 C7
Hedon Rd HU9 ....146 B6
Heigholm La HU25 ....34 A1
Heigholme La HU17 ..44 F8
Height Lands La YO23 ..24 D6
Heimdal Rd DN33 ....102 C1
Helen Cres **9** DN40 ..87 B1
Helene Gr DN32 ......153 B3
Heliport HU15 ....68 C4
Hellyers Ct HU4 ......144 D2
Helm Dr HU9 ....146 C6
Helms Ave **6** HU12 ..58 C1
Helmsdale HU24 ......132 C6
Helmsley Gr
  10 Haxby YO32 ......13 D5
  Kingston upon Hull HU5 .144 C7
Helsinki Rd HU7 ......140 F5
Helvellyn Cl **10** HU7 ..57 A6
Hemble Way HU7 ......56 F5
Hemingbrough CP Sch
  YO8 ....49 F1
Hemlock Ave YO31 ..127 E1
Hemmingway Wlk
  HU13 ....143 E3
Hempbridge CI **10** YO8 .148 A5
Hempbridge Rd YO8 .148 A5
Hempdyke Rd DN15 ..150 E8
Hempland Ave YO31 .130 F6
Hempland Dr YO31 ..131 A7
Hempland Inf Sch
  YO31 ....131 A6
Hempland Jun Sch
  YO31 ....131 B6
Hempland La YO31 ..131 A7
Hemsell Ave HU9 ....147 D8
Hemswell Cty Prim Sch
  DN21 ....119 D1
Hemswell Ave HU9 ..119 A1
Hemswell Dr **6** DN37 .102 C4
Hemswell La DN21 ..119 A1
Henderson Ave DN15 .150 F8
Henderson Avenue Prim Sch
  DN15 ....150 F8
Henderson Cres DN15 .150 F8
Henderson St DN31 ..153 A6
Henderson Way DN15 .83 A5
Hendon Garth YO30 ..127 A1
Heneage Rd DN32 ....152 F2
Hengate HU17 ....154 A3
Henley Ct **6** DN21 ..117 B1
Henley Dr HU9 ....141 E1
Henlow Cl **4** DN21 ..119 C8
Henry Ct **8** DN8 ......79 B1
Henry St Goole DN14 .149 B4
  Grimsby DN31 ......152 C4
  Scunthorpe DN15 ....150 F7
Hensall CP Sch DN14 ..62 C1
Hensall Sta DN14 ......62 C1
Henwick Hall La YO8 .148 C1
Hepworth's La DN14 ..63 C2
Herbert St **5** YO10 ..130 E3
Herberts Way YO31 ..130 F7
Herdsman Dr YO23 ..132 C3
Herdsman Rd **3** YO24 .132 B8
Herdwick Cl **1** YO30 .127 B1
Hereford Ave DN34 ..152 C1
Hereford Cl **4** HU17 .136 E1
Hereford Rd YO42 ....28 C3
Hereford St DN34 ....152 B1
Hereford St HU4 ......144 E3
Hereward Pl DN16 ..151 E3
Herman Wlk YO24 ..132 C8
Hermes CI HU9 ......142 C4
Hermitage Rd YO16 ..122 C4
Hermitage The **5** DN8 .79 B2
Heron Ave DN34 ......132 C8
Heron CI Grimsby DN32 .103 A2
  16 Hedon HU12 ......72 C7
  10 Scunthorpe DN15 ..96 B7
Heron Holt **1** DN20 ..97 D4
Heron Rise YO32 ......127 F5
Heron St HU3 ....145 B5
Heron Way **6** DN36 ..114 A6
Herrick Rd DN17 ....150 D3
Hersey Rd **24** LN7 ..111 B4
Hertfordshire CI **2**
  HU5 ....139 D1
Hesketh Bank YO10 ..131 D3
Hesketh Dr DN3 ......92 A2
Heslerton Ave HU16 .139 A4
Heslin CI **8** YO32 ....127 C8
Heslington Croft YO10 .133 F7
Heslington CI **2** YO10 .131 B1
Heslington La
  Heslington YO10 ....131 A1
  York YO10 ....133 E8
Heslington Prim Sch
  YO10 ....131 C1
Heslington Rd YO10 ..130 E3
Hessay Pl **2** YO26 ..129 A3
Hessle High Sch
  HU13 ....143 C2
Hessle Lower Sch
  HU13 ....143 E3
Hessle Mount Sch
  HU13 ....143 C3
Hessle Penshurst Prim Sch
  HU13 ....143 F3
Hessle Rd HU1 ......155 A1
Hessle View DN18 ....84 E8
Hessleskew La YO43 ..42 A4
Hetherton St YO30 ..156 A3
Hewde La DN15 ....83 A8

Hewitt's Ave DN36 ....114 A8
Hewitt's Cir DN36 ....103 B1
Hewitts Manor **3** DN35 .103 B1
Hewley Ave YO10 ....131 A4
Heworth YO31 ....131 A6
Heworth ARLFC YO31 .131 A8
Heworth C of E Prim Sch
  YO31 ....130 F6
Heworth Gn YO31 ....156 C4
Heworth Hall Dr YO31 .130 F6
Heworth Pl YO31 ....130 F6
Heworth Rd YO31 ....130 F6
Hewson Rd DN36 ....114 D8
Hewson St DN17 ....107 D7
Hey St DN35 ....153 F1
Heythrop Rd DN35 ..103 C2
Hibaldstow Cl **21** DN34 .102 C2
Hibaldstow Prim Sch
  DN20 ....109 A5
Hickman Cres DN21 ..117 B2
Hickman Gr DN21 ....117 E5
Hiderthorpe Cty Jun Sch
  YO15 ....122 C1
High Bridge Rd DN8 ..93 C7
High Brighton St **18**
  HU19 ....75 A6
High Burgage
  2 Winteringham DN15 .68 B1
  Winterringham DN15 ..83 B8
High Catton Rd YO41 ..27 D8
High Croft **7** YO14 ..2 F8
High Eggborough La
  DN14 ....62 A1
High Farm Ct HU11 ..142 F7
High Field YO10 ......131 D4
High Field Rd DN20 ..98 D3
High Garth DN17 ......96 C1
High Hazel Rd DN8 ....79 B2
High La Carnaby YO25 ..10 C3
  Sutton upon Derwent YO41 ....27 D3
High Levels Bank
  Belton DN8 ....94 A4
  Hatfield DN8 ....93 A6
High Leys Rd DN17 ....96 C2
High Mdw Gowdall DN14 .63 A1
  Selby YO8 ....148 B6
High Moor La YO30 ..12 C8
High Newbiggin St
  YO31 ....156 B3
High Oaks YO31 ......131 B7
High Ousegate YO1 ..156 B2
High Peter La YO25 ..20 D7
High Petergate YO1 ..156 B3
High Rd
  Elloughton-cum-Brough HU15 ....68 D6
  North Cave HU15 ....53 E3
High Ridge Comp Sch
  DN15 ....150 E7
High Risby Medieval
  Village* DN15 ....83 A1
High Row YO41 ....16 D4
High Sewerby Rd
  YO15 ....123 C7
High Side YO25 ....34 A8
High St Airmyn DN14 ..64 E3
  Aldbrough HU11 ......47 C1
  Barmby on the Marsh DN14 ....64 A7
  Barrow upon Humber DN19 ....85 D8
  Barton-upon-Humber DN18 ....69 E1
  Beckingham DN10 ..116 D1
  Belton DN9 ....94 E1
  Blyton DN21 ....117 F5
  Boynton YO16 ....10 D7
  Bridlington YO16 ..122 C4
  Broughton DN20 ....97 D3
  Buckton/Bempton YO15 ..4 C3
  Burringham DN17 ....95 D4
  Burton upon Stather DN15 ....82 B4
  Caistor LN7 ....111 B4
  Carlton DN14 ....63 C2
  Cawood YO8 ....48 B8
  Cleethorpes DN35 ..153 E2
  Corringham DN21 ..118 A1
  Cottam YO25 ....7 B7
  4 Crowle DN17 ......94 D7
  Easington HU12 ......90 F6
  East Butterwick DN17 .106 D8
  East Ferry DN21 ....106 B2
  Eastoft DN17 ....81 A3
  Eastrington DN14 ....65 F8
  Epworth DN9 ....105 E6
  7 Flamborough YO15 ..5 A2
  Flixborough DN15 ....82 B1
  Garthorpe & Fockerby DN17 ....81 E5
  Goole DN14 ....65 C4
  Great Limber DN37 ..100 D3
  Gringley on the Hill DN10 ....116 A1
  Hatfield DN7 ....92 C2
  Haxey DN9 ....105 D2
  Holme-on-Spalding-Moor YO43 ....40 A1
  Humberside Airport DN39 ....100 A6
  Kilham YO25 ....9 A8
  Kingston upon Hull HU1 .155 C1
  Kirby Grindalythe YO17 ..6 D8
  Kirton in Lindsey DN21 .108 B1
  Laceby DN37 ....101 F1
  Langtoft YO25 ....8 C8

High St continued
  Luddington & Haldenby DN17 ....81 C4
  Market Weighton YO43 .135 D4
  Messingham DN17 ..107 D2
  Misterton DN10 ......116 C5
  Nafferton YO25 ......125 E7
  Nettleton LN7 ......111 C2
  North Ferriby HU14 ..69 A5
  North Kelsey LN7 ....110 A4
  North Thoresby DN36 .114 A1
  Norton DN6 ....76 E2
  Owston Ferry DN9 ..106 B3
  Rawcliffe DN14 ......64 A1
  Redbourne DN21 ....108 F2
  Roxby cum Risby DN15 .82 E1
  Sancton YO43 ....41 D2
  Scotter DN21 ....107 C3
  Scotton DN21 ....107 C1
  Scunthorpe DN15 ..151 A7
  Snaith DN14 ....63 B1
  South Ferriby DN18 ..84 A7
  Swinefleet DN14 ......65 D1
  Ulceby DN39 ....86 A1
  Walkeringham DN10 .116 C3
  Waltham DN37 ......113 D6
  West/East Butterwick DN17 ....95 D1
  Wharram YO17 ....6 A6
  Winterton DN15 ......83 A5
  Witherwick HU11 ....46 D3
  Wootton DN39 ....85 E2
  Wroot DN9 ....104 D6
High St E DN15 ......151 C7
High St W DN21 ......107 C4
High Stile HU17 ......45 B8
High Thorpe Cres
  DN35 ....103 B2
High Trees Mount
  HU7 ....141 E6
Higham CI HU8 ......141 E7
Higham Way HU15 ..68 D5
Highcliff Gdns DN15 .150 E7
Highcliffe Ct YO30 ..130 A6
Highcourt HU6 ......139 E7
Highcroft HU17 ......43 C5
Highdales HU10 ......143 C8
Highfield
  Kingston upon Hull HU7 .141 D6
  Pollington DN14 ......77 F7
  Withernsea HU19 ....75 A6
Highfield Ave
  Great Driffield YO25 .124 E6
  22 Immingham DN40 ..87 B1
  Scunthorpe DN15 ..150 E7
Highfield CI
  Barnby Dun DN3 ......92 A4
  Fangfoss YO41 ....28 C8
  Gainsborough DN21 ..117 C1
  Kingston upon Hull HU7 .141 D6
  5 North Thoresby DN36 .114 B1
  Wold Newton YO25 ..2 A4
Highfield Cres
  Barlby with Osgodby YO8 .49 B5
  15 Barton-upon-Humber DN18 ....84 F8
  Kingston upon Hull HU11 ....142 F7
  9 Thorne/Moorends DN8 .79 A1
  2 Thorne/Moorends DN8 .93 A8
  2 Westwoodside DN9 .105 B2
Highfield Ct YO8 ....148 B1
Highfield Dr **1** DN21 .108 B1
Highfield Gr **4** DN20 ..98 C3
Highfield La
  Fangfoss YO41 ....16 B1
  Womersley DN6 ......76 B7
Highfield Rd
  Beverley HU17 ......136 F1
  North Thoresby DN36 .114 B1
Highfield Rise **1** HU12 .58 D1
Highfield View **3** YO8 ..49 B4
Highfield Way HU17 ..69 A4
Highfields
  10 Barrow upon Humber DN19 ....85 C8
  Crowle DN17 ....94 D8
  South Cave HU15 ....54 A2
Highgate Balne DN14 ..77 D6
  Beverley HU17 ......154 B2
  Cherry Burton HU17 ..42 E4
  Cleethorpes DN35 ..153 E1
Highgate CI HU8 ....142 A5
Highgrove DN17 ......107 D7
Highgrove CI **7** YO30 .126 E3
Highland Tarn **31** DN40 .87 B1
Highlands Ave **5** YO42 .14 B7
Highlands Prim Sch
  HU7 ....57 A6
Highmoor CI YO24 ..132 D8
Highmoor Rd YO24 ..132 D8
Highthorn Rd YO31 ..127 E2
Highwood YO25 ......124 E6
Hilary Gr HU4 ......144 B4
Hilary Rd **11** DN33 ..113 E8
Hilbeck Gr YO31 ....131 B6
Hilbra Ave YO32 ....127 D6
Hilda St Goole DN14 ..149 C5
  Grimsby DN32 ......153 A4
  6 Selby YO8 ....148 C5
  3 York YO10 ......130 E3
Hilderthorpe Cty Inf Sch
  YO15 ....122 C1
Hildyard CI
  19 Hedon HU12 ......72 D7
  1 Kingston upon Hull HU10 ....143 F6

Hildyard St DN32 ...153 A4
Hiles Ave DN15 ...83 A5
Hill Brow HU10 ...143 B6
Hill Crest YO19 ...14 F1
Hill Crest Gdns YO24 ...129 F1
Hill Field YO8 ...148 B8
Hill Rd DN21 ...118 B1
Hill Rise Brough HU15 ...68 C6
Market Weighton YO43 ...135 E4
Hill Rise Cl YO43 ...135 E4
Hill Rise Dr YO43 ...135 E4
Hill St Bridlington YO16 ...122 D3
Kingston upon Hull HU8 ...141 A2
York YO24 ...129 E3
Hill The DN20 ...98 D8
Hill Top La DN21 ...117 E5
Hill Top Pl DN34 ...102 B2
Hill Top Rd 4 YO8 ...48 D6
Hill View YO31 ...131 C7
Hillam Comm La LS25 ...61 B7
Hillam Hall La 4 LS25 ...61 A7
Hillam Hall View 3 LS25 ...61 A7
Hillam La LS25 ...61 A7
Hillam Rd YO8 ...61 F8
Hillary Garth 9 YO26 ...129 E4
Hillary Rd DN16 ...151 B1
Hillary Way DN37 ...102 C4
Hillcrest Beverley HU17 ...136 C6
8 Monk Fryston LS25 ...61 A8
Hillcrest Ave
Kingston upon Hull
HU13 ...143 C2
Poppleton YO26 ...126 A2
Hillcrest Dr
Beverley HU17 ...136 D6
Burton upon Stather
DN15 ...82 A4
Hillerby La HU18 ...134 B4
Hillfield Dr HU11 ...45 D2
Hillfoot Dr 22 DN17 ...96 C2
Hillgarth Ct 4 YO41 ...27 B2
Hilliam H Cl 5 LS25 ...61 A7
Hillman Rd HU13 ...143 F3
Hills Dr 6 DN36 ...114 D4
Hillsborough Terr 5
YO30 ...130 C7
Hillside Cl 9 LS25 ...61 A8
Hillside Cres DN38 ...99 B5
Hillside Dr DN18 ...84 E8
Hillside Gdns YO25 ...8 D5
Hillside Rd DN20 ...97 E4
Hillside Way YO17 ...7 B8
Hillsmere Gr 5 DN15 ...83 A5
Hillstead Cl 5 DN36 ...114 D4
Hillsyde Ave DN10 ...116 C5
Hilltop Ave DN15 ...150 E8
Hilston Gr HU9 ...142 B1
Hilton Ave DN15 ...150 B7
Hilton Cl DN9 ...94 E2
Hilton Ct DN35 ...103 D1
Hinch Garth HU12 ...60 B1
Hinderwell St HU5 ...140 C1
Hinkler St DN35 ...153 E1
Hinkley Dr 2 DN40 ...87 B2
Hinsley La DN14 ...63 C2
Hinton Ave 1 YO24 ...132 C8
Hirncroft Cl 10 HU8 ...141 E7
Hirst Courtney & Temple
Hirst CP Sch YO8 ...62 E3
Hirst Rd YO8 ...63 A3
Hive La DN14 ...52 B1
Hob Moor Dr YO24 ...129 E2
Hob Moor Inf Sch
YO24 ...129 D2
Hob Moor Jun Sch
YO24 ...129 E2
Hobart St HU3 ...145 D5
Hobb La 14 DN21 ...107 C3
Hobgate YO24 ...129 D3
Hobman La YO25 ...32 E7
Hobmoor Terr YO24 ...129 F1
Hobson Cl YO23 ...132 B1
Hobson Rd 5 HU15 ...68 C6
Hobson Way DN41 ...101 F8
Hodder Gr HU8 ...142 C6
Hoddesdon Cres 13 DN7 ...92 D3
Hoddy Cows La YO15 ...4 C3
Hodge Ct 3 HU9 ...146 C7
Hodge La WF8 ...76 B3
Hodgson Ave HU17 ...154 B4
Hodgson La Roos HU12 ...60 A1
Upper Poppleton YO26 ...24 F8
Hodgson St HU8 ...155 C3
Hodsow Fields YO42 ...28 E4
Hodsow La YO42 ...28 F3
Hogg La HU10 ...143 B8
Hoggard La DN14 ...81 E8
Hogsea La HU12 ...60 B4
Holbeck Pl 17 DN40 ...87 B1
Holborn St HU8 ...146 B7
Holbrook Cl 2 HU7 ...141 B4
Holburns Croft 3 YO10 ...131 B1
Holcombe Cl HU8 ...142 B7
Holcroft Garth 10 HU12 ...72 D7
Holden Gdns YO8 ...48 D2
Holderness Cres
HU17 ...154 B3
Holderness Rd HU9 ...146 C8
Holgate Bridge Gdn 7
YO24 ...130 A3
Holgate Cl 2 HU17 ...137 B3
Holgate Lodge Dr
YO26 ...129 E4
Holgate Pl 12 HU14 ...69 B7
Holgate Rd
Scunthorpe DN16 ...151 D4
York YO24 ...156 A1
Holland Ave DN15 ...150 E8
Holland St HU9 ...146 C8
Holles St DN32 ...152 E3
Hollicarrs Cl YO19 ...37 A2
Hollies The
Barlby with Osgodby YO8 ...49 C4
Beverley HU17 ...137 A7
Hornsea HU18 ...134 D2
Kingston upon Hull
HU10 ...138 E2
Snaith & Cowick DN14 ...78 C8
Hollin Bridge La DN7 ...93 A3
Hollingsworth Ave 12
DN40 ...87 B1
Hollingsworth Cl 14
DN35 ...103 B1
Hollingsworth La 22
DN9 ...105 E6
Hollis Cres YO32 ...14 B6
Hollowgate Hill DN21 ...119 A3
Hollows The 9 YO16 ...122 C5
Holly Bank Gr 3 YO24 ...129 F2
Holly Bank Rd YO24 ...129 F2
Holly Cl
Acaster Malbis YO23 ...36 C8
Full Sutton YO41 ...16 A2
13 Scunthorpe DN16 ...96 E2
Stallingborough DN41 ...101 D6
Holly Dr HU16 ...138 E5
Holly Gr Selby YO8 ...148 B3
8 Thorpe Willoughby YO8 ...48 B2
Holly Hill HU15 ...68 E6
Holly Rd DN8 ...79 B1
Holly Tree Croft 2 YO19 ...26 F7
Holly Tree Garth YO32 ...14 E3
Holly Tree La
Dunnington YO19 ...26 F7
Haxby YO32 ...127 D8
Hollycroft YO25 ...23 A6
Hollygarth La DN14 ...61 D4
Hollym Rd
Patrington HU19 ...74 F3
Withernsea HU19 ...75 A5
Hollyrood Rd YO30 ...126 E3
Hollytree Ave 2 HU4 ...144 B7
Hollywood YO8 ...148 B7
Holm Garth Dr HU8 ...142 B4
Holm Rd DN9 ...105 B2
Holme Ave DN36 ...114 A7
Holme Church La
HU17 ...154 C2
Holme Cl 18 Brigg DN20 ...98 C2
Holme-on-Spalding-Moor
YO43 ...40 A1
Paull HU12 ...72 A5
Holme Cres HU16 ...138 E6
Holme Dene DN9 ...105 C2
Holme Dr DN15 ...82 B5
Holme Farm Cl DN37 ...102 B5
Holme Gdns 11 DN7 ...92 C6
Holme Hall Ave DN16 ...96 D2
Holme Hill La YO10 ...26 C4
Holme Ind Est YO43 ...52 C6
Holme La Holme DN16 ...96 E2
Messingham DN17 ...107 D8
Scunthorpe DN16 ...96 D2
Selby YO8 ...148 D6
Holme Rd YO43 ...135 B3
Holme St DN32 ...152 E3
Holme Valley Prim Sch
DN16 ...96 E2
Holme Wood Ct 2 DN3 ...92 A1
Holmefield Cl 3 YO8 ...148 A1
Holmefield Ct 2 YO8 ...148 A1
Holmefield La YO10 ...131 A1
Holme-on-Spalding-Moor
Prim Sch YO43 ...40 A1
Holmes Dr 2 YO19 ...37 A1
Holmes House★ YO8 ...50 B3
Holmes La Bilton HU11 ...58 A4
Roxby cum Risby DN15 ...83 D5
Holmes Pk DN14 ...51 F1
Holmfirth Rd DN15 ...150 C8
Holmpton Gr HU9 ...142 B1
Holmpton Rd
Patrington HU12 ...74 E1
Withernsea HU19 ...75 A5
Holms La YO43 ...53 E7
Holray Pk DN14 ...63 C2
Holroyd Ave YO31 ...131 A5
Holstein Dr 2 DN16 ...96 D1
Holtby Gdns HU18 ...134 C6
Holtby La Holtby YO19 ...14 D1
Stockton-on-the-Forest
YO32 ...128 F2
Holtby's Yd YO16 ...122 C4
Holton Ct 8 DN36 ...114 A5
Holton le Clay Jun Sch
DN36 ...114 B5
Holton Mount 7 DN36 ...114 A5
Holton Rd
Holton le Moor LN7 ...110 F1
South Kelsey LN7 ...110 D1
Tetney DN36 ...114 C5
Holwell Rd HU7 ...141 A5
Holwick Mews HU5 ...139 D4
Holy Family CP Sch
DN7 ...92 D7
Holy Family RC High Sch
DN14 ...63 C3
Holy Name RC Prim Sch
HU6 ...139 E7
Holy Well★ DN15 ...83 C4
Holy Well La LN11 ...121 D4
Holydyke DN18 ...84 E8
Holyoake Rd DN32 ...153 C2
Holyrood Dr DN15 ...96 B7
Holyrood Ave YO15 ...122 F3
Home Beat Dr DN20 ...97 C3
Home Cl HU4 ...144 C5
Home Gn HU16 ...139 A5
Home Paddock 5 DN37 ...113 E6
Home St DN15 ...151 B8
Homefield Ave 8 DN33 ...102 E2
Homefield Cl YO23 ...132 A2
Homestead Cl
Eggborough DN14 ...62 A2
2 York YO32 ...127 F1
Homestead Garth 3
DN7 ...92 D4
Homestead Rd HU12 ...72 F5
Homethorpe HU6 ...140 A8
Honey Pot 5 YO8 ...50 D7
Honeypots La HU12 ...59 A2
Honeysuckle Cl YO8 ...148 C2
Honeysuckle Ct DN35 ...103 C1
Honiton Rd HU7 ...141 A8
Hood Gr DN14 ...149 B6
Hood Rd DN17 ...150 D2
Hood St HU8 ...155 C4
Hook La DN14 ...149 C8
Hook Pasture La
DN14 ...149 C1
Hook Rd DN14 ...149 E4
Hooks La Holmpton HU19 ...75 B2
Thorngumbald HU12 ...72 E4
Hoop End DN36 ...114 D4
Hop Hills La DN7 ...92 D5
Hope St
Cleethorpes DN35 ...103 D3
Grimsby DN32 ...152 F4
York YO10 ...156 C1
Hopewell Rd HU9 ...142 C3
Hopfield DN20 ...109 A5
Hopgarth DN9 ...105 D2
Hopgrove La N YO32 ...128 C3
Hopgrove La S YO32 ...128 E3
Hopkins Ave DN17 ...151 A3
Hopkins St HU9 ...142 A3
Hopwood Cl HU3 ...145 D8
Hopwood La HU15 ...52 F1
Horbury Cl DN15 ...150 D8
Hords La YO25 ...21 D4
Horkstow Rd DN18 ...84 A6
Hornbeam Ave DN16 ...151 A1
Hornbeam Dr HU16 ...139 C5
Hornbeam Wlk HU16 ...139 B5
Hornby Gr HU9 ...142 C3
Horner St YO30 ...130 B7
Hornsby Cres DN15 ...96 C7
Hornsea & District War Meml
Cottage Hospl HU18 ...134 C5
Hornsea Burton Rd
HU18 ...134 D3
Hornsea Leisure Ctr
HU18 ...134 D4
Hornsea Mus★ HU18 ...134 C4
Hornsea Par 5 HU9 ...146 C8
Hornsea Prim Sch
HU18 ...134 C4
Hornsea Rd
Aldbrough HU11 ...47 B2
Atwick HU18 ...134 A8
Hatfield HU11 ...46 D6
Leven HU17 ...45 B8
Seaton HU11 ...35 B1
Skipsea YO25 ...23 B1
Hornsea Sch HU18 ...134 B4
Hornsey Garth 25 YO32 ...13 E5
Hornsey Hill Rd DN21 ...106 D1
Horse Carr La YO25 ...10 B1
Horse Fair Gn 21 DN8 ...93 A8
Horse Mkt 17 LN7 ...111 B4
Horsefair La YO25 ...124 B5
Horsegate Field Rd
DN19 ...86 A8
Horseman Ave YO23 ...132 A3
Horseman Cl 2 YO23 ...132 A3
Horseman Dr YO23 ...132 A3
Horseman La YO23 ...132 A3
Horseshoe Cres YO43 ...40 A1
Horseshoe Dr YO15 ...123 C6
Horseshoe The
Great Driffield YO25 ...124 E3
York YO24 ...132 E7
Horsfield Way YO19 ...26 F7
Horsforth Ave YO15 ...122 D1
Horsman Ave YO10 ...156 C1
Horstead Ave DN20 ...98 C3
Hospital Fields Rd
YO10 ...130 D1
Hospital Hill 4 YO25 ...10 A2
Hospital La YO8 ...48 B4
Hospitium The★ YO30 ...156 A3
Hotham Ave YO26 ...129 B2
Hotham Dr HU5 ...144 B8
Hotham Rd
Hutton Cranswick YO25 ...32 E7
Kingston upon Hull HU5 ...144 A8
North Cave YO43 ...53 D4
Hotham Rd N HU5 ...139 E3
Hotham Rd S HU5 ...144 B8
Hotham Sq HU17 ...137 B4
Hotham St HU9 ...146 D7
Hotspur Rd 1 DN21 ...117 B1
Hotton Cl HU9 ...142 C1
Houghton La YO43 ...41 C1
Houndale La YO25 ...125 E8
Houndsway 6 YO24 ...132 B8
Houps Rd 10 DN8 ...93 B8
Hourne The HU13 ...143 E2
Housemartin Dr 4 HU8 ...141 D8
Houston Dr HU5 ...140 D3
Hove Rd HU5 ...139 D1
Hovedene Dr DN14 ...65 A6
Hovingham Cl 17 HU8 ...141 E7
Howard Dr YO30 ...126 E2
Howard Gr DN32 ...153 B2
Howard Link YO30 ...126 D2
Howard Rd YO32 ...14 B6
Howard St YO10 ...130 D2
Howdale Rd HU8 ...141 E7
Howden Croft Hill
HU15 ...68 A8
Howden Cty Jun & Inf Sch
DN14 ...65 B7
Howden La YO19 ...133 E1
Howden Rd 4 Barlby YO8 ...49 B4
Eastrington DN14 ...65 F8
Holme-on-Spalding-Moor
YO43 ...51 F6
Howden Sec Sch DN14 ...65 B7
Howdens Hill DN15 ...151 A6
Howdenshire Way
DN14 ...64 F6
Howe Hill★ DN39 ...85 D2
Howe Hill Cl YO26 ...129 E4
Howe Hill Rd YO26 ...129 E4
Howe La Goxhill DN19 ...85 F8
Kirby Underdale YO41 ...17 A5
Nafferton YO25 ...125 F7
Howe St YO24 ...129 D3
Howes La YO25 ...33 E8
Howes Rd 8 YO14 ...3 A8
Howgate La YO43 ...41 A8
Howl Gate YO41 ...27 E8
Howl La YO25 ...32 E8
Howlett Rd 4 DN35 ...103 D2
Howsham Cl HU9 ...142 D5
Howsham La DN38 ...110 C8
Howville Ave DN7 ...92 F3
Howville Rd DN7 ...92 F3
Hoylake Cl HU6 ...139 E5
Hoylake Dr 6 DN40 ...87 C2
Hoylake Rd DN17 ...96 B2
Hubert St
1 Withernsea HU19 ...74 F7
2 York YO23 ...130 B1
Hucknall Garth 16 HU7 ...57 A5
Huddleston Rd DN32 ...153 B3
Hudson Ave DN15 ...96 C7
Hudson Cl YO41 ...15 D2
Hudson Cres 2 YO30 ...130 A7
Hudson Gdns 2 HU5 ...140 D1
Hudson St
Kingston upon Hull HU3 ...145 D8
6 York YO30 ...130 C7
Hudson's La YO25 ...31 B7
Huggate Dikes★ YO42 ...17 F2
Huggate Hill YO17 ...17 E7
Huggate La YO25 ...18 B5
Huggin Carr Rd DN7 ...92 F1
Hugh Field La YO8 ...50 A8
Hugh Field N La YO8 ...38 A1
Hugh Hill La DN7 ...92 D6
Hulberry Cl 11 DN41 ...101 A4
Hull & E Riding Hospl
HU10 ...143 E5
Hull & East Riding Mus★
HU1 ...155 C2
Hull Arena★ HU1 ...145 E4
Hull Bridge Rd
Beverley HU17 ...154 B4
Tickton HU17 ...137 C7
Hull City AFC HU4 ...144 E5
Hull Coll HU3 ...144 F7
Hull Coll of F Ed HU6 ...56 C5
Hull Coll Park Street Ctr
HU2 ...145 D7
Hull College of F Ed
HU1 ...155 C3
Hull Gram Sch HU5 ...140 C3
Hull High Sch for Girls
HU10 ...143 C5
Hull Ionians RUFC
HU15 ...68 C7
Hull Kingston Rovers RLFC
HU9 ...142 C1
Hull Maritime Mus★
HU1 ...155 B2
Hull Maternity Hospl
HU9 ...147 A8
Hull Nuffield Hospl
HU5 ...140 B1
Hull Rd Aldbrough HU11 ...59 B7
Beverley HU17 ...137 B3
Cliffe YO8 ...49 E2
Coniston HU11 ...57 F5
Easington HU12 ...90 E6
Hatfield HU11 ...46 C5
Hemingbrough YO8 ...50 B1
Heslington YO19 ...131 E3
Hornsea HU11 ...46 D8
Hornsea HU18 ...134 B1
Howden DN14 ...65 B7
Keyingham HU12 ...73 C4
Kingston upon Hull
HU16 ...139 D5
Kingston upon Hull
HU13 ...143 F1
Kingston upon Hull
HU10 ...143 F6
Kingston upon Hull
HU12 ...147 F6
Preston HU12 ...72 A7
Rimswell HU19 ...74 E6
Woodmansey HU17 ...137 B2
York YO10 ...131 B3
Hull RLFC HU3 ...145 B5
Hull Road Ave 4 DN14 ...65 B7
Hull Royal Infmy HU3 ...145 C6
Hull RUFC HU7 ...140 D8
Hull Sta HU1 ...155 A2
Hull Trinity Ho Sch
HU1 ...155 B2
Humber Bank S DN31 ...153 A6
Humber Bridge★ HU13 ...69 E3
Humber Bridge Ctry Pk★
HU13 ...69 D4
Humber Bridge Rd
DN31 ...153 A5
Humber Cres
5 Brough HU15 ...68 C5
Scunthorpe DN17 ...150 F2
Humber Dock St HU1 ...155 B1
Humber Dr 5 YO32 ...14 B6
Humber La
Patrington HU12 ...74 D1
Skeffling HU12 ...90 D5
Welwick HU12 ...90 A7
Humber Pl HU1 ...155 B1
Humber Rd
Barton-upon-Humber
DN18 ...69 E1
North Ferriby HU14 ...69 A4
South Killingholme DN40 ...86 F3
Humber Side La
Easington HU12 ...90 F4
Welwick HU12 ...89 F6
Humber Side Rd HU12 ...90 B6
Humber St
Cleethorpes DN35 ...153 F1
Goole DN14 ...149 D1
Grimsby DN31 ...153 A5
Kingston upon Hull HU9 ...155 C1
Market Weighton YO43 ...135 F4
Humber Terr DN31 ...152 C4
Humber View
Barton-upon-Humber
DN18 ...84 E8
Kingston upon Hull
HU13 ...143 C2
5 Swanland HU14 ...69 B6
Humberdale Cl 4 HU14 ...69 B6
Humberdale Dr HU14 ...69 C5
Humberside Int Airport
DN38 ...99 F5
Humberston Ave
13 Humberston DN36 ...114 D8
New Waltham DN36 ...114 B7
Humberston C of E Prim Sch
DN36 ...114 D8
Humberston Cloverfields
Prim Sch DN36 ...114 C8
Humberston Comp Sch
DN36 ...114 C8
Humberston Rd DN36 ...103 B1
Humberstone Rd
DN32 ...153 A2
Humberville Rd DN40 ...87 C1
Humbleton Rd
East Garton HU12 ...59 C6
Elstronwick HU12 ...58 E3
Hume Brae DN40 ...87 B1
Hume St DN31 ...152 C3
Hund Oak Dr DN7 ...92 D4
Hungate
13 Barton-upon-Humber
DN18 ...69 E1
York YO1 ...156 C2
Hungate Ct
11 Hunmanby YO14 ...2 F8
Market Weighton YO43 ...135 D5
Hungate La YO14 ...2 F8
Hunger Hills Balk YO25 ...10 C4
Hungerhills Dr HU11 ...58 A4
Hunmanby CP Sch YO14 ...2 F8
Hunmanby Rd
Burton Fleming YO25 ...2 E3
Reighton YO14 ...3 C6
Hunmanby Sta YO14 ...3 A7
Hunsley Ave 3 HU5 ...139 B1
Hunsley Cres DN32 ...103 A2
Hunsley Dr DN41 ...101 E6
Hunsley Rd HU17 ...55 A7
Hunt Ct YO31 ...156 C3
Hunt Rd DN16 ...151 C1
Huntcliffe Comp Sch
DN21 ...108 C1
Hunter Cl
1 Patrington HU12 ...74 D1
5 Preston HU12 ...58 D1
Hunter Rd HU15 ...68 C6
Hunters Cl
Dunnington YO19 ...26 E7
10 Haxby YO32 ...127 C8
Hunter's Croft DN9 ...105 D3
Hunters Gate DN37 ...102 B5
Hunters Way
Selby YO8 ...148 B4
York YO24 ...132 F7
Hunters Wlk YO8 ...63 D7
Hunters Wood Way 21
YO19 ...26 F7
Huntingdon Cres 5
DN15 ...82 B4
Huntingdon St HU4 ...144 E3
Huntington Prim Sch
YO32 ...127 F4
Huntington Rd YO31 ...156 C4
Huntington Sch YO32 ...127 E3
Huntington Sports Club
YO32 ...128 A5
Huntley Dr HU5 ...140 A1
Hunts Cl 7 DN20 ...97 E4
Hunts La DN20 ...108 F5
Huntsmans La YO41 ...15 C2
Huntsman's Wlk YO24 ...129 B1
Hurford Pl DN37 ...113 E7
Hurley Cl HU8 ...141 F3

Hurn Cl HU8 . . . . .141 E6
Hurns La YO30 . . . . .126 A7
Hurricane Way YO30 . . . .126 E3
Hurst La DN17 . . . . .96 C2
Hurstlea Dr 19 DN36 . . . . .103 D1
Hurton's La LN11 . . . . .121 F6
Hushells La DN14 . . . . .78 C2
Hustler Rd YO16 . . . . .122 F5
Hutch La DN14 . . . . .66 C3
Hutchinson Rd DN35 . . . .153 D3
Hutchinson St 1 YO8 . . .148 B6
Huteson La DN15 . . . . .82 C8
Hutt St HU3 . . . . .145 D7
Hutton Balk YO25 . . . . .32 D8
Hutton Cl
  Kingston upon Hull HU5 .139 E2
  Poppleton YO26 . . . . .126 A2
Hutton Rd
  Grimsby DN31 . . . . .153 A6
  Hutton Cranswick YO25 . . .32 E7
Hutton St YO26 . . . . .24 A5
Huzzard St 5 DN14 . . . . . . .55 D8
Hykeham Cl 17 HU7 . . . . . .56 F6
Hymers Ave HU3 . . . . .145 B7
Hymers St 11 YO25 . . . . . . .34 B2
Hymers Coll HU3 . . . . .145 B7
Hyperion St HU9 . . . . .155 C3
Hyrst Gr YO31 . . . . .130 E6

I

Icehouse Rd HU3 . . . . .145 D6
Idas Cl HU9 . . . . .155 C1
Idle Bank Epworth DN9 . . . .94 A2
  Haxey DN9 . . . . .104 F4
  Wroot DN9 . . . . .104 E4
Ikin Way YO32 . . . . .127 F6
Ilchester Cl HU7 . . . . .141 B5
Ilford Rd HU5 . . . . .139 C1
Ilkeston Ave DN14 . . . . . . .149 B5
Ilthorpe HU6 . . . . .140 A8
Ilton Garth YO30 . . . . .127 A2
Immingham Dock
  DN40 . . . . .87 D3
Immingham Medieval
  Village★ DN40 . . . . .87 B2
Immingham Mus★
  DN40 . . . . .87 C1
Immingham Pelham Inf &
  Nursery Sch DN40 . . . . . .87 C1
Immingham Sch The
  DN40 . . . . .87 C1
Immingham Sports Ctr
  DN40 . . . . .87 C1
Immingham St Andrews C of
  E Jun Sch DN40 . . . . .87 C1
Immingham Swimming Pool
  DN40 . . . . .87 C1
Impala Way HU4 . . . . .144 D2
Imperial Ave DN35 . . . . . .153 C4
Imperial Ct 12 HU9 . . . . . .142 A3
Ing Nook Rd HU15 . . . . . . .52 C2
Inghams La 12 DN36 . . . . .114 D4
Inghams Rd DN36 . . . . . . .114 C4
Ingland Ct HU9 . . . . .142 B1
Ingleborough Ave
  YO10 . . . . .131 B4
Ingleby Hl HU9 . . . . .141 F7
Ingleby Rd DN17 . . . . .107 D7
Inglefield Cl 7 HU17 . . . . .55 E8
Inglemire Ave HU6 . . . . . .140 C5
Inglemire La HU6 . . . . .139 E5
Inglenook Dr 1 DN8 . . . . . .93 B8
Ingleton Ave HU4 . . . . . . .144 C4
Ingleton Wlk 3 YO31 . . . .131 A5
Inglewood Dr 4 HU4 . . . . .144 B5
Ingmires 3 HU15 . . . . .68 D6
Ingram Ave
  Kingston upon Hull
    HU11 . . . . .142 F6
  York YO30 . . . . .130 C8
Ingram Cres DN7 . . . . .92 C4
Ingram Gdns DN20 . . . . . .108 E8
Ingram Gr DN7 . . . . .92 C4
Ingram Pl DN35 . . . . .103 B2
Ingram Rd DN7 . . . . .92 C3
Ingrish La YO23 . . . . .24 C1
Ings Ct DN14 . . . . .61 F4
Ings Dr YO43 . . . . .53 F7
Ings La Beal DN14 . . . . .61 D2
  Bishop Wilton YO42 . . . . . .16 D2
  Brough HU15 . . . . .68 C5
  Carlton DN14 . . . . .63 E2
  Cawood YO8 . . . . .48 D8
  Cottingwith YO42 . . . . .38 C5
  Dunswell HU6 . . . . .56 D2
  Ellerker HU15 . . . . .67 F8
  Hensall DN14 . . . . .62 D2
  Hibaldstow DN20 . . . . . . .109 A5
  Immingham DN40 . . . . .87 D1
  Kellington DN14 . . . . .61 F4
  Keyingham HU12 . . . . .73 C4
  Kirk Bramwith DN7 . . . . . . .92 C7
  Nether Poppleton YO26 . . .126 B1
  North Coates DN36 . . . . . .115 A3
  North Ferriby HU14 . . . . . . .69 A4
  Patrington HU12 . . . . .74 C1
  Riccall YO19 . . . . .48 E8
  Riston HU11 . . . . .45 C2
  South Cave HU15 . . . . .67 E7
  Spaldington DN14 . . . . .51 C4
  Thorganby YO19 . . . . .38 B5
  Utterby LN11 . . . . .121 E4

Ings La continued
  Walkerith DN21 . . . . .116 F3
  Waltham DN37 . . . . .113 E6
  West Stockwith DN10 . . . .116 F6
  Wheldrake YO19 . . . . .38 B7
  Whitton DN15 . . . . .67 E3
  Winterton DN15 . . . . .83 D7
  Wistow YO8 . . . . .49 A6
Ings Prim Sch HU8 . . . . . .141 F4
Ings Rd Cliffe YO8 . . . . .49 D2
  Kingston upon Hull HU7 . .141 D5
  Kirton in Lindsey DN21 . . .107 F1
  Molescroft HU17 . . . . .136 D7
  Snaith DN14 . . . . .63 C1
  Thorganby YO19 . . . . .38 B4
  Wilberfoss YO41 . . . . .27 E6
Ings View YO30 . . . . .126 D2
Inmans Prim Sch HU12 . . . .72 D7
Inmans St HU12 . . . . .72 D7
Innescourt HU6 . . . . .139 E7
Innsworth Garth 17 HU7 . .57 A5
Inrea Hill YO42 . . . . .29 F5
Intake Ave YO30 . . . . .130 C8
Intake Hill YO43 . . . . .135 C8
Intake La
  Acaster Malbis YO23 . . . . .36 C7
  Beal WF11 . . . . .61 D5
  Dunnington YO19 . . . . .26 E7
  Heck DN14 . . . . .77 C8
  West Haddlesey YO8 . . . . .61 F6
Intakefield Rd YO8 . . . . . . .50 D7
Intakes La YO42 . . . . .39 A6
Inverewe Way 2 HU16 . . .138 F5
Inverness 24 DN7 . . . . .92 D4
Invicta Ct YO24 . . . . .132 B8
Iona Cl
  8 Gainsborough DN21 . . .117 C1
  Kingston upon Hull HU8 . .141 E7
Iona Dr DN36 . . . . .114 D8
Iona Rd YO16 . . . . .122 F4
Irby Ct 8 DN35 . . . . .103 B2
Irby Rd DN17 . . . . .150 E1
Irvine Rd DN16 . . . . .151 C1
Irwin Ave YO31 . . . . .130 E6
Isaac Newton Sch
  HU9 . . . . .142 D1
Isaac's Hill DN35 . . . . .153 E2
Isis Ct HU9 . . . . .146 B5
Island Carr Rd DN20 . . . . . .98 B2
Island St DN17 . . . . .81 E6
Isle Cl DN17 . . . . .94 D8
Isledane HU6 . . . . .139 C4
Itlings La HU13 . . . . .143 F1
Itterby Cres DN35 . . . . . . .103 B4
Ivanhoe Rd DN16 . . . . .151 C5
Iver Cl YO26 . . . . .129 C5
Iveson Cl 27 HU12 . . . . .72 C7
Ivy Cl DN7 . . . . .92 E4
Ivy Farm Ct 6 DN41 . . . . .101 F5
Ivy La Grainthorpe LN11 . .115 E1
  Hedon HU12 . . . . .72 C7
  Snaith & Cowick DN14 . . . .78 D8
Ivy Mdw HU12 . . . . .59 C2
Ivy Park Rd DN14 . . . . . . .149 E6
Ivy Rd DN8 . . . . .79 A1
Ivybridge Wlk 5 HU9 . . . .142 E1

J

Jack Rd YO43 . . . . .53 C8
Jack Row La DN7 . . . . .92 B8
Jack Taylor La HU17 . . . . .137 B4
Jackey La HU11 . . . . .58 B8
Jacklin La DN17 . . . . .81 C3
Jacklins App DN16 . . . . . . .96 D2
Jackson La YO41 . . . . .27 E4
Jackson Mews 7 DN40 . . . .87 B1
Jackson Rd DN15 . . . . .150 E7
Jackson St Goole DN14 . . .149 C4
  Grimsby DN31 . . . . .152 C4
  Kingston upon Hull HU3 . .145 D4
  York YO31 . . . . .156 C4
Jackson's Pl DN36 . . . . . . .103 B1
Jackson's Wlk YO23 . . . . . .24 D3
Jacksonville DN14 . . . . . . .149 C5
Jacobi Cl YO30 . . . . .130 A7
Jacques' La YO8 . . . . .49 E4
Jade Gr 1 HU3 . . . . .145 A4
Jalland St HU8 . . . . .141 C1
James Backhouse Pl
  YO24 . . . . .129 C3
James Cl 1 HU19 . . . . .75 A6
James Ct 5 DN8 . . . . .79 B1
James Nicholson Way
  YO30 . . . . .127 A2
James Niven Ct 1 HU9 . . .141 D1
James Pl DN39 . . . . .86 B1
James Reckitt Ave
  HU8 . . . . .141 B1
James St 22 Brigg DN20 . . . .98 B2
  Goole DN14 . . . . .149 D2
  Grimsby DN31 . . . . .152 C4
  Selby YO8 . . . . .148 C5
  York YO10 . . . . .130 E4
James Way 29 DN40 . . . . . .87 B1
Jameson Rd YO16 . . . . . . .122 C4
Jameson St HU1 . . . . .155 A2
Jamieson Terr YO23 . . . . . .130 B1
Janton Ct DN36 . . . . .114 A8
Japan Rd DN21 . . . . .117 A1
Japonica Hill 8 DN40 . . . . .87 C1
Jaque's Bank DN8 . . . . .94 A3
Jarratt Hill La HU15 . . . . . .67 C8
Jarratt St HU1 . . . . .155 B3
Jasmine Cl
  10 Snaith DN14 . . . . .63 C1

Jasmine Cl continued
  York YO32 . . . . .127 D2
Jasmine Gr 17 HU7 . . . . . . .56 F5
Jasmine Way DN40 . . . . . . .87 C1
Jason Cl YO16 . . . . .122 E6
Jason Garth 1 HU7 . . . . . . .57 B5
Jaywick Cl 3 YO32 . . . . . . .14 B8
Jedwell Cl YO32 . . . . .127 D5
Jefferson Cl Goole DN14 . .65 C4
  Molescroft HU17 . . . . .136 C6
Jefferson Dr HU15 . . . . .68 C6
Jefferson St DN14 . . . . . . .149 C4
Jeffrey La DN9 . . . . .94 E1
Jendale HU7 . . . . .140 F8
Jenkinson La YO25 . . . . .32 D8
Jenner Pl DN35 . . . . .153 B4
Jennifer Gr 4 YO24 . . . . . .129 F2
Jenning St HU8 . . . . .155 C4
Jenny Brough La
  HU13 . . . . .143 B3
Jenny Cl HU13 . . . . .143 B3
Jenny La DN14 . . . . .77 B5
Jenthorpe HU6 . . . . .140 A8
Jericho La DN40 . . . . .86 D7
Jervis Rd
  Kingston upon Hull HU9 . .142 D5
  York YO24 . . . . .132 E8
Jesmond Gdns HU9 . . . . . .141 D1
Jesmond Rd HU16 . . . . . . .139 C6
Jetcourt HU6 . . . . .139 E7
Jevans Ct 2 YO25 . . . . . . .124 F4
Jewbury YO31 . . . . .156 C3
Jewison La
  Bempton YO16 . . . . .4 D1
  Flamborough Maltings
    YO15 . . . . .123 B8
Jill Gr HU13 . . . . .143 F1
Jipdane HU6 . . . . .139 F8
Jobsons Cl 11 HU15 . . . . . .53 F1
Joby La HU17 . . . . .43 A2
Jockey La YO32 . . . . .127 F2
John Coupland Hospl
  DN21 . . . . .117 A2
John Gray Ct HU10 . . . . . .138 C1
John Harrison C of E Prim
  Sch DN19 . . . . .85 D8
John Harrison's Cl 1
  DN19 . . . . .85 D8
John Leggott Coll
  DN17 . . . . .150 E4
John Newton Way HU7 . . .56 E5
John St
  Kingston upon Hull HU2 . .155 B3
  Scunthorpe DN15 . . . . . . .151 B7
  Selby YO8 . . . . .148 B6
  York YO31 . . . . .130 E6
Johnny Moor Long La
  DN14 . . . . .79 B6
Johnson Cl DN9 . . . . .94 E2
Johnson St
  Cleethorpes DN35 . . . . . .153 B4
  Selby YO8 . . . . .148 B6
Johnson's La DN17 . . . . . . .94 C7
Johnston Ct HU17 . . . . . . .136 D7
Johnston's Rd DN7 . . . . . . .92 E7
Joiners La YO25 . . . . .19 B6
Jonquil Ave DN16 . . . . .96 E2
Jorvik Viking Ctr★
  YO1 . . . . .156 C2
Joscelyn Ave HU7 . . . . . . .141 B5
Joseph Ogle Cl
  6 New Waltham DN36 . . .113 F8
  3 New Waltham DN36 . . .114 A8
Joseph Rowntree Sch
  YO32 . . . . .127 E5
Joseph St DN31 . . . . .152 C4
Jowland Winn La YO8 . . . . .63 A4
Jubbergate YO1 . . . . .156 B2
Jubilee Ave YO16 . . . . .122 D4
Jubilee Cres 35 DN21 . . . .117 B1
Jubilee Gr 8 YO16 . . . . . .122 D5
Jubilee La HU12 . . . . .59 C2
Jubilee Rd YO8 . . . . .48 D6
Jubilee Terr YO26 . . . . .129 F5
Julia Ave YO32 . . . . .128 B2
Julian Cl HU4 . . . . .144 A7
Julian St DN32 . . . . .153 A3
Julian's Bower (Maze)★
  DN15 . . . . .82 C8
Julian's Wlk 8 HU10 . . . .143 F6
Junction Rd DN7 . . . . .92 C6
Junella Cl HU3 . . . . .145 A4
Juniper Cl YO32 . . . . .127 D3
Juniper Way DN33 . . . . . . .102 E1
Justice Hall La 3 DN17 . . . .94 D8
Justice La DN14 . . . . .81 B8
Jute Rd YO26 . . . . .129 B5
Jutland Ct 13 DN36 . . . . . .114 A8

K

Karen Ave 10 DN41 . . . . . .101 A4
Kathleen Ave
  Cleethorpes DN35 . . . . . .153 D4
  Scunthorpe DN16 . . . . . . .151 B1
Kathleen Dr DN32 . . . . . . .153 C3
Kathleen Rd HU8 . . . . .141 B2
Kathryn Ave YO32 . . . . . . .128 A2
Katrine Cl HU7 . . . . .141 D5
Kay Kendall Ct 16 HU19 . . .75 A6
Kaye Dr YO8 . . . . .49 B4
Kaymile Cl 15 DN36 . . . . .114 A7
Kealholme Rd DN17 . . . . . .107 D7
Keats Ave DN17 . . . . .150 D3
Keats Cl YO30 . . . . .129 F8
Keb La DN15 . . . . .83 D2
Keble Cl YO23 . . . . .133 B3

Keble Dr YO23 . . . . .133 A2
Keble Gdns YO23 . . . . .133 B2
Keble Park Cres YO23 . . . .133 A2
Keble Pk N YO23 . . . . .133 A3
Keble Pk S YO23 . . . . .133 A2
Keddington Rd 13 DN17 . . .96 C2
Kedrum Rd HU9 . . . . .141 F1
Keel Ct HU17 . . . . .137 B3
Keel Rd HU6 . . . . .140 C8
Keelby CP Sch DN41 . . . . .101 A5
Keelby Rd
  Scunthorpe DN17 . . . . . . .150 F1
  Stallingborough DN41 . . . .101 C6
Keelby View DN20 . . . . .98 D2
Keeper's Hill YO25 . . . . .7 A1
Keeper's Way 2 DN9 . . . . . .94 E1
Keepers Way 11 YO19 . . . . .26 F7
Keirhardie Wlk 4 DN32 . . .152 E1
Keith Ave YO32 . . . . .128 A4
Keith Cres DN37 . . . . .101 E1
Keldale 4 YO32 . . . . .13 F5
Keldgarth YO25 . . . . .32 F6
Keldgate HU17 . . . . .154 A2
Keldgate Cl HU17 . . . . .154 A2
Keldgate Rd
  Beverley HU17 . . . . .136 C2
  Cottingham HU16 . . . . . . .138 D7
Keldspring La YO42 . . . . . . .28 C3
Kelfield Rd 9 YO19 . . . . . . .48 F8
Kelgate Cl 11 HU8 . . . . . . .141 E7
Kelham Rd DN32 . . . . .153 D2
Kelk La YO25 . . . . .22 B6
Kellythorpe Ind Est
  YO25 . . . . .124 B3
Kellington La DN14 . . . . . . .61 F2
Kellington Prim Sch
  DN14 . . . . .61 F3
Kelsey Ave DN15 . . . . .150 B7
Kelsey Cl YO43 . . . . .135 D2
Kelsey Dr 3 HU12 . . . . .73 C4
Kelsey La DN17 . . . . .95 D4
Kelsey Rd LN7 . . . . .110 D1
Kelstern Ct DN34 . . . . .152 A1
Kelston Dr 2 HU13 . . . . . .144 A3
Kelvin Hall Sch HU5 . . . .139 E3
Kelvin St HU9 . . . . .141 E2
Kemp Rd
  Grimsby DN31 . . . . .153 A7
  North Ferriby HU14 . . . . . . .69 B6
Kempton Cl 2 YO24 . . . . . .129 D1
Kempton Dr DN7 . . . . .92 C2
Kempton Rd HU3 . . . . .144 E6
Kendal Cl 6 YO19 . . . . .26 F7
Kendal Rd DN40 . . . . .87 D1
Kendal Way HU4 . . . . .144 C7
Kendale Rd DN16 . . . . .151 E4
Kendale View YO25 . . . . . .124 E6
Kendon Gdns DN8 . . . . .93 B8
Kendrew Cl 3 YO32 . . . . . .127 F3
Kenerdales La YO43 . . . . . . .53 E8
Kenford Ct 1 DN36 . . . . . .114 A8
Kenilworth Ave HU5 . . . . .139 F3
Kenilworth Rd
  6 Cleethorpes DN35 . . . .103 B2
  Scunthorpe DN16 . . . . . . .151 C5
Kenlay Cl YO32 . . . . .127 D4
Kenmar Rd DN37 . . . . .101 F1
Kenmore Dr HU6 . . . . .56 D5
Kennedy Dr DN20 . . . . .98 C2
Kennedy Dr
  Goole DN14 . . . . .149 D5
  32 Haxby YO32 . . . . .13 E5
Kennet Rd HU8 . . . . .142 C6
Kenneth Ave 5 DN7 . . . . . .92 C6
Kennington Wlk HU16 . . . .139 D6
Kenrick Pl 5 YO26 . . . . . . .129 B5
Kensal Rise HU13 . . . . .130 D2
Kensington Ct 1 YO24 . . .132 F8
Kensington Gdns 14
  DN14 . . . . .65 A7
Kensington Pl 3 DN33 . . . .113 F8
Kensington Rd
  Rawcliffe DN15 . . . . .126 D2
  Scunthorpe DN15 . . . . . . .150 B7
Kensington St YO23 . . . . . .130 B1
Kent Cl HU9 . . . . .146 C7
Kent Dr DN20 . . . . .109 A5
Kent Rd
  Bridlington YO16 . . . . .122 A2
  Goole DN14 . . . . .149 B4
  Kingston upon Hull
    HU16 . . . . .139 A5
  Selby YO8 . . . . .148 A6
Kent Sq YO16 . . . . .122 A2
Kent St Grimsby DN32 . . . .152 F5
  York YO10 . . . . .156 C1
Kentmere Cl 2 HU7 . . . . . . .57 A7
Kentmere Dr YO30 . . . . . . .126 F1
Kents Gdns 14 DN8 . . . . . . .79 B2
Kenwardly Rd HU10 . . . . . .143 E8
Kenwood HU9 . . . . .75 A5
Kenya Dr 3 DN17 . . . . .96 C1
Keppel Dr YO16 . . . . .123 A8
Kerdane HU6 . . . . .139 F8
Kerries Wlk DN17 . . . . .150 C2
Kerry Dr HU10 . . . . .143 C6
Kerry Pit Way HU10 . . . . . .143 C6
Kerver La YO19 . . . . .26 F7
Kesgrave St DN31 . . . . .153 A5
Kesteven Ct 6 DN40 . . . . .100 E8
Kesteven Gr DN17 . . . . .94 D8
Kesteven Way HU7 . . . . . . .56 D5
Kestrel Ave HU7 . . . . .141 D8
Kestrel Dr YO15 . . . . .123 B7
Kestrel St DN31 . . . . .150 E2
Kestrel Wood Way
  YO31 . . . . .127 F2
Keswick Gdns HU6 . . . . . . .139 E6
Keswick Way 5 YO32 . . . .127 F5

Kettering Rd DN16 . . . . . . .151 C6
Kettlebridge La DN40 . . . . .86 D6
Kettleby La DN20 . . . . .98 E3
Kettleby View DN20 . . . . . .98 D2
Kettlestring La YO30 . . . . .127 A3
Kettlethorpe Hill HU15 . . . .53 C4
Kettlewell Cl 2 HU17 . . . . .56 F6
Kettlewell St DN32 . . . . . . .152 E1
Ketwell La 19 HU12 . . . . . .72 C7
Ketwell Lane Prim Sch
  HU12 . . . . .72 C7
Kew Rd DN35 . . . . .153 E2
Kexby Ave YO10 . . . . .130 F3
Kexby Bridge★ YO41 . . . . .27 C6
Kexby House★ YO41 . . . . . .27 C6
Kexby Stray YO41 . . . . .27 A5
Key Way YO19 . . . . .133 F5
Keyholme La DN36 . . . . . . .115 D2
Keyingham Cty Jun Sch
  HU12 . . . . .73 D4
Keyingham Inf Sch
  HU12 . . . . .73 C3
Keyingham Rd HU12 . . . . . .73 D3
Keyworth Dr 5 LN7 . . . . . .111 B4
Kidd La Brough HU15 . . . . . .68 D6
  Melbourne YO42 . . . . .39 A6
Kiddier Ave 12 DN33 . . . . .113 C8
Kidhill La HU17 . . . . .45 B2
Kilburn Ave HU2 . . . . .155 A4
Kilburn Rd YO10 . . . . .130 D2
Kildale Cl HU8 . . . . .141 E6
Kilham La Kilham YO25 . . . . .9 E5
  Thwing YO25 . . . . .9 B8
Kilham Prim Sch YO25 . . . .9 C3
Kilham Rd YO25 . . . . .8 D5
Kilkoy Dr 4 HU7 . . . . .56 F6
Killingholme High
  Lighthouse★ DN40 . . . . .87 B5
Killingholme N Low
  Lighthouse★ DN40 . . . . .87 C5
Killingholme Prim Sch
  DN40 . . . . .86 E3
Killingholme Rd DN40 . . . . .86 F1
Killingwoldgraves La
  HU17 . . . . .43 C2
Kiln La 18 Brigg DN20 . . . . .98 B2
  Patrington HU12 . . . . .74 D1
  Stallingborough DN41 . . . .101 D8
Kilnhouse La HU12 . . . . . . .60 C2
Kilnsea Gr HU9 . . . . .141 F2
Kilnwick Ave HU5 . . . . .139 C2
Kilnwick Garth 2 YO42 . . .29 A3
Kilnwick La YO25 . . . . .32 B2
Kilnwick Percy Hill
  YO42 . . . . .29 D4
Kilnwick Rd YO42 . . . . .29 B4
Kilpin Broad La DN14 . . . . .65 E6
Kilton Ct 12 HU8 . . . . .141 D7
Kilvin Dr HU7 . . . . .137 A6
Kimberley St HU3 . . . . . .145 C7
Kimberlows Wood Hill 3
  YO10 . . . . .131 C3
Kimmeridge Cl HU7 . . . . . .141 B6
Kinbrace Dr YO24 . . . . .132 B2
Kinderscout Cl 15 HU7 . . . .56 F6
King Charles Cl HU10 . . . .143 E7
King Edward Cres 9
  DN8 . . . . .79 B1
King Edward Fst Sch
  DN8 . . . . .93 B8
King Edward Rd DN8 . . . . . .93 A8
King Edward St
  Belton DN9 . . . . .94 E2
  Grimsby DN31 . . . . .152 E5
  Kingston upon Hull HU1 . .155 A3
  12 Kirton in Lindsey DN21 .108 B1
  Scunthorpe DN16 . . . . . . .151 A5
King Edwards Terr 4
  HU15 . . . . .68 C5
King George Dock
  HU9 . . . . .147 C6
King Georges Ct DN7 . . . . .92 C5
King Rudding Cl 6 YO19 . . .49 A6
King Rudding La YO19 . . . . .49 B6
King St
  1 Barton-upon-Humber
    DN18 . . . . .84 F8
  Bridlington YO15 . . . . .122 E2
  6 Cawood YO8 . . . . .48 B8
  East Halton DN40 . . . . .86 D7
  Goxhill DN19 . . . . .86 A8
  Great Driffield YO25 . . . . .124 F4
  1 Hornsea HU18 . . . . .134 C3
  19 Keelby DN41 . . . . .101 A4
  Kingston upon Hull
    HU16 . . . . .139 B6
  Kingston upon Hull HU1 . .155 B2
  Sancton YO43 . . . . .41 E2
  Scunthorpe DN15 . . . . . . .151 B8
  Thorne/Moorends DN8 . . . .93 A8
  Winterton DN15 . . . . .83 A5
  17 Withernsea HU19 . . . . .75 A6
  Woodmansey HU17 . . . . . .137 D1
  York YO1 . . . . .156 B2
Kingerby Rd DN17 . . . . . . .150 E1
Kingfisher HU7 . . . . .141 D6
Kingfisher Cl
  Kingston upon Hull HU7 . .141 D8
  1 Leven HU17 . . . . .45 A8
  Scunthorpe DN15 . . . . .96 B7
Kingfisher Rise HU7 . . . . . .141 E6
Kings Acre YO31 . . . . .131 B6
King's Ave DN20 . . . . .98 C2
King's Bench St HU3 . . . . .145 B5
Kings Cl YO8 . . . . .49 B5
King's Cl 7 DN7 . . . . .92 D4
Kings Cl 24 YO41 . . . . .29 A3
Kings Court Rd 4 DN8 . . . .79 B1

King's Cross Cl 2 HU3 .145 C6
King's Cswy
  Reedness DN14 . . . . .80 E8
  Swinefleet DN14 . . . . .65 D1
Kings Ct DN20 . . . . .108 F8
Kings Garth YO25 . . . . . . .125 F7
Kings Lea YO8 . . . . .50 A8
Kings Leigh 1 HU3 . . . . .145 C6
Kings Mdw YO25 . . . . . . .124 D3
Kings Mead
  Great Driffield YO25 . . . .124 D4
  Woodmansey HU17 . . . . .137 D1
Kings Mews DN35 . . . . . . .103 E1
Kings Mill Cl YO25 . . . . . .124 D4
Kings Mill Pk YO25 . . . . . .124 D4
Kings Mill Rd YO25 . . . . . .124 D3
Kings Mill Sch YO25 . . . . .124 E4
Kings Moor Rd YO32 . . . . . .14 D2
King's Pl 29 HU12 . . . . . . .72 C7
King's Rd
  Barnetby le Wold DN38 . . .99 B5
  Cleethorpes DN35 . . . . . .103 D2
Kings Rd DN40 . . . . .87 D1
King's Sq
  Beverley HU17 . . . . .154 B3
  York YO1 . . . . .156 C2
Kingsbury Way 7 HU7 . . . .56 F6
Kingsclere YO32 . . . . .127 F6
Kingscott Cl 10 HU7 . . . . .56 F5
Kingsdale DN17 . . . . .96 C1
Kingsgate
  Bridlington YO15 . . . . . .122 D1
  Carnaby YO15 . . . . .10 F2
Kingsland Terr 11 YO26 . .129 F5
Kingsley Ave HU9 . . . . . . .141 E2
Kingsley Cl 6 HU15 . . . . .68 B5
Kingsley Dr HU10 . . . . . . .138 C1
Kingsley Gr 4 DN33 . . . . .102 C2
Kingsport Cl HU3 . . . . . . .145 A7
Kingsthorpe YO24 . . . . . . .129 D2
Kingston Ave
  Grimsby DN34 . . . . .152 A2
  Kingston upon Hull
    HU13 . . . . .143 F1
Kingston Cl 8 DN35 . . . . .103 C1
Kingston General Hospl
    HU2 . . . . .140 E1
Kingston Lower Sch
    HU4 . . . . .144 C4
Kingston Rd
  Bridlington YO15 . . . . . . .11 B4
  Kingston upon Hull
    HU10 . . . . .138 D1
  Scunthorpe DN16 . . . . . .151 A3
Kingston Ret Pk HU1 . . . .155 C4
Kingston Rise HU10 . . . . .138 C1
Kingston Sq HU2 . . . . . . .155 B3
Kingston St
  Goole DN14 . . . . .149 C2
  Kingston upon Hull HU1 . .155 B1
Kingston upon Hull
  Swimming Club HU6 . . . .140 B7
Kingston Upper Sch
    HU4 . . . . .144 C4
Kingston View 27 DN18 . . .84 F8
Kingston Way HU7 . . . . . .140 F5
Kingston Wharf HU1 . . . . .155 A1
Kingsway 2 Brigg DN20 . .98 B2
  Cleethorpes DN35 . . . . . .103 C3
  Goole DN14 . . . . .149 D4
  Kingston upon Hull
    HU16 . . . . .139 B5
  Scunthorpe DN15 . . . . . .150 C7
  14 Stainforth DN7 . . . . . .92 C6
  6 Stamford Bridge YO41 . .15 D2
Kingsway Jun Sch
    YO30 . . . . .130 B7
Kingsway N YO30 . . . . . . .130 B7
Kingsway Prim Sch
    DN14 . . . . .149 E5
Kingsway W YO24 . . . . . .129 D3
Kingswood Gr YO24 . . . . .129 D3
Kingswood Ret Pk HU7 . . . .56 E5
Kingswood Way HU7 . . . . .57 A5
Kingtree Ave HU16 . . . . . .139 B6
Kinloch Way
  28 Immingham DN40 . . . . .87 B1
  2 Immingham DN40 . . . .101 B8
Kinloss Garth 2 HU7 . . . . .57 B5
Kinloss Prim Sch HU7 . . . . .57 B5
Kinsbourne Gn 37 DN7 . . .92 D4
Kinthorpe HU6 . . . . .140 A8
Kipling Ave DN17 . . . . . . .150 D3
Kipling Cl HU5 . . . . .31 C4
Kipling Cotes Medieval
  Village* YO25 . . . . .30 D2
Kipling Cotes Race Course*
  YO25 . . . . .30 E1
Kipling Wlk 1 HU4 . . . . .144 D2
Kiplingcotes La YO43 . . . .42 A5
Kiplingcotes Nature
  Reserve* YO43 . . . . .41 E6
Kiplington Cl HU3 . . . . . . .145 A7
Kir Cres YO24 . . . . .129 C3
Kirby Cl YO43 . . . . .135 E2
Kirby Dr HU16 . . . . .139 B6
Kirby La YO25 . . . . .7 A4
Kirk Balk YO17 . . . . .16 E8
Kirk Balk La YO60 . . . . . . .15 B7
Kirk Cl HU7 . . . . .141 D6
Kirk Croft HU16 . . . . .139 A6
Kirk Gate DN37 . . . . .113 E6
Kirk La Sykehouse DN14 . . .78 A4
  Walkington HU17 . . . . . . .55 B7
Kirk Rd DN21 . . . . .58 C1
Kirk Rise HU10 . . . . .143 D7
Kirk Smeaton C of E Prim
  Sch WF8 . . . . .76 B3

Kirk View 1 YO26 . . . . . .129 C3
Kirkby Rd
  Scunthorpe DN17 . . . . . . .96 C2
  Selby YO8 . . . . .148 B1
Kirkby St HU2 . . . . .155 B4
Kirkby Wlk HU23 . . . . . . .127 C8
Kirkcroft YO32 . . . . .127 C8
Kirkdale Rd YO10 . . . . . . .131 D4
Kirkden Paddocks DN9 . . . .94 C2
Kirkfield HU19 . . . . .75 A6
Kirkgate
  Bridlington YO16 . . . . . .122 D4
  8 Pocklington YO42 . . . . .29 A4
Kirkgate Mews YO16 . . . . .122 D5
Kirkham Ave 1 YO31 . . . .130 E8
Kirkham Cl HU13 . . . . . . .143 F2
Kirkham Ct DN14 . . . . . . .149 E6
Kirkham Dr HU5 . . . . .140 B2
Kirkham Rd YO16 . . . . . . .122 D7
Kirkholme Way HU17 . . . .137 B4
Kirkhouse Green Rd
    DN7 . . . . .92 A8
Kirkland St YO8 . . . . .148 D4
Kirkland St YO42 . . . . .29 A4
Kirklands YO32 . . . . .14 B6
Kirklands La YO41 . . . . . . .16 C2
Kirklands Rd HU5 . . . . . . .144 E8
Kirkside 2 DN37 . . . . . . .113 E6
Kirkstead Cres DN33 . . . .102 D2
Kirkstead St HU8 . . . . . . .141 A2
Kirkstone Dr YO31 . . . . . .131 A6
Kirkstone Rd HU5 . . . . . . .139 D2
Kirkway HU10 . . . . .143 B7
Kirkwell YO23 . . . . .133 A4
Kirman Cres 18 DN17 . . . .96 C2
Kirmington C of E Prim Sch
    DN39 . . . . .100 A6
Kirmington Gdns
    DN34 . . . . .152 A2
Kirncroft Cl 16 HU12 . . . .73 C4
Kirton in Lindsey Prim Sch
    DN21 . . . . .108 B1
Kirton La DN7 . . . . .92 E6
Kirton Lane Prim Sch
    DN7 . . . . .92 D7
Kirton Lindsey Sta
    DN21 . . . . .108 B2
Kirton Rd Blyton DN21 . . .117 F6
  Holme DN7 . . . . .97 B2
  Kirton in Lindsey DN21 . .108 A3
  Messingham DN17 . . . . .107 C6
  Scawby DN20 . . . . .108 C8
  Scotton DN21 . . . . .107 D2
Kishorn Ct
  30 Immingham DN40 . . . . .87 B1
  1 Immingham DN40 . . . .101 B8
Kissing Gate HU12 . . . . . . .59 D2
Kitchen Dr YO8 . . . . .148 D4
Kitchen La HU17 . . . . .154 A1
Kitchener St Selby YO8 . . .148 B6
  York YO31 . . . . .130 D7
Kitemere Pl 2 YO24 . . . . .132 B8
Kitty Garth YO19 . . . . .38 A7
Kitty Hill (Tumulus)*
    YO41 . . . . .16 E3
Knapton Ave 7 HU5 . . . . .139 E3
Knapton Cl 1 YO32 . . . . . .14 B6
Knapton La YO26 . . . . . . .129 B4
Knavesmire Cres
    YO23 . . . . .130 B1
Knavesmire Prim Sch
    YO23 . . . . .130 B1
Knavesmire Rd YO23 . . . .130 A1
Knedlington Rd DN14 . . . . .65 A6
Knight St DN32 . . . . .153 B2
Knightly Way HU7 . . . . . . .56 E5
Knights Cl Belton DN9 . . . .94 E2
  8 Laceby DN37 . . . . . . .101 F1
Knight's Ct 16 DN16 . . . . .96 C2
Knights Way HU17 . . . . . .154 B3
Knightsbridge 7 DN36 . . .114 A8
Knightsbridge Ct 7
    HU3 . . . . .140 D1
Knightsbridge Rd
    DN17 . . . . .107 D7
Knightscourt HU6 . . . . . . .139 E7
Knoll St DN35 . . . . .153 F2
Knoll The HU6 . . . . .139 E7
Knottingley England Lane
  Jun & Inf Sch WF11 . . . . .61 A2
Knottingley High Sch
    WF11 . . . . .61 A2
Knottingley Rugby Union
  Club WF11 . . . . .61 A3
Knowles Ave HU6 . . . . . . .140 C8
Knowsley Ave HU16 . . . . .139 A7
Kyffin Ave HU9 . . . . .142 D2
Kyle Cl HU8 . . . . .142 C6
Kyle Way YO26 . . . . .129 B8
Kyme St YO1 . . . . .156 B1

L

Labrador Dr 11 DN20 . . . . .97 E4
Laburnham Ave 21
    DN37 . . . . .113 D6
Laburnham Cl 22 DN37 . .113 D6
Laburnum Ave
  18 Gainsborough DN21 . . .117 B1
  Gunness DN15 . . . . .150 F7
  Hutton Cranswick YO25 . . .32 E7
  Kingston upon Hull HU8 . .141 C2
  11 Thorne/Moorends DN8 . .79 B2
Laburnum Cl
  Rufforth YO23 . . . . .24 C6
  7 Snaith DN14 . . . . .63 C1
  3 Thorpe Willoughby YO8 . .48 B1
Laburnum Ct 4 YO16 . . . .123 A6

Laburnum Dr
  Beverley HU17 . . . . .137 A7
  Grimsby DN34 . . . . .102 C4
  3 Kingston upon Hull
    HU4 . . . . .144 B7
Laburnum Garth 6
    YO31 . . . . .130 F8
Laburnum Gr
  Burton upon Stather
    DN15 . . . . .82 B5
  Crowle DN17 . . . . .94 D7
  Scunthorpe DN16 . . . . . .151 B3
  Stillingfleet YO19 . . . . . . .36 D4
Laburnum Wlk 17 HU15 . . .66 D8
Laceby Acres Prim Sch
    DN34 . . . . .102 B3
Laceby Rd
  Grimsby DN34 . . . . .102 C2
  Scunthorpe DN17 . . . . . .150 E1
Lady Frances Cres
    DN35 . . . . .153 C1
Lady Hamilton Gdns
    YO24 . . . . .129 E2
Lady Rd YO24 . . . . .130 B7
Ladybower Cl 4 HU7 . . . .141 D7
Ladygate HU17 . . . . .154 A3
Lady's Well* YO43 . . . . . .135 F7
Ladyside Cl 17 HU7 . . . . . .57 A6
Ladysmith Mews 13
    YO32 . . . . .14 A7
Ladysmith Rd
  Grimsby DN32 . . . . .152 F3
  Kingston upon Hull
    HU10 . . . . .138 E1
Ladywell Gate 3 HU15 . . .68 E6
Laforey Rd DN37 . . . . . . .102 C6
Lagoon Dr HU7 . . . . .141 D8
Lagoon Rd DN17 . . . . . . .150 B2
Lairgate HU17 . . . . .154 A2
Lairs La DN9 . . . . .30 A5
Lake Dr HU8 . . . . .141 E3
Lake View HU8 . . . . .141 E3
Lakeside HU23 . . . . .36 C7
Lakeside Dr DN17 . . . . . . .150 C1
Lakeside Gr
  Kingston upon Hull HU4 . .144 D4
  1 Strensall YO32 . . . . . . .14 B8
Lakeside Prim Sch
    YO30 . . . . .126 F2
Lakeside Ret Pk DN16 . . .151 F1
Laking La YO25 . . . . .2 A3
Lalrgate Pl 20 DN8 . . . . . .79 B2
Lamb Inn Rd 9 WF11 . . . .61 A2
Lamb La Newport HU15 . . . .67 B8
  Roos HU12 . . . . .60 A1
Lambert Ave 16 HU15 . . . .68 C6
Lambert Cl HU43 . . . . . . .135 E3
Lambert Ct YO1 . . . . .156 B1
Lambert Park Rd 23
    HU12 . . . . .72 C7
Lambert Rd
  Bridlington YO16 . . . . . .122 F5
  Grimsby DN32 . . . . .152 E2
Lambert St HU5 . . . . .140 D2
Lambourn Ct 25 DN35 . . .103 C1
Lambourne Rise 7 DN16 .96 D1
Lambton St HU5 . . . . .140 D2
Lambwath La HU11 . . . . . . .46 A3
Lambwath Rd HU8 . . . . . .141 C4
Lambwell Hill HU15 . . . . . .54 E2
Lamel St YO10 . . . . .131 A3
Lamorna Ave HU8 . . . . . . .141 B3
Lamplugh Cres YO33 . . . .133 B3
Lamplugh La 7 YO15 . . . .122 F4
Lamplugh Rd YO15 . . . . . .122 F4
Lamplugh Sq 6 YO15 . . . .122 F4
Lampton Gr DN32 . . . . . . .152 C2
Lamwath Prim Sch
    HU8 . . . . .141 F5
Lanark St HU5 . . . . .145 B8
Lancar Cl 18 YO32 . . . . . . .13 D5
Lancaster App DN40 . . . . . .86 D4
Lancaster Ave DN31 . . . . .152 B3
Lancaster Dr
  Kingston upon Hull HU8 . .141 D4
  2 Moorland Prison DN7 . .104 A8
Lancaster Gate DN36 . . . .114 A4
Lancaster Rd
  Carnaby YO25 . . . . .10 D2
  Gringley on the Hill
    DN10 . . . . .116 A2
  Pocklington Ind Est YO42 . .28 E3
  Scunthorpe DN16 . . . . . .151 A1
Lancaster Way YO30 . . . . .127 A1
Lancelot Ct HU9 . . . . .146 C6
Lancing Way 2 DN33 . . . .113 E8
Land Dike LN11 . . . . .115 A1
Land Ends Rd DN8 . . . . . . .78 E4
Land of Green Ginger
    HU1 . . . . .155 B2
Landalewood Rd YO30 . . .126 F2
Landau Ct YO30 . . . . .129 F8
Landeck Ave DN34 . . . . . .152 B2
Landing La
  Asselby DN14 . . . . .64 D6
  Barlby with Osgodby
    YO8 . . . . .148 F8
  Broomfleet HU15 . . . . . . .67 A7
  Gilberdyke HU15 . . . . . . .52 D1
  22 Haxby YO32 . . . . .13 F5
  Haxby YO32 . . . . .127 F8
  Hemingbrough YO8 . . . . .63 F8
  Newport HU15 . . . . .52 E1
  Riccall YO19 . . . . .48 F8
  York YO26 . . . . .129 E6
Landing Rd YO8 . . . . .62 A7
Landings The 21 YO32 . . . .13 F5
Landor Ave DN17 . . . . . . .150 D3

Landress La HU17 . . . . . . .154 A2
Lane The YO41 . . . . .15 B2
Laneham St DN31 . . . . . . .151 A7
Lanes The 7 DN36 . . . . . .114 C4
Lang Ave YO10 . . . . .131 A4
Lang Rd
  Bishopthorpe YO23 . . . . .132 F4
  York YO23 . . . . .127 F6
Langdale Ave
  Beverley HU17 . . . . .154 B3
  Grimsby DN33 . . . . .113 D8
  Kingston upon Hull HU5 . .139 E2
  York YO31 . . . . .131 B6
Langdale Cres HU16 . . . . .139 A5
Langdale Dr 4 HU12 . . . . .73 C4
Langdale Gr YO8 . . . . .148 B3
Langdale Rd DN40 . . . . . . .135 C4
Langford Wlk 1 HU4 . . . .144 B7
Langham St
  13 Thorngumbald HU12 . . .72 E5
  10 Thorngumbald HU12 . . .72 E5
Langholm Cl HU17 . . . . . .136 D5
Langholme Dr YO26 . . . . .129 C6
Langholme La DN9 . . . . . .116 B8
Langley Ct 1 YO32 . . . . . .127 C6
Langley Dr DN16 . . . . .96 D1
Langley Garth YO25 . . . . .124 C4
Langley Pk 25 HU7 . . . . . .56 F5
Langley Pl 5 DN35 . . . . . .103 C2
Langleys Rd 6 DN6 . . . . . .76 C3
Langrick Ave HU4 . . . . .65 B7
Langrickgate La YO42 . . . .38 C5
Langsett Gr YO30 . . . . . . .126 F3
Langsett Rd HU7 . . . . .141 D7
Langthorpe Rd HU11 . . . . .45 F2
Langtoft CP Sch YO25 . . . . .8 C5
Langtoft Gr HU6 . . . . .139 F5
Langton Cl 16 DN33 . . . . .102 D2
Langton Ct 1 YO32 . . . . . .14 A6
Langton Dr DN33 . . . . . . .102 D2
Langton Rd DN36 . . . . . . .114 B5
Langtree Cl HU7 . . . . .140 F8
Langwith Stray YO10 . . . . .26 C2
Lansdown Link 17 DN35 .103 C2
Lansdown Rd
  Goole DN14 . . . . .149 A5
  13 Immingham DN40 . . . . .87 B1
Lansdown Way 7 YO32 . . .13 D5
Lansdowne Ave DN33 . . .102 A2
Lansdowne Cres 9
    YO15 . . . . .122 F3
Lansdowne Rd YO15 . . . . .122 F2
Lansdowne St HU3 . . . . . .145 C4
Lansdowne Terr 5
    YO10 . . . . .130 E3
Lanshaw Croft YO30 . . . . .126 F1
Lanyon Cl HU7 . . . . .141 C7
Laporte Rd DN40 . . . . .87 E2
Lapwing Cl HU7 . . . . .141 D8
Larard Ave 2 HU6 . . . . . .140 C8
Larch Cl
  2 Immingham DN40 . . . . .87 B4
  Kingston upon Hull HU5 . .140 D2
Larch Cl 11 DN21 . . . . . .117 C1
Larch Dr HU12 . . . . .72 C5
Larch Gr Scawby DN20 . . .108 F8
  Scunthorpe DN16 . . . . . .151 B3
Larch Rd 6 DN35 . . . . . . .103 B1
Larchfield YO31 . . . . .131 C7
Larchmont Cl 7 HU15 . . . .68 C6
Larden Ave 1 DN33 . . . . .113 E8
Lark Rise 2 DN21 . . . . . .107 B3
Larkfield Cl 1 YO23 . . . . .132 A3
Larkfield Rd YO8 . . . . .148 A5
Larkspur Ave DN41 . . . . . .101 F5
Larmour Rd DN37 . . . . . . .102 B4
Larne Rd HU9 . . . . .142 B4
Larsen Rd DN40 . . . . .87 C2
Larsen Rd 24 HU4 . . . . . .149 A3
Lascelles Ave HU19 . . . . . .74 C4
Lashbrook Garth HU4 . . . .144 B4
Lastingham 12 HU15 . . . . .68 C6
Lastingham Cl HU6 . . . . . .139 F6
Laughton Endowed Sch
    DN21 . . . . .117 E8
Laughton Rd
  Beverley HU17 . . . . .154 B4
  Blyton DN21 . . . . .117 B4
Laundry La YO25 . . . . .124 E5
Laura St DN14 . . . . .149 C5
Laurel Ave DN8 . . . . .79 B2
Laurel Cl
  10 Gainsborough DN21 . . .117 C1
  Gateforth YO8 . . . . .48 B1
  3 Grimsby DN33 . . . . . .102 C1
  Kingston upon Hull HU4 . .144 B7
Laurels Cl 1 DN40 . . . . . .100 E8
Laurels The YO42 . . . . .28 D3
Laurier St DN35 . . . . .153 D4
Laurold Ave DN7 . . . . .93 A3
Lauty La HU11 . . . . .45 C5
Lavender Gr YO26 . . . . . . .129 E5
Lavender Wlk
  Beverley HU17 . . . . .154 A1
  1 Kingston upon Hull
    HU4 . . . . .144 C7
Lavenham Rd DN33 . . . . .113 D8
Laveracks Ind Est YO41 . . .27 B3
Lawn La DN6 . . . . .77 E3
Lawns The
  Beverley HU17 . . . . .136 C6
  Bridlington YO16 . . . . . .122 E7
  Grimsby DN34 . . . . .152 C2
  Kingston upon Hull HU7 . .141 D6
  Kingston upon Hull
    HU10 . . . . .143 D7
Lawnsgarth HU16 . . . . . . .139 A7
Lawnswood
  Kingston upon Hull HU7 . .141 D5

Lawnswood continued
  Kingston upon Hull
    HU13 . . . . .143 D2
Lawnswood Dr YO30 . . . . .129 F8
Lawnway YO31 . . . . .131 A7
Lawrence Ave
  Bewholme YO25 . . . . .34 E3
  Kingston upon Hull HU8 . .141 E7
Lawrence St
  Grimsby DN31 . . . . .152 C4
  York YO10 . . . . .130 E3
Lawson Ave
  Grimsby DN31 . . . . .152 B3
  Kingston upon Hull
    HU16 . . . . .139 B7
Lawson Cl
  Kingston upon Hull HU6 . .140 B5
  1 Walkington HU17 . . . . .55 B7
Lawson Rd
  Bridlington YO16 . . . . . .122 D4
  York YO24 . . . . .132 F7
Lawsons Cl YO14 . . . . .2 F7
Laxthorpe HU6 . . . . .140 A8
Laxton Garth HU10 . . . . . .138 B1
Laxton Gr 5 DN16 . . . . . . .96 D1
Layerthorpe YO31 . . . . . . .156 C3
Lea Cres HU16 . . . . .139 A5
Lea Croft 2 YO43 . . . . . . .135 E4
Lea Field Rd YO25 . . . . . . .31 E6
Lea Garth DN17 . . . . .107 D7
Lea The HU15 . . . . .54 A2
Lea Way YO32 . . . . .128 A4
Leaburn Rd DN17 . . . . . . .107 D7
Leaconfield Park House*
    HU17 . . . . .43 E5
Lead Mill La YO1 . . . . .156 C1
Leadhills Way 6 HU7 . . . . .57 B5
Leadley Croft YO23 . . . . . .132 A1
Leads Rd HU7 . . . . .141 C6
Leake St YO10 . . . . .130 E3
Lealholm Ct 11 HU8 . . . . .141 D7
Leame Cl HU3 . . . . .145 A7
Leamington Cl DN16 . . . .151 C5
Leander Rd HU9 . . . . .142 B3
Leas Cl DN37 . . . . .113 E7
Leas Jun & Inf Sch The
    DN37 . . . . .113 E7
Leas La HU11 . . . . .34 F1
Lease La DN40 . . . . .86 D6
Leases The HU17 . . . . .154 A2
Leatherdog La HU15 . . . . . .52 E1
Leathley Cl 1 HU17 . . . . .136 C1
Leavens La HU15 . . . . .52 D2
Leconfield Cl HU9 . . . . . . .142 D1
Leconfield Prim Sch
    HU17 . . . . .43 D6
Ledbury Dr 10 DN36 . . . .114 A8
Ledbury Rd HU5 . . . . .139 D2
Lee Ave HU19 . . . . .75 A6
Lee Fair Gdns DN17 . . . . . .96 C1
Lee Smith St HU9 . . . . . . .146 E7
Lee St HU8 . . . . .141 D3
Leeds Rd YO8 . . . . .148 A4
Leek Hill 9 DN15 . . . . .83 A5
Leeman Rd YO26 . . . . .156 A2
Leeming Garth 3 HU7 . . . .57 B5
Lees Wlk HU3 . . . . .145 A7
Leeside YO24 . . . . .132 E8
Legard Ave DN16 . . . . . . .151 B2
Legard Dr HU4 . . . . .143 F6
Legarde Ave HU4 . . . . . . .144 C6
Leggott Way 1 DN41 . . . .101 E6
Legion Cl 11 HU15 . . . . . .68 C5
Legsby Ave DN32 . . . . . . .152 E2
Legsby Pl DN32 . . . . .102 F2
Leicester St HU3 . . . . .145 D8
Leicester Way YO1 . . . . . .156 C1
Leighton Croft 3 YO30 . . .126 F1
Leighton Gr 2 DN33 . . . .102 E2
Leisure Pk YO32 . . . . .128 A2
Leitholm Cl 2 HU7 . . . . . .57 A6
Lelley Rd
  Humbleton HU11 . . . . . . .58 F5
  Preston HU12 . . . . .58 D2
Lendal YO1 . . . . .156 B2
Lenham La HU1 . . . . .155 A2
Leningrad Rd HU7 . . . . . . .140 F6
Lennox Cl 2 YO14 . . . . .3 A8
Leonard Cl HU12 . . . . .72 A5
Leonard Cres DN15 . . . . .150 F7
Leonard St
  4 Kingston upon Hull
    HU3 . . . . .145 D8
  Kingston upon Hull HU2 . .155 A4
Leopold Cl DN16 . . . . .151 A2
Lerecroft Rd YO24 . . . . . .132 D8
Lesley Ave YO10 . . . . .133 E8
Lestrange St DN35 . . . . . .153 C3
Levels La DN9 . . . . .104 A4
Leven C of E Sch HU17 . . . .45 A8
Leven Gr 4 YO32 . . . . . . .142 A2
Leven Rd
  Scunthorpe DN16 . . . . . .151 D2
  York YO24 . . . . .132 D7
Leverstock Gn 36 DN7 . . . .92 D4
Levington St DN32 . . . . . .153 A5
Levisham Cl HU6 . . . . .139 F6
Levisham St YO10 . . . . . . .130 D2
Levita Ave HU9 . . . . .142 C2
Levitt Lanes DN37 . . . . . . .31 F2
Lewis Rd DN35 . . . . .153 D4
Lexington Dr HU4 . . . . . . .144 C5
Leyburn Ave
  Hornsea HU18 . . . . .134 C2
  Kingston upon Hull HU6 . .139 E4

Leyden Cl [18] DN40 ....87 B1
Leyes The YO10 ....131 C4
Leyfield Cl [1] YO32 ......14 A7
Leyland Ave [6] DN7 ......92 E4
Leyland Rd YO31 ....131 A5
Leys Ct YO16 ....122 B4
Leys Farm Jun Sch
DN17 ....96 C2
Leys La Darrington WF11 ..76 A8
Little Smeaton WF8 ......76 B4
Skipsea YO25 ....23 A1
Winterton DN15 ....83 B6
Leys Rd
Bridlington YO16 ....122 B4
Darrington WF11 ....76 A7
Leys The HU18 ....134 B4
Liberty La HU1 ....155 C2
Lichfield Ave DN17 ....150 C3
Lichfield Cl
Beverley HU17 ....136 E1
Kingston upon Hull HU2 ..155 A4
Lichfield Ct [6] YO23 ...130 B1
Lichfield Rd
Grimsby DN32 ....153 B3
[40] Hatfield DN7 ....92 D4
Liddell St HU2 ....155 A3
Lidgard Rd DN36 ....103 D1
Lidgett Cl DN20 ....108 E8
Lidgett Gr YO26 ....129 B6
Lidgett Grove Sch
YO26 ....129 B6
Lidgett The [7] DN9 ....105 D6
Lidice Rd DN14 ....64 E2
Lighthouse Mus The★
HU19 ....74 F6
Lighthouse Rd YO15 ......5 B2
Lilac Ave
Beverley HU17 ....136 F7
Kingston upon Hull
HU10 ....138 D1
Kingston upon Hull HU8 ..141 B2
Scunthorpe DN16 ....151 C5
York YO10 ....131 B3
Lilac Cl YO25 ....124 D3
Lilac Gr YO32 ....127 D4
Lilacs The [10] YO42 .....29 A3
Lilbourne Dr YO30 .....130 A8
Lilling Ave [3] YO31 ....130 E8
Lily La YO15 ....5 A2
Lilywood Rd DN20 ....97 D3
Limber Ct DN34 ....152 A2
Limber Hill LN8 ....120 A4
Limber Rd
Humberside Airport
DN39 ....100 A6
Swallow LN7 ....112 A7
Limber Vale DN34 ......152 A2
Lime Ave
Kingston upon Hull
HU10 ....138 E1
Scunthorpe DN16 ....97 A3
York YO31 ....130 F7
Lime Cl YO25 ....124 F2
Lime Gr Goxhill DN19 ....86 A4
Holton le Clay DN36 ...114 A5
Humberston DN36 .....114 C7
Scunthorpe DN16 ......151 B3
Lime St Grimsby DN31 ..152 C4
Kingston upon Hull HU8 ..155 C4
Lime Tree [6] HU15 ......66 D7
Lime Tree Ave
Beverley HU17 ....137 A6
[21] Gainsborough DN21 ..117 B1
Goole DN14 ....149 D5
Kingston upon Hull HU8 ..141 C2
Kingston upon Hull
HU13 ....143 F2
York YO32 ....127 D3
Lime Tree Gdns DN14 ...149 D5
Lime Tree Gr
Selby YO8 ....148 A6
[4] Thorne/Moorends DN8 .93 A8
Lime Tree La HU11 .....142 F6
Lime Tree Mews [26] YO19 .26 F7
Limedale View [3] DN3 ...92 A3
Limedane HU6 ....139 F8
Limegarth [10] YO26 .....12 F1
Limekiln La YO16 ......123 A5
Limerick Cl HU8 ....142 B6
Limes The
[2] Beckingham DN10 ...116 D1
[3] South Cave HU15 .....53 F1
[3] Stallingborough DN41 .101 D6
Stockton-on-the-Forest
YO32 ....14 D2
Limetree Ave
[12] Grimsby DN33 ......102 E2
Kingston upon Hull HU7 .141 D6
Limetree Ct [2] YO8 .....48 B1
Lincoln Castle Way
DN19 ....70 D2
Lincoln Cl [11] DN17 .....94 D7
Lincoln Cres [2] DN21 ..119 C8
Lincoln Dr
[24] Barton-upon-Humber
DN18 ....84 F8
Caistor LN7 ....111 B4
Winterton DN15 ....83 A5
Lincoln Gate DN16 .....121 A5
Lincoln Gdns DN16 .....151 A4
Lincoln Gdns Inf Sch
DN16 ....151 B3
Lincoln Gdns Jun Sch
DN16 ....151 A2

Lincoln Gn HU4 ....144 C7
Lincoln Rd
Cleethorpes DN35 .....153 C1
Moorland Prison DN7 ...104 A8
Lincoln St
[23] Gainsborough DN21 ..117 B1
Kingston upon Hull HU2 .155 B4
Scunthorpe DN16 ......129 F5
Lincoln Way
[9] Beverley HU17 ....55 E8
Beverley HU17 ....154 A1
Lincolnshire Wolds Rly★
LN11 ....121 C7
Lindale [2] YO24 ......132 C7
Lindale Ave HU18 .....134 B2
Lindale Gdns DN16 ....151 C3
Linden Ave HU16 .....139 C6
Linden Cl [6] Hatfield DN7 .92 D4
York YO32 ....127 F5
Linden Gr [1] YO30 ...130 A8
Linden Way [9] YO8 .....48 B2
Lindengate Ave HU7 ...141 B4
Lindengate Way HU7 ..141 B5
Lindholme DN21 ....107 C3
Lindholme Bank Rd
DN7 ....93 B1
Lindisfarne Ave [4]
DN36 ....113 F7
Lindley Rd YO30 ......126 F1
Lindley St
Scunthorpe DN16 .....151 A2
York YO24 ....129 F3
Lindley Wood Gr
YO30 ....126 E3
Lindrick Wlk [8] DN37 ..113 D6
Lindsey DN36 ....114 A6
Lindsey Ave YO26 .....129 D4
Lindsey Ct [21] DN9 ...105 E6
Lindsey Dr Crowle DN17 .94 D8
Healing DN41 ....102 A5
Holton le Clay DN36 ...114 A6
Lindsey Lower Sch The
DN35 ....153 D2
Lindsey Pl HU4 ....144 D6
Lindsey Rd
[7] Cleethorpes DN35 ...103 C2
Cleethorpes DN35 .....153 F1
Lindsey Rise [30] DN33 .113 E8
Lindsey Sch The
DN35 ....103 C2
Lindsey St [2] DN16 ...151 C6
Lindum Ave [23] DN40 ...87 B1
Lindum Gr DN17 ....94 C7
Lindum Rd DN35 ......103 C2
Lindum St DN15 ......151 B7
Lindum Wlk LN7 ......110 A4
Linecroft La DN10 .....116 E4
Linegate [4] YO43 ....135 D4
Ling House La DN7 .....92 A5
Ling La YO41 ....27 F6
Lingcourt HU6 ....139 F7
Lingcroft Cl YO8 ....63 D4
Lingcroft La YO19 ....133 E3
Lingdale Rd HU9 ......142 E3
Lings La DN7 ....92 D3
Lings Rd HU17 ....42 E3
Lings Windmill★ DN7 ...92 E3
Link Ave YO30 ....130 C8
Link Rd
Huntington YO31 ......127 E2
Kingston upon Hull
HU16 ....139 B5
Link The
Copmanthorpe YO23 ..132 A3
Kingston upon Hull HU4 .145 C5
Selby YO8 ....148 A4
York YO10 ....133 E4
Linkfield Rd HU5 .....139 E4
Links Rd DN35 ....103 D2
Linkway Hatfield DN7 ...92 F3
Norton DN6 ....76 E2
Linley Cl HU17 ....45 A8
Linleyhill Rd HU17 .....33 C1
Linnaeus St HU3 .....145 C6
Linnet Cl DN15 ....96 B7
Linnet Dr HU7 ....141 D7
Linnet Way YO24 ....132 C8
Linthorpe Gr HU10 ...143 E8
Linton Cl HU17 ....154 A1
Linton Garth HU17 ....43 A5
Linton on Ouse Cty Prim Sch
YO30 ....12 A7
Linton Rd YO26 ......126 A1
Linton Rise DN15 ......82 A4
Linton St [5] YO26 ...129 E5
Linton Woods YO30 ...12 A7
Linton Woods La YO30 .12 A8
Linwith La DN14 ....63 C3
Linwood Ave [17] DN33 .113 E8
Lisburn Gr DN33 ......102 E1
Lisle Marsden C of E Prim
Sch DN32 ....102 F2
Lismore Ave HU9 .....142 A3
Lissett Cl HU17 ....43 D6
Lissett St HU6 ....140 C7
Lissett La DN15 ....22 C4
Lister Rd DN15 ....150 C7
Lister St Grimsby DN31 .152 B4
Kingston upon Hull HU1 .155 A1
Lister Way YO30 ......130 A7
Little Ave YO30 ......130 B8
Little Beck Rd HU16 ..122 B4
Little Belt The DN21 ..117 B2
Little Burton [3] YO25 ..34 B2
Little Clover HU17 ....136 F6
Little Coates Prim Sch
DN31 ....152 B5
Little Coates Rd DN34 .102 C2

Little Comm La DN14 ...77 C5
Little Dam La HU12 .....88 B8
Little Garth YO26 .....126 A2
Little George St HU8 ..155 C4
Little Grimsby La
LN11 ....121 D1
Little Hallfield Rd
YO31 ....130 E5
Little Heck Comm La
DN14 ....62 D1
Little John St DN34 ...152 B3
Little La
Broomfleet HU15 ......67 C6
Ellerton YO42 ....38 C1
[11] Haxby YO32 ....13 E5
Little Smeaton DN6 ....76 D4
Mappleton HU11 ......47 A5
Shipton Thorpe YO43 ..40 E5
Watton YO25 ....32 C5
Wrawby DN20 ....98 D3
Little London La DN14 ..78 D8
Little Mason St HU2 ..155 C3
Little Mdws YO32 ....127 D8
Little Michael St
DN34 ....152 B3
Little Moor La YO8 ...148 A8
Little Queen St HU1 ..155 A2
Little Reed St HU2 ...155 A3
Little Shore HU1 ......45 C2
Little Stonegate YO1 .156 B3
Little Weighton Rd
Skidby HU16 ....138 A4
Walkington HU17 ......55 B7
Little Westfield YO25 ...8 C3
Little Wlk DN21 ......116 E5
Little Wold La HU15 ...54 A2
Littlebeck Cl HU3 ....145 A7
Littlebeck Rd [4] DN36 114 C8
Littlefair Rd HU17 ...147 A7
Littlefield Cl [5] YO26 ..12 F1
Littlefield La
Grimsby DN34 ....152 B2
Marsh Chapel DN36 ..115 B1
Littleham Cl HU7 ....141 B8
Littlemoor Cl HU15 ...53 D3
Littlewood Rd
Rowley HU17 ....54 D7
[11] Thorne/Moorends DN8 93 B8
Littondale HU7 ......140 F7
Liverpool St HU3 ....145 A3
Livesey Rd DN36 ....121 B6
Livingstone Rd HU13 .69 F4
Livingstone St YO26 .129 F5
Lloyd Cl YO10 ....131 B1
Lloyds Ave HU17 ....150 F4
Lob La YO41 ....15 D2
Lochrin Pl YO26 .....129 B4
Lock Cl HU4 ....77 F6
Lock Hill DN8 ....93 A8
Lock La
Holme-on-Spalding-Moor
YO43 ....52 B8
Thorne/Moorends DN8 .93 A8
Lock Rd DN36 ......115 A4
Lockey Croft YO32 ..127 C8
Lockgate Rd DN14 ...77 C4
Lockham Rd HU12 ....90 F4
Lockhill DN31 ....152 E6
Lockington C of E Sch
YO25 ....32 B2
Lockington Rd YO25 .31 F3
Lockton Gr [1] HU4 ..144 D8
Lockwood Bank DN9 .105 E6
Lockwood Cl [6] DN8 ..93 B8
Lockwood Ct DN15 ..150 E8
Lockwood Dr HU17 ..136 E7
Lockwood Rd HU17 ..136 D7
Lockwood St
Great Driffield YO25 ..124 E4
Kingston upon Hull HU2 155 B4
York YO31 ....156 C3
Lodge Ave DN18 ......84 F8
Lodge Cl HU13 ......143 F1
Lodge Ct [35] DN7 ....92 D4
Lodge Farm Ct YO42 .39 B6
Lodge Gdns [5] DN14 .63 C1
Lodge La
Flixborough DN15 ....82 B2
Gowdall DN14 ....62 F1
Kirk Bramwith DN7 ...92 A8
Snaith DN14 ....78 D8
Lodge Rd DN15 .....150 C6
Lodge St HU9 ....141 E2
Lofthouse La YO41 ..27 D7
Loftsome Way [11] DN14 65 B7
Loftus Gr HU9 ......142 E3
Logan Cl HU7 ....141 C7
Loganberry Dr HU4 ..144 C4
Lombard St
Grimsby DN34 ....152 A3
Kingston upon Hull HU2 155 A3
Londesborough Ct
YO25 ....124 C4
Londesborough Gr [5]
YO8 ....48 B2
Londesborough Hill
YO43 ....41 A8
Londesborough Rd
Hutton Cranswick YO25 32 E7
Market Weighton YO43 135 D6
Londesborough St
Kingston upon Hull HU3 145 C7
[5] Selby YO8 ....148 C5

London La DN6 ....77 D1
London St [15] YO42 ..29 A4
Long Barrow★
Beelsby DN37 ....112 D4
Thixendale YO17 .....17 A7
Willerby YO12 ....1 E7
Long Close La YO10 .156 C1
Long Field Dr DN3 ...92 A1
Long Field Rd DN3 ...92 A2
Long Furrow YO32 ..127 C8
Long Hill YO42 ....29 D1
Long La Atwick YO25 .35 D6
Beverley HU17 ....154 B2
Bridlington YO16 ....122 C5
Catton YO41 ....27 D6
Cawood YO8 ....48 A6
Driffield YO25 ....124 F7
Eastrington DN14 ....65 D8
Ellerby HU11 ....58 B8
Ellerton YO42 ....38 C1
Foston YO25 ....22 A3
Goole DN14 ....149 E7
Great Driffield YO25 .124 F6
Heck DN14 ....77 D8
Heslington YO10 ....26 C3
Humbleton HU11 ....58 F5
Kirk Smeaton WF8 ..76 B1
Market Weighton YO43 41 B2
Nafferton YO25 .....20 E8
Pollington DN14 .....78 A7
Skeffling HU12 ......90 C5
Willoughton DN21 ..119 B3
Woodmansey HU17 .154 B1
Long Mann Hills Rd
YO8 ....148 B4
Long Marston C of E Prim
Sch YO26 ....24 A6
Long Rampart YO42 .38 D3
Long Rd DN15 ......150 E8
Long Ridge Dr YO26 126 A1
Long Ridge La YO26 126 A1
Long St YO25 ....9 F6
Long Trods [5] YO8 ..148 C6
Long Wood Rd DN21 117 D1
Longbrough La HU12 59 E4
Longcroft [2] YO32 ...13 E5
Longcroft Lower Sch
HU17 ....136 B5
Longcroft Pk HU17 ..136 C5
Longcroft Sch HU17 .136 C5
Longdales La HU11 ..142 E2
Longden St HU3 ....145 A7
Longfield Rd [4] DN34 102 C2
Longfield Terr YO30 .156 A3
Longford Gr HU9 ....142 E2
Longhill Prim Sch
HU8 ....142 C6
Longhorn Cl [1] DN37 113 C6
Longmans Hill CP Sch
YO8 ....148 C3
Longmans La HU16 .139 B6
Longmeadow Rise [7]
DN41 ....101 A4
Longmeadows Dr
DN37 ....101 F1
Longton Rd [13] DN3 .92 A3
Longwood Link [8] YO30 126 E3
Longwood Rd YO30 .126 F3
Lonsdale Cl DN36 ...114 D7
Lonsdale St [5] HU3 .145 A6
Lopham La DN37 ....112 F8
Lord Mayor's Wlk
YO31 ....156 B4
Lord Roberts Rd HU17 154 B2
Lord St Grimsby DN31 152 B4
Stainforth DN7 ......92 C6
Lords La DN19 ......85 D8
Lords Moor La YO32 14 C7
Lordship La YO8 ....148 B6
Lorenzo Way HU9 ..141 F2
Loriners Dr [7] YO23 132 B3
Lorne Cl HU2 ....155 B4
Lorne St YO23 ......130 B1
Lorraine Ave [3] YO41 27 B2
Lorraine St HU8 ....141 A3
Loten Dr HU18 .....134 D6
Lothian Way HU7 ....57 A6
Lotting's La YO42 ...28 C4
Louis Dr HU5 ....144 B8
Louis St HU3 ....145 A6
Louth Rd
Fotherby LN11 .....121 D3
Grimsby DN33 .....102 E1
[5] New Waltham DN36 113 F7
Louville Ave HU19 ...75 A6
Lovat Cl HU3 ....145 D5
Love La
Gainsborough DN21 117 B1
Hedon HU12 ....72 C7
Londesborough YO43 41 A8
York YO30 ....130 A2
Loveden Ct [7] DN35 103 D2
Lovell Rd [8] HU17 ..96 C2
Loveridge Ave HU5 .140 A2
Lovett St DN35 ....153 B4
Low Balk Rd HU17 ...42 F2
Low Burgage DN15 ..68 B1
Low Catton Rd YO41 27 C8
Low Comm La HU15 68 D4
Low Croft [6] YO32 ..14 A7
Low Cross St [7] DN17 94 D8
Low Deeps La DN10 104 C1
Low Farm Rd HU11 ..57 E5
Low Field La
Carnaby YO25 ....10 C3
Welton HU14 ....68 B5
Low Fields Dr YO24 129 C3
Low Garth DN17 ....96 C1

Low Gate DN36 ....115 C1
Low Gn
Copmanthorpe YO23 132 B2
[13] Knottingley WF11 .61 A2
Low La
Heslington YO10 ...131 D1
Kirk Bramwith DN7 ..92 A6
Low Levels Bank DN8 93 E3
Low Leys Rd DN17 ..96 C1
Low Mdw YO8 .....148 C6
Low Mill Cl YO10 ..131 D3
Low Mill La HU15 ...53 C2
Low Moor Ave [3] YO10 133 F8
Low Moor La
Askham Richard YO23 24 D3
Hessay YO23 ....24 C8
Low Ousegate YO1 .156 B2
Low Peter La YO25 .124 C8
Low Petergate YO1 .156 B3
Low Poppleton La
YO26 ....129 B7
Low Rd
Blyborough DN21 ...119 B6
Gowdall DN14 ....63 A1
Healing DN41 ......101 F5
Kellington DN14 ....61 F4
Kirby Grindalythe YO17 6 F7
Marsh Chapel DN36 115 A1
North Cave HU15 ...53 C2
Worlaby DN20 ......98 C8
Low St
Beckingham DN10 .116 E1
Carlton DN14 ....63 C2
Haxey DN9 ....105 D2
North Ferriby HU14 .69 A5
Sancton YO43 ......41 D2
South Ferriby DN18 84 A7
Winterton DN15 ....83 A5
Low Well Pk YO19 ..37 F7
Low Westfield Rd
YO23 ....132 A1
Lowcroft Ave [3] DN9 105 D2
Lowcroft Ct DN9 ...105 D2
Lowdale Cl HU5 ....139 E1
Lower Bridge St DN14 149 C3
Lower Burgess St
DN31 ....152 E4
Lower Darnborough St
YO23 ....156 B1
Lower Derwent Valley Nature
Reserve★ YO42 ......50 C8
Lower Friargate YO1 156 B2
Lower Kenyon St [6] DN8 93 A8
Lower Priory St YO1 156 A1
Lower Spring St DN31 152 E5
Lowerdale [13] HU15 68 C2
Loweswater Rd [5] YO30 126 E1
Lowfield YO43 ......40 B1
Lowfield Cl
[10] Barnby Dun DN3 92 A3
[18] Kirton in Lindsey DN21 108 B1
Lowfield Dr YO32 ..13 E5
Lowfield La
East Garton HU12 ..59 C5
Nunburnholme YO42 29 D3
Rufforth YO26 .....129 A4
Scrayingham YO41 .16 A7
Lowfield Rd
Barlby with Osgodby YO8 49 B5
Beverley HU17 ....137 A7
Hillam LS25 ....61 C8
Kingston upon Hull
HU10 ....143 E5
Lowfield Sch YO24 129 D3
Lowgate Balne DN14 77 D5
Kingston upon Hull HU1 155 C2
Lowhill DN8 ....78 F1
Lowick YO24 ......132 C7
Lowland Cl [3] HU7 141 D8
Lowmoor Rd YO8 ..49 E6
Lown Hill YO24 ....129 C2
Lowndes Pk YO25 .124 D5
Lowood Dr YO16 ..122 B4
Lowther Ct YO31 ..156 C4
Lowther Dr YO8 ...148 E3
Lowther St
Kingston upon Hull HU3 145 A7
York YO31 ....156 C4
Lowther Terr YO24 130 A3
Lowthorpe La YO25 125 F7
Loxley Cl YO30 ....126 F2
Loxley Gn HU4 ....144 B7
Loyds Ct [12] HU15 .53 F1
Lucas Ave YO30 ..130 C8
Lucas Ct DN41 ....101 F5
Luck La HU12 ......58 C1
Lucombe Way YO32 127 D4
Ludborough Pk DN36 121 B6
Ludborough Rd DN36 121 B8
Ludborough Way [21]
DN35 ....103 C2
Luddington & Garthorpe
Prim Sch DN17 ......81 C4
Luddington Rd DN17 81 E5
Ludford St DN32 ..152 E2
Ludgate Cl [4] DN37 113 D6
Ludlow Ave DN34 .152 A3
Ludlow Pl DN35 ...153 E1
Lulworth Ave HU4 .144 A3
Lumby Hill LS25 ....61 A8
Lumby La LS25 ....61 A8
Lumley Rd DN30 ..130 B7
Lumsden Cl YO25 .124 B2
Lund Ave HU16 ...138 E6
Lund Cl YO32 .....127 C8
Lund La Bubwith YO8 50 C4
Cliffe YO8 ....49 D4

Lund Rd YO25 . . . . .32 A2
Lunds The HU10 . . . . . . .143 C6
Lundy Cl 10 YO30 . . . . . .127 A1
Lundy Ct DN40 . . . . .101 C8
Luneburg Pl 14 DN15 . . .96 B7
Luneburg Way DN15 . . .96 B7
Lunedale Cl HU8 . . . . . .141 E7
Lunedale Rd DN16 . . . . .151 D1
Lunn La DN14 . . . . .61 D3
Lunn's Cres DN18 . . . . . .84 E8
Luton Rd HU5 . . . . .144 F8
Luttons CP Sch YO17 . . . .7 B8
Lycett Rd YO24 . . . . . . .132 F6
Lych Gate DN20 . . . . . . .97 D3
Lydbrook Rd DN16 . . . . .151 A5
Lydham Ct 2 YO24 . . . . .132 C8
Lydia Ct 6 DN40 . . . . . . .87 C1
Lygon St DN16 . . . . .151 B5
Lymington Garth HU4 . .144 A3
Lyndale Ave
 10 Kirk Sandall DN3 . . .92 A1
 York YO10 . . . . .131 C3
Lynden Way YO24 . . . . .129 D3
Lyndhurst Ave
 17 Grimsby DN33 . . . . .102 E2
 Kingston upon Hull
 HU16 . . . . .139 D6
Lyndhurst Cl
 Beverley HU17 . . . . . . .137 B4
 2 Norton DN6 . . . . .76 F2
 Thorne/Moorends DN8 . .92 F8
Lyndhurst Dr 1 DN6 . . . .76 F2
Lyndhurst Rise 3 DN6 . . .76 F2
Lynesykes Rd YO25 . . . . .21 F5
Lynhams Rd
 Bempton YO15 . . . . .4 E1
 Bridlington YO15 . . . . .123 B8
Lynmouth Cl 9 HU7 . . . . .57 A5
Lynmouth Dr DN17 . . . . .150 C4
Lynngarth Ave HU16 . . .139 C6
Lynton Ave
 Kingston upon Hull HU4 .144 B3
 Kingston upon Hull HU5 .145 A8
Lynton Cl Brayton YO8 . .148 B1
 Scunthorpe DN15 . . . . .150 C4
Lynton Gdns DN14 . . . . .148 B1
Lynton Rise 10 DN35 . . .103 C2
Lynwith Cl DN14 . . . . . . .63 C3
Lynwith Ct DN14 . . . . . . .63 C3
Lynwith Dr DN14 . . . . . . .63 C3
Lynwood Ave
 3 Copmanthorpe YO23 .132 A2
 Kingston upon Hull
 HU10 . . . . .143 E6
Lynwood View 4 YO23 . .132 A3
Lyric Cl 1 HU3 . . . . .145 C5
Lysaghts Way DN15 . . . . .82 C1
Lysander Cl YO30 . . . . . .127 A3
Lysander Dr YO43 . . . . . .135 E4
Lyth Cl 5 YO16 . . . . . . .123 A7
Lytham Dr
 Barnoldby le Beck DN37 .113 D6
 Kingston upon Hull
 HU16 . . . . .139 D6
Lythe Ave HU5 . . . . .139 E4

M

M62 Trad Est DN14 . . . .149 A3
Mablethorpe Rd DN36 . .115 A3
Macaulay St DN31 . . . . .152 B4
Macauley Jun & Inf Sch
 DN31 . . . . .152 B4
Macdonald Ct 12 YO42 . .29 A3
Mace View 154 B1
Machray Pl DN35 . . . . . .153 D3
Mackender Ct 3 DN16 . .151 B2
Mackenzie Pl 2 DN40 . . .87 B1
Maclagan Rd YO23 . . . . .132 F4
Maclure St DN31 . . . . . .152 F6
Madeley St HU3 . . . . . . .145 C4
Madison Gdns 4 HU5 . .140 A1
Madron Cl HU7 . . . . .141 B8
Magazine Cl HU8 . . . . . . .49 B3
Magazine Rd YO8 . . . . . .49 B4
Magdalen Cl 3 DN16 . . .96 C3
Magdalen Ct 8 HU12 . . .72 D7
Magdalen Gate HU12 . . .72 D7
Magdalen La HU12 . . . . .72 D7
Magdalene Rd 8 DN34 . .102 C3
Magnolia Cl YO25 . . . . . .124 D3
Magnolia Dr DN36 . . . . .114 A5
Magnolia Gr YO32 . . . . .127 C8
Magnolia Rise 9 DN40 . .87 C1
Magnolia Way DN16 . . . .151 A3
Magrath Ct 3 DN20 . . . . .98 C2
Maida Gr YO10 . . . . .130 D2
Maiden Cl 1 DN40 . . . . . .87 B1
Maiden Ct 8 HU7 . . . . . . .57 B5
Maidensgrave Henge ★
 YO25 . . . . .2 F1
Maidenwell La LN7 . . . . .110 A3
Maidwell Way 1 DN34 . .102 B2
Main App Rd DN16 . . . . .151 C7
Main Ave
 Scunthorpe DN17 . . . . .150 C2
 York YO31 . . . . .130 F4
Main Rd
 Ashby cum Fenby DN37 .113 D3
 Burton Agnes DN18 . . . .10 C3
 Burton Agnes YO25 . . . . .22 C6
 Burton Pidsea HU12 . . . .59 C2
 Drax YO8 . . . . .63 F5
 Gilberdyke DN14 . . . . . .66 B7
 Holmpton HU19 . . . . . . .75 C2
 Kilpin DN14 . . . . .65 D7

Main Rd continued
 Kingston upon Hull
 HU11 . . . . .142 E6
 Mappleton HU11 . . . . . . .47 A4
 Newport HU15 . . . . .53 A1
 Skeffling HU12 . . . . .90 D6
 Thorngumbald HU12 . . . .72 F5
 Ulrome YO25 . . . . .22 C6
 Utterby LN11 . . . . .121 C4

Main St
 Askham Bryan YO23 . . . .24 F3
 Asselby DN14 . . . . .64 D7
 Bainton YO25 . . . . .31 E7
 Barmby Moor YO42 . . . . .28 D3
 3 Beal DN14 . . . . .61 D4
 Beeford YO25 . . . . .22 C1
 Beswick YO25 . . . . .32 C4
 Bilbrough YO23 . . . . .24 C1
 Bishopthorpe YO23 . . . .133 A4
 Bonby DN20 . . . . .84 C2
 Boynton YO16 . . . . .10 D6
 Brandesburton YO25 . . . .34 B2
 Bridlington YO16 . . . . . .122 A1
 Bridlington YO15 . . . . . .123 C6
 Broomfleet HU15 . . . . . . .67 C6
 Brough HU15 . . . . .68 C6
 Bubwith YO8 . . . . .50 C7
 Buckton/Bempton YO15 . .4 C3
 Bugthorpe YO41 . . . . . . .16 D4
 Burstwick HU12 . . . . . . .73 A6
 Burton Agnes YO25 . . . . .10 A1
 Cadney DN20 . . . . .109 D6
 Cadney LN7 . . . . .110 A7
 Carnaby YO16 . . . . .10 E4
 Catwick HU17 . . . . .45 C8
 Cherry Burton HU17 . . . .43 A5
 Cliffe YO8 . . . . .49 E2
 Coniston HU11 . . . . .57 F6
 Copmanthorpe YO23 . . .132 A2
 Cottingwith YO42 . . . . . .38 C5
 Crowle DN17 . . . . .94 E6
 Dalton Holme HU17 . . . . .42 E8
 Deighton YO19 . . . . .37 A7
 East/West Stockwith
 DN10 . . . . .116 F6
 Ellerker HU15 . . . . .68 A8
 Ellerton YO42 . . . . .38 C1
 Elvington YO41 . . . . .27 C2
 Escrick YO19 . . . . .37 B5
 Etton HU17 . . . . .42 F6
 Fishlake DN7 . . . . .92 D8
 Foston YO25 . . . . .22 A4
 Fulstow LN11 . . . . .121 F8
 Ganton YO12 . . . . .1 A8
 Garton YO25 . . . . .19 F6
 Goodmanham YO43 . . . . .41 D6
 Gowdall DN14 . . . . .63 A1
 Grasby DN38 . . . . .110 E7
 Harpham YO25 . . . . .21 F8
 Hatfield HU11 . . . . .46 C5
 Hatfield DN7 . . . . .92 F3
 Heck DN14 . . . . .77 C8
 Hemingbrough YO8 . . . . .49 F1
 Hensall DN14 . . . . .62 D2
 Hessay YO26 . . . . .24 B8
 Horkstow DN18 . . . . .84 A5
 Hotham YO43 . . . . .53 D5
 Humberside Airport
 DN39 . . . . .100 A6
 Hutton Cranswick YO25 . .32 E7
 Keadby with Althorpe
 DN17 . . . . .95 D4
 Kelfield YO19 . . . . .36 D1
 Kelk YO25 . . . . .21 F6
 Kellington DN14 . . . . . . .61 F3
 Keyingham HU12 . . . . . . .73 C4
 Kingston upon Hull
 HU10 . . . . .138 C2
 Kingston upon Hull HU2 .140 F1
 Kirk Smeaton WF8 . . . . .76 B3
 Kirkburn YO25 . . . . .19 F1
 Leconfield HU17 . . . . . . .43 D6
 Long Riston/Arnold HU11 .45 C5
 Monk Fryston LS25 . . . . .61 A8
 1 Naburn YO19 . . . . . . .36 D8
 North Duffield YO8 . . . . .50 A8
 North Frodingham YO25 . .33 F8
 Ottringham HU12 . . . . . .73 E3
 Patrington HU12 . . . . . . .89 C8
 Paull HU12 . . . . .72 A5
 Pollington DN14 . . . . . . .77 F6
 Poppleton YO26 . . . . . . .12 F1
 Preston HU12 . . . . .58 C1
 Reighton YO14 . . . . .3 C5
 Riccall YO19 . . . . .49 A8
 Roos HU12 . . . . .60 A1
 Scawby DN20 . . . . .108 E7
 Searby cum Owmby
 DN38 . . . . .110 D8
 Seaton HU11 . . . . .35 A1
 Shipton YO30 . . . . .12 F5
 Sigglesthorne HU11 . . . .45 F8
 Skerne & Wansford YO25 .21 A2
 Skidby HU16 . . . . .138 B8
 Skipsea YO25 . . . . .23 A1
 Stamford Bridge YO41 . . .15 D2
 Swanland HU14 . . . . . . .69 B7
 Swine HU11 . . . . .57 D6
 Thornton Curtis DN39 . . .85 E5
 Thwing YO25 . . . . .2 B1
 Tibthorpe YO25 . . . . . . .19 D2
 Tickton HU17 . . . . .137 E8
 Ulrome YO25 . . . . .22 E5
 Watton YO25 . . . . .32 C4
 Wawne HU7 . . . . .56 F7
 Welwick HU12 . . . . .90 A7
 Wheldrake YO19 . . . . . . .37 F7
 Whitton DN15 . . . . .67 E3

Main St continued
 Wilberfoss YO41 . . . . . . .27 E5
 Withernwick HU11 . . . . . .46 D3
 Womersley DN6 . . . . .76 C6
 Worlaby DN20 . . . . .98 D8
 York YO26 . . . . .129 A5
 York YO10 . . . . .131 B1
 York YO10 . . . . .133 D8
Maine Ave DN15 . . . . . . .96 A7
Mains La YO42 . . . . .39 E3
Maister Rd 12 HU12 . . . .73 C4
Majestic Ct 7 HU9 . . . . .142 A3
Malbys Gr YO23 . . . . . . .132 B2
Malcolm Rd DN34 . . . . .102 C2
Maldon Dr HU9 . . . . .146 C6
Malet Lambert Sch
 HU8 . . . . .141 E4
Malham Ave HU4 . . . . . .144 E6
Malham Gr YO31 . . . . . .131 B5
Malkinson Cl 11 DN15 . . .83 A5
Mallalieu Ct DN15 . . . . .150 E8
Mallard Ave
 Barnby Dun DN3 . . . . . . .92 A4
 2 Leven HU17 . . . . .45 A8
Mallard Cl
 Beverley HU17 . . . . . . .136 F6
 2 Healing DN41 . . . . . .101 F5
 Ulrome YO25 . . . . .23 A3
Mallard Dr LN7 . . . . .111 A4
Mallard Mews DN32 . . . .152 E2
Mallard Rd
 Kingston upon Hull HU9 .142 B4
 Scunthorpe DN15 . . . . .150 E2
Mallard Way 11 YO32 . . .13 F5
Malling Wlk 13 DN16 . . .96 D1
Mallory Cl YO32 . . . . . . .127 C8
Mallory Rd DN16 . . . . . .151 D1
Mallyan Cl 15 HU8 . . . . .141 E7
Malm St HU3 . . . . .145 B6
Malmesbury Dr DN34 . . .152 C2
Malmo Rd HU7 . . . . .140 E5
Malpas Cl 8 HU7 . . . . . . .56 F5
Malt Kilns The DN14 . . . .149 D4
Maltby Ave DN37 . . . . . .102 B2
Maltby La 12 DN18 . . . . .69 E1
Maltby Rd DN17 . . . . . . .150 E1
Malthouse La 4 HU16 . . .96 D1
Malthouse Row DN14 . . .149 C3
Maltings Ct 6 YO8 . . . . .148 C5
Maltings The
 Beverley HU17 . . . . . . .154 C3
 Nafferton YO25 . . . . . . .125 F6
Maltkiln La 4 DN20 . . . . .98 F7
Maltkiln Rd DN18 . . . . . .69 F1
Malton Ave YO31 . . . . . .130 E6
Malton La YO17 . . . . .7 A8
Malton Rd
 Hunmanby YO14 . . . . . . .2 F8
 Huntington YO32 . . . . . .128 A1
 Molescroft HU17 . . . . . .136 B6
 York YO31 . . . . .130 F7
Malton St HU9 . . . . .155 C3
Malton Way YO30 . . . . .129 A4
Malvern Ave
 Grimsby DN33 . . . . .102 D2
 York YO26 . . . . .129 D5
Malvern Cl
 Huntington YO32 . . . . . .128 A5
 4 Thorne/Moorends DN8 .93 A7
Malvern Cres 9 HU5 . . .139 D2
Malvern Rd
 Goole DN14 . . . . .149 D5
 Kingston upon Hull HU5 .139 D2
 Scunthorpe DN17 . . . . .150 F3
Manby Rd
 Immingham DN40 . . . . . .87 B3
 Scunthorpe DN17 . . . . . .96 C2
Manchester Rd YO42 . . . .28 E3
Manchester St
 Cleethorpes DN35 . . . . .153 D4
 Kingston upon Hull HU3 .145 A4
Mancklin Ave HU8 . . . . .141 D5
Mancroft YO32 . . . . .127 C8
Mandela Link DN31 . . . .152 C3
Manderville Cl 18 HU12 . .72 D7
Manet Rd HU8 . . . . .141 C1
Manifold Rd DN16 . . . . .151 E1
Manlake Ave DN15 . . . . .83 A5
Manley Cl YO32 . . . . . . .127 D4
Manley Ct 1 DN9 . . . . . .105 D6
Manley Gdns
 Brigg DN20 . . . . .98 B2
 Cleethorpes DN35 . . . . .103 C2
Manley St DN15 . . . . . . .151 B7
Mann La DN9 . . . . .94 D2
Mannaberg Way DN15 . . .96 D7
Manor Ave DN32 . . . . . .152 D2
Manor Beeches The 3
 YO19 . . . . .26 E7
Manor C of E Sch
 YO26 . . . . .129 C7
Manor Cl
 Beverley HU17 . . . . . . .154 A4
 Great Driffield YO25 . . . .124 F4
 5 Hemingbrough YO8 . . .49 F1
 4 Keelby DN41 . . . . . . .101 A5
 Kirk Smeaton WF8 . . . . .76 B3
 6 North Duffield YO8 . . . .50 A7
 Nafferton YO25 . . . . . . .125 F6
 12 Norton DN6 . . . . .76 E2
 Skipsea YO25 . . . . .23 A2
 Sproatley HU11 . . . . .58 D5
Manor Court Rd 7 DN9 .105 E6
Manor Ct 6 Bubwith YO8 .50 D7
 Kingston upon Hull HU16 .69 C8
 Stallingborough DN41 . . .101 C2
 2 York YO32 . . . . .127 F6
Manor Dr Beeford YO25 . .22 C1

Manor Dr continued
 Bonby DN20 . . . . .84 C2
 Brough HU15 . . . . .68 C6
 Camblesforth YO8 . . . . . .63 C4
 4 Dunnington YO19 . . . .26 E7
 10 Gilberdyke HU15 . . . .66 D8
 5 North Duffield YO8 . . . .50 A7
 Scawby DN20 . . . . .108 E8
 Waltham DN37 . . . . .113 C4
Manor Dr N YO26 . . . . . .129 D4
Manor Dr S YO26 . . . . . .129 D4
Manor Farm Cl
 1 Brayton YO8 . . . . . . .148 A1
 Carlton DN14 . . . . .63 C2
 Copmanthorpe YO23 . . .132 A2
 Kellington DN14 . . . . . . .61 F3
 Messingham DN17 . . . . .107 D6
Manor Farm Ct YO8 . . . . .62 C4
Manor Farm La DN14 . . . .78 A3
Manor Farm Rd DN17 . . .150 E2
Manor Fields
 Kingston upon Hull HU10 .69 C8
 Market Weighton YO43 . .135 C4
Manor Garth
 Barmby Moor YO42 . . . . .28 D3
 Haxby YO32 . . . . .127 B8
 Kellington DN14 . . . . . . .61 F3
 Keyingham HU12 . . . . . .73 C4
 7 Norton DN6 . . . . .76 F2
 1 Riccall YO19 . . . . .49 A8
 Skidby HU16 . . . . .55 C4
Manor Gdns
 8 Hatfield DN7 . . . . .92 E4
 Hunmanby YO14 . . . . . . .3 A7
Manor Heath YO23 . . . . .132 A3
Manor House St HU1 . . .155 A1
Manor La
 Barrow upon Humber
 DN19 . . . . .85 D8
 Goxhill DN19 . . . . .85 F8
 Hollym HU19 . . . . .75 A4
 Rawcliffe YO30 . . . . . . .126 D2
Manor Mid Sch DN7 . . . .92 E4
Manor Park Cl YO30 . . . .126 E2
Manor Park Gr YO30 . . . .126 E2
Manor Park Rd YO30 . . . .126 E2
Manor Pk
 Beverley HU17 . . . . . . .154 A4
 Preston HU12 . . . . .58 D1
 Seaton HU11 . . . . .35 A1
Manor Rd Beal DN14 . . . .61 C4
 Beverley HU17 . . . . . . .154 A3
 Crowle DN17 . . . . .94 D7
 Goole DN14 . . . . .149 C1
 Hatfield DN7 . . . . .92 E4
 Kingston upon Hull HU5 .144 B8
 9 North Cave HU15 . . . .53 D5
 Northorpe DN21 . . . . . .118 D3
 Preston HU12 . . . . .58 C1
 Reedness DN14 . . . . . . .65 F3
 Scunthorpe DN16 . . . . . .96 D2
 South Cliffe YO43 . . . . . .53 B7
 Swanland HU14 . . . . . . .69 B6
 Thorngumbald HU12 . . . .72 F5
 Twin Rivers DN14 . . . . . .81 E7
Manor St
 6 Bridlington YO15 . . . .122 E2
 6 Keelby DN41 . . . . . . .101 A5
 Kingston upon Hull HU1 .155 B1
Manor Way
 Kingston upon Hull
 HU10 . . . . .143 F6
 York YO26 . . . . .126 E2
Manorfield Ave YO25 . . .124 F5
Manorfield Rd YO25 . . . .124 F4
Manorhouse La HU17 . . .55 B8
Mansel St DN32 . . . . . . .153 B4
Mansfield Pk HU5 . . . . . .140 B3
Mansfield Rd DN15 . . . . .150 B6
Mansfield St YO31 . . . . .156 C3
Mansgate Hill LN7 . . . . .111 B3
Mansion Court Gdns
 DN8 . . . . .93 A8
Manson Cl 13 DN9 . . . . .102 B2
Manston Garth 4 HU7 . . .57 B5
Manton Ct DN20 . . . . . . .108 F6
Manton La DN20 . . . . . . .108 F6
Manton Rd DN21 . . . . . .108 A4
Manuel St DN14 . . . . . . .149 B4
Manvers St HU5 . . . . . . .140 C3
Maple Ave
 Bishopthorpe YO23 . . . .133 A3
 Crowle DN17 . . . . .94 D7
 Flixborough DN15 . . . . . .96 B7
 Grimsby DN34 . . . . .102 C4
 Keelby DN41 . . . . .101 A4
 Kingston upon Hull
 HU16 . . . . .143 F8
Maple Cl
 2 Bridlington YO16 . . . .123 A6
 Brigg DN20 . . . . .98 D2
 Gainsborough DN21 . . . .117 A2
 Hambleton YO8 . . . . . . .48 B1
 12 Keelby DN41 . . . . . .101 A5
 5 Kingston upon Hull
 HU4 . . . . .144 C7
 Messingham DN17 . . . . .107 D6
Maple Ct YO10 . . . . .133 E6
Maple Dr
 Beverley HU17 . . . . . . .136 F6
 Goole DN14 . . . . .149 F5
Maple Gr 12 Brayton YO8 .48 D1
 8 Healing DN41 . . . . . .101 F5
 3 Immingham DN40 . . . .87 C2
 7 New Waltham DN36 . .113 F4
 York YO10 . . . . .130 D1
Maple Pk HU12 . . . . .72 D8

Lun - Mar 179

Maple Rd
 Bridlington YO16 . . . . . .123 A6
 1 Thorne/Moorends DN8 .79 B1
Maple St HU5 . . . . .140 D2
Maple Tree Ave YO8 . . . . .48 D1
Maple Tree Cl E DN16 . . .151 A5
Maple Tree Cl W
 DN16 . . . . .151 A5
Maple Tree Way DN16 . . .151 A5
Maple Wlk 8 YO25 . . . . . .34 B2
Mapleleaf Ct 9 HU16 . . .138 F5
Maplewood Ave HU4 . . .144 B7
Maplewood Paddock 2
 YO24 . . . . .129 C1
Mappleton Gr HU9 . . . . .142 A2
Mappleton Rd HU11 . . . . .46 D6
March St
 6 Kirton in Lindsey DN21 108 B1
 York YO31 . . . . .156 C4
Marchant Cl HU17 . . . . .136 D7
Marcus St Goole DN14 . .149 B4
 Grimsby DN34 . . . . .152 A2
Marfleet Ave HU9 . . . . . .147 B7
Marfleet Cnr DN36 . . . . .114 B1
Marfleet La HU9 . . . . . . .142 B3
Marfleet Prim Sch
 HU9 . . . . .147 C8
Margaret Ave DN17 . . . . .95 D5
Margaret Gr 1 HU13 . . .143 F1
Margaret Pl 18 DN36 . . .114 A7
Margaret St
 Grimsby DN32 . . . . .152 F3
 Immingham DN40 . . . . .101 C8
 York YO10 . . . . .156 C1
Margrave La
 Garthorpe & Fockerby
 DN17 . . . . .81 E5
 Reedness DN14 . . . . . . .80 E7
Marian Way DN37 . . . . .113 C6
Marigold Cl YO8 . . . . . . .148 C2
Marigold Wlk 22 DN35 . .103 C1
Marina Ave 3 DN14 . . . . .63 B1
Marina View 6 DN8 . . . . .93 A7
Marine Ave HU14 . . . . . .69 A4
Marine Dr HU18 . . . . . . .134 D5
Marine Valley 2 YO15 . . . .5 B3
Marine Wharf HU1 . . . . .155 B1
Mariners Arms Flats
 DN17 . . . . .95 D6
Mariners Cl HU9 . . . . . . .146 C6
Mariners St 9 DN14 . . . .149 C4
Mark Rise DN21 . . . . . . .117 F5
Market Ct 5 DN17 . . . . . .94 D7
Market Hall Sh Ctr
 DN31 . . . . .152 D3
Market La
 12 Barton-upon-Humber
 DN18 . . . . .84 F8
 6 Brigg DN20 . . . . .98 B2
 Selby YO8 . . . . .148 C5
Market Pl
 11 Barton-upon-Humber
 DN18 . . . . .84 F8
 Bridlington YO16 . . . . . .122 C5
 9 Brigg DN20 . . . . .98 B2
 11 Caistor LN7 . . . . . . .111 B4
 2 Cawood YO8 . . . . .48 B8
 5 Epworth DN9 . . . . . . .105 E6
 Great Driffield YO25 . . . .124 E4
 31 Hedon HU12 . . . . . . .72 C7
 Hornsea HU18 . . . . .134 B4
 Kingston upon Hull HU1 .155 C1
 Market Weighton YO43 . .135 D4
 Owston Ferry DN9 . . . . .106 B2
 Patrington HU12 . . . . . . .74 D1
 Pocklington YO42 . . . . . .29 A3
 11 Selby YO8 . . . . .148 C5
 9 Snaith DN14 . . . . .63 C1
 South Cave HU15 . . . . . .54 A2
Market St
 Cleethorpes DN35 . . . . .153 F2
 9 Pocklington YO42 . . . .29 A4
 14 Winterton DN15 . . . . .83 A5
 York YO1 . . . . .156 B2
Market Weighton Inf Sch
 YO43 . . . . .135 D3
Market Weighton Rd
 Barlby with Osgodby YO8 .49 B6
 Holme-on-Spalding-Moor
 YO43 . . . . .40 B2
 Market Weighton YO43 . .135 A2
 Sancton YO43 . . . . .41 D3
Market Weighton Sch Adult
 Ed & Sports Ctr
 YO43 . . . . .135 F4
Marketbridge La YO43 . . .39 E7
Markham Cres YO31 . . . .156 B4
Markham Mews DN37 . . .113 C6
Markham St YO31 . . . . . .156 B4
Markham Way DN20 . . . . .98 E4
Markhams Orch DN33 . . .113 E8
Marklew Ave DN34 . . . . .152 B3
Markman La YO25 . . . . . .125 D5
Marlborough Ave
 Goole DN14 . . . . .149 C5
 2 Haxey DN9 . . . . .105 D2
 Hornsea HU18 . . . . .134 C1
 Kingston upon Hull
 HU13 . . . . .143 D2
 Kingston upon Hull HU5 .145 A8
Marlborough Cl YO30 . . .126 D3
Marlborough Dr DN15 . . .151 B4
Marlborough Gr YO10 . . .130 D2
Marlborough Rd 9 DN8 . .93 B7

Marlborough Terr
8 Bridlington YO15 . . . .**122** F2
Kingston upon Hull HU2 . . . .**155** A3
Marlborough Way
DN35 . . . .**103** C1
Marlow Rd DN21 . . . . . .**117** C1
Marlowe Rd DN17 . . . . . .**150** D3
Marlowe St HU8 . . . .**141** C2
Marmaduke St 3 HU3 . .**145** C4
Marmiam Dr 2 YO32 . . . . . .**14** D2
Marmion Dr DN15 . . . .**83** A5
Marmion Rd DN16 . . . . . .**151** C3
Marne St HU5 . . . .**145** A8
Marquis Ave DN36 . . . . . .**114** A8
Marr La HU15 . . . .**66** F7
Marris Dr DN15 . . . .**83** B5
Marritt Way 9 HU12 . . . . .**73** C4
Marsdale HU7 . . . .**140** F7
Marsden Dr DN15 . . . .**150** D8
Marsden Gr 3 DN8 . . . . . .**93** A8
Marsh Dr HU17 . . . .**154** A1
Marsh End
17 Howden DN14 . . . .**65** A4
Knottingley WF11 . . . .**61** A4
Marsh Hill La DN14 . . . . . .**78** C4
Marsh La Asselby DN14 . . . .**64** D7
Barlow YO8 . . . .**63** B8
Barnetby le Wold DN38 . . . . . .**99** B4
Barrow upon Humber
DN19 . . . .**70** C2
Barton-upon-Humber
DN18 . . . .**69** F1
2 Beal DN14 . . . .**61** D4
Cawood YO8 . . . .**48** B3
Keyingham HU12 . . . .**73** B3
Knottingley WF11 . . . .**61** A2
Misterton DN10 . . . .**116** D5
New Holland DN19 . . . .**70** E2
Ryehill HU12 . . . .**73** A4
South Killingholme DN40 . . . . .**87** B4
Thorne DN8 . . . .**79** A2
Thorngumbald HU12 . . . .**73** A4
West Haddlesey YO8 . . . .**61** F5
Winteringham DN15 . . . .**68** A1
Marsh Lane Gdns DN14 . . .**61** F4
Marsh Rd Crowle DN17 . . . .**94** B7
Easington HU12 . . . .**90** E5
Keyingham HU12 . . . .**73** A2
Ottringham HU12 . . . .**88** C8
Walkeringham DN10 . . . .**116** E3
Marsh Way DN36 . . . .**115** C5
Marshall Ave
Bridlington YO15 . . . .**122** E2
Grimsby DN34 . . . .**152** B3
Kingston upon Hull
HU10 . . . .**143** A8
Preston HU12 . . . .**72** C8
Marshall Hill YO25 . . . .**19** D2
Marshall St HU5 . . . .**140** C2
Marshchapel Cl 20
DN35 . . . .**103** C2
**Marshchapel County Prim
Sch** DN36 . . . .**115** B2
Marshfield Ave DN14 . . . .**149** E4
Marshfield Rd
Goole DN14 . . . .**149** E4
Scunthorpe DN16 . . . .**151** C1
Marshland Rd
Thorne DN8 . . . .**79** B2
Thorne/Moorends DN8 . . . .**79** B1
Marshlands Prim Sch
DN14 . . . .**149** D1
Marske Wlk 1 HU5 . . . . . .**139** D4
Marston Ave YO26 . . . . . .**129** B3
Marston Cres YO26 . . . . . .**129** B3
Marten Cl 2 YO30 . . . . . .**130** A8
Marston La
Long Marston YO26 . . . .**24** A8
Moor Monkton YO26 . . . .**12** A1
Martin Cheeseman Ct 3
YO24 . . . .**132** C8
Martin Cl HU9 . . . .**142** B3
Martin La YO42 . . . .**29** C6
Martin St HU17 . . . .**137** B3
Martin Way
7 New Waltham DN36 . . . . . .**113** F8
4 New Waltham DN36 . . . .**114** A7
Martin's Cl DN19 . . . .**85** D8
Martins Rd DN39 . . . .**86** B1
Marton Ave YO16 . . . .**122** E5
Marton Ct 6 YO16 . . . .**123** A7
Marton Dr DN7 . . . .**92** D4
Marton Gate YO16 . . . . . .**123** A7
Marton Gr
8 Grimsby DN33 . . . .**102** D2
Kingston upon Hull HU6 . . . . .**139** F5
Marton La YO25 . . . .**9** F6
Marton Rd
Bridlington YO16 . . . .**122** D5
Ellerby HU11 . . . .**46** B1
Marton View YO15 . . . . . .**123** B8
Martongate Cty Prim Sch
YO16 . . . .**122** F6
Martyn Rd DN32 . . . .**153** D2
Marvel St HU9 . . . .**146** B7
Marvelgarth La HU11 . . . . .**35** A2
Mary St DN15 . . . .**151** A7
Mary Sumner Way
DN15 . . . .**150** E8
Marydene Dr HU6 . . . .**140** C5
Marygate YO30 . . . .**156** A3
Marygate La YO30 . . . . . .**156** A3

Marylebone Wlk 3
DN33 . . . .**102** D1
Mascotte Gdns HU18 . . . .**134** D3
Mask La YO41 . . . .**27** D4
Mason Dr DN17 . . . .**96** C2
Mason St HU2 . . . .**155** B3
Masons Ct 6 DN18 . . . .**84** E8
Maspin Cl 19 HU7 . . . .**56** F5
Maspin Moor Rd LS25 . . . . .**61** C7
Massey Cl
8 Epworth DN9 . . . .**105** D6
Kingston upon Hull HU3 . . . . .**145** A5
Massey St
Kingston upon Hull HU3 . . . . .**145** A4
Selby YO8 . . . .**148** C5
Mast Dr HU9 . . . .**146** C6
Mathews St DN35 . . . .**153** C3
Matlock Dr DN37 . . . .**102** C4
Matson Cl YO16 . . . .**122** C4
Matson Rd DN14 . . . .**149** B1
Matthew Humberstone Sch
DN35 . . . .**103** B2
Mattison Way YO24 . . . . . .**129** E2
Mattocks La HU12 . . . .**72** D8
Matty La 10 YO43 . . . .**53** F7
Maude Cl 10 HU12 . . . .**73** C4
Maulson Dr HU14 . . . .**58** A3
Maurice Ave HU8 . . . .**141** A2
Mavis Rd DN17 . . . .**150** E2
Mawson Gn La DN14 . . . . . .**78** C3
Maxwell Ct 9 DN34 . . . . . .**102** B3
Maxwell Rd YO42 . . . .**29** A4
Maxwell St HU8 . . . .**141** A2
May Gr HU13 . . . .**143** D2
May St
Cleethorpes DN35 . . . .**153** D4
Kingston upon Hull HU5 . . . . .**140** D3
May Tree Ave HU8 . . . .**141** C2
Maybury Prim Sch
HU9 . . . .**142** B3
Maybury Rd HU9 . . . .**141** F3
Mayfair Cres 18 DN37 . . . .**113** D6
Mayfair Ct 3 DN35 . . . . . .**103** D1
Mayfair Dr W DN37 . . . . . .**102** B4
Mayfield DN14 . . . .**149** E6
Mayfield Ave
2 Gainsborough DN21 . . . . .**117** B2
South Killingholme DN40 . . . . .**86** F2
Stainforth DN7 . . . .**92** D7
Mayfield Cl DN33 . . . .**113** D8
Mayfield Dr 5 YO8 . . . . . .**148** A1
Mayfield Gr YO24 . . . .**132** E8
Mayfield Rd
Brayton YO8 . . . .**148** A1
Bridlington YO15 . . . .**122** D1
Mayfield St HU3 . . . .**145** C8
Mayflower Ave 6 DN40 . . . .**87** C1
Mayflower Cl 2 DN40 . . . . .**86** E3
Mayland Ave HU5 . . . .**144** A8
Mayland Dr HU16 . . . .**138** E6
Maypole Gdns YO8 . . . .**48** B8
Maypole Gr 3 YO19 . . . . . .**36** D8
Maypole St DN21 . . . .**119** A2
Maysfield Ct DN20 . . . .**109** A5
Maythorn Rd YO31 . . . .**127** C4
Maythorpe YO23 . . . .**24** C6
Maythorpe Cl HU3 . . . .**145** A7
Mayville Ave HU8 . . . .**141** B3
McGrath Cl 25 YO42 . . . . . .**29** A4
McShane Ct 11 YO42 . . . . . .**29** A3
McVeigh Ct 10 DN41 . . . . .**101** F5
Mead Cl HU8 . . . .**141** D5
Mead The 7 DN37 . . . .**101** F1
Mead Wlk HU4 . . . .**144** C6
Meadlands YO31 . . . .**131** B6
Meadley Ct HU17 . . . .**137** C4
Meadow Ave DN39 . . . .**86** A2
Meadow Bank 2 HU17 . . . .**136** F7
Meadow Cl
5 Beeford YO25 . . . .**22** D1
Thorpe Willoughby YO8 . . . . . .**48** C2
**Meadow Court Greyhound
Stadium** DN7 . . . .**92** C5
Meadow Croft
Brayton YO8 . . . .**148** A2
16 Kirk Sandall DN3 . . . .**92** A2
Waltham DN37 . . . .**113** D7
Meadow Ct
Grimsby DN37 . . . .**102** C4
Hibaldstow DN20 . . . .**108** F5
3 York YO24 . . . .**132** E8
Meadow Dr
Barton-upon-Humber
DN18 . . . .**84** F8
Grimsby DN33 . . . .**113** D8
Healing DN41 . . . .**102** A5
Market Weighton YO43 . . . . . .**135** E4
Misterton DN10 . . . .**116** C5
Thorpe Willoughby YO8 . . . . . .**48** B2
Meadow Field YO43 . . . . . .**40** A1
Meadow Garth
Kingston upon Hull HU6 . . . . . .**56** D5
Thorpe Willoughby YO8 . . . . . .**48** C2
Meadow La
Driffield YO25 . . . .**125** B4
1 Haxby YO32 . . . .**127** D8
9 Newport HU15 . . . .**52** F1
Meadow Pl 5 YO8 . . . .**148** B6
Meadow Rd
Bridlington YO16 . . . .**122** B2
Great Driffield YO25 . . . .**125** A4
Scunthorpe DN17 . . . .**150** C2
Meadow Rise
Barnby Dun DN3 . . . .**92** A3
Blyton DN21 . . . .**117** F6
Meadow The LN7 . . . .**111** B3
Meadow Vale DN20 . . . . . .**108** F8

Meadow View
Bainton YO25 . . . .**31** E7
Bridlington YO16 . . . .**122** E7
28 Humberston DN35 . . . . . .**103** C1
Meadow Way
Kingston upon Hull
HU16 . . . .**138** F5
3 Walkington HU17 . . . .**55** C8
York YO32 . . . .**127** F4
York YO31 . . . .**130** F7
Meadow Wlk 6 HU14 . . . . . .**69** B7
Meadowbank
4 Belton DN9 . . . .**94** E1
Grimsby DN37 . . . .**102** E2
Meadowbank Rd HU3 . . . .**144** E7
Meadowbeck Cl YO10 . . . .**131** B4
Meadowcroft Rd
YO25 . . . .**125** A6
Meadowfield
Barnby Dun DN3 . . . .**92** A3
1 Bubwith YO8 . . . .**50** D7
Meadowfield Cl 6 YO42 . . .**28** A4
Meadowfield Rd YO15 . . . .**122** D1
Meadowfields Dr
YO31 . . . .**127** D2
Meadows The
Beverley HU17 . . . .**137** B2
4 Buckton/Bempton YO15 . . . .**4** C3
Burringham DN17 . . . .**95** D4
Carlton DN14 . . . .**63** C3
Cherry Burton HU17 . . . .**43** A4
Dunswell HU6 . . . .**56** D5
Great Driffield YO25 . . . .**125** A4
Howden DN14 . . . .**65** A6
Kingston upon Hull HU10 . . . . .**69** C8
Kingston upon Hull HU7 . . . . .**140** E7
Leven HU17 . . . .**45** A8
Messingham DN17 . . . .**107** D7
7 Monk Fryston LS25 . . . .**61** A8
Riccall YO19 . . . .**48** F8
2 Skelton YO30 . . . .**126** B5
13 South Cave HU15 . . . .**53** F1
5 Westwoodside DN9 . . . . .**105** A2
Meadway YO8 . . . .**48** C2
Meadway Dr YO8 . . . .**48** D2
Measham Dr DN7 . . . .**92** D7
Meaux Abbey (Site of) ★
HU17 . . . .**44** F2
Meaux La HU17 . . . .**44** F4
Meaux Rd HU7 . . . .**56** F8
Mechanic La 9 HU3 . . . . . .**145** D5
Medforth Rd YO16 . . . .**122** C4
Medina Ave YO16 . . . .**122** D3
Medina Rd HU8 . . . .**142** C5
Medium Section Rd
DN16 . . . .**97** A4
Medlar Dr 2 HU15 . . . .**68** D5
Medway Pl DN34 . . . .**152** A1
Meggison's Turnpike
YO25 . . . .**32** F7
Meggitt La DN15 . . . .**68** A1
Megson Way HU17 . . . .**55** D8
Melander Cl YO26 . . . .**129** B4
Melander Gdns 5 YO32 . .**127** D7
Melbourne Ave
Bridlington YO16 . . . .**122** D3
18 Grimsby DN33 . . . .**102** E2
Melbourne CP Sch
YO42 . . . .**39** A7
Melbourne Pk YO42 . . . .**39** A6
Melbourne Sq HU17 . . . .**43** D6
Melbourne St
4 Kingston upon Hull
HU5 . . . .**140** C3
York YO10 . . . .**130** D2
Melcombe Ave 11 YO42 . . . .**14** A7
Mellwood View DN9 . . . . . .**106** A3
Melrose Cl 1 YO31 . . . . . .**131** A5
Melrose Pk HU17 . . . .**154** A2
Melrose Rd 5 DN21 . . . . . .**117** B1
Melrose St HU3 . . . .**144** F6
Melrosegate YO31 . . . .**130** F5
Melton Ave YO30 . . . .**129** F8
Melton Bottom HU14 . . . . . .**68** E5
Melton Dr
Bishopthorpe YO23 . . . .**133** A3
York YO30 . . . .**129** F8
Melton Fields HU14 . . . .**68** F5
Melton Gallows DN38 . . . . . .**99** A5
Melton Old Rd HU14 . . . . . .**68** E5
Melton Rd
North Ferriby HU14 . . . .**69** A5
Wrawby DN20 . . . .**98** F4
Meltonby Ave HU5 . . . .**139** C2
Meltonby La YO42 . . . .**28** E6
Melville St HU12 . . . .**73** C4
Melville St HU1 . . . .**155** A1
Melwood Cl DN9 . . . .**105** F6
Melwood Dr
Kingston upon Hull HU5 . . . . .**140** D2
York YO26 . . . .**129** B5
Melwood Hill DN9 . . . .**105** F6
Melwood View DN9 . . . . . .**105** F6
Memorial Ave 14 HU19 . . . . .**75** A6
Menasha Way DN16 . . . . . .**151** E3
Mendip Ave
Goole DN14 . . . .**149** D5
Grimsby DN33 . . . .**113** E8
Mendip Cl 2 YO32 . . . .**127** D5
Mendip Rd DN17 . . . .**150** D4
Menson Dr DN7 . . . .**92** D4
Mercer Rd 1 DN21 . . . .**117** A1
Merchant Adventurers Hall ★
YO1 . . . .**156** C2
Merchant Taylors Hall ★
YO31 . . . .**156** C3
Merchant Way YO23 . . . . . .**132** B3
Merchantgate YO1 . . . .**156** C2

Mere Cres DN16 . . . .**151** D3
Mere La
Dalton Holme HU17 . . . .**42** F8
Edenthorpe DN3 . . . .**92** A1
Winterton DN15 . . . .**83** A7
Mere View Ave HU18 . . . . .**134** B2
Mere Way HU14 . . . .**69** B7
Mere Wlk 6 HU18 . . . .**134** C4
Meredith Ave DN17 . . . . . .**150** C2
Meredyke Rd DN17 . . . .**81** D3
Mereside 9 YO15 . . . .**5** A2
Mereside Terr HU18 . . . . . .**134** B4
Meridian Point ★
DN35 . . . .**103** D2
Merlin Cl HU7 . . . .**141** D7
Merlin Covert 4 YO31 . . . .**127** F3
Merlin Dr DN20 . . . .**99** A8
Merlin Rd DN17 . . . .**150** D2
Merrick St HU9 . . . .**146** B7
Merryman Garth HU12 . . . . .**72** C7
Merryweather Ct 14
HU16 . . . .**96** D1
Mersey Prim Sch HU8 . . . .**141** C1
Mersey St HU8 . . . .**141** C1
Merton Gr 5 HU9 . . . .**141** F1
Merton Rd DN16 . . . .**96** D2
Messingham Cty Prim Sch
DN17 . . . .**107** D7
Messingham Cty Sch
DN17 . . . .**107** D7
Messingham La DN20 . . . .**108** C7
Messingham Rd
East Butterwick DN17 . . . .**106** D8
Scotter DN21 . . . .**107** C4
16 Scunthorpe DN17 . . . .**96** C2
Scunthorpe DN16 . . . .**151** A1
Metcalfe La YO19 . . . .**131** C5
Metham La DN14 . . . .**65** F4
Mews The HU3 . . . .**145** C4
Meynell St DN17 . . . .**117** A8
Micklegate 1 Selby YO8 . .**148** D5
York YO1 . . . .**156** A2
Micklegate Bar Mus ★
YO24 . . . .**156** A1
Micklethwaite Gr 2 DN8 . . .**79** B3
Micklethwaite Rd 1 DN8 . . .**79** B3
Mickley Gr HU9 . . . .**142** C2
Middle Banks 24 YO32 . . . . .**13** C5
Middle Barn Hill DN20 . . . .**84** D1
Middle Cl DN31 . . . .**152** E4
Middle Dike La HU16 . . . . .**139** D7
Middle Garth Dr HU15 . . . . .**54** A2
Middle La Amcotts DN17 . . . .**95** D4
Brayton YO8 . . . .**148** C1
14 Knottingley WF11 . . . .**61** A2
Preston HU12 . . . .**58** B1
5 Seaton HU11 . . . .**35** A1
Middle St
Corringham DN21 . . . .**118** B2
Foggathorpe YO42 . . . .**39** A2
Kilham YO25 . . . .**9** B3
Nafferton YO25 . . . .**125** F7
North Kelsey LN7 . . . .**110** A4
Rudston YO25 . . . .**9** F6
Scotton DN21 . . . .**107** C1
Wilberfoss YO41 . . . .**27** F5
Willoughton DN21 . . . .**119** B3
Middle St N YO25 . . . .**124** E4
Middle St S YO25 . . . .**124** F3
Middle Thorpe Rd
DN35 . . . .**103** B2
Middlebrook Gdns
YO8 . . . .**148** A2
Middlebrook La 28 DN8 . . . .**93** A8
Middleburg St HU9 . . . . . .**146** B8
Middlecroft Dr YO32 . . . . . .**14** A7
Middlecroft Gr 2 YO32 . . . .**14** B7
Middlefield La WF8 . . . .**76** A2
Middlegate Cl 9 DN19 . . . . .**85** C8
Middlegate La
Saxby All Saints DN20 . . . .**84** B4
South Ferriby DN18 . . . .**84** B7
Middleham Ave YO31 . . . . .**130** E8
Middleham Cl 3 HU9 . . . . .**146** E8
Middlehowe Gn 2 HU17 . . . .**55** B8
Middlehowe Rd HU17 . . . . . .**55** A8
Middlemarsh Cl 3 HU8 . . .**141** B4
Middleplatt Rd DN40 . . . . . .**87** D2
Middlesex Rd HU8 . . . .**141** F5
Middlethorpe Cty Prim Sch
DN35 . . . .**103** B2
Middlethorpe Dr
YO24 . . . .**132** E7
Middlethorpe Gr YO24 . . . .**132** F7
Middleton Hall HU6 . . . . . .**140** B4
Middleton Cl
Beverley HU17 . . . .**154** C4
Messingham DN17 . . . .**107** D7
Middleton St HU3 . . . .**145** B8
Middleton Rd
Bainton YO25 . . . .**31** D5
Scunthorpe DN16 . . . .**96** D2
York YO24 . . . .**129** C2
Middleton St HU3 . . . .**145** C4
**Middleton-on-the-Wolds C
of E Sch** YO25 . . . .**31** C4
Middlewood Cl YO23 . . . . . .**24** C6
Midfield Pl DN36 . . . .**114** D8
Midfield Rd DN36 . . . .**114** D8
Midfield Way 1 DN41 . . . . .**101** A4
Midgley Cl
Kingston upon Hull HU3 . . . . .**145** C5
21 Stamford Bridge YO41 . . . .**15** D2
Midland Rd DN16 . . . .**151** D5
Midland St HU1 . . . .**155** A2
Midmere Ave HU7 . . . .**141** B7
Midmere Prim Sch
HU7 . . . .**141** C6

Midway Ave
Bridlington YO16 . . . .**122** D2
Poppleton YO26 . . . .**126** A1
Midway Gr HU4 . . . .**144** E4
Milcroft Cres 13 DN7 . . . . . .**92** D4
Mildred Gr 5 YO24 . . . .**129** F2
Mile End Ave DN7 . . . .**92** D3
Mile End Pk YO42 . . . .**29** A4
Mile The YO42 . . . .**29** A4
Miles La HU17 . . . .**43** C6
Milestone Ave YO23 . . . . . .**24** C6
Milford Ave YO16 . . . .**122** C5
Milford Cres 5 YO16 . . . . .**122** C5
Milford Gr HU9 . . . .**142** E1
Milford Mews 7 YO32 . . . .**127** D7
Milford Way 8 YO32 . . . . .**127** D7
Mill Ave DN31 . . . .**152** C4
Mill Balk DN14 . . . .**77** C8
Mill Balk Pl DN14 . . . .**78** B8
Mill Baulk Rd DN10 . . . . . .**116** C3
Mill Beck La HU16 . . . .**139** B8
Mill Cl Bridlington YO16 . . . .**122** C5
16 Broughton DN20 . . . .**98** B2
Great Driffield YO25 . . . .**124** D4
Marshchapel DN36 . . . .**115** C2
Monk Fryston LS25 . . . .**61** A8
7 Waltham DN37 . . . .**113** E6
Mill Cres 11 DN21 . . . .**107** C3
Mill Croft Scawby DN20 . . . .**108** F8
11 Scunthorpe DN16 . . . .**96** E2
Scunthorpe DN16 . . . .**151** D3
Mill Ct 10 YO16 . . . .**122** C5
Mill Dr HU17 . . . .**45** A8
Mill Falls YO25 . . . .**124** D4
Mill Field Rd
Chapel Haddlesey YO8 . . . .**62** B5
Fishlake DN7 . . . .**92** C8
Scunthorpe DN16 . . . .**151** E7
Mill Garth
12 Cleethorpes DN35 . . . . . .**103** B2
14 Hemingbrough YO8 . . . . . .**49** F1
Mill Gate YO16 . . . .**122** C5
Mill Hill Ellerker HU15 . . . . .**68** A8
Escrick YO19 . . . .**37** B5
Mill Hill Cres DN35 . . . . . .**153** E1
Mill Hill Dr
6 Scunthorpe DN16 . . . .**96** E2
York YO32 . . . .**127** F4
Mill Hill Rd DN7 . . . .**92** E3
Mill House La DN15 . . . .**83** B5
Mill House Way HU11 . . . . . .**45** D2
Mill La
Acaster Malbis YO23 . . . .**36** A3
Askham Richard YO23 . . . .**24** C2
Barlow YO8 . . . .**63** B7
Barrow upon Humber
DN19 . . . .**85** C8
Beverley HU17 . . . .**154** B4
Bielby YO42 . . . .**39** E6
Bishop Burton HU17 . . . .**43** B2
Brandesburton YO25 . . . .**34** B2
Brayton YO8 . . . .**62** C8
Bridlington YO16 . . . .**122** C5
Brigg DN20 . . . .**98** B1
Brough HU15 . . . .**68** C6
Broughton DN20 . . . .**97** E3
Caistor LN7 . . . .**111** C4
Carlton DN14 . . . .**63** D3
East Halton DN40 . . . .**86** D6
Eastrington DN14 . . . .**52** A1
Elstronwick HU12 . . . .**58** F3
Foston YO25 . . . .**21** F1
Gainsborough DN21 . . . .**117** A2
Gilberdyke HU15 . . . .**52** D1
Gilberdyke DN14 . . . .**66** B7
Goxhill DN19 . . . .**71** A1
Harpham YO25 . . . .**21** E7
Haxby YO32 . . . .**13** D5
Haxey DN9 . . . .**105** B2
Hayton YO42 . . . .**29** D1
2 Hemingbrough YO8 . . . .**49** F1
Hessay YO26 . . . .**24** B7
Holton le Clay DN36 . . . .**114** B4
Hornsea HU18 . . . .**134** B4
Huggate YO42 . . . .**18** B1
Immingham DN40 . . . .**87** A1
14 Keelby DN41 . . . .**101** A4
Kilpin DN14 . . . .**65** C3
Kingston upon Hull
HU16 . . . .**138** E7
Kingston upon Hull
HU10 . . . .**143** C6
Kirton in Lindsey DN21 . . . . . .**108** C1
Langtoft YO25 . . . .**8** C7
Laxton DN14 . . . .**65** F3
Marshchapel DN36 . . . .**115** C2
Newbald YO43 . . . .**53** E6
Newland YO8 . . . .**64** A3
Newport HU15 . . . .**52** E1
3 North Cave HU15 . . . .**53** D3
North Dalton YO25 . . . .**31** C7
North Kelsey LN7 . . . .**110** A4
Rawcliffe DN14 . . . .**63** F1
1 Riccall YO19 . . . .**37** A1
Rise HU11 . . . .**45** E6
Scawby DN20 . . . .**108** F8
Seaton HU11 . . . .**35** A2
Seaton Ross YO42 . . . .**39** D4
Skipsea YO25 . . . .**23** B2
Sledmere YO25 . . . .**6** F3
Snaith & Cowick DN14 . . . .**78** C8
South Ferriby DN18 . . . .**84** A7
Walkeringham DN10 . . . .**116** C3
Warter YO42 . . . .**30** A4
Watton YO25 . . . .**32** D4
Welwick HU12 . . . .**90** A7
Wilberfoss YO41 . . . .**27** E6

Mill La continued
Wrawby DN20 . . . .**98** E3
York YO31 . . . .**130** E6
Mill La W HU15 . . . .**68** B6
Mill Mere Rd DN21 . . . .**118** A2
Mill Mount YO24 . . . .**130** A3
Mill Mount Ct YO24 . . . . . .**130** A3
Mill Pl DN35 . . . .**153** F2
Mill Race DN36 . . . .**114** E4
Mill Rd Aldbrough HU11 . . .**47** C2
Burton Constable HU11 . . .**58** D7
Burton Fleming YO25 . . . . . .**2** D4
Cleethorpes DN35 . . . . . .**153** E1
Crowle DN17 . . . .**94** D8
Hibaldstow DN20 . . . .**108** E4
Keadby DN17 . . . .**95** D5
Keyingham HU12 . . . .**73** C4
Luddington & Haldenby
    DN17 . . . .**81** C4
Skidby HU16 . . . .**138** C7
Sproatley HU11 . . . .**58** D5
Swanland HU14 . . . .**69** A6
Mill Rise
Great Driffield YO25 . . .**124** D4
Skidby HU16 . . . .**138** B8
Swanland HU14 . . . .**69** A6
Mill Side YO25 . . . .**9** C3
Mill Side Cl YO25 . . . .**9** C3
Mill St
Great Driffield YO25 . . .**124** E4
Hutton Cranswick YO25 . . .**32** E8
Kingston upon Hull HU1 . .**155** A2
York YO1 . . . .**156** C1
Mill View DN37 . . . .**113** D6
Mill View Rd HU17 . . . . . .**137** B3
Mill Wlk YO16 . . . .**139** C5
Millard Ave DN7 . . . .**92** D4
Millard Nook 18 DN7 . . . . .**92** D4
Millbank 11 YO16 . . . .**122** C5
Millbank St DN14 . . . .**149** F5
Millbeck Bank HU15 . . . . . .**67** E4
Millbeck Cl YO43 . . . .**135** D5
Millbrook Way 23 DN18 . . .**84** E8
Millennium Way DN14 . . . .**149** F5
Miller Ave DN32 . . . .**153** C2
Miller Cl
Barmby Moor YO42 . . . . .**28** F4
10 Thorne/Moorends DN8 . .**93** B7
Miller La
Thorne/Moorends DN8 . . . .**93** B7
Yapham YO42 . . . .**29** A6
Millers Rd DN21 . . . .**117** D1
Millers Croft 6 YO23 . . . .**132** A3
Millers Quay 15 DN8 . . . . .**98** B2
Miller's Wlk HU5 . . . .**139** F2
Millfield Ave
16 Grimsby DN33 . . . . . .**102** E2
York YO10 . . . .**130** F3
Millfield Cl YO41 . . . .**27** E5
Millfield Dr YO8 . . . .**63** D4
Millfield Garth YO25 . . . . . .**31** C4
Millfield Gdns YO26 . . . . .**126** A2
Millfield La
Nether Poppleton YO26 . . .**129** B8
Poppleton YO26 . . . .**126** A2
York YO10 . . . .**131** A3
Millfield Rd
4 Bridlington YO16 . . . .**122** C5
17 Hemingbrough YO8 . . . .**49** F1
Hemingbrough YO8 . . . . . .**63** F8
Thorne/Moorends DN8 . . . .**93** B7
York YO23 . . . .**130** B2
Millfield The DN20 . . . . . .**109** A6
Millfields
Barton-upon-Humber
    DN18 . . . .**84** E8
23 Caistor LN7 . . . .**111** B4
Millfields Way 7 DN18 . . . .**85** C2
Millgate YO8 . . . .**148** C6
Millgates YO26 . . . .**129** C6
Millhill Rd DN14 . . . .**149** E5
Millhouse La DN14 . . . . . .**149** F5
Millhouse Street Rise 3
    DN40 . . . .**87** B1
Millhouse Woods La
    HU16 . . . .**139** B8
Millington Woods Nature
    Reserve★ YO42 . . . .**29** D8
Millom Way DN32 . . . . . .**152** F4
Millport Dr HU4 . . . .**144** B2
Mills Dr DN7 . . . .**104** A8
Mills Service Rd DN16 . . . .**97** A4
Millview Gdns DN20 . . . . .**98** E3
Milne Rd HU9 . . . .**142** C4
Milner Rd YO16 . . . .**122** D4
Milner St YO24 . . . .**129** D3
Milson Cl
4 Barton-upon-Humber
    DN18 . . . .**84** E8
Broughton DN20 . . . .**97** C4
York YO23 . . . .**130** C1
Milson Gr YO10 . . . .**131** A3
Milson Rd 8 DN34 . . . . . .**101** A4
Milton Carr 8 YO30 . . . . .**126** F1
Milton Cl
5 Gainsborough DN21 . . .**117** C1
12 Howden DN14 . . . . . .**65** A7
Milton Rd
3 Gainsborough DN21 . . .**117** C1
Grimsby DN33 . . . .**102** D2
Scunthorpe DN16 . . . . . .**151** B6
Milton St Goole DN14 . . . .**149** C4
York YO10 . . . .**130** F3
Minchin Cl 3 YO30 . . . . . .**127** B1
Minehead Rd HU7 . . . .**57** A5
Minerva Terr HU1 . . . .**155** B1
Minnow Cl 14 DN37 . . . . .**102** B4
Minshull 12 DN35 . . . . . .**103** C2

Minster Ave
Beverley HU17 . . . .**154** B2
York YO1 . . . .**127** F2
Minster Cl
3 Haxby YO32 . . . .**127** C8
Kingston upon Hull HU8 . .**141** D5
Minster Ct
Beverley HU17 . . . .**154** A2
11 Howden DN14 . . . . . .**65** A7
Minster Moorgate
    HU17 . . . .**154** A2
Minster Moorgate W
    HU17 . . . .**154** A2
Minster Rd
Misterton DN10 . . . .**116** C5
Scunthorpe DN15 . . . . . .**150** B6
Minster Sch The
Beverley HU17 . . . .**136** D3
York YO1 . . . .**156** B3
Minster The★ HU17 . . . . .**154** B3
Minster View YO32 . . . . .**127** C8
Minster Yd YO1 . . . .**156** B3
Minster Yd N HU17 . . . . . .**154** B2
Minster Yd S HU17 . . . . . .**154** B2
Mint Wlk HU17 . . . .**154** B1
Minter Cl 2 YO24 . . . . . .**129** B1
Mintfields Rd HU17 . . . . . .**154** C3
Minton St HU5 . . . .**140** D3
Mires La HU15 . . . .**53** D2
Mires The YO43 . . . .**53** F7
Mirfield Gr HU9 . . . .**142** C1
Mirfield Rd
Grimsby DN32 . . . .**102** F2
Scunthorpe DN15 . . . . . .**150** C8
Mirkhill Rd YO8 . . . .**148** B6
Misson Bank DN9 . . . . . .**104** C3
Misterton Prim Sch
    DN10 . . . .**116** C4
Mistral Ct YO31 . . . .**130** E8
Mitcham Rd HU8 . . . .**142** A3
Mitchell Cl DN7 . . . .**92** D5
Mitchell La YO41 . . . .**27** D8
Mitchel's La YO10 . . . . . .**133** F8
Miterdale 4 YO24 . . . . . .**132** C7
Mitford Cl 3 HU9 . . . .**2** E1
Mitford Rd 2 YO14 . . . .**2** E1
Mitten Ave 4 DN14 . . . . . .**78** C8
Mizzen Rd HU6 . . . .**140** B8
Moat Field YO10 . . . .**131** C4
Moat House Rd DN21 . . . .**108** A4
Moat La 4 DN40 . . . .**86** E3
Moat Way YO8 . . . .**48** D1
Moatside Ct YO31 . . . . . .**156** B3
Modder St DN16 . . . .**151** B2
Moffat Cl HU8 . . . .**141** C4
Moira Ct DN7 . . . .**92** D7
Moiser Cl YO32 . . . .**127** D4
Molescroft Ave 3
    HU17 . . . .**136** D6
Molescroft Cty Prim Sch
    HU17 . . . .**136** D6
Molescroft Dr HU17 . . . . .**136** D6
Molescroft Pk 4 HU17 . . . .**136** D6
Molescroft Rd HU17 . . . . .**136** D6
Molescroft West Cl 2
    HU17 . . . .**136** D6
Mollison Ave DN35 . . . . .**153** F1
Mollison Rd HU4 . . . .**144** A3
Mond Ave DN14 . . . .**149** D5
Money Hill (Tumulus)★
    YO43 . . . .**42** A8
Monic Ave HU13 . . . .**143** F2
Monk Ave YO31 . . . .**130** F7
Monk Bar Ct YO31 . . . . . .**156** B3
Monk Bar Mus★ YO31 . .**156** C3
Monk Fryston C of E Prim
    Sch LS25 . . . .**61** A8
Monk Fryston Prim Sch
    LS25 . . . .**61** A8
Monk La YO8 . . . .**148** C7
Monkbridge Ct YO31 . . . .**156** B4
Monkgate YO31 . . . .**156** C3
Monkgate Cloisters
    YO31 . . . .**156** C3
Monks Cl DN7 . . . .**92** D5
Monks Cross Dr YO32 . . .**128** A3
Monks Cross Link
    YO32 . . . .**128** B4
Monks Rd DN17 . . . .**150** F2
Monkton 11 HU15 . . . . . .**68** D6
Monkton Cl 10 DN14 . . . .**138** F5
Monkton Rd
5 York YO31 . . . .**127** F1
York YO31 . . . .**130** F8
Monmouth St HU4 . . . . . .**144** E3
Mons St HU5 . . . .**145** A8
Monson Rd DN21 . . . . . .**118** D8
Montague Rd YO23 . . . . .**133** A3
Montague St
Cleethorpes DN35 . . . . .**153** B5
Goole DN14 . . . .**149** C4
York YO23 . . . .**130** C1
Montague Wlk 6 YO26 . . .**12** F1
Montcalm Wlk 8 HU16 . . .**138** F5
Montgomery Rd DN35 . . .**153** D1
Montgomery Sq YO25 . . .**124** C2
Montreal Cres 4 HU16 . . .**138** F5
Montrose Ave DN30 . . . . .**98** D8
Montrose Ct DN14 . . . . . .**149** D5
Montrose Dr DN14 . . . . . .**149** F5
Montrose St
Kingston upon Hull HU8 . .**141** B1
Scunthorpe DN16 . . . . . .**151** B6
Moody La DN31 . . . .**152** A7
Mook St YO60 . . . .**16** B8
Moor Carr La YO8 . . . . . .**49** B5
Moor Cl YO19 . . . .**37** F8
Moor Cottage Rd YO25 . . .**34** D5

Moor Dike Rd DN7 . . . . .**104** A8
Moor Edges Rd DN8 . . . . .**93** B8
Moor End YO43 . . . .**52** B8
Moor Gn HU4 . . . .**144** B7
Moor Gr YO24 . . . .**132** E8
Moor La 6 Barlby YO8 . . . .**49** B5
Bilbrough LS24 . . . .**24** B1
Bishopthorpe YO23 . . . . .**132** E2
Burton Agnes YO25 . . . . .**10** C2
Caistor LN7 . . . .**111** A4
Carnaby YO16 . . . .**10** E4
Cliffe YO8 . . . .**49** F4
Copmanthorpe YO23 . . . .**132** A1
Earswick YO32 . . . .**128** C8
Full Sutton YO41 . . . .**15** F1
Hatfield DN8 . . . .**93** D3
Haxby YO32 . . . .**13** D7
Humbleton HU11 . . . .**58** E6
Kelfield YO19 . . . .**36** E2
Murton YO19 . . . .**131** F8
Naburn YO19 . . . .**36** D8
Newton-on-Ouse YO30 . . .**12** C7
Rufforth YO23 . . . .**24** E6
Skelton YO30 . . . .**126** D6
Strensall YO32 . . . .**14** B7
Sykehouse DN14 . . . .**78** A4
Thorne DN8 . . . .**79** B1
Wroot DN9 . . . .**104** C6
York YO24 . . . .**132** C6
Moor Lee La
Eggborough DN14 . . . . . .**77** B8
Heck DN14 . . . .**77** B8
Moor Owners Rd DN8 . . . .**93** D8
Moor Rd
Bottesford DN17 . . . .**96** B1
Bridlington YO15 . . . . . .**123** D7
Crowle DN17 . . . .**94** C8
Hunmanby YO14 . . . .**3** B7
Rawcliffe DN14 . . . .**79** B7
Sancton YO43 . . . .**53** C8
Stamford Bridge YO41 . . .**15** D2
Thorne DN8 . . . .**93** C7
Moor Way YO32 . . . .**128** A4
Moorbeck Cl HU6 . . . . . .**139** F4
Moorcroft Rd YO32 . . . . .**132** F4
Moore Ave YO10 . . . .**131** B4
Moorends Marshland Fst Sch
    DN8 . . . .**79** B2
Moorends Rd DN8 . . . . . .**79** A4
Moorfield Cty Jun Sch
    YO16 . . . .**122** D3
Moorfield Dr YO41 . . . . . .**27** E6
Moorfield Rd YO16 . . . . .**122** D3
Moorfield Way YO41 . . . . .**27** E6
Moorfields 3 DN14 . . . . . .**65** D3
Moorfields La
Kilpin DN14 . . . .**65** D3
Reedness DN14 . . . .**80** F7
Moorfoot Cl 8 HU7 . . . . . .**57** A6
Moorgarth Ave 3
    HU17 . . . .**154** A4
Moorgate Ave
10 York YO24 . . . .**129** F2
3 York YO24 . . . .**130** A2
Moorgate YO24 . . . .**129** D3
Moorhouse Rd 1 HU5 . . . .**139** B1
Moorings The DN20 . . . . . .**98** A2
Moorland Ave 3 DN10 . . .**116** C3
Moorland Cl 4 DN10 . . . .**116** C3
Moorland Dr 16 DN36 . . .**114** A8
Moorland Garth 2 YO32 . .**14** A7
Moorland Rd
Goole DN14 . . . .**149** D1
York YO10 . . . .**133** D8
Moorland Way 12 DN9 . . .**105** E6
Moorlands Skelton YO32 . .**13** B5
6 Westwoodside DN9 . . .**105** A2
Moorlands La YO30 . . . . .**126** C6
Moorlands The HU15 . . . . .**53** E1
Moors La HU15 . . . .**53** E2
Moors Rd DN15 . . . .**150** C7
Moortown Rd
Brandesburton YO25 . . . . .**34** B4
Nettleton LN7 . . . .**111** A3
Moorwell Rd DN17 . . . . . .**96** C1
Mordacks Dr YO16 . . . . .**123** B8
Mordacks Rd YO16 . . . . .**123** A7
Mordaunt Ave DN33 . . . .**113** D8
More Hall Dr HU7 . . . . . .**141** D7
Morecambe Ave DN16 . . .**151** A1
Morehall Cl YO30 . . . . . .**126** F2
Moreton Bay HU4 . . . . . .**142** E5
Moreton Rd DN9 . . . .**105** D6
Morfield Gr 3 DN9 . . . . .**105** D6
Morgan Way DN19 . . . . . .**70** D2
Morley Rd DN7 . . . .**150** F1
Morley St Goole DN14 . . .**149** D1
Kingston upon Hull HU8 . .**141** A2
Morley's Yd HU17 . . . . . .**154** A3
Morpeth St HU3 . . . .**145** D7
Morrets La YO8 . . . .**48** A1
Morrill St HU9 . . . .**141** D1
Morris Rd HU3 . . . .**144** E7
Morritt Cl 3 YO31 . . . . . .**130** F4
Morrow Ave HU18 . . . . . .**134** D5
Mortal Ash Hill DN16 . . . . .**97** C2
Mortimer Dr HU10 . . . . . .**143** F6
Mortlake Cl HU8 . . . .**141** E5
Morton Cl
4 Gainsborough DN21 . . .**117** A2
Immingham DN40 . . . . . .**87** B2
Morton La
Beverley HU17 . . . .**154** B3
Hambleton YO8 . . . .**62** A8
Morton Rd
Gainsborough DN21 . . . .**117** B2
Grimsby DN34 . . . .**152** B3
Laughton DN21 . . . .**117** E8

Morton St HU3 . . . .**145** C8
Morton Terr DN21 . . . . . .**117** B1
Morton Trentside CP Sch
    DN21 . . . .**117** A2
Moseley Hill HU11 . . . . . .**142** E6
Moss Green La
Brayton YO8 . . . .**148** A2
Hirst Courtney YO8 . . . . . .**62** F3
Moss Haven DN6 . . . .**77** D1
Moss Rd Grimsby DN32 . .**152** E3
Kirk Bramwith DN7 . . . . . .**92** A8
Moss DN6 . . . .**77** B1
Moss St YO24 . . . .**156** A1
Mosscroft La DN7 . . . .**92** C2
Motherwell Cl HU7 . . . . .**141** C4
Moulton Cl 6 DN34 . . . . .**102** B2
Mount Ave
13 Barton-upon-Humber
    DN18 . . . .**84** E8
Bridlington YO16 . . . . . .**122** E6
Kingston upon Hull
    HU13 . . . .**143** D2
Selby YO8 . . . .**148** B3
Winterton DN15 . . . .**83** B5
Mount Cres YO16 . . . . . .**122** E6
Mount Dr YO16 . . . .**122** E6
Mount Ephraim 6
    YO24 . . . .**130** A3
Mount Gr YO8 . . . .**148** B3
Mount Par YO24 . . . .**130** A3
Mount Pk YO16 . . . .**49** A8
Mount Pleasant
Aldbrough HU11 . . . .**47** D2
Harpham YO25 . . . .**9** D3
9 Holton le Clay DN36 . .**114** A5
1 Hornsea HU18 . . . . .**134** B4
Kingston upon Hull HU8 . .**141** A1
New Holland DN19 . . . . . .**70** E2
Waltham DN37 . . . .**113** D7
Mount Pleasant C of E Jun
    Sch YO43 . . . .**135** D3
Mount Pleasant Rd
Goole DN14 . . . .**149** D5
North Frodingham YO25 . .**34** A7
Thorne DN8 . . . .**79** A2
Mount Pleasant Windmill★
    DN21 . . . .**108** B2
Mount Royale Cl 4
    DN39 . . . .**86** A1
Mount Sch The YO24 . . .**130** A3
Mount The
Great Driffield YO25 . . .**124** F5
9 Kirk Sandall DN3 . . . .**92** A1
Selby YO8 . . . .**148** B3
York YO24 . . . .**156** A1
Mount Vale YO24 . . . . . .**130** A2
Mount Vale Dr YO24 . . . .**130** A2
Mount Vernon HU11 . . . .**142** E6
Mount View HU11 . . . . . .**69** A5
Mountbatten Cl 7 DN16 . .**96** D2
Mountbatten Prim Sch
    HU9 . . . .**142** E3
Mowbray Cl DN9 . . . . . .**105** D3
Mowbray Cr 20 DN9 . . . .**105** E6
Mowbray Dr YO26 . . . . .**129** C4
Mowbray Rd 18 DN8 . . . .**93** B7
Mowbray St
Epworth DN9 . . . .**105** E6
3 Gainsborough DN21 . .**117** B1
Mowthorpe Medieval
    Village★ YO17 . . . .**6** C6
Moy Ct HU6 . . . .**140** A6
Mucky La HU12 . . . .**59** C6
Muirfield 18 DN37 . . . . .**113** D6
Muirfield Croft 4 DN40 . . .**87** C1
Muirfield Way 6 YO26 . . .**129** B5
Mulberry Ave 12 DN8 . . . .**79** B2
Mulberry Cl
Great Driffield YO25 . . .**124** D3
North Thoresby DN36 . . .**114** B1
Mulberry Ct YO32 . . . . . .**127** F6
Mulberry Dr
10 Crowle DN17 . . . . . .**94** D7
7 Haxby YO32 . . . .**13** E5
Mulberry La HU11 . . . . . .**45** E2
Mulcourt HU6 . . . .**139** F7
Mulgrave St
Kingston upon Hull HU8 . .**155** C4
Scunthorpe DN15 . . . . . .**151** A8
Mull Way DN40 . . . .**101** C8
Mullion Cl HU7 . . . .**141** C7
Mulwith Cl YO31 . . . .**131** A6
Mumby Cl 7 DN36 . . . . .**114** B1
Muncastergate YO31 . . . .**130** E7
Munroe Cl HU8 . . . .**141** C6
Murham Ave DN14 . . . . .**149** C6
Murray Cl 3 YO42 . . . . . .**29** A4
Murray Cres HU16 . . . . . .**138** F5
Murray St
Grimsby DN31 . . . .**152** F6
York YO24 . . . .**129** F3
Murrayfield Rd HU5 . . . . .**139** F1
Murrough Wilson Pl 3
    YO31 . . . .**130** F7
Murton Garth YO19 . . . . .**131** F6
Murton La YO19 . . . .**26** D7
Murton Way YO19 . . . . . .**131** F6
Museum of Army Transport★
    HU17 . . . .**154** C2
Museum St YO1 . . . .**156** B2
Muston Ave HU16 . . . . . .**139** A5
Muston Rd YO14 . . . .**2** F8
Mutton La DN10 . . . .**116** C3
Mylor Cl 18 HU7 . . . .**57** A5
Myrtle Ave
Bishopthorpe YO23 . . . . .**133** B3
Selby YO8 . . . .**148** B3
Myrtle Rd DN7 . . . .**92** C4

Myton St HU1 . . . .**155** A2
Mytongate HU1 . . . .**155** A1

N

Nab Dr DN14 . . . .**149** C6
Nab La DN7 . . . .**92** C8
Naburn La
Deighton YO19 . . . .**37** A7
Fulford YO19 . . . .**133** D4
Naburn Pk Mews YO19 . . .**36** E8
Nacton St DN31 . . . .**152** F5
Nafferton Prim Sch
    YO25 . . . .**125** E6
Nafferton Sta YO25 . . . . .**125** F6
Nairn Cl YO23 . . . .**132** C6
Nalton Cl YO23 . . . .**132** A1
Nalton Ct HU16 . . . .**139** C5
Nalton St YO8 . . . .**148** C5
Nan Sampson Bank
    DN9 . . . .**104** B4
Nandike Cl 4 HU10 . . . . .**143** F6
Napier Cl 1 HU7 . . . .**154** A4
Narrow Boats The 14
    DN20 . . . .**98** B2
Narrow La
Cottingwith YO42 . . . . . .**38** D7
Eastrington DN14 . . . . . .**52** A2
Kilpin DN14 . . . .**65** D6
Twin Rivers DN14 . . . . . .**81** D3
Narvick Rd HU7 . . . .**140** E5
Naseby Cl 14 DN7 . . . . . .**92** D3
Naseby Dr DN31 . . . .**152** B3
Nashcourt HU6 . . . .**139** F7
National Ave HU5 . . . . . .**144** F8
National Fishing Heritage
    Ctr★ DN31 . . . .**152** A4
National Rly Mus★
    YO26 . . . .**130** A4
Navigation La LN7 . . . . . .**111** A4
Navigation Rd 1 YO1 . . . .**156** C2
Navigation Way HU9 . . . .**146** C6
Nayfield Cl 7 YO25 . . . . .**124** F4
Naylor's Row 3 HU9 . . . .**146** B2
Neap House Rd DN15 . . . .**95** E6
Neasden Cl 1 HU8 . . . . . .**141** E5
Neasden Prim Sch
    HU8 . . . .**141** E5
Neat Marsh Rd HU12 . . . .**58** B1
Neatgangs La DN19 . . . . .**71** A3
Neath Rd DN16 . . . .**151** A5
Neatshead Garth 9 HU7 . . .**57** B5
Nelson Cl HU1 . . . .**155** B1
Nelson Rd HU5 . . . .**144** B7
Nelson St
Bridlington YO15 . . . . . .**122** E2
Gainsborough DN21 . . . .**117** B1
Grimsby DN32 . . . .**152** F5
Kingston upon Hull HU1 . .**155** C1
York YO31 . . . .**156** C4
Nelson Way DN34 . . . . . .**102** B3
Nelson's La YO24 . . . . . .**129** F1
Nelthorpe Cl 6 DN39 . . . . .**86** A1
Neptune St
Bridlington YO15 . . . . . .**122** E1
Cleethorpes DN35 . . . . .**153** E3
Kingston upon Hull HU1 . .**145** D4
Ness La
Garthorpe & Fockerby
    DN17 . . . .**81** E6
1 Preston HU12 . . . . . .**58** C1
Ness Rd 5 YO8 . . . .**148** D6
Nessgate YO1 . . . .**156** B2
Nestor Gr HU9 . . . .**142** C5
Neswick La YO25 . . . .**31** F7
Nether Way 20 YO26 . . . . .**12** F1
Nethergate
Nafferton YO25 . . . .**125** F7
Westwoodside DN9 . . . . .**105** B2
Netherlands Way DN41 . . .**87** E1
Netherton Rd HU4 . . . . . .**144** B4
Netherwindings 18 YO32 . .**13** F5
Netherwoods 6 YO32 . . . .**14** B8
Nettleholme 2 DN7 . . . . . .**92** D4
Nettleton Garth 3 HU12 . .**73** A6
Nettleton Rd LN7 . . . . . .**111** B3
Nettleton St LN7 . . . .**111** A3
Neville Ave HU17 . . . . . .**154** C3
Neville Cl
2 Keadby with Althorpe
    DN17 . . . .**95** D4
Kingston upon Hull HU3 . .**145** D5
Neville Cres DN15 . . . . . .**83** A5
Neville Dr YO23 . . . .**133** A3
Neville Garth 27 HU12 . . . .**72** D7
Neville La DN7 . . . .**92** A4
Neville Pits La DN14 . . . . .**77** B4
Neville Rd DN16 . . . .**151** C6
Neville St
Cleethorpes DN35 . . . . .**153** D4
York YO31 . . . .**156** C4
Neville Terr YO31 . . . . . .**156** C4
Neville Turner Way 9
    DN37 . . . .**113** D6
Nevinson Gr YO10 . . . . . .**133** E8
Nevis Way YO24 . . . .**132** B7
New Bridge La YO25 . . . .**125** F5
New Bridge Rd HU9 . . . . .**146** C8
New Burlington Rd
    YO15 . . . .**122** D2
New Carr La DN14 . . . . . .**52** A3
New Cartergate 5
    DN31 . . . .**152** D3
New Chapel La 6 DN37 . .**101** F1

New Cl **1** DN33 . . . . 102 E2
New Clee Sta DN31 . . . 153 B5
New Cleveland St
HU8 . . . . 155 C4
New Cut YO25 . . . . 22 E5
New Delights DN36 . . . 114 F3
New Earswick Prim Sch
YO32 . . . . 127 D4
New Earswick Sports Club
YO32 . . . . 127 D3
New Fen La HU8 . . . . . . 48 F6
New Finkle Ct HU16 . . 139 A6
New Forge Ct **15** YO32 . . 13 F5
New Garden St HU1 . . . 155 B3
New George St HU2 . . . 155 B3
New Gn **2** DN7 . . . . 92 C6
New Haven Terr DN31 . . 152 B5
New Holland C of E &
Methodist Sch DN19 . . 70 E2
New Holland Rd DN19 . . 85 D8
New Holland Sta DN19 . . 70 E3
New Inn La DN7 . . . . . . 92 C7
New La Beal DN14 . . . . . 61 D3
Bishopthorpe YO23 . . . 133 A4
Holme-on-Spalding-Moor
YO43 . . . . 52 C4
Humbleton HU11 . . . . . 59 A5
Huntington YO32 . . . . . 128 A1
Laxton DN14 . . . . 65 E4
Long Marston YO23 . . . . 24 B3
Newland YO8 . . . . 64 A3
Rawcliffe DN14 . . . . . . 79 A8
Reedness DN14 . . . . . . 80 E8
Selby YO8 . . . . 148 C5
Strensall YO32 . . . . 14 B8
York YO32 . . . . 127 F1
York YO24 . . . . 129 E3
New Laids La HU12 . . . . 73 B7
New Michael St HU1 . . 155 A1
New Mill Field Rd DN7 . . 92 E3
New Millgate YO8 . . . . 148 C6
New Park Est DN7 . . . . . 92 D7
New Pasture Cl **6**
YO16 . . . . 122 C5
New Pasture La YO16 . . 122 B5
New Potter Grange Rd
DN14 . . . . 64 E2
New Rd
Beningbrough YO30 . . . . 12 C6
Brandesburton YO25 . . . 33 E3
Brantingham HU15 . . . . 68 C8
Burton Pidsea HU12 . . . 59 C2
Cleethorpes DN35 . . . . 153 F2
Etton HU17 . . . . 43 A6
Foggathorpe YO42 . . . . 39 A2
Great Driffield YO25 . . . 124 F4
Harpham YO25 . . . . 21 C8
Heck DN14 . . . . 62 D1
Hedon HU12 . . . . 72 C7
Hessay YO26 . . . . 24 C8
Holme-on-Spalding-Moor
YO43 . . . . 40 B1
Hornsea HU18 . . . . . . 134 D4
Hunmanby YO14 . . . . . . 2 F7
Keyingham HU12 . . . . . 73 D5
Kirby Grindalythe YO17 . . 6 B6
Laceby DN37 . . . . 113 A8
Long Drax YO8 . . . . 63 E6
Nafferton YO25 . . . . . 125 D7
Norton DN6 . . . . 76 F2
Ottringham HU12 . . . . . 73 E3
Reighton YO14 . . . . 3 E5
Roos HU12 . . . . 59 F3
Scunthorpe DN15 . . . . 150 B2
Stapleton WF8 . . . . 76 B5
Swinefleet DN14 . . . . . . 80 C4
Waltham DN37 . . . . . . 113 E6
Wheldrake YO19 . . . . . . 37 C7
Worlaby DN20 . . . . 98 D8
New Row DN17 . . . . . . 107 D7
New St **17** Brigg DN20 . . 98 C2
Elsham DN20 . . . . 98 F7
Gainsborough DN21 . . . 117 B1
Grimsby DN31 . . . . . . 152 E3
Pocklington YO42 . . . . . 29 A3
York YO1 . . . . 156 B2
New Trent St DN17 . . . . 94 E6
New Village Rd
Kingston upon Hull
HU16 . . . . 139 C7
Little Weighton HU20 . . . 55 A4
New Walkergate
HU17 . . . . 154 A3
New Waltham Cty Prim Sch
DN36 . . . . 114 A8
New Wlk
Beverley HU17 . . . . . . 136 D5
Great Driffield YO25 . . . 124 F4
North Ferriby HU14 . . . . 69 A4
New Wlk Cl YO25 . . . . 124 F4
New Wlk Terr YO10 . . . 130 D2
Newbald CP Sch YO43 . . 53 F8
Newbald Gr HU6 . . . . . 139 F6
Newbald Rd HU17 . . . . 136 A2
Newbald Way **1** HU16 . . 138 E6
Newbegin
Beverley HU17 . . . . . . 154 A3
Hornsea HU18 . . . . . . 134 C4
Newbigg Crowle DN17 . . 94 C8
Westwoodside DN9 . . . 105 B2
Newbolt Ave DN17 . . . 150 D3
Newbolt Cl LN7 . . . . . 111 A3
Newborn Ave DN15 . . . 150 E8
Newborough St YO30 . . 156 A4
Newbridge La YO41 . . . 28 A7

Newbridge Rd HU12 . . . 73 B6
Newbury Ave
Grimsby DN37 . . . . . . 102 C5
York YO24 . . . . 129 D1
Newbury Gr **2** DN34 . . 102 C2
Newby La DN14 . . . . 77 F8
Newby Rd DN31 . . . . . 152 C3
Newby Terr YO31 . . . . 130 C7
Newclose La DN14 . . . 149 D6
Newcomen St HU9 . . . 141 B1
Newcroft YO8 . . . . 148 B4
Newdale **3** HU3 . . . . . . 13 F5
Newdown Rd DN17 . . . . 96 B2
Newfield Cl DN3 . . . . . . 92 A3
Newfield La
Burstwick HU12 . . . . . . 58 F2
South Cave HU15 . . . . . 53 E1
Newfields Ave DN8 . . . . 79 B1
Newfields Cl DN8 . . . . . 79 B1
Newfields Dr DN8 . . . . . 79 B1
Newgate YO1 . . . . 156 B2
Newgate Ct YO1 . . . . . 156 B2
Newhall La HU16 . . . . . 139 B6
Newhall Rd **8** DN3 . . . . 92 A4
Newhay La YO8 . . . . . . 49 E1
Newholme Cl HU6 . . . . 139 F6
Newholme Dr **8** DN8 . . . 79 B2
Newington Ave HU4 . . . 144 E5
Newington Prim Sch
HU3 . . . . 145 A4
Newington St HU3 . . . 144 F4
Newland Ave
Great Driffield YO25 . . . 124 D4
Kingston upon Hull HU5 . 140 C2
Scunthorpe DN15 . . . . 150 E6
Newland Ave Sch
HU5 . . . . 140 C2
Newland Dr DN15 . . . . 150 D7
Newland Gr **1** HU5 . . . 140 C3
Newland Park Ave
HU6 . . . . 140 B4
Newland Park Cl
YO10 . . . . 131 A3
Newland Park Dr
YO10 . . . . 130 F3
Newland Pk HU5 . . . . . 140 A3
Newland Rd HU5 . . . . . 149 C5
Newland Sch for Girls
HU6 . . . . 140 A4
Newland St Johns C of E
Prim Sch HU6 . . . . . 140 C4
Newland View **11** DN9 . . 105 E6
Newland Wlk DN15 . . . 150 D7
Newlands **7** DN21 . . . . 117 C1
Newlands Dr YO26 . . . 129 B6
Newlands La Paull HU12 . . 72 B3
Upper Poppleton YO26 . . 24 E8
Newlands Pk **23** DN36 . . 103 D1
Newlands Rd
Bishopthorpe YO23 . . . 132 F4
Sunk Island HU12 . . . . . 89 D6
Newlands The HU6 . . . 140 C4
Newlyn Cl
Kingston upon Hull HU7 . 141 C7
4 Kingston upon Hull
HU13 . . . . 144 A2
Newmarket St DN32 . . 152 F4
Newnham Cres **12** DN16 . 96 D2
Newport Ave YO8 . . . . 148 B4
Newport Cl **4** HU3 . . . 145 D5
Newport Cty Prim Sch
HU15 . . . . 52 F1
Newport Dr DN15 . . . . . 83 A6
Newport Rd HU15 . . . . . 53 C2
Newport St
Barton-upon-Humber
DN18 . . . . 69 E1
Goole DN14 . . . . 149 B4
Newsam Cl **4** YO25 . . . 22 D1
Newsham Abbey (Site of)★
DN39 . . . . 100 C8
Newsham Dr DN34 . . . 152 A3
Newsham Gdns HU19 . . 75 A5
Newsham Hill La YO16 . . 4 C2
Newsham La DN39 . . . 100 D8
Newstead Ave DN36 . . 114 B5
Newstead Cres YO16 . . 122 D6
Newstead Rd DN35 . . . 103 C2
Newstead St HU5 . . . . 145 A8
Newthorpe Rd **2** DN6 . . 76 E2
Newton Dr HU17 . . . . . 154 A1
Newton La LN8 . . . . . . 120 A5
Newton Marsh La
DN36 . . . . 114 F6
Newton Pk YO30 . . . . . 12 B7
Newton Rd DN16 . . . . 151 E2
Newton St **3** HU3 . . . . 145 B4
Newton Terr YO1 . . . . 156 B1
Newtondale HU7 . . . . . 140 F7
Newtondale Garth
YO16 . . . . 122 F7
Newtown Sq HU9 . . . . 146 E7
Nicholas St **7** DN18 . . . 84 E8
Nicholas Gdns YO10 . . 130 F3
Nicholas St YO10 . . . . 130 F3
Nicholson Cl HU17 . . . 137 B4
Nicholson La **2** HU11 . . . 35 A1
Nicholson Rd
Healing DN41 . . . . 102 A5
Immingham DN40 . . . . . 86 E4
Nicholson St
Cleethorpes DN35 . . . . 153 F1
5 Kingston upon Hull
HU5 . . . . 140 E2
Nicholson Way **6** DN9 . 105 D7
Nicholson's La HU12 . . . 74 B3
Nickey Nackey La YO8 . . 48 B8

Nicolgate La **26** DN20 . . 98 C2
Nicolson Dr **16** DN18 . . . 84 F8
Nidd Cl YO26 . . . . 129 B8
Nidd Gr YO24 . . . . 132 E8
Nidd St DN14 . . . . 149 D1
Nidderdale HU7 . . . . . 140 F6
Nidderdale Cl **1** YO16 . 123 A4
Nigel Gr **7** YO24 . . . . . 129 F2
Nightingale Cl
Scunthorpe DN15 . . . . . 96 B7
4 Walkington HU17 . . . 55 D8
Nightingale Dr YO16 . . 122 F5
Nightingale Rd YO16 . . 122 F5
Nine Dikes Rd YO25 . . . . 9 D8
Ninescores La DN9 . . . 104 B4
Ninth Ave
Fixborough Ind Est. DN15 . 82 A1
York YO31 . . . . 130 F5
Nith Gr HU8 . . . . 142 C6
Nithdale Gdns HU5 . . . 140 B3
Noah's Wood Submarine
Forest★ HU19 . . . . . . 75 A7
Noddle Hill Way HU7 . . 141 D8
Noel St **2** DN21 . . . . . 117 B1
Nolloth Cres HU17 . . . 154 B4
Nooking La DN37 . . . . 101 D2
Nooking The DN9 . . . . 105 D3
Nookings Dr DN20 . . . 109 A5
Nordale Cl **9** HU8 . . . . 141 E7
Nordham HU15 . . . . 53 D3
Norfolk Ave DN15 . . . . . 82 B4
Norfolk Bank La HU15 . . 67 E8
Norfolk La DN35 . . . . . 153 E3
Norfolk St
Beverley HU17 . . . . . . 136 D5
Kingston upon Hull HU2 . 155 A3
York YO23 . . . . 130 C2
Norland Ave HU4 . . . . 144 C6
Norlands La YO16 . . . . . 4 A1
Norman Cl
Barton-upon-Humber
DN18 . . . . 84 F8
7 Thorpe Willoughby YO8 . 48 B1
Norman Cres DN17 . . . 150 F4
Norman Dr
3 Hatfield DN7 . . . . . . 92 D3
York YO26 . . . . 129 B6
Norman Rd
Grimsby DN34 . . . . . . 152 B3
Hatfield DN7 . . . . 92 D3
Norman St **5** YO10 . . . 131 A3
Normanby Hall★ 82 C3
Normanby Hall Ctry Pk★
DN15 . . . . 82 C3
Normanby Rd
Burton upon Stather
DN15 . . . . 82 B4
Nettleton LN7 . . . . 111 B2
Scunthorpe DN15 . . . . 151 A8
Normandy Ave HU17 . . . 55 E8
Normandy Cl **4** YO8 . . 148 B6
Normandy Rd DN35 . . . 153 D1
Normandy Way DN14 . . 149 C3
Normanton Rise HU4 . . 144 C7
Nornabell Dr HU17 . . . 136 E7
Nornabell St **1** HU8 . . 146 C8
Norrison Ave HU6 . . . . 140 C8
Norsefield Ave **1** DN37 . 113 E7
Norseman Cl **7** YO19 . . 48 F8
Norseway **2** YO41 . . . . . 15 D1
North Axholme Comp Sch
DN17 . . . . 94 D7
North Back La
2 Bridlington YO16 . . . 122 D4
Kilham YO25 . . . . 9 B3
North Bar Within
HU17 . . . . 154 A3
North Bar Without
HU17 . . . . 136 D4
North Bridge St DN32 . . 152 F5
North Burton La YO14 . . . 3 B4
North Carr Dales Rd
HU19 . . . . 74 F4
North Carr La
Saxby All Saints DN20 . . 83 F3
Tickton HU17 . . . . 44 D3
North Carr Rd
Scotter DN17 . . . . 106 E5
West Stockwith DN10 . . 116 E5
North Cave C of E Sch
HU15 . . . . 53 D3
North Cave Rd YO43 . . . 53 D4
North Church Side
1 Easington HU12 . . . . 90 F6
Kingston upon Hull HU1 . 155 B2
North Cliff Rd DN21 . . . 108 C2
North Cliffe Wood Nature
Reserve★ YO43 . . . . . 53 A7
North Coates Rd
DN36 . . . . 115 A4
North Coates C of E Sch
DN36 . . . . 115 B3
North Cotes Rd
Hunmanby YO25 . . . . . . 2 C5
Wold Newton YO25 . . . . . 1 E5
North Cty Ct **2** HU9 . . 141 F1
North Cty Prim Sch
DN21 . . . . 117 A1
North Dr
Kingston upon Hull
HU10 . . . . 143 E6
Swanland HU14 . . . . . . 69 B7
North Duffield CP Sch
YO8 . . . . 50 A8
North Eastern Rd DN8 . . 93 A8

North Elkington La
LN11 . . . . 121 B1
North End
5 Flamborough YO15 . . . 5 A2
Goxhill DN19 . . . . 86 A8
Seaton Ross YO42 . . . . . 39 D4
South Ferriby DN18 . . . . 84 A8
North End Cres **13**
DN36 . . . . 114 D4
North End La LN7 . . . . 110 A2
North End Rd
Halsham HU12 . . . . 73 F5
Roos HU12 . . . . 60 A2
1 Tetney DN36 . . . . . 114 D4
North Farm Rd DN17 . . . 96 B2
North Ferriby C of E Sch
HU14 . . . . 69 A5
North Field La
Askham Bryan YO23 . . . 24 F3
Upper Poppleton YO26 . . 24 F7
North Frodingham County
Prim Sch YO25 . . . . . 33 F8
North Frodingham Rd
YO25 . . . . 34 B8
North Holme **8** DN36 . . 114 D4
North Ings Rd DN7 . . . . 92 E5
North Intake La DN9 . . 116 B3
North Kelsey Cty Prim Sch
LN7 . . . . 110 A4
North Kelsey Rd LN7 . . 110 A2
North La
Huntington YO32 . . . . . 128 D5
Marsh Chapel DN36 . . . 115 C2
Sykehouse DN14 . . . . . . 78 B4
Wheldrake YO19 . . . . . . 37 F7
York YO32 . . . . 127 F5
North Leas Ave YO16 . . 122 E7
North Leas Dr YO16 . . . 122 E7
North Leys Rd HU19 . . . 75 B4
North Lincoln Rd
DN16 . . . . 151 D6
North Lindsey Coll
DN17 . . . . 150 E4
North Marine Dr
YO15 . . . . 123 A4
North Marine Rd **1** YO15 . 5 B3
North Marsh Rd HU12 . . 91 B3
North Moor **7** YO32 . . . 127 F5
North Moor Dr **1** DN10 . 116 C3
North Moor Gdns
YO32 . . . . 127 F5
North Moor La
Bottesford DN17 . . . . . 96 B1
Cottingham HU16 . . . . 139 D8
Messingham DN17 . . . . 107 B8
North Moor Rd
3 Flamborough YO15 . . . 5 B2
Messingham DN17 . . . . 107 C6
Walkeringham DN10 . . . 116 C3
York YO32 . . . . 127 F5
North Moss La DN41 . . 101 E8
North Ormsby Medieval
Village★ LN11 . . . . . 121 A3
North Par
Scunthorpe DN16 . . . . 151 D2
York YO30 . . . . 156 A3
North Pinfold Way 2
YO16 . . . . 122 D6
North Pk HU12 . . . . 58 F2
North Prom
Cleethorpes DN35 . . . . 153 E3
Withernsea HU19 . . . . . 75 A7
North Quay DN31 . . . . 153 A7
North Rd Atwick YO25 . . 35 C6
Bewholme YO25 . . . . . . 35 A5
Halsham HU12 . . . . 73 F6
Hatfield HU11 . . . . 46 C5
Keadby with Althorpe
DN17 . . . . 95 C6
Kingston upon Hull HU4 . 144 E4
Lund YO25 . . . . 31 F3
Ulrome YO25 . . . . 23 A4
Withernsea HU19 . . . . . 74 F7
North Rise **2** HU12 . . . . 73 A6
North Sea Aquarium★
YO15 . . . . 122 F2
North Sea La DN36 . . . 103 D1
North St Aldbrough HU11 . 47 C1
Barmby on the Marsh
DN14 . . . . 64 A7
Barrow upon Humber
DN19 . . . . 85 D8
Bridlington YO15 . . . . . 122 E2
Caistor LN7 . . . . 111 B4
Cleethorpes DN35 . . . . 153 F2
Crowle DN17 . . . . 94 D8
6 Gainsborough DN21 . . 117 A2
Goole DN14 . . . . 149 B6
Great Driffield YO25 . . . 124 E5
Kingston upon Hull
HU10 . . . . 143 E6
Kingston upon Hull HU2 . 155 A3
Leven HU17 . . . . 45 A8
Nafferton YO25 . . . . . . 125 E8
Owston Ferry DN9 . . . . 106 B3
Roxby cum Risby DN15 . . 83 A4
1 Scunthorpe DN15 . . . 151 B8
West Butterwick DN17 . . 95 D1
West/East Butterwick
DN17 . . . . 106 D8
York YO1 . . . . 156 B2
North Thoresby Prim Sch
DN36 . . . . 114 A1
North Townside Rd
YO25 . . . . 23 A4
North Turnpike YO25 . . . 23 A4
North View HU20 . . . . . 55 B4

North Walls HU1 . . . . . 155 C2
North Warren Rd
DN21 . . . . 117 A1
North Way DN36 . . . . . 115 B2
Northampton Rd
DN16 . . . . 151 C5
Northcote Ave YO24 . . 129 E3
Northcroft **5** YO32 . . . . 13 C5
Northcroft Dr **13** HU4 . . 141 E2
North-Dale Ct **2** DN21 . 108 B2
Northdale Pk **3** HU14 . . 69 B7
Northern Ave **3** DN20 . . 98 C3
Northferry La DN9 . . . . 94 C1
Northfield **3** Barlby YO8 . 49 B5
Rimswell HU19 . . . . 74 F7
Swanland HU14 . . . . . . 69 B7
Northfield Ave
Great Driffield YO25 . . . 124 F6
Kingston upon Hull
HU13 . . . . 143 E3
Northfield Cl
Driffield YO25 . . . . 124 F6
12 Pocklington YO42 . . . 28 F4
1 Scunthorpe DN16 . . . 151 C5
5 South Cave HU15 . . . . 53 F1
2 Tetney DN36 . . . . . . 114 D4
West Butterwick DN17 . . 95 D1
Womersley DN6 . . . . . . 76 C6
Northfield Cotts DN16 . . 96 C1
Northfield Cres YO25 . . 124 E5
Northfield Inf Sch
YO25 . . . . 124 F6
Northfield La
Amcotts DN17 . . . . 81 F2
3 Riccall YO19 . . . . 36 F1
Thornton Curtis DN39 . . 85 D5
Welwick HU12 . . . . 90 A8
Willoughton DN21 . . . . 119 A4
Womersley DN6 . . . . . . 76 C7
Northfield Rd
Beverley HU17 . . . . . . 136 C6
Bubwith YO8 . . . . 50 E8
Coniston HU11 . . . . 57 F7
Great Driffield YO25 . . . 124 E6
Kingston upon Hull HU3 . 144 E6
Market Weighton YO43 . 135 E4
Messingham DN17 . . . . 107 D8
Pocklington YO42 . . . . . 28 F4
Wetwang YO25 . . . . 19 A6
Northfield Rise **7** YO42 . 28 F4
Northfield Sch YO25 . . 129 B5
Northfield Wlk YO25 . . 124 F6
Northfields
Barmby Moor YO42 . . . . 28 D4
5 Strensall YO32 . . . . . 14 B8
Northgate
Hornsea HU18 . . . . . . 134 C5
Hunmanby YO14 . . . . 2 F7
Kingston upon Hull
HU16 . . . . 139 A7
Kingston upon Hull
HU13 . . . . 143 E2
Thorne/Moorends DN8 . . 79 B2
Walkington HU17 . . . . . 55 B8
Northgate Gr YO43 . . . 135 C4
Northgate La YO41 . . . . 15 A3
Northgate Vale YO43 . . 135 C4
Northlands Ave
1 Earswick YO32 . . . . 127 F7
2 Winterton DN15 . . . . 83 A5
Northlands Rd DN15 . . . 83 A6
Northlands Rd S DN15 . . 83 A5
Northminster Bsns Pk
YO26 . . . . 24 F7
Northmoor Rd DN17 . . . 80 C1
Northolme DN21 . . . . 117 B1
Northolme Circ 2
HU13 . . . . 143 E2
Northolme Cres
Kingston upon Hull
HU13 . . . . 143 E2
Scunthorpe DN15 . . . . 150 F7
Northolme Dr YO30 . . . 126 E1
Northolme Rd HU13 . . . 143 E2
Northolt Cl HU8 . . . . . 141 E6
Northorpe Cl HU9 . . . . 142 C1
Northorpe Rd DN21 . . . 107 D1
Northorpe Rise YO16 . . 122 B5
North's La DN37 . . . . . 112 D8
Northside Haxey DN9 . . 105 C2
Laxton DN14 . . . . 65 F4
Patrington HU12 . . . . . 74 D1
Northside Ct **6** HU12 . . 74 D1
Northside Rd HU19 . . . . 75 A4
Northstead Cl HU10 . . . 138 C1
Northumberland Ave
Hornsea HU18 . . . . . . 134 B5
Kingston upon Hull HU2 . 155 B4
Northumberland Cl
DN34 . . . . 152 B2
Northway Fulstow LN11 . 121 E8
Goole DN14 . . . . 149 B6
Northwood Dr HU13 . . 143 B3
Norton & Kirk Smeat
WF8 . . . . 76 C3
Norton Comm La DN6 . . 76 F2
Norton Comm Rd DN6 . . 77 A1
Norton Cty Jun & Inf Sch
DN6 . . . . 76 E2
Norton Gr HU4 . . . . . . 144 D4
Norton La LN8 . . . . . . 119 C6
Norton Mill La DN6 . . . 76 E2
Norton Priory DN6 . . . . 76 E2
Norton Rd DN16 . . . . . 151 B1
Norton St HU17 . . . . . 154 A2
Norway Dr YO10 . . . . . 133 D8
Norwich Ave **3** DN34 . . 102 D2
Norwich Ct HU17 . . . . 136 E1

Norwood HU17 ....154 B4
Norwood Ave DN15 ...150 F6
Norwood Cl 3 HU10 ...143 E7
Norwood Dale HU17 ...154 A3
Norwood Far Gr HU17 ..154 B4
Norwood Gr HU17 ....154 B4
Norwood Rd DN7 .....92 C5
Norwood St HU3 ....145 C7
Nostell Rd DN16 ....151 D5
Nostell Way YO16 ...122 D7
Nottingham Rd 6 HU11 .47 C1
Nova Scotia Way 4
  YO19 ....49 A8
Nuffield Cl 6 DN16 ...96 D2
Nun Monkton Prim Sch
  YO26 ....12 A5
Nunburnholme Ave
  HU14 ....69 A4
Nunburnholme Hill
  YO42 ....29 F3
Nunburnholme Pk
  HU4 ....144 B7
Nunmill St YO23 ....130 C2
Nunnery Hill★ YO25 ...21 F6
Nunnery La YO23 ...156 B1
Nunnery Wlk 4 HU15 ...53 F1
Nunnington Cl HU5 ..140 B2
Nuns Rd DN17 ....150 F2
Nunsthorpe Inf Sch
  DN33 ....102 D2
Nunsthorpe Jun Sch
  DN33 ....102 D2
Nunthorpe Ave YO23 ..130 B2
Nunthorpe Cl 17 DN7 ..92 D4
Nunthorpe Cres YO23 ..130 B1
Nunthorpe Gr YO23 ...130 B2
Nunthorpe Rd YO23 ...156 A1
Nurseries The HU17 ..136 D7
Nursery Cl
  3 Barton-upon-Humber
  DN18 ....69 F1
  Scunthorpe DN17 ....96 C2
Nursery Ct
  14 Brough HU15 ....68 C5
  Nether Poppleton YO26 .126 A2
Nursery Dr YO24 ...129 E3
Nursery Gdns
  Beverley HU17 ....154 A1
  York YO10 ....131 C3
Nursery Gr YO16 ...122 B5
Nursery Rd YO26 ...126 A2
Nursery Wlk HU16 ...139 D6
Nutana Ave HU18 ...134 C7
Nutfields Gr 12 DN7 ...92 C6
Nuttles La HU12 ....58 E2

O

Oak Ave Brough HU15 ..68 C6
  Goole DN14 ....149 D1
  Grimsby DN32 ....102 F4
  Kingston upon Hull
  HU10 ....138 D1
  Scawby DN20 ....108 F8
  Withernsea HU19 ....75 A5
Oak Cl Beverley HU17 ..137 A6
  Sproatley HU11 ....58 C5
Oak Cres 7 DN8 ....79 A1
Oak Dene DN14 ....149 E6
Oak Dr
  Kingston upon Hull HU4 .144 B7
  Newport HU15 ....52 F1
  5 Thorpe Willoughby YO8 ..48 B1
Oak Field YO8 ....148 A1
Oak Glade 6 YO31 ...127 F3
Oak Gr
  Barrow upon Humber
  DN19 ....85 C4
  9 Hedon HU12 ....72 C7
Oak Hill HU10 ....138 C2
Oak Rd Healing DN41 ..101 F5
  Kingston upon Hull HU6 .140 D5
  2 North Duffield YO8 ...50 A7
  Scunthorpe DN16 ....151 B3
  Thorne/Moorends DN8 ..79 A1
Oak Rise 4 YO26 ...129 C3
Oak Sq 3 HU7 ....56 E7
Oak St 3 YO26 ....129 E5
Oak Tree Ave 14 DN21 .117 C1
Oak Tree Cl
  Beverley HU17 ....136 D6
  Strensall YO32 ....14 B7
Oak Tree Ct 7 YO8 ...50 D7
Oak Tree Dr HU17 ...136 D6
Oak Tree Est 10 HU12 ..58 C1
Oak Tree Gr YO32 ...127 D3
Oak Tree La YO32 ...127 C2
Oak Tree Way 10 YO32 ..14 B7
Oak Way DN35 ....103 B1
Oakdale Ave 3 HU10 ..143 E8
Oakdale Cl 6 DN14 ...78 C8
Oakdale Rd YO30 ...126 F2
Oakdene HU16 ....139 B6
Oaken Grove Sch YO32 ..13 F5
Oakfield Cl DN20 ....98 C2
Oakfield Ct 11 HU6 ...139 F4
Oakford Cl DN17 ...150 F4
Oakhill Cres 3 YO32 ...14 A6
Oakington Garth HU7 ..141 D6
Oakland Ave
  33 Hatfield DN7 ....92 D4
  York YO31 ....131 A4
Oakland Dr YO31 ...131 A4
Oaklands
  Camblesforth YO8 ....63 C5
  Gilberdyke HU15 ....66 D8
  Hornsea HU18 ....134 D2

Oaklands continued
  Hutton Cranswick YO25 ..32 E6
  6 Strensall YO32 ....14 B7
Oaklands Ave 3 DN14 ..65 B7
Oaklands Cres YO8 ...63 C5
Oaklands Dr
  Kingston upon Hull
  HU10 ....138 C1
  Kingston upon Hull
  HU13 ....143 D3
Oaklands Rd DN40 ...87 C2
Oaklands Sch YO24 ..129 C2
Oaklands Small Sch
  DN14 ....64 E4
Oaklands Sports Ctr
  YO24 ....129 C2
Oakleigh 8 DN16 ....96 E2
Oakmoor Gr DN8 ....79 B2
Oakmoor Rd DN8 ....79 B2
Oakney Wood Dr YO8 ..148 D1
Oaks La HU10 ....116 C2
Oaktree Dr 4 HU7 ...141 D7
Oakwell Ave YO16 ...123 A6
Oakwell Gr 2 HU8 ...141 B1
Oakwood Cl HU4 ...144 A7
Oakwood Dr DN37 ...102 B3
Oakwood Pk DN14 ...77 F6
Oakwood Rise 1 DN16 ..96 D2
Oatlands Rd YO16 ...123 A6
Oban Ave HU9 ....142 A2
Oban Ct
  32 Immingham DN40 ...87 B1
  5 Immingham DN40 ..101 B8
Occupation La
  North Kelsey LN7 ....110 A4
  Swanland HU14 ....69 B8
Ocean Bvd HU9 ....146 B6
Ocean Dr 7 HU15 ....52 F1
Ochrepit Hill YO42 ...17 A2
Octon Rd YO25 ....9 A8
Ogilvy Dr DN17 ....96 C2
Ogle Rd 11 YO15 ....5 B2
Ogleforth YO31 ....156 B3
O'Hanlon Ave DN20 ...98 C2
Old Annandale Rd
  HU10 ....143 C8
Old Boys Sch La 4 YO8 .48 B8
Old Bridge Rd HU18 ..134 C2
Old Brumby St DN16 ..151 A4
Old Carpenter's Yd
  DN7 ....92 B6
Old Chapel La DN37 ..101 F1
Old Clee Jun & Inf Sch
  DN32 ....153 B2
Old Coppice 14 YO32 ..13 F5
Old Courts Rd 5 DN20 ..98 C2
Old Crosby DN15 ....96 D7
Old Dairy DN19 ....85 D8
Old Dike Lands YO32 ..127 C8
Old Epworth Rd E DN7 ..92 F4
Old Farm Cl HU12 ....73 E3
Old Farm Ct 5 DN37 ..113 D6
Old Farm Way YO8 ...148 B2
Old Field La DN7 ....92 A5
Old Fleet 2 DN37 ...102 B3
Old Fleet Prim Sch
  HU9 ....142 E2
Old Forge Rd 4 DN10 .116 C5
Old Forge Way HU11 ...45 D2
Old Green La YO41 ...28 A5
Old Hall La YO41 ....27 C5
Old Haxey La DN10 ..116 C6
Old Howe La YO25 ...22 A3
Old Ironside Rd DN16 .151 D7
Old La Blacktoft DN14 ..66 C4
  Hirst Courtney YO8 ...62 F3
  Long Marston YO26 ...24 A6
  Reedness DN14 ....80 E7
  Sigglesthorne HU11 ...45 F8
Old Lea YO43 ....40 B1
Old Leys La DN21 ...119 C3
Old Main Rd
  Barnetby Le Beck DN37 .113 B6
  Irby DN37 ....112 D7
Old Manor Dr DN20 ..108 E8
Old Manor Lawns
  HU17 ....154 B2
Old Market Pl 6 DN31 .152 D3
Old Mill Cl YO43 ....135 F3
Old Mill La
  7 Broughton DN20 ...97 E3
  Whitton DN15 ....67 E4
  Wrawby DN20 ....98 D4
Old Moor La YO24 ...132 E2
Old Orch YO32 ....127 D8
Old Orch The
  Fulford YO10 ....133 E7
  Shipton YO31 ....12 F5
Old Plumtree La 2
  DN36 ....114 B1
Old Pond Pl 16 HU14 ..69 A4
Old Post Office La
  Barnetby le Wold DN38 ..99 B4
  5 South Ferriby DN18 ..84 A7
Old Rd Healing DN37 ..102 B5
  Holme-on-Spalding-Moor
  YO43 ....40 B1
  Leconfield HU17 ....43 C6
  Ottringham HU12 ....73 E3
Old Rectory Gdns
  DN16 ....151 A1
Old Row DN15 ....82 A5
Old Sch The
  East Garton HU11 ....59 F6
  Kirk Bramwith DN7 ...92 A7
  Roxby cum Risby DN15 ..82 F4
Old School Dr DN20 ..108 F5

Old School La
  Barlby with Osgodby YO8 .49 B5
  North Kelsey LN7 ....110 A4
  20 Scunthorpe DN16 ...96 D2
Old School Yd 8 DN21 .108 B1
Old Showfields 8 DN21 .117 B1
Old Sunderlandwick La
  YO25 ....20 D1
Old Tatham YO43 ....40 B1
Old Thorne Rd DN7 ...92 E4
Old Trent Rd DN10 ..116 F1
Old Trough La HU15 ...52 C2
Old Vicarage La 5 LS25 ..61 A8
Old Vicarage Pk DN20 .108 E8
Old Village HU20 ....55 A4
Old Village St DN15 ...95 E6
Old Village The YO32 ..127 F5
Old Warp La DN18 ...84 A7
Old Waste HU17 ....154 A3
Oldbeck Rd HU17 ...137 C4
Oldfield Ave HU6 ...140 C6
Oldfield Cl
  Barnby Dun DN3 ....92 A4
  Stainforth DN7 ....92 B6
Oldfield Cres DN7 ...92 C6
Oldfield La HU12 ....92 B6
Oldfield Rd 11 DN8 ...93 B7
Oldlane Gate DN14 ...80 D4
Oldstead Ave HU6 ...139 F5
Olinda Rd 2 YO15 ...122 E2
Oliver Ct DN31 ....152 D4
Oliver St DN35 ....153 D4
Oliver's Cl 18 YO14 ....2 F8
Olivers La YO16 ....122 E3
Olivier Ct HU4 ....144 E3
Olympia Cres YO8 ...148 E6
Ombler Cl 11 HU12 ...73 C4
Omega Bvd DN8 ....92 F8
Omega Cl YO16 ....123 A5
Omega Cres YO16 ...122 F5
On Hill HU14 ....69 B6
Ontario Rd DN17 ....96 B2
Onyx Gr 2 HU3 ....145 A4
Oole Rd DN35 ....153 F2
Or The HU9 ....142 B4
Orb La DN15 ....96 D8
Orby Gr 5 DN33 ...102 D2
Orch The Leven HU17 ...45 A7
  14 New Waltham DN36 .114 A7
Orchard Ave 8 DN21 ..107 C3
Orchard Cl
  2 Barrow upon Humber
  DN19 ....85 C7
  13 Barton-upon-Humber
  DN18 ....84 F8
  Blyton DN21 ....117 F5
  Bridlington YO16 ...122 E7
  3 Burringham DN17 ...95 D4
  Burton upon Stather
  DN15 ....82 B5
  Great Driffield YO25 ..124 D5
  Hatfield DN7 ....92 C3
  Kingston upon Hull
  HU10 ....143 F7
  2 Kirton in Lindsey DN21 .108 B1
  Messingham DN17 ...107 D7
  6 Monk Fryston LS25 ...61 A8
  Morton DN21 ....117 A3
  9 Norton DN6 ....76 E2
  10 Pocklington YO42 ...28 F4
  Roos HU12 ....74 A8
  2 Scunthorpe DN16 ..151 B2
  Selby YO8 ....148 A4
  York YO24 ....129 E1
Orchard Cotts 4 YO19 ..26 F7
Orchard Croft
  8 Epworth DN9 ....105 D7
  10 Grimsby DN33 ...113 E8
  Kingston upon Hull
  HU16 ....139 B8
Orchard Ct
  3 Market Weighton YO43 .135 E4
  10 Waltham DN37 ...113 D6
Orchard Dr
  Burton upon Stather
  DN15 ....82 B5
  Goole DN14 ....65 C4
  Gunness DN15 ....95 E6
  Hatfield DN7 ....92 C3
  Kingston upon Hull
  HU13 ....143 E1
  Middleton-on-the-Wolds
  YO25 ....31 C4
  1 Winteringham DN15 ..68 B1
Orchard Garth HU17 ..136 D6
Orchard Gdns
  4 Pocklington YO42 ...28 F4
  York YO31 ....131 A4
Orchard Gr Hatfield DN7 .92 D5
  Misterton DN10 ....116 D4
Orchard La
  Great Driffield YO25 ..124 E5
  Hutton Cranswick YO25 ..32 E8
  Thorne/Moorends DN8 ..79 B2
Orchard Paddock
  34 Haxby YO32 ....13 E5
  28 Scunthorpe DN17 ...96 C2
Orchard Park Rd HU6 .139 D8
Orchard Pk YO42 ....39 B6
Orchard Rd
  Kingston upon Hull HU4 .144 B5
  Selby YO8 ....148 A4
  Skidby HU16 ....138 A8
  Upper Poppleton YO26 .126 A1
Orchard St DN8 ....93 B6
Orchard View 3 YO30 .126 B5
Orchard Way
  1 Gilberdyke HU15 ...66 D7

Orchard Way continued
  Hensall DN14 ....62 C2
  Howden DN14 ....65 A6
  9 Pocklington YO42 ...28 F4
  Selby YO8 ....148 A4
  Skirlaugh HU11 ....45 D2
  1 Strensall YO32 ....14 B7
  Thorpe Willoughby YO8 ..48 B2
  York YO24 ....129 E1
Orchards The YO25 ...32 E8
Orchid Rise DN15 ...150 F6
Ordnance La YO10 ...130 D1
Ore Blending Rd DN16 ..97 A4
Oribi Cl HU4 ....144 C2
Oriel Cl 6 HU17 ....55 D8
Oriel Gr
  Kingston upon Hull HU9 .142 A1
  York YO30 ....130 A8
Oriole Cl DN17 ....150 E2
Orion Cl 8 HU3 ....145 B5
Orion Way DN34 ...102 B2
Orkney Cl 7 HU8 ...141 E7
Orkney Pl
  11 Immingham DN40 ...87 C1
  3 Immingham DN40 ...101 C8
Ormerod Cres HU5 ..139 D2
Ormerod Rd HU5 ...139 D2
Ormonde Ave HU6 ...140 D4
Ormsby Cl 9 DN35 ...103 B2
Ormsby Rd DN17 ...150 E1
Orniscourt HU6 ....139 F7
Orrin Cl YO24 ....132 C7
Orwell St DN31 ....152 F5
Osbaldwick La YO10 ..131 B4
Osbaldwick Link Rd
  YO19 ....131 D4
Osbaldwick Prim Sch
  YO10 ....131 C4
Osbaldwick Village
  YO10 ....131 C4
Osborne Dr DN36 ...114 A5
Osborne Rd DN41 ...101 E8
Osborne St
  Cleethorpes DN35 ...153 F2
  Grimsby DN31 ....152 D3
  Kingston upon Hull HU1 .155 A2
Osbourne Dr
  Keyingham HU12 ....73 C4
  4 York YO30 ....126 E3
Oshawa Dell YO42 ...29 A2
Oslear Cres DN35 ...153 E1
Oslo Rd HU7 ....140 F5
Osmington Gdns 10 YO32 14 A7
Osprey Cl
  Kingston upon Hull HU6 .140 B8
  4 York YO24 ....132 B8
Ostler's Cl YO23 ...132 C3
Ostler's La DN18 ....84 A5
Ostman Rd YO26 ...129 C5
Oswald Rd DN15 ...151 A7
Otley Cl HU4 ....142 C2
Ottawa Cl 6 HU16 ...138 F5
Ottawa Rd DN17 ....96 C2
Otterburn St 6 HU3 ..145 A4
Otterwood Bank 6
  YO24 ....129 B1
Otterwood La YO24 ..129 B1
Otterwood Paddock
  YO41 ....15 D2
Ottringham Rd HU12 ..73 D4
Oubrough La HU11 ...57 F8
Oundle Cl 5 DN36 ...96 E2
Our Ladys RC Prim Sch
  YO24 ....129 E1
Ouse Acres YO26 ...129 D6
Ouse Bank YO8 ....148 B6
Ouse Carr La DN14 ...65 A5
Ouseburn Ave YO26 ..129 C6
Ousecliffe Gdns YO30 .130 A6
Ousegate YO8 ....148 D5
Out Gates Foston YO25 ..22 B3
  Harpham YO25 ....21 E6
Out Holme La DN36 ..114 C3
Out Newton Rd
  Holmpton HU19 ....75 C1
  Skeffling HU12 ....90 B6
Outer Trinities HU17 ..154 B2
Outgaits Cl 4 YO14 ....2 F8
Outgaits La YO14 ....3 A8
Outgang La YO19 ...131 D6
Outgang The
  Brantingham HU15 ...68 B4
  South Cliffe YO43 ...53 B6
Outgate DN17 ....94 E6
Outlands Rd HU16 ...139 D5
Outram Cl HU2 ....155 A4
Outstray Rd HU12 ...89 C7
Oval The Brough HU15 ..68 C6
  Grimsby DN33 ....102 E1
  Hatfield DN7 ....92 C5
  Kellingley DN14 ....61 C3
  Kingston upon Hull HU8 .141 C2
  Kingston upon Hull
  HU10 ....143 E8
  Pocklington YO42 ...29 A4
  28 Scunthorpe DN17 ...96 C2
Overdale Cl YO24 ...132 D8
Overland Rd HU16 ...139 C5
Overstrand Dr HU7 ..141 D6
Overton Ave HU10 ...143 E8
Overton Ct 6 DN18 ...69 F1
Overton Rd YO30 ....12 F3
Ovington Terr YO23 ..130 B2
Owen Ave HU13 ....144 A1
Owlwood Ct 7 YO19 ...26 F7
Owlwood La 6 YO19 ...26 F7
Owmby Hill DN38 ...110 D8
Owmby La LN7 ....110 C5

Owmby Mount DN38 ..110 D8
Owmby Rd DN38 ...110 D8
Owmby Wold La DN38 .110 E8
Owst Rd HU12 ....73 C4
Owsthorpe La DN14 ...52 A1
Owston Ave 2 YO10 ..131 A3
Owston Ferry Rd DN9 .116 E8
Owston Rd
  1 Hunmanby YO14 ....2 F1
  West Stockwith DN10 .116 E6
Owthorne Cl YO16 ...122 B6
Owthorne Grange
  HU19 ....74 F6
Owthorne Wlk HU19 ...74 F7
Ox Calder Cl 16 YO19 ..26 F7
Ox Carr La YO32 ....14 B6
Ox Cl YO41 ....15 D2
Ox Pasture La DN17 ...81 C2
Oxen La YO8 ....49 E3
Oxenhope Rd HU6 ...140 D7
Oxford Cl 6 HU17 ...136 E1
Oxford Rd DN14 ...149 C5
Oxford St
  Bridlington YO16 ...122 D3
  Cleethorpes DN35 ...153 F1
  Grimsby DN32 ....153 A4
  Kingston upon Hull HU2 .155 C4
  Scunthorpe DN16 ...151 D2
  5 York YO24 ....130 A3
Oxmardyke La HU15 ...66 E6
Oxmarsh La DN19 ...70 E2

P

Packman La HU10 ...143 B8
Paddock Cl YO23 ...132 A2
Paddock Ct
  Bridlington YO16 ...122 E7
  Great Driffield YO25 ..124 F5
  33 Immingham DN40 ...87 B1
Paddock La
  Blyton DN21 ....117 F5
  West Butterwick DN17 ..95 C1
Paddock La E DN17 ..117 F5
Paddock Rise 8 DN19 ..85 C8
Paddock The
  14 Airmyn DN14 ....64 E4
  Beverley HU17 ....136 D6
  1 Buckton/Bempton YO15 ..4 D3
  3 Burton upon Stather
  DN15 ....82 B4
  13 Gilberdyke HU15 ...66 D8
  Kingston upon Hull
  HU16 ....139 C6
  Kingston upon Hull HU4 .144 B5
  North Ferriby HU14 ...69 A5
  8 Selby YO8 ....148 C6
  2 Swanland HU14 ....69 C2
  Wilberfoss YO41 ....27 E5
  York YO26 ....129 C6
Paddock Way YO26 ..129 C6
Paddocks The
  Barnoldby le Beck DN37 .113 B6
  Beckingham DN10 ...116 D1
  6 Crowle DN17 ....94 D7
  Great Driffield YO25 ..124 D3
  Hutton Cranswick YO25 ..32 E7
  Kingston upon Hull
  HU10 ....143 B7
  Middleton YO25 ....31 C4
Pademoor Terr DN17 ...81 A2
Padstow Cl 7 HU7 ...56 F5
Pagehall Cl DN33 ...102 E1
Paghill Est HU12 ...72 A5
Pagnell Ave YO8 ...148 B4
Paignton Ct DN33 ...113 E4
Painsthorpe La YO41 ...17 B5
Paisley Prim Sch HU3 .145 A6
Paisley St HU3 ....145 A7
Palace Ave YO15 ...122 E2
Palanza Terr 8 YO15 .122 E2
Pale La YO8 ....61 F7
Palmcourt HU6 ....139 F7
Palmer Gr YO8 ....148 A3
Palmer La
  Barrow upon Humber
  DN19 ....85 C4
  York YO1 ....156 C2
Palmes Cl YO19 ....36 E8
Pam Cl 19 DN40 ....87 C1
Pamela Rd DN40 ...87 C1
Panama Dr HU11 ....45 D2
Panman La YO19 ...26 F8
Paper Mill Rd DN14 ...79 B8
Parade Cl YO31 ...130 F6
Parade The HU5 ...140 D1
Paradise Cotts YO17 ...17 D8
Paradise Pl 10 Brigg DN20 98 B2
  3 Goole DN14 ....149 D4
Paragon Sq HU1 ...155 A2
Paragon St
  Kingston upon Hull HU1 .155 A2
  York YO1 ....156 C1
Parish Church Prim Sch The
  DN21 ....117 B1
Park Ave Barlow YO8 ...63 C7
  Barton-upon-Humber
  DN18 ....84 E8
  Beverley HU17 ....154 A4
  1 Brandesburton YO25 ..34 B2
  Bridlington YO15 ...122 F3
  Crowle DN17 ....94 D7

Park Ave *continued*
Goole DN14 .....149 B5
Great Driffield YO25 .....124 E6
Grimsby DN32 .....152 D1
Kingston upon Hull HU16 .....139 A7
Kingston upon Hull HU5 ..140 A1
Kingston upon Hull HU13 .....143 E3
New Earswick YO32 .....127 D5
Scunthorpe DN17 .....96 C2
Snaith DN14 .....78 D8
Withernsea HU19 .....75 A6
Park Ave W HU5 .....140 A1
Park Cl 6 Airmyn DN14 ....64 E4
Great Driffield YO25 .....124 E5
Immingham DN40 .....87 C1
Melbourne YO42 .....39 A7
Skelton YO30 .....126 B4
Westwoodside DN9 .....105 A2
Park Cres
11 Thorne/Moorends DN8 .93 A7
York YO31 .....156 C4
Park Dr Campsall DN6 ....76 E1
Grimsby DN32 .....152 E1
4 Westwoodside DN9 ...105 A2
Park Farm Rd DN15 .....96 C8
Park Gate YO32 .....14 B8
Park Gdns 5 DN14 .....78 C8
Park Gr
Kingston upon Hull HU5 ..140 C1
Selby YO8 .....148 B3
York YO31 .....156 C4
Park Grove Sch YO31 ..156 C4
Park Hill DN21 .....108 B1
Park La Balne DN14 .....77 C5
Barlow YO8 .....63 C7
Bishop Wilton YO42 .....16 F1
Burn YO8 .....62 D7
Humberston DN35 .....103 C1
Kingston upon Hull HU16 .....139 A7
Kingston upon Hull HU5 ..140 D1
Luttons YO17 .....7 C8
Redbourne DN21 .....108 F3
Rowley HU17 .....55 B6
Saxby All Saints DN20 .....84 A3
Scawby DN20 .....108 F8
Snaith & Cowick DN14 .....78 C6
Tickton HU17 .....44 D2
Westwoodside DN9 .....105 A2
Wilberfoss YO41 .....27 E5
Womersley DN6 .....76 D6
York YO24 .....129 F3
Park La E HU4 .....144 C6
Park La W HU4 .....144 C5
Park Lane Cl
Bishop Wilton YO42 .....16 F1
Hatfield DN7 .....92 C4
Park Lane Rd DN7 .....92 C2
Park Rd Airmyn DN14 .....64 E4
Barlow YO8 .....63 C7
Brough HU15 .....68 E5
Dalton Holme HU17 .....42 C8
Kingston upon Hull HU3 ..140 D1
Sproatley HU11 .....58 C5
Thorne/Moorends DN8 .....79 B2
Park Rise 17 YO14 .....2 F8
Park Rose Pottery & L Park★ YO15 .....10 F3
Park Row
Hornsea HU18 .....134 D4
Kingston upon Hull HU3 ..145 D7
Selby YO8 .....148 D5
Sproatley HU11 .....58 C5
Park St
Cleethorpes DN35 .....153 B4
Hotham YO43 .....53 D5
Kingston upon Hull HU3 ..145 D6
Messingham DN17 .....107 D7
Selby YO8 .....148 D5
Swinefleet DN14 .....80 D8
Winterton DN15 .....83 B5
York YO24 .....156 A1
Park View
Barton-upon-Humber DN18 .....84 F8
2 Bridlington YO16 .....122 F4
Cleethorpes DN35 .....153 C3
Crowle DN17 .....94 D6
Kingston upon Hull HU4 ..144 E4
Messingham DN17 .....107 D7
10 Thorne/Moorends DN8 .93 A7
Park View Cl DN19 .....85 C7
Park View Terr DN17 .....106 C8
Park Wlk HU4 .....144 B5
Parkdale 15 DN18 .....84 E8
Parker Ave YO26 .....129 B2
Parker Rd DN36 .....114 D8
Parker St
8 Cleethorpes DN35 ....103 C2
Cleethorpes DN35 .....153 F1
Parker's La DN16 .....151 C2
Parkfield Ave HU14 .....69 A4
Parkfield Dr
Bridlington YO16 .....122 B5
Kingston upon Hull HU3 ..144 F6
Parkhill Cres DN3 .....92 A4
Parkhill Rd DN3 .....92 A4
Parkhill Rise DN15 .....83 B5
Parkhurst Cl 4 HU8 .....142 C6
Parkin Ave YO8 .....148 E4
Parkin Rd DN17 .....96 C2
Parkinson Ave DN15 .....151 A7
Parkland Way YO32 ....127 D8
Parklands Beeford YO25 ..34 C8
3 West/East Butterwick DN17 .....106 D8
Parklands Cres 10 HU14 .69 A5
Parklands Dr 9 HU14 ...69 A5
Parklands The 2 HU15 ..54 A2
Parks Cl 8 DN39 .....86 A1
Parks Rd DN7 .....92 C4
Parkside Cl
Kingston upon Hull HU16 .....138 F6
Kingston upon Hull HU5 ..140 B1
York YO24 .....129 E3
Parkside Prim Sch DN14 .....149 B6
Parkstone Gr 8 DN7 ....92 D4
Parkstone Prim Sch HU6 .....140 D7
Parkstone Rd HU6 .....140 C7
Parkway The
Kingston upon Hull HU16 .....139 A5
Kingston upon Hull HU10 .....143 E8
9 Snaith DN14 .....78 C8
Parkways 12 Hatfield DN7 .92 D4
Selby YO8 .....148 B3
Parkwood Jun & Inf Sch DN17 .....150 C4
Parkwood Rise DN3 .....92 A3
Parliament St
8 Brough HU15 .....68 D6
Goole DN14 .....149 C4
Kingston upon Hull HU1 ..155 B2
York YO1 .....156 B2
Parris Pl DN35 .....153 D3
Parsonage Cl YO25 .....125 E7
Parsons Cl 10 DN14 .....64 E4
Parson's La DN14 .....65 A7
Parsons La YO26 .....12 E1
Parson's Wlk 11 DN14 ....64 E4
Parthian Rd HU9 .....142 C3
Partridge Cl
Caistor LN7 .....111 B4
Scunthorpe DN17 .....150 E2
Partridge Dr LN7 .....111 F2
Parva Rd HU18 .....134 D4
Pashley Rd Thorne DN8 ...93 B8
20 Thorne/Moorends DN8 .93 B7
Pasture Ave
5 Burringham DN17 .....95 D4
Goole DN14 .....149 D5
Pasture Cl Kilham YO25 ....9 B3
2 Leconfield HU17 .....43 D6
Market Weighton YO43 ...135 E4
Skelton YO30 .....126 B5
2 Strensall YO32 .....14 B6
Wistow YO8 .....48 D6
Pasture Farm Cl YO10 ..133 D6
Pasture Hill YO17 .....16 E8
Pasture La
Amcotts DN17 .....81 D1
Beverley HU17 .....136 D4
Ellerton YO42 .....38 C1
Garthorpe & Fockerby DN17 .....81 D6
Heworth YO31 .....131 B8
Sproatley HU11 .....58 D6
Pasture Prim Sch DN14 .....149 C5
Pasture Rd
Barton-upon-Humber DN18 .....69 F1
Goole DN14 .....149 C4
Hornsea HU18 .....134 D4
Pasture Rd N DN18 .....69 F1
Pasture Rd S DN18 .....69 F1
Pasture Rise YO16 .....122 B5
Pasture St DN32 .....152 E3
Pasture Terr HU17 .....136 D4
Pasture Way YO8 .....48 D6
Pastures Ct DN17 .....107 D7
Pastures La HU12 .....60 B4
Pastures The
Carlton DN14 .....63 C3
Hutton Cranswick YO25 ...32 F7
4 York YO24 .....132 E8
Pately Pl 1 YO26 .....129 D4
Patrick Pool YO1 .....156 B2
Patrick St DN32 .....152 E1
Patricks Cl LN7 .....110 A4
Patrington C of E Sch HU12 .....74 D1
Patrington Garth HU7 ..141 C8
Patrington Rd
Holmpton HU19 .....75 C2
Ottringham HU12 .....73 F3
Patterdale Dr YO30 .....126 E1
Patterdale Rd HU5 .....144 E8
Paul Cres 5 DN36 .....114 C8
Paul La DN15 .....83 D1
Paull Lands Rd HU12 ....72 D5
Paull Prim Sch HU12 ....72 A5
Paull Rd HU12 .....72 B6
Pavement YO1 .....156 B2
Paver La YO1 .....156 C2
Pavilion Cl HU8 .....141 B2
Pavilion Gdns DN17 .....150 F6
Paxdale HU7 .....140 E8
Payton Cl 17 YO42 .....29 A4
Peace Haven 3 DN37 ...113 D7
Peace Wlk 6 HU12 .....58 D1
Peacehaven Cl 2 HU7 ..141 B7
Peach Tree Ct 5 HU3 ...145 D5
Peacock St DN17 .....150 F1
Peaks Ave DN36 .....114 A8
Peaks La Grimsby DN32 ..152 F1
New Waltham DN36 .....114 A8
Peaks Parkway DN32 ...152 E2
Pear Tree Ave
Long Drax YO8 .....63 F7
8 Poppleton YO26 .....12 F1
Pear Tree Cl
Kingston upon Hull HU8 ..141 D4
11 Waltham DN37 .....113 D6
York YO32 .....127 F4
Pear Tree La
Covenham St Bartholomew LN11 .....121 E6
Kirk Bramwith DN7 .....92 A8
Utterby DN36 .....121 B5
Pearson Ave HU5 .....140 D1
Pearson Park Prim Sch HU3 .....145 D8
Pearson Rd DN35 .....103 C2
Pearson St HU2 .....155 A3
Peartree Ct YO1 .....156 C3
Peartree Pk 19 DN14 ....65 A7
Pease St HU3 .....155 A2
Peaseholme HU13 .....143 C1
Peasholme Gn YO1 .....156 C2
Peat Carr Bank DN9 ...104 C3
Peckham Cl HU8 .....141 E5
Peckitt St YO1 .....156 B1
Peel Castle Rd 8 DN8 ...93 B7
Peel Cl YO10 .....131 A1
Peel Hill Rd 5 DN8 .....93 B7
Peel Pl HU17 .....136 D4
Peel St
Kingston upon Hull HU3 ..145 D8
York YO1 .....156 C1
Pefham La YO17 .....17 F4
Pegasus Rd DN20 .....99 A8
Pelham Ave 8 DN33 ...102 E1
Pelham Cl
5 Barton-upon-Humber DN18 .....84 E8
5 Beverley HU17 .....55 F8
Pelham Cres 15 DN41 ...101 A4
Pelham Dr 1 HU9 .....146 C7
Pelham Pl
9 Grimsby DN33 .....102 E1
15 Strensall YO32 .....14 A7
Pelham Rd
Cleethorpes DN35 .....153 D3
Grimsby DN34 .....152 C2
1 Holton le Clay DN36 ...114 A5
Immingham DN40 .....87 C1
Pelham Sq DN35 .....153 E3
Pelham View DN20 .....108 F5
Pelham's Pillar★ DN37 .....111 C6
Pem La 7 YO42 .....29 A4
Pemberton Dr 3 DN36 .113 F7
Pemberton St 1 HU8 ..146 B7
Pembroke Ave 13 DN16 ..96 D2
Pembroke Gr HU9 .....142 A1
Pembroke Rd DN34 .....152 A1
Pembroke St YO30 .....130 B7
Pembroke Terr YO15 ...122 E1
Pendeen Cl 7 DN21 ....117 C1
Pendeen Gr HU8 .....141 B3
Pendle Cl 18 HU7 .....57 A6
Pendreth Pl DN35 .....153 D3
Pendrill St HU3 .....140 E1
Penistone Ct 2 HU9 ...146 D7
Penley's Gr St YO31 ...156 C4
Pennine Cl
Immingham DN40 .....87 B2
York YO32 .....127 F4
Pennine Rd DN8 .....93 A7
Pennine Way HU7 .....57 A6
Pennington St HU8 .....146 B7
Pennyman Rd HU17 ....154 C4
Penrose Cl 9 HU7 .....56 F5
Penshurst Ave HU13 ...143 F3
Penshurst Rd DN35 ....103 B2
Pentland Ave DN14 ....149 D5
Pentland Cl HU8 .....141 F7
Pentland Dr YO32 .....127 E3
Penwith Dr HU10 .....143 F7
Penyghent Ave YO31 ...131 A5
Peploe Cres 6 DN19 .....70 E2
Peploe La DN19 .....70 E2
Peppercorn Cl 6 YO26 .129 E4
Peppercorn Wlk
Grimsby DN32 .....152 E3
11 Holton le Clay DN36 .114 A5
Peppercorns The 2 HU15 .....66 D8
Peppermint Way YO8 ..148 A5
Peppin La LN11 .....121 D2
Peppleton Cl HU8 .....141 C4
Percival St DN15 .....151 A8
Percy Cl HU17 .....43 C6
Percy Dr 4 DN14 .....64 E4
Percy Rd
14 Hunmanby YO14 .....3 A8
Pocklington YO42 .....29 A4
Percy St Goole DN14 ...149 C1
Kingston upon Hull HU2 ..155 A3
Scunthorpe DN16 .....151 B6
York YO31 .....156 B3
Percy's La YO1 .....156 C2
Peregrine Cl HU4 .....144 D2
Perivale Cl HU8 .....142 A5
Perkins Cl DN37 .....102 C4
Perran Cl HU7 .....141 B7
Perry St HU3 .....145 A6
Pershore Ave DN34 .....102 B2
Perth St HU5 .....144 F8
Perth Way 3 DN40 .....101 B8
Petchell Way DN32 .....152 E4
Peter Hill Dr YO30 .....130 A8
Peter La YO1 .....156 B2
Peterborough Rd DN16 .....151 B3
Petercroft Cl 5 YO19 ....26 F7
Petercroft La YO19 .....26 F7
Peterhouse Rd DN34 ...152 A1
Petersfield Cl HU7 .....141 B6
Petersham Cl 1 HU8 ...142 A5
Petersway YO30 .....156 A4
Petre Ave YO8 .....148 E3
Petuaria Cl HU15 .....68 B6
Pevensey Cl 1 HU7 ....141 B7
Peveril Ave DN17 .....150 F4
Pheasant Cl DN17 .....150 E2
Pheasant Ct 1 LN7 .....111 B4
Pheasant Dr 5 YO24 ...132 B8
Phelps Pl DN32 .....153 C1
Phelps St DN35 .....153 B5
Philadelphia Terr 2 YO23 .....130 B2
Philip Ave
Cleethorpes DN35 .....103 B2
5 Waltham DN37 .....113 E7
Philip Gr DN35 .....103 B2
Philips Cres DN15 .....150 F7
Phillips La 4 DN37 .....101 F1
Phoenix Cl HU8 .....141 F4
Phoenix House Sch DN32 .....153 B4
Phoenix Parkway DN15 ..96 B7
Phoenix St Goole DN14 ..149 D4
Grimsby DN32 .....152 E3
Phyllis Ave DN34 .....152 B3
Piccadilly
8 New Waltham DN36 ...114 A7
York YO1 .....156 C2
Pick Haven Garth DN14 ..61 F3
Pickering Ave HU18 ....134 D2
Pickering Gr 9 DN8 .....93 A7
Pickering Pk YO25 .....31 C4
Pickering Rd HU4 .....144 C3
Pickerings The 17 HU14 ..69 A4
Picksley Cres DN36 ....114 A5
Pidgeon Cote La 3 DN19 .....86 A8
Pier Rd HU19 .....75 A6
Pier St HU1 .....155 B1
Piggy La 4 HU19 .....75 A6
Pighill La HU17 .....136 D7
Pighill Nook Rd LS25 ....61 C7
Pike Hills Mount YO23 .....132 A3
Pilgrim Ave DN40 .....87 C1
Pilgrim St YO31 .....156 B4
Pilgrim's Cl 5 DN40 ....86 E3
Pilgrims Way DN40 .....87 B1
Pilham La DN21 .....117 E4
Pilmar La HU12 .....60 B1
Pilots Way HU9 .....155 C1
Pimpernel Way 15 DN16 .96 E2
Pinchbeck Ave DN16 ...151 C6
Pincheon Gn La DN14 ...78 D4
Pine Cl DN37 .....102 B5
Pine Ct 8 DN35 .....103 B1
Pine Hall Rd DN3 .....92 A3
Pine Mdws HU10 .....143 B8
Pine Tree Cl YO8 .....48 B2
Pine Tree La 1 LS25 ....61 A7
Pine Wlk 4 Brough HU15 .68 C6
Healing DN41 .....102 A5
Pinefield Ave 4 DN3 ....92 A3
Pinefield Rd DN3 .....92 A3
Pinelands 4 YO32 .....127 D7
Pinelands Way YO10 ....131 C3
Pinetree Ave 5 DN21 ...107 C3
Pinetree Cl 4 DN20 .....97 E4
Pinewood Cl 5 YO42 ....29 A3
Pinewood Cres DN33 ...102 C2
Pinewood Ct 4 YO42 ....29 A3
Pinewood Dr YO8 .....63 D4
Pinewood Gr
2 Kingston upon Hull HU4 .....144 C7
6 York YO31 .....127 E2
Pinewood Hill 4 YO10 .131 C3
Pinewood Rd 3 YO42 ....29 A3
Pinfold 10 Epworth DN9 ..105 E6
South Cave HU15 .....53 F1
Pinfold Cl
4 Bridlington YO16 .....122 D6
5 Riccall YO19 .....37 A1
Pinfold Ct
3 Bridlington YO16 .....122 D6
4 Preston HU12 .....58 C1
4 York YO30 .....130 A7
Pinfold Gdns
Bridlington YO16 .....122 D6
14 Holton le Clay DN36 ...114 B5
Pinfold Gr YO16 .....122 C6
Pinfold Hill YO8 .....48 D6
Pinfold La Asselby DN14 .64 F6
Bempton YO16 .....4 B1
Bridlington YO16 .....122 C7
Burstwick HU12 .....73 A6
Fishlake DN7 .....92 D8
10 Grimsby DN33 .....102 E1
Holton le Clay DN36 .....114 A5
Kirk Smeaton WF8 .....76 B3
Moss DN6 .....77 D1
Norton DN6 .....76 E2
Pollington DN14 .....77 F6
Roos HU12 .....60 A1
Stallingborough DN41 .....101 D6
25 Thorne/Moorends DN8 .93 A8
Pinfold Mdws YO16 .....122 C6
Pinfold Mews HU17 .....154 B3
Pinfold St
Bridlington YO16 .....122 D5
Eastrington DN14 .....51 F1
Pinfold St *continued*
Howden DN14 .....65 A6
Pinfold View DN14 .....77 F6
Pinfold Way S 2 YO16 .122 D5
Pingley La DN20 .....98 C1
Pingley Mdw DN20 .....98 C1
Pinkney's La YO25 .....124 D4
Pinney's Ct 7 DN41 ....101 F5
Piper Rd YO25 .....32 E8
Piper's La HU11 .....46 C2
Pippin Ct 11 DN15 .....96 B7
Pippin Dr 16 DN16 .....96 D1
Pit La HU12 .....73 A4
Pitbalk Hill YO43 .....53 E4
Pitman Ave DN18 .....84 E8
Pitmoor La 5 DN39 .....86 A1
Pitsfold Cl 11 HU7 .....57 A5
Pitt St HU3 .....144 F7
Plains La DN8 .....93 F3
Plane St HU3 .....145 A5
Plantain Cl 14 DN16 .....96 E2
Plantation Cl HU17 .....137 B4
Plantation Dr
Barlby with Osgodby YO8 ..49 B5
1 South Cave HU15 .....53 F1
Welton HU14 .....68 F5
York YO26 .....129 C6
Plantation Gr YO26 ....129 C6
Plantation Rd 22 DN8 ....93 A8
Plantation View YO16 ..123 A8
Plantation Way 23 YO32 .13 E5
Plaxton Bridge Rd HU17 .....56 C7
Pleasure Island Theme Pk★ DN35 .....103 E1
Plimsoll Way HU9 .....146 B6
Plough Garth The DN14 ..61 F3
Plough Hill 12 LN7 .....111 B4
Ploughlands 1 YO32 ...127 C7
Ploughman's Cl YO23 ..132 C3
Ploughmans' La YO32 ..127 C7
Plover Dr 9 HU15 .....68 C6
Plover Sq 2 LN7 .....111 B4
Plowden Rd HU3 .....144 F5
Plum Tree Dr DN36 ....115 C2
Plum Tree Rd HU11 .....58 D5
Plum Tree Way DN16 ...151 A5
Plum Tree Wlk HU15 .....54 A2
Plumer Ave YO31 .....131 A5
Plumtree Hill Rd DN7 ...92 C7
Plumtree La 1 DN36 ...114 B1
Plumtree Rd HU12 .....72 E4
Plym Gr HU8 .....142 C6
Plymouth Cl 8 DN15 ....83 A5
Plymouth Rd DN17 .....150 D4
Poacher's Croft 3 DN9 ..94 E1
Pochard Cl 3 HU15 .....52 F1
Pocklington C of E Infants Sch YO42 .....29 A4
Pocklington Ind Est YO42 .....28 F3
Pocklington La
Bishop Wilton YO42 .....16 F2
Huggate YO42 .....18 A1
Pocklington Sch YO42 ...28 F3
Pockthorpe La YO25 .....8 F2
Poffinder Wood Rd DN7 .....92 E7
Poles Bank DN9 .....104 E6
Pollard Cl YO32 .....127 E3
Pollington Balne C of E Sch DN14 .....77 F6
Polton Cl DN7 .....92 D7
Polton Toft DN7 .....92 D7
Pomona Way YO25 .....124 D3
Pond Side DN39 .....85 E3
Pond St 3 YO8 .....148 D6
Ponds Way 6 DN18 .....69 E1
Pontefract Rd DN14 .....78 A8
Pool Ct 7 DN14 .....149 C4
Pool Dr DN17 .....96 C2
Poolbank La HU15 .....68 E5
Poorhouse La HU9 .....142 C1
Poplar Cl
Burstwick HU12 .....73 A6
Kingston upon Hull HU4 ..144 A5
Skirlaugh HU11 .....45 E2
Poplar Ct HU7 .....141 C6
Poplar Dr
Beverley HU17 .....136 F6
Bridlington YO16 .....123 A6
Brigg DN20 .....98 C3
3 Broughton DN20 .....97 D3
Goole DN14 .....65 C3
21 Humberston DN36 ....103 D1
Poplar Gdns Drax YO8 ....63 F5
Scunthorpe DN16 .....151 B3
Poplar Gr
Cleethorpes DN35 .....153 E3
10 Hedon HU12 .....72 C7
1 Scotter DN21 .....107 C3
York YO32 .....127 E3
Poplar La DN21 .....118 A2
Poplar Rd
Cleethorpes DN35 .....153 E3
Hatfield DN7 .....92 C4
Healing DN41 .....101 F5
Poplar St YO26 .....129 E5
Poplars The
15 Brandesburton YO25 ...34 B2
11 Brayton YO8 .....48 D1
Knottingley WF11 .....61 A1
5 Leconfield HU17 .....43 D6
Poplars Way HU17 .....136 D1
Popple St HU9 .....146 B6
Poppleton Hall Gdn YO26 .....126 A3
Poppleton Rd YO26 ....129 E4

Poppleton Road Prim Sch
YO26 . . . .**129** E5
Poppleton Sta YO26 . . . .**24** F8
Popplewell Cl DN9 . . . . .**94** E2
Popplewell Terr **14** DN9 .**105** E6
Poppy Cl
2 Scunthorpe DN15 . . .**96** B7
Selby YO8 . . . .**148** C2
Porlock Dr HU7 . . . .**57** A5
Port Ave HU6 . . . .**140** C8
Portal Rd YO26 . . . .**129** B6
Porter St
Kingston upon Hull HU3 .**155** A8
Scunthorpe DN15 . . . . .**151** A8
Portholme Cres **7** **148** C5
Portholme Dr YO8 . . . . .**148** C4
Portholme Rd YO8 . . . . .**148** C5
Portington Rd DN14 . . . .**51** F1
Portisham Pl **12** DN14 . . .**14** A7
Portland Ave DN32 . . . . .**152** E1
Portland Pl
Bridlington YO16 . . . . . .**122** C3
Grimsby DN32 . . . .**102** F2
Kingston upon Hull HU2 .**155** A3
Portland St
Kingston upon Hull HU2 .**155** A8
Rawcliffe DN14 . . . .**79** B8
York YO31 . . . .**156** B4
Portmadoc Cl **5** HU7 . . .**56** F7
Portman Rd DN15 . . . . . .**96** C7
Portobello St HU9 . . . . .**141** F3
Post Office La
Ashby cum Fenby DN37 . .**113** D2
Humberside Airport
DN39 . . . .**100** A4
Whitton DN15 . . . .**67** F3
Post Office Row DN14 . . .**64** A1
Post Office **12** YO15 . . . . .**5** A1
Postern Cl YO23 . . . . . .**156** B1
Postern La YO42 . . . .**38** D6
Posterngate HU1 . . . . . .**155** B2
Postill Sq YO16 . . . .**122** C4
Potterdale Dr HU20 . . . . .**55** A4
Potterill La HU7 . . . .**141** D6
Potters Dr HU7 . . . .**57** A4
Potters La HU17 . . . .**94** D7
Potters Way HU18 . . . . .**134** C1
Pottery La YO31 . . . .**130** E2
Pottinger Gdns LN7 . . . .**111** A2
Potts La DN17 . . . .**94** D7
Poultney Garth **4** HU12 . .**72** D7
Powell St YO8 . . . .**148** B6
Powells Cres DN16 . . . . .**151** B5
Pratt's La HU11 . . . .**46** D3
Precentor's Ct YO31 . . . .**156** B3
Prescott Ave **9** HU15 . . .**68** C5
Prescott Gr **23** DN17 . . . . .**92** D4
Preston Cty Prim Sch
HU12 . . . .**58** D1
Preston Dr **1** DN20 . . . . .**98** C2
Preston La DN18 . . . .**84** F8
Preston Rd Hedon HU12 . .**72** C8
Kingston upon Hull HU9 .**141** F1
Prestwick Ct YO26 . . . . .**129** B5
Pretoria St HU3 . . . .**144** F5
Pretymen Cres DN36 . . . .**114** A7
Price's La YO23 . . . .**156** B1
Prickett Rd YO16 . . . . . .**122** C4
Priest Cl YO14 . . . .**2** E8
Priest La YO19 . . . .**26** F5
Priestgate
3 Barton-upon-Humber
DN18 . . . .**84** F8
Kingston upon Hull HU7 .**141** D6
Nafferton YO25 . . . .**125** F6
Priestgate **3** DN15 . . . . .**125** F6
Primitive Chapel La
DN40 . . . .**86** F2
Primrose Dr **1** HU5 . . . .**144** C8
Primrose Gr YO8 . . . . . .**148** A6
Primrose Hill **9** WF11 . . .**61** A3
Primrose Vale **1** WF11 . . .**61** A2
Primrose Way
Humberston DN35 . . . . .**103** C1
1 Scunthorpe DN15 . . .**96** B7
Prince Albert Gdns
DN32 . . . .**152** E5
Prince Charles Dr **20**
DN18 . . . .**84** F8
Prince Philip Dr **21** DN18 .**84** F8
Prince St
Bridlington YO16 . . . . . .**122** F2
Kingston upon Hull HU1 .**155** B2
Princes Ave
1 Hedon HU12 . . . . . .**72** C7
Kingston upon Hull
HU13 . . . .**143** E1
Kingston upon Hull HU5 .**145** E4
Prince's Ave HU17 . . . . .**75** A6
Prince's Dock St HU1 . . .**155** B2
Princes Gdns HU17 . . . .**154** C4
Prince's Rd
Cleethorpes DN35 . . . . .**153** E2
Kingston upon Hull HU5 .**140** C2
Princes St **16** DN20 . . . .**98** C2
Princess Alexandra Co **14**
DN17 . . . .**96** C2
Princess Ave DN7 . . . . . .**92** C6
Princess Cl YO43 . . . . . .**135** D3
Princess Dr **22** DN18 . . . .**84** F8
Princess Rd
Market Weighton YO43 . .**135** D3
Strensall YO32 . . . .**14** B7
Princess Royal Hospl The
HU8 . . . .**142** A6
Princess St
4 Bridlington YO15 . . .**122** F2
Goole DN14 . . . .**149** C2
Immingham DN40 . . . . . .**87** C1

Princess St continued
Kingston upon Hull HU2 .**155** B3
Princess Terr **5** YO15 . . .**122** F2
Princess Way
8 Beverley HU17 . . . . .**55** E8
Woodmansey HU17 . . . .**136** D1
Printing Office La **6**
DN17 . . . .**94** D8
Priors Cl DN36 . . . .**114** A7
Prior's Wlk YO26 . . . . . .**129** D6
Priory Ave **18** HU12★ **69** A4
Priory Cell (Rems of)★
DN37 . . . .**113** A2
Priory Cl
Bridlington YO16 . . . . . .**122** E5
10 Swanland HU14 . . . .**69** B7
Wilberfoss YO41 . . . .**27** F6
Priory Cres
Bridlington YO16 . . . . . .**122** E4
Kingston upon Hull
HU16 . . . .**139** B5
Scunthorpe DN17 . . . . .**151** A3
Ulceby DN39 . . . .**86** A2
Priory Dr HU5 . . . .**139** D2
Priory Farm Dr **4** HU4 . .**144** D2
Priory Gr HU4 . . . .**144** D3
Priory La
Barrow upon Humber
DN19 . . . .**85** D8
Scunthorpe DN17 . . . . .**150** E2
1 Snaith DN14 . . . .**63** C1
Priory Lane Inf Sch
DN17 . . . .**150** E2
Priory Park Cl **3** LS25 . . .**61** A8
Priory Park Gr **5** LS25 . . .**61** B8
Priory Prim Sch HU5 . . .**139** D1
Priory Rd
Beverley HU17 . . . .**154** C2
Cottingham HU5 . . . . . .**139** C3
Grimsby DN37 . . . .**102** B3
Kingston upon Hull
HU16 . . . .**139** B5
Scunthorpe DN17 . . . . .**151** A2
Priory Rd or H DN6 . . . . .**76** C2
Priory St YO1 . . . .**156** A1
Priory Way
Kingston upon Hull HU4 .**144** A1
1 Snaith DN14 . . . .**63** B1
Priory Wlk YO16 . . . . . .**122** D4
Priory Wood Way
YO31 . . . .**127** F2
Proctor's Way DN20 . . . .**109** A5
Promenade YO15 . . . . . .**122** F2
Promenades Sh Ctr The
YO15 . . . .**122** F2
Prospect Cl
Camblesforth YO8 . . . . . .**63** D5
Pollington DN14 . . . .**77** F6
Prospect Pl
Kingston upon Hull HU9 .**146** B7
Wistow YO8 . . . .**48** D6
Prospect Rd DN14 . . . . . .**79** B8
Prospect St
Bridlington YO15 . . . . . .**122** E2
Kingston upon Hull HU2 .**155** A3
Prospect Terr
Fulford YO10 . . . .**133** D6
York YO1 . . . .**156** B1
Prospect Way YO8 . . . . .**148** B6
Providence Cres DN18 . . .**84** E8
Providence Pl
10 Bridlington YO15 . . .**122** F3
1 Great Driffield YO25 .**124** F4
Providence Row HU2 . . .**155** A4
Prunus Ave HU17 . . . . . .**143** F8
Pryme Rd DN16 . . . .**151** C4
Pryme St
Kingston upon Hull
HU10 . . . .**143** F6
Kingston upon Hull HU2 .**155** A3
Prystie Pl **1** DN35 . . . . .**103** B1
Puddiners La DN14 . . . . .**80** E7
Pudding Gate **8** HU17 . . .**43** C4
Pulcroft Rd HU13 . . . . . .**143** D2
Pulham La YO25 . . . .**19** B5
Pulleyn Cl **3** YO32 . . . . .**14** C8
Pulleyn Dr YO24 . . . . . .**129** F1
Pulman St HU3 . . . .**145** A7
Pump Hill DN20 . . . .**109** D6
Pump La YO15 . . . .**4** C3
Purbeck Rd
Grimsby DN33 . . . .**113** E8
Scunthorpe DN17 . . . . .**150** E2
Purey Cust Nuffield Hospl
The YO31 . . . .**156** B3
Purton Gr HU7 . . . .**141** A7
Putney Cl HU8 . . . .**141** E5
Pyewipe Rd DN31 . . . . .**152** C5
Pykestone Cl **15** HU7 . . . .**57** A6
Pyruss Dr HU4 . . . .**144** B2
Pytchley Wlk **1** DN35 . . .**103** C1

Q

Quadrant The HU6 . . . . .**139** F4
Quaker Gn **1** YO24 . . . .**132** C2
Quaker La HU17 . . . . . .**136** D1
Quaker Rd HU12 . . . .**59** F4
Quales Mews **2** HU18 . .**134** C4
Quant Mews YO10 . . . . .**131** B3
Quantock Cl
7 Kingston upon Hull
HU3 . . . .**145** D5
Scunthorpe DN17 . . . . .**150** D4
5 Thorne/Moorends DN8 .**93** A4
Quantock Rd DN33 . . . . .**113** E8
Quarrington Gr **19** HU7 . .**56** F6

Quarry Ave **20** WF11 . . . . .**61** A2
Quarry Rd DN6 . . . .**76** F2
Quart La
Eastrington DN14 . . . . . .**65** F7
Reedness DN14 . . . .**80** D6
Quay La DN14 . . . .**80** C7
Quay Rd
Bridlington YO16 . . . . . .**122** D3
4 Thorne DN8 . . . .**78** F1
Quay St HU1 . . . .**155** B2
Quay The YO8 . . . .**148** D6
Quayside **1** DN8 . . . .**78** F1
Quebec Dr HU16 . . . . . .**138** E5
Quebec Rd DN17 . . . .**96** C2
Queen Anne's Rd
YO30 . . . .**156** A3
Queen Dike★ YO17 . . . . . .**17** B8
Queen Elizabeth Ave **4**
DN18 . . . .**84** A7
Queen Elizabeth High Sch
DN21 . . . .**117** B2
Queen Elizabeth Rd **6**
DN36 . . . .**114** C8
Queen Elizabeth Way **19**
DN18 . . . .**84** F8
Queen Margarets Sch
YO19 . . . .**37** A5
Queen Mary Ave
DN35 . . . .**153** C3
Queen Mary Ave Inf Sch
DN35 . . . .**153** C3
Queen St
Barton-upon-Humber
DN18 . . . .**69** F1
Bridlington YO15 . . . . . .**122** E2
14 Brigg DN20 . . . .**98** C2
13 Epworth DN9 . . . . . .**105** E6
Great Driffield YO25 . . . .**124** F4
Grimsby DN32 . . . .**152** E3
Kingston upon Hull HU1 .**155** B1
Kirton in Lindsey DN21 . .**108** B1
Scunthorpe DN17 . . . . . .**96** B7
16 Thorne/Moorends DN8 .**93** A8
15 Winterton DN15 . . . .**83** A5
Withernsea HU19 . . . . . .**75** A6
York YO24 . . . .**156** A2
Queen St N HU19 . . . . . .**74** F7
Queen St S **15** HU19 . . . .**75** A6
Queen Victoria Sq
HU1 . . . .**155** B2
Queen Victoria St
YO23 . . . .**130** B1
Queen's Alley HU1 . . . . .**155** C1
Queen's Ave **5** DN8 . . . . .**69** F1
Queen's Cl Goole DN14 . .**149** C4
2 Kingston upon Hull
HU16 . . . .**139** B7
Queens Cres DN17 . . . . . .**95** D6
Queen's Cres DN7 . . . . . .**92** C6
Queen's Ct **17** DN8 . . . . .**93** A8
Queens Dock Ave
HU1 . . . .**155** B2
Queens Dock Mus★
HU1 . . . .**155** B2
Queens Dr DN14 . . . . . .**149** D6
Queen's Dr HU16 . . . . . .**139** A4
Queen's Gate HU16 . . . .**139** B7
Queen's Gate St HU3 . . .**145** B5
Queens Gdns HU18 . . . .**134** B3
Queen's Par DN35 . . . . .**153** F1
Queen's Rd DN38 . . . . . .**99** B4
Queens Rd
Beverley HU17 . . . .**154** C4
Immingham DN40 . . . . . .**87** D1
Kingston upon Hull HU5 .**140** C2
Queen's Staith Rd
YO1 . . . .**156** B2
Queen's View Cres
DN16 . . . .**151** D3
Queen's Way HU16 . . . . .**139** B7
Queensbury Way **2**
HU14 . . . .**69** B6
Queensfield LN7 . . . . . .**110** A1
Queensgate
Beverley HU17 . . . .**154** A1
Bridlington YO16 . . . . . .**122** E4
Queensgate Sq YO16 . . .**122** D3
Queensmead
Aldbrough HU11 . . . .**47** C1
Beverley HU17 . . . .**55** E8
Lund YO25 . . . .**31** F2
Queensway
Goole DN14 . . . .**149** D4
Grimsby DN37 . . . .**102** C4
Scunthorpe DN16 . . . . .**151** C3
Woodmansey HU17 . . . . .**56** B8
Queensway The HU6 . . .**140** B8
Queenswood Gr YO24 . . .**129** D2
Queenswood Rd **7** DN16 .**96** C5
Quillcourt HU6 . . . .**139** E7
Quilter Ave HU4 . . . . . .**144** B5
Quilter Dr HU4 . . . .**142** F7
Quinton Rd DN32 . . . . . .**102** F2
Quorn Mews **26** DN35 . .**103** C2
Quorum The HU4 . . . . . .**144** A2

R

Racca Ave **11** WF11 . . . . .**61** A2
Racca Gn WF11 . . . .**61** A2
Race La Carlton YO8 . . . . .**63** B4
Wootton DN39 . . . .**85** D3
Racecourse Rd YO23 . . .**133** B8
Rachel Cl **3** DN21 . . . . .**117** B2
Radcliffe Rd DN41 . . . . .**101** F5
Radcroft La YO43 . . . . . .**53** D5
Raglan St HU5 . . . .**140** C3

Raich Carter Way HU6 . . .**56** D5
Railway Cres **2** HU19 . . . .**75** A6
Railway Pl DN31 . . . . . .**152** F5
Railway St
Barnetby le Wold DN38 . . .**99** B4
Beverley HU17 . . . .**154** B2
Grimsby DN32 . . . .**152** F4
Hornsea HU18 . . . .**134** D4
Kingston upon Hull HU1 .**155** B1
Railway Terr
Grimsby DN32 . . . .**152** D3
York YO24 . . . .**130** A4
Raincliffe St **4** YO8 . . . .**148** C5
Raines Cl HU12 . . . .**73** A6
Rainham Cl HU8 . . . . . .**141** E7
Rainhill Rd **2** HU5 . . . . .**140** A2
Rainsborough Way **3**
YO30 . . . .**130** A8
Rainsburgh La YO25 . . . . . .**2** A3
Rainsbutt Rd DN17 . . . . . .**94** C8
Rainswood Ct **8** HU7 . . .**56** F6
Raithby Ave **3** DN41 . . .**101** A4
Raithby Gr **12** DN33 . . . .**102** D2
Rake Bridge Bank DN7 . . .**92** D1
Raker Cl YO19 . . . .**37** F7
Rakes Rd HU7 . . . .**42** E2
Raleigh Dr
Kingston upon Hull HU9 .**146** D6
Sproatley HU11 . . . .**58** D5
Ralph Butterfield Sch
YO32 . . . .**13** F5
Ram Bvd DN15 . . . .**96** C8
Ramsay Cl YO31 . . . . . .**156** C4
Ramsden Ave DN18 . . . . .**84** E8
Ramsden Cl YO25 . . . . . .**124** A1
Ramsden Ct HU17 . . . . .**154** C3
Ramsden Pl **11** HU16 . . .**138** F5
Ramsey Ave DN33 . . . . .**113** B2
Ramsey Cl YO16 . . . . . .**122** C4
Ramsey Rd YO16 . . . . . .**122** B2
Ramsgate Cl HU8 . . . . . .**141** E7
Ramskir La DN7 . . . .**92** C7
Ranby Cres HU18 . . . . . .**134** C2
Ranby Dr HU18 . . . .**134** C2
Ranby Rd DN17 . . . .**150** E4
Rands Est **7** HU12 . . . . . .**58** D1
Randsfield Ave **17** HU15 . .**68** C5
Rangely Cl **9** HU7 . . . . . .**57** A6
Rannoch Cl **6** HU7 . . . . . .**57** A6
Ransom Ct DN39 . . . . . .**100** A4
Ransome Way **14** HU15 . . .**68** C6
Ratcliffe Ct YO30 . . . . . .**126** C5
Ratcliffe St YO30 . . . . . .**130** B7
Rattan Row YO25 . . . .**8** C6
Ratten Row
4 Bishop Burton HU17 . .**43** A2
12 North Newbald YO43 . .**53** F7
Rauceby Cl **10** HU7 . . . . .**56** F6
Raven Cl DN20 . . . .**97** D4
Raven Gr YO26 . . . .**129** C4
Raven St HU9 . . . .**146** D7
Ravencroft La **1** DN10 . .**116** D1
Ravendale **18** DN18 . . . . .**84** F8
Ravendale Rd **10** DN35 . .**103** D2
Ravendale St N DN15 . . .**151** A4
Ravendale St S DN15 . . .**151** B7
Ravenfleet Rd DN21 . . . .**116** F6
Ravenhill Cl **14** DN35 . . .**103** B4
Ravenscar Rd **9** DN37 . .**102** C5
Ravenspur Rd HU11 . . . . .**58** A4
Ravenspurn Rd YO25 . . .**122** B6
Ravenspurn Gr **1** HU9 . .**142** A2
Ravenspurn Rd HU12 . . . .**89** C8
Ravenspurn St DN31 . . .**152** D4
Raventhorpe Medieval
Village★ HU17 . . . .**97** B2
Rawcliffe Ave YO30 . . . .**129** F8
Rawcliffe Cl YO30 . . . . .**126** E2
Rawcliffe Croft YO30 . . .**126** D8
Rawcliffe Dr YO30 . . . . .**129** F8
Rawcliffe Gr HU4 . . . . . .**144** D5
Rawcliffe in Snaith Prim Sch
DN14 . . . .**64** A2
Rawcliffe Inf Sch
YO30 . . . .**126** E1
Rawcliffe La YO30 . . . . .**126** E1
Rawcliffe Rd DN14 . . . . .**149** A4
Rawcliffe Sta DN14 . . . . .**79** A8
Rawdale Cl HU15 . . . .**54** A2
Rawdon Ave YO10 . . . . .**130** F4
Rawling Way HU3 . . . . . .**145** C5
Rawlinson Ave **22** LN7 . .**111** B4
Ray Dike Cl YO32 . . . . . .**127** C2
Raymond Rd DN15 . . . . .**151** C3
Raywell Cl HU10 . . . . . .**143** F7
Raywell St HU2 . . . .**155** A3
Read Cl YO8 . . . .**63** F5
Read Sch YO8 . . . .**63** F5
Reading Gate
Reedness DN17 . . . .**80** C3
Swinefleet DN14 . . . .**80** D7
Reading Room Yd **4**
HU14 . . . .**69** A4
Real Aeroplane Mus The★
YO8 . . . .**50** D5
Reangamoor La YO42 . . . .**39** D2
Reaper's Rise **15** DN9 . . .**105** E6
Reaper's Way **3** DN9 . . .**105** D2
Recreation Rd **2** YO8 . . .**148** D6
Recto Ave DN17 . . . .**150** F2
Rectory Ave **34** DN21 . . .**117** B2
Rectory Cl YO25 . . . .**125** F7
Rectory Gdns
3 Beckingham DN10 . . .**116** D1
York YO23 . . . .**130** B1

Rectory La
Beeford YO25 . . . .**22** C1
Preston HU12 . . . .**58** C1
Roos HU12 . . . .**60** C3
Rectory Rd HU12 . . . .**74** A8
Rectory St DN9 . . . .**105** E6
Rectory View YO25 . . . . .**32** C3
Rectory Way YO43 . . . . .**40** B1
Red House La YO43 . . . .**135** A4
Red House Prep Sch
YO26 . . . .**12** D3
Red La
Market Weighton YO43 . .**135** E5
South Ferriby DN18 . . . . .**83** F7
Red Lion St **2** DN14 . . . .**149** C4
Red Tower★ YO1 . . . . . .**130** E4
Redbourn Cl DN16 . . . . .**151** B5
Redbourn E Rd DN16 . . . .**97** A6
Redbourn Way DN16 . . . .**151** B6
Redbourne Mere
DN21 . . . .**108** E2
Redbourne Rd
Grimsby DN33 . . . .**102** D2
Hibaldstow DN20 . . . . . .**108** F4
Waddingham DN21 . . . . .**119** F8
Redbourne St
Kingston upon Hull HU3 .**145** B5
3 Scunthorpe DN16 . . .**151** B5
Redcap La YO42 . . . .**38** C5
Redcar Gr DN32 . . . .**153** A1
Redcar St HU8 . . . .**155** C4
Redcliff Dr **19** HU14 . . . . .**69** A4
Redcliff Rd HU13 . . . .**69** E4
Redcoat W **1** YO24 . . . .**132** B8
Redcombe La DN20 . . . . .**98** B2
Redeness St YO31 . . . . .**130** E5
Redfern Cl HU3 . . . .**145** D5
Redgates HU17 . . . .**55** B7
Redhall Cl **7** DN3 . . . . . .**92** A2
Redhill Field La YO23 . . . .**24** D1
Redhouse La YO8 . . . .**63** F6
Redland Cres **2** DN8 . . . .**93** B8
Redland Dr HU10 . . . . . .**143** C8
Redman Cl
15 Gainsborough DN21 .**117** C1
York YO10 . . . .**133** C8
Redmayne Sq YO32 . . . . .**14** B8
Redmire Cl HU7 . . . .**57** A6
Redmires Cl YO30 . . . . .**127** A2
Redruth Cl HU7 . . . .**141** C6
Redthorn Dr YO31 . . . . .**127** F1
Redwing Cl YO25 . . . . . .**125** A5
Redwood Cl YO16 . . . . . .**122** E6
Redwood Cl DN16 . . . . . .**96** E2
Redwood Dr
7 Cleethorpes DN35 . . .**103** B1
6 Haxby YO32 . . . .**13** E5
Redwood Gdns YO25 . . .**124** F3
Redwood Way YO16 . . . .**122** D6
Redwoods The HU10 . . . .**138** C2
Reed St HU2 . . . .**155** A3
Reedholme La DN8 . . . . . .**78** F4
Reedness Prim Sch
DN14 . . . .**66** A1
Reedsway **12** YO25 . . . . .**34** B2
Reeves The YO24 . . . . . .**129** C1
Refinery Rd DN16 . . . . . .**151** F6
Reform St HU2 . . . .**155** B3
Regency Ct **8** DN16 . . . . .**69** E1
Regency Mews **2** YO24 . .**132** C3
Regent Cl
Kingston upon Hull
HU10 . . . .**138** E1
Kingston upon Hull HU10 .**145** C6
Regent Dr **13** DN17 . . . . .**94** D7
Regent St
Beverley HU17 . . . .**154** B2
York YO10 . . . .**130** E3
Regent St Pavement **8**
YO42 . . . .**29** A3
Regent Terr **7** YO15 . . . .**122** F2
Regents Ct **14** YO26 . . . .**129** F5
Regina Cres **2** HU5 . . . .**140** A1
Reginald Gr YO23 . . . . . .**130** C1
Reginald Rd DN15 . . . . . .**96** C7
Regis Ct HU9 . . . .**142** B3
Register Sq HU1 . . . . . .**154** A2
Reigate Cl HU8 . . . .**142** A4
Reighton Ave YO30 . . . .**129** F8
Reldene Dr **10** YO30 . . . .**126** E1
Remello Ave DN16 . . . . .**152** F1
Remington Ave YO25 . . . .**34** E3
Remple Ave DN7 . . . .**93** A3
Remple Comm Rd DN7 . . .**92** F2
Remple La DN7 . . . .**93** A3
Rendel St DN31 . . . .**152** D5
Rensburg St HU9 . . . . . .**141** D1
Renshaw Gdns **2** YO26 .**129** E4
Reporto Ave DN32 . . . . .**152** F1
Repton Dr
Kingston upon Hull HU7 .**141** D5
21 Scunthorpe DN16 . . .**96** D2
Reservoir Rd HU6 . . . . . .**140** F3
Responso Ave DN32 . . . .**152** F1
Reston Ct **8** DN15 . . . . .**103** D2
Reston Gr **25** DN33 . . . .**102** D2
Retford Gr HU9 . . . .**142** E1
Retreat Hospl The
YO10 . . . .**130** F2
Revesby Ave
13 Grimsby DN34 . . . .**102** C2
Scunthorpe DN16 . . . . .**151** A3
Revesby Ct DN16 . . . . . .**151** A4
Revigo Ave DN32 . . . . . .**152** F1

Revill Cl 17 DN21 ......107 C3
Reygate Gr YO23 ......132 B2
Reynolds Cl HU14 ......68 E5
Reynolds Inf Sch
  DN35 ......153 D3
Reynolds Jun Sch
  DN35 ......153 D3
Reynolds St DN35 ......153 D2
Reynoldson St HU5 ......140 C2
Rhodena Ave YO16 ......122 D2
Rhodes St HU3 ......144 F5
Rhyl Cl 4 HU7 ......56 F7
Rialto Ave DN32 ......152 E1
Ribble St 4 HU3 ......145 B4
Ribblesdale 3 HU7 ......141 A6
Ribblesdale Cl HU16 ......122 F7
Ribston Cl 9 DN16 ......96 D1
Ribstone Gr YO31 ......131 B6
Riby Ct DN36 ......114 B5
Riby Rd Cabourne LN7 ......111 D6
  Keelby DN41 ......101 A4
  Scunthorpe DN17 ......150 E1
  Stallingborough DN41 ......101 C4
  Swallow LN7 ......112 A7
Riby Sq DN32 ......152 F5
Riby St DN31 ......153 A5
Ribycourt HU6 ......139 E7
Riccall Cl HU6 ......140 A6
Riccall CP Sch YO19 ......36 F1
Riccall La YO19 ......36 D1
Richard Cooper St
  DN14 ......149 E4
Richard St
  Grimsby DN31 ......152 C4
  Selby YO8 ......148 B5
Richardson Cl DN36 ......114 D8
Richardson St YO23 ......130 C2
Richdale Ave DN21 ......108 B1
Richmond Cl YO43 ......135 F3
Richmond Dr
  Goole DN14 ......149 F5
  10 Scunthorpe DN16 ......96 E2
Richmond Gdns HU17 ......136 D1
Richmond Rd
  Cleethorpes DN35 ......153 E1
  Grimsby DN34 ......152 A2
  Kingston upon Hull
    HU13 ......143 E2
  Thorne/Moorends DN8 ......79 B2
Richmond St
  Bridlington YO15 ......122 D1
  2 Kingston upon Hull
    HU5 ......145 B8
  York YO31 ......130 E5
Richmond Way 2 HU17 ......55 E8
Richmond Wlk HU17 ......136 D1
Rickaby Cl YO16 ......122 D4
Ridding Cres DN14 ......64 A1
Ridding La DN14 ......64 A1
Riddings Infants Sch
  DN17 ......96 C2
Riddings Jun Sch DN17 ......96 C2
Ridge View DN20 ......98 C4
Ridgeway YO26 ......129 B3
Ridgeway Rd HU5 ......144 B7
Ridgeway The 102 B2
Ridgewood Ave 8 DN3 ......92 A1
Ridgewood Dr DN15 ......82 A4
Riding Fields Sq
  HU17 ......154 C3
Ridings The
  Beverley HU17 ......136 C6
  Great Driffield YO25 ......125 A6
  Kingston upon Hull
    HU16 ......138 E6
  Kingston upon Hull HU5 ......144 A8
  15 North Ferriby HU14 ......69 A4
Ridsdale HU7 ......140 F7
Rigby Cl HU17 ......136 D7
Rileston Pl 12 DN16 ......96 D1
Rillington Ave HU16 ......139 A5
Rimswell Gr HU9 ......142 A2
Ring Beck La HU15 ......68 A8
Ringley Mdws 5 YO15 ......4 C3
Ringrose St HU3 ......144 F5
Ringstead Garth 4 HU7 ......57 A6
Ringstone Rd YO30 ......126 F3
Ringwood Cl DN16 ......151 B1
Ripley Cl
  Bridlington YO16 ......122 D5
  Kingston upon Hull HU6 ......140 B7
Ripley Gr 3 YO32 ......13 E5
Riplingham Rd
  Kingston upon Hull
    HU10 ......143 A8
  Kingston upon Hull HU10 ......55 C1
  Skidby HU10 ......138 A1
Ripon Ave HU17 ......136 E1
Ripon Cl DN17 ......150 C3
Ripon St DN31 ......152 C3
Ripon Way HU9 ......146 C8
Risby Garth YO16 ......55 C4
Risby Gr HU6 ......139 F5
Risby Hill HU20 ......55 A4
Risby La HU17 ......55 B7
Risby Medieval Village *
  DN15 ......83 A2
Risby Pl HU17 ......154 A1
Risby Rd DN15 ......82 F1
Rise Cl HU11 ......45 C5
Rise La Catwick HU17 ......45 D8
  Rise HU11 ......45 D5
Rise Rd HU11 ......45 F7

Rise The
  7 North Ferriby HU14 ......69 A5
  Scunthorpe DN17 ......96 C2
  South Ferriby DN18 ......84 A8
Risedale 21 LN7 ......111 B4
Riseway HU11 ......45 C5
Risewood YO41 ......15 B2
Rishworth Cl 5 HU7 ......57 A6
Rishworth Gr YO30 ......126 F2
Riston C of E Sch HU11 ......45 C5
Riston Rd HU17 ......45 C7
Riston St HU3 ......145 C5
Rivan Ave 5 DN33 ......113 E8
Rivan Gr 6 DN33 ......113 E8
Rivelin Cres DN16 ......151 A4
Rivelin Pl DN16 ......151 A4
Rivelin Rd DN16 ......151 A3
Rivelin Way YO30 ......126 F2
River Cl 2 Barlby YO8 ......49 B5
  Goole DN14 ......149 F5
River Gr HU4 ......144 E3
River Head YO25 ......124 F3
River Head Dr 3 YO25 ......124 F3
River La Fishlake DN7 ......92 D8
  Market Weighton YO43 ......40 F2
  West Haddlesey YO8 ......62 A5
River Mdw DN20 ......98 B1
River St 1 Selby YO8 ......148 D6
  York YO23 ......156 B1
River View 1 Barlby YO8 ......49 B5
  26 Barton-upon-Humber
    DN18 ......84 F8
  Goole DN14 ......65 C3
River Wlk DN14 ......65 C4
Riverdale 4 DN14 ......61 D4
Riverdale Rd
  Kilpin DN14 ......65 C1
  Scunthorpe DN16 ......151 A3
Riversdale 17 YO32 ......13 F5
Riversdale Dr DN14 ......149 F5
Riversdale Rd HU6 ......140 D6
Riverside
  12 Broughton DN20 ......98 B2
  Great Driffield YO25 ......124 F3
  Rawcliffe DN14 ......64 A2
  Scotter DN21 ......107 C3
Riverside Area Specl Sch
  DN14 ......149 E5
Riverside Cl
  1 Elvington YO41 ......27 C2
  6 Great Driffield YO25 ......124 F3
Riverside Cres YO32 ......127 F6
Riverside Ct
  5 Hessle HU13 ......69 E4
  Rawcliffe DN14 ......64 A2
Riverside Dr DN35 ......103 D1
Riverside Gdns
  1 Elvington YO41 ......27 C2
  2 Poppleton YO26 ......12 F1
Riverside Mews 5
  YO25 ......124 F3
Riverside Wlk
  1 Poppleton YO26 ......12 F1
  5 Strensall YO32 ......14 A7
Riversvale Dr 21 YO26 ......12 F1
Riverview Ave HU14 ......69 A4
Riverview Gdns HU7 ......140 E7
Riverview Rd HU17 ......137 C4
Rivesby Ave DN16 ......151 A3
Riviera Dr YO15 ......123 B6
Rix Rd HU7 ......141 A3
Roall La DN14 ......61 F4
Robert Cl
  Immingham DN40 ......87 B1
  3 Withernsea HU19 ......75 A6
Robert Wilkinson Prim Sch
  YO32 ......14 A7
Robert Wood Ave
  HU17 ......154 A2
Roberts St DN32 ......153 A3
Robin Gr 6 YO24 ......129 F3
Robin Hood Cres 7 DN3 ......92 A1
Robin Hood Rd 5 DN3 ......92 A1
Robinia Dr HU4 ......144 C2
Robinson Cl DN15 ......150 E8
Robinson Dr YO24 ......129 B2
Robinson La DN31 ......153 A6
Robinson Rd DN40 ......87 D2
Robinson Row HU1 ......155 B2
Robinson St E DN32 ......152 E3
Robinson's Gr DN20 ......109 A5
Robinson's La DN36 ......114 B1
Roborough Cl HU7 ......141 B8
Robson Ave HU6 ......140 B8
Robson Rd DN35 ......153 D3
Robson Way
  Kingston upon Hull HU7 ......141 D7
  6 Preston HU12 ......72 C7
Rochdale Rd DN16 ......151 A1
Rochdale Road Jun Sch
  DN16 ......151 A1
Roche Ave YO31 ......130 E8
Roche Dr DN14 ......149 E6
Rochester Ave HU4 ......144 A3
Rochester Cl DN17 ......150 C3
Rochester Ct 3 DN15 ......103 D1
Rockford Ave HU8 ......141 B3
Rockford Gr HU8 ......141 B3
Rockingham Ave
  YO31 ......131 A6
Rockingham Ct 10
  DN34 ......102 B2
Rod Mill Rd DN16 ......151 E5
Rodney Cl HU2 ......155 A4
Roe La LS25 ......61 C7
Rokeby Ave HU4 ......144 B5

Rokeby Cl
  Beverley HU17 ......154 A4
  Kingston upon Hull HU4 ......144 B5
Rokeby Pk HU4 ......144 B5
Rokeby Prim Sch HU4 ......144 B4
Roland Simpson Cl 1
  DN14 ......78 C8
Rolston Ave 3 YO31 ......127 E3
Rolston Cl HU9 ......142 C1
Rolston Rd HU18 ......134 C2
Roman Ave N 17 YO41 ......15 D2
Roman Ave S 4 YO41 ......15 D1
Roman Camps * YO30 ......127 B2
Roman Rigg YO43 ......53 D8
Romans Cl YO19 ......48 F3
Romford Gr HU9 ......142 E1
Romney Gdns 4 HU5 ......140 E2
Romsey Ct 11 DN34 ......102 B3
Romyn Cl YO16 ......122 B2
Ronaldsway Cl 6 HU9 ......142 A3
Ronson Cl HU9 ......142 D3
Rookery Ave 10 DN33 ......102 E2
Rookery Croft 9 DN9 ......105 E6
Rookery Rd DN41 ......101 F5
Rookery The DN20 ......108 F8
Rooklands 2 DN21 ......107 C3
Rookley Cl 3 HU8 ......142 C5
Rook's La HU10 ......116 C5
Roos Cl HU17 ......136 F7
Rootas La HU17 ......43 A6
Rope Wlk
  Bridlington YO15 ......122 E2
  Thorne/Moorends DN8 ......93 A8
Roper St HU1 ......155 A2
Ropers Ct YO23 ......132 C3
Ropery Cl 3 YO25 ......9 C3
Ropery La 1 DN18 ......69 E1
Ropery Rd DN21 ......117 A2
Ropery St
  Grimsby DN32 ......152 F3
  Kingston upon Hull HU3 ......145 D5
Ropewalk The
  9 Caistor LN7 ......111 B4
  York YO31 ......130 E5
Rosaire Pl DN33 ......113 E8
Rosalind Ave DN34 ......152 B3
Rosamond St 7 HU3 ......145 B4
Rose Gdns 4 DN40 ......87 C2
Rose La HU17 ......43 C5
Rose Lea Cl 2 LS25 ......61 A7
Rose St YO31 ......130 C7
Rose Tree Gr YO32 ......127 D4
Rose Wlk DN35 ......151 C7
Roseacres DN14 ......65 C4
Roseberry Ave
  Bridlington YO15 ......122 C1
  15 Hatfield DN7 ......92 D4
Roseberry Gr YO30 ......126 F3
Rosebery St YO26 ......129 F6
Rosecomb Way 6
  YO32 ......127 D7
Rosecroft Way YO30 ......129 E8
Rosedale Leven HU17 ......45 B8
  Scunthorpe DN17 ......96 C1
  Waltham DN37 ......113 D7
Rosedale Ave
  Kingston upon Hull HU9 ......141 E1
  York YO26 ......129 C4
Rosedale Gr HU5 ......144 D7
Rosedale St YO10 ......130 D2
Rosemary Ave DN34 ......102 C3
Rosemary Ct YO1 ......156 C2
Rosemary Pl YO1 ......156 C2
Rosemary Way
  Beverley HU17 ......154 C1
  Humberston DN36 ......103 C1
Rosemoor Cl 19 YO14 ......2 E8
Rosemount Cl 3 HU6 ......140 B8
Rosemount Dr DN16 ......151 B2
Rosemount Grange
  HU13 ......143 C3
Roseveare Ave DN34 ......152 A3
Rosewood Cl
  3 Bridlington YO16 ......123 A6
  4 Kingston upon Hull
    HU4 ......144 B7
Rosewood Way 25 DN16 ......96 D2
Rosey Row 44 HU4 ......146 C7
Rosina Gr N DN32 ......153 B2
Rosina Gr S DN32 ......153 B2
Roslyn Cres HU12 ......72 C7
Roslyn Rd HU3 ......144 E7
Rosmead St HU9 ......146 D8
Rosper Rd DN40 ......87 A4
Ross La Bainton YO25 ......31 D7
  Winterton DN15 ......83 B5
Ross Rd DN31 ......153 B5
Rossall Cl 4 DN16 ......96 E2
Rosslyn St 1 YO30 ......130 A6
Rostun Rd YO16 ......60 B2
Rothbury Rd DN17 ......150 F3
Rothesay Cl 1 HU9 ......141 E1
Rothwell Ave HU18 ......134 C5
Rothwell 15 DN33 ......102 D2
Rothwell Rd
  Cabourne LN7 ......111 C3
  Scunthorpe DN15 ......150 D8
Rotsea La YO25 ......33 B7
Rotterdam Rd HU7 ......141 A5
Rotton Sykes La DN15 ......67 F2
Rougier St YO1 ......156 A2
Round Hill Link YO30 ......126 F2
Roundhay Rd YO15 ......122 D1
Roundway
  Grimsby DN34 ......152 C1
  7 Immingham DN40 ......87 C1
Roundway The HU4 ......144 C5

Routh Ave HU17 ......154 C3
Roval Dr DN40 ......87 B1
Row La HU12 ......90 A7
Rowan Ave
  Beverley HU17 ......136 F7
  York YO32 ......127 D4
Rowan Cl
  3 Barrow upon Humber
    DN19 ......85 C8
  Gateforth YO8 ......48 B1
  2 Keelby DN41 ......101 A4
  10 Thorne/Moorends DN8 ......79 B2
Rowan Cres 2 DN16 ......96 E2
Rowan Dr
  Healing DN41 ......101 F5
  6 Humberston DN36 ......114 D8
Rowan Garth HU16 ......55 C4
Rowan Pl YO32 ......127 D4
Rowan Wlk HU18 ......134 D2
Rowans The 1 DN9 ......105 A2
Rowedale Cl 15 YO14 ......2 F8
Rowland Rd DN16 ......151 A6
Rowlandhall La DN14 ......50 E1
Rowlandson St DN31 ......152 F6
Rowley C of E Sch
  HU20 ......55 A4
Rowley Ct 2 YO32 ......127 F7
Rowley Gr HU6 ......139 F5
Rowley Rd HU20 ......54 F3
Rowlston Gr HU9 ......142 A2
Rowmans The YO30 ......126 C4
Rowmills Rd DN16 ......151 C4
Rowntree Ave YO30 ......130 C8
Rowpit La HU17 ......45 C8
Rowston Cl 7 DN21 ......117 B1
Rowston St DN35 ......103 D3
Rowton Dr HU11 ......45 D2
Roxburgh St 1 HU5 ......145 B8
Roxby Ave YO31 ......127 E3
Roxby Cswy DN15 ......83 C4
Roxby Rd DN15 ......82 F4
Roxton Ave DN41 ......101 A5
Roxton Hall Dr 13 HU4 ......69 A5
Roxton Medieval Village *
  DN40 ......101 A7
Royal Chase YO24 ......132 F8
Royal Cres YO15 ......122 F2
Royal Ct 25 DN35 ......103 D1
Royal Dr DN14 ......79 A8
Royal Dragoon Guard
  Association Regimental
  Mus * YO1 ......156 B2
Royal Garth HU17 ......154 A1
Royal Hull Hospitals NHS
  Trust HU16 ......145 C6
Royal St DN31 ......152 E6
Royal Wlk HU16 ......139 D5
Royd's Rd YO8 ......61 F6
Royston Gr HU8 ......141 B1
Ruard Rd DN19 ......86 B8
Ruards La DN19 ......71 A1
Ruby St 3 YO23 ......130 B1
Rudcarr La YO19 ......14 E1
Rudding Dr YO16 ......122 D7
Ruddings YO19 ......38 A8
Ruddings Cl 9 YO32 ......127 C8
Ruddings La YO42 ......38 E2
Ruddings The YO8 ......148 A4
Rudgate La DN14 ......78 E4
Rudham Ave DN32 ......102 F2
Rudston Beacon * YO25 ......9 F4
Rudston Monolith *
  YO25 ......9 F6
Rudston Rd YO25 ......9 F2
Rue De Nozay 2 DN20 ......97 E4
Ruffhams Cl YO19 ......37 F8
Rufford Rd 3 DN35 ......103 C2
Rufforth Dr HU7 ......43 D5
Rufforth Garth HU7 ......141 C8
Rufforth Prim Sch
  YO23 ......24 C6
Rugby Rd DN16 ......151 A4
Rugby St 5 HU3 ......145 B4
Ruislip Cl HU8 ......142 A5
Runcorn Garth HU4 ......144 B3
Runner End YO43 ......40 A1
Runswick Ave YO26 ......129 B4
Runswick Rd DN32 ......153 B2
Rupert Rd 9 DN33 ......102 E2
Rushcarr La DN17 ......95 C1
Rusholme La YO8 ......64 A5
Rushtons Way DN20 ......108 F5
Rushwood Cl 6 YO32 ......13 F5
Ruskin St HU3 ......145 B6
Russell Ct 18 DN35 ......103 D1
Russell Dr 20 HU12 ......73 C4
Russell Rd DN14 ......149 B4
Russell St
  Kingston upon Hull HU2 ......155 A3
  York YO23 ......130 B2
Russell Wlk DN17 ......107 D7
Russet Cl 12 DN15 ......96 B7
Russet Dr YO31 ......131 B5
Rustenburg St HU9 ......141 E6
Rustic La DN17 ......117 F6
Ruswarp Gr HU6 ......139 E6
Rutherglen Dr HU9 ......142 A3
Rutland Cl YO23 ......132 A3
Rutland Dr 18 DN36 ......114 A7
Rutland Rd
  Goole DN14 ......149 D6
  Kingston upon Hull HU5 ......144 E8
  Scunthorpe DN16 ......151 D3
Rutland St DN32 ......153 A4
Ryburn Cl YO30 ......126 F2
Rydal Ave
  11 Grimsby DN33 ......113 D8
  York YO31 ......131 A6

Rydal Gr HU16 ......138 E6
Rydale Ct HU5 ......140 E3
Rydales The HU5 ......140 E3
Ryde Ave HU5 ......140 D3
Ryde St HU5 ......140 D2
Rye Cl YO32 ......127 C8
Ryecroft 7 YO32 ......14 A6
Ryecroft Ave
  10 Norton DN6 ......76 E2
  York YO24 ......132 C7
Ryecroft Cl YO31 ......131 C8
Ryecroft Dr HU19 ......75 A6
Ryecroft Gdns DN14 ......62 A2
Ryecroft Rd DN6 ......76 E1
Ryedale 12 HU15 ......68 D6
Ryedale Ave DN15 ......83 A6
Ryedale Way YO8 ......148 C3
Ryehill Cl YO32 ......127 D5
Ryehill Gr HU9 ......141 F2
Ryehill La HU12 ......73 A4
Ryelands Ave YO16 ......123 A6
Ryemoor Rd YO32 ......127 C8
Rylatt Pl YO26 ......129 B3
Rymer Pl DN35 ......103 D2
Rysome La HU19 ......75 C1
Rysome Rd HU12 ......90 B7

S

Sable Cl HU4 ......144 C2
Sackville Cl
  5 Beverley HU17 ......55 E8
  14 Immingham DN40 ......87 C1
Sackville Rd 15 DN40 ......87 C1
Sackville St DN34 ......152 C3
Sacred Gate HU12 ......72 D6
Sadberge Ct YO10 ......131 C3
Saddlers Cl
  1 Copmanthorpe YO23 ......132 B3
  Huntington YO32 ......127 F2
Saddler's Way DN9 ......105 D3
Saddlers Way YO26 ......24 A4
Saddleworth Cl 19 HU7 ......57 A6
Saffron Dr 6 DN14 ......63 C1
Saffron Garth 15 HU12 ......74 D1
Saffrondale HU10 ......143 E7
Sage Cl HU17 ......154 B1
Sagefield Cl 5 DN33 ......113 D8
Sailors Wharf HU9 ......146 C6
Sails Dr YO10 ......131 B3
Sainsbury Way HU4 ......144 A1
St Abbs Cl HU9 ......155 C1
St Aelreds Cl YO31 ......130 F4
St Aelreds RC Prim Sch
  YO31 ......131 B5
St Aidan Cres YO16 ......122 E4
St Aidan Ct YO16 ......122 E4
St Aidan Rd YO16 ......122 E4
St Aiden Cl YO43 ......135 E3
St Alban Cl YO16 ......122 E4
St Alban Rd YO16 ......122 E4
St Albans Ave DN31 ......152 A4
St Albans Cl
  7 Beverley HU17 ......136 E1
  Hibaldstow DN20 ......108 F5
  Scunthorpe DN17 ......150 C3
St Alban's Cl HU11 ......46 D3
St Alban Way HU9 ......141 F2
St Andrew Pl YO1 ......156 C2
St Andrew St HU17 ......154 B4
St Andrewgate YO1 ......156 B2
St Andrews Ave DN17 ......96 C1
St Andrews C of E Prim Sch
  HU7 ......140 E7
St Andrew's Cl
  Middleton-on-the-Wolds
    YO25 ......31 C4
  Paull HU12 ......72 A5
  Redbourne DN21 ......108 E3
St Andrew's Dr DN15 ......82 A4
St Andrews Gr 10 DN7 ......92 D4
St Andrews La 5 DN40 ......87 B2
St Andrew's Mount
  HU10 ......143 C8
St Andrews Prim Sch
  HU10 ......143 C7
St Andrews Quay *
  HU3 ......145 A2
St Andrew's St DN21 ......108 A1
St Andrew's Terr 6
  DN14 ......149 C4
St Andrew's Way
  2 Barnby Dun DN3 ......92 A3
  Epworth DN9 ......105 E7
St Andrews Way HU8 ......141 C3
St Anne's Cl HU17 ......137 B5
St Anne's Dr HU16 ......139 C7
St Annes Rd YO15 ......122 F3
St Anne's Rd 8 DN41 ......101 A5
St Annes Specl Sch
  HU15 ......68 E5
St Anne's Wlk 9 HU15 ......68 D6
St Ann's Ave DN34 ......152 B2
St Ann's Ct YO10 ......130 D2
St Anthony Rd YO16 ......122 E4
St Anthony's Dr 24 HU12 ......72 D7
St Anthony's Pk 25 HU12 ......72 D7
St Antony's Pl YO24 ......130 A2
St Augustine Ave
  DN32 ......152 E1
St Augustine Cres
  DN16 ......151 B1
St Augustine Rd HU11 ......45 E2
St Augustine Webster RC
  Prim Sch DN15 ......150 D8

St Augustine's Ct 2 HU5 ....140 D3
St Augustine's Dr YO16 ....122 E5
St Augustine's Gate 30 HU12 ....72 C7
St Augustine's Gr YO16 ....122 E5
St Barbara's Cres 8 DN15 ....82 B4
St Barnabas Ct
4 Kingston upon Hull HU3 ....145 C4
18 York YO26 ....129 F5
St Barnabas Dr HU14 ...69 C7
St Barnabas Rd DN38 ...99 B4
St Bartholomew's Cl 17 DN41 ....101 A4
St Bedes RC Comp Sch DN16 ....151 B2
St Benedict Rd YO23 ...156 A1
St Bernadettes RC Sch DN16 ....151 C2
St Bernard's Cl 9 DN20 ...97 E4
St Boltophs Cl 4 WF11 ...61 A2
St Botolph's Rd DN16 ...151 C3
St Catherines YO30 ...126 D6
St Catherines Cl YO30 ...126 C5
St Catherines Cres 8 DN16 ....96 D2
St Catherines Ct
6 Grimsby DN34 ...102 C3
Kingston upon Hull HU5 ...140 E2
St Catherine's Dr DN7 ...92 C2
St Catherines Dr HU17 ...43 C6
St Chad DN19 ....85 D8
St Chad Cres YO16 ...122 E4
St Chad Gr YO16 ....122 E4
St Chad Rd YO16 ....122 E4
St Chad's Rd DN16 ...151 D3
St Chads Wharf YO23 ...133 C8
St Charles RC Prim Sch HU2 ....155 A3
St Christopher Rd YO16 ....122 E4
St Christopher's Rd DN36 ....114 C8
St Clares Wlk 11 DN20 ...98 C2
St Clement's Gr YO32 ...130 C2
St Columba Rd YO16 ...122 F5
St Crispins Cl DN40 ...86 E4
St Cuthbert Rd YO16 ...122 E4
St David Cl HU17 ...154 B2
St David La YO15 ....5 B3
St David's Cl HU16 ...139 D6
St Davids Cres DN17 ...96 C2
St David's View 9 DN14 ...64 E4
St Deny's Cl 1 DN40 ...86 E3
St Denys' Rd YO1 ...156 C2
St Edmunds's Ct 4 HU5 ....139 D2
St Edward's Cl YO24 ...132 F8
St Edwins Cl 27 DN7 ...92 D4
St Ellens Ct HU17 ...154 B2
St Francis Ave DN31 ...152 A4
St Francis Ct 1 HU5 ...139 D2
St Francis Gr DN37 ...101 E1
St Francis Prep Sch YO25 ....125 E7
St George's Ave
Bridlington YO15 ...122 E3
Hatfield DN7 ....92 C3
St Georges Cl 19 DN8 ...93 B7
St George's Cl DN21 ...108 F3
St Georges Gn DN14 ...149 D6
St George's Pl YO24 ...129 F2
St Georges Prim Sch HU3 ....145 A6
St Georges RC Prim Sch YO10 ....130 D2
St George's Rd HU5 ...145 A5
St Georges Rd 16 DN8 ...93 B7
St George's Wlk HU9 ...142 E6
St Giles' Ave DN33 ...102 E1
St Giles Ct
Kingston upon Hull HU9 ...142 C1
York YO31 ....156 B3
St Giles Rd YO26 ...126 B5
St Giles Way YO23 ...132 A3
St Giles's Croft HU17 ...154 A2
St Hedda's Ct 6 HU5 ...139 D2
St Helena Gdns 3 HU5 ...140 E2
St Helens Ave 18 DN33 ...102 E1
St Helen's Ave YO42 ...29 B4
St Helen's Cl YO42 ...29 B4
St Helen's Cres DN37 ...113 D5
St Helen's Dr 10 HU5 ...68 D6
St Helen's La YO14 ....3 C6
St Helen's Rd
Brigg DN20 ....98 C2
Pocklington YO42 ...29 B4
5 York YO24 ....132 E8
St Helen's Rise YO19 ...38 A7
St Helen's Sq
Barmby Moor YO42 ...28 D4
3 Market Weighton YO43 ....135 D4
York YO1 ....156 B2
St Helens Way DN21 ...119 B2
St Helen's Well * YO43 ...41 D5
St Hilda St
3 Bridlington YO15 ...122 E2
Kingston upon Hull HU3 ...145 B5
St Hilda's Ave DN34 ...152 B2
St Hugh's Ave DN16 ...153 D2
St Hugh's Cres DN16 ...151 C4
St Hughs Hospl DN32 ...102 F2

St Hughs Sch DN16 ...151 B5
St Hybald's Dr DN20 ...108 F7
St Ives Cl HU7 ...141 C7
St Ives Cres DN34 ...102 C3
St James Ave
Grimsby DN34 ...152 A2
Hatfield DN7 ....92 C3
St James C of E Prim Sch HU7 ....141 C6
St James Cl
9 Crowle DN17 ...94 D7
Kingston upon Hull HU7 ...141 D7
York YO30 ....126 E3
St James' Ct DN34 ...152 C2
St James Ct
Rawcliffe DN14 ...64 A1
Scunthorpe DN15 ...151 A6
St James Mount YO24 ...130 A2
St James Pl 5 YO24 ...129 D1
St James' Rd YO15 ...122 D1
St James Rd
21 Brigg DN20 ....98 C2
Welton HU14 ....68 F5
St James Sch DN34 ...152 C2
St James St HU3 ...145 D5
St James Terr YO8 ...148 C5
St James's Rd DN20 ...108 E8
St Joan's Dr DN20 ...108 E8
St John Mews YO8 ...148 B7
St John St
Beverley HU17 ...154 B2
York YO31 ....156 B3
St John's Ave YO16 ...122 C3
St John's Ave W YO16 ...122 C3
St Johns Cl 1 HU17 ...55 F8
St John's Cl
Bridlington YO16 ...122 C2
11 Pocklington YO42 ...28 F4
St John's Cres YO31 ...156 C4
St Johns Ct HU6 ...140 C4
St John's Gdns YO25 ...124 E3
St John's Gr HU9 ...141 F1
St John's Pl 2 YO25 ...124 F3
St John's Rd
Great Driffield YO25 ...124 E3
8 Humberston DN36 ...114 C8
Scunthorpe DN16 ...151 C2
9 Stamford Bridge YO41 ...15 D2
St Johns Sch HU17 ...154 C4
St John's St
Bridlington YO16 ...122 D4
15 Howden DN14 ...65 A7
St John's Well *
Harpham YO25 ...21 F8
Scunthorpe DN16 ...96 D1
St John's Wlk
Bridlington YO16 ...122 C3
1 Great Driffield YO25 ...124 F3
Kingston upon Hull HU13 ...143 F2
St Joseph Dr HU4 ...144 C5
St Josephs RC Prim Sch
Cleethorpes DN35 ...103 B2
Goole DN14 ....149 D5
St Jude Gr YO16 ...122 D4
St Jude Rd YO16 ....122 D4
St Jude's Ct 3 HU5 ...139 D2
St Julian's Wells HU10 ....143 D7
St Katherine's Rd 2 HU15 ....53 F1
St Lawrence Ave
Kingston upon Hull HU16 ...138 E5
Snaith DN14 ....78 B8
St Lawrence Rd DN7 ...92 C4
St Lawrence Sq HU11 ...45 F8
St Lawrences C of E Prim Sch YO10 ....130 E3
St Lawrence's Pl DN16 ...151 D3
St Lawrence's Rd DN16 ...151 D2
St Leonards Ave DN31 ...152 A4
St Leonard's Cl 2 YO25 ...22 D1
St Leonard's Pl YO30 ...156 B3
St Leonard's Rd
Beverley HU17 ...136 C6
Kingston upon Hull HU5 ...140 D2
St Luke's Cl DN7 ...92 C2
St Luke's Cres 12 DN36 ...114 C8
St Luke's Ct DN32 ...152 F4
St Luke's Gr YO30 ...130 B7
St Lukes Sch DN16 ...151 D3
St Luke's St HU3 ...155 A2
St Margarets Ave HU16 ....138 E6
St Margarets Cl
Driffield YO25 ...124 E3
Kingston upon Hull HU16 ...138 E6
St Margaret's Cl 9 DN37 ....101 F1
St Margaret's Cres 4 DN40 ....100 E8
St Margaret's Ct 3 HU8 ...142 C4
St Margaret's Terr YO1 ....130 E4
St Margaret's Wlk DN16 ....151 C1
St Mark St HU8 ...155 C4
St Mark's Gr YO16 ...126 E2
St Mark's Rd 18 DN36 ...114 C8
St Mark's Sq HU3 ...145 D4
St Martins Ave 2 HU4 ...144 E6

St Martins C of E Sch DN9 ....106 A3
St Martin's Cl
Blyton DN21 ...117 F5
2 Burton Agnes YO25 ...10 A3
Fangfoss YO41 ....28 C8
St Martin's Cres
6 Grimsby DN33 ...102 E2
Scawby DN20 ....108 E8
St Martin's Ct HU17 ...154 B2
St Martins Dr YO16 ...122 C2
St Martin's Dr 1 YO25 ...10 A2
St Martin's Gr YO16 ...122 C2
St Martin's La YO1 ...156 A2
St Martin's Pl 16 DN41 ...101 A4
St Martins Prep Sch DN32 ....152 D1
St Martin's Rd
Scawby DN20 ....108 E8
Thorngumbald HU12 ...72 E5
St Mary Queen of Martyrs RC Prim Sch HU7 ...140 F7
St Mary's Ave
1 Barnetby le Wold DN38 ...99 B4
12 Hemingbrough YO8 ...49 F1
Kingston upon Hull HU5 ...139 D4
St Marys C of E Jun & Inf Sch HU17 ....154 A4
St Marys C of E Prim Sch YO23 ....24 D3
St Mary's Cl
Beverley HU17 ...136 D5
Brough HU15 ....68 C7
St Marys Cl YO42 ....38 C5
St Mary's Cl
Grimsby DN32 ...153 C2
15 Haxby YO32 ....127 B8
7 Thorngumbald HU12 ...72 E5
St Marys Coll HU6 ...140 C5
St Mary's Ct
9 Scunthorpe DN15 ...96 B7
York YO24 ....156 A1
St Mary's Dr
Hatfield DN7 ....92 C2
Hedon HU12 ....72 D7
St Mary's Gr YO16 ...131 C4
St Mary's La 5 DN18 ...84 F8
St Mary's La HU17 ...154 A3
St Marys RC High Sch DN33 ....102 D2
St Marys RC Prim Sch
Brigg DN20 ....98 C3
Grimsby DN32 ...152 F4
Market Weighton YO43 ...135 E3
Selby YO8 ....148 B2
St Marys RC Sch YO15 ....122 C2
St Mary's Rd DN7 ...92 C2
St Mary's Terr
Beverley HU17 ...154 A3
York YO30 ....156 A3
St Mary's Wlk
Beverley HU17 ...154 A4
Bridlington YO16 ...122 D4
St Matthew St HU3 ...145 B5
St Matthew's Cl 4 YO19 ...36 D8
St Matthews Ct HU17 ...154 B2
St Matthew's Rd 11 DN36 ....114 C8
St Maurice's Rd YO31 ...156 C3
St Mawes Cres DN34 ...152 A3
St Michael's Cl
Kingston upon Hull HU8 ...142 B5
Skidby HU16 ....138 A8
13 Thorne/Moorends DN8 ...93 B7
St Michael's Cres DN16 ....151 C1
St Michael's Ct DN19 ...86 A8
St Michael's Dr
Hedon HU12 ....72 D7
Thorne DN8 ....93 B7
St Michael's Mount
Kingston upon Hull HU6 ...140 C5
14 Swanland HU14 ...69 B7
St Michael's Rd DN34 ...102 B2
St Michael's Wlk 3 YO15 ...4 D3
St Monicas YO42 ....39 B6
St Monica's Ct 3 HU5 ...140 C3
St Nectan Cl 9 HU3 ...145 A4
St Nicholas Ave HU4 ...144 C4
St Nicholas C of E Sch DN39 ....86 A1
St Nicholas Cl
Copmanthorpe YO23 ...132 A3
8 Newbald YO43 ...53 F7
St Nicholas Cres YO23 ....132 A3
St Nicholas Croft 2 YO23 ...24 D3
St Nicholas Cty Prim Sch HU17 ....154 C2
St Nicholas Dr
Beverley HU17 ...154 C2
Grimsby DN37 ...102 B3
Hornsea HU18 ....134 C6
St Nicholas Gate HU12 ...72 D7
St Nicholas Pk 6 HU19 ...75 A6
St Nicholas Pl 1 YO10 ...130 F3
St Nicholas Prim Sch HU6 ....140 C4
St Nicholas Rd
Beverley HU17 ...154 C2
Copmanthorpe YO23 ...132 A3
Thorne/Moorends DN8 ...93 A8
St Nicholas Way 22 YO32 ...13 E5

St Norberts RC Sch DN17 ....94 D7
St Olaf's Dr DN32 ...152 D2
St Olave's Rd YO30 ...156 A4
St Olave's Sch YO30 ...156 A3
St Oswald Ct 5 HU5 ...139 D2
St Oswald Rd HU5 ...139 D2
St Oswalds C of E Prim Sch YO10 ....133 E7
St Oswald's Cl YO41 ...27 F6
St Oswald's Rd YO10 ...133 D8
St Patrick's Gn 14 HU12 ...74 D1
St Paul St HU2 ...155 A4
St Pauls C of E Prim Sch 130 A3
St Pauls Dr HU17 ...137 E8
St Pauls Mews YO24 ...130 A3
St Paul's Rd
Gainsborough DN21 ...117 A2
Scunthorpe DN16 ...151 B2
St Paul's Sq YO24 ...130 A3
St Paul's Terr YO24 ...130 A3
St Pauls Way HU17 ...137 E8
St Peter Ave HU9 ...155 C2
St Peter's Ave
Cleethorpes DN35 ...153 E2
Kingston upon Hull HU10 ...143 E6
Scunthorpe DN16 ...96 D2
St Peters C of E Prim Sch DN35 ....153 E2
St Peters Cl DN21 ...116 E5
St Peter's Cl
10 Holton le Clay DN36 ...114 A5
16 Howden DN14 ...65 A7
St Peters Cl
Hutton Cranswick YO25 ...32 E8
Rufforth YO26 ....129 A5
St Peter's Cres 7 DN36 ...114 C8
St Peters Gr DN37 ...101 E1
St Peter's Gr
9 Scotter DN21 ...107 C3
York YO30 ....156 A4
St Peter's Rd Drax YO8 ...63 F5
19 Scotter DN21 ...107 C3
St Peters Sch YO30 ...156 A4
St Peter's Sq 14 YO42 ...29 A4
St Peters View HU11 ...142 F6
St Peters Wlk HU17 ...59 D2
St Philip's Gr YO30 ...130 A8
St Philips Rd HU12 ...73 C4
St Quintin Field YO25 ...125 F7
St Quintin Pk YO25 ...34 B2
St Quintins Cl 6 HU9 ...146 C8
St Richards RC Prim Sch HU9 ....142 C1
St Sampsons Sq YO1 ...156 B2
St Saviourgate YO1 ...156 C2
St Saviour's Pl YO1 ...156 C2
St Silas St HU2 ...155 B4
St Stephen Rd YO16 ...122 E4
St Stephens Cl YO25 ...124 E3
St Stephen's Cl HU10 ...138 C2
St Stephen's Cres 4 HU15 ....66 D8
St Stephen's Rd YO24 ...129 C2
St Stephen's Sq YO24 ...129 C1
St Stephens HU2 ...145 D6
St Swithin's Wlk YO26 ...129 E4
St Thomas Moore Rd HU4 ....144 A4
St Thomas More RC Prim Sch HU4 ....144 A4
St Thomas' Pl YO31 ...156 B4
St Thomas Rd YO16 ...122 E4
St Thomas's Rd 1 HU8 ...146 B7
St Thomas's Cl 2 YO10 ...131 C4
St Thomas's Grange 2 HU5 ....139 D2
St Vincent's Ave DN15 ...96 D4
St Vincents Prim Sch HU5 ....140 D2
St Wilfred Rd HU16 ...122 E3
St Wilfrids Cl HU12 ...73 E3
St Wilfrid's Cl 7 YO32 ...14 B6
St Wilfrid's Cres YO8 ...48 D1
St Wilfrids RC Prim Sch YO31 ....156 C3
St Wilfrid's Rd 8 YO32 ...14 B6
St Williams Coll YO31 ...156 B3
St Wulstan Cl YO31 ...130 C7
Saints Cl HU9 ...141 E2
Salacon Way 1 DN34 ...153 A5
Salamander Cl DN31 ...152 B4
Salcey Cl 23 HU7 ...56 F6
Sales La DN14 ...78 B3
Salisbury Ave
Beverley HU17 ...136 E1
Goole DN14 ....149 E4
Hornsea HU18 ....134 C2
24 Waltham DN37 ...113 D6
Salisbury Cl DN17 ...150 C3
Salisbury Rd YO26 ...129 F5
Salisbury St
6 Gainsborough DN21 ...117 B2
Kingston upon Hull HU5 ...140 D2
Kingston upon Hull HU13 ...143 D1
Salmon Gr HU6 ...140 B4
Salmonby Rd
1 Scunthorpe DN17 ...96 C2
Scunthorpe DN17 ...150 C1
Salmond Rd 5 YO24 ...129 B1
Salisbury Ave DN34 ...152 B2
Salt End La HU12 ...72 A4
Saltash Rd HU4 ...144 A2
Saltaugh Rd HU12 ...88 B8
Saltburn Gr DN32 ...153 A1

Saltergate Rd DN17 ...107 D7
Salters' La LN11 ...120 E4
Saltford Ave HU9 ...147 F8
Saltgrounds Rd HU15 ...68 B5
Salthouse La HU1 ...155 C2
Saltmarsh La HU12 ...89 D8
Saltmarshe Sta DN14 ...65 E4
Salton Ave 4 HU5 ...139 E3
Saltshouse Rd HU8 ...141 E6
Saltwell Pk 29 HU7 ...56 F6
Salvesen Rd DN35 ...153 B5
Salvesen Way HU3 ...145 A3
Samman Cl HU10 ...143 D6
Samman Rd HU17 ...154 C4
Samphire Cl DN35 ...115 C4
Sample Ave HU17 ...154 E4
Sampson St DN17 ...81 A3
Samuel Ave DN32 ...153 B2
Sanbeds La DN9 ...105 B2
Sancton Cl HU16 ...138 E6
Sancton Rd YO43 ...135 C4
Sanctuary Way DN37 ...102 B3
Sand Hutton C of E Prim Sch YO41 ....15 B5
Sand Hutton Ct YO41 ...15 B5
Sand La
Barlby with Osgodby YO8 ...49 B4
Broughton DN20 ...97 D3
Bubwith YO8 ....50 D5
Caistor LN7 ....110 E4
Manton DN21 ...108 A5
Messingham DN17 ...107 A7
Newton on Derwent YO41 ...28 B5
North Cave HU15 ...53 D2
Sancton YO43 ....53 D8
South Cliffe YO43 ...52 E8
Thornton YO42 ....39 D7
Wistow YO8 ....48 E6
Wroot DN9 ....104 C6
Sand Rd DN17 ...106 B8
Sandacre Dr YO26 ...129 D5
Sandale Ct HU5 ...139 E1
Sandbeck La DN21 ...117 E6
Sandcroft Cl 4 YO24 ...132 D8
Sandcroft Rd YO24 ...132 D8
Sanderson Cl YO25 ...124 D2
Sanderson's Bank DN10 ....104 C2
Sandfield Cl
Market Weighton YO43 ...135 B3
Scunthorpe DN17 ...150 D1
Sandfield Dr 3 HU15 ...68 C5
Sandford Cl HU7 ...56 F5
Sandford St DN31 ...152 B4
Sandgate Rd YO16 ...123 A6
Sandhall Dr DN14 ...149 F5
Sandhall Rd DN14 ...65 C3
Sandhill La Brayton YO8 ...48 D2
Sutton upon Derwent YO41 ....27 E2
Sandhill Rd DN14 ...81 B6
Sandholme 2 YO32 ...13 F5
Sandholme Cl 1 HU15 ...66 D8
Sandholme La HU7 ...44 F8
Sandholme Rd HU15 ...66 C8
Sandholme Way 4 DN14 ...65 A7
Sandhouse Cres DN16 ...151 C5
Sandiacres 5 YO8 ...48 D1
Sandlemere Cl 3 HU3 ...145 A5
Sandmartin Ct YO24 ...132 D8
Sandmoor Cl HU8 ...142 B6
Sandown Cl YO24 ...129 E2
Sandpiper Cl HU18 ...134 D6
Sandpiper Dr HU4 ...144 B1
Sandpits La HU11 ...47 C1
Sandringham Cl
6 Bridlington YO16 ...122 D6
Haxby YO32 ....127 C7
Kingston upon Hull HU16 ...139 A7
Sandringham Cres 15 DN17 ....96 C2
Sandringham Dr DN14 ....149 B6
Sandringham Rd DN35 ....103 B2
Sandringham St
2 Kingston upon Hull HU3 ...145 A6
York YO10 ....130 D2
Sands Keadby DN17 ...95 D6
Reighton YO14 ....3 D7
Sands Cl 3 HU14 ...69 A4
Sands La Barmston YO25 ...22 F5
Bridlington YO15 ...122 F3
Brough HU15 ....68 C6
Ellerker HU15 ....67 F6
Holme-on-Spalding-Moor YO43 ....39 F1
Hornsea HU18 ....134 D4
Hunmanby YO14 ....3 A8
Scotter DN21 ....107 C3
South Ferriby DN18 ...84 A7
Ulrome YO25 ....23 B3
Sands Rd Barmston YO15 ...22 F7
Hunmanby YO14 ....3 B7
Sands Top YO43 ...53 E7
Sandsacre Ave YO16 ...123 A6
Sandsacre Dr 1 YO16 ...123 A6
Sandsacre Rd YO16 ...123 A6
Sandsacre Way YO16 ...123 F6
Sandsfield Ave YO43 ...40 E6
Sandstock Rd
Pocklington YO42 ...29 A4
York YO31 ....131 B7

Sandtoft Rd
Epworth DN9 ....94 B3
Hatfield DN7 ....93 A4
Sandtoft Transport Ctr Mus★
DN8 ....94 A3
Sandwalk YO43 ....135 C3
Sandway Ave 12 YO8 ....48 B1
Sandway Cl 11 YO8 .....48 B1
Sandway Dr
Camblesforth YO8 ....63 D4
1 Thorpe Willoughby YO8 .48 B1
Sandwith La YO8 ....63 B4
Sandy Cl DN36 ....115 C5
Sandy Gap YO32 ....127 C7
Sandy La Harpham YO25 ...9 E2
Harton YO60 ....15 B8
16 Haxby YO32 ....13 C5
North Duffield YO8 ....49 F8
Stockton on the Forest
YO32 ....14 E4
Sandy Point HU9 ......142 E5
Sandy Rise YO8 ....148 C3
Sandycroft Cl HU10 ....139 A1
Sandyland 29 YO32 .....13 C5
Sandyridge YO26 ......126 A1
Saner St HU3 ....145 B6
Saner's Cl HU16 ....139 B5
Sapperton Cl 18 HU7 ....56 F6
Sapphire Gr 7 HU3 .....145 A4
Sarah Rhodes La DN14 ..65 C3
Sargent Ave YO23 .....132 F4
Sargon Way DN17 ......102 C6
Sassaby Cl HU4 ....144 C3
Saunby Gr DN35 ....153 E3
Saunders Cres 21 YO42 ..29 A3
Saunders Croft 4 HU17 ..55 B8
Saunders La HU17 ......55 B7
Saunders St DN31 ......152 C2
Savage Rd YO15 ....122 D2
Savery St HU9 ....141 D1
Savile Cl HU17 ....136 E6
Saville Gr YO30 ....130 A8
Saville St HU1 ....155 B2
Savoy Cl 12 DN36 ......114 A7
Savoy Rd HU8 ....141 F4
Sawcliffe Medieval Village★
DN15 ....82 E1
Sawley Cl HU18 ....134 C5
Sawmill Yd 5 YO15 ....122 E2
Sawston Ave HU5 ......139 C2
Sawyer's Cres YO23 ...132 C2
Sawyers Wlk 9 YO19 ....26 F7
Saxby 17 DN33 ....102 D2
Saxby Hill DN20 ....84 B3
Saxby Rd Bonby DN20 ...84 A2
Kingston upon Hull HU8 ..142 A5
Scunthorpe DN17 ....150 E1
Saxcourt HU6 ....139 E7
Saxford Way 8 YO32 ...13 C5
Saxon Cl
Barton-upon-Humber
DN18 ....84 F8
Shipton YO30 ....12 F5
6 Thorpe Willoughby YO8 .48 B1
Saxon Cres DN35 ......153 D2
Saxon Ct Blyton DN21 ..117 F5
Scunthorpe DN16 ....96 D2
Saxon Pl YO31 ....130 E7
Saxon Rd YO41 ....15 D2
Saxon Rise HU17 ......136 D7
Saxon Vale YO30 ....12 F5
Saxon Way
4 Caistor LN7 ....111 B4
Kingston upon Hull
HU13 ....143 F1
Saxondale HU4 ....144 B7
Saxonfield LN7 ....111 A4
Scafell Cl 4 YO30 ......126 E1
Scaife Garth YO42 .....28 F3
Scaife Gdns YO31 .....130 C7
Scaife St YO31 ....130 C7
Scalby Gr HU5 ....144 D8
Scalby La HU15 ....66 D8
Scalby Pl HU18 ....134 B4
Scale La HU1 ....155 C2
Scale La Staith HU1 ...155 C2
Scallow La DN17 ......107 D6
Scalm La YO8 ....63 D4
Scampton Cl DN34 ....152 A1
Scampton Garth HU7 ...141 C8
Scandinavian Way
DN41 ....87 E1
Scarborough Cres 8
YO16 ....122 C5
Scarborough Rd
Bempton YO16 ....4 A1
Blyton DN17 ....117 E5
7 Bridlington YO16 .....122 C5
Great Driffield YO25 ....124 E6
Langtoft YO25 ....8 C7
Scarborough St HU3 ...145 A4
Scarborough Terr
YO30 ....156 B4
Scarcroft Hill YO24 ....130 B2
Scarcroft La YO23 .....156 A1
Scarcroft Prim Sch
YO23 ....156 A1
Scarcroft Rd YO24 ....156 A1
Scardale Ct YO8 ....148 A2
Scargate Cl YO16 ......123 A7
Scarrington Cres HU4 ..144 B6
Scarrow Cl YO8 ....145 A2
Scarsea Way YO15 ......4 C3
Scartho Jun & Inf Sch
DN33 ....102 E1

Scartho Pk DN33 ......102 D1
Scartho Rd DN33 ......102 E2
Scaudercroft 13 YO19 ..26 F7
Scawby Hall★ DN20 ...108 F8
Scawby Prim Sch
DN20 ....108 E8
Scawby Rd Brigg DN20 ..98 A1
Broughton DN20 ....97 E2
Scunthorpe DN17 ....150 E1
Scawton Ave 1 YO31 ...127 E2
Schiphol Way DN38 .....99 E5
Schofield Ave HU17 ...154 C3
Schofield Cl 5 DN19 ....85 C8
Scholefield Ave HU17 ..56 B8
School Cl Selby YO8 ...148 B3
16 Stamford Bridge YO41 ..15 D2
School Dr DN17 ....107 D7
School Hill YO16 ....10 C1
School House La 2
DN10 ....116 C3
School Houses 6 DN20 ..97 E4
School La Appleby DN15 .83 D1
Askham Richard YO23 ...24 D3
Beswick YO25 ....32 B4
Beverley HU17 ....154 B3
Bishopthorpe YO23 .....133 A4
Bonby DN20 ....84 C2
Buckton/Bempton YO15 ...4 C3
Burton Fleming YO25 .....2 E3
Cabourne LN7 ....111 D5
Copmanthorpe YO23 ...132 A2
10 Flamborough YO15 .....5 A2
Goxhill DN19 ....86 A8
Grayingham DN21 ......119 B7
Holmpton HU19 ....75 D2
Irby DN37 ....112 D7
15 Keyingham HU12 ......73 C4
Kingston upon Hull
HU10 ....143 C8
New Holland DN19 ......70 E2
5 North Ferriby HU14 ....69 A4
North Kelsey LN7 ......110 A5
5 Pocklington YO42 .....29 A4
23 Poppleton YO26 ......12 F1
Redbourne DN21 ......108 F2
Rothwell LN7 ....111 E2
South Ferriby DN18 .....84 A7
Tetney DN36 ....114 C3
West/East Butterwick
DN17 ....106 D8
York YO10 ....131 B1
York YO10 ....133 E7
School St
Kingston upon Hull HU1 ..155 A2
York YO24 ....129 D3
School Wlk DN35 .....153 C1
Schooner Ct HU4 .....144 B3
Schubert Cl HU9 ......142 A3
Scorborough La YO25 ...43 D8
Scoreby La YO41 ......15 B1
Scotchman La YO60 ....15 A8
Scotney Cl 5 DN37 ....140 E1
Scott Ave DN17 ....150 C2
Scott Cl 7 DN37 ......102 C4
Scott Gdns 7 DN19 .....75 A6
Scott Moncrieff Rd
YO32 ....14 B6
Scott Rd YO8 ....148 C6
Scott St
28 Gainsborough DN21 ..117 B1
Kingston upon Hull HU2 ..155 B3
York YO23 ....130 C2
Scotter Cty Sch DN21 ..107 C3
Scotter Rd
Laughton DN21 ....117 F8
Messingham DN17 ......107 D5
Scotton DN21 ....107 C2
Scunthorpe DN17 ......150 C3
Scotter Rd S
Bottesford DN17 ....96 B1
Scunthorpe DN17 ......150 C1
Scotterthorpe Rd
DN21 ....107 B4
Scotton Rd DN21 ......107 C3
Scotts Croft YO43 .....135 D3
Scotts Garth Cl HU17 ..137 F8
Scotts Garth Dr HU17 ...44 C5
Scrap Bay Rd DN16 ....97 A3
Scrivelsby Ct 9 DN35 ..103 D2
Scriven Gr 8 YO32 .....13 F5
Scrope Ave 4 YO31 ....130 E5
Scrub La DN40 ....86 E5
Scrubwood La HU17 ...136 E6
Sculcoates La HU5 .....140 E2
Scunthorpe General Hospl
DN15 ....150 E6
Scunthorpe Leisure Ctr
DN15 ....151 B7
Scunthorpe Mus & Art Gall★
DN15 ....151 A6
Scunthorpe Sta DN16 ..151 B1
Scunthorpe United Football
Club DN15 ....150 A6
Sea La DN36 ....115 B3
Sea Rd
Cleethorpes DN35 ......153 F2
Holmpton HU19 ....75 D3
Sea View St DN35 .....153 F1
Seabrook Dr DN16 ......96 D1
Seacroft Rd
Cleethorpes DN35 ......103 D3

Seacroft Rd continued
Withernsea HU19 ....75 A6
Seafield Ave HU9 ......141 F5
Seafire Cl YO30 ....127 A3
Seaford Rd DN35 ......103 D1
Seagate YO15 ....123 C6
Seagull Cl HU4 ....144 E2
Seakel La YO23 ....24 C1
Seamer Gr DN32 ......153 A1
Sean La DN14 ....65 F4
Searby Hill DN38 ......110 B8
Searby Rd DN17 ....96 C2
Searby Wold La DN38 ...99 E1
Seaside La HU12 ....60 C2
Seaside Rd
Aldbrough HU11 ....47 C2
Easington HU12 ....91 A5
Holmpton HU19 ....75 C2
Withernsea HU19 ....75 A7
Seathorne HU19 ....74 F7
Seathorne Rd 1 YO16 ..122 C5
Seaton Cl DN17 ....131 C4
Seaton Gr
Grimsby DN32 ....153 A1
Kingston upon Hull HU4 ..144 E5
Seaton Rd
Bewholme YO25 ....35 A4
Hornsea HU18 ....134 A4
Kingston upon Hull
HU13 ....143 F2
Scunthorpe DN17 ......150 D4
Seavy Carr La HU15 ....52 F2
Seavy Rd DN14 ....149 B3
Seawall La DN36 ......115 C5
Second Ave
Bridlington YO15 ....123 A4
Fixborough Ind Est. DN15 .81 F1
4 Goole DN14 ....149 C4
Grimsby DN33 ....102 D2
Scunthorpe DN17 ......150 C2
York YO31 ....130 F6
Second Common La
YO8 ....48 C4
Sedbergh Ave HU5 ....139 D3
Sedbury Cl HU7 ....56 F6
Sedge Cl 4 DN18 ......69 F1
Sedgebrook Gr 18 HU7 ..56 F6
Sedgewood Way 13
DN15 ....96 B7
Seed Close La 3 DN37 .101 F1
Sefton Ave YO31 ......130 F8
Sefton St 3 HU3 ......145 B4
Seg La YO8 ....63 F3
Segmere St DN35 .....103 D3
Segrave Gr HU5 ......144 D8
Segrave Wlk 10 YO26 ..129 E4
Selbourne Rd 5 DN34 ..102 C2
Selby Abbey YO8 ......148 D5
Selby Abbey Prim Sch
YO8 ....148 C5
Selby Coll Selby YO8 ..148 C5
Selby YO8 ....148 F3
Selby High Sch YO8 ...148 B4
Selby Rd
Eggborough DN14 ....61 F1
Fulford YO19 ....133 E6
Holme-on-Spalding-Moor
YO43 ....39 F1
Howden DN14 ....65 A7
Riccall YO19 ....49 A8
Snaith DN14 ....63 C1
Thorne DN8 ....92 F8
Wistow YO8 ....48 D6
Womersley DN14 ....77 A4
Selby Rly Sports & Social
Club YO8 ....148 B3
Selby St HU3 ....145 A5
Selby Sta YO8 ....148 D5
Selby Town Football Club
YO8 ....148 B5
Seldon Rd YO26 ......129 E5
Selge Way DN17 ......102 C1
Selkirk St HU5 ....145 A8
Sellers Dr HU17 ....43 D6
Selsey Cl 2 HU5 ....140 D2
Selvage La DN14 ......78 A6
Selwick Dr YO15 ......5 D2
Selworthy Cl 3 HU7 ....57 A5
Selwyn Ave 14 HU14 ...69 A4
Seraphim App Rd
DN16 ....151 E5
Seraphim Rd DN16 ....151 F4
Service Rd 1 12 DN37 ..102 C5
Service Rd 10 3 DN37 ..102 C5
Service Rd 11 4 DN37 ..102 C5
Service Rd 12 5 DN37 ..102 C5
Service Rd 13 6 DN37 ..102 C4
Service Rd 14 7 DN37 ..102 C5
Service Rd 15 19 DN37 ..102 C4
Service Rd 16 19 DN37 ..102 C4
Service Rd 17 10 DN37 ..102 C4
Service Rd 18 11 DN37 ..102 C4
Service Rd 19 18 DN37 ..102 C4
Service Rd 2 15 DN37 ..102 C4
Service Rd 20 14 DN37 ..102 C4
Service Rd 21 13 DN37 ..102 B4
Service Rd 22 1 DN37 ..102 C4
Service Rd 23 2 DN37 ..102 C4
Service Rd 24 4 DN37 ..102 C4
Service Rd 25 5 DN37 ..102 C4
Service Rd 26 8 DN37 ..102 C5
Service Rd 3 17 DN37 ..102 C5
Service Rd 4 3 DN37 ..102 C4
Service Rd 5 4 DN37 ..102 C4
Service Rd 6 5 DN37 ..102 C4
Service Rd 7 9 DN37 ..102 C4
Service Rd 8 1 DN37 ..102 C5
Service Rd 9 2 DN37 ..102 C5
Service Rd No 1 DN32 ..152 F5

Service Rd No 2 DN32 ..152 F5
Services Rd DN16 .....151 E6
Setterwood Garth 2
HU10 ....143 E8
Setting Cres 8 HU5 ....139 D2
Setting Rd HU5 ....139 D2
Seven Corners La
HU17 ....136 D4
Seven Quay Rd DN40 ...87 D3
Seventh Ave
3 Bridlington YO15 .....122 F4
York YO31 ....130 F5
Severn Gn YO26 ......129 C8
Severn St HU3 ....141 C1
Severus Ave YO24 ....129 D4
Severus St YO24 .....129 D3
Sewer La HU1 ....155 B1
Sewerby Ave YO16 ....122 D5
Sewerby Cres YO16 ....122 D5
Sewerby Ct 6 YO16 ....122 D5
Sewerby Hall Mus & Art
Gall★ YO15 ....123 C7
Sewerby Headlands
YO15 ....122 F5
Sewerby Heads YO16 ..122 F5
Sewerby Park Cl
YO15 ....123 C7
Sewerby Rd YO16 .....122 D5
Sewerby Rise YO16 ....122 D5
Sextant Rd HU6 ......140 C8
Seymour Gr YO31 .....130 F6
Seymour Rd 6 HU12 ...73 C4
Seymour St HU3 ......144 F5
Shadwell Rise 5 DN18 ..69 E1
Shady La 3 YO25 ......10 A2
Shaftesbury Ave
Goole DN14 ....149 A5
Grimsby DN34 ....152 B3
Hornsea HU18 ....134 C5
Kellingley DN14 ....61 C3
Kingston upon Hull HU8 ..141 F4
Shaftesbury Mews 1
DN36 ....114 A7
Shaftesbury Rd YO15 ..122 C1
Shakespeare Ave
2 Campsall DN6 ....76 E1
Scunthorpe DN17 ......150 C2
Shakespeare Cl 6 HU3 ..145 D8
Shallowdale Gr 1 YO10 .131 C3
Shambles YO1 ....156 B2
Shannon Rd HU8 ......142 C6
Shardeloes HU9 ......142 E5
Shardlow Rd HU18 ....134 C5
Sharp Ave HU12 ......73 A6
Sharp Hill La YO8 ......63 F6
Sharp St HU5 ....140 B2
Sharpe Cl 20 DN18 ....84 E8
Sharpe Howe★ YO11 ...2 A8
Sharps La HU17 ......55 B7
Shaw Dr 1 DN33 ......113 F8
Shaw La DN6 ....77 D2
Shaw Park Prim Sch
HU6 ....139 F8
Shaw Rd DN10 ....116 A2
Shaw St HU9 ....146 B7
Shawfield Cl 7 DN3 ....92 A3
Shaw's Terr YO24 .....156 A1
Shears Ct DN14 ....113 E7
Sheep Cote La DN7 ....92 D2
Sheep Dip La DN7 .....92 D2
Sheep Marsh La DN36 ..115 B3
Sheep Rake La YO25 ....8 F4
Sheep Trod La HU12 ...89 F6
Sheepdike La YO25 ....21 F2
Sheepdyke La
Bonby DN20 ....84 C2
Hunmanby YO14 ....3 A8
Sheepfold St DN32 ....152 E3
Sheepman La YO25 .....32 F7
Sheeprake La YO25 ....123 B8
Sheepswarth La HU20 ..54 F3
Sheepwalk La YO17 .....7 B7
Sheepwash La DN14 ...77 A4
Sheffield Park Ave
DN15 ....96 C7
Sheffield St DN15 .....151 A8
Sheffield St E DN15 ...151 A8
Sheffield St W DN15 ...150 F8
Sheldon Cl HU7 ....141 B8
Sheldrake Way HU17 ..136 F6
Shelford Ave DN14 ....65 A7
Shelford St DN15 .....151 A7
Shelley Ave
Grimsby DN33 ....102 D2
Kingston upon Hull HU9 ..142 C2
Shelley Gr YO30 ......126 F1
Shelroy Cl DN15 ......96 B7
Shenley Cl 11 DN7 ....92 D3
Shepherd La HU17 .....55 F8
Shepherd's Croft DN9 ..105 D7
Shepherds Lea 6 HU17 ..55 B8
Shepherdton Mere YO25 ..9 B1
Sheraton Dr 3 DN36 ...114 D8
Sherbrooke Ave HU5 ...139 E4
Sherburn Cres DN15 ...150 D8
Sherburn Rd YO8 .....148 A8
Sherburn St
1 Cawood YO8 ....48 B8
Cleethorpes DN35 ......153 F1
Kingston upon Hull HU9 ..146 C7
Sherbuttgate Dr 13 YO42 .28 F4
Sherbuttgate Rd 14 YO42 .28 F4
Sheriff Highway HU12 ..72 C6
Sherringham Dr YO24 ..132 D8
Sherwood Ave HU9 ....141 E1
Sherwood Cl
13 Norton DN6 ....76 E1
4 Walkington HU17 .....55 C8

Sherwood Ct HU9 .....142 D5
Sherwood Dr HU4 .....144 A7
Sherwood Gr
Huntington YO32 ....127 F1
York YO26 ....129 B6
Sherwood Rd DN34 ....102 C2
Sherwood Vale DN15 ..150 D7
Shetland Cl 6 HU7 ....141 E7
Shetland Way 4 DN40 ..101 C8
Shields Rd 2 HU12 ....72 C7
Shildon Gr DN8 ....79 C2
Shildon Garth Cl 3
YO32 ....127 F7
Shipcote Rd DN14 ....149 D1
Shipley Cl HU3 ....142 C2
Shipton Cres 6 HU17 ...43 D6
Shipton La YO43 ....40 E3
Shipton Low Rd YO30 ..12 C3
Shipton Rd
Clifton YO30 ....129 F8
Rawcliffe YO30 ....126 D2
Scunthorpe DN16 ......151 C1
York YO30 ....130 A7
Shipton St 3 YO30 ....130 B7
Shipton Street Inf Sch
YO30 ....130 B7
Shipyard Rd YO8 ......148 E5
Shirbutt La YO26 ......24 C8
Shirley Ave YO26 .....129 C6
Shirley Cres DN16 ....151 B4
Shoemaker's La DN21 ..107 D5
Shopeth Way HU17 ....56 B8
Shore Rd DN17 ....81 F5
Shoreditch Cl 2 HU8 ..141 F5
Short La Bempton YO16 ..4 C1
12 Bridlington YO16 ....122 C5
Fotherby LN11 ....121 C2
Market Weighton YO43 ..41 B2
West Haddlesey YO8 ....61 F6
West Halton DN15 ......82 E8
Short St
Cleethorpes DN35 ......153 E2
Kingston upon Hull HU1 ..155 A2
Shortacre La YO42 ....38 E2
Shorthill Croft HU17 ...154 A1
Shorwell Cl 2 HU8 ....142 C5
Shotel Cl YO30 ....129 F8
Shropshire Cl HU5 ....139 D1
Shrubberies The YO8 ...49 E2
Sibelius Rd HU4 ......144 B4
Sicey La HU6 ....56 D7
Side La DN33 ....113 F8
Sidebottom St DN31 ...152 F6
Siding La YO8 ....49 E5
Sidings Ct HU15 ......68 C3
Sidmouth Prim Sch
HU5 ....140 B3
Sidmouth St HU5 .....140 C3
Sidney Pl DN35 ....153 B4
Sidney Rd
Grimsby DN34 ....152 D1
Scunthorpe DN17 ......150 D2
Sidney St DN35 ......153 B4
Sidney Way DN35 .....153 B4
Sidsaph Hill 2 DN10 ...118 A8
Sigglesthorne C of E Prim
Sch HU11 ....45 F8
Sigglesthorne Rd HU11 ..46 B6
Signhills Ave 1 DN35 ..103 D2
Signhills Jun & Inf Sch
DN35 ....103 D2
Sigston Rd
2 Beverley HU17 ....137 A6
Beverley HU17 ....154 C4
Silica Cres DN17 ......150 D1
Silkstone Oval 15 DN8 ..79 B2
Sills La YO30 ....12 B6
Silsden Ave 5 HU6 ....140 C7
Silver Birch Rise 22
DN16 ....96 D2
Silver St
Barnetby le Wold DN38 ..99 B4
Barrow upon Humber
DN19 ....85 C7
Holton le Clay DN36 ....114 A5
Huggate YO42 ....18 C2
Kingston upon Hull HU1 ..155 B2
Owston Ferry DN9 .....106 B2
3 Riccall YO19 ....49 A8
1 Stainforth DN7 ......92 C6
24 Thorne/Moorends DN8 ..93 A8
Whitley DN14 ....77 A7
Winteringham DN15 ....68 B1
York YO1 ....156 B2
Silverdale Ct YO24 ....132 D7
Silverdale Rd HU6 ....140 C6
Silvergarth DN32 .....153 A1
Silversides La DN20 ...98 A1
Sim Balk La YO24 .....132 E5
Simon Howe YO12 .....1 A5
Simons Pl DN35 ......153 D3
Simpson Ave 6 YO14 ...2 F8
Simpson Cl DN19 .....85 D8
Simpson's Yd 3 YO8 ...148 C6
Sinclair Cres HU8 .....141 F6
Sinderson Rd 18 DN36 .103 D1
Sir Henry Cooper Sch
HU6 ....56 D5
Sir John Nelthorpe Lower
Sch DN20 ....98 C2
Sir John Nelthorpe Sch
DN20 ....98 C2
Sirius Cl 3 HU3 ....145 B5
Sirocco Ct YO31 ......130 D8
Siskin Cres DN16 .....96 D1
Sissons La HU15 ......53 B1
Sissons Way HU5 .....140 E3

Sittingbourne CI HU8 ...141 E8
Sitwell Gr YO26 ......129 C5
Sitwell St HU8 ....155 C4
Siward St YO10 ......131 A3
Siwards How★ YO10 ..131 B1
Sixhills St DN32 ......152 F3
Sixth Ave
  Bridlington YO15 ......122 F4
  Fixborough Ind. Est. DN15 ..82 A1
  Scunthorpe DN17 ......150 B2
  York YO31 ....130 E5
Skeckling CI HU12 .....73 A6
Skeffling Rd HU12 .....90 B7
Skeldergate YO1 ......156 B2
Skelton Ave HU5 ......139 E2
Skelton Broad La DN14 ..65 C4
Skelton Cres YO43 ....135 C4
Skelton Ct 3 YO30 ...130 A6
Skelton Prim Sch
  YO30 ....126 C5
Skelton Rd DN17 ......150 C3
Skern Gr HU9 ....142 E2
Skerne Rd YO25 ......124 F2
Skewsby Gr YO31 .....127 F1
Skidby C of E Prim Sch
  HU16 ....138 E7
Skidby Carr La HU6 ....56 C6
Skidby Gr HU6 ....139 F5
Skidby Rd HU20 ....55 A4
Skidby Windmill & Mus of E
  Riding Rural Life★
  HU16 ....138 C7
Skiddaw YO24 ....132 C7
Skiff La YO43 ....52 C7
Skiff Lane Ind Est YO43 .52 B6
Skilgate CI 7 HU7 .....57 A5
Skillings La HU15 ......68 C5
Skinners La
  3 South Ferriby DN18 ...84 A7
  Waltham DN37 ....113 E6
Skipper La YO25 ....1 E3
Skippingdale Rd DN15 ..96 C7
Skipsea Castle★ YO25 ..23 A1
Skipsea CP Sch YO25 ...23 B1
Skipsea La YO25 ....23 A3
Skipsea Rd Atwick YO25 ..35 C7
  Beeford YO25 ....22 D1
  Bewholme YO25 ....35 A5
Skipwith CI HU8 ......140 B6
Skipwith Comm Nature
  Reserve★ YO8 ....49 E8
Skipwith Rd YO19 .....37 B6
Skirbeck Rd HU8 .....141 D5
Skirlaugh C of E Sch
  HU11 ....45 E2
Skirlaugh Rd
  Ellerby HU11 ....45 F1
  Swine HU11 ....57 E8
Skirlaw CI 18 DN14 ....65 A7
Skitter Rd DN40 ....86 D8
Skylark Dr DN16 ....96 D1
Slack The DN17 ....94 D8
Slates The★ LN11 ....121 B4
Slay Pit CI DN7 ....92 A4
Slay Pit La DN7 ....92 F3
Sleaford Ave 3 HU9 ...142 E4
Sledmere Gr HU4 .....144 E5
Sledmere Rd YO25 ......8 B6
Sledmere Sch YO25 .....7 B3
Sleightholme CI 21 HU7 .56 F6
Sleights CI HU3 ......145 A4
Sleights La Acklam YO17 ..16 E7
  Broomfleet HU15 ....67 B6
  Eastrington DN14 ......51 E3
Slessor Rd YO24 ......129 B1
Slingsby CI HU5 ......139 D2
Slingsby Gr YO24 .....132 E8
Sloe La HU17 ....136 D2
Sluice La DN18 ....83 D8
Sluice Rd DN18 ....83 F8
Smales' St YO1 ....156 B1
Small Sch at Winestead Hall
  HU12 ....74 C4
Smary La YO19 ....26 D7
Smeatley's La DN6 .....76 C4
Smeaton Gr YO26 .....129 C5
Smeaton Rd YO41 ......27 D1
Smedley CI HU17 .....154 C2
Smith CI YO10 ....133 F8
Smith Field 4 DN36 ...114 B1
Smith St Grimsby DN31 ..152 F6
  Scunthorpe DN15 ......150 F8
Smithall Rd HU17 .....136 E7
Smithfield Rd DN16 ...151 D2
Smithie CI YO32 ......127 D5
Smithy La
  7 Barnetby le Wold DN38 ..99 B4
  Bigby DN38 ....99 B2
Smitton St DN31 ......153 A6
Smook Hills Rd HU19 ...75 A4
Smythy La YO25 ....1 D4
Snainton Gr 4 HU5 ...144 D8
Snaith Prim Sch DN14 ..78 C8
Snaith Rd
  Pollington DN14 ....77 F7
  Rawcliffe DN14 ....64 A1
  Snaith DN14 ....78 D8
Snaith Sec Sch DN14 ...78 B8
Snaith Sta DN14 ....63 C1
Snatchells La DN14 ....78 C2
Snowdon CI YO23 ......24 D3
Snowdon Way HU7 .....57 A7
Snowdonia Ave DN15 ...96 B8
Snowhill CI 4 HU7 .....57 A6
Snuff Mill La HU16 ...139 B6
Sober Hill Dr YO43 .....40 A1
Soft La DN19 ....86 A6
Solomon Ct DN35 ....153 D1

Somerby Rd DN17 ....150 D1
Somerby Wold La
  DN38 ....99 C1
Somerden Rd HU9 ....147 E7
Somersby St DN31 ....152 D4
Somerscales St HU2 ...155 A4
Somerset CI 6 YO30 ..126 E3
Somerset Dr 6 DN15 ...82 B4
Somerset Rd YO31 ....130 D8
Somerset St HU3 .....145 A5
Somerton Dr DN7 ......92 F4
Somerton Rd DN40 ....87 C1
Somervell Rd DN16 ...151 C1
Sonia Crest DN40 ......87 B1
Sophia Ave 7 DN33 ...102 E1
Sorbus CI 5 HU3 .....145 D6
Sorbus View 4 HU4 ...144 C7
Sorrel CI HU17 ....136 C1
Sorrel Dr 5 HU5 .....144 D8
Sorrel Way DN15 ......96 B7
Sorrell La DN14 ....78 D1
Soss La DN10 ....116 D5
Sotheron St DN14 ....149 D4
Sour La DN8 ....92 A4
Soutergate 12 DN18 ...69 F1
South Axholme Sch
  DN9 ....105 D6
South Back La HU6 ...122 B4
South Bank DN17 ......95 D6
South Bank Ave YO23 .130 B1
South Bridge Rd HU9 ..155 C1
South Carr Dales Rd
  HU19 ....74 F3
South Carr La DN20 ...109 B4
South Carr Rd DN20 ..109 A3
South Carrs HU17 .....45 A8
South Cave Prim Sch
  HU15 ....53 F1
South Church Side
  2 Easington HU12 .....90 F6
  Kingston upon Hull HU1 .155 B2
South CI 7 YO25 ....9 C1
South Cliff Rd
  4 Bridlington YO15 ...122 E2
  Kirton in Lindsey DN21 ..108 B1
South Dale LN7 ....111 B4
South Down Rd 3 YO32 127 F5
South Dr YO25 ....31 C4
South Duffield Rd YO8 ..49 C4
South Ella Dr HU10 ...143 D7
South Ella Way HU10 .143 D7
South End
  Seaton Ross YO42 .....39 E3
  Thorne/Moorends DN8 ..93 A4
South End La DN14 .....77 B4
South End Rd
  Ottringham HU12 ......73 E3
  Roos HU12 ....60 B1
South Ferriby Cty Sch
  DN18 ....84 A7
South Field Ct 5 HU16 .138 F5
South Furlong Croft 17
  DN9 ....105 E6
South Gate YO25 ......32 E6
South Glebe YO25 .....32 B1
South Gr 8 YO25 ....9 C3
South Holderness Sch
  HU12 ....72 D8
South Hunsley Sch
  HU14 ....68 E5
South Ings La HU15 ....53 C2
South Intake La DN9 ..116 F7
South La
  Bishop Wilton YO42 ....16 F1
  Cawood YO8 ....48 B7
  Kingston upon Hull
  HU13 ....143 E1
South Leys Comp Sch
  DN17 ....96 C2
South Leys Rd HU19 ...75 A4
South Marine Dr
  YO15 ....122 D1
South Marsh Rd DN41 .101 F7
South Moor Rd DN10 .116 C3
South Newbald Rd
  YO43 ....53 F7
South Par
  Grimsby DN31 ....152 D4
  Leven HU17 ....45 A7
  8 Selby YO8 ....148 C5
  Thorne DN8 ....93 A4
  York YO24 ....156 A1
South Par Inf Sch
  DN31 ....152 D4
South Par Jun Sch
  DN31 ....152 D4
South Park Rd DN17 ...96 B2
South Parkway 4 DN14 .78 C8
South Pk HU12 ....60 B1
South Prom HU18 ....134 C4
South Rd
  Keadby with Althorpe
  DN17 ....95 C6
  Thorne/Moorends DN8 ..79 B2
South Rise HU16 .....138 B8
South Rise Cres 20 DN17 96 C2
South Ruddings La
  YO19 ....37 F7
South Sea Ave 28 YO15 ..5 A2
South Sea La DN36 ...114 D7
South Sea Rd YO15 ....5 A2
South Side Kilham YO25 ..9 B3
  Winteringham DN15 ....68 A1
South Side La YO25 ....9 F6
South St
  Barmby on the Marsh
  DN14 ....64 A7

South St continued
  Barnetby le Wold DN38 ...99 B4
  Bridlington YO15 .....122 E1
  Burton Fleming YO25 ....2 E2
  8 Gainsborough DN21 ..117 A2
  Goole DN14 ....149 C2
  Keelby DN41 ....101 A5
  Kingston upon Hull
  HU16 ....139 A6
  Kingston upon Hull HU1 .155 A6
  Leven HU17 ....45 A7
  Middleton-on-the-Wolds
  YO25 ....31 C4
  North Kelsey LN7 .....110 A4
  Owston Ferry DN9 ....106 B2
  Roxby cum Risby DN15 ..82 F3
  West Butterwick DN17 .106 D8
  Winterton DN15 ....83 A5
South St Mary's Gate 4
  DN31 ....152 D3
South Townside Rd
  YO25 ....34 A8
South View
  Broughton DN20 ......97 D4
  Healaugh LS24 ....24 A2
  Holton le Clay DN36 ..114 B5
  6 Humberston DN36 ..103 D1
South View Ave
  Brigg DN20 ....98 C2
  Burringham DN17 ......95 D4
South Wold HU20 ......55 A4
South Wolds Sch HU17 .43 A7
South Wood Dr 8 DN8 ..93 A7
Southburn Ave HU4 ...144 E7
Southburn Rd YO25 ....20 A1
Southcliff Rd HU19 ....75 A6
Southcliffe Rd 12 DN21 107 C3
Southcoates Ave HU9 .141 E2
Southcoates La HU9 ..146 E8
Southcoates Prim Sch
  HU9 ....141 F1
Southcote CI 4 HU15 ..34 A2
Southcroft Dr 8 HU8 ..141 E7
South-Dale CI 7 DN21 .108 B2
Southern Dr HU4 .....144 C5
Southern Rd DN40 .....87 C3
Southern Wlk DN33 ...113 E8
Southfield 1 Belton DN9 .94 E1
  Kingston upon Hull HU13 ..69 E4
Southfield CI
  Great Driffield YO25 ..124 F6
  Rufforth YO23 ....24 D6
  14 Thorne/Moorends DN8 .93 B7
  Ulceby DN39 ....86 B1
  Wetwang YO25 ....19 B5
Southfield Cres 2
  YO24 ....132 E8
Southfield Dr
  1 Beverley HU17 .....137 A6
  4 Epworth DN9 ......105 D6
  North Ferriby HU14 ....69 A4
Southfield La
  Barmston YO25 ....23 A6
  Elstronwick HU12 ......59 C3
  Everingham YO42 ......40 B4
  Kellington DN14 ......61 E2
  Roos HU12 ....60 C1
  Seaton Ross YO42 .....39 D1
  Skipsea YO25 ....23 B2
  Willoughton DN21 ....119 A3
Southfield Pk YO43 ...135 D3
Southfield Rd
  1 Broughton DN20 ....97 D3
  7 Crowle DN17 ....94 D7
  Elstronwick HU12 ......59 A2
  Great Driffield YO25 ..124 F6
  Grimsby DN33 ....113 E8
  15 Holton le Clay DN36 .114 A5
  Kingston upon Hull HU5 .140 D4
  North Kelsey LN7 .....109 C2
  Pocklington YO42 .....28 F4
  Scunthorpe DN16 .....151 C1
  Thorne/Moorends DN8 ..93 B7
  Wetwang YO25 ....19 A5
  Winterton DN15 ....82 F5
Southfield Well Balk
  YO25 ....19 B5
Southfields HU15 ......52 E1
Southfields Rd YO32 ...14 B7
Southgate
  Hornsea HU18 ....134 C3
  Kingston upon Hull
  HU13 ....143 E1
  Market Weighton YO43 .135 E3
Southgate CI HU10 ...138 E2
Southgate Gdns 2
  HU18 ....134 C3
Southlands
  4 Haxby YO32 ....13 E5
  16 Hemingbrough YO8 ..49 F1
Southlands Ave 1
  DN21 ....117 A2
Southlands CI YO19 ...37 B6
Southlands Dr 3 DN21 .117 A2
Southlands Gdns 2
  DN21 ....117 A2
Southlands Rd YO23 ..130 B2
Southmoor La WF11 ...61 B1
Southmoor Rd
  Crowle DN17 ....94 C8
  Thorganby YO19 ......37 F5
Southolme Dr 7 YO30 .126 F1
Southorpe La DN21 ...118 D7
Southorpe Rd HU11 ...134 A1
Southside HU12 ....74 D1
Southside Rd HU12 ....73 F5

Southwell Ave HU9 ...147 E8
Southwell CI HU17 ....136 C1
Southwold Cres 25
  DN33 ....113 E8
Southwood Ave HU16 .138 F6
Southwood Dr HU16 ..139 A6
Southwood Gdns
  HU16 ....138 F5
Southwood Rd
  Kingston upon Hull
  HU16 ....138 F5
  Sutton upon Derwent
  YO41 ....38 C8
Soutter Gate HU12 ....72 C7
Sovereign CI 14 DN34 .102 E2
Sow Hill Rd HU17 .....154 A3
Sowerby Rd YO26 ....129 D4
Sowers La DN15 ....83 A5
Spa Hill DN21 ....108 B1
Spa Well La DN14 .....78 C8
Spalding Ave YO30 ...130 B7
Spalding Rd DN16 ....151 B4
Spark Mill La HU17 ...154 C1
Sparrowcroft La DN14 ..66 E3
Speculation St YO1 ...130 E4
Speedwell Cres DN15 ..96 B7
Speedwell La 1 HU17 ..55 D8
Speeton Gate YO15 .....4 D3
Spellowgate YO25 .....20 C7
Spellowgate CI YO25 .124 D5
Spen La
  Holme-on-Spalding-Moor
  YO43 ....39 F2
  York YO1 ....156 C3
Spencer Ave DN15 ...150 F8
Spencer CI
  22 Hedon HU12 ....72 C7
  Kingston upon Hull
  HU16 ....138 F6
Spencer St
  Beverley HU17 ....154 A3
  Grimsby DN31 ....153 B5
  Kingston upon Hull HU2 .155 A3
  3 York YO23 ....156 B1
Spencer Way 1 HU16 .139 B7
Spencers Mead YO25 .124 E3
Spencers Way YO25 ..124 E4
Speng La YO26 ....24 B4
Spenser St DN14 .....149 C5
Sperrin CI 2 HU9 .....142 A3
Spey Bank YO24 .....132 C6
Spilsby Rd DN17 .....150 E1
Spindle CI YO24 .....132 C8
Spindlewood 1 HU15 ..68 C7
Spinnaker CI HU9 ....146 C6
Spinney CI 2 DN40 ....87 C1
Spinney Croft CI 12 HU14 69 A5
Spinney The
  1 Barnby Dun DN3 ....92 A3
  Grimsby DN34 ....152 C3
  Kingston upon Hull
  HU16 ....139 A5
  6 Newport HU15 .....52 F1
  7 Swanland HU14 ....69 B7
  York YO24 ....132 F7
Spinney Wlk HU4 ....144 C6
Spire View 1 HU13 ...143 E1
Spital Hill DN21 ......117 B1
Spital Terr DN21 .....117 B1
Spittlerush La DN6 ....76 C7
Spout H YO42 ....28 D3
Spout Hill HU15 ....68 C8
Spratton Ct 2 DN37 ..102 B2
Spring Bank
  Grimsby DN34 ....152 A3
  Kingston upon Hull HU2 .155 A3
  4 North Newbald YO43 .53 F7
Spring Bank W HU4 ..144 D7
Spring CI YO25 ......124 D5
Spring Cottage Prim Sch
  HU8 ....141 F6
Spring Dale Rd YO43 .135 E5
Spring Field CI HU11 ..45 F8
Spring Gdns HU8 ....141 D5
Spring Gdns E HU4 ..144 B6
Spring Gdns S HU4 ..144 B6
Spring Gdns W HU4 ..144 B6
Spring Gr HU3 ....145 A7
Spring La
  2 Buckton/Bempton YO15 .4 D3
  11 Laceby DN37 .....101 F1
  Long Marston YO26 ....24 A5
  York YO10 ....131 A1
Spring Rd 1 YO43 ....135 E4
Spring St
  Immingham DN40 ......87 C1
  Kingston upon Hull HU2 .155 A3
Spring Vale HU9 .....142 D5
Spring Wlk HU3 ......148 A1
Springbank DN20 ......98 C2
Springbank Ave
  Dunnington YO19 ......26 E7
  Hornsea HU18 ....134 B4
Springbok CI HU4 ....144 D2
Springburn St HU3 ...145 A4
Springdale CI YO16 ..122 D3
Springdale Way HU17 .154 C1
Springfield
  Holme-on-Spalding-Moor
  YO43 ....40 A1
  6 Howden DN14 ......65 B7
Springfield Ave
  Bridlington YO15 .....122 E2
  18 Brough HU15 ......68 C6
  5 Hatfield DN7 ....92 D4
Springfield CI
  Barlby with Osgodby YO8 ..49 B5

Springfield CI continued
  Heworth YO31 ....131 C7
  2 Scunthorpe DN16 ..151 C2
Springfield Cres 3 WF8 .76 C3
Springfield Dr
  1 Barlby YO8 ....49 B5
  Beverley HU17 ....137 A6
Springfield Gdns YO43 .40 A1
Springfield Prim Sch
  DN33 ....113 D8
Springfield Rd
  25 Brigg DN20 ....98 C2
  Grimsby DN33 ....113 D8
  Kingston upon Hull HU3 .144 F6
  Pocklington YO42 .....29 B3
  4 Poppleton YO26 ....12 F1
Springfield Rise DN20 ..98 C2
Springfield Way
  Hook DN14 ....149 F6
  Kingston upon Hull
  HU10 ....143 E7
  York YO31 ....131 B7
Springfields 18 WF11 ..61 A2
Springfields Ave 17
  WF11 ....61 A2
Springhead Ave HU5 .144 A7
Springhead CI 6 DN14 .65 A7
Springhead Ct HU16 .144 A6
Springhead Gdns
  HU10 ....144 A7
Springhead La HU4 ..144 A7
Springhead Prim Sch
  HU10 ....143 F7
Springs Rd DN10 ....104 C1
Springs Way DN20 ....98 B2
Springthorpe Rd
  DN21 ....118 B1
Springville Ave HU13 .143 F2
Springway Cres DN34 .152 A3
Springwood YO32 ....127 D7
Springwood Cres 7
  DN33 ....113 D8
Sproatley Endowed Sch
  HU11 ....58 D5
Sproatley Rd HU12 ....58 D3
Spruce CI YO32 ......127 D2
Spruce La DN39 ....86 A1
Spruce Rd
  Kingston upon Hull HU1 .155 A1
  Leven HU17 ....45 B8
Spurn Ave 16 DN33 ..113 E8
Spurn Lightship★
  YO23 ....156 B1
Spurn Rd HU12 ....91 B2
Spurriergate YO1 .....156 B2
Spyvee St HU8 ......155 C3
Square The
  4 Easington HU12 .....90 F6
  Goxhill DN19 ....86 A8
  Kingston upon Hull
  HU13 ....143 E1
  Skerne & Wansford YO25 .21 C3
  Yapham YO42 ....28 C3
Squire La YO16 ......122 C4
Stable La
  4 Barton-upon-Humber
  DN18 ....69 E1
  Barton-upon-Humber
  DN18 ....69 E1
Stable Rd YO8 ....63 D7
Stabler CI 15 YO32 ....13 D5
Stablers Wlk YO32 ...127 F7
Staddlethorpe Broad La
  HU15 ....66 D7
Stafford St HU2 .....155 A4
Staindale CI YO30 ...126 E2
Staindale Rd DN16 ...151 E1
Staines CI HU8 ......142 A4
Stainforth Mid Sch
  DN7 ....92 C6
Stainforth Moor Rd
  DN7 ....93 C3
Stainforth Rd DN7 ....92 A5
Stainton Dr
  Grimsby DN33 ....102 C2
  15 Immingham DN40 ..87 B1
  9 Scunthorpe DN17 ..96 C2
Staithe St 3 YO8 ......50 D7
Staithes CI 4 YO26 ..129 B4
Staithes Rd HU12 .....72 B8
Stallingborough C of E Prim
  Sch DN41 ....101 E6
Stallingborough Rd
  Healing DN41 ....101 E5
  Immingham DN40 ......87 B1
  Keelby DN41 ....101 A5
Stallingborough Sta
  DN41 ....101 E6
Stalybridge Ave HU9 .142 E1
Stamford Bridge Prim & Inf
  Sch YO41 ....15 D2
Stamford Bridge Rd
  YO19 ....26 E7
Stamford Bridge W
  YO41 ....15 C2
Stamford Gr HU9 .....142 E1
Stamford St E 10 YO26 129 C5
Stamford St W 9 YO26 129 C5
Stan Valley 2 WF8 .....76 C3
Stanbury Rd HU6 ....140 C7
Standage Rd 12 HU12 ..72 C7
Standidge Dr HU8 ...142 A5
Standish La LN7 ......110 A2
Stanfield Rd 2 DN9 ..105 D6
Stanford CI DN37 ....101 F1

Stanford Sch DN37 101 F1
Stanholme La DN36 114 A1
Stanhope Ave HU9 141 E2
Stanhope Pl DN35 153 C3
Stanhope St DN14 149 C4
Stanhurst La DN7 93 A5
Staniland Dr YO8 148 A5
Staniland Way 1 DN36 114 D8
Staniwell Rise DN17 150 D3
Staniwells Dr 9 DN20 97 D3
Stanley Ave
Haxby YO32 127 D7
Hornsea HU18 134 C2
Stanley Gdns 15 DN7 92 C6
Stanley Rd
Scunthorpe DN15 150 C7
16 Stainforth DN7 92 C6
Stanley St Goole DN14 149 D4
Grimsby DN32 153 A4
Kingston upon Hull HU3 145 C7
York YO31 156 C4
Stannington Dr HU8 142 D6
Stansfield Cl HU9 142 D1
Stansted St DN31 152 B5
Staple Rd DN40 86 F3
Stapleford Cl 4 HU9 142 E2
Star Carr La DN20 98 C4
Star Hill Rd YO25 124 F5
Starboard Ave HU6 140 C8
Starcarr La YO25 34 A1
Starella Gr HU3 145 A4
Starham Rd LN7 109 C4
Starkbridge La DN14 78 A3
Starkey Cres YO31 131 A5
Stather Rd
Burton upon Stather DN15 82 A5
Flixborough DN15 82 A1
Stathers Wlk 3 HU10 143 F6
Station App YO15 122 E2
Station Ave
Bridlington YO16 122 D2
New Waltham DN36 114 A7
York YO32 127 D3
York YO1 156 A2
Station Ct HU18 134 D4
Station Dr HU3 140 D1
Station Hill YO25 19 B6
Station La
Barmby on the Marsh DN14 64 B7
Cliffe YO8 49 E3
Hedon HU12 72 C8
Holme-on-Spalding-Moor YO43 39 F1
Searby cum Owmby DN38 110 D7
Shipton YO30 12 E5
Station Mews HU18 134 D4
Station Rd Bainton YO25 31 E6
Blyton DN21 117 F6
Bridlington YO15 122 D2
Brough HU15 68 B5
Burringham DN17 95 D4
7 Burstwick HU12 73 A6
Burton Agnes YO25 10 A1
Carlton DN14 63 C3
Cleethorpes DN35 153 E3
Copmanthorpe YO23 132 B2
East Halton DN40 86 D7
Eastrington DN14 65 F8
Epworth DN9 105 D7
Fulstow LN11 121 D7
Garthorpe & Fockerby DN17 81 E6
Garton YO25 20 A5
Gilberdyke HU15 66 D8
Grasby DN38 110 E6
Grimsby DN37 102 B5
Gunness DN15 95 E5
Habrough DN40 100 E8
Harpham YO25 21 E8
Hatfield DN7 92 D4
Haxby YO32 13 F5
Haxey DN9 116 C7
Healing DN41 101 F5
Hensall DN14 62 C1
Holton le Clay DN36 114 A4
Howden DN14 65 B8
Hutton Cranswick YO25 32 E7
Keadby with Althorpe DN17 95 D6
Keyingham HU12 73 C4
Killingholme High DN40 87 B5
Kingston upon Hull HU16 139 C7
Kingston upon Hull HU13 143 E1
Kirton in Lindsey DN21 108 B2
Lockington YO25 32 D1
Ludborough DN36 121 B6
Market Weighton YO43 135 D4
Middleton YO25 31 C5
Middleton-on-the-Wolds YO25 31 C4
Misterton DN10 116 D5
Nafferton YO25 125 F6
New Waltham DN36 114 A7
North Cave HU15 53 D3
North Ferriby HU14 69 A4
North Kelsey LN7 110 A4
North Thoresby DN36 114 B1
Norton DN6 76 F2
Ottringham HU12 73 F4
Owston Ferry DN9 106 A2
Station Rd *continued*
Patrington HU12 74 C2
Pocklington YO42 29 A3
24 Poppleton YO26 12 F1
Poppleton YO26 24 F8
Preston HU12 72 C8
Rawcliffe DN14 64 A1
Riccall YO19 49 A8
Scawby DN20 108 F7
Scunthorpe DN15 151 B6
Selby YO8 148 D5
South Cave HU15 54 A2
South Kelsey LN7 110 D2
South Killingholme DN40 87 A5
Stainforth DN7 92 C5
Stallingborough DN41 101 D6
Thorngumbald HU12 73 A5
Thornton Curtis DN39 85 F5
Ulceby DN39 86 B1
Walkeringham DN10 116 D3
Waltham DN37 113 E7
Wharram YO17 6 A4
Whitton DN15 67 D3
Wistow YO8 48 C6
5 Withernsea HU19 75 A6
Womersley DN6 76 D5
York YO1 156 A2
Station Rise YO1 156 A2
Station Sq 4 YO32 14 B7
Station St DN10 116 C5
Station View YO8 49 D3
Staveley Rd HU9 142 C3
Staves Ct 10 DN36 114 D4
Staxton Ct HU9 146 D8
Staxton Hill YO12 1 C8
Staynor Ave YO8 148 E3
Steadings The DN15 82 B1
Steele Cl YO43 135 D3
Steep Hill HU15 54 B2
Steeping Dr 11 DN40 87 B1
Steeple Cl 4 YO32 13 D5
Steeton Ave 4 HU6 140 C7
Stembridge Cl 1 HU9 142 E1
Stephen Cl 2 DN39 86 A1
Stephen Cres
14 Barton-upon-Humber DN18 84 F8
Grimsby DN34 102 C2
10 Humberston DN36 114 C8
Stephen's Wlk YO8 148 B1
Stephenson Cl
Market Weighton YO43 135 C3
York YO31 127 E1
Stephenson St HU9 141 E1
Stephenson Way YO26 129 F5
Stephenson's Wlk HU16 139 D6
Stephenwath La YO41 16 C5
Stepney Ave 13 YO16 122 C5
Stepney Gr YO16 122 C4
Stepney La HU5 140 E1
Sterling Cres DN37 113 D6
Sterne Ave
7 Broughton DN20 97 D3
York YO31 131 A5
Stevenson Pl DN35 153 D1
Stevenson's Way 18 DN18 84 E8
Stewart Garth HU16 138 E6
Stewart La YO19 36 C4
Steynburg St HU9 141 D1
Stirling Cl 2 DN21 117 C1
Stirling Gr YO10 133 F8
Stirling Rd
Barmby Moor YO42 28 E3
York YO30 126 F3
Stirling St
Grimsby DN31 153 B5
Kingston upon Hull HU3 144 F6
Stirrup Cl YO24 132 B8
Stockbridge Ave HU9 142 E1
Stockbridge La YO25 32 F6
Stockbridge Pk 2 HU15 68 C7
Stockbridge Rd HU15 68 B7
Stockhill Cl 1 YO19 26 E7
Stockholm Cl 1 YO10 133 D8
Stockholm Pk 23 HU12 72 D7
Stockholm Rd
Kingston upon Hull HU7 140 E5
16 Thorngumbald HU12 73 A5
Stocking La Hillam LS25 61 B7
Knottingley WF11 61 B2
Stockleigh Cl HU7 140 F8
Stocks Dr DN14 79 B8
Stocks Hill Belton DN9 94 E1
Huggate YO42 18 C1
Stockshill Rd DN16 151 C2
Stockton Hall YO32 14 D3
Stockton La
Heworth YO32 128 D1
York YO31 131 A7
Stockton on the Forest Cty Prim Sch YO32 14 D3
Stockwell Gr HU9 147 E8
Stockwell La 13 YO25 34 B2
Stockwell Prim Sch HU9 147 E8
Stockwith La YO8 63 A4
Stockwith Rd
Haxey DN9 105 E1
Owston Ferry DN9 116 E8
Walkeringham DN10 116 D3
Walkerith DN21 116 E4
Stoke St HU2 155 A4
Stone Bridge Dr YO41 27 F5
Stone Dale YO42 17 D3
Stone Hill DN7 93 A4
Stone Hill Rd DN7 93 A4
Stone La DN17 95 D4
Stone Riggs YO32 14 D2
Stonebow The YO1 156 C2
Stonebridge Ave HU9 142 D1
Stonecarr Ct 2 HU7 56 F7
Stoneferry Prim Sch HU8 141 A3
Stoneferry Rd HU8 141 A2
Stonegate
Hunmanby YO14 2 F8
Thorne/Moorends DN8 93 A8
York YO1 156 B2
Stonegate Cl 3 HU7 141 D7
Stoneknowle Hill YO43 54 A8
Stonelands Ct 2 YO30 127 A1
Stonepit Balk YO17 6 C5
Stonepit Hill YO17 6 C4
Stonepit La YO15 4 E3
Stonepit Rd
Ellerker HU15 54 A1
Welton HU15 68 E6
Stones Mount HU16 139 A7
Stonesdale HU7 141 A6
Stonethwaite 5 YO24 132 C7
Stoney La HU15 53 A3
Stoney Way DN36 114 D4
Stony La HU15 53 A3
Stool Close Rd DN9 94 E1
Stoop Cl YO32 127 C8
Storkhill Rd HU17 154 C4
Storking La YO41 27 F6
Stornaway Sq HU8 141 F7
Stortford St DN31 152 B5
Story St HU1 155 A3
Stothards La 1 DN19 86 A8
Stottlebink 17 YO15 5 A2
Stovin Cres DN15 83 A5
Stow Cl 11 DN37 102 B4
Stow Ct YO32 127 E3
Stow Rd Atwick YO25 35 D5
Scunthorpe DN16 151 B3
Straight La YO19 26 F8
Straits Rd HU11 46 D2
Strand Cl HU2 155 A4
Strand Inf Sch DN32 153 A5
Strand Jun Sch DN32 152 F5
Strand St DN32 152 F5
Stratford Ave 4 DN33 102 D2
Stratford Dr DN16 151 C5
Stratford Way YO32 127 E3
Strathcona Ave HU5 139 E4
Strathearn St 1 HU5 140 D3
Strathmore Ave
Burstwick HU12 73 A7
Kingston upon Hull HU6 140 C6
Stratton Cl HU8 142 B7
Stratton Pk 3 HU14 69 B6
Strawberry Gdns HU18 134 C1
Strawberry Hill 2 DN37 113 C6
Strawberry St HU9 146 B7
Stray Garth YO31 130 F7
Stray Rd
Sunk Island HU12 89 B6
York YO31 131 B6
Stray The HU15 54 A2
Straylands Gr YO31 130 F8
Street YO25 9 E1
Street La Bubwith YO8 50 F5
North Kelsey LN7 110 B4
Street Life Mus of Transport★ HU1 155 C2
Street The YO42 28 A2
Strensall Pk YO32 14 A5
Strensall Rd
Earswick YO32 128 A7
Kingston upon Hull HU5 139 C1
York YO32 127 F6
Strickland Rd
Eastoft DN17 81 A2
13 Hunmanby YO14 3 A8
Strickland St HU3 145 C4
Strines Gr 9 HU7 141 D7
Stripe La YO30 126 B5
Stromness Way HU8 141 F7
Stroud Cres E HU7 141 A7
Stroud Cres W HU7 141 A8
Strouther Cl YO42 29 A3
Strubby Cl 6 DN35 103 D2
Stuart Cl
Bridlington YO15 122 C1
Scunthorpe DN17 96 C1
4 Strensall YO32 14 C8
Stuart Gr
Eggborough DN14 62 A2
9 Thorpe Willoughby YO8 48 B1
Stuart Rd YO24 129 D1
Stuart Wortley St DN31 152 F6
Stub Ings La DN40 87 D1
Stubbs La
Cridling Stubbs WF11 76 A8
Norton DN6 76 E2
Stubbs Rd DN6 76 D3
Stubden Gr YO30 126 F2
Studcross DN9 105 D6
Studley Mdws YO16 122 D7
Studley St HU8 146 B8
Stump Cross★ HU17 43 C2
Sturdee Gr YO31 130 D7
Sturmer Ct 15 DN16 96 D1
Sturton Gr 23 DN33 102 D2
Sturton La DN20 108 E7
Stygate La DN6 76 E1
Stylefield Rd 15 YO15 5 A2
Styles Croft HU14 69 C7
Subway St HU3 145 B3
Subway The DN16 97 A4
Suddaby Cl HU9 141 F2
Suddle Way 4 DN41 101 A4
Sudforth La DN14 61 C3
Suffolk St HU5 140 D3
Suggitt's Ct DN35 153 D4
Suggitt's La DN35 153 D4
Suggitt's Orch DN35 153 D4
Sullivan Rd HU4 144 B4
Summer Hill DN21 117 C1
Summerdale DN18 84 E8
Summerfield Ave 3 DN37 113 E7
Summerfield Cl
Great Driffield YO25 124 D5
4 Waltham DN37 113 E7
Summerfield Rd
Bridlington YO15 122 D1
York YO24 132 C7
Summergangs Dr 17 HU12 72 E5
Summergangs Rd HU8 141 C3
Summergroves Way HU4 144 B2
Sunbeam Rd HU4 144 D5
Sunk Island Rd HU12 88 E8
Sunningdale 12 DN37 113 D6
Sunningdale Ave 1 DN20 98 C3
Sunningdale Cl 1 YO26 129 B5
Sunningdale Dr 7 DN40 87 C2
Sunningdale Rd
Kingston upon Hull HU13 143 F2
Kingston upon Hull HU4 144 E4
Scunthorpe DN17 96 B2
Sunny Bank
Kingston upon Hull HU3 145 B7
3 Knottingley WF11 61 A2
Sunny Cnr 18 DN33 102 E1
Sunny Hill 9 DN21 108 B1
Sunnybank 1 DN18 84 E8
Sunnydale 3 YO32 127 D7
Sunway Gr DN16 151 A1
Sunway Infants Sch DN16 151 A1
Surbiton Cl HU8 141 F5
Surrey Garth HU4 144 B4
Surrey Way YO30 129 F8
Surtees St
Grimsby DN31 152 F6
York YO30 130 B7
Sussex Cl
5 Kingston upon Hull HU5 139 D1
York YO10 131 C2
Sussex Rd YO10 131 C2
Sussex St DN35 153 B4
Sussex Way 14 YO32 14 A7
Susworth Rd DN17 106 D4
Sutcliffe Ave 18 DN33 102 D2
Sutherland Ave HU6 140 B6
Sutherland St YO23 130 B1
Sutor Cl YO23 132 B3
Sutton Bridge★ YO41 27 C2
Sutton C of E Sch HU7 141 D7
Sutton Cl HU7 141 B8
Sutton Ct HU8 141 E6
Sutton Gdns HU7 141 B7
Sutton Ho Rd HU8 141 D5
Sutton La
Barmby Moor YO42 28 B3
Byram cum Sutton WF11 61 A4
Sutton on Derwent C of E Prim Sch YO41 27 C2
Sutton Park Prim Sch HU7 140 F7
Sutton Pl DN20 108 F7
Sutton Rd Howden DN14 65 A6
Kingston upon Hull HU6 140 D6
12 Kirk Sandall DN3 92 A3
Wawne HU7 56 F7
Sutton St DN14 149 D4
Sutton Way
Kingston upon Hull HU9 142 B2
York YO30 130 B8
Swaby Dr DN35 103 B2
Swaby's Yd HU17 154 A3
Swaddale Ave HU10 138 F2
Swainby Cl HU7 141 D7
Swale Ave YO24 132 E8
Swaledale Ave HU9 141 E1
Swaledale Mews YO16 122 F6
Swaledale Pl DN16 151 D2
Swales Rd DN36 114 D8
Swallow Ct 4 DN9 105 D7
Swallow Dr 3 DN41 101 F5
Swallow Grange 6 HU8 141 D7
Swallow La DN39 85 E2
Swallowfield Dr HU4 144 B2
Swan Cl YO19 37 A7
Swan Farm Ct YO19 37 A7
Swan Hill★ HU11 142 F6
Swan Syke Dr 8 DN6 76 F2
Swanella Gr HU3 145 A4
Swanfield Rd HU9 142 C2
Swanland Ave 3 YO15 122 F3
Swanland Butts Cl HU10 143 C6
Swanland Cl 17 DN8 93 B7
Swanland CP Sch HU14 69 B6
Swanland Dale HU14 69 B8
Swanland Garth 4 HU14 69 A5
Swanland Hill HU14 69 B5
Swanland Rd HU13 143 C2
Swanland Way 3 HU16 138 E6
Swann St
Kingston upon Hull HU2 155 C4
York YO23 156 A1
Swannacks View DN20 108 F7
Sweet Briar Cl 7 DN37 113 D7
Sweet Dews Gr HU9 146 D8
Sweyne Garth DN14 65 D1
Swift Rd DN17 150 D2
Swiftsure Cres 16 DN34 102 B2
Swinburne La DN17 150 D3
Swinburne St HU8 141 D2
Swinderby Garth 19 HU7 57 A5
Swinderby Gdns DN34 152 A1
Swindon St YO16 122 D3
Swine Bank HU5 139 B2
Swine La HU11 57 E5
Swine Rd HU11 45 C1
Swinefleet Prim Sch DN14 65 C1
Swinefleet Rd
Goole DN14 149 D2
Goole Fields DN14 80 C8
Swinegate
Kingston upon Hull HU13 143 E1
York YO1 156 B2
Swinemoor Cty Inf Sch HU17 154 C4
Swinemoor Cty Prim Sch HU17 154 C4
Swinemoor La HU17 137 B5
Swineridge Hill YO42 29 B6
Swineridge La YO42 29 C6
Swinescaif Hill Swine HU15 54 A3
Swinescaif Rd HU15 54 A3
Swinhope Brats★ LN8 120 B6
Swinster La DN40 86 E6
Swinsty Ct YO30 126 F1
Switchback LN8 120 A1
Swithin Cl HU13 144 A2
Sycamore Ave
15 Grimsby DN33 102 E2
York YO32 127 D4
Sycamore Cl
3 Barnetby le Wold DN38 99 B4
2 Broughton DN20 97 D3
14 Gilberdyke HU15 66 D8
Goole DN14 149 E6
1 Haxby YO32 127 D7
Kingston upon Hull HU4 144 C7
Nafferton YO25 125 F7
8 Preston HU12 58 C1
Selby YO8 148 A4
Skelton YO30 126 C5
12 Snaith & Cowick DN14 78 C8
Sycamore Cres YO25 32 E7
Sycamore Dr
9 Gainsborough DN21 117 C1
3 Thorngumbald HU12 72 E5
Sycamore Pl YO30 156 A3
Sycamore Rd YO8 49 B5
Sycamore Terr YO30 156 A3
Sycamore View 17 YO26 12 F1
Sycamores The HU17 137 B3
Sydney Smith Sch HU10 144 A5
Sykehouse Rd DN14 78 C4
Sykes Balk YO25 21 E8
Sykes Cl 6 HU10 143 F6
Sykes La Garton YO25 124 A5
Goxhill DN19 71 A2
Sykes St HU2 155 B3
Sylvan Falls YO25 124 C4
Sylvan Lea YO25 124 C4
Sylvan Mead YO25 124 C4
Sylvester St 18 DN21 108 B1
Sylvia Cl HU6 139 F5
Symmons Cl 4 HU17 137 A6
Symons Cl HU2 155 A4
Symons Way 13 YO42 29 A3

T

Tabard Hamlet 5 DN14 61 F2
Tabard Rd 6 DN14 61 F2
Tabards The 7 DN14 61 F2
Tadcaster Rd YO24 132 F8
Tadcaster Rd Dringhouses YO23 132 E5
Tadman Cl HU17 136 E7
Tadman St HU3 145 D4
Talbot Circ DN3 92 A4
Talbot Rd DN40 87 C1
Talisman Dr 6 DN16 96 D1
Tall Trees HU13 143 C3
Tallert Way 28 DN33 102 C2
Tamar Dr 14 DN36 114 A8
Tamar Gr HU8 142 C7
Tamarisk Way DN16 96 E2
Tamworth Rd 9 YO30 127 A1
Tan Dyke Way HU17 154 C2
Tanashi Dori DN17 150 E5
Tanfield Gr HU9 142 C2
Tang Hall La YO31 131 A5
Tang Hall Prim Sch YO31 130 F5
Tanner Row YO1 156 A2
Tanner's Moat YO1 156 A2
Tanpit La DN6 76 E3
Tansley La HU18 134 D1
Tansterne La HU11 59 A7
Tarbert Cres 2 YO24 132 B7

Tardrew Cl HU17 . . . . . . .136 E6
Target La 16 YO42 . . . . . . .29 A4
Tarleton Cl 3 DN3 . . . . .92 A2
Tarran Ave HU6 . . . . . . .140 B8
Tasburgh St DN32 . . . . . .152 F2
Tate Cl YO8 . . . . .48 D6
Tattersall Dr 1 HU17 . .137 B3
Tattershall Ave 14 DN32 102 C2
Tattershall Cl HU2 . . . . .140 E1
Tatton Cl YO30 . . . . . . .127 A1
Taunton Rd HU4 . . . . . .144 A3
Taunton Way 19 DN33 . .113 E8
Tavella Ct 1 DN9 . . . . .105 B2
Tavistock St HU5 . . . . . .140 C3
Taylor Ave HU9 . . . . . . .142 C3
Taylor Cl DN9 . . . . .94 E2
Taylor St DN35 . . . . . . .153 B5
Taylor's Ave DN35 . . . . .103 C2
Taylors Field YO25 . . . . .124 E4
Taylor's La HU19 . . . . . . .75 C2
Teal Cl 13 Broughton DN20 .98 B2
Walkington HU17 . . . . . . .55 B7
Teal Dr YO24 . . . . .132 C8
Teal Pl LN7 . . . . .111 A4
Teal Rd 1 HU15 . . . . . . .52 F1
Tealby Gr 19 DN33 . . . . .102 D2
Tealby Rd DN17 . . . . . . .150 D1
Teale St DN15 . . . . .151 A8
Team Gate 1 DN37 . . . .102 B3
Teanby Dr DN15 . . . . . . .83 A5
Tedder Rd YO24 . . . . . . .129 B1
Teddington Cl HU8 . . . . .141 E6
Tedworth Rd HU9 . . . . . .142 C5
Tee La DN15 . . . . .82 B5
Tees Gr HU8 . . . . .142 C7
Teesdale Ave HU9 . . . . .146 E8
Teesdale Mews YO16 . . .122 F7
Telford St HU9 . . . . .141 E2
Telford Terr 1 YO24 . . .130 B2
Temper Rd DN16 . . . . . .151 F4
Temperance Ave
  DN17 . . . . .107 D7
Temperton's La DN9 . . . .106 A2
Templar Cl DN14 . . . . . . .61 F1
Templar Ct 17 DN16 . . . . .96 D2
Templar Way YO8 . . . . .148 C2
Templar's Bath ★ DN16 . .96 D1
Temple Ave YO10 . . . . . .131 B4
Temple Cl Belton DN9 . . .94 E2
  Welton HU15 . . . . .68 E6
Temple Garth YO23 . . . .132 C1
Temple La
  Aylesby DN37 . . . . .101 E1
  Carnaby YO16 . . . . .10 E5
  Copmanthorpe YO23 . . .132 C1
Temple Manor ★ YO8 . . .62 D4
Temple Rd YO23 . . . . . . .132 F4
Temple St HU5 . . . . .140 E1
Temple Wlk 2 HU15 . . . .68 E6
Templefield Rd DN21 . . .119 A3
Templemead YO31 . . . . .130 E8
Temsdale 2 HU7 . . . . . .141 A6
Ten Thorn La YO26 . . . . .129 A4
Tennant St YO8 . . . . . . .148 B6
Tennent Rd YO24 . . . . . .129 B2
Tennison Ct HU16 . . . . . .139 A7
Tennyson Ave
  Bridlington YO15 . . . . . .122 E3
  1 Campsall DN6 . . . . . .76 E1
  Kingston upon Hull HU5 . .140 A1
  7 Thorne/Moorends DN8 . .93 B8
  York YO30 . . . . .130 C7
Tennyson Cl Brigg DN20 .98 C1
  Caistor LN7 . . . . .111 A3
Tennyson Rd
  Cleethorpes DN35 . . . . .153 D5
  Scunthorpe DN16 . . . . .151 D3
Tennyson St
  33 Gainsborough DN21 . .117 B1
  Goole DN14 . . . . .149 C5
  Grimsby DN31 . . . . . . .152 D4
Tensing Rd DN16 . . . . . .151 C1
Tenterden Cl HU7 . . . . . .141 A6
Tern Gr HU8 . . . . .142 C5
Terrington Pl 4 DN35 . .103 B2
Terry Ave YO1 . . . . .156 B1
Terry St
  Kingston upon Hull HU3 . .140 D1
  York YO23 . . . . .130 C1
Teskey King Sch HU6 . . .140 A5
Tetley Rd DN16 . . . . . . .151 C3
Tetley View 2 DN17 . . . .94 E6
Tetney CP Sch DN36 . . .114 D4
Tetney La DN36 . . . . . . .114 B5
Tetney Lock Rd DN36 . . .114 D6
Tetney Rd DN36 . . . . . . .114 C8
Tewkesbury Dr DN34 . . .152 C2
Thanet Prim Sch HU9 . . .142 D6
Thanet Rd
  Kingston upon Hull HU9 . .142 D5
  York YO24 . . . . .129 D1
Thatch Cl YO8 . . . . .148 C4
Thatchers Croft YO23 . . .132 C3
Theaker Ave DN21 . . . . .117 C1
Thealby La HU15 . . . . . . .82 D5
Thearne Cl 7 HU5 . . . . .140 C3
Thearne La HU17 . . . . . . .56 D7
Theodore Rd DN15 . . . . .150 E8
Theresa Cl 6 YO31 . . . .127 F1
Therm Rd HU8 . . . . .155 C4
Thesiger St DN32 . . . . . .152 F5
Thief La Barlow YO8 . . . .148 F1
  York YO10 . . . . .130 F3
Thimblehall La HU15 . . . .52 E2
Thinholme La DN9 . . . . .105 A1
Third Ave
  Bridlington YO15 . . . . . .123 A4
  Fixborough Ind Est. DN15 .82 A1

Third Ave continued
  Goole DN14 . . . . .149 C4
  Scunthorpe DN17 . . . . .150 C2
  York YO31 . . . . .130 F5
Third La DN37 . . . . .113 D3
Thirkleby Cres DN32 . . . .103 A2
Thirkleby Way YO10 . . . .146 B7
Thirlmere Ave DN33 . . . .113 E8
Thirlmere Dr YO31 . . . . .131 A6
Thirlmere Wlk DN14 . . . .149 F6
Thirsk Mews HU5 . . . . . .139 D4
Thirtle Bridge La HU19 . . .74 C8
Thirtleby La HU11 . . . . . . .57 F6
Thirty Acre La 13 HU12 . .72 D7
Thiseldine Cl 6 YO43 . . . .53 F7
Thistle Cl YO8 . . . . .148 C2
Thistleton Gdns 6 HU5 .140 E2
Thixendale Rd YO25 . . . . .18 A7
Thomas Clarkson Way
  HU7 . . . . .140 E8
Thomas Rd
  Scunthorpe DN17 . . . . .150 F4
  17 Stainforth DN7 . . . . . .92 C5
Thomas St
  Grimsby DN32 . . . . . . .152 F3
  Kingston upon Hull HU9 . .146 D7
  6 Selby YO8 . . . . .148 D6
  York YO10 . . . . .130 E3
Thomas Sumpter Comp Sch
  DN17 . . . . .150 E3
Thompson Ave HU17 . . . .154 C3
Thompson Cl 9 YO8 . . . .49 B4
Thompson Dr
  16 Hatfield DN7 . . . . .92 D4
  2 Strensall YO32 . . . . . .14 B8
Thompson Nook 14 DN7 . .92 D4
Thompson Pl 6 YO26 . . .129 E5
Thompson St
  Bridlington YO16 . . . . . .122 D3
  Scunthorpe DN15 . . . . .151 B7
Thonock Rd DN21 . . . . . .117 D4
Thoresians Rugby Club
  DN8 . . . . .93 B8
Thoresby Ave YO16 . . . .122 C6
Thoresby Cl YO16 . . . . . .122 D6
Thoresby Mews 7
  YO16 . . . . .122 D6
Thoresby Pl 2 DN35 . . .103 C2
Thoresby Prim Sch
  HU5 . . . . .145 B8
Thoresby Rd
  Fulstow LN11 . . . . .121 D8
  North Coates DN36 . . . .115 A2
  Scunthorpe DN17 . . . . .150 D1
  Tetney DN36 . . . . .114 D3
  York YO24 . . . . .129 B1
Thoresby St HU5 . . . . . .145 B8
Thoresway Gr 9 DN33 . .102 C2
Thorganby Rd DN35 . . . .103 C2
Thorgill Gr HU5 . . . . . . .139 E3
Thorn Bank DN9 . . . . . . .104 E4
Thorn Barn Cl 2 HU12 . . .72 F5
Thorn La DN19 . . . . .86 A8
Thorn Leigh 3 HU3 . . . .145 C6
Thorn Marsh Rd HU12 . . .72 E2
Thorn Nook YO31 . . . . . .130 F8
Thorn Rd HU12 . . . . .72 D7
Thornbridge Cl HU9 . . . .142 B3
Thornbury Rd DN40 . . . . .87 C1
Thorncroft 8 YO19 . . . . . .26 F7
Thorndale HU7 . . . . .140 E8
Thorndale Croft YO25 . . . .19 B5
Thorndale La YO25 . . . . . .19 A5
Thornden Bldgs YO8 . . . .148 D5
Thorndike Way DN21 . . . .117 D1
Thorne & Dikesmarsh
  DN8 . . . . .79 A2
Thorne Gram Sch DN8 . .93 B8
Thorne North Sta DN8 . .93 A8
Thorne Rd Hatfield DN7 . .92 F5
  Kirk Sandall DN3 . . . . . .92 A1
  3 Stainforth DN7 . . . . . .92 C6
Thorne South Comm Fst Sch
  DN8 . . . . .93 B7
Thorne South Sta DN8 . .93 B7
Thorne Swimming Baths
  DN8 . . . . .93 B8
Thorne Waste Drain Rd
  DN8 . . . . .79 D1
Thorneycroft 14 HU12 72 E5
Thornfield Ave 5 YO31 .130 F8
Thornfield Dr 7 YO31 . .127 E2
Thorngarth La DN19 . . . . .85 C8
Thorngumbald Inf Sch
  HU12 . . . . .72 E5
Thorngumbald Jun Sch
  HU12 . . . . .72 F5
Thorngumbald Rd
  HU12 . . . . .72 B4
Thornham Cl HU15 . . . . . .53 F1
Thornham's Way 6
  HU15 . . . . .68 C2
Thornhill Ave HU8 . . . . .141 C4
Thornhill Cres 19 DN17 . .96 C2
Thornhill Gdns DN34 . . .152 A3
Thornhills 19 YO32 . . . . . .13 F5
Thornholme Dr 14 DN16 .96 D2
Thornleys HU17 . . . . .43 A4
Thornton 10 HU15 . . . . . .68 C6
Thornton Abbey (Rems of) ★
  DN39 . . . . .86 B5
Thornton Abbey Sta
  DN39 . . . . .86 A5
Thornton Cl DN16 . . . . . .151 A3
Thornton Cl DN13 . . . . . .143 D1
Thornton Cres DN35 . . . .103 C2
Thornton Ct DN36 . . . . . .114 A4
Thornton Dam La HU15 . . .66 D8

Thornton Gdns 5 DN41 101 A4
Thornton Gr
  7 Grimsby DN34 . . . . . .102 C2
  3 Preston HU12 . . . . . . .58 C1
Thornton Hall ★ DN39 . .85 F5
Thornton La YO25 . . . . . . .20 A1
Thornton Moor Cl
  YO30 . . . . .126 F2
Thornton Pl DN40 . . . . . . .87 B1
Thornton Rd
  Barrow upon Humber
    DN19 . . . . .85 D6
  Bridlington YO16 . . . . . .122 B2
  Goxhill DN19 . . . . .85 F6
  South Kelsey LN7 . . . . .110 A1
Thornton St DN19 . . . . . . .85 C7
Thorntondale Dr YO16 . . .122 F7
Thorntree Cl DN14 . . . . . .149 E6
Thorntree La
  Balne DN14 . . . . .77 C6
  Goole DN14 . . . . .149 E6
Thornwick Ave HU10 . . . .143 E8
Thornwick Cl 2 HU3 . . . .145 C5
Thornwick Rd YO15 . . . . . .5 B3
Thornwood Covert 1
  YO24 . . . . .129 C1
Thorny La YO42 . . . . .16 F2
Thorold Pl 11 DN31 . . . . .92 A3
Thorold St DN31 . . . . . . .153 A5
Thorpe YO25 . . . . .32 B1
Thorpe La YO8 . . . . .48 B8
Thorpe Leys YO25 . . . . . .32 B2
Thorpe Rd
  6 Brough HU15 . . . . . . .68 C5
  Howden DN14 . . . . .65 C8
Thorpe Rd Ave 2 HU15 . .65 B7
Thorpe St
  9 Bridlington YO15 . . . .122 E2
  York YO23 . . . . .130 B2
Thorpe Willoughby Cty Prim
  Sch YO8 . . . . .48 B1
Thorpehall Rd DN3 . . . . . .92 A2
Thorpepark Prim Sch
  HU6 . . . . .140 A8
Thorpepark Rd HU6 . . . .139 F8
Thrislington Sq 19 DN8 . .79 B2
Throughleys La YO42 . . . .39 A5
Thrunscoe Inf Sch & Nursery
  DN35 . . . . .153 F1
Thrunscoe Rd DN35 . . . .153 F1
Thrussendale Rd YO17 . . .16 E8
Thurlow Ave
  Beverley HU17 . . . . . . .136 E6
  22 Pocklington YO42 . . . .29 A3
Thurlow Garth YO25 . . . .125 F7
Thurlstone Cl 18 HU7 . . .56 F6
Thurstan Rd HU17 . . . . . .136 D2
Thurstan Rd HU17 . . . . . .154 A2
Thwaite St HU16 . . . . . . .139 C6
Thwing Rd
  Burton Fleming YO25 . . . .2 E2
  Kilham YO25 . . . . .9 B5
Thyme Way HU17 . . . . . . .55 F8
Tibby La YO25 . . . . .32 C4
Tichbourne Cl 6 HU3 . .145 C5
Tickton C of E Prim Sch
  HU17 . . . . .137 F8
Tickton Gr HU6 . . . . .139 F4
Tickton Mdws HU17 . . . .137 F8
Tideworth Hague La
  DN14 . . . . .78 C3
Tiger La HU17 . . . . .44 D8
Tilbury Prim Sch HU4 . .144 B3
Tilbury Rd HU4 . . . . .144 B3
Tilia Cl
  Kingston upon Hull HU4 . .144 B2
  Scunthorpe DN16 . . . . . .96 E2
Tilmire Cl 2 YO10 . . . . .133 F8
Tilworth Rd HU8 . . . . . . .141 F4
Timberland DN16 . . . . . . .96 C2
Timberley Dr 7 DN37 . . .102 B4
Tindale Bank Rd
  DN10 . . . . .116 C7
Tinker La YO23 . . . . .24 D6
Tinkler's La WF11 . . . . . . .61 D6
Tinley Cl HU16 . . . . .139 B7
Tintagel Way DN36 . . . . .114 A8
Tippaty La WF11 . . . . . . .61 A4
Tippet La HU17 . . . . .44 F2
Tisbury Rd YO26 . . . . . . .129 E4
Tison Garth HU16 . . . . . .139 A6
Tithe Barn Cl 9 HU12 . . .74 D1
Tithe Barn La
  8 Patrington HU12 . . . . .74 D1
  13 Thorne/Moorends DN8 . .93 B8
Tithe Barn Rd 2 WF11 . .61 A4
Tithe Barn Way DN14 . . . .61 F3
Tithe La YO24 . . . . .129 B1
Tithe La YO25 . . . . .22 E5
Tithe Rd HU12 . . . . .58 A1
Tiverton Rd HU7 . . . . . . .141 A8
Tiverton St DN35 . . . . . .153 C4
Toadham La DN14 . . . . . . .77 C5
Toby Ct YO32 . . . . .14 A7
Todd La DN21 . . . . .117 F4
Todds Cl HU14 . . . . .69 C6
Todds Cl DN17 . . . . .107 D7
Todds La DN15 . . . . .82 A4
Todd's La HU15 . . . . .68 A8
Toft Gn YO1 . . . . .156 A2
Tofts Rd 2 DN18 . . . . . . .84 E8
Toll Bar Ave DN36 . . . . .113 F7
Toll Gavel HU17 . . . . . . .154 A3
Tollerton Rd YO30 . . . . . .12 B1
Tollesby La 9 DN7 . . . . . .92 D4
Tomline Rd 2 DN41 . . . .101 A5
Tomline St DN31 . . . . . . .152 F5
Tomlinson Ave DN15 . . . .150 E7

Tonbridge 21 DN33 . . . . .113 E8
Tonbridge Gr 2 HU9 . . . .142 E2
Tongue La HU15 . . . . .66 E6
Tonnant Way 6 DN34 . . .102 B3
Toogood St HU2 . . . . . . .155 B4
Toothill Gdns 2 DN34 . . .102 B3
Toothill Rd 1 DN34 . . . . .102 C3
Top La
  Copmanthorpe YO23 . . .132 B3
  Kirk Bramwith DN7 . . . . .92 A7
Top Rd
  South Killingholme DN40 . .86 E3
  Winterton DN15 . . . . . . .82 F6
  Worlaby DN20 . . . . .98 D8
Topaz Gr 3 HU3 . . . . . . .145 A4
Topcliff Ct YO8 . . . . .148 B7
Topcliffe Garth HU7 . . . .141 C8
Torbay Dr DN33 . . . . . . .113 E4
Torchil Cl HU3 . . . . .143 C6
Toremill Cl YO32 . . . . . . .127 C4
Torksey Dr DN33 . . . . . . .102 D2
Torksey Pl 28 DN33 . . . .102 D2
Torksey St DN21 . . . . . . .108 B2
Tornville Cres DN14 . . . . .79 B8
Torridge Rd HU8 . . . . . . .142 C6
Torridon Pl YO24 . . . . . . .132 B7
Torrington Rd DN4 . . . . .150 C4
Torrington St
  Grimsby DN32 . . . . . . .152 F1
  5 Kingston upon Hull
    HU5 . . . . .140 C3
Tostig Ave YO26 . . . . . . .129 C5
Tostig Cl 14 YO41 . . . . . .15 D2
Totnes Rd DN33 . . . . . . .113 E7
Tottenham Cl 3 HU8 . . .141 F5
Tottering La YO42 . . . . . . .51 B5
Tottermire La DN9 . . . . . .105 C2
Towan Cl 11 HU7 . . . . . . .56 F5
Tower Hill
  Kingston upon Hull
    HU13 . . . . .143 E1
  Westwoodside DN9 . . . .105 B2
Tower Hill Dr HU13 . . . . .143 E1
Tower Hill Mews 2
  HU13 . . . . .143 E1
Tower House La HU12 . . .147 F7
Tower Rd
  Rimswell HU12 . . . . .74 C6
  Roos HU11 . . . . .60 A4
Tower St
  Flamborough YO15 . . . . . .5 A2
  32 Gainsborough DN21 . .117 B1
  Kingston upon Hull HU9 . .155 C2
  York YO1 . . . . .156 B1
Tower View
  Carlton DN14 . . . . .63 C2
  Kingston upon Hull
    HU10 . . . . .143 C5
Town End Ave DN14 . . . . .63 C3
Town End Gdns 3 YO32 .13 D5
Town End La YO42 . . . . . .18 C2
Town End Rd HU12 . . . . . .72 A5
Town Farm Ct YO25 . . . . .23 A2
Town Hall Sq DN31 . . . . .152 E3
Town Hall St 1 DN31 . . .152 E3
Town Hill DN20 . . . . .97 E4
Town Hill Dr DN20 . . . . . .97 E4
Town Rd DN36 . . . . .114 D4
Town St Hayton YO42 . . . .40 C8
  Immingham DN40 . . . . . .86 E4
  Nunburnholme YO42 . . . .29 A1
  Shiptonthorpe YO43 . . . .40 F6
Townend Cswy HU15 . . . .66 D2
Townend La HU15 . . . . . . .53 C3
Townend Rd
  Ellerton YO42 . . . . .38 D7
  13 Newbald YO43 . . . . . .53 F7
  Walkington HU17 . . . . . .55 B8
Townend St HU17 . . . . . .156 B4
Townsend CI DN36 . . . . .103 E1
Townside HU12 . . . . .86 D6
Townside Cl 1 YO43 . . . .53 F7
Townside Rd YO43 . . . . . .53 F7
Towthorpe La YO43 . . . . .135 B7
Towthorpe Medieval
  Village ★ YO43 . . . . . . .135 B8
Towthorpe Moor La
  YO32 . . . . .14 C5
Towthorpe Rd YO32 . . . . .13 D2
Towton Ave
  9 York YO24 . . . . .129 F2
  1 York YO24 . . . . .130 A2
Toynton Rd 27 DN33 . . . .102 D2
Trafalgar Ave 10 DN34 . .102 B3
Trafalgar Pk DN36 . . . . .114 A8
Trafalgar St
  5 Kingston upon Hull
    HU3 . . . . .145 D7
  Kingston upon Hull HU2 . .155 A4
  York YO23 . . . . .130 B1
Trafford Rd
  Kingston upon Hull
    HU10 . . . . .143 E8
  4 Norton DN6 . . . . .76 E2
Trafford St DN15 . . . . . . .151 B8
Traffords Way DN20 . . . .108 F6
Train Ave HU6 . . . . .140 C7
Train Gate DN21 . . . . . . .108 B1
Tranby Ave
  Kingston upon Hull
    HU13 . . . . .143 C3
  York YO10 . . . . .131 D4
Tranby Dr DN32 . . . . . . .103 A2
Tranby La Hessle HU10 . .143 B5
  Swanland HU14 . . . . . . .69 B6

Tranby Mdws Pk
  HU13 . . . . .143 C3
Tranby Ride HU10 . . . . . .143 C5
Trandy La DN14 . . . . .65 C5
Tranmere Cl HU3 . . . . . .145 B5
Tranmere Pk HU18 . . . . .134 C3
Tranmore La DN14 . . . . . .62 B3
Travis Ave 18 DN8 . . . . . .93 B8
Travis St DN8 . . . . .93 B8
Travis Cty Prim Sch
  DN8 . . . . .92 F4
Travis Gr 17 DN8 . . . . . . .93 B8
Travis Rd HU16 . . . . .138 F5
Travis St YO15 . . . . .122 E3
Traviss Cl DN16 . . . . . . .151 B4
Trawden Cl HU7 . . . . .56 F6
Tree Cl 9 DN9 . . . . .105 D6
Treece Gdns 5 DN18 . . . .69 E1
Trees The HU6 . . . . .140 C4
Treeton Rd DN14 . . . . . . .65 A6
Tremayne Ave 2 HU15 . . .68 C5
Trenchard Cl 3 DN40 . . . .87 D2
Trenchard Rd YO26 . . . . .129 B6
Trent Ave 4 YO32 . . . . . .127 F6
Trent Pk HU7 . . . . .56 F6
Trent Rd DN17 . . . . .95 D6
Trent Side
  4 Amcotts DN17 . . . . . . .81 F1
  Keadby with Althorpe
    DN17 . . . . .95 D6
Trent St DN16 . . . . .151 B6
Trent View DN17 . . . . . . .95 D5
Trent Way YO24 . . . . . . .132 D7
Trentham Cl YO16 . . . . . .122 D6
Trentham Dr YO16 . . . . . .122 D6
Trentham Mews 1
  YO16 . . . . .122 D6
Trentholme Dr
  Messingham DN17 . . . . .107 D7
  2 York YO24 . . . . .130 A2
Trenton Ave HU4 . . . . . .144 B6
Trentside
  Keadby with Althorpe
    DN17 . . . . .95 D3
  Morton DN21 . . . . .117 A2
Trentvale Prep Sch
  DN17 . . . . .95 D6
Trevor Cl 15 DN37 . . . . .101 F1
Trevor Gr 13 YO24 . . . . .129 F2
Trevor St HU2 . . . . .155 B4
Triangle Dr HU14 . . . . . . .69 A4
Triangle The 11 HU14 . . .69 A4
Trinity Ave YO15 . . . . . . .122 F3
Trinity Cl
  Burstwick HU12 . . . . . . .73 A6
  Goxhill DN19 . . . . .86 A8
  Leven HU17 . . . . .45 B8
Trinity Ct 5 DN20 . . . . . .97 D4
Trinity Garth HU16 . . . . .138 A8
Trinity Gr
  Beverley HU17 . . . . . . .154 B3
  1 Bridlington YO15 . . . .122 F3
  3 Kingston upon Hull
    HU9 . . . . .141 F1
  Kingston upon Hull
    HU13 . . . . .143 E2
Trinity House La HU1 . . .155 B2
Trinity La
  Beverley HU17 . . . . . . .154 B2
  York YO1 . . . . .156 A2
Trinity Mews 2 YO15 . . .122 F3
Trinity Rd
  Bridlington YO15 . . . . . .122 F3
  Cleethorpes DN35 . . . . .153 E1
  Hornsea HU18 . . . . . . .134 C2
  10 Scunthorpe DN16 . . . .96 D2
Trinity St
  Grimsby DN31 . . . . . . .152 A5
  Kingston upon Hull HU3 . .145 C7
Trinity Wlk 2 DN18 . . . . .69 E1
Trippett St HU2 . . . . .155 C3
Triton Rd HU9 . . . . .142 D3
Troon Cl 2 YO26 . . . . . . .129 B5
Troon Ct HU8 . . . . .142 B6
Troon Rd DN7 . . . . .92 D4
Troutbeck 7 YO24 . . . . .132 C7
Troutsdale Ave YO30 . . .126 E2
Troutsdale Cl YO16 . . . . .122 F7
Troutsdale Gr HU9 . . . . .146 F8
Trumfleet La DN6 . . . . . . .77 D1
Trundle Gate YO43 . . . . . .53 F6
Trundle La DN7 . . . . .92 C8
Trundle St HU1 . . . . .155 A2
Trundles La 7 WF11 . . . . .61 A2
Trunkass La DN37 . . . . . .112 D6
Truro Cl HU7 . . . . .141 C6
Tudor Cl
  Bridlington YO15 . . . . . .122 C1
  10 Thorpe Willoughby YO8 . .48 B1
Tudor Ct HU11 . . . . .138 C1
Tudor Dr HU6 . . . . .140 B8
Tudor Rd YO24 . . . . .129 C2
Tudor Way YO32 . . . . . . .14 C8
Tudworth Field Rd DN7 . .93 B5
Tudworth Rd DN7 . . . . . .93 A5
Tuke Ave YO10 . . . . .131 B4
Tulip Rd DN15 . . . . .151 C7
Tummel Ct 4 DN40 . . . . .101 B8
Tune St YO8 . . . . .49 B4
Tunis St HU5 . . . . .140 E2
Tunnard St DN32 . . . . . .153 A4
Tunnel Rd DN20 . . . . .98 D4
Turbary Rd
  Epworth DN9 . . . . .105 B6
  Haxey DN9 . . . . .105 C3

Turf Moor Rd DN7 . . . . . .93 A3
Turkey La YO16 . . . . .10 E4
Turks Head Gdns 10
  HU15 . . . . .52 F1
Turmar View HU11 . . . . .58 A4
Turmarr Rd HU12 . . . . . .89 C8
Turner Ave YO15 . . . . .122 F3
Turnberry App DN37 . . .113 D6
Turnberry Dr YO26 . . . . .129 B4
Turnbull Dr 18 YO42 . . . .29 A3
Turner Ave HU19 . . . . . .75 A5
Turner Cl YO43 . . . . . . .135 D3
Turner Ct HU3 . . . . .155 A2
Turner Rd HU17 . . . . . . .154 B4
Turner Cl 5 DN21 . . . . .108 B1
Turner's Croft YO10 . . . .131 A1
Turner's La 15 HU14 . . . .69 A5
Turners Sq 9 YO8 . . . . .148 C5
Turnham La YO8 . . . . . . .49 C2
Turnhead Cres YO8 . . . . .49 B5
Turnhead Ct YO8 . . . . . .49 B6
Turnmire Rd 1 YO24 . . .132 E8
Turpin Cl DN21 . . . . . . .117 C1
Turpit La HU12 . . . . .72 A5
Turrets The 15 HU12 . . . .72 E5
Turver's La Beal WF11 . . .61 C2
  Kellingley WF11 . . . . . . .61 C2
Tuxford Dr HU9 . . . . . . .142 E2
Tweed Gr HU8 . . . . .142 B5
Tween Dykes Rd HU7 . . .141 D6
Twickenham Cl 2 HU8 . .142 A5
Twin Pike Way 14 YO32 . .13 D5
Twyford Cl 5 HU9 . . . . .142 E2
Twyning Pl DN35 . . . . . .153 D3
Tydeman Cl 1 DN16 . . . .96 D1
Tyler Ave DN34 . . . . . . .152 A3
Tyn Garth YO19 . . . . . . .36 D8
Tyne St HU3 . . . . .145 B4
Tynedale 1 HU7 . . . . . .141 A6
Tynedale Ct 1 DN3 . . . . .92 A2
Tysons Cl 7 DN18 . . . . .69 F1
Tythe Garth 8 HU15 . . . .53 D3

U

Ulceby Rd
  Scunthorpe DN17 . . . . . .96 B2
  South Killingholme DN39 . .86 C2
  Wootton DN39 . . . . .85 F3
Ulceby Sta DN39 . . . . . .86 C2
Ullswater YO24 . . . . . . .132 D7
Ullswater Cl HU8 . . . . . .141 D4
Ullswater Gr DN14 . . . . .149 E5
Ulrome Ct 1 HU9 . . . . . .142 B1
Ulster Ave 5 DN33 . . . . .102 C1
Ulster Rd DN21 . . . . . . .117 B1
Ulverston Rd HU4 . . . . . .144 A3
Ulyett La DN17 . . . . . . .106 C8
Undercroft 7 YO19 . . . . .26 F7
Underwit Rd YO8 . . . . . . .63 C4
Unicorn Row 10 DN21 . . .108 B1
Union La YO8 . . . . .148 C4
Union Rd DN8 . . . . .93 A8
Union St
  Great Driffield YO25 . . . .124 E4
  Kingston upon Hull HU2 . .155 B3
  Pocklington YO42 . . . . . .29 A4
Union Terr YO31 . . . . . . .156 B4
Unity Ave HU13 . . . . . . .143 F1
Unity Rd DN32 . . . . .153 C2
University of Hull
  Cottingham HU16 . . . . . .138 F8
  Kingston upon Hull
    HU16 . . . . .139 C5
  Kingston upon Hull HU6 . .140 B4
University of Humberside
  Kingston upon Hull HU6 . .140 A4
  Kingston upon Hull HU6 . .140 C4
  Kingston upon Hull 155 C2
University of Lincolnshire &
  Humberside HU1 . . . . . .155 A2
University of York
  Heslington YO10 . . . . . .130 F1
  York YO10 . . . . .130 E3
  York YO10 . . . . .131 B2
  York YO30 . . . . .156 A3
University Rd YO10 . . . . .130 F2
Upavon Garth HU7 . . . . .141 C7
Upper Burgess St
  DN31 . . . . .152 D4
Upper Hanover St 6
  YO26 . . . . .129 F5
Upper Kenyon St 5 DN8 .93 A8
Upper Newborough St 1
  YO30 . . . . .130 C2
Upper Poppleton Jun Sch
  YO26 . . . . .12 F1
Upper Price St YO23 . . . .156 A1
Upper St Paul's Terr
  YO24 . . . . .130 A4
Upper Union St HU1 . . . .155 A2
Uppercommon La
  DN14 . . . . .61 F3
Uppercroft 4 YO32 . . . . .127 C8
Upperthorpe Hill DN9 . . .105 A2
Upton St HU8 . . . . .141 B1
Uredale Pl DN16 . . . . . . .151 E1
Usher La YO32 . . . . .13 F6
Utgard Way 4 DN33 . . . .102 E1
Utterby Cty Prim Sch
  DN36 . . . . .121 B5
Utterby Dr DN34 . . . . . .152 C1

V

Valda Vale 34 DN40 . . . . .87 B1
Vale Cres YO42 . . . . .16 F2
Vale of Ancholme Sch
  DN20 . . . . .98 B2
Vale The
  Beverley HU17 . . . . . . .137 B2
  Kingston upon Hull
    HU10 . . . . .143 B7
  Skelton YO30 . . . . .126 B5
Valentine Cl
  1 Kingston upon Hull
    HU4 . . . . .144 A2
  6 Pocklington YO42 . . . .29 A3
Valiant Dr HU9 . . . . .142 D4
Valletta St HU9 . . . . . . .147 D7
Valley Dr HU10 . . . . . . .143 B7
Valley View YO19 . . . . . .37 F7
Valley View Dr DN16 . . . .96 D1
Vanbrugh Dr YO10 . . . . .131 C3
Vancouver Cres 5 DN17 . .96 C2
Vane St HU3 . . . . .145 D7
Vanessa Dr DN21 . . . . . .117 B2
Varah Cl DN18 . . . . .84 E8
Varlow Rd LN7 . . . . .111 B4
Varsity Cl 6 DN7 . . . . . .104 A8
Vaughan Ave DN36 . . . . .103 A2
Vaughan Rd
  10 Campsall DN6 . . . . . .76 E1
  1 Kingston upon Hull HU13 69 F4
Vavasour Ct YO23 . . . . . .132 B2
Veal St DN31 . . . . .152 C3
Ventnor St HU5 . . . . . . .140 C3
Vere Terr DN31 . . . . . . .152 C4
Vermont St HU5 . . . . . . .140 D3
Vermuyden Rd DN8 . . . . .79 C2
Vermuyden Sch DN14 . . .149 B5
Vermuyden Terr
  DN14 . . . . .149 D2
Vernon Cl YO23 . . . . . . .133 A3
Vernon Rd
  Bridlington YO15 . . . . . .122 F3
  York YO30 . . . . .126 E2
Vernon St HU1 . . . . .155 B3
Vesper Dr YO24 . . . . . . .129 B3
Vesper Wlk YO32 . . . . . .127 F6
Vicar La Beverley HU17 . .154 A3
  Eastrington DN14 . . . . . .51 F1
  Hollym HU19 . . . . .75 A4
  Kingston upon Hull 155 B1
Vicarage Ave DN20 . . . . .98 D3
Vicarage Cl
  Beswick YO25 . . . . .32 D4
  2 Bubwith YO8 . . . . . . .50 D7
  12 Hunmanby YO14 . . . . .2 F8
Vicarage Cres DN15 . . . . .82 B5
Vicarage Gdns
  2 Brough HU15 . . . . . . .68 C6
  Scunthorpe DN15 . . . . . .150 F6
  Wrawby DN20 . . . . .98 E4
  1 York YO10 . . . . .131 C4
Vicarage La
  Beckingham DN10 . . . . .116 D1
  Bishop Wilton YO42 . . . . .16 F7
  8 Buckton/Bempton YO15 . .4 D3
  Cadney DN20 . . . . .109 D6
  Elsham DN20 . . . . .98 F7
  Grasby DN38 . . . . .110 E7
  Immingham DN40 . . . . . .86 E4
  3 Kingston upon Hull
    HU13 . . . . .143 E1
  Naburn YO19 . . . . .36 E8
  Redbourne DN21 . . . . . .108 F2
  Scawby DN20 . . . . .108 E8
  Skirlaugh HU11 . . . . . . .45 D2
  Wootton DN39 . . . . .85 E3
Vicarage Pk DN15 . . . . . .83 D1
Vicarage Rd
  Willoughton DN21 . . . . .119 B4
  Wrawby DN20 . . . . .98 D3
Vicars Cl YO23 . . . . .132 B2
Vicar's La HU12 . . . . . . .91 A6
Vicar's Wlk 1 DN17 . . . . .94 D7
Viceroy Cl HU2 . . . . . . .155 B4
Vickerman's La HU12 . . . .59 A3
Victor St Grimsby DN32 . .153 A4
  2 Kingston upon Hull
    HU9 . . . . .146 C8
  York YO1 . . . . .156 B1
Victoria Ave
  Hatfield DN7 . . . . .92 D4
  Hornsea HU18 . . . . .134 D5
  Kingston upon Hull
    HU10 . . . . .138 C2
  Kingston upon Hull HU5 . .140 A1
  12 Withernsea HU19 . . . .75 A6
Victoria Cl
  Marshchapel DN36 . . . . .115 C2
  Stainforth DN7 . . . . .92 C5
Victoria Ct
  Burton upon Stather
    DN15 . . . . .82 B5
  15 York YO26 . . . . .129 F5
Victoria Dock Prim Sch
  HU9 . . . . .146 B6
Victoria Dr
  3 Barton-upon-Humber
    DN18 . . . . .69 E1
  3 Gilberdyke HU15 . . . . .66 D8
Victoria Farm Ct YO23 . . .24 C1
Victoria Gdns
  Hornsea HU18 . . . . .134 C6
  1 Kingston upon Hull
    HU5 . . . . .140 A1

Victoria Pier* HU1 . . . .155 C1
Victoria Rd
  Barnetby le Wold DN38 . . .99 B4
  Beverley HU17 . . . . . . .154 A1
  Bridlington YO15 . . . . . .122 E3
  Great Driffield YO25 . . . .124 D5
  5 Keelby DN41 . . . . . . .101 A5
  2 Pocklington YO42 . . . .29 A4
  Scunthorpe DN16 . . . . . .151 A1
  Woodmansey HU17 . . . . .55 E8
Victoria St Goole DN14 . .149 D4
  Kingston upon Hull
    HU13 . . . . .144 A1
  1 York YO23 . . . . .156 B1
Victoria St N DN31 . . . . .152 E4
Victoria St S 3 DN31 . . .152 E3
Victoria St W
  7 Grimsby DN31 . . . . . .152 D3
  2 Grimsby DN31 . . . . . .152 E3
Victoria Way
  Grimsby DN31 . . . . .152 A6
  2 York YO32 . . . . .130 E8
Victoria's Way HU16 . . . .139 B6
Victory Way
  1 Barton-upon-Humber
    DN18 . . . . .69 F1
  9 Grimsby DN37 . . . . . .102 B2
Viking Cl
  2 Immingham DN40 . . . .87 B1
  Kingston upon Hull
    HU10 . . . . .138 C2
  20 Stamford Bridge YO41 . .15 D2
Viking Dr 5 YO19 . . . . . .48 F8
Viking Rd
  Bridlington YO16 . . . . . .123 B6
  Stamford Bridge YO41 . . .15 D2
  York YO26 . . . . .129 C5
Villa Cl HU9 . . . . .49 F1
Villa Fields 4 DN14 . . . . .63 C1
Villa Gr 2 YO31 . . . . . . .130 E6
Village Farm Cl 11 HU15 . .52 F1
Village Farm Ct 2 DN14 . .61 D4
Village Farm Rd 5 HU12 . 58 C1
Village Garth 1 YO32 . . .13 E5
Village Rd
  Kingston upon Hull HU8 . .141 D1
  Sunk Island HU12 . . . . . .88 C5
Village St YO30 . . . . . . .126 E3
Village The Haxby YO32 . .13 E5
  Skelton YO30 . . . . .126 B5
  Stockton on the Forest
    YO32 . . . . .14 D3
  Strensall YO32 . . . . .14 B7
Ville Rd DN16 . . . . .151 D2
Villiers Ct 7 HU12 . . . . .72 D7
Vincent Cl 3 HU4 . . . . . .144 A2
Vincent Way YO24 . . . . .132 C8
Vine Cl HU16 . . . . .139 A7
Vine St YO23 . . . . .130 C2
Vinegarth 2 DN9 . . . . . .105 E6
Vinehall Rd DN9 . . . . . . .105 C2
Vinery The 13 DN14 . . . . .65 A7
Vineyards The 3 HU17 . . .45 A8
Violet Cl 16 DN35 . . . . . .103 C1
Viscount Way 12 DN36 . .114 D8
Vivars Way YO8 . . . . . . .148 D5
Vivian Ave DN32 . . . . . .153 B1
Voases Cl HU10 . . . . . . .143 E6
Voases La HU10 . . . . . . .143 E6
Volage Ct 18 YO42 . . . . .29 A4
Volta St HU9 . . . . .148 E4
Vulcan St HU6 . . . . .140 F4
Vulcan Way DN7 . . . . . . .93 A1
Vyner St YO31 . . . . .130 C7

W

Waby Cl DN37 . . . . .102 B4
Waddingham Pl
  3 Habrough DN40 . . . . .100 E8
  19 New Waltham DN36 . .114 A7
Waddingham Rd LN7 . . . .109 F1
Waddington Ct HU5 . . . .140 B3
Waddington Dr 24 DN17 . .96 C2
Waddington Pl DN34 . . . .152 A1
Wade Ave HU18 . . . . . . .134 C6
Wade House La YO8 . . . . .63 F4
Wadebridge Gr 4 HU9 . .142 E1
Wadham Gr 4 HU9 . . . . .141 F1
Wadhurst Cl HU7 . . . . . .141 A6
Wadsworth Ave HU6 . . . .140 E4
Wadsworth Rd YO25 . . . .124 B3
Waggoners Dr 3 YO23 . .132 B3
Waincroft 8 YO32 . . . . . .14 A6
Wainers Cl 5 YO23 . . . . .132 B3
Wainfleet Ave HU16 . . . .139 A6
Wainfleet Rd 33 DN33 . .102 D2
Wain's Gr YO24 . . . . . . .132 D7
Wain's Rd YO24 . . . . . . .132 D8
Waite Cl 17 YO42 . . . . . .29 A3
Waithe La DN37 . . . . . . .113 E4
Wake Ave HU16 . . . . . . .139 A5
Wakefield Ave
  Kingston upon Hull HU9 . .142 C2
  Scotter DN21 . . . . .107 D4
Wakefield La HU19 . . . . . .75 A2
Wakerley Rd 13 DN21 . . .107 C3
Walcot Rd DN15 . . . . . . .82 B8
Walcott St HU3 . . . . . . .145 C4
Waldby Garth Rd HU12 . . .73 C4
Waldegrave Ave HU8 . . . .142 A4
Walden Stubbs Rd DN6 . . .76 E2
Waldorf Rd DN35 . . . . . .103 C1
Walesby Cl 8 DN33 . . . . .113 D8
Walesby Rd
  2 Scunthorpe DN17 . . . . .96 C2
  Scunthorpe DN17 . . . . . .150 E1

Walgrave St HU5 . . . . . .140 C3
Walk La
  Humberston DN36 . . . . .114 C7
  Irby DN37 . . . . .112 D7
Walker Ave DN33 . . . . . .113 E8
Walker Cl DN15 . . . . .82 E7
Walker Dr
  Winterton DN15 . . . . . . .83 A5
  York YO24 . . . . .132 C8
Walker La YO19 . . . . .37 F7
Walker St HU3 . . . . .145 C5
Walkergate HU17 . . . . . .154 A3
Walkergate Inf Sch
  HU17 . . . . .154 A3
Walkeringham Cty Prim Sch
  DN10 . . . . .116 C3
Walkeringham Rd
  Beckingham DN10 . . . . .116 D2
  Gringley on the Hill
    DN10 . . . . .116 A2
Walkerith Rd 11 DN21 . .117 A2
Walker's Cl 2 DN38 . . . . .99 B4
Walkers Ct DN17 . . . . . .107 D7
Walkers Way DN39 . . . . .86 B2
Walkington Dr YO43 . . . .135 C5
Walkington Heads
  HU17 . . . . .54 D8
Walkington La YO30 . . . . .12 B8
Walkington Prim Sch
  HU17 . . . . .55 C7
Walkington Rd
  Beverley HU17 . . . . . . .136 C2
  Rowley HU20 . . . . .55 A5
Wall St DN34 . . . . .152 A3
Waller St
  3 Hornsea HU18 . . . . .134 C3
  Kingston upon Hull HU9 . .146 C8
Walliker St HU3 . . . . . . .145 A6
Wallingfen La HU15 . . . . .53 A1
Walmgate YO1 . . . . .156 C2
Walmsgate DN33 . . . . . .102 D2
Walmsgate Pl 24 DN33 . .102 D2
Walmsley Cl 1 YO15 . . . . .4 C3
Walmsley St HU3 . . . . . .145 D7
Walney Rd YO31 . . . . . . .131 A5
Walnut Cl
  Kingston upon Hull
    HU16 . . . . .139 D5
  York YO10 . . . . .131 A1
Walnut Cres
  9 Cleethorpes DN35 . . .103 B1
  11 Snaith & Cowick DN14 . .78 C8
Walnut Dr DN20 . . . . . . .108 F7
Walnut Gr YO25 . . . . . . .125 F8
Walnut Rd 1 DN8 . . . . . .79 A1
Walnut Way DN17 . . . . . .107 C7
Walpole St YO31 . . . . . .130 D7
Walsall Garth HU4 . . . . .144 A4
Walsham Grange 24
  DN35 . . . . .103 C2
Waltham La DN14 . . . . . .154 A3
Waltham Rd
  Barnoldby le Beck DN37 . .113 C6
  Brigsley DN37 . . . . .113 D5
  Grimsby DN33 . . . . .113 E8
  Kingston upon Hull HU1 . .155 B2
Waltham Toll Bar Sch
  DN36 . . . . .113 F7
Waltham Windmill*
  DN37 . . . . .113 D6
Walton Ct HU17 . . . . . . .154 B4
Walton Gr 3 DN33 . . . . .102 E2
Walton La YO43 . . . . .53 E6
Walton Pl YO26 . . . . . . .129 B3
Walton St HU3 . . . . .145 A7
Walton Street L Ctr
  HU3 . . . . .145 A6
Walworth Cl HU17 . . . . .154 B4
Walworth St N 4 YO26 . .129 F5
Walworth St S 9 YO26 . .129 F5
Wand La DN14 . . . . .62 C3
Wandell's View HU15 . . . .68 C8
Wandhill 31 YO32 . . . . . .13 E5
Wandle The YO26 . . . . . .129 A2
Wanlass Dr HU16 . . . . . .139 C7
Wansbeck 3 YO24 . . . . .132 B7
Wansbeck Prim Sch
  HU8 . . . . .142 D7
Wansbeck Rd HU8 . . . . .142 C7
Wansford Gr HU9 . . . . . .142 A1
Wansford Rd
  Driffield YO25 . . . . .125 B3
  Nafferton YO25 . . . . . . .125 F5
Ward Ave HU11 . . . . . . .142 F7
Ward Ct YO23 . . . . .156 B1
Ward Lea YO25 . . . . . . .124 E4
Ward St DN35 . . . . .153 C4
Wardall St DN35 . . . . . . .153 F1
Wareham Cl HU7 . . . . . .141 B6
Warley Ave DN16 . . . . . .151 C4
Warley Dr DN16 . . . . . . .151 C4
Warley Rd DN16 . . . . . . .151 C3
Warmer La HU12 . . . . . . .90 E7
Warn Ave 18 HU12 . . . . .72 C7
Warping Way DN15 . . . . .150 B7
Warren Farm Cotts
  YO42 . . . . .28 C1
Warren Rd DN15 . . . . . . .96 D7
Warrendale DN18 . . . . . .84 E8
Warrenne Rd 31 DN7 . . . .92 D4
Warrenne Rd DN7 . . . . . .92 D4
Warter C of E Sch
  YO42 . . . . .30 A5

Warter Rd Etton HU17 . . .42 F6
  Middleton YO25 . . . . . . .31 A4
Warthill C of E Prim Sch
  YO19 . . . . .14 F2
Warton Rd HU17 . . . . . .137 B4
Warwick Ave 5 DN33 . . .102 D2
Warwick Cl DN7 . . . . . . .92 F4
Warwick Dr
  Barton-upon-Humber
    DN18 . . . . .84 E8
  Molescroft HU17 . . . . . .136 E6
Warwick Rd
  Cleethorpes DN35 . . . . .153 D1
  Scunthorpe DN16 . . . . . .151 C5
Warwick St
  Kingston upon Hull HU9 . .146 B7
  York YO31 . . . . .130 D7
Warwickshire Cl 6
  HU5 . . . . .139 D1
Wascana Cl HU4 . . . . . . .144 B3
Wasdale Ave HU9 . . . . . .142 D4
Wasdale Cl 2 YO30 . . . . .126 E1
Wasdale Gn 4 HU16 . . . .139 B7
Washdyke La
  Elsham DN20 . . . . .98 E6
  Immingham DN40 . . . . . .87 B2
Washinghall La DN17 . . . .81 A2
Washington St
  Great Driffield YO25 . . . .124 E4
  Kingston upon Hull HU5 . .140 D3
Wassand Balk HU11 . . . . .46 A8
Wassand Rd HU11 . . . . . .35 B1
Wassand St HU3 . . . . . . .145 C4
Water Bank DN9 . . . . . . .104 E5
Water End YO26 . . . . . . .129 E5
Water Garth DN14 . . . . . .61 F4
Water Hill La YO8 . . . . . .148 D6
Water La
  Bewholme YO25 . . . . . . .35 A5
  Camblesforth YO8 . . . . . .63 D5
  8 Clifton YO30 . . . . . . .127 A1
  Dunnington YO19 . . . . . .26 F7
  Eggborough DN14 . . . . . .62 A2
  20 Flamborough YO15 . . . .5 A2
  Goole DN14 . . . . .65 C4
  Harpham YO25 . . . . .21 E7
  Hemingbrough YO8 . . . . .49 F1
  Kirby Grindalythe YO17 . . .6 B6
  Kirby Underdale YO41 . . . .17 A5
  Kirk Bramwith DN7 . . . . .92 C7
  Kirk Smeaton WF8 . . . . . .76 C3
  South Cave HU15 . . . . . .53 F1
  West Halton DN15 . . . . . .82 E8
  York YO30 . . . . .130 A7
Water Side DN15 . . . . . . .68 A2
Water Way Garth DN14 . . .77 F6
Waterdale HU7 . . . . .140 E8
Waterdale Pk YO31 . . . . .127 E1
Waterhouse La HU1 . . . . .155 A1
Wateringdike La YO43 . . .135 F7
Waterings 19 YO32 . . . . .13 D5
Waterland Ct 15 HU12 . . .72 D7
Waterloo St HU2 . . . . . . .155 A4
Waterlow Dr 7 DN35 . . . .83 A5
Waterman Ct 3 YO24 . . .129 B1
Waters Edge DN20 . . . . . .98 B2
Watersedge YO25 . . . . . .124 F3
Waterside Goole DN14 . . .65 C4
  3 Thorne DN8 . . . . .78 F1
  Thorne DN8 . . . . .92 F8
Waterside Dr DN31 . . . . .152 C4
Waterside Rd
  Barton-upon-Humber
    DN18 . . . . .69 E2
  Beverley HU17 . . . . . . .137 B3
  2 Thorne DN8 . . . . .78 F1
Waterton La DN7 . . . . . . .92 F2
Waterways Mus & Adventure
  Ctr The* DN14 . . . . . . .149 B2
Waterworks La HU11 . . . .142 E6
Waterworks St DN40 . . . .87 C2
Watford Ave DN34 . . . . .102 C2
Wath Gr HU8 . . . . .141 C1
Wath La YO41 . . . . .27 C8
Watkin St N DN31 . . . . .152 C5
Watkin St S DN31 . . . . .152 D5
Watkinson Cl 8 HU12 . . . .58 D1
Watson Cl HU9 . . . . .142 C2
Watson Cl 3 YO14 . . . . . . .3 A8
Watson Dr 30 HU12 . . . . .72 D7
Watson St
  Kingston upon Hull HU7 . .141 D6
  York YO24 . . . . .130 A3
Watson Terr 2 YO24 . . . .130 A3
Watsons Ave YO16 . . . . .122 D5
Watsons Croft DN7 . . . . .92 D6
Watson's La YO14 . . . . . . .3 D6
Watt St HU9 . . . . .141 E1
Wattlers Cl YO23 . . . . . .132 C3
Watton Abbey* YO25 . . . .32 E4
Watton Gr HU6 . . . . .140 A5
Watton Nature Reserve*
  YO25 . . . . .33 C2
Watts Rd HU17 . . . . .154 B4
Waudby Cl 2 HU17 . . . . .55 C8
Wauldby Cl 4 HU10 . . . .143 E7
Wauldby View 2 HU14 . . .69 B7
Wavell St YO8 . . . . .148 A6
Waveney Cl DN15 . . . . . .82 B5
Waveney Gr YO30 . . . . . .130 B8
Waveney Rd HU8 . . . . . .142 B6
Waverley Cl DN14 . . . . . .63 C2
Waverley St
  Kingston upon Hull HU1 . .155 A1
  York YO31 . . . . .156 C3
Wawne CP Sch HU7 . . . . .56 F6
Wawne Lodge HU7 . . . . .56 F6
Wawne Rd HU7 . . . . . . .141 C8

Waxholme Rd HU19 .....74 E8
Wayfbain La [20] HU12 ....72 C7
Waynefleet Gr [3] YO10 .131 A3
Wayside Cl
  Holton le Clay DN36 ....114 A5
  [15] Scunthorpe DN16 ......96 D2
Wayside Cres YO16 .....122 B4
Wayside Dr DN36 ......114 A8
Wayside Rd YO16 ......122 B4
Weald Pk HU7 ....56 F5
Weardale HU7 ....140 F8
Weatherill St DN14 ....149 C4
Weaver Gr HU8 ....142 C7
Weavers Cl YO23 ......132 B3
Weavers Croft [8] DN9 .105 A2
Webb Cl DN18 ....84 E8
Webster Ave DN15 ....150 E7
Weddall Cl YO24 ......129 F1
Weekes Rd [18] DN35 ..103 C2
Weel Rd HU17 ....137 D8
Weeland Ct [16] WF11 ..61 A2
Weeland Rd Beal DN14 .61 E3
  Hensall DN14 ....62 E2
Weelsby Ave DN32 ....152 E1
Weelsby Gr DN32 .....102 F2
Weelsby Prim Sch
  DN32 ....153 A4
Weelsby Rd DN32 .....152 E1
Weelsby St DN32 .....153 A4
Weelsby St S DN32 ...153 A3
Weelsby View DN36 ...114 A8
Weelsby Way HU13 ...143 C2
Weeping Elm Way
  DN16 ....96 E2
Weeton Cl HU11 ....58 A4
Weeton Dr YO25 ......19 B5
Weeton North La HU12 .90 B8
Weeton Rd HU12 ......90 C7
Weeton Way [5] HU10 .143 E7
Weghill Rd HU12 ......58 D1
Weighton Ct [9] DN14 .65 A7
Weighton Gr HU6 .....139 F5
Weighton Hill YO43 ...135 F4
Weir Cl DN9 ....105 A2
Weir Rd DN9 ....105 A2
Weir The HU13 ....143 E1
Welbeck Pl [9] DN34 ..102 C2
Welbeck Rd DN35 ....153 C1
Welbeck St HU5 ......145 B8
Welborn Cl YO10 .....131 A4
Welbourn Wlk HU4 ...144 B6
Welburn Ct [8] YO25 ..22 D1
Welburn Gr HU5 ......139 E2
Welbury Gr HU4 ......142 C2
Weldon Rd DN21 .....119 B1
Welgarth YO25 ....31 B7
Welham Cl [10] DN14 ..65 B7
Welholme Ave DN32 ..152 D1
Welholme Fst Sch
  DN32 ....152 F2
Welholme Mid Sch
  DN32 ....152 F2
Welholme Mus & Gall★
  DN32 ....152 E2
Welholme Rd DN32 ...152 E2
Well La Beverley HU17 .154 B2
  Bridlington YO16 ......122 B4
  Kingston upon Hull
  HU10 ....138 E8
Well St
  Messingham DN17 .....107 A4
  Tibthorpe YO25 ....19 D2
Well Vale [3] DN33 ....113 D8
Welland Ave DN34 ....102 C2
Welland Dr DN15 ......82 B5
Welland Rd HU8 ......142 F4
Welland Rise YO26 ...129 D5
Wellbeck Cl [19] DN20 ..98 C4
Wellbeck Rd DN34 ....102 C2
Wellesley Ave HU6 ...140 D4
Wellesley Cl YO30 ...127 A2
Wellgarth DN32 ......153 B1
Wellington Ave HU18 .134 C2
Wellington Cl [5] YO42 .28 F4
Wellington La HU3 ...145 D8
Wellington Rd
  Beverley HU17 ....154 B4
  Bridlington YO15 .....122 E2
  Pocklington Ind Est YO42 .28 E3
Wellington Row YO1 ..156 A2
Wellington St
  Grimsby DN32 ....152 F4
  Kingston upon Hull HU1 .155 B1
  York YO10 ....130 E4
Wellington St W HU1 .155 B1
Wellington Way DN20 .99 A8
Wellingtonia Dr [5] DN6 .76 E1
Wellowgate DN32 ....152 D3
Wells Cl YO8 ....148 A5
Wells Cres [3] DN35 ..103 C1
Wells Gr DN14 ......149 B6
Wells La [3] 61 E3
Wells Rd DN37 ......101 D4
Wells St Grimsby DN34 .152 B3
  Kingston upon Hull HU3 .145 A5
  Scunthorpe DN15 .....151 B8
Wellsted St HU3 .....145 C5
Welshpool Cl [3] HU7 .56 F7
Welton Ave
  [2] Kingston upon Hull
  HU16 ....138 E6
  York YO10 ....129 D5
Welton Cl
  [17] Barton-upon-Humber
  DN18 ....84 E8
  [9] Beverley HU17 ....136 E1
Welton Gr HU6 ......139 F4
Welton Low Rd HU15 .68 C6

Welton Mill★ HU15 ....68 E6
Welton Old Rd HU15 ..68 E6
Welton Prim Sch HU15 .68 D5
Welton Rd HU15 .....68 C5
Welwick Rd HU12 ....74 D1
Welwyn Park Ave
  HU6 ....140 C7
Welwyn Park Dr HU6 .140 C7
Welwyn Park Rd HU6 .140 C7
Wembley Park Ave
  HU8 ....141 E5
Wembley Rd DN8 .....79 B2
Wenchirst La DN14 ...78 D2
Wendan Rd [7] DN8 ..93 A7
Wendover Cl
  Humberston DN36 ....114 D8
  Messingham DN17 ....107 D7
Wendover Rd DN17 ..107 D7
Wendover Rise
  [6] Cleethorpes DN35 .103 C2
  Cleethorpes DN35 ....153 C1
Wendron Cl HU7 .....141 C6
Wenham Rd YO24 ...132 C3
Wenlock Dr YO19 ....37 B6
Wenlock St HU3 .....145 C7
Wenlock Terr
  Kingston upon Hull HU9 .141 E1
  York YO10 ....130 D1
Wenning Ave YO26 ..29 A3
Wensley Ave HU6 ....139 E4
Wensleydale HU7 ....140 F8
Wensleydale Cl YO16 .122 F6
Wensleydale Dr YO10 .131 D4
Wensleydale Rd DN16 .151 E2
Wentdale [1] WF8 ....76 C3
Wentworth Cl
  [3] Beverley HU17 ....55 E8
  Camblesforth YO8 ....63 D4
  Kellington DN14 .....62 A2
  Kingston upon Hull
  HU10 ....143 F8
Wentworth Cres [1] DN19 .70 E2
Wentworth Dr
  Goole DN14 ....149 E5
  Messingham DN17 ....107 D7
Wentworth Gr [5] HU11 .47 C1
Wentworth Rd
  Bottesford DN17 ......96 B1
  Bridlington YO16 ....122 C4
  Grimsby DN34 ....152 B3
  York YO24 ....130 B2
Wentworth Way
  [5] Hunmanby YO14 ...2 F8
  Kingston upon Hull HU9 .146 C7
Werneth Rd DN32 ...152 F4
Wesley Cl
  [3] Epworth DN9 .....105 E6
  South Cave HU15 .....54 A2
  Winterton DN15 ......83 A5
Wesley Cres [15] DN35 .103 C2
Wesley Ct [7] HU3 ...145 C5
Wesley Pl YO1 ......156 C2
Wesley Rd [4] Brigg DN20 .98 C2
  Scunthorpe DN16 ....151 E3
Wesley St DN21 .....108 B1
West Acridge DN18 ..69 E1
West Ave
  Burton Fleming YO25 .2 E3
  Stainforth DN7 ....92 C6
West Back Side YO25 .10 C4
West Bank
  Stainforth DN7 ....92 B7
  York YO24 ....129 E3
West Butterwick C of E Sch
  DN17 ....106 D8
West Carr La HU7 ...140 F6
West Cl Fangfoss YO41 .28 C8
  Nafferton YO25 .....125 E6
  Newport HU15 ....52 E1
West Coates Rd DN31 .152 B6
West Comm Cres
  DN17 ....150 F4
West Comm Gdns
  DN17 ....150 F2
West Comm La DN17 .150 F3
West Comm N Rd
  DN17 ....107 A8
West Comm Rd DN17 .150 F3
West Crayke YO16 ...122 F6
West Cross St [16] DN21 .108 B1
West Ct [8] Riccall YO19 .48 F8
  [8] Thorne/Moorends DN8 .93 A7
West Dale Cres DN21 .108 B2
West Dock Ave HU3 .145 B4
West Dock St HU3 ...145 B3
West Dr YO25 ....125 F6
West Edge Rd WF8 ..76 A3
West Ella Rd
  Kingston upon Hull
  HU10 ....143 A7
  Swanland HU14 ......69 C7
West Ella Way HU10 .143 C7
West End Bainton YO25 .31 E7
  Dalton Holme HU17 ...42 E8
  Garthorpe & Fockerby
  DN17 ....81 E6
  Kilham YO25 ....9 B3
  Lund YO25 ....31 E2
  Pollington DN14 .....77 F6
  Rawcliffe DN14 ......64 A2
  Seaton Ross YO42 ....39 D4
  South Cave HU15 .....53 F1
  Strensall YO32 ....14 A7
  Swanland HU14 ......69 B6
  Ulceby DN39 ....86 A1
  Walkington HU17 ....55 B7
  Winteringham DN15 ..68 A1

West End Cl
  North Duffield YO8 ...50 A8
  [9] Strensall YO32 ...14 B7
West End Farm Cl [6]
  HU15 ....53 F1
West End Gdns DN14 .77 F6
West End La DN36 ...115 B1
West End Rd
  Epworth DN9 ....105 C7
  [2] Habrough DN40 ..100 E8
  [5] Habrough DN40 ..100 E8
  Kingston upon Hull
  HU16 ....138 F7
  Norton DN6 ....76 E2
  Ulceby DN39 ....85 F1
West Field La
  [1] Swanland HU14 ...69 B6
  Upper Poppleton YO26 .12 E1
West Garth Kilham YO25 .9 B3
  Rowley HU20 ....55 A4
West Gate YO25 .....124 E5
West Gn
  Kingston upon Hull HU10 .143 A7
  Messingham DN17 ....107 D7
  Pocklington YO42 ....28 F3
West Gr
  Barton-upon-Humber
  DN18 ....69 E1
  Kingston upon Hull HU4 .144 D4
West Green DN17 ....29 A3
West Hall Garth [10] HU15 .53 E7
West Halton La DN15 .82 C8
West Hann La DN19 ..70 C1
West Haven Way DN40 .87 B3
West Ings Cl [4] WF11 .61 A3
West Ings Cres [5] WF11 .61 A3
West Ings Ct [1] WF11 .61 A3
West Ings La [2] WF11 .61 A3
West Ings Mews [6]
  WF11 ....61 A3
West Ings Way [8] WF11 .61 A3
West La Burn YO8 ....62 C6
  Burton Fleming YO25 .2 E3
  Keelby DN41 ....101 A4
  Laxton DN14 ....65 D2
  Sykehouse DN14 .....77 F2
  Winterton DN15 ......83 B5
West Lambwath Rd
  HU11 ....46 D3
West Lea DN33 ......113 E8
West Leys Pk HU14 ..69 B6
West Leys Rd HU14 .69 B6
West Marsh La
  Barrow upon Humber
  DN19 ....70 B1
  Goxhill DN19 ....71 A3
West Mid Mere Rd
  DN40 ....86 D3
West Mill Rise [4] HU17 .55 B7
West Moor Rd DN10 .116 C3
West Newton Rd HU11 .58 D6
West Par HU3 ....145 C7
West Parklands Dr [8]
  HU14 ....69 A5
West Pk YO8 ....148 A4
West Prom YO25 ....124 D4
West Rd
  Keadby with Althorpe
  DN17 ....95 C6
  Sigglesthorne HU11 ..34 E1
  Thorne/Moorends DN8 .79 B2
West Road Fst Sch
  DN8 ....79 B2
West St Mary's Gate
  DN31 ....152 D3
West St
  Barnetby le Wold DN38 .99 B4
  Beverley HU17 ....137 C4
  Bridlington YO15 ....122 C4
  Cleethorpes DN35 ...153 F2
  [21] Flamborough YO15 .5 A2
  [9] Gainsborough DN21 .117 A2
  Goole DN14 ....149 C5
  Hibaldstow DN20 ....108 F5
  Kingston upon Hull HU1 .155 A2
  Leven HU17 ....44 F8
  North Kelsey LN7 ....110 A4
  Roxby cum Risby DN15 .82 F3
  Scawby DN20 ....108 E8
  Scunthorpe DN15 ...151 A7
  Thorne/Moorends DN8 .93 A7
  West Butterwick DN17 .106 C8
  West Halton DN15 ...82 C7
  Winterton DN15 .....83 A5
West Terr
  Beverley HU17 ....154 C2
  [19] Brigg DN20 .....98 B2
West Terrace St [3] DN17 .94 B2
West Thorpe YO24 ..132 D8
West View
  Messingham DN17 ....107 C7
  [12] North Ferriby HU14 .69 A4
  Scunthorpe DN17 .....96 C2
West View Ul [3] DN41 .101 A4
West Wood La YO23 .24 E4
Westbeck Hill YO42 ..30 A5
Westbeck La DN21 ...118 F5
Westborough Way
  HU4 ....144 B6
Westbourne Ave
  Bridlington YO16 ....122 D3
  Kingston upon Hull HU5 .140 A1
  [3] Kingston upon Hull
  HU13 ....143 E2
Westbourne Ave W
  HU5 ....140 A1
Westbourne Dr DN17 .94 D7

Westbourne Gdns
  YO8 ....148 C4
Westbourne Gr
  Goole DN14 ....149 D6
  [15] Grimsby DN33 ..113 E8
  Kingston upon Hull
  HU13 ....143 D2
  Selby YO8 ....148 C4
Westbourne Rd
  Hornsea HU18 ....134 D4
  Selby YO8 ....148 C4
Westbourne St [5] HU3 .145 A4
Westbrook Cres [3] HU15 .66 D7
Westbrook Rd [12] HU15 .66 D7
Westbrooke Gr [18] LN7 .111 B4
Westburn Ave [2] DN19 .70 E2
Westbury Pk [10] DN35 .103 D1
Westbury Rd DN35 ..103 C1
Westcliff Rd [5] DN17 .150 F3
Westcliffe Jun & Inf Sch
  DN17 ....150 D2
Westcliffe Rd [16] DN21 .107 C3
Westcott Prim Sch
  HU8 ....141 C3
Westcott St HU8 ....141 D2
Westcroft [11] YO43 ..53 F7
Westend Falls YO25 .125 E6
Westend La YO25 ....77 B6
Westenders Way HU1 .155 A1
Westerdale [4] HU14 .69 B7
Westerdale Cl [8] HU12 .73 C4
Westerdale Ct [2] YO30 .130 A6
Westerdale Gr HU9 ..146 E8
Westerdale Rd DN16 .151 D1
Western Ave DN20 ..98 C3
Western Comp Sch
  DN34 ....102 C3
Western Dr [7] DN18 .69 E1
Western Gailes Way
  HU8 ....142 B5
Western Gn DN15 ...68 A1
Western Outway
  DN34 ....102 D2
Western Rd DN14 ...149 C6
Westfield
  Patrington HU12 .....74 C1
  Selby YO8 ....148 B4
Westfield Ave
  Beverley HU17 ....136 D6
  [3] Eggborough DN14 .61 F2
  Goole DN14 ....149 D5
  [11] Grimsby DN33 ..102 E2
  Rawcliffe DN14 ......64 A1
  Selby YO8 ....148 B4
Westfield Cl
  Easington HU12 ......90 F6
  [2] Eggborough DN14 .61 F2
  [21] Haxby YO32 ....13 E5
  Kingston upon Hull
  HU16 ....138 F6
  Nafferton YO25 .....125 E6
  [3] Pocklington YO42 .28 F4
Westfield Cres HU15 .135 C4
Westfield Cty Inf Sch
  YO24 ....129 B2
Westfield Cty Jun Sch
  YO26 ....129 A2
Westfield Dr
  Messingham DN17 ....107 D7
  York YO10 ....133 D8
Westfield Garth
  [1] Crowle DN17 .....94 E6
  [1] Walkington HU17 .55 B8
Westfield Gr
  [4] Eggborough DN14 .61 F2
  Grimsby DN35 ....153 D2
  [12] Haxby YO32 ....13 D5
Westfield La
  East Garton HU12 ....59 D5
  Fishlake DN7 ....92 B4
  Hook DN14 ....149 B8
  Kirk Bramwith DN7 ...78 B1
  Norton WF8 ....76 C2
  Preston HU12 ....58 B1
  Thorganby YO19 .....38 A5
Westfield Pk HU15 ...68 C6
Westfield Pl
  [19] Haxby YO32 ....13 E5
  York YO24 ....129 A1
Westfield Prim Sch
  HU16 ....138 F6
Westfield Rd
  Barton-upon-Humber
  DN18 ....69 C1
  Easington HU12 ......90 F5
  [1] Eggborough DN14 .61 F2
  [4] Goxhill DN19 .....86 A4
  [4] Hatfield DN7 .....92 E4
  [20] Haxby YO32 ....13 D5
  Kingston upon Hull
  HU16 ....138 F6
  Kingston upon Hull HU4 .144 D5
  Kirk Bramwith DN7 ...92 A4
  Market Weighton YO43 .135 C4
  [3] North Duffield YO8 .50 A7
  Pocklington YO42 ....28 F4
  Rawcliffe DN14 ......64 A1
  Scunthorpe DN17 ...150 D2
  Scunthorpe DN16 ...151 C2
  Selby YO8 ....148 B4
  Skidby HU16 ....138 A5
  Waltham DN37 ......113 D6
Westfield Rise
  Beeford YO25 ....34 B8
  Kingston upon Hull
  HU13 ....143 D2
  [13] Withernsea HU19 .75 A6
Westfield Sq DN14 ..149 D5

Westfield Terr YO43 .135 C4
Westfield Villas [3] DN7 .92 C4
Westgarth Ave HU6 .139 F5
Westgate
  Bridlington YO16 ....122 B4
  Grimsby DN31 ....152 D5
  Hornsea HU18 ....134 B4
  Nafferton YO25 .....125 E6
  North Cave HU15 .....53 D3
  North Newbald YO43 .53 E7
  Patrington HU12 .....74 D1
  Scotton DN21 ....107 C1
Westgate Manor [4]
  YO12 ....74 D1
Westgate Mdws YO25 .125 E6
Westgate Rd DN9 ...94 D2
Westhill Rd DN34 ...152 A1
Westholme Ave HU4 .134 C7
Westholme Cl [10] DN15 .82 B4
Westholme Dr YO30 .126 B3
Westholme La DN38 .99 C5
Westkirke Ave [2] DN33 .113 F8
Westland Rd
  Kingston upon Hull
  HU10 ....143 B7
  [3] Westwoodside DN9 .105 B2
Westlands Ave
  Grimsby DN34 ....152 C1
  Tetney DN36 ....114 D4
Westlands Cl [13] HU12 .72 C7
Westlands Dr HU12 .72 C7
Westlands Gr YO31 .130 F7
Westlands Mews
  YO25 ....124 D5
Westlands Rd
  Hedon HU12 ....72 C7
  Kingston upon Hull HU5 .144 B8
  Sproatley HU11 ......58 C5
Westlands Way HU17 .45 A8
Westminster Ave HU8 .141 E3
Westminster Ct DN14 .149 E6
Westminster Dr
  Grimsby DN34 ....152 C2
  Hatfield DN7 ....92 C2
Westminster Rd
  [2] Broughton DN20 .97 D4
  York YO30 ....130 A6
Westmoreland Ave [3]
  YO15 ....122 F2
Westmoreland Cl DN9 .105 A2
Westmoreland Gr [2]
  YO15 ....122 F2
Westmoreland St
  [1] Kingston upon Hull
  HU2 ....140 F1
  Kingston upon Hull HU2 .155 B4
Westoby La
  Barrow upon Humber
  DN19 ....85 C7
  Rowley HU15 ....54 E3
Weston Gr [3] DN40 .87 B2
Westover Dr DN15 ...82 A4
Westparkside DN14 .149 A6
Westpit La YO32 .....14 A7
Westport Rd [27] DN35 .103 C3
Westrum La DN20 ...98 C1
Westside Rd DN31 ..152 C6
Westview YO16 .....129 B7
Westward Cl DN34 ..152 C1
Westward Ho DN34 .152 B1
Westway Ave HU6 ..139 F6
Westwick [28] HU12 .72 C7
Westwinds Gdns DN15 .83 A5
Westwinds Rd [10] DN15 .83 A5
Westwold Rd [20] LN7 .111 B4
Westwood [4] DN20 .97 D4
Westwood Ave HU18 .134 B4
Westwood Cl HU7 ...141 C6
Westwood Dr [3] HU4 .144 B6
Westwood Gate HU17 .154 A1
Westwood Hospl
  HU17 ....136 D3
Westwood Mews [12]
  YO19 ....26 F7
Westwood Rd
  Beverley HU17 ....154 A3
  [12] Healing DN41 ..101 F5
Westwood Terr YO23 .130 B1
Westwoodside C of E Sch
  DN9 ....105 B2
Wetherby Cl HU6 ....139 F7
Wetherby Rd YO26 .129 B3
Wetwang C of E Sch
  YO25 ....19 B5
Wexford Ave HU9 ..142 E1
Weyford Rd [9] DN35 .103 D1
Weymouth Cl HU7 ..141 B6
Weymouth Cres DN17 .150 C5
Whales La DN14 ....61 E3
Wharf Rd Crowle DN17 .94 D7
  Misterton DN10 .....116 C5
Wharf The DN36 ....115 A5
Whardale Cl DN15 ..95 E5
Wharfe Dr YO24 ....132 D8
Wharfedale Ave HU9 .141 E1
Wharfedale Dr YO16 .122 F7
Wharfedale Pl DN16 .151 D2
Wharncliffe Rd N
  DN31 ....153 A7
Wharncliffe St HU5 .153 A7
Wharncliffe Dr YO30 .126 F2
Wharram Field [3] YO25 .22 D1
Wharram St HU2 ....140 F1
Wharton Ave YO30 .130 B7

Wharton Rd
Blyton DN21 ....117 D5
🖼 Stamford Bridge YO41 ..15 D2
Wharton St DN31 ....152 B3
Wheatcroft 🖼 YO32 .....14 A6
Wheatcroft Ave HU10 .138 E2
Wheatfield Cl
🖼 Barnby Dun DN3 ....92 A3
Epworth DN9 ....105 F6
🖼 Kingston upon Hull
HU4 ....144 D2
Wheatfield Dr 🖼 DN37 .113 D6
Wheatfield La YO32 ...127 C8
Wheatland Cl YO42 .....29 B3
Wheatlands Dr HU17 ..136 C6
Wheatlands Dr YO26 ..129 C6
Wheatley Dr
Bridlington YO16 ....123 A6
Haxby YO32 ....127 C8
Wheatley Gdns HU8 ...141 D3
Wheeldale Cl 🖼 HU7 ...141 D7
Wheeler Prim Sch
HU3 ....144 F5
Wheeler St HU3 ....144 F6
Wheelhouse The 🖼
YO30 ....126 B5
Wheels La YO8 ....63 F3
Wheelwright Cl
Copmanthorpe YO23 ...132 B2
Sutton upon Derwent
YO41 ....27 C1
Wheldrake C of E Prim Sch
YO19 ....38 A3
Wheldrake Ings Nature
Reserve ★ YO19 ....38 C7
Wheldrake La
Deighton YO19 ....26 B1
Escrick YO19 ....37 B5
Whenby Gr YO31 ....127 F1
Whernside Ave YO31 ..131 A5
Whernside Cl 🖼 HU7 ...57 A6
Whimbrel Ave HU18 ...134 C2
Whimbrel Way 🖼 DN36 .114 A8
Whin Cl 🖼 Strensall YO32 .14 B6
York YO24 ....132 F7
Whin Garth YO24 ....132 F6
Whin La Burstwick HU12 .73 C7
South Cave YO43 ....54 B6
Whin Moor La HU15 ....68 A7
Whin Rd YO24 ....132 F6
Whincroft Ave DN14 ..149 C6
Whinhill La HU12 ....73 F4
Whinns The HU17 ....154 C1
Whinny Hagg La YO8 ...48 A2
Whinny La YO60 ....15 A7
Whins Gate DN17 ....81 A4
Whins La HU11 ....45 D6
Whip-ma-whop-ma-gate
YO1 ....156 C2
Whisby Ct DN36 ....114 B5
Whiston Way 🖼 DN18 ...69 F1
Whitby Ave YO31 ......131 A7
Whitby Dr
Grimsby DN32 ....153 A1
York YO31 ....131 A7
Whitby St HU8 ....146 B8
White Cross ★ HU11 ....45 A6
White Cross Rd YO31 ..130 D7
White Cross Way YO41 ..16 A2
White Gap La HU20 .....54 C5
White Gap Rd HU20 ....54 F4
White Horse Cl 🖼 YO32 .127 F5
White Horse La HU12 ...73 E3
White House Cl
🖼 Hatfield DN7 ....92 D4
Kingston upon Hull
HU10 ....138 C2
Kirk Bramwith DN7 .....92 C7
White House Dale
YO24 ....129 F1
White House Dr YO24 ..129 F1
White House Gdns 🖼
YO24 ....130 A2
White House Gr 🖼 YO41 .27 B2
White House La DN15 ..82 E8
White House Rise
YO24 ....129 F1
White La DN8 ....92 F8
White Ley Rd DN6 ......76 C1
White Lodge YO8 ....148 B4
White Rose Ave 🖼
YO32 ....127 D3
White Rose Cl DN34 ...126 C1
White Rose Gr 🖼 YO32 .127 C3
White Rose Way YO26 .129 C8
White Sprunt Hill YO17 ..1 A1
White St
Kingston upon Hull HU3 .144 F5
Selby YO8 ....148 B6
White Wlk HU10 ....143 C6
Whitebeam Cl HU3 .....145 D6
Whitecarr La YO42 ......39 E8
Whitecross Rd HU11 ....45 B6
Whitecross St HU3 ......84 F8
Whitefield Bglws DN14 ..76 F8
Whitefield La DN14 ......61 E1
Whitefields HU17 ......136 E7
Whitefriargate HU1 ....155 B2
Whitegate Hill LN7 .....111 C3
Whitehall Gdns 🖼 HU5 .140 A1
Whitehall Rd 🖼 DN35 ..103 D1
Whitehead Cl 🖼 HU7 ...57 A6
Whitehouse Wlk HU6 ...56 D5
Whitelands YO25 ....124 D5

Whitemoor La YO8 ......49 C6
Whiterose Dr YO41 ......15 D2
White's Close La HU12 ..59 A2
White's Rd DN35 ....153 F1
Whitestone Dr YO31 ...127 E2
Whitestone Rd DN17 ...150 C2
Whitethorn Ave 🖼 HU19 .75 A6
Whitethorn Cl YO31 ....127 E2
Whitethorn Way HU8 ..141 D4
Whitewell Cl 🖼 DN21 ..108 B1
Whitfield Rd DN17 .....150 C2
Whitgift Cl 🖼 DN37 ....101 F1
Whitgift Sch DN37 .....102 B4
Whitley & Eggborough Cty
Prim Sch DN14 ....61 F1
Whitley Bridge Sta
DN14 ....61 F1
Whitley Cl YO30 ....127 A1
Whitley Rd YO41 ....27 A3
Whitley Thorpe La
DN14 ....76 F7
Whitman Rd DN17 .....150 C2
Whitstable Cl 🖼 HU8 ...141 E7
Whitstone Cl HU7 ......140 F8
Whitton Pl YO10 ....131 C4
Whitton Rd DN15 ....82 C8
Whitworth St HU9 .....141 E2
Whoofer La DN21 ......117 B7
Wickenby Cl 🖼 DN34 ..102 C2
Wickenby Garth HU7 ..141 C8
Wickham Rd DN31 .....153 A6
Wicklow Ave 🖼 DN33 .113 E8
Wickwane Rd HU17 ....137 A6
Wicstun Way YO43 ....135 C3
Wide La YO14 ....3 E5
Widford Gn 🖼 DN7 ......92 D5
Widop St DN14 ....149 C5
Wigginton Prim Sch
YO32 ....13 D5
Wigginton Rd YO31 ....156 B4
Wigginton Terr YO31 ..130 C8
Wike Gate Cl 🖼 DN8 ....93 B7
Wike Gate Gr 🖼 DN8 ...93 B7
Wike Gate Rd DN8 ......93 B8
Wilbar Gr HU5 ....140 B2
Wilberforce Ave YO30 .130 B7
Wilberforce Coll HU8 ..142 A5
Wilberforce Cres
HU17 ....154 C4
Wilberforce Dr HU1 ....155 C3
Wilberforce House Mus ★
HU1 ....155 C2
Wilberforce Monument ★
HU1 ....155 C3
Wilberforce St HU3 ....145 D6
Wilberfoss Sch YO41 ...27 E6
Wilbert Gr HU17 ....154 B3
Wilbert Gr HU17 ....154 B3
Wiles Ct HU17 ....154 C4
Wilfholme Rd YO25 .....32 F3
Wilflete Ct HU9 ....142 B3
Wilfreds Gr 🖼 YO8 ......49 B4
Wilfreds Rd 🖼 YO8 .....49 B4
Wilkie Cl DN15 ....150 C7
Wilkinson Ave DN8 .....79 B1
Wilkinson Way 🖼 YO32 .14 A7
Willerby Carr Cl 🖼 HU5 139 B1
Willerby Dr 🖼 DN14 ....65 A7
Willerby Low Rd
HU10 ....138 D3
Willerby Rd HU5 ....144 C8
Willesden Cl 🖼 HU8 ....141 F5
William Barcroft Jun Sch
DN32 ....153 C3
William Gee High Sch
HU5 ....139 D3
William Jacques Dr
YO8 ....49 E2
William Plows Ave
YO10 ....130 E2
William Rd YO8 ....49 B4
William St
Cleethorpes DN35 .....153 E1
Kingston upon Hull HU1 .155 A1
Scunthorpe DN16 ......151 B6
Williams Dr DN39 ....86 B1
Williamson St HU9 ....146 C7
Willing Way DN32 .....152 F4
Willingham Garth 🖼
HU12 ....72 E5
Willingham St DN32 ...152 E2
Willingham Way HU10 .138 B1
Willis St YO10 ....130 E3
Willitoft Rd YO8 ....50 F6
Willoughby Gr 🖼 DN34 .102 C2
Willoughby Rd DN17 ..150 E1
Willoughby Way YO24 .132 B8
Willoughton CP Sch
DN21 ....119 A4
Willow Ave
🖼 Misterton DN10 ......116 C5
Thorne/Moorends DN8 .79 A1
Willow Bank YO32 .....127 E4
Willow Cl
🖼 Gainsborough DN21 ...117 A2
Laceby DN37 ....101 E1
Pollington DN14 ....78 A6
Snaith DN14 ....78 B8
Willow Cres DN8 ....79 A1
Willow Ct
Hutton Cranswick YO25 ..32 E6
Kexby YO41 ....15 C2
Kingston upon Hull
HU10 ....138 E1
🖼 Pocklington YO42 .....29 A3
Willow Dr
🖼 Barton-upon-Humber
DN18 ....69 F1

Willow Dr continued
Bridlington YO16 ....123 A6
Goole DN14 ....65 C3
Kingston upon Hull
HU10 ....143 D8
Messingham DN17 .....107 D7
🖼 North Duffield YO8 ...50 A7
🖼 Thorngumbald HU12 ..72 E5
Willow Garth
Eastrington DN14 ......51 F1
Pollington DN14 ....78 A6
Willow Garth La DN6 ...77 A1
Willow Gdns 🖼 DN19 ....85 D8
Willow Glade YO32 ....127 F3
Willow Gn 🖼 HU15 ......66 D8
Willow Gr
🖼 Aldbrough HU11 ......47 C1
Beverley HU17 ....136 D4
Earswick YO32 ....128 A7
Keadby DN17 ....95 D6
Kingston upon Hull HU5 .140 C2
Pollington DN14 ....78 A6
Scawby DN20 ....108 F8
Scunthorpe DN16 .....151 B3
🖼 Thorne/Moorends DN8 .79 B1
York YO31 ....130 F7
Willow La Goxhill DN19 .86 A8
Pollington DN14 ....78 A6
Woodmansey HU17 ....154 B1
Willow Park Rd YO41 ...27 F5
Willow Rd
Burstwick HU12 ....73 B6
🖼 Campsall DN6 ....76 E1
🖼 Knottingley WF11 ....61 A3
🖼 Thorne/Moorends DN8 .79 A1
Willow Rise YO8 ....48 B1
Willow Tree Garth 🖼
HU17 ....136 F7
Willowbridge Rd WF8 ...76 C2
Willowbrook Dr DN20 ...98 D2
Willowdale HU7 ....140 F8
Willowfield HU6 ....140 A6
Willows Ave HU9 ....141 F3
Willows Dr HU18 ......134 C4
Willows Prim Sch
DN37 ....102 C4
Willows The
Kingston upon Hull
HU13 ....143 E4
🖼 Strensall YO32 ....14 B7
Willy Howe ★ YO25 ......2 C3
Wilson Cl
Market Weighton YO43 .135 D3
🖼 North Ferriby HU14 ...69 A4
Wilson St
Cleethorpes DN35 .....153 D4
Gainsborough DN21 ...117 A1
🖼 Goole DN14 ....149 C4
Kingston upon Hull
HU10 ....143 E6
🖼 Kingston upon Hull
HU9 ....146 B7
Wilstrop Gr 🖼 YO10 ...133 F8
Wilstrop Farm Rd
YO23 ....132 A2
Wilton Rd
Hornsea HU18 ....134 D3
Humberston DN36 ....114 B8
Wilton Rise YO24 ......129 F3
Wilton St HU8 ....146 B8
Wiltshire Ave DN15 ....82 B4
Wiltshire Rd HU4 ......144 E2
Wimbledon Cl 🖼 HU8 ..142 A5
Wimborn Ave DN34 ...152 B2
Wimbourne Cl HU7 ....141 C6
Wimpole Cl 🖼 YO30 ...127 A1
Winceby Ave DN31 ....152 A4
Winchcombe Ave 🖼
DN34 ....102 C2
Winchester Ave
🖼 Beverley HU17 ....136 E1
Grimsby DN33 ....102 D2
Kingston upon Hull HU9 .142 B4
🖼 York YO26 ....129 E4
Winchester Cl HU9 ....142 B4
Winchester Dr DN16 ...96 E2
Winchester Gr 🖼 YO26 .129 E4
Winchester Rd 🖼 DN7 ..92 C4
Wincolmlee HU2 ....155 C3
Windermere YO24 ....132 D7
Windermere Ave
DN33 ....113 D8
Windermere Cres
🖼 Humberston DN36 ...103 C1
🖼 Kirk Sandall DN3 ....92 A2
Windermere Dr DN14 .149 E5
Windgate Hill La YO8 ..48 B6
Windham Cres 🖼 HU7 ..56 F7
Windle Ave HU6 ....140 C7
Windlesham Ave 🖼
DN33 ....113 D8
Windlestone Sq 🖼 DN8 .79 B2
Windmill Gdns YO8 ....148 B7
Windmill Hill YO25 ....124 C5
Windmill La Norton DN6 ..76 D1
York YO10 ....131 B2
Windmill Mdws YO41 ...27 C6
Windmill Rise YO26 ...129 C3
Windmill Way HU13 ...143 F1
Windsor Ave HU10 ....143 E7
Windsor Cl
Beverley HU17 ....137 B5
🖼 Keelby DN41 ....101 A5
Kingston upon Hull
HU16 ....139 B5
Windsor Cres
Bridlington YO15 ......122 E2
Crowle DN17 ....94 C7

Windsor Cres continued
Scunthorpe DN17 ......96 C1
Windsor Ct DN7 ....92 C2
Windsor Dr
Caistor LN7 ....111 B4
Goole DN14 ....149 B5
🖼 Haxby YO32 ....13 D5
Windsor Garth YO24 ..129 D1
Windsor Gr DN19 ....71 A1
Windsor La DN17 ....94 C7
Windsor Rd
Cleethorpes DN35 .....153 C1
Crowle DN17 ....94 C7
Kingston upon Hull HU5 .139 F1
Windsor St 🖼 YO23 ....130 B1
Windsor Way
Barnetby le Wold DN38 ..99 B5
Broughton DN20 ......97 E4
Winestead Gr 🖼 HU7 ..142 A2
Winestead Ings La
HU12 ....74 A1
Winestead La HU12 ....74 B3
Wingate Rd DN37 .....102 B4
Wingfield Rd HU9 .....142 C2
Wingfield Way HU17 ...55 E8
Winifred Holtby Sch
HU7 ....141 B7
Winn St 🖼 DN16 ....151 B6
Winscar Croft 🖼 HU7 ..141 D7
Winscar Gr 🖼 YO30 ...126 E3
Winsetts Rd HU12 ......90 D5
Winship Cl 🖼 HU3 .....145 C5
Winslow Dr DN40 ....87 B1
Winslow Gr 🖼 DN34 ...102 C2
Winston Ave DN34 .....152 B2
Winston Cl HU12 ....73 A7
Winston Dr HU16 ......138 F5
Winston Way DN20 .....98 D2
Winterham County Prim
Sch DN15 ....68 A1
Winteringham La DN15 .82 E8
Winteringham Rd DN15 .83 B6
Winterscale St YO10 ..130 D2
Winterton C of E Inf Sch
DN15 ....83 A5
Winterton Comp Sch
DN15 ....83 A6
Winterton Rd
Roxby cum Risby DN15 ..82 F2
Scunthorpe DN15 .....151 B8
Winteringham DN15 ...83 B8
Winthorpe Rd
Grimsby DN33 ....102 D1
🖼 Kingston upon Hull
HU13 ....144 A3
Wintringham Rd DN32 .152 E2
Wintringham Sch
DN32 ....102 F2
Wirral Ave 🖼 DN34 ....102 C2
Wise Cl HU17 ....136 E7
Wisker La YO32 ....128 C2
Wisteria Dr DN41 ......101 E5
Wisteria Way HU16 ....151 E1
Wistow Gr HU4 ....144 D5
Wistow Paruchial C of E Prim
Sch YO8 ....48 D6
Wistow Rd YO8 ....148 A6
Wistowgate YO8 ....48 B8
Witch La YO25 ....3 B2
Witham HU9 ....155 C3
Witham Dr
Burton upon Stather
DN15 ....82 B5
York YO32 ....128 A6
Withern Rd DN33 ......102 D2
Withernsea Cty Jun Sch
HU19 ....74 F7
Withernsea High Sch
HU19 ....74 F7
Withernsea Hospl
HU19 ....75 A6
Withernsea Inf Sch
HU19 ....74 F7
Withernsea Rd
Hollym HU19 ....75 A4
Holmpton HU19 ....75 C3
Rimswell HU19 ....74 D8
Roos HU19 ....60 C1
Withernsea St HU8 ....141 A1
Withernwick La HU11 ...47 A4
Withernwick Prim Sch
HU11 ....46 D3
Witherwick Rd
Aldbrough HU11 ....47 A2
Hatfield HU11 ....46 C5
Witty St HU3 ....145 A3
Wittys Paddock 🖼 HU11 .35 A1
Wivell Dr DN41 ....101 A5
Wivern Rd HU9 ....142 D3
Woad La DN37 ....102 C5
Woburn Dr DN14 ......149 E5
Woburn St HU3 ....144 F4
Wold Ave YO43 ....135 E3
Wold Garth YO42 ....29 A3
Wold Hill HU15 ....53 E4
Wold La YO12 ....1 E8
Wold Newton GM Sch
YO25 ....2 A4
Wold Newton Rd YO25 ..2 E3
Wold Prim Sch HU5 ...139 B1
Wold Rd
Barrow upon Humber
DN19 ....85 D7
Kingston upon Hull HU5 .139 B1
Kirby Grindalythe YO17 ..6 C1
Market Weighton YO43 .135 F2
Nafferton YO25 ....125 E8
Pocklington YO42 ......29 A4

Wold Rd continued
Walkington HU17 ....54 E7
Worlaby DN20 ....84 E1
Wold Rise YO43 ....41 E2
Wold View Brigg DN20 ..98 C2
Caistor LN7 ....111 B4
Elloughton-cum-Brough
HU15 ....68 C6
Fotherby LN11 ....121 D2
Fridaythorpe YO25 .....18 B5
🖼 Holton le Clay DN36 .114 A5
Rothwell LN7 ....111 F2
🖼 South Cave HU15 ....54 A2
Wold View Rd N YO25 .124 E3
Wold View Rd S YO25 .124 E3
Woldcarr Rd HU3 ......144 F6
Woldcroft YO41 ....27 C2
Woldgate
Bridlington YO16 ......122 A3
Carnaby YO16 ....10 E6
Harpham YO25 ....9 D3
🖼 North Newbald YO43 .53 F7
Woldgate Sch YO42 ....29 B4
Woldgate View 🖼 YO42 .29 A3
Woldholme Ave YO25 .124 D3
Wolds Cl 🖼 DN17 ....94 D7
Wolds Gliding Club
YO42 ....28 F3
Wolds The HU16 ....138 E6
Wolfe Ave YO31 ....130 F5
Wolfe Cl 🖼 HU16 ......138 F5
Wolfreton Dr HU10 ....143 F6
Wolfreton Garth
HU10 ....143 D8
Wolfreton La HU10 ....143 F6
Wolfreton Lower Sch
HU10 ....138 D1
Wolfreton Rd HU10 ....143 F7
Wolfreton Sch HU10 ..138 D1
Wollaston Rd DN35 ...153 E2
Wolsey Ave YO8 ....48 B8
Wolsey Dr
🖼 Barrow upon Humber
DN19 ....85 C7
Bishopthorpe YO23 ...133 A3
Wolsley St YO10 ....130 E3
Wolviston Ave YO10 ...131 C3
Wombwell Gr 🖼 HU8 ..141 B1
Womersley C of E Prim Sch
DN6 ....76 C6
Womersley Rd
Grimsby DN31 ....153 A6
Knottingley WF11 ......61 A2
Wood Carr La DN9 ......94 C2
Wood Cl
🖼 Grimsby DN33 ....113 E8
🖼 Strensall YO32 ....14 A7
🖼 Thorpe Willoughby YO8 .48 B1
Wood Dr 🖼 HU14 ....69 A4
Wood Gate YO42 ....29 D7
Wood Hill Rd DN21 ...107 A3
Wood Hill Way HU16 ..138 C8
Wood La
Acaster Selby YO23 ....36 B2
Beverley HU17 ....154 A3
Birkin WF11 ....61 D6
Bubwith DN14 ....51 A5
Cottingham HU16 .....139 B4
Fishlake DN7 ....92 D8
🖼 Thorpe Willoughby YO8 .48 B1
Wressle DN14 ....51 B2
Wood St Grimsby DN32 .152 F4
York YO31 ....130 E6
Wood Vale DN16 ....96 E2
Wood View Airmyn DN14 .64 E3
Messingham DN17 ....107 D8
Swanland HU14 ....69 B7
Wood Way YO32 ....128 A4
Woodale Cl 🖼 DN15 ....96 B3
Woodall Ct 🖼 YO8 ......48 D6
Woodapple Ct 🖼 DN41 .101 E6
Woodbine Ave DN20 ....98 C2
Woodbine Cl HU2 ......155 A4
Woodclose Rd DN17 ...150 D2
Woodcoates Cl 🖼 HU7 136 F7
Woodcock Cl 🖼 YO32 ..13 C5
Woodcock Rd 🖼 YO15 ...5 A2
Woodcock St HU3 ......145 A4
Woodcroft Ave HU6 ...139 F5
Wooden Beck Hill
DN10 ....116 B2
Woodfield Cl 🖼 DN36 ..114 D8
Woodfield La HU13 ....143 C1
Woodfield Rd
Gainsborough DN21 ...117 C1
Goole DN14 ....149 B6
Woodford L Ctr HU8 ...141 E2
Woodford Pl 🖼 YO24 ..129 D1
Woodgarr Ave 🖼 DN17 .95 D6
Woodgate La HU5 .....144 F8
Woodgate Rd
Kingston upon Hull HU5 .144 F7
Newbald YO43 ....54 A8
Woodgates Cl 🖼 HU14 .69 A5
Woodgates La HU14 ....69 A5
Woodgates Mount 🖼
HU14 ....69 A5
Woodhall Dr
🖼 Beverley HU17 ....136 D6
Waltham DN37 ....113 D6
Woodhall La
Hemingbrough YO8 .....50 B3
Womersley DN6 ....76 D6
Woodhall Pk HU17 ....136 D7
Woodhall St HU8 ......141 A2
Woodhall Way HU17 ..154 A4
Woodhill Ave DN21 ...117 C1
Woodhill Cl 🖼 HU10 ..143 E7

Woodhill Rise HU13 ....143 C2
Woodhouse Gr 4 YO31 .131 A5
Woodhouse Green Rd
  DN7 ....92 B8
Woodhouse La
  Beeford YO25 ....22 C1
  Belton DN9 ....94 E2
  Hatfield DN7 ....92 D2
  Pocklington YO42 ....29 A5
  Riston HU11 ....45 B3
Woodhouse Rd
  Scunthorpe DN16 .....151 E4
  Thorganby YO19 ....38 A3
Woodhouse St HU9 ...146 D2
Woodings Ct 5 DN14 ..65 A7
Woodland Ave
  17 Brough HU15 ....68 C6
  14 Gainsborough DN21 ..117 A2
  Goole DN14 ....149 C6
Woodland Chase
  YO30 ....127 B1
Woodland Dr
  Broughton DN20 ....97 D4
  1 Elsham DN20 ....98 F7
  Kingston upon Hull
    HU10 ....143 C6
Woodland End HU4 ....144 C5
Woodland Pl YO32 ....127 E4
Woodland Rise YO25 ..125 A6
Woodland View
  5 Barnetby le Wold DN38 ..99 B4
  Scunthorpe DN15 ......150 C7
Woodland Way
  8 Airmyn DN14 ....64 E4
  19 Epworth DN9 ....105 E6
  York YO32 ....127 F4
Woodland Wlk 6 DN35 .103 C1
Woodlands
  Beverley HU17 ....136 D4
  Escrick YO19 ....37 B5
Woodlands Ave
  Haxby YO32 ....127 C8
  Immingham DN40 ....87 C2
  Keelby DN41 ....101 A4
Woodlands Cl
  4 Barrow upon Humber
    DN19 ....85 C7
  Bridlington YO15 ......123 B7
Woodlands Dr DN17 ...136 D4
Woodlands Gr YO31 ...131 A7
Woodlands La
  8 Brough HU15 ....68 C6
  Hillam LS25 ....61 B7
Woodlands Prim Sch
  DN33 ....102 D1
Woodlands Rd HU5 ...144 B7
Woodlands Rise
  5 North Ferriby HU14 ..69 A5
  Norton DN6 ....76 B1
Woodlands Sports Ctr
  DN40 ....87 C2
Woodlands The
  Kingston upon Hull
    HU16 ....138 F7
  Kingston upon Hull HU5 .140 B2
  Preston HU12 ....72 B7
  2 Stallingborough DN41 .101 D6
Woodlands View YO8 ...49 B4
Woodlea Ave YO26 ....129 C4

Woodlea Bank YO26 ..129 D4
Woodlea Cres YO26 ..129 D4
Woodlea Gr YO26 .....129 D5
Woodleigh Cl 2 YO32 ...14 A6
Woodleigh Dr HU7 ....141 C5
Woodmansey C of E Sch
  HU17 ....56 C8
Woodmarketgate 26
  HU12 ....72 C7
Woodrow Pk DN33 ....102 E1
Wood's La HU1 ....155 A1
Woods La DN40 ....86 F2
Woods Mdw DN20 ....108 F6
Woods Terr 7 DN21 ...117 B2
Woodside
  10 Gilberdyke HU15 ....66 D7
  Kingston upon Hull
    HU13 ....143 D1
Woodside Ave YO31 ..131 A6
Woodside La DN9 .....104 D6
Woodside Rd YO12 ......1 A8
Woodsley Ave
  5 Cleethorpes DN35 ..153 C2
  Cleethorpes DN35 ....153 E1
Woodstock Cl HU16 ..138 F6
Woodstock Rd DN16 ..151 D4
Woodthorpe Prim Sch
  YO24 ....132 C7
Woodville Terr YO8 ..148 E3
Woolam Hill HU12 .....73 A6
Woollin Ave DN17 ....151 A2
Woolnough Ave YO10 .131 B3
Woolsthorpe Gr 20 HU7 ..56 F6
Woolwich Dr 2 HU4 ...144 B2
Wootton C of E Sch
  DN39 ....85 E3
Wootton Rd
  Grimsby DN33 ....102 D2
  Wootton DN39 ....85 F2
Worcester Ave DN35 .153 E1
Worcester Cl 11 DN16 .96 D1
Worcester Dr YO31 ...131 B5
Worcester Rd HU5 ...139 C1
Worcestershire Cl 1
  HU5 ....139 D1
Wordsworth Ave 4 DN6 .76 E1
Wordsworth Cres
  YO24 ....132 D7
Wordsworth St HU8 ..141 D2
Workington Ave 8 HU4 144 B6
Worlaby Prim Sch
  DN20 ....98 D8
Worlaby Rd 1 DN33 ..113 D8
Worldwide Way
  Immingham DN41 .....101 F8
  Stallingborough DN41 ..87 F1
Wormley Hill La DN14 ..78 E2
Worral Ct 1 DN3 ......92 A1
Worsborough Cl 10
  HU7 ....141 D7
Worsendale Rd YO42 ..16 F2
Worship St HU2 ......155 B3
Worsley Cl
  7 Holton le Clay DN36 .114 A5
  Immingham DN40 ......87 D1
Worsley Fst Sch DN34 .102 C4
Worsley Rd DN40 ......87 C1
Worthing St HU5 .....140 D3

Wortley St DN16 .....151 A6
Wragby Rd DN17 .....150 D1
Wragby St DN32 .....152 F3
Wrangbrook Cl 3 DN14 .65 A7
Wrangham Dr 1 YO14 ...3 A8
Wrangman Dale Rd
  YO43 ....54 A8
Wrawby C E Sch DN20 ..98 E3
Wrawby La HU12 ......58 D2
Wrawby Postmill ★
  DN20 ....98 E3
Wrawby Rd Brigg DN20 .98 C2
  Scunthorpe DN17 .....150 E1
Wrawby St 7 DN20 ....98 C2
Wray Cl Beverley HU17 .154 B4
  9 Waltham DN37 ......113 D7
Wray St 14 DN21 .....108 B1
Wray's Ave YO31 .....127 E1
Wren Cl 4 Healing DN41 101 F5
  17 Scunthorpe DN16 ...96 D1
Wren Cres DN33 .....102 C3
Wren Cres DN33 .....102 D1
Wren Hall La YO8 .....63 E6
Wren La 2 YO8 ....148 D5
Wressle Rd DN20 ......97 E4
Wressle Sta YO8 ......50 D2
Wright Cl YO16 ......122 B2
Wright Cres YO16 ...122 B2
Wright St HU2 ....155 A3
Wrights Gdns 1 DN10 .116 D3
Wrights La WF11 ......76 B8
Wroot Rd DN9 ....104 A2
Wroot Travis Charity Sch
  DN9 ....104 D5
Wroots Ave DN14 ....149 D1
Wroxham Ave DN34 ..102 C3
Wrygarth Ave 7 HU15 .68 C5
Wyatt Ave DN20 ......97 D3
Wybeck Rd DN15 ......96 D7
Wybers Way DN37 ...102 B4
Wybers Wood Jun & Inf Sch
  DN37 ....102 B4
Wycliffe Ave YO10 ...131 B3
Wycliffe La YO15 ....122 E2
Wydale Rd YO10 .....131 D4
Wyham Medieval Village ★
  DN36 ....120 F5
Wyke Coll HU5 ....139 E2
Wyke St HU9 ....146 B2
Wykeham Cl
  2 Bridlington YO16 ...122 C4
  1 Kingston upon Hull
    HU7 ....141 D7
Wykeman Cl YO25 ...124 D3
Wylies Rd HU17 ......154 A3
Wymark View 28 DN33 .102 C2
Wymersley Rd HU5 ...144 A8
Wynburg St HU9 .....141 D1
Wyndham Cl 4 HU17 ..43 D6
Wyndham Rd 10 DN36 .114 A7
Wyndham St HU3 ....145 C7
Wynmoor Rd DN17 ...150 F3
Wyntryngham Cl 14
  HU12 ....72 D7
Wyredale Rd DN16 ...151 D1
Wysteria Way HU8 ...141 E7
Wytherstone Cl 3 HU7 .56 F6
Wyton Gr HU9 ....142 A2
Wyton Rd HU12 ......58 B2
Wyvern Cl DN17 ......94 D8

Y

Yapham Rd
  Pocklington YO42 .....28 F5
  Yapham YO42 ....28 E5
Yarborough Camp ★
  DN39 ....99 E7
Yarborough Cl 2 DN36 114 A5
Yarborough Cres 6
  DN20 ....97 D4
Yarborough Dr DN31 .152 C4
Yarborough Mid Sch
  DN34 ....152 A3
Yarborough Prim Sch
  DN34 ....102 C4
Yarborough Rd
  24 Brigg DN20 ....98 C2
  Grimsby DN34 ....152 A3
  Keelby DN41 ....101 A5
  Scunthorpe DN16 .....97 A5
Yarburgh Cl 4 DN14 ..63 B1
Yarburgh Gr 2 YO26 .129 E5
Yarburgh Way YO10 .131 C3
Yardley Way 3 DN34 .102 B2
Yarmouth Ave 3 HU4 .144 A3
Yarra Rd DN35 ....153 C2
Yarrow Rd DN34 .....102 C4
Yatesbury Garth 18 HU7 .57 A5
Yeadon Garth HU7 ...141 C8
Yearsley Cres YO31 .130 D7
Yearsley Gr YO31 ....127 E1
Yearsley Grove Jun Sch
  YO31 ....127 F1
Yearsley Swimming Baths
  YO31 ....130 D8
Yew Tree Cl
  Acaster Malbis YO23 ...36 C8
  Rufforth YO23 ....24 C6
  Selby YO8 ....148 C6
Yew Tree Mews YO19 .131 C5
Yew Tree Pk DN14 .....77 A7
Yews La DN37 ....101 E1
Yewtree Dr HU4 .....144 B7
Yiewsley Cl HU8 .....141 E6
Yokegate DN14 ....51 E3
Yordas Ct 3 YO16 ...123 A7
York Abbey ★ YO30 ..156 A3
York Ave DN16 ....96 D2
York Barbican Leisure Ctr
  YO10 ....156 C1
York Castle Mus ★
  YO1 ....156 C1
York City Art Gall ★
  YO30 ....156 B3
York City Football Club
  YO30 ....156 A4
York Cl YO43 ....135 D4
York Coll of F & H Ed
  YO24 ....132 E6
York Cricket & RUFC
  YO30 ....129 F7
York District Hospl
  YO30 ....156 B4
York Dungeon ★ YO1 .156 B2
York La Flaxton YO60 ..14 E8
  Huggate YO42 ....18 A2
York Minster ★ YO1 .156 B3
York Pl DN35 ....103 B2

York Race Course (The
  Knavesmire) ★ YO24 ..130 A1
York Rd Barlby YO8 ...49 B5
  Beverley HU17 ....136 D4
  Bilbrough YO23 ....24 B2
  Bishop Burton HU17 ..42 F3
  Bridlington YO15 ....122 F3
  Brigg DN20 ....98 C2
  Cliffe YO8 ....49 E3
  Cottam YO25 ....8 B2
  Driffield YO25 ....124 B5
  Dunnington YO19 .....26 D6
  Fridaythorpe YO25 ...18 B5
  Garton YO25 ....19 D8
  Great Driffield YO25 .124 D5
  28 Hatfield DN7 ......92 D4
  Haxby YO32 ....127 D7
  Kilham YO25 ....8 F3
  Kingston upon Hull HU6 139 F7
  1 Kirton in Lindsey DN21 119 C8
  Long Marston YO26 ...24 A6
  Market Weighton YO43 135 A5
  Naburn YO19 ....36 D8
  North Duffield YO8 ...50 A8
  Riccall YO19 ....37 A1
  Shipton Thorpe YO43 .40 E6
  Sledmere YO25 ....7 E1
  Stillingfleet YO19 ....36 D4
  Strensall YO32 ....14 A6
  Sutton-on-the-Forest
    YO61 ....13 C8
  York YO26 ....129 C3
York Rd Gallows Hill
  YO43 ....135 A6
York Rugby League Club
  YO32 ....128 A2
York Sixth Form Coll
  YO24 ....132 E6
York St
  5 Dunnington YO19 ...26 E7
  Grimsby DN31 ....152 C4
  Kingston upon Hull HU2 155 C4
  1 Selby YO8 ....148 C5
York Sta YO24 ....156 A2
York Steiner Sch
  YO10 ....130 D1
York Terr DN10 ......116 D5
Yorklands YO25 ......124 D5
Yorkshire Air Mus ★
  YO41 ....26 F3
Yorkshire Cl 3 HU5 ..139 D1
Yorkshire Mus ★ YO30 .156 A3
Yorkshire Mus of Farming ★
  YO19 ....131 F5
Yorkshireside DN17 ...81 A3
Young Pl DN35 ......153 B3
Young St HU19 ....75 A7
Youth Ctr YO25 .....125 A5

Z

Zeigfield Ct 11 HU9 ..142 A3
Zetland St HU3 .....145 A5

FISH & CHIPS.

14a Marton Rd Bridlington

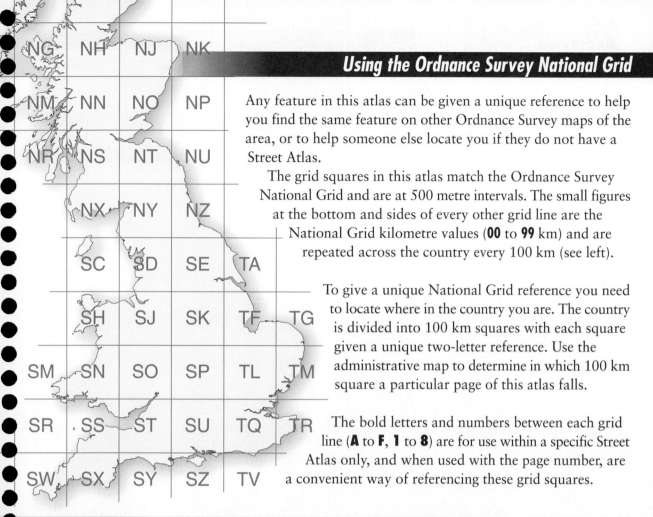

Any feature in this atlas can be given a unique reference to help you find the same feature on other Ordnance Survey maps of the area, or to help someone else locate you if they do not have a Street Atlas.

The grid squares in this atlas match the Ordnance Survey National Grid and are at 500 metre intervals. The small figures at the bottom and sides of every other grid line are the National Grid kilometre values (**00** to **99** km) and are repeated across the country every 100 km (see left).

To give a unique National Grid reference you need to locate where in the country you are. The country is divided into 100 km squares with each square given a unique two-letter reference. Use the administrative map to determine in which 100 km square a particular page of this atlas falls.

The bold letters and numbers between each grid line (**A** to **F**, **1** to **8**) are for use within a specific Street Atlas only, and when used with the page number, are a convenient way of referencing these grid squares.

Example   The railway bridge over DARLEY GREEN RD in grid square B1

Step 1: Identify the two-letter reference, in this example the page is in **SP**

Step 2: Identify the 1 km square in which the railway bridge falls. Use the figures in the southwest corner of this square: Eastings **17**, Northings **74**. This gives a unique reference: **SP 17 74**, accurate to 1 km.

Step 3: To give a more precise reference accurate to 100 m you need to estimate how many tenths along and how many tenths up this 1 km square the feature is (to help with this the 1 km square is divided into four 500 m squares). This makes the bridge about **8** tenths along and about **1** tenth up from the southwest corner.

This gives a unique reference: **SP 178 741**, accurate to 100 m.

Eastings (read from left to right along the bottom) come before Northings (read from bottom to top). If you have trouble remembering say to yourself "Along the hall, THEN up the stairs"!

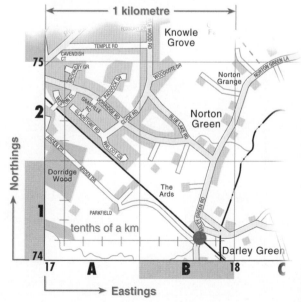

Name and Address	Telephone	Page	Grid reference

Name and Address	Telephone	Page	Grid reference

PHILIP'S MAPS

the Gold Standard for serious driving

◆ Philip's street atlases cover every county in England, plus much of Wales and Scotland

◆ All our atlases use the same style of mapping, with the same colours and symbols, so you can move with confidence from one atlas to the next

◆ Widely used by the emergency services, transport companies and local authorities

◆ Created from the most up-to-date and detailed information available from Ordnance Survey

◆ Based on the National Grid

BEST BUY • BEST BUY
Auto EXPRESS
• BEST BUY • BEST BUY •

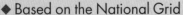

PHILIP'S
STREET ATLAS
London
The definitive Lon...
from Britain's national ma...
PHILIP'S

PHILIP'S
STREET ATLAS
Devon
Unique comprehensive coverage
BEST BUY
with time-saving through-routes
Includes Lyme Regis, Sidbouth and Wellington, plus Exeter and Plymouth centres at extra-large scale

PHILIP'S
STREET ATLAS
Norfolk
Unique comprehensive coverage
BEST BUY
with time-saving through-routes
Includes Norwich city centre at extra-large scale, plus town maps of Bury St Edmunds and Lowestoft

PHILIP'S
STREET ATLAS
Cumbria
Unique comprehensive coverage
BEST BUY
Every named street, road and lane
Plus town maps of Dumfries and Morecambe, with Carlisle city centre at extra-large scale

PHILIP'S
BRITAIN'S MOST DETAILED ROAD ATLAS
NAVIGATOR Britain
Ultra-large scale mapping
1½ miles to 1 inch
50 fully indexed town plans
'Extremely clear mapping with the most detail by far'
Auto Express
Recommended by the Institute of Advanced Motorists

For national mapping, choose **Philip's Navigator Britain** – the most detailed road atlas available of England, Wales and Scotland. Hailed by Auto Express as 'the ultimate road atlas', this is the only one-volume atlas to show every road and lane in Britain.

England	
Bedfordshire	
Berkshire	
Birmingham and West Midlands	
Bristol and Bath	
Buckinghamshire	
Cambridgeshire	
Cheshire	
Cornwall	
Cumbria	
Derbyshire	
Devon	
Dorset	
County Durham and Teesside	
Essex	
North Essex	
South Essex	
Gloucestershire	
North Hampshire	
South Hampshire	
Herefordshire Monmouthshire	
Hertfordshire	
Isle of Wight	
East Kent	
West Kent	
Lancashire	
Leicestershire and Rutland	
Lincolnshire	
London	
Greater Manchester	
Merseyside	
Norfolk	
Northamptonshire	
Nottinghamshire	
Oxfordshire	
Shropshire	

All-England coverage

- **Somerset**
- **Staffordshire**
- **Suffolk**
- **Surrey**
- **East Sussex**
- **West Sussex**
- **Tyne and Wear Northumberland**
- **Warwickshire**
- **Birmingham and West Midlands**
- **Wiltshire and Swindon**
- **Worcestershire**
- **East Yorkshire Northern Lincolnshire**
- **North Yorkshire**
- **South Yorkshire**
- **West Yorkshire**

Wales
- **Anglesey, Conwy and Gwynedd**
- **Cardiff, Swansea and The Valleys**
- **Denbighshire, Flintshire, Wrexham**
- **Herefordshire Monmouthshire**

Scotland
- **Edinburgh and East Central Scotland**
- **Fife and Tayside**
- **Glasgow and West Central Scotland**

How to order

Philip's maps and atlases are available from bookshops, motorway services and petrol stations. You can order direct from the publisher by phoning **01903 828503** or online at **www.philips-maps.co.uk**

For bulk orders only, phone 020 7644 6940 and quote Philip's 35